Readings for Writers

second edition

Readings for Writers

second edition

Jo Ray McCuen

GLENDALE COLLEGE

Anthony C. Winkler

HARCOURT BRACE JOVANOVICH, INC.

NEW YORK   CHICAGO   SAN FRANCISCO   ATLANTA

ISBN: 0-15-575827-6
Library of Congress Catalog Card Number: 76-50463
Printed in the United States of America

COPYRIGHTS AND ACKNOWLEDGMENTS

For permission to use the selections reprinted in this book, the authors are grateful to the following publishers and copyright holders:

CYRILLY ABELS   For "Who Decides What's Fit to Print?" from *The Sugar Pill* by T. S. Matthews. Copyright © 1959 by T. S. Matthews. Reprinted by permission of Cyrilly Abels, Literary Agent. First appeared in *Saturday Review*, January 24, 1959.

AMERICAN ASSOCIATION FOR THE ADVANCEMENT OF SCIENCE   For an excerpt from "On Being Sane in Insane Places" by D. L. Rosenhan from *Science*, vol. 179, pp. 250–258 (January 19, 1973). Copyright 1973 by the American Association for the Advancement of Science. Reprinted by permission.

AMERICAN ASSOCIATION OF UNIVERSITY PROFESSORS   For "Composition and Linguistic Revolution" by Maxwell Fullerton from *American Association of University Professors Bulletin*, vol. 44, no. 3 (autumn 1958). Reprinted by permission.

APPLETON-CENTURY-CROFTS   For an excerpt from *Autobiography and Selected Letters* by T. H. Huxley, edited by Sarah E. Simons. Reprinted by permission.

EDWARD ARNOLD (PUBLISHERS) LTD.   For "My Wood" from *Abinger Harvest* by E. M. Forster.

ASSOCIATED BOOK PUBLISHERS   For "A Funeral" by E. V. Lucas. Reprinted by permission of the Trustees of the Estate of E. V. Lucas and by Associated Book Publishers.

LAURA BOHANNAN   For "Shakespeare in the Bush" by Laura Bohannan from *Natural History*, August-September 1966. Copyright © 1966 by Laura Bohannan.

BROADCAST MUSIC, INC.   For "Grant and Lee: A Study in Contrasts" by Bruce Catton from *The American Story*, edited by Earl Schenk Miers. Copyright, 1956, by Broadcast Music, Inc.

CURTIS BROWN, LTD.   For "Thinking as a Hobby" by William Golding from *Holiday*, August 1961. Copyright © 1961 by William Golding. Reprinted by permission of Curtis Brown, Ltd.

CHARLES BUKOWSKI   For "The Twins" by Charles Bukowski. Reprinted by permission.

MERVYN L. CADWALLADER   For "Marriage as a Wretched Institution" by Mervyn L. Cadwallader from *The Atlantic Monthly*, vol. 218 (November 1966). Copyright © 1966, by The Atlantic Monthly Company, Boston, Mass. Reprinted by permission.

CHATTO AND WINDUS LTD.   For "The New Villa" from *The Witch and Other Stories* by Anton Chekhov, translated by Constance Garnett. Reprinted by permission of David Garnett and Chatto and Windus Ltd.

MARCHETTE CHUTE   For "Getting At the Truth" by Marchette Chute from *Saturday Review*, September 19, 1953. By permission of the author and the publisher.

COWARD, MCCANN & GEOGHEGAN, INC.   For Chapter 10 from *The Little Locksmith* by Katherine Butler Hathaway. Copyright 1943 by Coward, McCann & Geoghegan, Inc. Renewed © 1971 by Warren H. Butler. Reprinted by permission of Coward, McCann & Geoghegan, Inc.

MALCOLM COWLEY   For "Sociological Habit Patterns in Linguistic Transmogrification" by Malcolm Cowley from *The Reporter*, September 20, 1956, pp. 257–261. Copyright © 1956 by Malcolm Cowley. Reprinted by permission.

J. M. DENT & SONS LTD.   For an excerpt from the Everyman's Library edition of *Great Expectations* by Charles Dickens.

ANDRE DEUTSCH LTD.   For an excerpt from *The Coming of Age* by Simone de Beauvoir, translated by Patrick O'Brian.

DOUBLEDAY & COMPANY, INC.   For excerpts from *The Summing Up* by W. Somerset Maugham. Copyright 1938 by W. Somerset Maugham. Reprinted by permission of Doubleday & Company, Inc.

SHIRLEY GRAHAM DU BOIS   For "On Being Crazy" from *An ABC of Color* by W. E. B. Du Bois. Reprinted by permission.

DUN-DONNELLEY PUBLISHING CORPORATION   For "The Thesis" from *The Complete Stylist* by Sheridan Baker. New York: Thomas Y. Crowell Company, Inc., 1972. Reprinted by permission.

Continued on page 557.

PREFACE TO THE SECOND EDITION

This new edition of *Readings for Writers* is essentially a fine-tuning of the first. We have continued to label each selection *Model, Example,* and so on, according to the purpose for its inclusion. The original chapters remain, a few considerably changed, some merely tinkered with, and one—Chapter 6, "What's the Best Way of Following Through?: Development"—greatly expanded. We have been guided in our additions and deletions primarily by comments from users of the first edition.

That edition contained a total of 122 selections—articles, paragraphs, stories, and poems. Twenty-five of those have been dropped, and forty-three new selections have been added. Because so many users of the first edition suggested that we enlarge our examples of the use of the various rhetorical modes, the chief beneficiary of the additions is Chapter 6, on development. Here only three selections have been dropped, while seventeen have been added. We have also included in that chapter some original advice to students on how to write papers by description, example, definition, comparison/contrast, division, and causal analysis. Another new feature of this edition is an appendix of annotated student papers that exemplify the use of the rhetorical modes in the brief essay.

Every change has been made with the intent of increasing the practicality and usefulness of *Readings for Writers*. For instance, in Chapter 11, "Writing About Literature," we have added examples of a book review, a movie review, and a play review, since students are often assigned to write one or all of these. Despite the changes, however, the average length of selections remains essentially the same, and instructors will find the second edition of *Readings for Writers* as compact and accessible as the first.

JO RAY MC CUEN AND ANTHONY C. WINKLER

FROM THE PREFACE TO THE FIRST EDITION

"'Facts are stupid things,' [Professor Louis Agassiz] would say, 'until brought into connection with some general law.'"* In this anthology of readings for freshman composition we have tried to suggest how the laws of writing are constituted by answering the questions "What do you mean by rhetoric?" "What's a thesis?" "How do I get from outline to paragraph?"

The chapters are structured in this manner:

A *Model* selection: a short piece that serves as a model of excellence for the chapter topic. All chapters dealing with actual writing performance open with a model.

An *Advice* selection: an article that offers practical advice on the chapter topic.

Discussion selections: two or three articles, for most chapters, that further discuss the chapter topic.

Example selections: a variety of examples that demonstrate mastery of the chapter topic.

Each selection, except for the advice articles, is preceded by a headnote and followed by a list of vocabulary words and by questions about both the content and the form of the selection. There are writing assignments for each selection as well as for each chapter as a whole, and suggestions for research papers are liberally sprinkled throughout the book. An instructor's manual containing answers to the questions is available.

We have included chapters on writing research papers, writing for the sciences, and writing reports, in the belief that they will be of benefit to students in classes other than freshman composition, and even in their years ahead.

Our special thanks to Robert Pawlik of Harcourt Brace Jovanovich for his helpful survey of readings for freshman composition, to William Parker for letting us tap three articles in his collection, and to our colleagues for listening and suggestions.

JO RAY MC CUEN AND ANTHONY C. WINKLER

*From "Take This Fish and Look at It" by Samuel H. Scudder, p. 103.

CONTENTS

part 2 Writing

THEMATIC TABLE OF CONTENTS

Man and Woman

American Values

Education

Literature and the Arts

Philosophy and Religion

Thinking

Social Problems

Portrait of the Individual

Readings for Writers

second edition

part 1
Prewriting

What Do You Mean by Rhetoric?

advice

PAUL ROBERTS

HOW TO SAY NOTHING IN FIVE HUNDRED WORDS

The author of this article was a well-known linguist and teacher. In it he describes the common enemy of the freshman, the five-hundred-word essay, and gives some advice on how to write it.

1 It's Friday afternoon, and you have almost survived another week of classes. You are just looking forward dreamily to the weekend when the English instructor says: "For Monday you will turn in a five-hundred-word composition on college football."

2 Well, that puts a good hole in the weekend. You don't have any strong views on college football one way or the other. You get rather excited during the season and go to all the home games and find it rather more fun than not. On the other hand, the class has been reading Robert Hutchins in the anthology and perhaps Shaw's "Eighty-Yard Run," and from the class discussion you have got the idea that the instructor thinks college football is for the birds. You are no fool. You can figure out what side to take.

3 After dinner you get out the portable typewriter that you got for high school graduation. You might as well get it over with and enjoy Saturday and Sunday. Five hundred words is about two double-spaced pages with normal margins. You put in a sheet of paper, think up a title, and you're off:

WHY COLLEGE FOOTBALL SHOULD BE ABOLISHED

4   College football should be abolished because it's bad for the school and also bad for the players. The players are so busy practicing that they don't have any time for their studies.

This, you feel, is a mighty good start. The only trouble is that it's only thirty-two words. You still have four hundred and sixty-eight to go, and you've pretty well exhausted the subject. It comes to you that you do your best thinking in the morning, so you put away the typewriter and go to the movies. But the next morning you have to do your washing and some math problems, and in the afternoon you go to the game. The English instructor turns up too, and you wonder if you've taken the right side after all. Saturday night you have a date, and Sunday morning you have to go to church. (You can't let English assignments interfere with your religion.) What with one thing and another, it's ten o'clock Sunday night before you get out the typewriter again. You make a pot of coffee and start to fill out your views on college football. Put a little meat on the bones.

WHY COLLEGE FOOTBALL SHOULD BE ABOLISHED

5   In my opinion, it seems to me that college football should be abolished. The reason why I think this to be true is because I feel that football is bad for the colleges in nearly every respect. As Robert Hutchins says in his article in our anthology in which he discusses college football, it would be better if the colleges had race horses and had races with one another, because then the horses would not have to attend classes. I firmly agree with Mr. Hutchins on this point, and I am sure that many other students would agree too.

6   One reason why it seems to me that college football is bad is that it has become too commercial. In the olden times when people played football just for the fun of it, maybe college football was all right, but they do not play football just for the fun of it now as they used to in the old days. Nowadays college football is what you might call a big business. Maybe this is not true at all schools, and I don't think it is especially true here at State, but certainly this is the case at most colleges and universities in America nowadays, as Mr. Hutchins points out in his very interesting article. Actually the coaches and alumni go around to the high schools and offer the high school stars large salaries to come to their colleges and play football for them. There was one case where a high school star was offered a convertible if he would play football for a certain college.

7   Another reason for abolishing college football is that it is bad for the players. They do not have time to get a college education, because they are so busy playing football. A football player has to practice every afternoon from three to six and then he is so tired that he can't concentrate on his studies. He just feels like dropping off to sleep after dinner, and then the next day he goes to his classes without having studied and maybe he fails the test.

(Good ripe stuff so far, but you're still a hundred and fifty-one words from home. One more push.)

8   Also I think college football is bad for the colleges and the universities because not very many students get to participate in it. Out of a college of ten thousand students only seventy-five or a hundred play football, if that many. Football is what you might call a spectator sport. That means that most people go to watch it but do not play it themselves.

(Four hundred and fifteen. Well, you still have the conclusion, and when you retype it, you can make the margins a little wider.)

9   These are the reasons why I agree with Mr. Hutchins that college football should be abolished in American colleges and universities.

10 On Monday you turn it in, moderately hopeful, and on Friday it comes back marked "weak in content" and sporting a big "D."

11 This essay is exaggerated a little, not much. The English instructor will recognize it as reasonably typical of what an assignment on college football will bring in. He knows that nearly half of the class will contrive in five hundred words to say that college football is too commercial and bad for the players. Most of the other half will inform him that college football builds character and prepares one for life and brings prestige to the school. As he reads paper after paper all saying the same thing in almost the same words, all bloodless, five hundred words dripping out of nothing, he wonders how he allowed himself to get trapped into teaching English when he might have had a happy and interesting life as an electrician or a confidence man.

12 Well, you may ask, what can you do about it? The subject is one on which you have few convictions and little information. Can you be expected to make a dull subject interesting? As a matter of fact, this is precisely what you are expected to do. This is the writer's essential task. All subjects, except sex, are dull until somebody makes them interesting. The writer's job is to find the argument, the approach, the angle, the wording that will take the reader with him. This is seldom easy, and it is particularly hard in subjects that have been much discussed: College Football, Fraternities, Popular Music, Is Chivalry Dead?, and the like. You will feel that there is nothing you can do with such subjects except repeat the old bromides. But there are some things you can do which will make your papers, if not throbbingly alive, at least less insufferably tedious than they might otherwise be.

Avoid the Obvious Content

13 Say the assignment is college football. Say that you've decided to be against it. Begin by putting down the arguments that come to your mind: it is too commercial, it takes the students' minds off their studies, it is hard on the players, it makes the university a kind of circus instead of an intellectual center, for most schools it is financially ruinous. Can you think of any more arguments, just off hand? All right. Now when you write your paper, *make sure that you don't use any of the material on this list*. If these are the points that leap to your mind, they will leap to everyone else's too, and whether you get a "C" or a "D" may depend on whether the instructor reads your paper early when he is fresh and tolerant or late, when the sentence "In my opinion, college football has become too commercial," inexorably repeated, has brought him to the brink of lunacy.

14 Be against college football for some reason or reasons of your own. If

they are keen and perceptive ones, that's splendid. But even if they are trivial or foolish or indefensible, you are still ahead so long as they are not everybody else's reasons too. Be against it because the colleges don't spend enough money on it to make it worthwhile, because it is bad for the characters of the spectators, because the players are forced to attend classes, because the football stars hog all the beautiful women, because it competes with baseball and is therefore un-American and possibly Communist-inspired. There are lots of more or less unused reasons for being against college football.

15 Sometimes it is a good idea to sum up and dispose of the trite and conventional points before going on to your own. This has the advantage of indicating to the reader that you are going to be neither trite nor conventional. Something like this:

16   We are often told that college football should be abolished because it has become too commercial or because it is bad for the players. These arguments are no doubt very cogent, but they don't really go to the heart of the matter.

Then you go to the heart of the matter.

Take the Less Usual Side

17 One rather simple way of getting into your paper is to take the side of the argument that most of the citizens will want to avoid. If the assignment is an essay on dogs, you can, if you choose, explain that dogs are faithful and lovable companions, intelligent, useful as guardians of the house and protectors of children, indispensable in police work—in short, when all is said and done, man's best friends. Or you can suggest that those big brown eyes conceal, more often than not, a vacuity of mind and an inconstancy of purpose; that the dogs you have known most intimately have been mangy, ill-tempered brutes, incapable of instruction; and that only your nobility of mind and fear of arrest prevent you from kicking the flea-ridden animals when you pass them on the street.

18 Naturally personal convictions will sometimes dictate your approach. If the assigned subject is "Is Methodism Rewarding to the Individual?" and you are a pious Methodist, you have really no choice. But few assigned subjects, if any, will fall in this category. Most of them will lie in broad areas of discussion with much to be said on both sides. They are intellectual exercises, and it is legitimate to argue now one way and now another, as debaters do in similar circumstances. Always take the side that looks to you hardest, least defensible. It will almost always turn out to be easier to write interestingly on that side.

19 This general advice applies where you have a choice of subjects. If you are to choose among "The Value of Fraternities" and "My Favorite High School Teacher" and "What I Think About Beetles," by all means plump for the beetles. By the time the instructor gets to your paper, he will be up to his ears in tedious tales about the French teacher at Bloombury High and assertions about how fraternities build character and prepare one for life.

Your views on beetles, whatever they are, are bound to be a refreshing change.

20 Don't worry too much about figuring out what the instructor thinks about the subject so that you can cuddle up with him. Chances are his views are no stronger than yours. If he does have convictions and you oppose him, his problem is to keep from grading you higher than you deserve in order to show he is not biased. This doesn't mean that you should always cantankerously dissent from what the instructor says; that gets tiresome too. And if the subject assigned is "My Pet Peeve," do not begin, "My pet peeve is the English instructor who assigns papers on 'my pet peeve.'" This was still funny during the War of 1812, but it has sort of lost its edge since then. It is in general good manners to avoid personalities.

Slip Out of Abstraction

21 If you will study the essay on college football [near the beginning of this essay], you will perceive that one reason for its appalling dullness is that it never gets down to particulars. It is just a series of not very glittering generalities: "football is bad for the colleges," "it has become too commercial," "football is a big business," "it is bad for the players," and so on. Such round phrases thudding against the reader's brain are unlikely to convince him, though they may well render him unconscious.

22 If you want the reader to believe that college football is bad for the players, you have to do more than say so. You have to display the evil. Take your roommate, Alfred Simkins, the second-string center. Picture poor old Alfy coming home from football practice every evening, bruised and aching, agonizingly tired, scarcely able to shovel the mashed potatoes into his mouth. Let us see him staggering up to the room, getting out his econ textbook, peering desperately at it with his good eye, falling asleep and failing the test in the morning. Let us share his unbearable tension as Saturday draws near. Will he fail, be demoted, lose his monthly allowance, be forced to return to the coal mines? And if he succeeds, what will be his reward? Perhaps a slight ripple of applause when the third-string center replaces him, a moment of elation in the locker room if the team wins, of despair if it loses. What will he look back on when he graduates from college? Toil and torn ligaments. And what will be his future? He is not good enough for pro football, and he is too obscure and weak in econ to succeed in stocks and bonds. College football is tearing the heart from Alfy Simkins and, when it finishes with him, will callously toss aside the shattered hulk.

23 This is no doubt a weak enough argument for the abolition of college football, but it is a sight better than saying, in three or four variations, that college football (in your opinion) is bad for the players.

24 Look at the work of any professional writer and notice how constantly he is moving from the generality, the abstract statement, to the concrete example, the facts and figures, the illustrations. If he is writing on juvenile delinquency, he does not just tell you that juveniles are (it seems to him)

delinquent and that (in his opinion) something should be done about it. He shows you juveniles being delinquent, tearing up movie theatres in Buffalo, stabbing high school principals in Dallas, smoking marijuana in Palo Alto. And more than likely he is moving toward some specific remedy, not just a general wringing of the hands.

25 It is no doubt possible to be *too* concrete, too illustrative or anecdotal, but few inexperienced writers err this way. For most the soundest advice is to be seeking always for the picture, to be always turning general remarks into seeable examples. Don't say, "Sororities teach girls the social graces." Say, "Sorority life teaches a girl how to carry on a conversation while pouring tea, without sloshing the tea into the saucer." Don't say, "I like certain kinds of popular music very much." Say, "Whenever I hear Gerber Sprinklittle play 'Mississippi Man' on the trombone, my socks creep up my ankles."

Get Rid of Obvious Padding

26 The student toiling away at his weekly English theme is too often tormented by a figure: five hundred words. How, he asks himself, is he to achieve this staggering total? Obviously by never using one word when he can somehow work in ten.

27 He is therefore seldom content with a plain statement like "Fast driving is dangerous." This has only four words in it. He takes thought, and the sentence becomes:

> In my opinion, fast driving is dangerous.

Better, but he can do better still:

> In my opinion, fast driving would seem to be rather dangerous.

If he is really adept, it may come out:

> In my humble opinion, though I do not claim to be an expert on this complicated subject, fast driving, in most circumstances, would seem to be rather dangerous in many respects, or at least so it would seem to me.

Thus four words have been turned into forty, and not an iota of content has been added.

28 Now this is a way to go about reaching five hundred words, and if you are content with a "D" grade, it is as good a way as any. But if you aim higher, you must work differently. Instead of stuffing your sentences with straw, you must try steadily to get rid of the padding, to make your sentences lean and tough. If you are really working at it, your first draft will greatly exceed the required total, and then you will work it down, thus:

29   It is thought in some quarters that fraternities do not contribute as much as might be expected to campus life.

30   Some people think that fraternities contribute little to campus life.
    The average doctor who practices in small towns or in the country must toil night and day to heal the sick.

31   Most country doctors work long hours.
      When I was a little girl, I suffered from shyness and embarrassment in the presence of others.
32   I was a shy little girl.
      It is absolutely necessary for the person employed as a marine fireman to give the matter of steam pressure his undivided attention at all times.
      The fireman has to keep his eye on the steam gauge.

33 You may ask how you can arrive at five hundred words at this rate. Simple. You dig up more real content. Instead of taking a couple of obvious points off the surface of the topic and then circling warily around them for six paragraphs, you work in and explore, figure out the details. You illustrate. You say that fast driving is dangerous, and then you prove it. How long does it take to stop a car at forty and at eighty? How far can you see at night? What happens when a tire blows? What happens in a head-on collision at fifty miles an hour? Pretty soon your paper will be full of broken glass and blood and headless torsos, and reaching five hundred words will not really be a problem.

Call a Fool a Fool

34 Some of the padding in freshman themes is to be blamed not on anxiety about the word minimum but on excessive timidity. The student writes, "In my opinion, the principal of my high school acted in ways that I believe every unbiased person would have to call foolish." This isn't exactly what he means. What he means is, "My high school principal was a fool." If he was a fool, call him a fool. Hedging the thing about with "in-my-opinion's" and "it-seems-to-me's" and "as-I-see-it's" and "at-least-from-my-point-of-view's" gains you nothing. Delete these phrases whenever they creep into your paper.

35 The student's tendency to hedge stems from a modesty that in other circumstances would be commendable. He is, he realizes, young and inexperienced, and he half suspects that he is dopey and fuzzy-minded beyond the average. Probably only too true. But it doesn't help to announce your incompetence six times in every paragraph. Decide what you want to say and say it as vigorously as possible, without apology and in plain words.

36 Linguistic diffidence can take various forms. One is what we call *euphemism*. This is the tendency to call a spade "a certain garden implement" or women's underwear "unmentionables." It is stronger in some eras than others and in some people than others but it always operates more or less in subjects that are touchy or taboo: death, sex, madness, and so on. Thus we shrink from saying "He died last night" but say instead "passed away," "left us," "joined his Maker," "went to his reward." Or we try to take off the tension with a lighter cliché: "kicked the bucket," "cashed in his chips," "handed in his dinner pail." We have found all sorts of ways to avoid saying *mad*: "mentally ill," "touched," "not quite right upstairs," "feeble-minded," "innocent," "simple," "off his trolley," "not in his right mind." Even such a now plain word as *insane* began as a euphemism with the meaning "not healthy."

37 Modern science, particularly psychology, contributes many polysyllables in which we can wrap our thoughts and blunt their force. To many writers there is no such thing as a bad schoolboy. Schoolboys are maladjusted or unoriented or misunderstood or in the need of guidance or lacking in continued success toward satisfactory integration of the personality as a social unit, but they are never bad. Psychology no doubt makes us better men and women, more sympathetic and tolerant, but it doesn't make writing any easier. Had Shakespeare been confronted with psychology, "To be or not to be" might have come out, "To continue as a social unit or not to do so. That is the personality problem. Whether 'tis a better sign of integration at the conscious level to display a psychic tolerance toward the maladjustments and repressions induced by one's lack of orientation in one's environment or—" But Hamlet would never have finished the soliloquy.

38 Writing in the modern world, you cannot altogether avoid modern jargon. Nor, in an effort to get away from euphemism, should you salt your paper with four-letter words. But you can do much if you will mount guard against those roundabout phrases, those echoing polysyllables that tend to slip into your writing to rob it of its crispness and force.

Beware of Pat Expressions

39 Other things being equal, avoid phrases like "other things being equal." Those sentences that come to you whole, or in two or three doughy lumps, are sure to be bad sentences. They are no creation of yours but pieces of common thought floating in the community soup.

40 Pat expressions are hard, often impossible, to avoid, because they come too easily to be noticed and seem too necessary to be dispensed with. No writer avoids them altogether, but good writers avoid them more often than poor writers.

41 By "pat expressions" we mean such tags as "to all practical intents and purposes," "the pure and simple truth," "from where I sit," "the time of his life," "to the ends of the earth," "in the twinkling of an eye," "as sure as you're born," "over my dead body," "under cover of darkness," "took the easy way out," "when all is said and done," "told him time and time again," "parted the best of friends," "stand up and be counted," "gave him the best years of her life," "worked her fingers to the bone." Like other clichés, these expressions were once forceful. Now we should use them only when we can't possibly think of anything else.

42 Some pat expressions stand like a wall between the writer and thought. Such a one is "the American way of life." Many student writers feel that when they have said that something accords with the American way of life or does not they have exhausted the subject. Actually, they have stopped at the highest level of abstraction. The American way of life is the complicated set of bonds between a hundred and eighty million ways. All of us know this when we think about it, but the tag phrase too often keeps us from thinking about it.

43 So with many another phrase dear to the politician: "this great land of

ours," "the man in the street," "our national heritage." These may prove our patriotism or give a clue to our political beliefs, but otherwise they add nothing to the paper except words.

Colorful Words

44 The writer builds with words, and no builder uses a raw material more slippery and elusive and treacherous. A writer's work is a constant struggle to get the right word in the right place, to find that particular word that will convey his meaning exactly, that will persuade the reader or soothe him or startle or amuse him. He never succeeds altogether—sometimes he feels that he scarcely succeeds at all—but such successes as he has are what make the thing worth doing.

45 There is no book of rules for this game. One progresses through everlasting experiment on the basis of ever-widening experience. There are few useful generalizations that one can make about words as words, but there are perhaps a few.

46 Some words are what we call "colorful." By this we mean that they are calculated to produce a picture or induce an emotion. They are dressy instead of plain, specific instead of general, loud instead of soft. Thus, in place of "Her heart beat," we may write, "Her heart *pounded, throbbed, fluttered, danced.*" Instead of "He sat in his chair," we may say, "He *lounged, sprawled, coiled.*" Instead of "It was hot," we may say, "It was *blistering, sultry, muggy, suffocating, steamy, wilting.*"

47 However, it should not be supposed that the fancy word is always better. Often it is as well to write "Her heart beat" or "It was hot" if that is all it did or all it was. Ages differ in how they like their prose. The nineteenth century liked it rich and smoky. The twentieth has usually preferred it lean and cool. The twentieth century writer, like all writers, is forever seeking the exact word, but he is wary of sounding feverish. He tends to pitch it low, to understate it, to throw it away. He knows that if he gets too colorful, the audience is likely to giggle.

48 See how this strikes you: "As the rich, golden glow of the sunset died away along the eternal western hills, Angela's limpid blue eyes looked softly and trustingly into Montague's flashing brown ones, and her heart pounded like a drum in time with the joyous song surging in her soul." Some people like that sort of thing, but most modern readers would say, "Good grief," and turn on the television.

Colored Words

49 Some words we would call not so much colorful as colored—that is, loaded with associations, good or bad. All words—except perhaps structure words—have associations of some sort. We have said that the meaning of a word is the sum of the contexts in which it occurs. When we hear a word, we hear with it an echo of all the situations in which we have heard it before.

50 In some words, these echoes are obvious and discussable. The word *mother*, for example, has, for most people, agreeable associations. When you hear *mother* you probably think of home, safety, love, food, and various other pleasant things. If one writes, "She was like a mother to me," he gets an effect which he would not get in "She was like an aunt to me." The advertiser makes use of the associations of *mother* by working it in when he talks about his product. The politician works it in when he talks about himself.

51 So also with such words as *home, liberty, fireside, contentment, patriot, tenderness, sacrifice, childlike, manly, bluff, limpid.* All of these words are loaded with associations that would be rather hard to indicate in a straightforward definition. There is more than a literal difference between "They sat around the fireside" and "They sat around the stove." They might have been equally warm and happy around the stove, but *fireside* suggests leisure, grace, quiet tradition, congenial company, and *stove* does not.

52 Conversely, some words have bad associations. *Mother* suggests pleasant things, but *mother-in-law* does not. Many mothers-in-law are heroically lovable and some mothers drink gin all day and beat their children insensible, but these facts of life are beside the point. The point is that *mother* sounds good and *mother-in-law* does not.

53 Or consider the word *intellectual.* This would seem to be a complimentary term, but in point of fact it is not, for it has picked up associations of impracticality and ineffectuality and general dopiness. So also such words as *liberal, reactionary, Communist, socialist, capitalist, radical, schoolteacher, truck driver, undertaker, operator, salesman, huckster, speculator.* These convey meaning on the literal level, but beyond that—sometimes, in some places—they convey contempt on the part of the speaker.

54 The question of whether to use loaded words or not depends on what is being written. The scientist, the scholar, try to avoid them; for the poet, the advertising writer, the public speaker, they are standard equipment. But every writer should take care that they do not substitute for thought. If you write, "Anyone who thinks that is nothing but a Socialist (or Communist or capitalist)" you have said nothing except that you don't like people who think that, and such remarks are effective only with the most naive readers. It is always a bad mistake to think your readers more naive than they really are.

Colorless Words

55 But probably most student writers come to grief not with words that are colorful or those that are colored but with those that have no color at all. A pet example is *nice,* a word we would find it hard to dispense with in casual conversation but which is no longer capable of adding much to a description. Colorless words are those of such general meaning that in a particular sentence they mean nothing. Slang adjectives like *cool* ("That's real cool") tend to explode all over the language. They are applied to everything, lose their original force, and quickly die.

56 Beware also of nouns of very general meaning, like *circumstances,*

cases, instances, aspects, factors, relationships, attitudes, eventualities, etc. In most circumstances you will find that those cases of writing which contain too many instances of words like these will in this and other aspects have factors leading to unsatisfactory relationships with the reader resulting in unfavorable attitudes on his part and perhaps other eventualities, like a grade of "D." Notice also what "etc." means. It means "I'd like to make this list longer, but I can't think of any more examples."

VOCABULARY*

contrive (11)	diffidence (36)
bromides (12)	euphemism (36)
inexorably (13)	jargon (38)
cogent (16)	polysyllables (38)
vacuity (17)	elusive (44)
warily (33)	induce (46)

discussion

JOHN E. JORDAN

RHETORIC

This article describes how we slander rhetoric by downgrading its value. It then gives a historical and etymological definition of rhetoric, argues our need for more of it, and shows how it differs from grammar or usage. (From *Using Rhetoric*.)

1 Some readers will be nearly as surprised to be told that they regularly practice the ancient art of rhetoric as was Molière's famous character to learn that all his life he had been speaking prose. For the word "rhetoric" is likely· to be associated vaguely in our memories with elocutionary posturing and to survive chiefly in the pejorative sense of flowery rhetoric. Or remembering that a rhetorical question does not really intend an answer, we may stigmatize rhetoric as suspiciously sophistical. Thus rhetoric may connote to us either something empty or something false, and at any rate something remote from our affairs, all the while that we are using it, well or badly.

2 Historically, rhetoric has been much respected and cultivated. Aristotle wrote a treatise on it, and in Athens of the second century the sophist, or professor of rhetoric, was one of the leading citizens. Cicero and Quintilian were famous Roman rhetoricians. Undergraduate education in medieval times consisted chiefly of the *trivium:* grammar, logic, and rhetoric. Training in rhetoric was an important part of the university curriculum in the Renais-

*Number in parentheses indicates paragraph in which word is found.

sance, and as late as the nineteenth century, colleges had departments of rhetoric. Nowadays, aspects of the subject are distributed among departments of philosophy, psychology, sociology, English, speech, and dramatic arts, and although deprived of its prominence among the academic disciplines and scarcely recognized by its old name, rhetoric still continues to be an important activity.

3 Etymologically, rhetoric meant the art of oratory; it came to mean the art or science of persuasion. Now it is apparent that we all use language to persuade—ourselves as well as others. Even if our primary purpose is to express ourselves or to communicate information, in so far as we have a hearer or reader, we are seeking to persuade him to take a certain attitude toward what we say. All of the marshaling of an argument, the structuring of a statement, the shaping of a paragraph, the molding of a sentence, and the choosing of a word toward a purposeful end is rhetoric.

The Place of Rhetoric

4 Anywhere, except possibly in a Trappist monastery, rhetoric is one of the facts of life. For most people there is a better, more effective way to speak and write—and a need to know how to find it. On one level we recognize the success of the smooth talker, although our traditional image of ourselves as laconic men of action makes us scorn and fear his verbal felicity. One of the paradoxes of our culture is that we admire the strong silent types, while the yap of our radio and TV chokes the ether. We have to realize that an apotheosis of the power of our physical action is not adequate to our needs as individuals or as a nation. Gradually, I think, we are coming to this awareness. I was asked some time ago to teach courses in writing at a research corporation because their scientists, highly trained and intelligent men most of whom were Ph.D.'s, could not get their discoveries across to the vice presidents! Quintilian would have said that they needed to study rhetoric. The term has gone out of favor, but the need remains to be able to express our ideas, to communicate our wishes, to sell our concepts. We are recognizing now that the United States is not gaining friends around the world or making known what is really important about our way of life by producing better refrigerators. The Peace Corps program includes, along with training in techniques of irrigation and other operations valuable to undeveloped areas, training in language—in how to talk about democracy with meaning and persuasion. Aristotle would have said that these young people need a course in rhetoric.

5 A student once protested to me that he did not want to learn to write like Shakespeare. Although I assured him that he was in no such danger, I regretted his attitude, for what he meant was that he did not think it important for him to make any special effort to rise above the routine and trite. Aside from the small group who perennially aspire to write the great American novel, most Americans are modest in their attitude toward writing. They do not expect to write like Shakespeare or even very well at all. If they do not exactly feel the ancestral contempt for the smooth talker, they are likely to

leave writing to Bohemian eggheads. One of the interesting phenomena of recent years has been the articulateness of the "beat" fringe of college generations. Student publications have tended to be *avant garde* partly because the solid, conservative elements in the student body did not feel that writing was their business. My scientist students at the research corporation had erroneously felt that writing was not their business. Probably the young people who join the Peace Corps, for the most part, have not realized the extent to which writing and speaking must be their business.

6 In our culture effective communication is nearly everybody's business, and from politics to love rhetoric shows a power we must recognize. We Americans tend to scoff at political oratory; nevertheless, we have seen a presidential election influenced materially, perhaps crucially, by a series of television debates. We have never fancied ourselves as great lovers, but we bestow that distinction on the French—a more articulate people. A nation which has built its economy on the persuasion of the "hard sell" and the "soft sell" cannot afford the belittling point of view expressed by one of Alberto Moravia's heroes: "And I am, in fact, inclined to rhetoric—that is, to the substitution of words for deeds."[1] Rhetoric *is* action, a more subtle kind of action, by which words often beget deeds.

7 At one end of its range rhetoric is concerned with the ordering of ideas: Aristotle said that rhetoric was merely popular logic. At the other end it is concerned with the presentation of ideas in language. Except perhaps in symbolic logic, the two ends are interrelated. Because rhetoric is concerned with the best use of language, it has connections with grammar. Some of these relations will appear later in this book, although we shall be concerned primarily with rhetoric.

8 The use of language is controlled by three factors: grammar, rhetoric, and usage. Grammar is the science of what is *permissible* in the language, rhetoric is the art of what is *effective*. Grammar concerns itself with the possible ways of saying something, rhetoric with the best way. A writer or speaker in choosing the best way must necessarily select from among the possible ways—he must know grammar. His choice must also be influenced by usage, the pattern of ways in which people actually use the language in any time, place, and circumstance. Over the history of the language, usage is the source of grammar; but in any given circle, usage rarely involves all the grammatical resources of the language.

9 For a simple example of the way in which these three elements work, suppose that a man wanted to say that he was named John. A Frenchman would find it natural to say, "I call myself John"; an American might say, "My name is John." One is no better than the other absolutely, but in English "I call myself John" would not mean the same thing as "My name is John"; it would suggest an assumed name or some other peculiarity in the situation. "I call myself John" is not ungrammatical, but it is outside the idioms sanctioned

[1] Alberto Moravia, *Conjugal Love* (New York: Signet Books, New American Library of World Literature, Inc., 1961), p. 11.—Ed.

by usage. "I John myself call" would be ungrammatical because it would be meaningless; it does not conform to any English pattern. "John is my name," on the other hand, would be a possible English formulation, not essentially different in meaning from "My name is John," but different in emphasis. Modern usage makes no distinction between the two forms, and a choice between them would have to be made entirely on rhetorical grounds— probably on whether "my" was important. Usage would influence the rhetorical decision, however, in the choice between "I am named John," "I am John," and "I'm John." For here is a range from formal to informal usage.

10 Rhetoric, then, exploits grammar and usage. The writer who seeks the most effective expression must know the resources of the language; he must know the rules of grammar and usage.

VOCABULARY

pejorative (1)	felicity (4)
stigmatize (1)	ether (4)
sophistical (1)	apotheosis (4)
sophist (2)	aspire (5)
etymologically (3)	avant garde (5)
marshaling (3)	articulate (adj.) (6)
laconic (4)	idioms (9)

QUESTIONS ON CONTENT

1. What is rhetoric? What are its uses?
2. Why are most Americans modest in their attitude toward writing?
3. What three factors determine the use of language?
4. What is the difference between grammar and rhetoric?
5. What influences a writer's rhetorical choices? Explain how the influence works.

QUESTIONS ON FORM

1. The author sets out to define the meaning of "rhetoric." How does he accomplish this? Does he give a dictionary definition? Does he give examples of "rhetoric"?
2. What is the purpose of the first paragraph in this essay?
3. The author writes: "A student once protested to me that he did not want to learn to write like Shakespeare. Although I assured him that he was in no such danger, I regretted his attitude." What tone is the author using here?
4. In paragraph 3 the author gives the etymological meaning of the word "rhetoric." What is an etymological meaning? What use has such a meaning in the context of this essay?

SUGGESTIONS FOR WRITING

1. Definitions will frequently give a lexical meaning of a term, state its history, show its function, and give examples of it. Analyze and discuss the structure of this article with the above in mind.

2. The author says that the word "rhetoric" has been stigmatized unfairly. Note the meanings of the word "rhetoric" in the following contexts:

(a) as it is used to describe a political speech

(b) as it is used by a woman to characterize her lover's verbal ardor

(c) as it is used by a buyer to describe the spiel of a used car salesman

Discuss these meanings and what they have in common.

MAXWELL FULLERTON

COMPOSITION AND LINGUISTIC REVOLUTION

A MODEST PROPOSAL FOR REFORMING THE TEACHING OF ENGLISH COMPOSITION

In this humorous article the author, who is in fact an English teacher, suggests a shortcut method of writing to avoid the drudgery of grammar, rhetoric, or thinking. He points out, by implication, some of the difficulties in learning how to write well.

1 It may seem strange that this proposal should come from one who is neither a teacher nor a linguist, but a businessman; and it is with respect for the better judgment of those actually engaged in teaching composition that I offer my proposal. But we in business do have a direct interest in the training colleges give their graduates, and it sometimes happens that a more detached view will offer clear solutions to problems that seem insoluble close at hand.

2 Universities have recently sent thousands of questionnaires to alumni, employers, faculty members, and students, asking them to evaluate the training students receive in college. For the most part, the results of these questionnaires confirm the colleges in their present practices. But there is one striking exception: no one is satisfied with the training in English composition. Alumni and employers agree that the graduates of our colleges are unable to do the writing required of the average businessman. Students themselves complain that they "don't know what the instructor wants" or they "don't get anything out of the course." Faculty members in other departments are unanimous in their judgment that the students seem to have learned nothing in their composition courses; they write abominably. And even the English faculty—and I have interviewed a number of them—agree that the English composition program is not a success. They say, variously, that the high schools send out students totally unprepared for college English, that the students have no interest in the subject, or that they refuse to be taught.

3 Finding this universal dissatisfaction with the English composition program, are we not justified in looking for a cause more fundamental than the teaching methods practiced by a given instructor or the pattern of assignments established by a given department? The cause, I submit, is not educational—i.e., methodological—at all; it is linguistic. In the past fifty years a profound change has taken place in the structure of the English language. The change

has not gone unobserved by philologists, but its significance for the teaching of English has never been recognized. Perhaps an analogy will best illustrate this change. In industry, we have moved into an age of prefabrication. Buildings are no longer constructed stud by stud and nail by nail; parts are delivered in assembled units—whole sides or floors or roofs—needing only to be fitted together. A similar change has affected the use of language. In the world of business and politics, where men are alert to the latest and most economical practices, sentences are no longer constructed of single words, slowly and laboriously put together. Instead, sentences are built of prefabricated units; indeed, whole sentences may be plant-assembled, as it were, for the convenience of the user. Take this sentence, for example: "In reference to your request concerning a consignment of assembly units (Catalogue No. BP-17369), I regret to inform you that we are unable to comply with your wishes at this time due to unforeseen delays in meeting our production schedules." Note that there are only two units here: the one preceding the comma and the one following. The first of these makes clear the subject under discussion, and the insertion of the catalogue number in the proper place is all that is required of the user. The second unit simply indicates a negative response and will apply to any situation. Should the response be positive, the sentence would run this way: "In reference to your request concerning a consignment of assembly units (Catalogue No. BP-17369), we shall be happy to comply with your wishes with as much dispatch as our crowded production schedule will permit."

4 It is hardly necessary to argue the advantages of the new system of sentence construction. The prefabricated sentence now allows business executives to dictate as many as fifty-four letters an hour, a performance inconceivable as little as thirty-five years ago. I have estimated—I believe conservatively—that this device saves thirteen and one-half billion dollars annually in the salaries of business executives alone. If the saving could be calculated for the entire population, the figure, I am convinced, would exceed the annual budget of the federal government.

5 Considering the economy accruing to both the writer and the reader (for the prefabricated sentence has the same advantages for the reader as for the writer), it is no wonder that this device has been universally adopted by men in every occupation. English instructors are themselves enthusiastic merchants of prefabricated sentences, though there has been an almost unbelievable lag separating their own usage from their theory and practice in the classroom.

6 This brings us back to the problem at hand. It should now be clear why conventional English composition courses have produced universal dissatisfaction. Students, when they enter the classroom, have already learned, by an instinctive awareness of contemporary practice, to use the prefabricated sentence, albeit in a haphazard and clumsy way. Now, instead of encouraging this instinctive tendency and helping students to become really skillful users of this most modern of linguistic tools, the English instructor insists that the students go back to the old stud-and-nail method, putting single word beside single word and fitting them painstakingly to a grammatical blueprint. This is

like insisting that a student who is beginning to master the slide rule do all his problems by long division and multiplication. He is naturally confused. He wants to solve his problems as quickly and efficiently as possible, his time being valuable; yet he must please the instructor who corrects him every time he begins to use the slide rule—or the prefabricated sentence. He knows, subconsciously at least, that the instructor is wrong, that the economical way is the right way; yet he has been taught to respect, or at least to follow, the teacher's directions. The result in practice is that he wavers between the two systems, taking an inordinate amount of time with his writing and succeeding only in hammering together preshaped parts and loose units into a completely formless and unintelligible structure.

7 The only question remaining is how to bring this new linguistic development most effectively into the classroom. A plan suggests itself which will be as much a boon to the instructor as to the student. In my interviews with English faculty members, I have frequently heard instructors express envy for members of the mathematics department, for instance, where questions have definite answers and problems are either right or wrong. Precision of that sort is now possible in composition—for one of the byproducts of the linguistic revolution is the emergence of the science of composition. Here, it seems to me, is the natural classroom procedure: After explaining to the students the nature of the modern linguistic tools they are already familiar with in practice, the instructor should drill the students on specific problems: for instance, a letter expressing thanks for a donation to the Red Cross, or an interoffice memo requesting a new typewriter for a secretary. To problems of this sort, there can be only one right answer—though there may be some minor variations until standard texts have been adopted. Thus the instructor will be able to grade papers as rapidly as the mathematics instructor—indeed, more rapidly, because there are no thought processes to be traced through the problem. The advantage to the student will be immeasurable. He will now know what is expected of him. Language will no longer be something to piece together, revise, and polish until, mysteriously, a lucid whole emerges—or, more often, does not emerge. And when the student leaves college, equipped with a full complement of euphonious phrases for every occasion, he will really be prepared to take a responsible place in business.

8 I have discussed this proposal with several members of an English faculty, and though they admit the many conveniences of the plan, they raise one objection, which, at first glance, would seem to be formidable: that the plan would put an end to individual thought on the part of students. But a closer examination will show that this objection has little force. Employers have frequently been asked what particular quality they look for in college graduates seeking employment. The answer, without variation, is "personality" or "the ability to get along with people." Now, who will get along with people more successfully, the graduate who has learned to think for himself and is thus in danger of disagreeing with his fellow workers or disapproving of what they are doing, or the graduate who, laboring under no such handicap, can agree with everyone he meets and look with equal enthusiasm on every

enterprise? Thus, in addition to reducing the work of the instructor by at least three fourths and providing the student with some really useful language skills, this plan will greatly increase the student's chances for a happy adjustment in society.

VOCABULARY

philologists (3)   unintelligible (6)
accruing (5)   boon (7)
albeit (6)   euphonious (7)
inordinate (6)

QUESTIONS ON CONTENT

1. What is the prefabricated sentence?
2. According to paragraph 6, why do students write badly? Why do composition courses fail?
3. The author satirically writes: "Thus the instructor will be able to grade papers as rapidly as the mathematics instructor—indeed, more rapidly, because there are no thought processes to be traced through the problem." What does this imply about the real nature of writing?
4. What objection, according to the satire, do English teachers raise to this plan? How does the author answer these objections?
5. The author is in fact an English teacher. What, by implication, is he saying about the way businessmen use and write English?

QUESTIONS ON FORM

1. The author assumes the persona of a businessman. Why? What does the assumed persona contribute to the satire?
2. What is the significance of the subtitle of this article?
3. Examine the analogy in paragraphs 3 and 6. What is its purpose in the satire? What does its use tell about the persona?
4. The author writes: "English instructors are themselves enthusiastic merchants of prefabricated sentences, though there has been an almost unbelievable lag separating their own usage from their theory and practice in the classroom." Bearing in mind that the author is himself an English teacher, what tone do you think he is using here?
5. The success of this kind of satire depends on the reader's belief that the persona is sincerely well-meaning, if naive. What techniques does the author use to convince us that his persona is well-meaning?

SUGGESTIONS FOR WRITING

1. Discuss the idea, implicit in this satire, that good writing is based on clear and independent thinking.
2. By its inversion of the true state of things, satire usually implies the reality while

making fun of it. What is here being implied about Freshman English? Why is it so difficult to teach students how to write well? Are any real solutions implied in this satire? Reconstruct and discuss what seems to be the author's real view of the role of Freshman English.

examples

JOHN FITZGERALD KENNEDY

INAUGURAL ADDRESS

Language level and content will vary with the audience and occasion of its use. In this presidential Inaugural Address, we see an example of the formal use of language on a formal occasion.

1 Vice President Johnson, Mr. Speaker, Mr. Chief Justice, President Eisenhower, Vice President Nixon, President Truman, Reverend Clergy, fellow citizens: We observe today not a victory of party but a celebration of freedom—symbolizing an end as well as a beginning—signifying renewal as well as change. For I have sworn before you and Almighty God the same solemn oath our forebears prescribed nearly a century and three-quarters ago.

2 The world is very different now. For man holds in his mortal hands the power to abolish all forms of human poverty and all forms of human life. And yet the same revolutionary beliefs for which our forebears fought are still at issue around the globe—the belief that the rights of man come not from the generosity of the state but from the hand of God.

3 We dare not forget today that we are heirs of that first revolution. Let the word go forth from this time and place, to friend and foe alike, that the torch has been passed to a new generation of Americans—born in this century, tempered by war, disciplined by a hard and bitter peace, proud of our ancient heritage—and unwilling to witness or permit the slow undoing of those human rights to which this nation has always been committed, and to which we are committed today at home and around the world.

4 Let every nation know, whether it wishes us well or ill, that we shall pay any price, bear any burden, meet any hardship, support any friend, oppose any foe to assure the survival and the success of liberty.

5 This much we pledge—and more.

6 To those old allies whose cultural and spiritual origins we share, we pledge the loyalty of faithful friends. United, there is little we cannot do in a host of new cooperative ventures. Divided, there is little we can do—for we dare not meet a powerful challenge at odds and split asunder.

7 To those new states whom we welcome to the ranks of the free, we pledge our word that one form of colonial control shall not have passed away merely to be replaced by a far more iron tyranny. We shall not always expect

to find them supporting our view. But we shall always hope to find them strongly supporting their own freedom—and to remember that, in the past, those who foolishly sought power by riding the back of the tiger ended up inside.

8 To those peoples in the huts and villages of half the globe struggling to break the bonds of mass misery, we pledge our best efforts to help them help themselves, for whatever period is required—not because the Communists may be doing it, not because we seek their votes, but because it is right. If a free society cannot help the many who are poor, it cannot save the few who are rich.

9 To our sister republics south of our border, we offer a special pledge—to convert our good words into good deeds—in a new alliance for progress—to assist free men and free governments in casting off the chains of poverty. But this peaceful revolution of hope cannot become the prey of hostile powers. Let all our neighbors know that we shall join with them to oppose aggression or subversion anywhere in the Americas. And let every other power know that this hemisphere intends to remain the master of its own house.

10 To that world assembly of sovereign states, the United Nations, our last best hope in an age where the instruments of war have far outpaced the instruments of peace, we renew our pledge of support—to prevent it from becoming merely a forum for invective—to strengthen its shield of the new and the weak—and to enlarge the area in which its writ may run.

11 Finally, to those nations who would make themselves our adversary, we offer not a pledge but a request: that both sides begin anew the quest for peace, before the dark powers of destruction unleashed by science engulf all humanity in planned or accidental self-destruction.

12 We dare not tempt them with weakness. For only when our arms are sufficient beyond doubt can we be certain beyond doubt that they will never be employed.

13 But neither can two great and powerful groups of nations take comfort from our present course—both sides overburdened by the cost of modern weapons, both rightly alarmed by the steady spread of the deadly atom, yet both racing to alter that uncertain balance of terror that stays the hand of mankind's final war.

14 So let us begin anew—remembering on both sides that civility is not a sign of weakness, and sincerity is always subject to proof. Let us never negotiate out of fear. But let us never fear to negotiate.

15 Let both sides explore what problems unite us instead of belaboring those problems which divide us.

16 Let both sides, for the first time, formulate serious and precise proposals for the inspection and control of arms—and bring the absolute power to destroy other nations under the absolute control of all nations.

17 Let both sides seek to invoke the wonders of science instead of its terrors. Together let us explore the stars, conquer the deserts, eradicate disease, tap the ocean depths and encourage the arts and commerce.

18 Let both sides unite to heed in all corners of the earth the command of Isaiah—to "undo the heavy burdens . . . [and] let the oppressed go free."

19 And if a beach-head of co-operation may push back the jungles of suspicion, let both sides join in creating a new endeavor—not a new balance of power, but a new world of law, where the strong are just and the weak secure and the peace preserved.

20 All this will not be finished in the first 100 days. Nor will it be finished in the first 1000 days, nor in the life of this Administration, nor even perhaps in our lifetime on this planet. But let us begin.

21 In your hands, my fellow citizens, more than mine, will rest the final success or failure of our course. Since this country was founded, each generation of Americans has been summoned to give testimony to its national loyalty. The graves of young Americans who answered the call to service surround the globe.

22 Now the trumpet summons us again—not as a call to bear arms, though arms we need—not as a call to battle, though embattled we are—but a call to bear the burden of a long twilight struggle year in and year out, "rejoicing in hope, patient in tribulation"—a struggle against the common enemies of man: tyranny, poverty, disease and war itself.

23 Can we forge against these enemies a grand and global alliance, north and south, east and west, that can assure a more fruitful life for all mankind? Will you join in that historic effort?

24 In the long history of the world, only a few generations have been granted the role of defending freedom in its hour of maximum danger. I do not shrink from this responsibility—I welcome it. I do not believe that any of us would exchange places with any other people or any other generation. The energy, the faith, the devotion which we bring to this endeavor will light our country and all who serve it—and the glow from that fire can truly light the world.

25 And so, my fellow Americans: ask not what your country can do for you—ask what you can do for your country.

26 My fellow citizens of the world: ask not what America will do for you, but what together we can do for the freedom of man.

27 Finally, whether you are citizens of America or citizens of the world, ask of us here the same high standards of strength and sacrifice which we ask of you. With a good conscience our only sure reward, with history the final judge of our deeds, let us go forth to lead the land we love, asking His blessing and His help, but knowing that here on earth God's work must truly be our own.

VOCABULARY

forebears (1)	invective (10)
prescribed (1)	civility (14)
asunder (6)	eradicate (17)
aggression (9)	

QUESTIONS ON CONTENT

1. What is the revolutionary belief our forebears fought for and which, according to the President, is still at issue around the world? What is our attitude toward this belief? By implication, what is the opposite side's attitude toward it?
2. The President says that this generation is "unwilling to witness or permit the slow undoing of those human rights to which this nation has always been committed." What does he mean by that? Do "human rights" vary from one culture to another, or are "human rights" absolute and the same for all cultures and all peoples?
3. What is the President's message to "those nations who would make themselves our adversary"? Is it militant? Defiant? Conciliatory? Characterize its tone.
4. Why, according to the President, should we help poorer nations? Because the Communists are helping them? How would you characterize our implied motive? As selfless? As self-interested? Explain.
5. The President ends his speech by saying that "here on earth God's work must truly be our own." What does he mean by that? Is he saying that God is on our side? That we are on God's side? What does that phrase imply about our self-image as a people at the time the speech was delivered?

QUESTIONS ON FORM

1. Who is the intended audience of this speech? Is it meant to be heard only by those people mentioned in the opening paragraph? Only by Americans? Explain.
2. What is the effect of the references to God in the speech? What purpose do they serve?
3. How would you characterize the diction and phrasing of this speech? As simple and direct? Lofty and metaphorical? How is its diction affected by the occasion and audience of this speech?
4. Here is a balanced sentence: "The memory of other authors is kept alive by their works; but the memory of Johnson keeps many of his works alive"—Macaulay. Find an example of a balanced sentence in the Inaugural Address.
5. A rhetorical question is a question asked for effect rather than in expectation of an answer. Are there any rhetorical questions in the text of the Inaugural Address? Cite them.

SUGGESTIONS FOR WRITING

1. Without substantially altering its message, rewrite paragraphs 18 through 27 of the Inaugural Address in the style, diction, and idiom of your everyday informal speech.
2. Discuss the following statement pro or con: Human rights come not from the state, but from God.

MARK TWAIN

ADVICE TO YOUTH, ABOUT 1882

In contrast to the Inaugural Address, this speech by Mark Twain (the pen name of Samuel Clemens) was given to an audience of young people. In it Twain skillfully focuses his humor to appeal to the interests of his audience.

This speech exemplifies how the good speaker (and writer) will vary his content and style to meet the demands of his audience.

1 Being told I would be expected to talk here, I inquired what sort of a talk I ought to make. They said it should be something suitable to youth—something didactic, instructive, or something in the nature of good advice. Very well. I have a few things in my mind which I have often longed to say for the instruction of the young; for it is in one's tender early years that such things will best take root and be most enduring and most valuable. First, then, I will say to you, my young friends—and I say it beseechingly, urgingly—

2 Always obey your parents, when they are present. This is the best policy in the long run, because if you don't they will make you. Most parents think they know better than you do, and you can generally make more by humoring that superstition than you can by acting on your own better judgment.

3 Be respectful to your superiors, if you have any, also to strangers, and sometimes to others. If a person offend you, and you are in doubt as to whether it was intentional or not, do not resort to extreme measures; simply watch your chance and hit him with a brick. That will be sufficient. If you shall find that he had not intended any offense, come out frankly and confess yourself in the wrong when you struck him; acknowledge it like a man and say you didn't mean to. Yes, always avoid violence; in this age of charity and kindliness, the time has gone by for such things. Leave dynamite to the low and unrefined.

4 Go to bed early, get up early—this is wise. Some authorities say get up with the sun; some others say get up with one thing, some with another. But a lark is really the best thing to get up with. It gives you a splendid reputation with everybody to know that you get up with the lark; and if you get the right kind of a lark, and work at him right, you can easily train him to get up at half past nine, every time—it is no trick at all.

5 Now as to the matter of lying. You want to be very careful about lying; otherwise you are nearly sure to get caught. Once caught, you can never again be, in the eyes of the good and the pure, what you were before. Many a young person has injured himself permanently through a single clumsy and illfinished lie, the result of carelessness born of incomplete training. Some authorities hold that the young ought not to lie at all. That, of course, is putting it rather stronger than necessary; still, while I cannot go quite so far as that, I do maintain, and I believe I am right, that the young ought to be temperate in the use of this great art until practice and experience shall give them that confidence, elegance, and precision which alone can make the accomplishment graceful and profitable. Patience, diligence, painstaking attention to detail— these are the requirements; these, in time, will make the student perfect; upon these, and upon these only, may he rely as the sure foundation for future eminence. Think what tedious years of study, thought, practice, experience, went to the equipment of that peerless old master who was able to impose upon the whole world the lofty and sounding maxim that "truth is mighty and will prevail"—the most majestic compound fracture of fact which any of

woman born has yet achieved. For the history of our race, and each individual's experience, are sown thick with evidence that a truth is not hard to kill and that a lie told well is immortal. There is in Boston a monument of the man who discovered anaesthesia; many people are aware, in these latter days, that that man didn't discover it at all, but stole the discovery from another man. Is this truth mighty, and will it prevail? Ah no, my hearers, the monument is made of hardy material, but the lie it tells will outlast it a million years. An awkward, feeble, leaky lie is a thing which you ought to make it your unceasing study to avoid; such a lie as that has no more real permanence than an average truth. Why, you might as well tell the truth at once and be done with it. A feeble, stupid, preposterous lie will not live two years—except it be a slander upon somebody. It is indestructible, then, of course, but that is no merit of yours. A final word: begin your practice of this gracious and beautiful art early—begin now. If I had begun earlier, I could have learned how.

6 Never handle firearms carelessly. The sorrow and suffering that have been caused through the innocent but heedless handling of firearms by the young! Only four days ago, right in the next farmhouse to the one where I am spending the summer, a grandmother, old and gray and sweet, one of the loveliest spirits in the land, was sitting at her work, when her young grandson crept in and got down an old, battered, rusty gun which had not been touched for many years and was supposed not to be loaded, and pointed it at her, laughing and threatening to shoot. In her fright she ran screaming and pleading toward the door on the other side of the room; but as she passed him he placed the gun almost against her very breast and pulled the trigger! He had supposed it was not loaded. And he was right—it wasn't. So there wasn't any harm done. It is the only case of that kind I ever heard of. Therefore, just the same, don't you meddle with old unloaded firearms; they are the most deadly and unerring things that have ever been created by man. You don't have to take any pains at all with them; you don't have to have a rest, you don't have to have any sights on the gun, you don't have to take aim, even. No, you just pick out a relative and bang away, and you are sure to get him. A youth who can't hit a cathedral at thirty yards with a Gatling gun in three-quarters of an hour, can take up an old empty musket and bag his grandmother every time, at a hundred. Think what Waterloo would have been if one of the armies had been boys armed with old muskets supposed not to be loaded, and the other army had been composed of their female relations. The very thought of it makes one shudder.

7 There are many sorts of books; but good ones are the sort for the young to read. Remember that. They are a great, an inestimable, an unspeakable means of improvement. Therefore be careful in your selection, my young friends; be very careful; confine yourselves exclusively to Robertson's Sermons, Baxter's *Saint's Rest, The Innocents Abroad,* and works of that kind.

8 But I have said enough. I hope you will treasure up the instructions which I have given you, and make them a guide to your feet and a light to your understanding. Build your character thoughtfully and painstakingly upon

these precepts, and by and by, when you have got it built, you will be surprised and gratified to see how nicely and sharply it resembles everybody else's.

VOCABULARY

didactic (1)
diligence (5)
eminence (5)

QUESTIONS ON CONTENT

1. Twain begins his speech by identifying its audience and announcing his intention to be didactic. Why does he do this? What does this opening have to do with the remainder of his speech?
2. What does this speech imply about Twain's view of man? About his view of the way adults moralize to the young?
3. Twain says that if the young follow his advice, they will turn out like everybody else. What does this speech imply about the character of men in general?
4. Why, according to Twain, did he not learn to lie? Why is he mentioning that?
5. Reread the ending of this speech. How is it related to the beginning?

QUESTIONS ON FORM

1. Twain ends his first paragraph thus: "First, then, I will say to you, my young friends—and I say it beseechingly, urgingly—" What tone is he using here? What is its purpose?
2. Periphrasis is defined as "an indirect, abstract, roundabout method of stating ideas," and is frequently used by writers and speakers for humor. Which sentence in paragraph 5 is an obvious example of periphrasis?
3. Anticlimax is "the arrangement of descriptive or narrative details in such an order that the lesser, the trivial, or the ludicrous confront the reader at the point when he expects something greater and more serious." Which sentence in paragraph 2 meets this definition?
4. Reread paragraph 6. How would you characterize the ending of this story?
5. Twain writes: "A youth who can't hit a cathedral at thirty yards with a Gatling gun in three-quarters of an hour, can take up an old empty musket and bag his grandmother every time, at a hundred." Why does he use the word "bag"?

SUGGESTIONS FOR WRITING

1. Analyze and discuss this speech as reflecting Twain's well-known hatred of hypocrisy.
2. Identify, analyze, and discuss Twain's use in this speech of anticlimax as a source of humor and satire.

E. E. CUMMINGS

SINCE FEELING IS FIRST

Writers frequently debate the value of feeling over form, and vice versa. This poem advocates "feeling as first," and by implication praises inspiration over structure.

> since feeling is first
> who pays any attention
> to the syntax of things
> will never wholly kiss you;
>
> wholly to be a fool
> while Spring is in the world
>
> my blood approves,
> and kisses are a better fate
> than wisdom
> lady i swear by all flowers. Don't cry
> —the best gesture of my brain is less than
> your eyelids' flutter which says
>
> we are for each other: then
> laugh, leaning back in my arms
> for life's not a paragraph
>
> And death i think is no parenthesis

QUESTIONS ON CONTENT

1. What does the phrase "the syntax of things" mean in the context of this poem?
2. The poet says that "feeling is first." What, by implication, is therefore second? What is being implied as the opposite to feeling?
3. The poet says that "kisses are a better fate/than wisdom." What does that mean? What would be a reasonable paraphrase of that line?
4. What does the line "And death i think is no parenthesis" mean?
5. What is the overall theme of the poem?

QUESTIONS ON FORM

1. How many sentences is this poem written in? Write out the sentences of the poem in prose form with no stanza breaks.
2. What, if any, is the effect on the reader of the poem's arrangement into stanzas? Is the poem made more powerful because of the arrangement of its stanzas? Is its stanza arrangement arbitrary?

3. What images are used in the poem to represent feeling? (Hint: examine the paired images in the third stanza.)
4. How many images in the poem have something to do with the conventions of grammar or writing? Identify these images.
5. The poet says, "wholly to be a fool/while Spring is in the world/my blood approves." Is this the usual grammatical arrangement for this sentence? If not, write out the sentence in conventional grammar, supplying any missing words. How does your version differ from the poet's? Which is more effective, and why?

SUGGESTIONS FOR WRITING

1. Write an essay on yourself beginning with either of these lines: "For me feeling is first and syntax is second," or "For me syntax is first and feeling is second."
2. Write an analysis of the meaning of this poem.

SAMUEL JOHNSON

LETTER TO LORD CHESTERFIELD

In 1747 Samuel Johnson, the English critic, poet, and lexicographer, was asked by several publishers to prepare a dictionary of the English language. Johnson drew up a plan for the dictionary which, at the request of Robert Dodsley, one of its publishers, he dedicated to Lord Chesterfield. Chesterfield ignored Johnson and his project until seven years later, when the dictionary was on the verge of publication. Then he wrote two flattering articles in the *World* magazine praising Johnson and his forthcoming dictionary. By this time, however, Johnson felt angered at Chesterfield's neglect and wrote the following letter, making it plain that the dictionary would not be dedicated to him. This letter is one of the most famous literary rebuffs in history.

February 7, 1755.

My lord,

1 I have been lately informed, by the proprietor of the *World,* that two papers, in which my Dictionary is recommended to the publick, were written by your Lordship. To be so distinguished, is an honour, which, being very little accustomed to favours from the great, I know not well how to receive, or in what terms to acknowledge.

2 When, upon some slight encouragement, I first visited your Lordship, I was overpowered, like the rest of mankind, by the enchantment of your address; and could not forbear to wish that I might boast myself *Le vainqueur du vainqueur de la terre;*—that I might obtain that regard for which I saw the world contending; but I found my attendance so little encouraged, that neither pride nor modesty would suffer me to continue it. When I had once addressed your Lordship in publick, I had exhausted all the art of pleasing which a retired and uncourtly scholar can possess. I had done all that I could; and no man is well pleased to have his all neglected, be it ever so little.

3 Seven years, my Lord, have now past, since I waited in your outward rooms, or was repulsed from your door; during which time I have been pushing on my work through difficulties, of which it is useless to complain, and have brought it, at last, to the verge of publication, without one act of assistance, one word of encouragement, or one smile of favour. Such treatment I did not expect, for I never had a Patron before.

4 The shepherd in Virgil grew at last acquainted with Love, and found him a native of the rocks.[1]

5 Is not a Patron, my Lord, one who looks with unconcern on a man struggling for life in the water, and, when he has reached ground, encumbers him with help? The notice which you have been pleased to take of my labours, had it been early, had been kind; but it has been delayed till I am indifferent, and cannot enjoy it; till I am solitary, and cannot impart it;[2] till I am known, and do not want it. I hope it is no very cynical asperity not to confess obligations where no benefit has been received, or to be unwilling that the Publick should consider me as owing that to a Patron, which Providence has enabled me to do for myself.

6 Having carried on my work thus far with so little obligation to any favourer of learning, I shall not be disappointed though I should conclude it, if less be possible, with less; for I have been long wakened from that dream of hope, in which I once boasted myself with so much exultation,

My Lord,
Your Lordship's most humble,
Most obedient servant,
Sam. Johnson

VOCABULARY

repulsed (3)	asperity (5)
encumbers (5)	exultation (6)

QUESTIONS ON CONTENT

1. What is the occasion prompting Johnson to write this letter? Where is it stated?
2. What, specifically, are Johnson's complaints against Chesterfield? Where does he enumerate them?
3. How many years have passed since Johnson first approached Chesterfield for his patronage?
4. According to Johnson in paragraph 5, who or what has been his real patron?
5. How would you characterize Johnson's closing address?

QUESTIONS ON FORM

1. Johnson uses irony in his rebuff of Chesterfield. Locate and identify an ironic sentence in the first paragraph.

[1]*Eclogues* of Virgil, Book 8, lines 44–46.—Ed.
[2]Johnson is evidently referring to the loss of his wife.—Ed.

2. In paragraph 3 Johnson writes: "Such treatment I did not expect, for I never had a Patron before." What tone is he evidently using here?
3. How would you characterize Johnson's definition of a patron in paragraph 5?
4. This sentence is found in paragraph 5: "The notice which you have been pleased to take of my labours, had it been early, had it been kind; but it has been delayed till I am indifferent, and cannot enjoy it; till I am solitary, and cannot impart it; till I am known, and do not want it." What characteristic does this sentence have?
5. Paragraph 4 consists of a single sentence in which a reference is made to the *Eclogues* by the Roman poet Virgil. What is this sort of literary reference called?

SUGGESTIONS FOR WRITING

1. Chesterfield, as befitting his rank and class, did not venture a reply to Johnson's letter, although in private conversation he conceded, "This man has great powers." Imagine you are Lord Chesterfield. Write a suitable reply to Johnson.
2. Johnson's letter is a model of anger restrained by manners. Imagine you are Johnson, living in our more vitriolic twentieth century. Write a letter to Chesterfield expressing your anger the way it might be done today.

TERM PAPER SUGGESTIONS

1. Write a term paper on the patronage system in the arts, tracing its rise and decline.
2. Johnson's dictionary was the first great dictionary of the English language. Write a term paper on Johnson and his dictionary, covering the events leading up to his preparation of it, and the critical reception it received.

SYLVIA PLATH

LETTER TO HER MOTHER

This lovely, exuberant letter was written by the American poet Sylvia Plath (1932–63) to her mother and illustrates the use of private, intimate language. The "Ted" referred to in the letter is Ted Hughes, the English poet who was Sylvia Plath's husband. In 1963 Sylvia Plath took her own life.

Whitstead, Barton Road
Cambridge, England
October 2, 1956

Dearest darling Mother,

1 Something very wonderful has happened. On my return to Whitstead in rain, weariness, and general numb sadness yesterday, I received a lovely letter from *Poetry* magazine, Chicago, saying they found my poems admirable and are buying six (!) for publication! Do you know what this means! First, about $76 (they pay 50 cents a line) . . . then, they are all my *new* poems, written after "Pursuit" and glorifying love and Ted. They are obviously in the market for a new lyrical woman. And they are *happy* poems.

2 This also means that my manuscript of poetry which I am going to get ready to submit to the Yale Series of Younger Poets Contest this January will have a terrific list of introductory credits. Already, nine of my poems were

published; add seven, this fall, and perhaps more this winter, and it's rather impressive. My manuscript should have much more chance; and, bless it, *Poetry* is a magazine of poets. . . . That, combined with my commercial publications, is also fine. . . . They are publishing "Two Sisters of Persephone," "Metamorphosis," "Wreath for a Bridal," "Strumpet Song," "Dream with Clam-Diggers," and "Epitaph for Fire and Flower," a longish one which I began on the beach in Benidorm, Spain! I'll enclose a copy.

3 Also got a lovely letter from Peter Davison, who is now associate editor of the Atlantic Monthly Press, saying he wants to encourage me from his new position and wouldn't it be nice if they could publish a novel by me some day? I wrote him a colossal letter, telling him of Ted's stuff and my novel plans, asking advice, etc. He can be a most valuable friend. Your little daughter will be a writer yet!

4 . . . I want to type up a poem-book Ms. for each of us. Ted is producing terrifically—the *Atlantic* has had his poems for four months; I have fingers crossed. You would be so touched—he wants to get his fables printed especially for you, so you would not worry that he can support me! He thinks you would be pleased. The dear one.

5 Naturally, it will be hard work here, but I am happy alone, want to see no one, but live in the spirit of Ted, writing daily. I'll see him in London before he leaves for Spain, so there is that to look forward to. He waits now word from the BBC.

6 You must tell Mrs. Prouty[1] about my new poem acceptances! It shows what true love can produce!

7 If only you knew how happy I am with Ted. I have been with him every minute for over four months, and every day I love him more and more. We . . . never run out of growing conversation. We talked the whole day on our bus trip to London, and it is so exciting, both of us writing, producing something new every day, criticizing, dreaming, encouraging, mulling over common experiences. I am walking on air; I love him more than the world and would do anything for him. . . . We want to work and work . . . success will never spoil either of us. We are not dependent on the social arty world, but scorn it, for those who are drinking and calling themselves "writers" at parties should be home writing and writing. Every day one has to *earn* the name of "writer" over again, with much wrestling.

8 Our last days at Ted's were lovely, even under the strain of coming parting. We listened to Beethoven after dinner by the light of the coal fire, the stars shining outside the big windows, and read in bed together quietly and happily. I finished my drawing of Wuthering Heights and will do a little article on it. . . .

9 *Do* write a lot this year.

Much love,
Your happy Sivvy

---

[1]Benefactress of Plath's scholarship at Smith College.—Ed.

VOCABULARY

metamorphosis (2)
strumpet (2)

QUESTIONS ON CONTENT

1. What wonderful thing is Sylvia Plath reporting to her mother?
2. Why was Sylvia so ecstatic about this news?
3. What encouraging news does she also report in paragraph 3?
4. How does Sylvia Plath characterize the poems accepted by *Poetry* magazine?
5. To what does Sylvia attribute the success of her new poems?

QUESTIONS ON FORM

1. This letter represents language used in private communication between intimates. Point out some of the informalities in its language which reflect this.
2. Locate and identify a sentence fragment in this letter. Is the fragment used effectively? Why, or why not?
3. What do the ellipses mean?
4. How would you characterize the paragraphing in this letter? What purpose does this paragraphing serve?
5. Examine the last sentence in this letter. What effect does its phrasing convey?

SUGGESTIONS FOR WRITING

1. Write a short essay characterizing the tone and feeling of this letter, saying as much as you think can be inferred about its writer, and giving quotes to substantiate your impressions of her.
2. Imagine yourself also in love or recall a time when you were. Write a letter to your mother telling about your love and your life.

CHAPTER WRITING ASSIGNMENTS

1. Select any two paragraphs, one from an article in the *Reader's Digest* and another from one in the *New Yorker*. Analyze the differences in their language (diction, phrasing, sentence style, and length), and speculate on the intended audience of each magazine.
2. Analyze the effects of their different audiences on the language and content of the "Inaugural Address" and "Advice to Youth." Point out how each speech is adapted to its intended audience.
3. Compare and contrast the Plath letter with the Johnson letter, focusing primarily on the use of language to convey the writer's purpose.

What Should I Sound Like?
Finding a Voice

model

CHIEF JOSEPH OF THE NEZ PERCÉ

I AM TIRED OF FIGHTING

(SURRENDER SPEECH)

I am tired of fighting. Our chiefs are killed. Looking Glass is dead. Toohulsote is dead. The old men are all dead. It is the young men who say no and yes. He who led the young men is dead. It is cold and we have no blankets. The little children are freezing to death. My people, some of them, have run away to the hills and have no blankets, no food. No one knows where they are—perhaps they are freezing to death. I want to have time to look for my children and see how many of them I can find. Maybe I shall find them among the dead. Hear me, my chiefs, I am tired. My heart is sad and sick. From where the sun now stands I will fight no more forever.

This speech by Chief Joseph of the Nez Percé Indians reads with the grace and elegance of simplicity; it rings with "sincerity." Whenever a writer succeeds in really sharing himself with a reader, he will project the sincere and indefinable qualities of his personality into his writing: that is the quality we call his "voice."

How does a writer know his own voice and how can he cultivate it? Various ideas are held by various theorists. Some say that voice must be contrived, that a writer has, not one, but a range of voices within him which he must modulate to suit his audience; others say that a writer needs only to be sincere and he will write naturally in his own voice. The compromise view contends

34

that neither theory excludes the other, that a writer has various voices but he must be sincere if he is to use the appropriate voice.

Students, however, do not have to write surrender speeches, they have to write themes. Many students hold to a national belief that Freshman English assignments require them to write on humdrum themes with oratorical thunder. Contrary to this mythology, most teachers want their students to write not with loftiness and thunder, but with clarity and directness. If the student imitated the eloquent roll of the Gettysburg Address in a freshman theme, his writing would sound grotesquely inappropriate. The appropriate voice should be direct, clear, and unstrained—it should be the student's own voice, the way he would naturally turn a phrase if left to write a diary in the privacy of himself. This is the voice that teachers attempt to draw out of their students, because it is the only one that can finally be made articulate.

We can only dispense what Jacqueline Berke in "The Qualities of Good Writing" calls "kindly advice": be yourself. Avoid the oratorical phrase, the high-flown word, the drum-roll sentence. Avoid these and you avoid the fake and the artificial: phrase your sentences plainly until they lie like varnish on your content. If you write like this, you will practice the first requirement of any sincere voice: consistency.

advice

JACQUELINE BERKE

THE QUALITIES OF GOOD WRITING

This selection examines the characteristics of "good" writing, defines the fundamental principle of rhetoric, and explains the rhetorical stance which a writer must assume for his writing.

1 Even before you set out, you come prepared by instinct and intuition to make certain judgments about what is "good." Take the following familiar sentence for example: "I know not what course others may take, but as for me, give me liberty or give me death." Do you suppose this thought of Patrick Henry's would have come ringing down through the centuries if he had expressed this sentiment not in one tight, rhythmical sentence but as follows:

It would be difficult, if not impossible, to predict on the basis of my limited information as to the predilections of the public, what the citizenry at large will regard as action commensurate with the present provocation, but after arduous consideration I personally feel so intensely and irrevocably committed to the position of social, political, and economic independence, that rather than submit to foreign and despotic control which is anathema to me, I will make the ultimate sacrifice of which man is capable—under the aegis of personal honor, ideological conviction, and existential commitment, I will sacrifice my own mortal existence.

2 How does this rambling, "high-flown" paraphrase measure up to the bold "Give me liberty or give me death"? Who will deny that something is "happening" in Patrick Henry's rousing challenge that not only fails to happen in the paraphrase but is actually negated there? Would you bear with this long-winded, pompous speaker to the end? If you were to judge his statement strictly on its rhetoric (its choice and arrangement of words), you might aptly call it more boring than brave. Perhaps a plainer version will work better. Let us consider this one:

> Liberty is a very important thing for a man to have. Most people—at least the people I've talked to or that other people have told me about—know this and therefore are very anxious to preserve their liberty. Of course I can't be absolutely sure about what other folks are going to do in this present crisis, what with all these threats and everything, but I've made up my mind that I'm going to fight because liberty is really a very important thing to me; at least that's the way I feel about it.

3 This flat, "homely" prose, weighted down with what Flaubert called "fatty deposits," is grammatical enough. As in the pompous paraphrase, every verb agrees with its subject, every comma is in its proper place; nonetheless it lacks the qualities that make a statement—of one sentence or one hundred pages—pungent, vital, moving, memorable.

4 Let us isolate these qualities and describe them briefly. . . . The first is *economy*. In an appropriately slender volume entitled *The Elements of Style,* authors William Strunk and E. B. White state concisely the case for economy: "A sentence should contain no unnecessary words, a paragraph no unnecessary sentences, for the same reason that a drawing should have no unnecessary lines and a machine no unnecessary parts. This requires not that the writer make all his sentences short or that he avoid all detail . . . but that every word tell." In other words, economical writing is *efficient* and *aesthetically satisfying*. While it makes a minimum demand on the energy and patience of the reader, it returns to him a maximum of sharply compressed meaning. The writer should accept this as his basic responsibility: that he inflict no unnecessary words on the reader—just as a dentist inflicts no unnecessary pain, a lawyer no unnecessary risk. Economical writing avoids strain and at the same time promotes pleasure by producing a sense of form and right proportion, a sense of words that fit the ideas that they embody—with not a line of "deadwood" to dull the reader's attention, not an extra, useless phrase to clog the free flow of ideas, one following swiftly and clearly upon another.

5 Another basic quality of good writing is *simplicity*. Here again this does not require that the writer make all his sentences primerlike or that he reduce complexities to bare bones, but rather that he avoid embellishment or embroidery. "All affectation is bad," said Cervantes, and most writers agree. The natural, unpretentious style is best. But, paradoxically, simplicity or naturalness does not come naturally. By the time a person is old enough to write, he has usually grown so self-conscious that he stiffens, sometimes to the point of rigidity, when he is called upon to make a statement—in speech or in writing.

It is easy to offer the kindly advice "be yourself," but many people do not feel like themselves when they take a pencil in hand or sit down at a typewriter. Thus during the early days of the Second World War when air raids were feared in New York City and "black-outs" instituted, an anonymous writer—probably a young civil service worker at City Hall—produced and distributed to stores throughout the city the following poster:

Illumination
is Required
to be
Extinguished
on These Premises
after Nightfall

6 What he meant, of course, was simply "Lights Out After Dark"; but apparently that direct imperative—clear and to the point—did not sound "official" enough. And so, under a common misapprehension, the writer resorted to long Latinate words and involved syntax (note the awkward passives "*is* Required" and "*to be* Extinguished") to establish a tone of dignity and authority. In contrast, how beautifully simple are the words of the translators of the King James Version of the Bible, who felt no need for flourish, flamboyance, or grandiloquence. The Lord did not loftily or bombastically proclaim that universal illumination was required to be instantaneously installed. Simply but majestically "God said, Let there be light: and there was light. . . . And God called the light Day, and the darkness he called Night."

7 In this same tradition most memorable declarations have been spare and direct. Abraham Lincoln and John Kennedy seem to "speak to each other across the span of a century," notes French author André Maurois, for both men embodied noble themes in eloquently simple terms. Said Lincoln in his second Inaugural Address: "With malice towards none, with charity for all, with firmness in the right as God gives us the right, let us strive on to finish the work we are in . . ." One hundred years later President Kennedy made his Inaugural dedication: "With a good conscience our only sure reward, with history the final judge of our deeds, let us go forth to lead the land we love. . . ."

8 The third fundamental element of good writing is *clarity*—a basic commandment of every responsible writer. Some people question whether it is always possible to be clear; after all, certain ideas are inherently complicated and inescapably difficult. True enough. But the responsible writer recognizes that his writing should not add to the complications nor increase the difficulty; his writing should not set up an additional roadblock to understanding. Indeed, the German philosopher Wittgenstein goes so far as to say that "whatever can be said can be said clearly." If a writer understands his own idea and wants to convey it to others, he is obliged to render it in clear, orderly, readable, understandable prose—else why bother writing in the first place? Actually the writer who is obscure is usually confused himself; uncer-

tain of what he wants to say or what he means, he has not yet completed that process of thinking through and reasoning into the heart of his subject. He is still working toward his thesis: he has not yet discovered it.

9 Suffice it to say that whatever the topic, whatever the occasion, expository writing should be readable, informative, and, wherever possible, engaging. At its best it may even be poetic, as Nikos Kazantzakis suggests in *Zorba the Greek,* where he draws an analogy between good prose and a beautiful landscape:

> To my mind, the Cretan countryside resembled good prose, carefully ordered, sober, free from superfluous ornament, powerful and restrained. It expressed all that was necessary with the greatest economy. It had no flippancy nor artifice about it. It said what it had to say with a manly austerity. But between the severe lines one could discern an unexpected sensitiveness and tenderness; in the sheltered hollows the lemon and orange trees perfumed the air, and from the vastness of the sea emanated an inexhaustible poetry.

10 Even in technical fields where the range of styles is necessarily limited (and poetry is neither possible nor appropriate), the writer must always be aware of "the reader over his shoulder." Take such topics as how to follow postal regulations for overseas mail, how to change oil in an engine, how to produce aspirin from salicylic acid. Here are technical expository descriptions that defy a memorable turn of phrase; here is writing that is of necessity cut-and-dried, dispassionate, and bloodless. But it need not be difficult, tedious, confusing, or dull to those who want to find out about mailing letters, changing oil, or making aspirin. Those who seek such information should have reasonably easy access to it, which means that written instructions should be clear, simple, spare, direct, and most of all, *human:* for no matter how technical a subject, all writing is done *for* human beings *by* human beings. Writing in other words, like language itself, is a strictly human enterprise. Machines may stamp letters, measure oil, and convert acids, but only human beings talk and write *about* these procedures so that other human beings may better understand them. It is always appropriate, therefore, to be human in one's statement.

Rhetorical Stance

11 Part of this humanity must stem from the writer's sense of who his readers are. He must assume a "rhetorical stance." Indeed this is a fundamental principle of rhetoric: *nothing should ever be written in a vacuum.* The writer should identify his audience, hypothetical or real, so that he may speak to them in an appropriate voice. A student, for example, should never "just write," without visualizing a definite group of readers—his fellow students, perhaps, or the educated community at large (intelligent nonspecialists). Without these definite readers in mind, the writer cannot assume a suitable and appropriate relationship to his material, his purpose, and his audience. A

proper rhetorical stance, in other words, requires that the writer have an active sense of:

1. Who he is as a writer.
2. Who his readers are.
3. Why he is addressing them and on what occasion.
4. His relationship to his subject matter.
5. How he wants his readers to relate to the subject matter.

VOCABULARY

predilections (1)

commensurate (1)

arduous (1)

irrevocably (1)

despotic (1)

anathema (1)

aegis (1)

paraphrase (2)

pungent (3)

aesthetically (4)

embellishment (5)

flamboyance (6)

grandiloquence (6)

bombastically (6)

flippancy (9)

artifice (9)

discern (9)

emanated (9)

dispassionate (10)

hypothetical (11)

examples

BARTOLOMEO VANZETTI

from LAST SPEECH TO THE COURT

Bartolomeo Vanzetti and Nicola Sacco, two Italian immigrants, were executed for murder on August 23, 1927, after a controversial trial. Many people, including Albert Einstein and Anatole France, protested that Sacco and Vanzetti were being executed for their political beliefs. The trial took place during the "Red Scare" of the 1920s.

This selection is from Vanzetti's last speech to the court. It illustrates the lyricism and elegance of simple words cast into idiomatic sentences.

1 I have talk a great deal of myself but I even forgot to name Sacco. Sacco too is a worker from his boyhood, a skilled worker lover of work, with a good job and pay, a good and lovely wife, two beautiful children and a neat little home at the verge of a wood, near a brook. Sacco is a heart, a faith, a character, a man; a man lover of nature and of mankind. A man who gave all, who sacrifice all to the cause of Liberty and to his love for mankind; money, rest, mundane ambitions, his own wife, his children, himself and his own life. Sacco has never dreamt to steal, never to assassinate. He and I have never

brought a morsel of bread to our mouths, from our childhood to today—which has not been gained by the sweat of our brows. Never.

2 Oh, yes, I may be more witful, as some have put it, I am a better babbler than he is, but many, many times in hearing his heartful voice ringing a faith sublime, in considering his supreme sacrifice, remembering his heroism I felt small small at the presence of his greatness and found myself compelled to fight back from my throat to not weep before him—this man called thief and assassin and doomed. But Sacco's name will live in the hearts of the people and in their gratitude when Katzmann's[1] and your bones will be dispersed by time, when your name, his name, your laws, institutions, and your false god are but a dim rememoring of a cursed past in which man was wolf to the man. . . .

3 If it had not been for these thing, I might have live out my life talking at street corners to scorning men. I might have die, unmarked, unknown, a failure. Now we are not a failure. This is our career and our triumph. Never in our full life could we hope to do such work for tolerance, for joostice, for man's onderstanding of man as now we do by accident. Our words—our lives—our pains—nothing! The taking of our lives—lives of a good shoe-maker and a poor fish-peddler—all! That last moment belongs to us—that agony is our triumph.

VOCABULARY

mundane (1)
sublime (2)

QUESTIONS ON CONTENT

1. What kind of a man does the speech make Sacco out to be?
2. Because of his beliefs, the author of this speech was labeled a philosophical anarchist. What does this speech reveal about him? What is a philosophical anarchist?
3. In this speech, the author talks more about Sacco than about himself. What effect does this have on the listener or reader?
4. In the final paragraph the author calls their impending execution "our triumph." What does he mean by that?

QUESTIONS ON FORM

1. The author was an Italian with a frail grasp of the American speech idiom. What effect do his grammatical errors have on the speech?
2. How would you characterize the diction of this speech? Is it lofty? Plain?
3. The first paragraph ends with a single word. What effect does this produce?

[1] Frederick G. Katzmann was the district attorney who prosecuted the case.—Ed.

4. Why do some editors include this speech in poetry anthologies? What is poetic about it?

SUGGESTIONS FOR WRITING

1. Copy this speech, correcting its grammatical and spelling errors as you go. Add any words which are necessary to make the speech grammatical. Write a paragraph on which version you think is more effective, the original or the corrected one, giving your reasons.
2. Without doing any further research into Vanzetti, and using his speech as your only evidence, write an impressionistic description of the kind of man you think he was. Be specific in your references to passages in the speech.

TERM PAPER SUGGESTION

Write a term paper on the Sacco-Vanzetti trial. Come to your own conclusion as to whether or not they had a fair trial, and support your belief.

LANGSTON HUGHES

SALVATION

In this selection from *The Big Sea* Langston Hughes (1902–67) recounts a dramatic incident from his childhood. The incident is narrated from the perspective of Hughes as a twelve-year-old boy and demonstrates a skillful writer's use of language to re-create the innocent voice of childhood.

1 I was saved from sin when I was going on thirteen. But not really saved. It happened like this. There was a big revival at my Auntie Reed's church. Every night for weeks there had been much preaching, singing, praying, and shouting, and some very hardened sinners had been brought to Christ, and the membership of the church had grown by leaps and bounds. Then just before the revival ended, they held a special meeting for children, "to bring the young lambs to the fold." My aunt spoke of it for days ahead. That night I was escorted to the front row and placed on the mourners' bench with all the other young sinners, who had not yet been brought to Jesus.

2 My aunt told me that when you were saved you saw a light, and something happened to you inside! And Jesus came into your life! And God was with you from then on! She said you could see and hear and feel Jesus in your soul. I believed her. I had heard a great many old people say the same thing and it seemed to me they ought to know. So I sat there calmly in the hot, crowded church, waiting for Jesus to come to me.

3 The preacher preached a wonderful rhythmical sermon, all moans and shouts and lonely cries and dire pictures of hell, and then he sang a song about the ninety and nine safe in the fold, but one little lamb was left out in the cold.

Then he said: "Won't you come? Won't you come to Jesus? Young lambs, won't you come?" And he held out his arms to all us young sinners there on the mourners' bench. And the little girls cried. And some of them jumped up and went to Jesus right away. But most of us just sat there.

4 A great many old people came and knelt around us and prayed, old women with jet-black faces and braided hair, old men with work-gnarled hands. And the church sang a song about the lower lights are burning, some poor sinners to be saved. And the whole building rocked with prayer and song.

5 Still I keep waiting to *see* Jesus.

6 Finally all the young people had gone to the altar and were saved, but one boy and me. He was a rounder's son named Westley. Westley and I were surrounded by sisters and deacons praying. It was very hot in the church, and getting late now. Finally Westley said to me in a whisper: "God damn! I'm tired o' sitting here. Let's get up and be saved." So he got up and was saved.

7 Then I was left all alone on the mourners' bench. My aunt came and knelt at my knees and cried, while prayers and songs swirled all around me in the little church. The whole congregation prayed for me alone, in a mighty wail of moans and voices. And I kept waiting serenely for Jesus, waiting, waiting—but he didn't come. I wanted to see him, but nothing happened to me. Nothing! I wanted something to happen to me, but nothing happened.

8 I heard the songs and the minister saying: "Why don't you come? My dear child, why don't you come to Jesus? Jesus is waiting for you. He wants you. Why don't you come? Sister Reed, what is this child's name?"

9 "Langston," my aunt sobbed.

10 "Langston, why don't you come? Why don't you come and be saved? Oh, Lamb of God! Why don't you come?"

11 Now it was really getting late. I began to be ashamed of myself, holding everything up so long. I began to wonder what God thought about Westley, who certainly hadn't seen Jesus either, but who was now sitting proudly on the platform, swinging his knickerbockered legs and grinning down at me, surrounded by deacons and old women on their knees praying. God had not struck Westley dead for taking his name in vain or for lying in the temple. So I decided that maybe to save further trouble, I'd better lie, too, and say that Jesus had come, and get up and be saved.

12 So I got up.

13 Suddenly the whole room broke into a sea of shouting, as they saw me rise. Waves of rejoicing swept the place. Women leaped in the air. My aunt threw her arms around me. The minister took me by the hand and led me to the platform.

14 When things quieted down, in a hushed silence, punctuated by a few ecstatic "Amens," all the new young lambs were blessed in the name of God. Then joyous singing filled the room.

15 That night, for the last time in my life but one—for I was a big boy twelve years old—I cried. I cried, in bed alone, and couldn't stop. I buried my head

under the quilts, but my aunt heard me. She woke up and told my uncle I was crying because the Holy Ghost had come into my life, and because I had seen Jesus. But I was really crying because I couldn't bear to tell her that I had lied, that I had deceived everybody in the church, and I hadn't seen Jesus, and that now I didn't believe there was a Jesus any more, since he didn't come to help me.

VOCABULARY

gnarled (4)
punctuated (14)
ecstatic (14)

QUESTIONS ON CONTENT

1. How does Westley's attitude differ from the narrator's? Is Westley more realistic and less gullible, or is he simply more callous and less sensitive than the narrator? Comment.
2. The narrator holds out to the last minute and finally submits to being saved. What is his motive for finally giving in? Because of group pressure? Because Westley did it, too?
3. Who has been deceived in the story? The aunt by the narrator? The narrator by the aunt? Both the narrator and the aunt by the minister? Everybody by the demands of religion? Comment.
4. What insight does the narrator come to at the end of the story? What has he learned?
5. The story is told as a flashback to when Hughes was a boy. What is his attitude toward the experience as he retells it? Is he cynical and bitter? Sympathetic? Neutral?

QUESTIONS ON FORM

1. The story is narrated from the point of view of a twelve-year-old boy. What techniques of language does the story use to create the perspective of a boy? How is the vocabulary appropriate to a boy?
2. In his article on "How to Say Nothing in Five Hundred Words," Paul Roberts urges the use of specific detail in writing. How does Hughes make use of such detail?
3. The description in paragraph 4 is vivid but compressed. How does Hughes achieve this effect?

SUGGESTIONS FOR WRITING

1. Describe an experience of your own where group pressure forced you into doing something you did not believe in.
2. Write a brief biographical sketch of Westley, fantasizing on the kind of man you believe he grew into and the kind of life he eventually led.

HENRY DAVID THOREAU

WHY I WENT TO THE WOODS

In this excerpt from *Walden,* Henry David Thoreau (1817–62) explains why he went to the woods to live by himself. Unlike many of the writers in this section, Thoreau writes in a voice rich with metaphors, allusions, and images.

1 I went to the woods because I wished to live deliberately, to front only the essential facts of life, and see if I could not learn what it had to teach, and not, when I came to die, discover that I had not lived. I did not wish to live what was not life, living is so dear; nor did I wish to practise resignation, unless it was quite necessary. I wanted to live deep and suck out all the marrow of life, to live so sturdily and Spartan-like as to put to rout all that was not life, to cut a broad swath and shave close, to drive life into a corner, and reduce it to its lowest terms, and, if it proved to be mean, why then to get the whole and genuine meanness of it, and publish its meanness to the world; or if it were sublime, to know it by experience, and be able to give a true account of it in my next excursion. For most men, it appears to me, are in a strange uncertainty about it, whether it is of the devil or of God, and have *somewhat hastily* concluded that it is the chief end of man here to "glorify God and enjoy him forever."

2 Still we live meanly, like ants; though the fable tells us that we were long ago changed into men; like pygmies we fight with cranes; it is error upon error, and clout upon clout, and our best virtue has for its occasion a superfluous and evitable wretchedness. Our life is frittered away by detail. An honest man has hardly need to count more than his ten fingers, or in extreme cases he may add his ten toes, and lump the rest. Simplicity, simplicity, simplicity! I say, let your affairs be as two or three, and not a hundred or a thousand; instead of a million count half a dozen, and keep your accounts on your thumb-nail. In the midst of this chopping sea of civilized life, such are the clouds and storms and quicksands and thousand-and-one items to be allowed for, that a man has to live, if he would not founder and go to the bottom and not make his port at all, by dead reckoning, and he must be a great calculator indeed who succeeds. Simplify, simplify. Instead of three meals a day, if it be necessary eat but one; instead of a hundred dishes, five; and reduce other things in proportion. Our life is like a German Confederacy, made up of petty states, with its boundary forever fluctuating, so that even a German cannot tell you how it is bounded at any moment. The nation itself, with all its so-called internal improvements, which, by the way are all external and superficial, is just such an unwieldy and overgrown establishment, cluttered with furniture and tripped up by its own traps, ruined by luxury and heedless expense, by want of calculation and a worthy aim, as the million households in the lands; and the only cure for it, as for them, is in a rigid economy, a stern and more than Spartan simplicity of life and elevation of purpose. It lives too fast. Men think that it is essential that the

Nation have commerce, and export ice, and talk through a telegraph, and ride thirty miles an hour, without a doubt, whether *they* do or not; but whether we should live like baboons or like men, is a little uncertain. If we do not get our sleepers, and forge rails, and devote days and nights to the work, but go to tinkering upon our *lives* to improve *them,* who will build railroads? And if railroads are not built, how shall we get to heaven in season? But if we stay at home and mind our business, who will want railroads? We do not ride on the railroad; it rides upon us. Did you ever think what those sleepers are that underlie the railroad? Each one is a man, an Irishman, or a Yankee man. The rails are laid on them, and they are covered with sand, and the cars run smoothly over them. They are sound sleepers, I assure you. And every few years a new lot is laid down and run over; so that, if some have the pleasure of riding on a rail, others have the misfortune to be ridden upon. And when they run over a man that is walking in his sleep, a supernumerary sleeper in the wrong position, and wake him up, they suddenly stop the cars, and make a hue and cry about it, as if this were an exception. I am glad to know that it takes a gang of men for every five miles to keep the sleepers down and level in their beds as it is, for this is a sign that they may sometimes get up again.

3 Why should we live with such hurry and waste of life? We are determined to be starved before we are hungry. Men say that a stitch in time saves nine, and so they take a thousand stitches to-day to save nine to-morrow. As for *work,* we haven't any of any consequence. We have the Saint Vitus' dance, and cannot possibly keep our heads still. If I should only give a few pulls at the parish bell-rope, as for a fire, that is, without setting the bell, there is hardly a man on his farm in the outskirts of Concord, notwithstanding that press of engagements which was his excuse so many times this morning, nor a boy, nor a woman, I might almost say, but would foresake all and follow that sound, not mainly to save property from the flames, but, if we will confess the truth, much more to see it burn, since burn it must, and we, be it known, did not set it on fire,—or to see it put out, and have a hand in it, if that is done as handsomely; yes, even if it were the parish church itself. Hardly a man takes a half-hour's nap after dinner, but when he wakes he holds up his head and asks, "What's the news?" as if the rest of mankind had stood his sentinels. Some give directions to be waked every half-hour, doubtless for no other purpose; and then, to pay for it, they tell what they have dreamed. After a night's sleep the news is as indispensable as the breakfast. "Pray tell me anything new that has happened to a man anywhere on this globe,"—and he reads it over his coffee and rolls, that a man has had his eyes gouged out this morning on the Wachito River; never dreaming the while that he lives in the dark unfathomed mammoth cave of this world, and has but the rudiment of an eye himself.

4 For my part, I could easily do without the post-office. I think that there are very few important communications made through it. To speak critically, I never received more than one or two letters in my life—I wrote this some years ago—that were worth the postage. The penny-post is, commonly, an institution through which you seriously offer a man that penny for his thoughts which is so often safely offered in jest. And I am sure that I never read any

memorable news in a newspaper. If we read of one man robbed, or murdered, or killed by accident, or one house burned, or one vessel wrecked, or one steamboat blown up, or one cow run over on the Western Railroad, or one mad dog killed, or one lot of grasshoppers in the winter,—we never need read of another. One is enough. If you are acquainted with the principle, what do you care for a myriad instances and applications? To a philosopher all *news,* as it is called, is gossip, and they who edit and read it are old women over their tea. Yet not a few are greedy after this gossip. There was such a rush, as I hear, the other day at one of the offices to learn the foreign news by the last arrival, that several large squares of plate glass belonging to the establishment were broken by the pressure,—news which I seriously think a ready wit might write a twelvemonth, or twelve years, beforehand with sufficient accuracy. As for Spain, for instance, if you know how to throw in Don Carlos and the Infanta, and Don Pedro and Seville and Granada, from time to time in the right proportions,—they may have changed the names a little since I saw the papers,—and serve up a bullfight when other entertainments fail, it will be true to the letter, and give us as good an idea of the exact state or ruin of things in Spain as the most succinct and lucid reports under this head in the newspapers: and as for England, almost the last significant scrap of news from that quarter was the revolution of 1649; and if you have learned the history of her crops for an average year, you never need attend to that thing again, unless your speculations are of a merely pecuniary character. If one may judge who rarely looks into the newspapers, nothing new does ever happen in foreign parts, a French revolution not excepted.

5 What news! how much more important to know what that is which was never old! "Kieou-he-yu (great dignitary of the state of Wei) sent a man to Khoung-tseu to know his news. Khoung-tseu caused the messenger to be seated near him, and questioned him in these terms: What is your master doing? The messenger answered with respect: My master desires to diminish the number of his faults, but he cannot come to the end of them. The messenger being gone, the philosopher remarked: What a worthy messenger! What a worthy messenger!" The preacher, instead of vexing the ears of drowsy farmers on their day of rest at the end of the week,—for Sunday is the fit conclusion of an ill-spent week, and not the fresh and brave beginning of a new one,—with this one other draggle-tail of a sermon, should shout with thundering voice, "Pause! Avast! Why so seeming fast, but deadly slow?"

6 Shams and delusions are esteemed for soundless truths, while reality is fabulous. If men would steadily observe realities only, and not allow themselves to be deluded, life, to compare it with such things as we know, would be like a fairy tale and the Arabian Nights' Entertainments. If we respected only what is inevitable and has a right to be, music and poetry would resound along the streets. When we are unhurried and wise, we perceive that only great and worthy things have any permanent and absolute existence, that petty fears and petty pleasures are but the shadow of the reality. This is always exhilarating and sublime. By closing the eyes and slumbering, and consenting to be deceived by shows, men establish and confirm their daily life

of routine and habit everywhere, which still is built on purely illusory foundations. Children, who play life, discern its true law and relations more clearly
than men, who fail to live it worthily, but who think that they are wiser by
experience, that is, by failure. I have read in a Hindoo book, that "there was a
king's son, who, being expelled in infancy from his native city, was brought up
by a forester, and, growing up to maturity in that state, imagined himself to
belong to the barbarous race with which he lived. One of his father's ministers
having discovered him, revealed to him what he was, and the misconception
of his character was removed, and he knew himself to be a prince. So soul,"
continues the Hindoo philosopher, "from the circumstances in which it is
placed, mistakes its own character, until the truth is revealed to it by some
holy teacher, and then it knows itself to be *Brahme.*" I perceive that we
inhabitants of New England live this mean life that we do because our vision
does not penetrate the surface of things. We think that that *is* which *appears*
to be. If a man should walk through this town and see only the reality, where,
think you, would the "Mill-dam" go to? If he should give us an account of the
realities he beheld there, we should not recognize the place in his description.
Look at the meeting-house, or a court-house, or a jail, or a shop, or a dwelling-
house, and say what that thing really is before a true gaze, and they would all
go to pieces in your account of them. Men esteem truth remote, in the
outskirts of the system, behind the farthest star, before Adam and after the
last man. In eternity there is indeed something true and sublime. But all these
times and places and occasions are now and here. God himself culminates in
the present moment, and will never be more divine in the lapse of all the ages.
And we are enabled to apprehend at all what is sublime and noble only by the
perpetual instilling and drenching of the reality that surrounds us. The universe constantly and obediently answers to our conceptions; whether we
travel fast or slow, the track is laid for us. Let us spend our lives in conceiving
then. The poet or the artist never yet had so fair and noble a design but some
of his posterity at least could accomplish it.

7 Let us spend one day as deliberately as Nature, and not be thrown off the
track by every nutshell and mosquito's wing that falls on the rails. Let us rise
early and fast, or breakfast, gently and without perturbation; let company
come and let company go, let the bells ring and the children cry,—determined
to make a day of it. Why should we knock under and go with the stream? Let
us not be upset and overwhelmed in that terrible rapid and whirlpool called a
dinner, situated in the meridian shallows. Weather this danger and you are
safe, for the rest of the way is down hill. With unrelaxed nerves, with morning
vigor, sail by it, looking another way, tied to the mast like Ulysses.[1] If the
engine whistles, let it whistle till it is hoarse for its pains. If the bell rings, why
should we run? We will consider what kind of music they are like. Let us settle
ourselves, and work and wedge our feet downward through the mud and slush
of opinion, and prejudice, and tradition, and delusion, and appearance, that

[1]tied . . . Ulysses: In Homer's *Odyssey,* Ulysses had himself tied to the mast of his boat so that
he could listen to the irresistible songs of the Sirens, who were believed to lure ships to their
doom.—Ed.

alluvion which covers the globe, through Paris and London, through New York and Boston and Concord, through Church and State, through poetry and philosophy and religion, till we come to a hard bottom and rocks in place, which we can call *reality,* and say, This is, and no mistake; and then begin, having a *point d'appui,*[2] below freshet and frost and fire, a place where you might found a wall or a state, or set a lamp-post safely, or perhaps a gauge, not a Nilometer, but a Realometer, that future ages might know how deep a freshet of shams and appearances had gathered from time to time. If you stand right fronting and face to face to a fact, you will see the sun glimmer on both its surfaces, as if it were a cimeter, and feel its sweet edge dividing you through the heart and marrow, and so you will happily conclude your mortal career. Be it life or death, we crave only reality. If we are really dying, let us hear the rattle in our throats and feel cold in the extremities; if we are alive, let us go about our business.

8 Time is but the stream I go a-fishing in. I drink at it; but while I drink I see the sandy bottom and detect how shallow it is. Its thin current slides away, but eternity remains. I would drink deeper; fish in the sky, whose bottom is pebbly with stars. I cannot count one. I know not the first letter of the alphabet. I have always been regretting that I was not as wise as the day I was born. The intellect is a cleaver; it discerns and rifts its way into the secret of things. I do not wish to be any more busy with my hands than is necessary. My head is hands and feet. I feel all my best faculties concentrated in it. My instinct tells me that my head is an organ for burrowing, as some creatures use their snout and fore paws, and with it I would mine and burrow my way through these hills. I think that the richest vein is somewhere hereabouts; so by the divining-rod and thin rising vapors, I judge; and here I will begin to mine.

VOCABULARY

superfluous (2)	succinct (4)
evitable (2)	pecuniary (4)
supernumerary (2)	posterity (6)
rudiment (3)	perturbation (7)
myriad (4)	freshet (7)

QUESTIONS ON CONTENT

1. Why did Thoreau go to the woods? What, in his opinion, is wrong with the nation?
2. Thoreau writes: "We do not ride on the railroad; it rides upon us." What does he mean?
3. What is Thoreau's definition of "news"? What is his definition of gossip? How, in his view, does news differ from gossip?
4. What does Thoreau mean when he says that the "universe constantly and obediently answers to our conceptions"? How, then, is truth possible?

[2]*point d'appui:* point of stability.—Ed.

5. Where, according to Thoreau, is truth to be found? What prevents us from finding it?

QUESTIONS ON FORM

1. Reread the final sentence of paragraph 1. What tone is Thoreau using?
2. Thoreau uses two anecdotes in this excerpt (paragraphs 5 and 6). What do these have in common? What do they indicate about the writer's philosophy?
3. "We have the Saint Vitus' dance, and cannot possibly keep our heads still" (paragraph 3).—What figure of speech is this? Can you find other examples of this same figure of speech in the text? What effect do they have on Thoreau's writing?
4. "Our life is like a German Confederacy, made up of petty states, with its boundary forever fluctuating, so that even a German cannot tell you how it is bounded at any moment" (paragraph 2).—What figure of speech is this? How does it differ from the example in the preceding question?
5. An allusion is a figure of speech in which some famous historical or literary figure or event is casually mentioned. Can you find an allusion in Thoreau's text? (Hint: examine paragraph 7.) What effect does the allusion have on the writer's style?

SUGGESTIONS FOR WRITING

1. Write an essay describing the clutter of pettiness in your own life. Say what you hope to do to remove it.
2. Pretend that you are Thoreau and that you have just been brought back to life and introduced to twentieth-century America. Write a diary putting down your first impressions of it.

TERM PAPER SUGGESTION

Thoreau was once sent to jail for refusing to pay his taxes. Research this episode and write about it.

NICANOR PARRA

Translated by W. S. Merwin

THE VIPER

Some poetry is written through the voice of a "persona," a character the poet assumes in the poem like a mask. In this poem, the persona reveals a bittersweet love affair with a mysterious woman.

1 For years I was doomed to worship a contemptible woman
Sacrifice myself for her, endure endless humiliations and sneers,
Work night and day to feed her and clothe her,
Perform several crimes, commit several misdemeanors,
Practice petty burglary by moonlight,
Forge compromising documents,

For fear of a scornful glance from her bewitching eyes.
During brief phases of understanding we used to meet in parks
And have ourselves photographed together driving a motorboat,
Or we would go to a nightclub
And fling ourselves into an orgy of dancing
That went on until well after dawn.
For years I was under the spell of that woman.
She used to appear in my office completely naked
And perform contortions that defy the imagination,
Simply to draw my poor soul into her orbit
And above all to wring from me my last penny.
She absolutely forbade me to have anything to do with my family.
To get rid of my friends this viper made free with defamatory libels
Which she published in a newspaper she owned.
Passionate to the point of delirium, she never let up for an instant,
Commanding me to kiss her on the mouth
And to reply at once to her silly questions
Concerning, among other things, eternity and the afterlife,
Subjects which upset me terribly,
Producing buzzing in my ears, recurrent nausea, sudden fainting spells
Which she turned to account with that practical turn of mind that
     distinguished her,
Putting her clothes on without wasting a moment
And clearing out of my apartment, leaving me flat.

2 This situation dragged on for five years and more.
There were periods when we lived together in a round room
In a plush district near the cemetery, sharing the rent.
(Some nights we had to interrupt our honeymoon
To cope with the rats that streamed in through the window.)
The viper kept a meticulous account book
In which she noted every penny I borrowed from her,
She would not let me use the toothbrush I had given her myself,
And she accused me of having ruined her youth:
With her eyes flashing fire she threatened to take me to court
And make me pay part of the debt within a reasonable period
Since she needed the money to go on with her studies.
Then I had to take to the street and live on public charity,
Sleeping on park benches
Where the police found me time and again, dying,
Among the first leaves of autumn.
Fortunately that state of affairs went no further,
For one time—and again I was in a park,
Posing for a photographer—
A pair of delicious feminine hands suddenly covered my eyes
While a voice that I loved asked me: Who am I.

You are my love, I answered serenely.
My angel! she said nervously.
Let me sit on your knees once again!
It was then that I was able to ponder the fact that she was now wearing
   brief tights.
It was a memorable meeting, though full of discordant notes.
I have bought a plot of land not far from the slaughterhouse, she
   exclaimed.
I plan to build a sort of pyramid there
Where we can spend the rest of our days.
I have finished my studies, I have been admitted to the bar,
I have a tidy bit of capital at my disposal;
Let's go into some lucrative business, we two, my love, she added,
Let's build our nest far from the world.
Enough of your foolishness, I answered, I have no confidence in your
   plans.
Bear in mind that my real wife
Can at any moment leave both of us in the most frightful poverty.
My children are grown up, time has elapsed,
I feel utterly exhausted, let me have a minute's rest,
Get me a little water, woman,
Get me something to eat from somewhere,
I'm starving,
I can't work for you any more,
It's all over between us.

QUESTIONS ON CONTENT

1. Who is the viper? Describe her nature: is she real? Imaginary? Symbolic?
2. How would you characterize his attitude toward the viper? What feelings does she inspire in him?
3. How does the viper treat him? What kinds of acts does she involve him in?
4. Where does he live with the viper? When she returns to him, where does she want him to live? What do these two locales have in common?
5. Does he return to the viper? Does he give her up? What do you think happens at the end of the poem?

QUESTIONS ON FORM

1. What is the overall tone of the poem? Is it serious? Ironic?
2. A catalogue in poetry is a listing of things or events for effect. Can you find a catalogue in this poem? (Hint: note the opening of the first stanza.) What effect does it have on the poem?
3. In poetry, a break within a line is called a "caesura." Are there any caesuras in this poem? What effect do they have on the poem?
4. Study the sentences making up the first stanza. Do they conform to any pattern? What? (Hint: examine sentence length.) What do they contribute to the poem?

SUGGESTIONS FOR WRITING

1. Write an imaginary sequel to this poem, saying what happened to the speaker and the viper, how they spent the rest of their lives together, where they lived, and whether or not they had any children. Invent as much detail as you can.
2. Write an essay arguing either that
   (a) the viper is a real person;
   (b) the viper is "symbolic."
   If (b), say what she symbolizes. In either case, make specific references to the poem in support of your argument.

PAT MAINARDI

POLITICS OF HOUSEWORK

The following article, written as a staccato interior monologue, is an analysis of the avoidance strategies that men sometimes use to get out of doing housework.

> Though women do not complain of the power of husbands, each complains of her own husband, or of the husbands of her friends. It is the same in all other cases of servitude; at least in the commencement of the emancipatory movement. The serfs did not at first complain of the power of the lords, but only of their tyranny.
>
> —JOHN STUART MILL
> *On the Subjection of Women*

1 Liberated women—very different from Women's Liberation! The first signals all kinds of goodies, to warm the hearts (not to mention other parts) of the most radical men. The other signals—HOUSEWORK. The first brings sex without marriage, sex before marriage, cozy housekeeping arrangements ("I'm living with this chick") and the self-content of knowing that you're not the kind of man who wants a doormat instead of a woman. That will come later. After all, who wants that old commodity anymore, the Standard American Housewife, all husband, home and kids? The New Commodity, the Liberated Woman, has sex a lot and has a Career, preferably something that can be fitted in with the household chores—like dancing, pottery, or painting.

2 On the other hand is Women's Liberation—and housework. What? You say this is all trivial? Wonderful! That's what I thought. It seemed perfectly reasonable. We both had careers, both had to work a couple of days a week to earn enough to live on, so why shouldn't we share the housework? So I suggested it to my mate and he agreed—most men are too hip to turn you down flat. You're right, he said. It's only fair.

3 Then an interesting thing happened. I can only explain it by stating that we women have been brainwashed more than even we can imagine. Probably too many years of seeing television women in ecstasy over their shiny waxed floors or breaking down over their dirty shirt collars. Men have no such

conditioning. They recognize the essential fact of housework right from the very beginning. Which is that it stinks.

4 Here's my list of dirty chores: buying groceries, carting them home and putting them away; cooking meals and washing dishes and pots; doing the laundry, digging out the place when things get out of control; washing floors. The list could go on but the sheer necessities are bad enough. All of us have to do these things, or get someone else to do them for us. The longer my husband contemplated these chores, the more repulsed he became, and so proceeded the change from the normally sweet, considerate Dr. Jekyll into the crafty Mr. Hyde who would stop at nothing to avoid the horrors of—housework. As he felt himself backed into a corner laden with dirty dishes, brooms, mops and reeking garbage, his front teeth grew longer and pointier, his fingernails haggled and his eyes grew wild. Housework trivial? Not on your life! Just try to share the burden.

5 So ensued a dialogue that's been going on for several years. Here are some of the high points:

6 • "I don't mind sharing the housework, but I don't do it very well. We should each do the things we're best at." MEANING: Unfortunately I'm no good at things like washing dishes or cooking. What I do best is a little light carpentry, changing light bulbs, moving furniture (how often do *you* move furniture?). ALSO MEANING: Historically the lower classes (black men and us) have had hundreds of years experience doing menial jobs. It would be a waste of manpower to train someone else to do them now. ALSO MEANING: I don't like the dull, stupid, boring jobs, so you should do them.

7 • "I don't mind sharing the work, but you'll have to show me how to do it." MEANING: I ask a lot of questions and you'll have to show me everything every time I do it because I don't remember so good. Also don't try to sit down and read while I'M doing my jobs because I'm going to annoy hell out of you until it's easier to do them yourself.

8 • "We used to be so happy!" (Said whenever it was his turn to do something.) MEANING: I used to be so happy. MEANING: Life without housework is bliss. No quarrel here. Perfect Agreement.

9 • "We have different standards, and why should I have to work to your standards? That's unfair." MEANING: If I begin to get bugged by the dirt and crap I will say, "This place sure is a sty" or "How can anyone live like this?" and wait for your reaction. I know that all women have a sore called "Guilt over a messy house" or "Household work is ultimately my responsibility." I know that men have caused that sore—if anyone visits and the place *is* a sty, they're not going to leave and say, "He sure is a lousy housekeeper." You'll take the rap in any case. I can outwait you. ALSO MEANING: I can provoke innumerable scenes over the housework issue. Eventually doing all the housework yourself will be less painful to you than trying to get me to do half. Or I'll suggest we get a maid. She will do my share of the work. You will do yours. It's women's work.

10 • "I've got nothing against sharing the housework, but you can't make me do it on your schedule." MEANING: Passive resistance. I'll do it when I damned well please, if at all. If my job is doing dishes, it's easier to do them once a week. If taking out laundry, once a month. If washing the floors, once a year. If you don't like it, do it yourself oftener, and then I won't do it at all.

11 • "I hate it more than you. You don't mind it so much." MEANING: Housework is garbage work. It's the worst crap I've ever done. It's degrading and humiliating for someone of *my* intelligence to do it. But for someone of *your* intelligence . . .

12 • "Housework is too trivial to even talk about." MEANING: It's even more trivial to do. Housework is beneath my status. My purpose in life is to deal with matters of significance. Yours is to deal with matters of insignificance. You should do the housework.

13 • "This problem of housework is not a man-woman problem. In any relationship between two people one is going to have a stronger personality and dominate." MEANING: That stronger personality had better be *me*.

14 • "In animal societies, wolves, for example, the top animal is usually a male even where he is not chosen for brute strength but on the basis of cunning and intelligence. Isn't that interesting?" MEANING: I have historical, psychological, anthropological and biological justification for keeping you down. How can you ask the top wolf to be equal?

15 • "Women's liberation isn't really a political movement." MEANING: The revolution is coming too close to home. ALSO MEANING: I am only interested in how I am oppressed, not how I oppress others. Therefore the war, the draft and the university are political. Women's liberation is not.

16 • "Man's accomplishments have always depended on getting help from other people, mostly women. What great man would have accomplished what he did if he had to do his own housework?" MEANING: Oppression is built into the system and I, as the white American male, receive the benefits of this system. I don't want to give them up.

17 Participatory democracy begins at home. If you are planning to implement your politics, there are certain things to remember:

18 1. He *is* feeling it more than you. He's losing some leisure and you're gaining it. The measure of your oppression is his resistance.

19 2. A great many American men are not accustomed to doing monotonous, repetitive work which never issues in any lasting, let alone important, achievement. This is why they would rather repair a cabinet than wash dishes. If human endeavors are like a pyramid with man's highest achievements at the top, then keeping oneself alive is at the bottom. Men have always had servants (us) to take care of this bottom stratum of life while they have confined their efforts to the rarefied upper regions. It is thus ironic when they ask of women—Where are your great painters, statesmen, etc.? Mme Matisse ran a millinery shop so he could paint. Mrs. Martin Luther King kept his house and raised his babies.

20 3. It is a traumatizing experience for someone who has always thought

of himself as being against any oppression or exploitation of one human being by another to realize that in his daily life he has been accepting and implementing (and benefiting from) this exploitation; that his rationalization is little different from that of the racist who says, "Black people don't feel pain" (women don't mind doing the shitwork); and that the oldest form of oppression in history has been the oppression of 50 percent of the population by the other 50 percent.

21 4. Arm yourself with some knowledge of the psychology of oppressed peoples everywhere, and a few facts about the animal kingdom. I admit playing top wolf or who runs the gorillas is silly but as a last resort men bring it up all the time. Talk about bees. If you feel really hostile bring up the sex life of spiders. They have sex. She bites off his head.

22 The psychology of oppressed peoples is not silly. Jews, immigrants, black men and all women have employed the same psychological mechanisms to survive: admiring the oppressor, glorifying the oppressor, wanting to be like the oppressor, wanting the oppressor to like them, mostly because the oppressor held all the power.

23 5. In a sense, all men everywhere are slightly schizoid—divorced from the reality of maintaining life. This makes it easier for them to play games with it. It is almost a cliché that women feel greater grief at sending a son off to a war or losing him to that war because they bore him, suckled him, and raised him. The men who foment those wars did none of those things and have a more superficial estimate of the worth of human life. One hour a day is a low estimate of the amount of time one has to spend "keeping" oneself. By foisting this off on others, man has seven hours a week—one working day more to play with his mind and not his human needs. Over the course of generations it is easy to see whence evolved the horrifying abstractions of modern life.

24 6. With the death of each form of oppression, life changes and new forms evolve. English aristocrats at the turn of the century were horrified at the idea of enfranchising working men—were sure that it signaled the death of civilization and a return to barbarism. Some working men were even deceived by this line. Similarly with the minimum wage, abolition of slavery, and female suffrage. Life changes but it goes on. Don't fall for any line about the death of everything if men take a turn at the dishes. They will imply that you are holding back the revolution (their revolution). But you are advancing it (your revolution).

25 7. Keep checking up. Periodically consider who's actually *doing* the jobs. These things have a way of backsliding so that a year later once again the woman is doing everything. After a year make a list of jobs the man has rarely if ever done. You will find cleaning pots, toilets, refrigerators and ovens high on the list. Use time sheets if necessary. He will accuse you of being petty. He is above that sort of thing (housework). Bear in mind that the worst jobs are, namely the ones that have to be done every day or several times a day. Also the ones that are dirty—it's more pleasant to pick up books, newspapers, etc., than to wash dishes. Alternate the bad jobs. It's the daily grind that gets you

down. Also make sure that you don't have the responsibility for the housework with occasional help from him. "I'll cook dinner for you tonight" implies it's really your job and isn't he a nice guy to do some of it for you.

26 8. Most men had a rich and rewarding bachelor life during which they did not starve or become encrusted with crud or buried under the litter. There is a taboo that says women mustn't strain themselves in the presence of men—we haul around 50 pounds of groceries if we have to but aren't allowed to open a jar if there is someone around to do it for us. The reverse side of the coin is that men aren't supposed to be able to take care of themselves without a woman. Both are excuses for making women do the housework.

27 9. Beware of the double whammy. He won't do the little things he always did because you're now a "Liberated Woman," right? Of course he won't do anything else either . . .

28 I was just finishing this when my husband came in and asked what I was doing. Writing a paper on housework. Housework? he said. *Housework?* Oh my god how trivial can you get? A paper on housework.

VOCABULARY

ecstasy (3)	rationalization (20)
conditioning (3)	schizoid (23)
repulsed (4)	cliché (23)
haggled (4)	foment (23)
stratum (19)	foisting (23)
rarefied (19)	enfranchising (24)
traumatizing (20)	suffrage (24)

QUESTIONS ON CONTENT

1. According to the first paragraph, what is the distinction between "liberated women" and "Women's Liberation"? Which do men prefer, and why?
2. What was the initial reaction of the author's husband to her suggestion that they share housework? What was his second reaction?
3. Why, according to the author, did her husband resist doing his share of housework?
4. Why, according to the author, are there so few great women painters, statesmen, etc.?
5. What is the "double whammy"?

QUESTIONS ON FORM

1. What function does the parenthetical expression in paragraph 1 serve?
2. How does the author use sentence fragments in this essay? What function do these fragments serve?
3. Why does the author give so many quotations throughout the essay? What function do these serve?
4. In paragraph 7 the author writes: "I ask a lot of questions and you'll have to show

me everything every time I do it because I don't remember so good." What is grammatically wrong with this sentence? Why is it worded this way?

5. What function does the final paragraph serve?

SUGGESTIONS FOR WRITING

1. Write an essay arguing for or against the author's thesis that men strive mightily to get out of doing their share of housework.
2. The author claims that women are brainwashed into being ecstatic about housework. Write an essay agreeing or disagreeing with this notion, giving specific examples to support your views.

CHAPTER WRITING ASSIGNMENTS

1. Analyze the concept of "reality" in the Thoreau article and the Hughes story.
2. Present your own ideas on how a writer finds his "voice" in his writing. Apply these ideas to any one of the selections in this section.

three

What's a Thesis?
The Controlling Idea

model

At the heart of most good nonfiction prose there is a general statement that *controls* the development of the composition, *predicts* its content, and *obligates* the writer to a certain restricted topic. This general statement is called a *thesis*.

The most convenient place for the thesis is somewhere near the beginning of the essay. Consider the following placements:

1. Thesis as opening sentence

    Forget about reform; it's time to talk about abolishing jails and prisons in American society.

Arthur I. Waskow, " . . . I Am Not Free," *Saturday Review,* January 8, 1972.

2. Thesis in middle of first paragraph

    As long as women were brought up and educated very differently from men and as long as their whole mode of life was different, it was safe and suitable to uphold the traditional beliefs as to certain mental sex differences. But as the differentiation in the education of the two sexes lessened so have the actual differences in their abilities and interest. *Today the survival of some of these stereotypes is a psychological strait jacket for both sexes.* Witness the fact that some 40 per cent of women undergraduates have confessed (the proportion was confirmed in two studies on widely separated college campuses) that they have occasionally "played dumb" on dates; that is, concealed some academic honor, pre-

58

tended ignorance of a subject, "threw games," played down certain skills in obedience to the unwritten law that the man must be superior in those particular areas. If he *were* superior, the stratagem would not be necessary. "It embarrassed me that my 'steady' in high school," recalled a college junior in an interview, "got worse marks than I. A boy should naturally do better in school. I would never tell him my marks and would often ask him to help me with my homework." Confront the belief "a boy should naturally do better in school" with the fact that the marks of high school girls are generally somewhat superior to those of boys, probably because girls study more conscientiously. Could a surer recipe for trouble be invented?

Mirra Komarovsky, "The Bright Girl's Dilemma," in *Women in the Modern World.*

3. Thesis at end of introduction (often first paragraph)

What has happened to sex during the last fifteen years? Among those over thirty-five, there is a feeling, half-envious and half-appalled, that the younger generation is calmly but insatiably erotic. What was tense sexual melodrama twenty years ago seems to be little more than reflex action today. If the sophisticated young are no longer agitated about sex, it is because sex is no longer a problem for them. *We appear to be living through a sexual revolution.* It is a quiet revolution—not a rebellion—without ideological fireworks or flamboyance or protest.

David Boroff, "The Quiet Revolution," *Esquire,* July 1961.

4. Statement of purpose as thesis

My aim in this essay is to raise the question "Is there such a thing as mental illness?" and to argue that there is not. Since the notion of mental illness is extremely widely used nowadays, inquiry into the ways in which this term is employed would seem to be especially indicated. Mental illness, of course, is not literally a "thing"—or physical object—and hence it can "exist" only the same sort of way in which other theoretical concepts exist. Yet, familiar theories are in the habit of posing, sooner or later—at least to those who come to believe in them—as "objective truths" (or "facts"). During certain historical periods, explanatory conceptions such as deities, witches, and microorganisms appeared not only as theories but as self-evident *causes* of a vast number of events. I submit that today mental illness is widely regarded in a somewhat similar fashion, that is, as the cause of innumerable diverse happenings. As an antidote to the complacent use of the notion of mental illness—whether as a self-evident phenomenon, theory, or cause—let us ask this question: What is meant when it is asserted that someone is mentally ill?

In what follows I shall describe briefly the main uses to which the concept of mental illness has been put. I shall argue that this notion has outlived whatever usefulness it might have had and that it now functions merely as a convenient myth.

Thomas S. Szasz, "The Myth of Mental Illness," *American Psychologist,* February 1960.

5. Controlling question as thesis

Why has your marriage failed? No doubt you have asked yourself this question many times. Perhaps your questioning has led you farther, and you have asked why marriage in general seems so impermanent at this mid-point in the twentieth century.

J. Louise Despert, M.D., "Why Do Marriages Fail?" in *Children of Divorce.*

advice

SHERIDAN BAKER

THE THESIS

Many good essays are launched by stating clearly in a sharp-edged thesis the controlling purpose. (From *The Complete Stylist.*)

You can usually blame a bad essay on a bad beginning. If your essay falls apart, it probably has no primary idea to hold it together. "What's the big idea?" we used to ask. The phrase will serve as a reminder that you must find the "big idea" behind your several smaller thoughts and musings before you start to write. In the beginning was the *logos,* says the Bible—the idea, the plan, caught in a flash as if in a single word. Find your *logos,* and you are ready to round out your essay and set it spinning.

The big idea behind our ride in the speeding car was that in adolescence, especially, the group can have a very deadly influence on the individual. If you had not focused your big idea in a thesis, you might have begun by picking up thoughts at random, something like this:

Everyone thinks he is a good driver. There are more accidents caused by young drivers than any other group. Driver education is a good beginning, but further practice is very necessary. People who object to driver education do not realize that modern society, with its suburban pattern of growth, is built around the automobile. The car becomes a way of life and a status symbol. When a teen-ager goes too fast he is probably only copying his own father.

A little reconsideration, aimed at a good thesis-sentence, could turn this into a reasonably good beginning:

Modern society is built on the automobile. Every child looks forward to the time when he can drive; every teen-ager, to the day when his father lets him take out the car alone. Soon he is testing his skill at higher and higher speeds, especially with a group of friends along. One final test at extreme speeds usually suffices. The teen-ager's high-speed ride, if it does not kill him, will probably open his eyes to the deadly dynamics of the group.

Thus the central idea, or thesis, is your essay's life and spirit. If your thesis is sufficiently firm and clear, it may tell you immediately how to organize your supporting material and so obviate elaborate planning. If you do not find a thesis, your essay will be a tour through the miscellaneous. An essay replete with scaffolds and catwalks—"We have just seen this; now let us turn to this"—is an essay in which the inherent idea is weak or nonexistent. A purely expository and descriptive essay, one simply about "Cats," for instance, will have to rely on outer scaffolding alone (some orderly progression from Persia to Siam) since it really has no idea at all. It is all subject, all cats, instead of being based on an idea *about* cats.

The Argumentative Edge

FIND YOUR THESIS

The *about*-ness puts an argumentative edge on the subject. When you have something to say *about* cats, you have found your underlying idea. You have something to defend, something to fight about: not just "Cats," but "The cat is really man's best friend." Now the hackles on all dog men are rising, and you have an argument on your hands. You have something to prove. You have a thesis.

"What's the big idea, Mac?" Let the impudence in that time-honored demand remind you that the best thesis is a kind of affront to somebody. No one will be very much interested in listening to you deplete the thesis "The dog is man's best friend." Everyone knows that already. Even the dog lovers will be uninterested, convinced that they know better than you. But the cat . . .

So it is with any unpopular idea. The more unpopular the viewpoint and the stronger the push against convention, the stronger the thesis and the more energetic the essay. Compare the energy in "Democracy is good" with that in

"Communism is good," for instance. The first is filled with platitudes, the second with plutonium. By the same token, if you can find the real energy in "Democracy is good," if you can get down through the sand to where the roots and water are, you will have a real essay, because the opposition against which you generate your energy is the heaviest in the world: boredom. Probably the most energetic thesis of all, the greatest inner organizer, is some tired old truth that you cause to jet with new life, making the old ground green again.

To find a thesis and to put it into one sentence is to narrow and define your subject to a workable size. Under "Cats" you must deal with all felinity from the jungle up, carefully partitioning the eons and areas, the tigers and tabbies, the sizes and shapes. The minute you proclaim the cat the friend of man, you have pared away whole categories and chapters, and need only think up the arguments sufficient to overwhelm the opposition. So, put an argumentative edge on your subject—and you will have found your thesis.

Simple exposition, to be sure, has its uses. You may want to tell someone how to build a doghouse, how to can asparagus, how to follow the outlines of relativity, or even how to write an essay. Performing a few exercises in simple exposition will no doubt sharpen your insight into the problems of finding orderly sequences, of considering how best to lead your readers through the hoops, of writing clearly and accurately. It will also illustrate how much finer and surer an argument is.

You will see that picking an argument immediately simplifies the problems so troublesome in straight exposition: the defining, the partitioning, the narrowing of the subject. Actually, you can put an argumentative edge on the flattest of expository subjects. "How to build a doghouse" might become "Building a doghouse is a thorough introduction to the building trades, including architecture and mechanical engineering." "Canning asparagus" might become "An asparagus patch is a course in economics." "Relativity" might become "Relativity is not so inscrutable as many suppose." You have simply assumed that you have a loyal opposition consisting of the uninformed, the scornful, or both. You have given your subject its edge; you have limited and organized it at a single stroke. Pick an argument, then, and you will automatically be defining and narrowing your subject, and all the partitions you don't need will fold up. Instead of dealing with things, subjects, and pieces of subjects, you will be dealing with an idea and its consequences.

SHARPEN YOUR THESIS

Come out with your subject pointed. Take a stand, make a judgment of value. Be reasonable, but don't be timid. It is helpful to think of your thesis, your main idea, as a debating question—"Resolved: Old age pensions must go"—taking out the "Resolved" when you actually write the subject down. But your resolution will be even stronger, your essay clearer and tighter, if you can sharpen your thesis even further—"Resolved: Old age pensions must go because——." Fill in that blank and your worries are practically over. The main idea is to put your whole argument into one sentence.

Try, for instance: "Old age pensions must go because they are making people irresponsible." I don't know at all if that is true, and neither will you until you write your way into it, considering probabilities and alternatives and objections, and especially the underlying assumptions. In fact, no one, no master sociologist or future historian, can tell absolutely if it is true, so multiplex are the causes in human affairs, so endless and tangled the consequences. The basic assumption—that irresponsibility is growing—may be entirely false. No one, I repeat, can tell absolutely. But by the same token, your guess may be as good as another's. At any rate, you are now ready to write. You have found your *logos*.

Now you can put your well-pointed thesis-sentence on a card on the wall in front of you to keep from drifting off target. But you will now want to dress it for the public, to burnish it and make it comely. Suppose you try:

Old age pensions, perhaps more than anything else, are eroding our heritage of personal and familial responsibility.

But is this true? Perhaps you had better try something like:

Despite their many advantages, old age pensions may actually be eroding our heritage of personal and familial responsibility.

This is really your thesis, and you can write that down on a scrap of paper too.

discussion

HARRY CROSBY AND GEORGE ESTEY

THE CONTROLLING CONCEPT

By supplying appropriate examples and commenting on them, the excerpt below demonstrates how a thesis works. (From *College Writing: The Rhetorical Imperative*.)

"A speech has two parts. You must state your thesis, and you must prove it."

—ARISTOTLE

1 Most of the writing in serious magazines, in military, professional, political, scientific, and literary reports, in college term papers, and in all other forms of nonfiction prose is composed of a mixture of definitive and generative sentences. Each composition has at its core a generative sentence that is the broadest or most complex idea in the work. It is this sentence that gives unity and purpose to the total effort.

2 That prose literature has unity is easily seen by examining almost any book or magazine article. Thomas Macaulay, in *The History of England from the Accession of James II* (1849–1861), does not merely present a vivid and detailed history of England from the reign of James II to the death of William

III; he tried to prove that England under the influence of a Whig government and the Protestant religion was the best of all possible worlds. Another famous work of history, Frederick Jackson Turner's speech at the American Historical Association's meeting in Chicago in 1893, "The Significance of the Frontier in American History," set out to prove that America is the product of a series of developments accompanying the new type of frontier.

3 Almost invariably the central idea is expressly stated. The monumental *Main Currents in American Thought,* by Vernon L. Parrington, contains in its introduction this sentence:

> I have undertaken to give some account of the genesis and development in American letters of certain germinal ideas that have come to be reckoned traditionally American—how they came into being here, how they were exposed, and what influence they have exerted in determining the form and scope of our characteristic ideals and institutions.

4 This is Professor Parrington's purpose statement; it controls the entire work. The work is divided into three volumes, and each volume is broken into books. Part One of the first book in Volume I is called "The Puritan Heritage." Preceding it is a brief introduction that ends with the book's thesis or generative statement: "The Puritan was a contribution of the old world, created by the rugged idealism of the English Reformation; the Yankee was a product of native conditions, created by practical economics."

5 Thorstein Veblen's *The Theory of the Leisure Class* (1899) attempts to prove that the leisure class represents a continuing maladjustment of modern institutions that causes a reversion to an archaic scheme of life. He expresses this idea in a thesis sentence in the first chapter of his work.

6 Shorter prose literature also has the characteristic of stating the central idea. Francis Bacon's essay "Of Studies" begins, "Studies serve for delight, for ornament, and for ability," thus giving the reader cause to anticipate three reasons why study is valuable. "The Method of Scientific Investigation," an essay by Thomas Henry Huxley,[1] contains in its introduction the sentence, "The method of scientific investigation is nothing but the expression of the necessary mode of working of the human mind"; the rest of the essay describes the scientific method and shows why the human mind must use the method to arrive at sound ideas. In an article in the *Saturday Evening Post* (July 13, 1957), a testy English baron, Lord Conesford, put his thesis in his title, "You Americans Are Murdering the Language," and you can anticipate what followed. In a *New Yorker* article (December 16, 1950), John Hersey wrote, "This conference caused frightful headlines all over the world about the possible use of the atomic bomb in Korea and China, and it also provided a hair-raising example of how bad news can be manufactured." Hersey's statement is another example of the generative sentence that predicts and obligates the rest of the article.

[1] Huxley's essay follows this one.—Ed.

7 This characteristic of good writing is known to skilled readers. According to Mortimer Adler and almost every other reading expert, the first requirement of effective reading is that you must be able to put in a single sentence the central message or thesis of the material you are reading. Very often, when skilled students read a book, they underline certain passages. This is a good technique—if the proper sections are selected. Too often, students underline only the sections they find interesting. The single sentence that should be underlined is the thesis or purpose statement of the book, its generative sentence. Almost every author, either in the introduction, the first chapter, or the final chapter, sums up his central idea. When you locate the sentence you aid comprehension. Take, for instance, the very difficult *Education of Henry Adams.* Many readers start out with Chapter 1; instead, they should begin with the preface, for in it are found these two sentences: "Except in the abandoned sphere of dead languages, no one has discussed what part of education has, in his personal experience, turned out to be useful, and what not. This volume attempts to discuss it." From these sentences the reader has a frame on which to hang all subsequent material. Reviewers frequently have misunderstood Adams's purpose; in spite of its title, they have perceived his book to be an autobiography and have criticized it because it makes no reference to such personal matters as his marriage and the suicide of his wife.

8 As Walter Pater has said, one of the delights of reading worthwhile prose is to detect the point of the composition, and then to follow an orderly mind through the content that must follow. If the thesis is not established and the content does not fulfill its obligation, we do not have effective, valuable writing.

VOCABULARY

definitive (1)	genesis (3)
generative (1)	germinal (3)
accession (2)	idealism (4)
Whig (2)	reversion (5)
expressly (3)	mode (6)
monumental (3)	

QUESTIONS ON CONTENT

1. What is the synonym used by Crosby and Estey for thesis? Why is this word appropriate?
2. What is the purpose of the thesis?
3. Suggest a circumstance in which a thesis would not need to be "expressly" stated.
4. Who is Mortimer Adler? Why do the authors quote him?
5. According to the authors, what passages in books do students tend to underline? Which passages ought they to underline? Comment on your own habits in this regard.

QUESTIONS ON FORM

1. What two words in the opening paragraph require further defining before you can fully understand the paragraph?
2. Judging from the thesis, at what level of student has Vernon L. Parrington aimed his book *Main Currents in American Thought?*
3. Where is the thesis of this essay located?

SUGGESTIONS FOR WRITING

1. Locate and copy down the thesis of at least three books at your library. This thesis must be stated expressly in one sentence. Follow Crosby and Estey's suggestion of checking the preface or introduction in each book.
2. Using any article of your choice taken from this book, supply the following: (a) a thesis, (b) a controlling question as thesis, (c) a statement of purpose as thesis.

examples

T. H. HUXLEY

THE METHOD OF SCIENTIFIC INVESTIGATION

In a series of closely knit paragraphs from his *Autobiography and Selected Letters,* the English biologist T. H. Huxley (1825–95) explains the logical processes of deduction and induction, indicating that these terms are merely technical names for thought habits we all use.

1 The method of scientific investigation is nothing but the expression of the necessary mode of working of the human mind. It is simply the mode at which all phenomena are reasoned about, rendered precise and exact. There is no more difference, but there is just the same kind of difference, between the mental operations of a man of science and those of an ordinary person, as there is between the operations and methods of a baker or of a butcher weighing out his goods in common scales and the operation of a chemist in performing a difficult and complex analysis by means of his balance and finely graduated weights. It is not that the action of the scales in the one case and the balance in the other differ in the principles of their construction or manner of working; but the beam of one is set on an infinitely finer axis than the other, and of course turns by the addition of a much smaller weight.

2 You will understand this better, perhaps, if I give you some familiar example. You have all heard it repeated, I dare say, that men of science work by means of induction and deduction, and that by the help of these operations, they, in a sort of sense, wring from Nature certain other things, which are called natural laws and causes, and that out of these, by some cunning skill of their own, they build up hypotheses and theories. And it is imagined by many that the operations of the common mind can be by no means compared with

these processes, and that they have to be acquired by a sort of special apprenticeship to the craft. To hear all these large words, you would think that the mind of a man of science must be constituted differently from that of his fellow men; but if you will not be frightened by terms, you will discover that you are quite wrong, and that all these terrible apparatus are being used by yourselves every day and every hour of your lives.

3 There is a well-known incident in one of Molière's[1] plays, where the author makes the hero express unbounded delight on being told that he has been talking prose during the whole of his life. In the same way, I trust that you will take comfort, and be delighted with yourselves, on the discovery that you have been acting on the principles of inductive and deductive philosophy during the same period. Probably there is not one here who has not in the course of the day had occasion to set in motion a complex train of reasoning, of the very same kind, though differing of course in degree, as that which a scientific man goes through in tracing the causes of natural phenomena.

4 A very trivial circumstance will serve to exemplify this. Suppose you go into a fruiterer's shop, wanting an apple—you take one up, and, on biting, you find it is sour; you look at it, and see that it is hard, and green. You take up another one and that too is hard, green, and sour. The shop man offers you a third; but, before biting it, you examine it, and find that it is hard and green, and you immediately say that you will not have it, as it must be sour, like those that you have already tried.

5 Nothing can be more simple than that, you think; but if you will take the trouble to analyze and trace out into its logical elements what has been done by the mind, you will be greatly surprised. In the first place, you have performed the operation of induction. You found, that, in two experiences, hardness and greenness in apples went together with sourness. It was so in the first case, and it was confirmed by the second. True, it is a very small basis, but still it is enough to make an induction from; you generalize the facts, and you expect to find sourness in apples where you get hardness and greenness. You found upon that a general law, that all hard and green apples are sour; and that, so far as it goes, is a perfect induction. Well, having got your natural law in this way, when you are offered another apple which you find is hard and green, you say, "All hard and green apples are sour; this apple is hard and green, therefore this apple is sour." That train of reasoning is what logicians call a syllogism and has all its various parts and terms—its major premise, its minor premise, and its conclusion. And, by the help of further reasoning, which, if drawn out, would have to be exhibited in two or three other syllogisms, you arrive at your final determination: "I will not have that apple." So that, you see, you have, in the first place, established a law by induction, and upon that you have founded a deduction and reasoned out the special conclusion of the particular case. Well now, suppose, having got your law, that at some time afterwards, you are discussing the qualities of apples

---

[1]Pen name of Jean-Baptiste Poquelin (1622–73), French playwright.—Ed.

with a friend; you will say to him, "It is a very curious thing—but I find that all hard and green apples are sour!" Your friend says to you, "But how do you know that?" You at once reply, "Oh, because I have tried them over and over again and have always found them to be so." Well, if we were talking science instead of common sense, we should call that an experimental verification. And, if still opposed, you go further and say, "I have heard from the people in Somersetshire and Devonshire, where a large number of apples are grown, that they have observed the same thing. It is also found to be the case in Normandy, and in North America. In short, I find it to be the universal experience of mankind wherever attention has been directed to the subject." Whereupon your friend, unless he is a very unreasonable man, agrees with you and is convinced that you are quite right in the conclusion you have drawn. He believes, although perhaps he does not know he believes it, that the more extensive verifications are—that the more frequently experiments have been made and results of the same kind arrived at—that the more varied the conditions under which the same results are attained, the more certain is the ultimate conclusion, and he disputes the question no further. He sees that the experiment has been tried under all sorts of conditions, as to time, place, and people, with the same result; and he says with you, therefore, that the law you have laid down must be a good one, and he must believe it.

6 In science we do the same thing; the philosopher exercises precisely the same faculties, though in a much more delicate manner. In scientific inquiry it becomes a matter of duty to expose a supposed law to every possible kind of verification and to take care, moreover, that this is done intentionally and not left to a mere accident, as in the case of the apples. And in science, as in common life, our confidence in a law is in exact proportion to the absence of variation in the result of our experimental verifications. For instance, if you let go your grasp of an article you may have in your hand, it will immediately fall to the ground. That is a very common verification of one of the best established laws of nature—that of gravitation. The method by which men of science established the existence of that law is exactly the same as that by which we have established the trivial proposition about the sourness of hard and green apples. But we believe it in such an extensive, thorough, and unhesitating manner because the universal experience of mankind verifies it, and we can verify it ourselves at any time; and that is the strongest possible foundation on which any natural law can rest.

VOCABULARY

phenomena (1)	exemplify (4)
analysis (1)	logicians (5)
induction (2)	syllogism (5)
deduction (2)	premise (5)
hypotheses (2)	faculties (6)
theories (2)	inquiry (6)
apparatus (2)	variation (6)

QUESTIONS ON CONTENT

1. What is Huxley's thesis? State it in your own words.
2. What is the strongest possible foundation on which any natural law can rest?
3. Based on the analogy of the baker, butcher, and chemist in paragraph 1, what is the difference between our own investigations and those of science?
4. A familiar example of induction is the conclusion, from a few tastes, that hard, green apples are sour; a familiar example of deduction is the decision not to buy the untasted hard, green apple because it is sour. Can you draw an inductive and deductive conclusion about the following: (a) ice cubes, (b) boiling water, (c) measles?
5. Huxley proposes the following syllogism:

   All hard and green apples are sour.
   This apple is hard and green.
   This apple is sour.

   Set up the same kind of syllogism with the following major premise: All human beings are mortal.
6. Now analyze the following syllogism:

   All redheads are passionate.
   This girl is a readhead.
   This girl is passionate.

   Does the syllogism have the same validity as Huxley's example of the green apple? Explain.

QUESTIONS ON FORM

1. What makes Huxley's article understandable to readers who are not professional scientists?
2. What is the purpose of the allusion to a character in one of Molière's plays?
3. Huxley is careful to illustrate all his scientific terms. Test yourself: explain the meaning of "inductive," "deductive," "verification," and "experiment."

SUGGESTIONS FOR WRITING

1. Write a summary of a notable experiment made by some famous scientist. (Examples: Madame Curie, Kepler, Galileo, Darwin, Newton.)
2. Describe the inductive logic that led you to some important conclusion in your life.

JOSEPH WOOD KRUTCH

THE SHODDY ETHICS OF ALIENATION

Through careful details and numerous illustrations, Krutch supports his thesis that the best way to help a society in turmoil is to improve oneself, not to rebel in a self-destructive, alienated way.

1 Some years ago a distinguished playwright told me how he had taken his

East Side mother-in-law to see Maurice Evans in *Richard III*. The old lady—whose experience with both literature and the theatre was extremely limited—listened intently in silence for half an hour, then waved a derisive thumb in the direction of the mellifluously complaining Richard and announced firmly: "I don't sympathize."

2 Now this was, of course, a fine tribute to the purely dramatic skill of Shakespeare. He had provoked the reaction he aimed at without any direct indication of what his own attitude was. I remember the anecdote at the moment for a simple reason. "I don't sympathize" vigorously sums up my own response to certain modern Richards, namely those who enlarge with too much self-pity upon their "alienation" from modern society, modern man and, indeed, from the universe as a whole. On the one hand I find myself ready to agree with a good deal of their criticism; on the other I am irritated by their chronic reaction to the things we both abhor.

3 To take the most obvious and least significant case, consider the beatniks. I dislike—almost if not quite as much as they do—the dominant middle-class and organization-man concept of the Good Life. Although we can't all be philosophers, scholars, artists or monks, I agree that too many moderns aspire to nothing more than the "status symbols" that money can buy, and far too few to what George N. Shuster recently defined as the ultimate aim of education: "sharing the life of the scholar, poet and saint." But to respond to this situation by taking a shot of heroin and driving a car at ninety miles an hour seems unlikely either to improve society or, what is more relevant, lead to a Good Life.

4 Sympathetic interpreters of the beatniks have described them as "taking a revenge on society." For example, the hero of a recent novel is described by a reviewer thus: "Seeing too well in a world dazed by the bomb, Renaud undertakes an alcoholic strike against humanity." But the phrase "an alcoholic strike," like "a revenge on society," seems to me merely comic. It suggests the popular saying about "biting off your nose to spite your face," that being precisely what some intellectuals (including many somewhat above the beatnik level) are doing—as though turning into a dope addict does not hurt oneself even more than it hurts anyone else. It seems only slightly less obvious that the more respectable intellectuals who devote themselves exclusively to exploring and exploiting their "alienation" are doing much the same thing. Surely it is more productive of personal happiness and even "more useful to society" to be a candle throwing its beams into a naughty world than a beatnik crying "revenge, revenge" from the gutter. We hear a great deal about the responsibility of society toward the individual. The individual also has a responsibility toward society. And if things are as bad as the alienated say, the only way one can discharge that responsibility is by being an honorable man.

5 I presume that this thesis hardly needs elaboration and is not likely to be contested outside beatnik circles. But a considerable number of the most talented novelists, poets, painters and composers of the present day reveal, even if they do not proclaim, their alienation; and it seems to me that their most frequent response is only less grotesque, not more fruitful, than that of

the beatniks. Even granted, as most of them proclaim in some version of Yeats's often quoted words that "Things fall apart; the centre cannot hold,"[1] is there still nothing for a wise man to do except take heroin with the beatniks or, as is usual among the alienated squares, elaborate in more and more complicated phrases their dark convictions?

6 To this question the hearty do-gooder will of course reply: "Why obviously the thing to do is to work for social improvement. Join the party of your choice and the church of your choice; be sure to register for all elections and attend the meetings of your local P.T.A." Without entering into any question concerning the ultimate effectiveness of such a method of employing one's time, it must be admitted that your alienated artist or philosopher is no more likely than a beatnik to undertake it. Let us suppose, therefore, that he has, like Thoreau, both "signed off" from the church and wished that he could as easily sign off from society as a whole. Of course he will be thoroughly disapproved of almost everywhere outside the circle of the completely alienated; but he might, like a few others besides Thoreau, find in this determination to stand alone the possibility of making for himself a private world from which he was *not* alienated, instead of devoting himself exclusively to the task of saying just how alienated he is. He could even find a few justifications formulated in the past for doing just what he had done.

7 I seem to remember somewhere in Plato the opinion that when times are thoroughly bad a wise man will merely stand by the wall. Similarly, it would appear from the *Meditations* of Marcus Aurelius that although the Emperor was no less aware than Yeats of a world in which "things fall apart," he spent relatively little time in either elaborating or bemoaning the lack of wisdom or virtue in society. He determined instead to cultivate them in himself. Then there is even a wholehearted defense of the mere slacker, which is quoted by Montaigne from one Theodorus who held that "It is not just that a wise man should risk his life for the good of his country and imperil wisdom for fools."

8 As I see it, the question is not so much whether the alienated would do better to imitate Marcus Aurelius rather than Baudelaire and Apollinaire, for it is a larger and, so many will think, an outrageous question. Is it possible that present-day civilization would be in some important respects better than it is if more people had thought less about how to improve society and more about how to improve themselves?

9 No doubt the medieval monk was too exclusively concerned with his private salvation. But we have gone to the other extreme and are so obsessed with the idea of society as a whole that it no longer seems quite respectable to seek even intellectual or spiritual self-improvement. I am not saying that we are, in actual fact, excessively unselfish. But the cant of the time requires that we should always be asking of any proposed good, "Can everybody have it?" or "Is it an answer to the general problem?" With astonishing regularity I get letters from people who comment on something I have written with a "well that's the answer so far as you are concerned; I guess it could be the answer so

---

[1]See W. B. Yeats's poem "The Second Coming."—Ed.

far as I am concerned. But only the privileged, or the lucky, or the well educated, or the intelligent, or the whatnot, can do what you and I can. So what is the answer for society as a whole?"

10 No doubt it would be fine if we could find a universal formula for salvation. I would welcome a convincing one if I ever heard it. But I never have, and I see no reason why, this being true, the individual should not save himself so long as he is not doing so at somebody else's expense. After all, society is composed of individuals. It cannot be "saved" except insofar as the individuals who compose it are.

11 I am not preaching universal indifference to society and social action as the highest wisdom. I am saying simply that if and when one individual feels (as so many articulate people do seem to feel) that the world is hopeless, then it is wiser to see what one can do about oneself than to give up all hope of that also. "I came into this world," said Thoreau, "not primarily to make it better but to live in it be it good or bad." If you insist, you may soften that a little by substituting "exclusively" for "primarily," but the meaning will still point in the same direction. Or as the same argument was recently discussed in that excellent "little magazine" called *Manas:* "If an artist can find nothing but bad brushes to paint with, he will not dissipate all his energies leading a revolution against bad brushes—but will develop techniques which make it possible for him to paint with bad brushes. He may even discover things that bad brushes do better than good brushes. It is one thing to fight the good fight for good brushes, and another to start to paint."

12 During the thirties, when most intellectuals moved leftward, quite a number of those who confessed (at least to their friends) that they had embraced communism were nevertheless engaged in writing movies for Hollywood or advertisements for Madison Avenue, while at the same time professing to regard both the movies and advertising as poisonous exhalations from a deliquescent society. Often (and I report from my own experience) they justified themselves by saying that there was no use trying to be anything but rotten in a rotten society. Comes the revolution and we will all be decent. Meanwhile, since we live in an evil society, we submit to it without any bourgeois nonsense about merely personal decency.

13 Such an attitude is only a logical extreme of the one taken by those who may not completely renounce either personal integrity or personal happiness, but insist upon our duty to think primarily in terms of what can be done for "society," and who sink into despair if we do not know an answer. I will even go so far as to suggest the possibility that society may be in a bad way partly because we have laid so much stress on public education—to take one example—and so little upon self-education. (Perhaps it also has something to do with the fact that I have met "educators" who were not and made no effort to be educated themselves.)

14 "Philanthropy," so Thoreau wrote, "is almost the only virtue which is sufficiently appreciated by mankind. . . . The kind uncles and aunts of the race are more esteemed than its true spiritual fathers and mothers. I once

heard a reverend lecturer on England, a man of learning and intelligence, after enumerating her scientific, literary and political worthies, Shakespeare, Bacon, Cromwell, Milton, Newton and others, speak next of her Christian heroes, whom, as if his profession required it of him, he elevated to a place far above all the rest, as the greatest of the great. They were Penn, Howard and Mrs. Fry. Everyone must feel the falsehood and cant of this. The last were not England's best men and women; only, perhaps, her best philanthropists.'' This is a tough-minded opinion. It is stated with characteristic exaggeration. But at least there is something to be said for those who do their best even though they do not see at the moment just what practical good it is going to do "for the common man.''

15 After all the medieval monk did perform a service. Neither the God he served nor the learning he preserved counted for much in the world from which he had retired. But he did exemplify in himself virtues that might otherwise have ceased to exist entirely, and he did preserve learning that without him would have been lost.

16 What it all comes down to in practice is simply this: if you despair of the world, don't despair of yourself. And it is because so many of the alienated critics of our society with whose criticisms I agree seem unable to do anything of the sort that I find myself alienated from them also.

17 Thirty years ago when I published a book much more pessimistic than I could possibly write now, I received a good many letters that might have been boiled down to a sentence in one of them: "If these are your convictions why don't you go hang yourself?'' The answer was, and has continued to be through all such changes of opinion as I have undergone, that there is a private world of thought and endeavor which society has never been able to take away from me.

18 Perhaps the most curious and shocking result of the exclusive stress upon social rather than upon private ethics is the disappearance of the concept of honor as distinct from that of morality. One of the differences between the two is simply that honor is relevant to the individual only. True, society may be more affected than some social scientists seem to think by the prevalence or scarcity of honor in the code of the individuals who make it up. But the man of honor always asks first whether or not an action would dishonor him personally, and he is not influenced by an argument that his dishonorable act would have no bad (perhaps even some good) effect upon society and is therefore "moral'' even if dishonorable.

19 The world would not now be as profoundly shocked as it was a generation ago by the phrase "a scrap of paper.'' We are used to having promises so treated. But the Junkers were merely a little ahead of us in their willingness to believe that since the triumph of Germany would promote the advent of the superman, there was nothing immoral in a broken oath.

20 Many college students, so the pollsters tell us, see nothing wrong about cheating on examinations. "Everybody does it and it doesn't really *hurt* anyone.''

21 In such statements it is easy to see a reasonable application of the two leading principles of ethics-without-absolutes-and-without-honor, which is sometimes called "socialized morality." These two leading principles are: (1) What everybody does must be permissible since the *mores* determine morality; and (2) Wrong can mean only "socially harmful."

22 If you believe all this and also that the only difference between, let us say, an honest man and a thief is the difference between a man who has been "conditioned" to act honestly and one who has not, then there isn't much basis for argument with the student opinion.

23 When some scandal breaks in government or journalism or business or broadcasting, the usual reaction of even that part of the public which is shocked by it is to say that it could not have happened if there had been adequate laws supervising this or that activity. But, usually, is it not equally true that it could not have happened if a whole group of men, often including the supposed guardians of public morality, had not been devoid of any sense of the meaning and importance of individual integrity? May one not go further and ask whether any amount of "social consciousness" and government control can make decent a society composed of people who have no conception of personal dignity and honor? It was a favorite and no doubt sound argument among early twentieth-century reformers that "playing the game" as the gentleman was supposed to play it was not enough. But has the time not come to add that it is, nevertheless, indispensable?

24 If the relevance of all this to the first part of the present discussion is not obvious, please allow me to dot the *i*'s. To those who believe that society is corrupt beyond redemption I propose the ancient but neglected concept of personal integrity, virtue and honor accompanied, if they feel it necessary, with the contempt and scorn recently advocated in a telling article in the [*American*] *Scholar* itself.

25 Those who hold that "social morality" is the only kind worth considering tend to assume that the end justifies the means. If a broken promise or a cynical invasion of a private right promotes "the greatest good of the greatest number" then it is an act of "higher morality." That seems to me a curiously inverted, soft-hearted and soft-headed Machiavellianism. The man of honor is reluctant to use dishonorable means no matter what ends seem to justify them. And he seems to be a safer member of society.

VOCABULARY

derisive (1)	deliquescent (12)
mellifluously (1)	bourgeois (12)
alienation (2)	philanthropy (14)
beatniks (3)	prevalence (18)
exploiting (4)	mores (21)
grotesque (5)	inverted (25)
cant (9)	Machiavellianism (25)

QUESTIONS ON CONTENT

1. What is Krutch's thesis and where is it expressly stated?
2. What about the "beatniks" does Krutch condemn? Do you agree or disagree with Krutch? Explain.
3. What is the danger in thinking more about improving oneself than about improving society?
4. Comment on the value of the ways to improve society mentioned in paragraph 6. Which activity do you consider the most important?
5. What is the meaning of Plato's opinion that "when times are thoroughly bad a wise man will merely stand by the wall"?
6. Krutch's article was published in 1960. Do you believe that today the majority of people are more concerned with personal improvement than they were a decade ago? Think especially of your college friends. Support your answer with examples.

QUESTIONS ON FORM

1. Krutch uses numerous allusions throughout his essay. How many of the following can you identify:

   (a) Yeats (5)   (h) Bacon (14)
   (b) Thoreau (6)   (i) Cromwell (14)
   (c) Plato (7)   (j) Milton (14)
   (d) Marcus Aurelius (7) (k) Newton (14)
   (e) Montaigne (7)   (l) Junkers (19)
   (f) Baudelaire (8)   (m) Machiavelli (25)
   (g) Apollinaire (8)

2. What two rhetorical devices does Krutch use to give his essay an effective beginning?
3. In what way are paragraphs 5 and 6 related to each other?
4. What is the analogy implied in the story of the painter in paragraph 11?
5. Do you consider the author's personal experience cited in paragraph 17 an effective part of the essay? Give your reasons why.
6. What is the tone of Krutch's essay?

SUGGESTIONS FOR WRITING

1. Choose a specific condition that you find intolerable in our society (violence, materialism, dishonesty, shoddy craftsmanship, pollution, laziness, and so on). Formulate a thesis that serves as an answer to the problem, then support that thesis with convincing details.
2. Choose a person from the past or present whom you consider ethical. Formulate a thesis about him and support the thesis with convincing details.

TERM PAPER SUGGESTION

Write a paper synthesizing the ethics proposed in some of the works written by a major writer. Suggestions: Bacon, Thoreau, Emerson, Montaigne.

T. S. MATTHEWS

THE POWER OF THE PRESS?

Matthews' essay is a succinct view of the power of the press and the limitations of that power. Matthews gives the American people credit for a basic common sense that cannot be manipulated by the press. (From *The Sugar Pill*.)

1 The biggest piece of clap-trap about the press is that it deals almost exclusively, or even mainly, with news.

2 And the next-biggest piece of clap-trap is that the press has enormous power. This delusion is persistent and widespread. It is taken for granted by the public-at-large, who are apt to be impressed by anything that is said three times; it is continually advertised by the press itself, and it is cherished by press lords, some of whom, at least, should know better. The Hutchins Commission of the Freedom of the Press, which represented a more-than-usually-intelligent public-at-large in the united States, not only took the power of the press at the press's own valuation, but thought it very alarming:

We have the impression that the American people do not realize what has happened to them. They are not aware that the communications revolution has occurred. They do not appreciate the tremendous power which the new instruments and the new organization of the press place in the hands of a few men.

3 In what way is the press supposed to be so powerful? The general notion is that the press can form, control or at least strongly influence public opinion. Can it really do any of these things? Hugh Cudlipp, editorial director of *The London Daily Mirror,* and a man who should know something about the effect of newspapers on public opinion, doesn't share this general notion about their power. He thinks newspapers can echo and stimulate a wave of popular feeling, but that's all. "A newspaper may successfully accelerate but never reverse the popular attitude that common sense has commended to the public." In short, it can jump aboard the bandwagon, once the bandwagon's under way, and exhort others to jump aboard too; but it can't start the bandwagon rolling, or change its direction after it's started.

4 Like other habit-forming pills, the press can stimulate or depress, but it cannot cure. It can fan fear and hatred of another nation (when the fear and hatred are there, waiting to be fanned) but it cannot make peace. As more and more people have painful reason to know, the press has a nasty kind of power—the same kind of power a bully has, of hurting somebody smaller and weaker than himself. An individual's only defense against the press is the law of libel, but considerable harm and much pain can be caused without going as far as to commit an actionable libel. Journalists themselves generally have a horror of being interviewed, "written up" or even noticed by the press—they know too well from their own experience how inept and cruel a distortion the

result is likely to be. Nine times out of ten, as they know, ineptness is to blame rather than conscious cruelty; but there is always that tenth case. And a blundering friendly hand can be as heavy as an unfriendly fist. The press is often like a clumsy giant who gives you a pat on the back and knocks the wind out of you, if he doesn't cause internal injuries. I remember once coming upon an elderly professor of my university who had just been "written up" by the paper I worked on. When he saw me, tears came into his eyes, and he said, "What have I done to them? What have I done to deserve this?" He was deeply wounded by the article, and regarded it as an extremely unkind caricature. Knowing that it had been written by one of his former students who liked and admired the professor, I tried to reassure him that it was at least kindly meant; I don't think I succeeded.

5 The press has a negative power—to titillate, alarm, enrage, amuse, humiliate, annoy, even to drive a person out of his community or his job. But of the positive power to which it pretends, and of which the press lords dream—to make and break governments, to swing an election, to stop a war or start a revolution—there is no tangible evidence. Its vaunted might is a gigantic spoof. Professor David Mitrany, speaking in 1932 on "The Press and International Relations," put the case with delicate irony:

> There is no need to spend time in an attempt to show how great is the influence of the press. It is greater in certain fields than in others. It is greater, one could say, in any field in which the knowledge and interest of the man in the street is lesser. For in that case the reading public is apt to think that the press speaks with authority; while the authorities are apt to assume that the press is speaking with the voice of the people.

6 Everyone has heard of the "power of the press"; no one has seen it. The greatest believers in this exaggerated "power" and the loudest promoters of it are, naturally, the press lords themselves. One of the most deluded of these, not even excepting Northcliffe or Beaverbrook, was Robert McCormick, publisher of *The Chicago Tribune* (still emblazoned with his modest motto: "The world's greatest newspaper"). McCormick, and of course his paper, were always in bitter opposition to the Roosevelt Democrats, as well as to the liberal element in his own Republican Party. A story used to be told about the *Tribune*—no doubt apocryphal but in essence true—that one of the janitors in the *Tribune* building always bet against any political candidate the paper supported, and gave odds to boot; and that he found this sideline so profitable that he was able to buy two sizable blocks of flats.

7 The people in Chicago who bought the *Tribune* didn't buy it to find out how to cast their votes: they bought it in spite of its advice and its bias, because on the whole they liked its personality and found it entertaining. Does this seem to argue a too shrewd, calm and sensible attitude on the part of the ordinary newspaper reader? The press is generally appreciated by the public for what it is rather than for what it pretends to be. They don't feel it as a power in their lives, but as a working-day prerequisite.

VOCABULARY

clap-trap (1)	titillate (5)
delusion (2)	vaunted (5)
exhort (3)	apocryphal (6)
libel (4)	prerequisite (7)
caricature (4)	

QUESTIONS ON CONTENT

1. What is the question that controls Matthews's essay? In which paragraph is it located?
2. How is the controlling question answered? Refer to specific passages.
3. What, according to Matthews, is the dominant reason why the press has limited powers only?
4. What is the meaning of the last sentence of the essay? In what way is the press a "prerequisite"?
5. Do you agree with Matthews's view of the limited power of the press? Explain your answer.

QUESTIONS ON FORM

1. In paragraph 4 Matthews uses two analogies to illustrate the power of the press. Explain both analogies.
2. In paragraph 5 Matthews refers to the vaunted might of the press as "a gigantic spoof." What figure of speech is this?
3. Matthews uses several quotations from other people. What is usually the effect of these quotations?
4. Paragraph 6 alludes to "press lords." Give an example of a past or present press lord in America.
5. How does Matthews introduce the quotation in paragraph 5? What is the stylistic function of this introduction?

SUGGESTIONS FOR WRITING

1. Summarize a newspaper article that you believe now has or once had the power to stimulate or depress the public. State reasons for your view.
2. Write a five-hundred-word essay arguing either for or against unrestricted freedom of the press. Begin with a clear thesis.
3. In a five-hundred-word essay answer the question, "What is the danger of filling the news with uninterpreted raw facts?"

JAMES BOSWELL

THE CHARACTER OF SAMUEL JOHNSON

This description is taken from the final pages of the famous biography by James Boswell (1740–95) of Samuel Johnson (1709–84). Having given a highly detailed account of Johnson's life, Boswell now proceeds with an overall descriptive summary of the man.

> "No need of Latin or of Greek to grace
> Our JOHNSON's memory, or inscribe his grave;
> His native language claims this mournful space,
> To pay the immortality he gave."

1 The character of SAMUEL JOHNSON has, I trust, been so developed in the course of this work, that they who have honored it with a perusal, may be considered as well acquainted with him. As, however, it may be expected that I should collect into one view the capital and distinguishing features of this extraordinary man, I shall endeavor to acquit myself of that part of my biographical undertaking,[1] however difficult it may be to do that which many of my readers will do better for themselves.

2 His figure was large and well formed, and his countenance of the cast of an ancient statue; yet his appearance was rendered strange and somewhat uncouth by convulsive cramps, by the scars of that distemper which it was once imagined the royal touch could cure, and by a slovenly mode of dress. He had the use only of one eye; yet so much does mind govern and even supply the deficiency of organs, that his visual perceptions, as far as they extended, were uncommonly quick and accurate. So morbid was his temperament that he never knew the natural joy of a free and vigorous use of his limbs: when he walked, it was like the struggling gait of one in fetters; when he rode, he had no command or direction of his horse, but was carried as if in a balloon. That with his constitution and habits of life he should have lived seventy-five years, is a proof that an inherent *vivida vis*[2] is a powerful preservative of the human frame.

3 Man is, in general, made up of contradictory qualities; and these will ever show themselves in strange succession, where a consistency in appearance at least, if not reality, has not been attained by long habits of philosophical discipline. In proportion to the native vigor of the mind, the contradictory qualities will be the more prominent, and more difficult to be adjusted; and, therefore, we are not to wonder that Johnson exhibited an eminent example of this remark which I have made upon human nature. At different times he seemed a different man, in some respects; not, however, in any great or essential article, upon which he had fully employed his mind, and settled certain principles of duty, but only in his manners, and in the display of argument and fancy in his talk. He was prone to superstition, but not to credulity. Though his imagination might incline him to a belief of the marvellous and the mysterious, his vigorous reason examined the evidence with jealousy. He was a sincere and zealous Christian, of high Church-of-England

---

[1] As I do not see any reason to give a different character of my illustrious friend now, from what I formerly gave, the greatest part of the sketch of him in my "Journal of a Tour to the Hebrides" is here adopted.—B.
[2] Lucretius, i. 72.

and monarchial principles, which he would not tamely suffer to be questioned; and had, perhaps, at an early period, narrowed his mind somewhat too much, both as to religion and politics. His being impressed with the danger of extreme latitude in either, though he was of a very independent spirit, occasioned his appearing somewhat unfavorable to the prevalence of that noble freedom of sentiment which is the best possession of man. Nor can it be denied, that he had many prejudices; which, however, frequently suggested many of his pointed sayings, that rather show a playfulness of fancy than any settled malignity. He was steady and inflexible in maintaining the obligations of religion and morality; both from a regard for the order of society, and from a veneration for the GREAT SOURCE of all order; correct, nay, stern in his taste; hard to please, and easily offended, impetuous and irritable in his temper, but of a most humane and benevolent heart,[1] which showed itself not only in a most liberal charity, as far as his circumstances would allow, but in a thousand instances of active benevolence. He was afflicted with a bodily disease which made him often restless and fretful; and with a constitutional melancholy, the clouds which darkened the brightness of his fancy, and gave a gloomy cast to his whole course of thinking: we, therefore, ought not to wonder at his sallies of impatience and passion at any time; especially when provoked by obtrusive ignorance, or presuming petulance; and allowance must be made for his uttering hasty and satirical sallies even against his best friends. And, surely, when it is considered, that, "amidst sickness and sorrow," he exerted his faculties in so many works for the benefit of mankind, and particularly that he achieved the great and admirable DICTIONARY of our language, we must be astonished at his resolution. The solemn text, "of him to whom much is given, much will be required," seems to have been ever present to his mind, in a rigorous sense, and to have made him dissatisfied with his labors and acts of goodness, however comparatively great; so that the unavoidable consciousness of his superiority was, in that respect, a cause of disquiet. He suffered so much from this, and from the gloom which perpetually haunted him and made solitude frightful, that it may be said of him, "If in this life only he had hope, he was of all men most miserable." He loved praise, when it was brought to him; but was too proud to seek for it. He was somewhat susceptible of flattery. As he was general and unconfined in his studies, he cannot be considered as master of any one particular science; but he had accumulated a vast and various collection of learning and knowledge, which was so arranged in his mind, as to be ever in readiness to be brought forth. But his superiority over other learned men consisted chiefly in what may be called the art of thinking, the art of using his mind: a certain continual power of seizing the useful substance of all that he knew, and exhibiting it in a clear and forcible manner; so that knowledge, which we often see to be no better than lumber in

[1]In the *Olla Podrida*, a collection of essays published at Oxford, there is an admirable paper upon the character of Johnson, written by the Reverend Dr. Horne, the last excellent Bishop of Norwich. The following passage is eminently happy:"To reject wisdom, because the person of him who communicates it is uncouth, and his manners are inelegant; what is it but to throw away a pine-apple, and assign for a person the roughness of its coat?"—B.

men of dull understanding, was in him true, evident, and actual wisdom. His moral precepts are practical; for they are drawn from an initimate acquaintance with human nature. His maxims carry conviction; for they are founded on the basis of common sense, and a very attentive and minute survey of real life. His mind was so full of imagery, that he might have been perpetually a poet; yet it is remarkeable, that, however rich his prose is in this respect, his poetical pieces, in general, have not much of that splendor, but are rather distinguished by strong sentiment, and acute observation, conveyed in harmonious and energetic verse, particularly in heroic couplets. Though usually grave, and even awful in his deportment, he possessed uncommon and peculiar powers of wit and humor; he frequently indulged himself in colloquial pleasantry; and the heartiest merriment was often enjoyed in his company; with this great advantage, that as it was entirely free from any poisonous tincture of vice or impiety, it was salutary to those who shared in it. He had accustomed himself to such accuracy in his common conversation,[1] that he at all times expressed his thoughts with great force, and an elegant choice of language, the effect of which was aided by his having a loud voice and a slow deliberate utterance. In him were united a most logical head with a most fertile imagination, which gave him an extraordinary advantage in arguing: for he could reason close or wide, as he saw best for the moment. Exulting in his intellectual strength and dexterity, he could, when he pleased, be the greatest sophist that ever contended in the lists of declamation; and, from a spirit of contradiction and a delight in showing his powers, he would often maintain the

---

[1]Though a perfect resemblance of Johnson is not to be found in any age, parts of his character are admirably expressed by Clarendon in drawing that of Lord Falkland, whom the noble and masterly historian describes at his seat near Oxford: "Such an immenseness of wit, such a solidity of judgment, so infinite a fancy bound in by a most logical ratiocination. His acquaintance was cultivated by the most polite and accurate men, so that his house was a University in less volume, whither they came, not so much for repose as study, and to examine and refine those grosser propositions, which laziness and consent made current in conversation." Bayle's account of *Menage* may also be quoted as exceedingly applicable to the great subject of this work. "His illustrious friends erected a very glorious monument to him in the collection entitled "Menagiana." Those who judge of things aright, will confess that this collection is very proper to show the extent of genius and learning which was the character of Menage. And I may be bold to say, that *the excellent works he published will not distinguish him from other learned men so advantageously as this.* To publish books of great learning, to make Greek and Latin verses exceedingly well turned, is not a common talent, I own; neither is it extremely rare. It is incomparably more difficult to find men who can furnish discourse about an infinite number of things, and who can diversify them an hundred ways. How many authors are there who are admired for their works, on account of the vast learning that is displayed in them, who are not able to sustain a conversation. Those who know Menage only by his books, might think he resembled those learned men; but if you show the MENAGIANA, you distinguish him from them, and make him known by a talent which is given to very few learned men. There it appears that he was a man who spoke offhand a thousand good things. His memory extended to what was ancient and modern; to the court and to the city; to the dead and to the living languages; to things serious and things jocose; in a word, to a thousand sorts of subjects. That which appeared a trifle to some readers of the "Menagiana," who did not consider circumstances, caused admiration in other readers, who minded the difference between what a man speaks without preparation. and that which he prepares for the press. And, therefore, we cannot sufficiently commend the care which his illustrious friends took to erect a monument so capable of giving him immortal glory. They were not obliged to rectify what they had heard him say; for, in so doing, they had not been faithful historians of his conversation."—B.

wrong side with equal warmth and ingenuity; so that when there was an audience, his real opinions could seldom be gathered from his talk; though when he was in company with a single friend, he would discuss a subject with genuine fairness; but he was too conscientious to make error permanent and pernicious by deliberately writing it; and, in all his numerous works he earnestly inculcated what appeared to him to be the truth; his piety being constant, and the ruling principle of all his conduct.

4 Such was SAMUEL JOHNSON, a man whose talents, acquirements, and virtues, were so extraordinary, that the more his character is considered, the more he will be regarded by the present age, and by posterity, with admiration and reverence.

VOCABULARY

distemper (2)	colloquial (3)
inherent (2)	tincture (3)
credulity (3)	impiety (3)
malignity (3)	exulting (3)
impetuous (3)	sophist (3)
sallies (3)	declamation (3)
petulance (3)	pernicious (3)
precepts (3)	inculcated (3)
maxims (3)	posterity (4)
deportment (3)	

QUESTIONS ON CONTENT

1. Boswell says that Johnson had many contradictory qualities. In what areas of his life were these contradictory qualities apparent? Give one example.
2. What was Johnson's religion? What was his political belief?
3. Boswell says that there was a solemn text ever present to Johnson's mind. What was this text?
4. What was Johnson's superiority over other learned men?
5. What distinguished Johnson's poetry?

QUESTIONS ON FORM

1. What is the thesis of this selection? Where is it found?
2. Examine the structure of the third paragraph. How are unity and coherence achieved?
3. Paragraphs are typically structured to proceed either from the general to the specific, or from the specific to the general. What is the structure of paragraph 3?
4. Boswell's summary description of Johnson is delivered in two paragraphs. What aspect of Johnson does paragraph 2 describe? What does paragraph 3 describe? What is the logic of this presentation?
5. Boswell writes: "Exulting in his intellectual strength and dexterity, he could, when he pleased, be the greatest sophist that ever contended in the lists of declamation." What figure of speech is "the lists of declamation"? Why is it appropriate?

SUGGESTIONS FOR WRITING

1. Write an essay describing the physical appearance and character of a relative, friend, or acquaintance.
2. Write an essay describing the ideal human being as you envision him or her to be.

TERM PAPER SUGGESTION

Boswell has been called the "Shakespeare of biography." Research and write a term paper on Boswell's relationship with Johnson, and the biography which came out of it.

FLANNERY O'CONNOR

A GOOD MAN IS HARD TO FIND

This story proceeds with grim, irresistible logic from the thesis contained in its title, "A Good Man Is Hard to Find." Flannery O'Connor (1925–64) was a Christian humanist writer and a member of the so-called Southern Renaissance in literature.

1 The grandmother didn't want to go to Florida. She wanted to visit some of her connections in east Tennessee and she was seizing at every chance to change Bailey's mind. Bailey was the son she lived with, her only boy. He was sitting on the edge of his chair at the table, bent over the orange sports section of the *Journal*. "Now look here, Bailey," she said, "see here, read this," and she stood with one hand on her thin hip and the other rattling the newspaper at his bald head. "Here this fellow that calls himself The Misfit is aloose from the Federal Pen and headed toward Florida and you read here what it says he did to these people. Just you read it. I wouldn't take my children in any direction with a criminal like that aloose in it. I couldn't answer to my conscience if I did."

2 Bailey didn't look up from his reading so she wheeled around then and faced the children's mother, a young woman in slacks, whose face was as broad and innocent as a cabbage and was tied around with a green headkerchief that had two points on the top like a rabbit's ears. She was sitting on the sofa, feeding the baby his apricots out of a jar. "The children have been to Florida before," the old lady said. "You all ought to take them somewhere else for a change so they would see different parts of the world and be broad. They never have been to east Tennessee."

3 The children's mother didn't seem to hear her but the eight-year-old boy, John Wesley, a stocky child with glasses, said, "If you don't want to go to Florida, why dontcha stay at home?" He and the little girl, June Star, were reading the funny papers on the floor.

"She wouldn't stay at home to be queen for a day," June Star said without raising her yellow head.

"Yes and what would you do if this fellow, The Misfit, caught you?" the grandmother asked.

"I'd smack his face," John Wesley said.

"She wouldn't stay at home for a million bucks," June Star said. "Afraid she'd miss something. She has to go everywhere we go."

"All right, Miss," the grandmother said. "Just remember that the next time you want me to curl your hair."

4 June Star said her hair was naturally curly.

The next morning the grandmother was the first one in the car, ready to go. She had her big black valise that looked like the head of a hippopotamus in one corner, and underneath it she was hiding a basket with Pitty Sing, the cat, in it. She didn't intend for the cat to be left alone in the house for three days because he would miss her too much and she was afraid he might brush against one of the gas burners and accidentally asphyxiate himself. Her son, Bailey, didn't like to arrive at a motel with a cat.

5 She sat in the middle of the back seat with John Wesley and June Star on either side of her. Bailey and the children's mother and the baby sat in front and they left Atlanta at eight forty-five with the mileage on the car at 55890. The grandmother wrote this down because she thought it would be interesting to say how many miles they had been when they got back. It took them twenty minutes to reach the outskirts of the city.

6 The old lady settled herself comfortably, removing her white cotton gloves and putting them up with her purse on the shelf in front of the back window. The children's mother still had on slacks and still had her head tied up in a green kerchief, but the grandmother had on a navy blue straw sailor hat with a bunch of white violets on the brim and a navy blue dress with a small white dot in the print. Her collars and cuffs were white organdy trimmed with lace and at her neckline she had pinned a purple spray of cloth violets containing a sachet. In case of an accident, anyone seeing her dead on the highway would know at once that she was a lady.

7 She said she thought it was going to be a good day for driving, neither too hot nor too cold, and she cautioned Bailey that the speed limit was fifty-five miles an hour and that the patrolmen hid themselves behind billboards and small clumps of trees and sped out after you before you had a chance to slow down. She pointed out interesting details of the scenery: Stone Mountain; the blue granite that in some places came up to both sides of the highway; the brilliant red clay banks slightly streaked with purple; and the various crops that made rows of green lace-work on the ground. The trees were full of silver-white sunlight and the meanest of them sparkled. The children were reading comic magazines and their mother had gone back to sleep.

8 "Let's go through Georgia fast so we won't have to look at it much," John Wesley said.

"If I were a little boy," said the grandmother, "I wouldn't talk about my native state that way. Tennessee has the mountains and Georgia has the hills."

"Tennessee is just a hillbilly dumping ground," John Wesley said, "and Georgia is a lousy state too."

"You said it," June Star said.

"In my time," said the grandmother, folding her thin veined fingers, "children were more respectful of their native states and their parents and everything else. People did right then. Oh look at the cute little pickaninny!" she said and pointed to a Negro child standing in the door of a shack. "Wouldn't that make a picture, now?" she asked and they all turned and looked at the little Negro out of the back window. He waved.

"He didn't have any britches on," June Star said.

"He probably didn't have any," the grandmother explained. "Little niggers in the country don't have things like we do. If I could paint, I'd paint that picture," she said.

9 The children exchanged comic books.

The grandmother offered to hold the baby and the children's mother passed him over the front seat to her. She set him on her knee and bounced him and told him about the things they were passing. She rolled her eyes and screwed up her mouth and stuck her leathery thin face into his smooth bland one. Occasionally he gave her a faraway smile. They passed a large cotton field with five or six graves fenced in the middle of it, like a small island. "Look at the graveyard!" the grandmother said, pointing it out. "That was the old family burying ground. That belonged to the plantation."

"Where's the plantation?" John Wesley asked.

"Gone With the Wind," said the grandmother. "Ha. Ha."

10 When the children finished all the comic books they had brought, they opened the lunch and ate it. The grandmother ate a peanut butter sandwich and an olive and would not let the children throw the box and the paper napkins out the window. When there was nothing else to do they played a game by choosing a cloud and making the other two guess what shape it suggested. John Wesley took one the shape of a cow and June Star guessed a cow and John Wesley said, no, an automobile, and June Star said he didn't play fair, and they began to slap each other over the grandmother.

11 The grandmother said she would tell them a story if they would keep quiet. When she told a story, she rolled her eyes and waved her head and was very dramatic. She said once when she was a maiden lady she had been courted by a Mr. Edgar Atkins Teagarden from Jasper, Georgia. She said he was a very good-looking man and a gentleman and that he brought her a watermelon every Saturday afternoon with his initials cut in it, E. A. T. Well, one Saturday, she said, Mr. Teagarden brought the watermelon and there was nobody at home and he left it on the front porch and returned in his buggy to Jasper, but she never got the watermelon, she said, because a nigger boy ate it when he saw the initials, E. A. T.! This story tickled John Wesley's funny bone and he giggled and giggled but June Star didn't think it was any good. She said she wouldn't marry a man that just brought her a watermelon on Saturday. The grandmother said she would have done well to marry Mr.

Teagarden because he was a gentleman and had bought Coca-Cola stock when it first came out and that he had died only a few years ago, a very wealthy man.

12 They stopped at The Tower for barbecued sandwiches. The Tower was a part stucco and part wood filling station and dance hall set in a clearing outside of Timothy. A fat man named Red Sammy Butts ran it and there were signs stuck here and there on the building and for miles up and down the highway saying, TRY RED SAMMY'S FAMOUS BARBECUE. NONE LIKE FAMOUS RED SAMMY'S! RED SAM! THE FAT BOY WITH THE HAPPY LAUGH! A VETERAN! RED SAMMY'S YOUR MAN!

13 Red Sammy was lying on the bare ground outside The Tower with his head under a truck while a gray monkey about a foot high, chained to a small chinaberry tree, chattered nearby. The monkey sprang back into the tree and got on the highest limb as soon as he saw the children jump out of the car and run toward him.

14 Inside, The Tower was a long dark room with a counter at one end and tables at the other and dancing space in the middle. They all sat down at a board table next to the nickelodeon and Red Sam's wife, a tall burnt-brown woman with hair and eyes lighter than her skin, came and took their order. The children's mother put a dime in the machine and played "The Tennessee Waltz," and the grandmother said that tune always made her want to dance. She asked Bailey if he would like to dance but he only glared at her. He didn't have a naturally sunny disposition like she did and trips made him nervous. The grandmother's brown eyes were very bright. She swayed her head from side to side and pretended she was dancing in her chair. June Star said play something she could tap to so the children's mother put in another dime and played a fast number and June Star stepped out onto the dance floor and did her tap routine.

15 "Ain't she cute?" Red Sam's wife said, leaning over the counter. "Would you like to come be my little girl?"

"No I certainly wouldn't," June Star said. "I wouldn't live in a broken-down place like this for a million bucks!" and she ran back to the table.

"Ain't she cute?" the woman repeated, stretching her mouth politely.

"Aren't you ashamed?" hissed the grandmother.

16 Red Sam came in and told his wife to quit lounging on the counter and hurry up with these people's order. His khaki trousers reached just to his hip bones and his stomach hung over them like a sack of meal swaying under his shirt. He came over and sat down at a table nearby and let out a combination sigh and yodel. "You can't win," he said. "You can't win," and he wiped his sweating red face off with a gray handkerchief. "These days you don't know who to trust," he said. "Ain't that the truth?"

"People are certainly not nice like they used to be," said the grandmother.

"Two fellers come in here last week," Red Sammy said, "driving a Chrysler. It was a old beat-up car but it was a good one and these boys looked all right to me. Said they worked at the mill and you know I let them fellers charge the gas they bought? Now why did I do that?"

"Because you're a good man!" the grandmother said at once.

"Yes'm, I suppose so," Red Sam said as if he were struck with this answer.

17 His wife brought the orders, carrying the five plates all at once without a tray, two in each hand and one balanced on her arm. "It isn't a soul in this green world of God's that you can trust," she said. "And I don't count nobody out of that, not nobody," she repeated, looking at Red Sammy.

"Did you read about that criminal, The Misfit, that's escaped?" asked the grandmother.

"I wouldn't be a bit surprised if he didn't attact this place right here," said the woman. "If he hears about it being here, I wouldn't be none surprised to see him. If he hears it's two cent in the cash register, I wouldn't be a tall surprised if he . . ."

"That'll do," Red Sam said. "Go bring these people their Co'-Colas," and the woman went off to get the rest of the order.

"A good man is hard to find," Red Sammy said. "Everything is getting terrible. I remember the day you could go off and leave your screen door unlatched. Not no more."

18 He and the grandmother discussed better times. The old lady said that in her opinion Europe was entirely to blame for the way things were now. She said the way Europe acted you would think we were made of money and Red Sam said it was no use talking about it, she was exactly right. The children ran outside into the white sunlight and looked at the monkey in the lacy chinaberry tree. He was busy catching fleas on himself and biting each one carefully between his teeth as if it were a delicacy.

19 They drove off again into the hot afternoon. The grandmother took cat naps and woke up every few minutes with her own snoring. Outside of Toombsboro she woke up and recalled an old plantation that she had visited in this neighborhood once when she was a young lady. She said the house had six white columns across the front and that there was an avenue of oaks leading up to it and two little wooden trellis arbors on each side in front where you sat down with your suitor after a stroll in the garden. She recalled exactly which road to turn off to get to it. She knew that Bailey would not be willing to lose any time looking at an old house, but the more she talked about it, the more she wanted to see it once again and find out if the little twin arbors were still standing. "There was a secret panel in this house," she said craftily, not telling the truth but wishing that she were, "and the story went that all the family silver was hidden in it when Sherman came through but it was never found . . ."

20 "Hey!" John Wesley said. "Let's go see it! We'll find it! We'll poke all the woodwork and find it! Who lives there? Where do you turn off at? Hey Pop, can't we turn off there?"

"We never have seen a house with a secret panel!" June Star shrieked. "Let's go to the house with the secret panel! Hey Pop, can't we go see the house with the secret panel!"

"It's not far from here, I know," the grandmother said. "It wouldn't take over twenty minutes."

Bailey was looking straight ahead. His jaw was as rigid as a horseshoe. "No," he said.

21 The children began to yell and scream that they wanted to see the house with the secret panel. John Wesley kicked the back of the front seat and June Star hung over her mother's shoulder and whined desperately into her ear that they never had any fun even on their vacation, that they could never do what THEY wanted to do. The baby began to scream and John Wesley kicked the back of the seat so hard that his father could feel the blows in his kidney .

"All right!" he shouted and drew the car to a stop at the side of the road. "Will you all shut up? Will you all just shut up for one second? If you don't shut up, we won't go anywhere."

"It would be very educational for them," the grandmother murmured.

"All right," Bailey said, "but get this: This is the only time we're going to stop for anything like this. This is the one and only time."

"The dirt road that you have to turn down is about a mile back," the grandmother directed. "I marked it when we passed."

"A dirt road," Bailey groaned.

22 After they had turned around and were headed toward the dirt road, the grandmother recalled other points about the house, the beautiful glass over the front doorway and the candle-lamp in the hall. John Wesley said that the secret panel was probably in the fireplace.

"You can't go inside this house," Bailey said. "You don't know who lives there."

"While you all talk to the people in front, I'll run around behind and get in a window," John Wesley suggested.

"We'll all stay in the car," his mother said.

23 They turned onto the dirt road and the car raced roughly along in a swirl of pink dust. The grandmother recalled the times when there were no paved roads and thirty miles was a day's journey. The dirt road was hilly and there were sudden washes in it and sharp curves on dangerous embankments. All at once they would be on a hill, looking down over the blue tops of trees for miles around, then the next minute, they would be in a red depression with the dust-coated trees looking down on them.

24 "This place had better turn up in a minute," Bailey said, "or I'm going to turn around."

The road looked as if no one had traveled on it in months.

"It's not much farther," the grandmother said and just as she said it, a horrible thought came to her. The thought was so embarrassing that she turned red in the face and her eyes dilated and her feet jumped up, upsetting her valise in the corner. The instant the valise moved, the newspaper top she had over the basket under it rose with a snarl and Pitty Sing, the cat, sprang onto Bailey's shoulder.

25 The children were thrown to the floor and their mother, clutching the baby, was thrown out the door onto the ground; the old lady was thrown into the front seat. The car turned over once and landed right-side-up in a gulch off

the side of the road. Bailey remained in the driver's seat with the cat—gray-striped with a broad white face and an orange nose—clinging to his neck like a caterpillar.

26 As soon as the children saw they could move their arms and legs, they scrambled out of the car, shouting, "We've had an ACCIDENT!" The grand-mother was curled up under the dashboard, hoping she was injured so that Bailey's wrath would not come down on her all at once. The horrible thought she had had before the accident was that the house she had remembered so vividly was not in Geogia but in Tennessee.

27 Bailey removed the cat from his neck with both hands and flung it out the window against the side of a pine tree. Then he got out of the car and started looking for the children's mother. She was sitting against the side of the red gutted ditch, holding the screaming baby, but she only had a cut down her face and a broken shoulder. "We've had an ACCIDENT!" the children screamed in a frenzy of delight.

28 "But nobody's killed," June Star said with disappointment as the grand-mother limped out of the car, her hat still pinned to her head but the broken front brim standing up at a jaunty angle and the violet spray hanging off the side. They all sat down in the ditch, except the children, to recover from the shock. They were all shaking.

"Maybe a car will come along," said the children's mother hoarsely.

"I believe I have injured an organ," said the grandmother, pressing her side, but no one answered her. Bailey's teeth were clattering. He had on a yellow sport shirt with bright blue parrots designed in it and his face was as yellow as the shirt. The grandmother decided that she would not mention that the house was in Tennessee.

29 The road was about ten feet above and they could see only the tops of the trees on the other side of it. Behind the ditch they were sitting in there were more woods, tall and dark and deep. In a few minutes they saw a car some distance away on top of a hill, coming slowly as if the occupants were watching them. The grandmother stood up and waved both arms dramatically to attract their attention. The car continued to come on slowly, disappeared around a bend and appeared again, moving even slower, on top of the hill they had gone over. It was a big black battered hearselike automobile. There were three men in it.

30 It came to a stop just over them and for some minutes, the driver looked down with a steady expressionless gaze to where they were sitting, and didn't speak. Then he turned his head and muttered something to the other two and they got out. One was a fat boy in black trousers and a red sweat shirt with a silver stallion embossed on the front of it. He moved around on the right side of them and stood staring, his mouth partly open in a kind of loose grin. The other had on khaki pants and a blue striped coat and a gray hat pulled down very low, hiding most of his face. He came around slowly on the left side. Neither spoke.

31 The driver got out of the car and stood by the side of it, looking down at

them. He was an older man than the other two. His hair was just beginning to gray and he wore silver-rimmed spectacles that gave him a scholarly look. He had a long creased face and didn't have on any shirt or undershirt. He had on blue jeans that were too tight for him and was holding a black hat and a gun. The two boys also had guns.

"We've had an ACCIDENT!" the children screamed.

32 The grandmother had the peculiar feeling that the bespectacled man was someone she knew. His face was as familiar to her as if she had known him all her life but she could not recall who he was. He moved away from the car and began to come down the embankment, placing his feet carefully so that he wouldn't slip. He had on tan and white shoes and no socks, and his ankles were red and thin. "Good afternoon," he said. "I see you all had you a little spill."

"We turned over twice!" said the grandmother.

"Oncet," he corrected. "We seen it happen. Try their car and see will it run, Hiram," he said quietly to the boy with the gray hat.

"What you got that gun for?" John Wesley asked. "Whatcha gonna do with that gun?"

"Lady," the man said to the children's mother, "would you mind calling them children to sit down by you? Children make me nervous. I want all you all to sit down right together there where you're at."

33 "What are you telling US what to do for?" June Star asked.

Behind them the line of woods gaped like a dark open mouth. "Come here," said their mother.

"Look here now," Bailey began suddenly, "we're in a predicament! We're in . . ."

The grandmother shrieked. She scrambled to her feet and stood staring. "You're The Misfit!" she said, "I recognized you at once!"

"Yes'm," the man said, smiling slightly as if he were pleased in spite of himself to be known, "but it would have been better for all of you, lady, if you hadn't of reckernized me."

34 Bailey turned his head sharply and said something to his mother that shocked even the children. The old lady began to cry and The Misfit reddened.

"Lady," he said, "don't you get upset. Sometimes a man says things he don't mean. I don't reckon he meant to talk to you thataway."

"You wouldn't shoot a lady, would you?" the grandmother said and removed a clean handkerchief from her cuff and began to slap at her eyes with it.

35 The Misfit pointed the toe of his shoe into the ground and made a little hole and then covered it up again. "I would hate to have to," he said.

"Listen," the grandmother almost screamed, "I know you're a good man. You don't look a bit like you have common blood. I know you must come from nice people!"

"Yes mam," he said, "finest people in the world." When he smiled he showed a row of strong white teeth. "God never made a finer woman than my

mother and my daddy's heart was pure gold,'' he said. The boy with the red
sweat shirt had come around behind them and was standing with his gun at his
hip. The Misfit squatted down on the ground. "Watch them children, Bobby
Lee," he said. "You know they make me nervous." He looked at the six of
them huddled together in front of him and he seemed to be embarrassed as if
he couldn't think of anything to say, "Ain't a cloud in the sky," he remarked,
looking up at it. "Don't see no sun but don't see no cloud neither."

36 "Yes, it's a beautiful day," said the grandmother. "Listen," she said,
"you shouldn't call yourself The Misfit because I know your're a good man at
heart. I can just look at you and tell."

"Hush!" Bailey yelled. "Hush! Everybody shut up and let me handle this!"
He was squatting in the position of a runner about to sprint forward but he
didn't move.

"I pre-chate that, lady," The Misfit said and drew a little circle in the
ground with the butt of his gun.

"It'll take a half a hour to fix this here car," Hiram called, looking over the
raised hood of it.

"Well, first you and Bobby Lee get him and that little boy to step over
yonder with you," The Misfit said, pointing to Bailey and John Wesley. "The
boys want to ast you something," he said to Bailey. "Would you mind
stepping back in them woods there with them?"

"Listen," Bailey began, "we're in a terrible predicament! Nobody realizes
what this is," and his voice cracked. His eyes were as blue and intense as the
parrots in his shirt and he remained perfectly still.

37 The grandmother reached up to adjust her hat brim as if she were going
to the woods with him but it came off in her hand. She stood staring at it and
after a second she let it fall on the ground. Hiram pulled Bailey up by the arm
as if he were assisting an old man. John Wesley caught hold of his father's
hand and Bobby Lee followed. They went off toward the woods and just as
they reached the dark edge, Bailey turned and supporting himself against a
gray naked pine trunk, he shouted, "I'll be back in a minute, Mamma, wait on
me!"

"Come back this instant!" his mother shrilled but they all disappeared into
the woods.

"Bailey Boy!" the grandmother called in a tragic voice but she found she
was looking at The Misfit squatting on the ground in front of her. "I just know
you're a good man," she said desperately. "You're not a bit common!"

38 "Nome, I ain't a good man," The Misfit said after a second as if he had
considered her statement carefully, "but I ain't the worst in the world neither.
My daddy said I was a different breed of dog from my brothers and sisters.
'You know,' Daddy said, 'it's some that can live their whole life out without
asking about it and it's others has to know why it is, and this boy is one of the
latters. He's going to be into everything!'" He put on his black hat and looked
up suddenly and then away deep into the woods as if he were embarrassed
again. "I'm sorry I don't have on a shirt before you ladies," he said, hunching

his shoulders slightly. "We buried our clothes that we had on when we escaped and we're just making do until we can get better. We borrowed these from some folks we met," he explained.

39 "That's perfectly all right," the grandmother said. "Maybe Bailey has an extra shirt in his suitcase."

"I'll look and see terrectly," The Misfit said.

"Where are they taking him?" the children's mother screamed.

"Daddy was a card himself," The Misfit said. "You couldn't put anything over on him. He never got in trouble with the Authorities though. Just had the knack of handling them."

"You could be honest too if you'd only try," said the grandmother. "Think how wonderful it would be to settle down and live a comfortable life and not have to think about somebody chasing you all the time."

40 The Misfit kept scratching in the ground with the butt of his gun as if he were thinking about it. "Yes'm, somebody is always after you," he murmured.

The grandmother noticed how thin his shoulder blades were just behind his hat because she was standing up looking down on him. "Do you ever pray?" she asked.

He shook his head. All she saw was the black hat wiggle between his shoulder blades. "Nome," he said.

There was a pistol shot from the woods, followed closely by another. Then silence. The old lady's head jerked around. She could hear the wind move through the tree tops like a long satisfied insuck of breath. "Bailey Boy!" she called.

41 "I was a gospel singer for a while," The Misfit said. "I been most everything. Been in the arm service, both land and sea, at home and abroad, been twicet married, been an undertaker, been with the railroads, plowed Mother Earth, been in a tornado, seen a man burnt alive oncet," and looked up at the children's mother and the little girl who were sitting close together, their faces white and their eyes glassy; "I even seen a woman flogged," he said.

"Pray, pray," the grandmother began, "pray, pray . . ."

"I never was a bad boy that I remember of," The Misfit said in an almost dreamy voice, "but somewheres along the line I done something wrong and got sent to the penitentiary. I was buried alive," and he looked up and held her attention to him by a steady stare.

42 "That's when you should have started to pray," she said. "What did you do to get sent to the penitentiary that first time?"

"Turn to the right, it was a wall," The Misfit said, looking up again at the cloudless sky. "Turn to the left, it was a wall. Look up it was a ceiling, look down it was a floor. I forget what I done, lady. I set there and set there, trying to remember what it was I done and I ain't recalled it to this day. Oncet in a while, I would think it was coming to me, but it never come."

"Maybe they put you in by mistake," the old lady said vaguely.

"Nome," he said. "It wasn't no mistake. They had the papers on me."

"You must have stolen something," she said.

43 The Misfit sneered slightly. "Nobody had nothing I wanted," he said. "It was a head-doctor at the penitentiary said what I had done was kill my daddy but I known that for a lie. My daddy died in nineteen ought nineteen of the epidemic flu and I never had a thing to do with it. He was buried in the Mount Hopewell Baptist churchyard and you can go there and see for yourself."

"If you would pray," the old lady said, "Jesus would help you."

"That's right," The Misfit said.

"Well then, why don't you pray?" she asked trembling with delight suddenly.

"I don't want no hep," he said, "I'm doing all right by myself."

44 Bobby Lee and Hiram came ambling back from the woods. Bobby Lee was dragging a yellow shirt with bright blue parrots in it.

"Thow me that shirt, Bobby Lee," The Misfit said. The shirt came flying at him and landed on his shoulder and he put it on. The grandmother couldn't name what the shirt reminded her of. "No, lady," The Misfit said while he was buttoning it up, "I found out the crime don't matter. You can do one thing or you can do another, kill a man or take a tire off his car, because sooner or later you're going to forget what it was you done and just be punished for it."

45 The children's mother had begun to make heaving noises as if she couldn't get her breath. "Lady," he asked, "would you and that little girl like to step off yonder with Bobby Lee and Hiram and join your husband?"

"Yes, thank you," the mother said faintly. Her left arm dangled helplessly and she was holding the baby, who had gone to sleep, in the other. "Hep that lady up, Hiram," The Misfit said as she struggled to climb out of the ditch, "and Bobby Lee, you hold onto that little girl's hand."

"I don't want to hold hands with him," June Star said. "He reminds me of a pig."

The fat boy blushed and laughed and caught her by the arm and pulled her off into the woods after Hiram and her mother.

46 Alone with The Misfit, the grandmother found that she had lost her voice. There was not a cloud in the sky nor any sun. There was nothing around her but woods. She wanted to tell him that he must pray. She opened and closed her mouth several times before anything came out. Finally she found herself saying, "Jesus, Jesus," meaning, Jesus will help you, but the way she was saying it, it sounded as if she might be cursing.

"Yes'm," The Misfit said as if he agreed. "Jesus thown everything off balance. It was the same case with Him as with me except He hadn't committed any crime and they could prove I had committed one because they had the papers on me. Of course," he said, "they never shown me my papers. That's why I sign myself now. I said long ago, you get you a signature and sign everything you do and keep a copy of it. Then you'll know what you done and you can hold up the crime to the punishment and see do they match and in the end you'll have something to prove you ain't been treated right. I call myself The Misfit," he said, "because I can't make what all I done wrong fit what all I gone through in punishment."

47 There was a piercing scream from the woods, followed closely by a pistol report. "Does it seem right to you, lady, that one is punished a heap and another ain't punished at all?"

"Jesus!" the old lady cried. "You've got good blood! I know you wouldn't shoot a lady! I know you come from nice people! Pray! Jesus, you ought not to shoot a lady, I'll give you all the money I've got!"

"Lady," The Misfit said, looking beyond her far into the woods, "there never was a body that give the undertaker a tip."

There were two more pistol reports and the grandmother raised her head like a parched old turkey hen crying for water and called, "Bailey Boy, Bailey Boy!" as if her heart would break.

48 "Jesus was the only One that ever raised the dead." The Misfit continued, "and He shouldn't have done it. He thrown everything off balance. If He did what He said, then it's nothing for you to do but throw away everything and follow Him, and if He didn't, then it's nothing for you to do but enjoy the few minutes you got left the best way you can—by killing somebody or burning down his house or doing some other meanness to him. No pleasure but meanness," he said and his voice had become almost a snarl.

"Maybe He didn't raise the dead," the old lady mumbled, not knowing what she was saying and feeling so dizzy that she sank down in the ditch with her legs twisted under her.

49 "I wasn't there so I can't say He didn't," The Misfit said. "I wisht I had of been there," he said, hitting the ground with his fist. "It ain't right I wasn't there because if I had of been there I would of known. Listen lady," he said in a high voice, "if I had of been there I would of known and I wouldn't be like I am now." His voice seemed about to crack and the grandmother's head cleared for an instant. She saw the man's face twisted close to her own as if he were going to cry and she murmured, "Why you're one of my babies. You're one of my own children!" She reached out and touched him on the shoulder. The Misfit sprang back as if a snake had bitten him and shot her three times through the chest. Then he put his gun down on the ground and took off his glasses and began to clean them.

50 Hiram and Bobby Lee returned from the woods and stood over the ditch, looking down at the grandmother who half sat and half lay in a puddle of blood with her legs crossed under her like a child's and her face smiling up at the cloudless sky.

Without his glasses, The Misfit's eyes were red-rimmed and pale and defenseless-looking. "Take her off and throw her where you thrown the others," he said, picking up the cat that was rubbing itself against his leg.

"She was a talker, wasn't she?" Bobby Lee said, sliding down the ditch with a yodel.

"She would of been a good woman," The Misfit said, "if it had been somebody there to shoot her every minute of her life."

"Some fun!" Bobby Lee said.

"Shut up, Bobby Lee," The Misfit said. "It's no real pleasure in life."

VOCABULARY

asphyxiate (4)	jaunty (28)
sachet (6)	embossed (30)
bland (9)	ambling (44)
dilated (24)	parched (47)

QUESTIONS ON CONTENT

1. Why didn't the grandmother want to go to Florida? Where did she want to go instead?
2. Why does the family turn off on the lonely dirt road?
3. What caused the accident?
4. For what crime was The Misfit sent to the penitentiary?
5. Why does he call himself "The Misfit"?

QUESTIONS ON FORM

1. The Misfit is mentioned in the first paragraph. Why does the author introduce him so early?
2. What does the initial dialogue between the grandmother and the children accomplish?
3. In paragraph 29 The Misfit's automobile is described as "a big black battered hearse-like automobile." What is the author doing in this description?
4. At a climactic part of the story, the grandmother has a sudden dramatic recognition of responsibility. When does it occur? Whom does it involve?
5. In paragraph 33 the author writes: "Behind them the line of woods gaped like a dark open mouth." What does this description accomplish? What does it signal to the reader?

SUGGESTIONS FOR WRITING

1. Write an interpretation of this story.
2. The author, Flannery O'Connor, has written of this story that The Misfit is the devil, and the grandmother a Christian who confronts the devil. Write an essay justifying or refuting this interpretation.

CHAPTER WRITING ASSIGNMENTS

1. Convert one of the following general subjects into a thesis that controls, obligates, and predicts:

    (a) college   (d) politics

    (b) parents   (e) sports

    (c) motion pictures   (f) work

    Now develop your thesis into a well-supported, unified five-hundred-word essay.
2. Using the thesis of any one of the essays in this chapter, develop your own essay. Do not lose sight of your thesis.

four

How Do I Organize?
Organization

model

E. M. FORSTER

MY WOOD

A few years ago I wrote a book which dealt in part with the difficulties of the English in India. Feeling that they would have had no difficulties in India themselves, the Americans read the book freely. The more they read it the better it made them feel, and a cheque to the author was the result. I bought a wood with the cheque. It is not a large wood—it contains scarcely any trees, and it is intersected, blast it, by a public footpath. Still, it is the first property that I have owned, so it is right that other people should participate in my shame, and should ask themselves, in accents that will vary in horror, this very important question: What is the effect of property upon the character? Don't let's touch economics; the effect of private ownership upon the community as a whole is another question—a more important question, perhaps, but another one. Let's keep to psychology. If you own things, what's their effect on you? What's the effect on me of my wood?

In the first place, it makes me feel heavy. Property does have this effect. Property produces men of weight, and it was a man of weight who failed to get into the Kingdom of Heaven. He was not wicked, that unfortunate millionaire in the parable, he was only stout; he stuck out in front, not to mention behind, and as he wedged himself this way and that in the crystalline entrance and bruised his well-fed flanks, he saw beneath him a comparatively slim camel passing through the eye of a needle and being woven into the robe of God. The Gospels all through couple stoutness and slowness. They point out what is perfectly obvious, yet seldom realized: that if you have a lot of things you cannot move about a lot, that furniture requires dusting, dusters require servants, servants require insurance stamps,[1] and the whole tangle of them makes you think twice before you accept an invitation to dinner or go for a bathe in the Jordan. Sometimes the Gospels proceed further and say with Tolstoy that property is sinful; they approach the difficult ground of asceticism here, where I cannot follow them. But as to the immediate effects of property on people, they just show straightforward logic. It produces men of weight. Men of weight cannot, by definition, move like the lightning from the East unto the West, and the ascent of a fourteen-stone bishop into a pulpit is thus the exact antithesis of the coming of the Son of Man. My wood makes me feel heavy.

In the second place, it makes me feel it ought to be larger.

The other day I heard a twig snap in it. I was annoyed at first, for I thought that someone was blackberrying, and depreciating the value of the undergrowth. On coming nearer, I saw it was not a man who had trodden on the twig and snapped it, but a bird, and I felt pleased. My bird. The bird was not equally pleased. Ignoring the relation between us, it took fright as soon as it saw the shape of my face, and flew straight over the boundary hedge into a field, the property of Mrs. Henessy, where it sat down with a loud squawk. It had become Mrs. Henessy's bird. Something seemed grossly amiss here, something that would not have occurred had the wood been larger. I could not afford to buy Mrs. Henessy out, I dared not murder her, and limitations of this sort beset me on every side. Ahab did not want that vineyard—he only needed it to round off his property, preparatory to plotting a new curve—and all the land around my wood was become necessary to me in order to round off the wood. A boundary protects. But—poor little thing—the boundary ought in its turn to be protected. Noises on the edge of it. Children throw stones. A little more, and then a little more, until we reach the sea. Happy Canute! Happier Alexander! And after all, why should even the world be the limit of possession? A rocket containing a Union Jack, will, it is hoped, be shortly fired at the moon. Mars. Sirius. Beyond which . . . But these immensities ended by saddening me. I could not suppose that my wood was the destined nucleus of universal dominion—it is so very small and contains no mineral wealth beyond the blackberries. Nor was I comforted when Mrs. Henessy's bird took alarm for the second time and flew clean away from us all, under the belief that it belonged to itself.

In the third place, property makes its owner feel that he ought to do something to it. Yet he isn't sure what. A restlessness comes over him, a vague sense that he has a personality to express—the same sense which, without any vagueness, leads the artist to an act of creation. Sometimes I think I will cut down such trees as remain in the wood, at other times I want to fill up the gaps between them with new trees. Both impulses are

[1]In England. —Ed.

pretentious and empty. They are not honest movements towards money-making or beauty. They spring from a foolish desire to express myself and from an inability to enjoy what I have got. Creation, property, enjoyment form a sinister trinity in the human mind. Creation and enjoyment are both very good, yet they are often unattainable without a material basis, and at such moments property pushes itself in as a substitute, saying, "Accept me instead—I'm good enough for all three." It is not enough. It is, as Shakespeare said of lust, "The expense of spirit in a waste of shame": it is "Before, a joy proposed; behind, a dream." Yet we don't know how to shun it. It is forced on us by our economic system as the alternative to starvation. It is also forced on us by an internal defect in the soul, by the feeling that in property may lie the germs of self-development and of exquisite or heroic deeds. Our life on earth is, and ought to be, material and carnal. But we have not yet learned to manage our materialism and carnality properly; they are still entangled with the desire for ownership, where (in the words of Dante) "Possession is one with loss."

And this brings us to our fourth and final point: the blackberries.

Blackberries are not plentiful in this meagre grove, but they are easily seen from the public footpath which traverses it, and all too easily gathered. Foxgloves, too—people will pull up the foxgloves, and ladies of an educational tendency even grub for toad stools to show them on the Monday in class. Other ladies, less educated, roll down the bracken in the arms of their gentlemen friends. There is a paper, there are tins. Pray, does my wood belong to me or doesn't it? And, if it does, should I not own it best by allowing no one else to walk there? There is a wood near Lyme Regis, also cursed by a public footpath, where the owner has not hesitated on this point. He has built high stone walls each side of the path, and has spanned it by bridges, so that the public circulate like termites while he gorges on the blackberries unseen. He really does own his wood, this able chap. Dives in Hell did pretty well, but the gulf dividing him from Lazarus could be traversed by vision, and nothing traverses it here. And perhaps I shall come to this in time. I shall wall in and fence out until I really taste the sweets of property. Enormously stout, endlessly avaricious, pseudo-creative, intensely selfish, I shall weave upon my forehead the quadruple crown of possession until those nasty Bolshies come and take it off again and thrust me aside into the outer darkness.

A well-organized essay is one in which all the parts are assembled to form a well-constructed whole. The paragraphs are arranged in logical, clear sequence, with an introduction, a body, and a conclusion. Every sentence within a paragraph is carefully laid out so that it makes sense and is a necessary part of the paragraph. The total impression is one of purpose, clarity, and harmony.

"My Wood" is an example of a well-organized essay. If you study the outline below and then compare it with the essay, you will see how Forster's ideas build up sentence by sentence and paragraph by paragraph into a close-knit purposeful essay.

My Wood

Thesis: *Property has four effects on a person.*

Introduction: What is the effect of property upon the character?

   I. Property makes me feel heavy.
     A. A man of weight failed to get into the Kingdom of Heaven.
     B. The Gospels couple stoutness and slowness.
     C. Sometimes the Gospels say that property is sinful.

  II. Property makes me feel it ought to be larger.
     A. *My* bird flew into Mrs. Henessy's property and became *her* bird.
     B. Ahab did not need that vineyard; he just wanted it.
     C. The more you have, the more you want.
       1. Happy Canute!
       2. Happier Alexander!
       3. Next the moon, Mars, Sirius, and finally universal dominion.

 III. Property makes its owner feel that he ought to do something to it.
     A. A restlessness comes over him.
     B. Property takes the place of genuine creativity.
     C. Creation, property, and enjoyment form a sinister trinity.
       1. They are often unattainable without a material basis.
       2. Property imposes itself as a substitute for all three.
     D. We don't know how to shun property.
       1. It is forced on us by our economic system.
       2. It is forced on us by a defect in the soul.

 IV. Property makes me selfish.
     A. No one else should eat my blackberries.
     B. The owner of a wood near Lyme Regis has built high stone walls to keep out the public.

Conclusion: Perhaps I shall become stout, avaricious, pseudo-creative, and intensely selfish—until the Bolshies come and take off my property.

advice

NORMAN COUSINS

ARE YOU MAKING YOURSELF CLEAR?

With his usual discernment, one of America's noted editors insists that students must learn to express themselves purposefully and with a recognizable sequence of ideas.

1 In the present scratchy and undiscriminating national mood, education is an easy target. I deplore the tendency but would like to get into the act nonetheless. One of the prime weaknesses of education, it seems to me, is that it doesn't give enough attention to the need for developing the individual's communications skills. It is concerned with his ability to absorb knowledge but it assigns somewhat lesser importance to his need to make himself clear. This is less a matter of vocabulary range than of vocabulary control. It has to do with the entire process by which an individual organizes his thoughts for purposes of transmission.

2 The prime element in this process is sequence. Ideas have to be fitted together. The movement of a concept or an image from the mind of the speaker to the mind of the listener is retarded when words become random chunks rather than sequential parts of an organized and ordered whole. This doesn't rule out unhurried allusions; these can give color to an account and help to make a claim on the imagination and memory. But it does rule out ungoverned circling and droning, reminiscent of buzzards hovering and swooping over a victim until he drops.

3 It contributes nothing to a conversation to have an individual interrupt himself in order to insert sudden thoughts. The abuse is compounded when these obtrusive thoughts are invaded by yet others so that nothing is complete, neither the sentence, nor the paragraph, nor any of the vagrant incidents or ideas that are strewn around like fragments of an automobile wreck.

4 The following quotation is a fair approximation drawn from a recent conversation:

"This book I want to talk to you about," a visitor told me, "is one of the finest novels that I—well, let me put it this way, when I first heard about it I said to myself—actually, I told my wife, who asked me if we were publishing anything exciting; you know, my wife is one of the finest assets I have in my job. She doesn't come to the office or anything like that, you know, but—well, first let me tell you that she did disagree with me about two manuscripts I turned down and they were published by another house and of course they became best sellers. First let me tell you I once had a manuscript reader who was working for me and, well, she was two years out of Radcliffe but she had taken Levin's course in writing at Yale. I don't agree that writing can't be taught. I remember my own lit course with Jenney, who told me—well, you know, he had the highest standards and I was really pleased to see him publish last month in *Saturday Review*. What I meant was, someone always publishes the manuscript that everyone considers unpublishable, and this is what one always hears about and it is what always comes up in conversation. One always hears about *A Tree Grows in Brooklyn*—it was rejected by a dozen publishers—or *The Naked and the Dead*—it must have been turned down by ten publishers. Of course, Norman Mailer has turned out to be quite different from what everyone expected. His report on the Chicago convention was one of the finest—I don't know whether you saw it in *Harper's*—it was better, you know, than his piece on the Pentagon riots in *Commentary* which—well, let me put it this way, the best writing is being done by—I mean the best reporting—no one has come close, you know, to Truman Capote and this is where we go, you know, when we want to find out what is really—you know, nothing in any of the newspapers can tell us what it is like, especially if you want to know what the real facts were . . .''

5 He was at least two hundred words and three minutes beyond his topic sentence, and I had yet to hear the title of the book. The passage quoted is not a parody. If you want its equivalent, I suggest you take a tape recording of a cross section of an average day's office interviews or serious conversations. Chances are you will be appalled by the sprawling and fragmented character of the transcript. Complete sentences will be largely nonexistent; central ideas will emerge as from a deep mist. The surprise will not be that the meaning should be as obscured as it is by the unrelated turnings and self-interruptions, but that there should be any meaning at all. Oral communications in our society come close to being a complete bust. . . .

6 If there is no excuse for blurring and meandering in conversation, there is even less excuse for it in written forms of communication. The daily correspondence basket is a greater source of fatigue than anything that has been invented to harass a man whose work requires him to be in almost constant communication. I have a vivid picture in my mind of Dr. Albert Schweitzer at the age of eighty-four spending most of his time struggling with his correspondence. Every day two sacks of mail would arrive at the hospital at Lambarene—letters from people who wanted to visit the hospital or work there; letters from Schweitzer Fellowship members all over the world; letters from admirers and readers of his books; letters from doctors and theologians, musicologists, and scientists, all of them writing on matters within his professional competence.

7 Late at night, long after the hospital was put to bed, Schweitzer would be bent over his desk, working on his correspondence. One night, during my visit in 1958, I was unable to sleep. I left my bunk and walked toward the river. I saw a light in Dr. Schweitzer's quarters and peeked in. There was Le Grand Docteur, struggling with his correspondence at 2 A.M.

8 We discussed the matter the next day.

"My correspondence is killing me," he said, "I try to answer all my letters, but I keep falling further and further behind. I get great joy out of reading my letters. It keeps me in touch with the outside world. I like to hear from people.

But most of the time, I don't really know what my letters are trying to tell me. They wander so!"

9 Is it unreasonable to expect education to attach primary importance to the techniques of clarity, either oral or written? Is it unreasonable to suggest that respect for the next man's time is one of the most essential and useful lessons a person can learn? Time is capital. Time is finite. Clarity is a coefficient of Time.

10 I should like to think that the school provided an environment conducive to the development of habits of clarity. But I am troubled by what I know. A recent high school test in English composition that came to my attention called upon the student to write descriptive material of 1,000 words or more in ninety minutes. If the school allowed (or even required) the student to spend half a day thinking about such a writing assignment, and a full day for the actual writing, the time would not be excessive. A writer like Thomas Mann felt he had put in a productive day if he had been able to write 500 words. Good writing, most of all, is clear writing. This is painstaking and often painful work. It requires time. It requires sustained and sequential thought. . . .

11 But the school itself is not yet a model of organization, either in its internal structure or in its relationship to the student. I see very little evidence of total time-management in the demands made by the school on the student. Each course of study has its own claim. Unable to get it all in, the student is often under pressure to cut corners. He finds himself forced into a strategy of intellectual merchandising and packaging; he becomes more concerned with the voluminous trappings and the appurtenances of surface scholarship than with genuine achievement. He learns the tricks of glibness. . . .

12 All this has to do with the student's ability to organize his time, to give his total attention to a difficult problem or objective, and to make himself clear. The school is not the only conditioning agent in the thought patterns and habits of the student, but it is possibly the dominant one.

13 Meanwhile, there is the ongoing problem of all those who are beyond the reach of the school. It is churlish and absurd to take the position that a poor communicator is locked into his low-level condition. The key to his liberation is the realization that effective communications, oral and written, depend absolutely on a clear understanding of his purpose. That purpose should be clearly defined and identified. It should not be cluttered with extensive comment or side excursions. It should be developed point by point, with the rigorous attention to sequence of a professional bead-stringer at work.

14 In verbal communication, the prime requisite is to anticipate the circumstances of a meeting or encounter. If it seems likely that the time available for meeting will be limited, then it is obviously suicidal to use up most of the time in clearing one's throat. Nor does it seem especially perspicacious to have overly long agenda, saving the most important items for last, when there is every likelihood that time will run out long before the main event.

15 In written communication, no better advice can be offered than to cite the favorite six-word question of Harold Ross, late editor of the *New Yorker:*

"What the hell do you mean?"

VOCABULARY

transmission (1)	coefficient (9)
sequential (2)	voluminous (11)
compounded (3)	trappings (11)
obtrusive (3)	appurtenances (11)
vagrant (3)	churlish (13)
parody (5)	perspicacious (14)

discussion

SAMUEL H. SCUDDER

TAKE THIS FISH AND LOOK AT IT

Most of us tend to look at things without really seeing what is there. In everyday life this lack of observation may not be noticed, but in science it would be considered a serious failing. Louis Agassiz (1807–73), the distinguished Harvard professor of natural history, knew this and used to subject his students to a rigorous but useful exercise in minute observation. One of his students was Samuel Scudder, who has left us the following account.

1 It was more than fifteen years ago that I entered the laboratory of Professor Agassiz, and told him I had enrolled my name in the Scientific School as a student of natural history. He asked me a few questions about my object in coming, my antecedents generally, the mode in which I afterwards proposed to use the knowledge I might acquire, and, finally, whether I wished to study any special branch. To the latter I replied that, while I wished to be well grounded in all departments of zoology, I purposed to devote myself specially to insects.

"When do you wish to begin?" he asked.

"Now," I replied.

2 This seemed to please him, and with an energetic "Very well!" he reached from a shelf a huge jar of specimens in yellow alcohol. "Take this fish," he said, "and look at it; we call it a haemulon; by and by I will ask what you have seen."

3 With that he left me, but in a moment returned with explicit instructions as to the care of the object entrusted to me.

"No man is fit to be a naturalist," said he, "who does not know how to take care of specimens."

4 I was to keep the fish before me in a tin tray, and occasionally moisten the surface with alcohol from the jar, always taking care to replace the stopper tightly. Those were not the days of ground-glass stoppers and elegantly shaped exhibition jars; all the old students will recall the huge neckless glass bottles with their leaky, wax-besmeared corks, half eaten by insects, and begrimed with cellar dust. Entomology was a cleaner science than ichthyology, but the example of the Professor, who had unhesitatingly plunged to the

bottom of the jar to produce the fish, was infectious; and though this alcohol had a "very ancient and fishlike smell," I really dared not show any aversion within these sacred precincts, and treated the alcohol as though it were pure water. Still I was conscious of a passing feeling of disappointment, for gazing at a fish did not commend itself to an ardent entomologist. My friends at home, too, were annoyed when they discovered that no amount of eau-de-Cologne would drawn the perfume which haunted me like a shadow.

5 In ten minutes I had seen all that could be seen in that fish, and started in search of the Professor—who had, however, left the Museum; and when I returned, after lingering over some of the odd animals stored in the upper apartment, my specimen was dry all over. I dashed the fluid over the fish as if to resuscitate the beast from a fainting fit, and looked with anxiety for a return of the normal sloppy appearance. This little excitement over, nothing was to be done but to return to a steadfast gaze at my mute companion. Half an hour passed—an hour—another hour; the fish began to look loathsome. I turned it over and around; looked it in the face—ghastly; from behind, beneath, above, sideways, at a three-quarters' view—just as ghastly. I was in despair; at an early hour I concluded that lunch was necessary; so, with infinite relief, the fish was carefully replaced in the jar, and for an hour I was free.

6 On my return, I learned that Professor Agassiz had been at the Museum, but had gone, and would not return for several hours. My fellow-students were too busy to be disturbed by continued conversation. Slowly I drew forth that hideous fish, and with a feeling of desperation again looked at it. I might not use a magnifying-glass; instruments of all kinds were interdicted. My two hands, my two eyes, and the fish: it seemed a most limited field. I pushed my finger down its throat to feel how sharp the teeth were. I began to count the scales in the different rows, until I was convinced that that was nonsense. At last a happy thought struck me—I would draw the fish; and now with surprise I began to discover new features in the creature. Just then the Professor returned.

"That is right," said he; "a pencil is one of the best of eyes. I am glad to notice, too, that you keep your specimen wet, and your bottle corked."

With these encouraging words, he added:

"Well, what is it like?"

7 He listened attentively to my brief rehearsal of the structure of parts whose names were still unknown to me: the fringed gill-arches and movable operculum; the pores of the head, fleshy lips and lidless eyes; the lateral line, the spinous fins and forked tail; the compressed and arched body. When I finished, he waited as if expecting more, and then, with an air of disappointment:

"You have not looked very carefully; why," he continued more earnestly, "you haven't even seen one of the most conspicuous features of the animal, which is as plainly before your eyes as the fish itself; look again, look again!" and he left me to my misery.

8 I was piqued; I was mortified. Still more of that wretched fish! But now I set myself to my task with a will, and discovered one new thing after another,

until I saw how just the Professor's criticism had been. The afternoon passed quickly; and when, towards its close, the Professor inquired:

"Do you see it yet?"

"No," I replied, "I am certain I do not, but I see how little I saw before."

"That is next best," said he, earnestly, "but I won't hear you now; put away your fish and go home; perhaps you will be ready with a better answer in the morning. I will examine you before you look at the fish."

9 This was disconcerting. Not only must I think of my fish all night, studying, without the object before me, what this unknown but most visible feature might be; but also, without reviewing my discoveries, I must give an exact account of them the next day. I had a bad memory; so I walked home by Charles River in a distracted state, with my two perplexities.

10 The cordial greeting from the Professor the next morning was reassuring; here was a man who seemed to be quite as anxious as I that I should see for myself what he saw.

"Do you perhaps mean," I asked, "that the fish has symmetrical sides with paired organs?"

11 His thoroughly pleased "Of course! of course!" repaid the wakeful hours of the previous night. After he had discoursed most happily and enthusiastically—as he always did—upon the importance of this point, I ventured to ask what I should do next.

"Oh, look at your fish!" he said, and left me again to my own devices. In a little more than an hour he returned, and heard my new catalogue.

"That is good, that is good!" he repeated; "but that is not all; go on"; and so for three long days he placed that fish before my eyes, forbidding me to look at anything else, or to use any artificial aid. "Look, look, look," was his repeated injunction.

12 This was the best entomological lesson I ever had—a lesson whose influence has extended to the details of every subsequent study; a legacy the Professor had left to me, as he has left it to many others, of inestimable value, which we could not buy, with which we cannot part.

13 A year afterward, some of us were amusing ourselves with chalking outlandish beasts on the Museum blackboard. We drew prancing starfishes; frogs in mortal combat; hydra-headed worms; stately crawfishes, standing on their tails, bearing aloft umbrellas; and grotesque fishes with gaping mouths and staring eyes. The Professor came in shortly after, and was as amused as any at our experiments. He looked at the fishes.

"Haemulons, every one of them," he said; "Mr.———drew them."

True; and to this day, if I attempt a fish, I can draw nothing but haemulons.

14 The fourth day, a second fish of the same group was placed beside the first, and I was bidden to point out the resemblances and differences between the two; another and another followed, until the entire family lay before me, and a whole legion of jars covered the table and surrounding shelves; the odor had become a pleasant perfume; and even now, the sight of an old, six-inch, worm-eaten cork brings fragrant memories.

15 The whole group of haemulons was thus brought in review; and, whether

engaged upon the dissection of the internal organs, the preparation and examination of the bony framework, or the description of the various parts, Agassiz's training in the method of observing facts and their orderly arrangement was ever accompanied by the urgent exhortation not to be content with them.

"Facts are stupid things," he would say, "until brought into connection with some general law."

16 At the end of eight months, it was almost with reluctance that I left these friends and turned to insects; but what I had gained by this outside experience has been of greater value than years of later investigation in my favorite groups.

VOCABULARY

antecedents (1)	spinous (7)
explicit (3)	piqued (8)
entomology (4)	catalogue (11)
ichthyology (4)	injunction (11)
aversion (4)	inestimable (12)
resuscitate (5)	hydra-headed (13)
interdicted (6)	exhortation (15)
operculum (7)	

QUESTIONS ON CONTENT

1. What is the most important lesson Scudder learned from his experiment with observation? In what paragraph is the lesson stated?
2. What relevance does Scudder's experience have to organizing your essay?
3. Why is the title of the essay appropriate? Comment.
4. What common characteristics do good writers and good scientists share?
5. Why did drawing the fish help Scudder in his task of observing?
6. How does Scudder's essay prove that he has become an observer of details?

QUESTIONS ON FORM

1. What is the level of diction used in this essay? What kind of audience is it aimed at?
2. This is not the kind of essay that lends itself to outlining, but it does follow a pattern. What is the pattern that gives organization to the essay?
3. Despite the academic and scientific setting of this experience, humor abounds. How is this humor achieved? Point out specific examples.
4. Which passage do you consider the most descriptive in terms of details supplied? Explain your selection.

SUGGESTIONS FOR WRITING

1. Following Scudder's example, write about an experience in which one of your teachers taught you an important lesson. Relate the experience according to an organized sequence.

2. Write an essay in which you start with the thesis, "Facts are stupid things until brought into connection with some general law." Illustrate this thesis with examples from your own experience.

STANLEY KUNITZ

ORGANIC BLOOM

"Organic Bloom" is a statement about the capacity of the human brain to organize experience.

> The brain constructs its systems to enclose
> The steady paradox of thought and sense;
> Momentously its tissued meaning grows
> To solve and integrate experience.
> But life escapes closed reason. We explain
> Our chaos into cosmos, cell by cell,
> Only to learn of some insidious pain
> Beyond the limits of our charted hell,
> A guilt not mentioned in our prayers, a sin
> Conceived against the self. So, vast and vaster
> The plasmic circles of gray discipline
> Spread outward to include each new disaster.
> Enormous floats the brain's organic bloom
> Till, bursting like a fruit, it scatters doom.

VOCABULARY

organic (title)	integrate
paradox	cosmos
momentously	insidious
tissued	plasmic

QUESTIONS ON CONTENT

1. What is the thesis (or theme) of this poem? Summarize it in one sentence.
2. According to the poem, what specific duties does the brain discharge?
3. Despite the brain's enormous capacity for rationalizing and reasoning, it can never make complete sense of experience. Why?
4. The final line of Kunitz's poem is loaded with ambiguity. Can you suggest a meaning?

QUESTIONS ON FORM

1. The entire poem is based on a figure of speech. Can you identify it? What words in the poem suggest this figure of speech?
2. In what way do "thought" and "sense" form a paradox?

3. What is the effect of "vast and vaster" in line 10?
4. What special significance, if any, does the rhyming of "bloom" and "doom" have?

SUGGESTIONS FOR WRITING

1. Write an account of how the organizing ability of the brain allows a person to cope with life. Make your account more optimistic than the poem "Organic Bloom."
2. Write a paragraph explaining the phrase "a sin conceived against the self." Develop your essay by the use of one or more examples.

examples

BERTRAND RUSSELL

WHAT GOOD IS PHILOSOPHY?

In answering the question "What good is philosophy?" the English philosopher Bertrand Russell (1872–1970) also draws our attention to what is meant by the philosophical approach. (From *The Art of Philosophizing and Other Essays*.)

1 If you wish to become a philosopher, you must try, as far as you can, to get rid of beliefs which depend solely upon the place and time of your education, and upon what your parents and schoolmasters told you. No one can do this completely, and no one can be a perfect philosopher, but up to a point we can all achieve it if we wish to. "But why should we wish to?" you may ask. There are several reasons. One of them is that irrational opinions have a great deal to do with war and other forms of violent strife. The only way in which a society can live for any length of time without violent strife is by establishing social justice, and social justice appears to each man to be injustice if he is persuaded that he is superior to his neighbors. Justice between classes is difficult where there is a class that believes itself to have a right to more than a proportionate share of power or wealth. Justice between nations is only possible through the power of neutrals, because each nation believes in its own superior excellence. Justice between creeds is even more difficult, since each creed is convinced that it has a monopoly of the truth of the most important of all subjects. It would be increasingly easier than it is to arrange disputes amicably and justly if the philosophic outlook were more widespread.

2 A second reason for wishing to be philosophic is that mistaken beliefs do not, as a rule, enable you to realize good purposes. In the middle ages, when there was an epidemic of plague, people crowded into the churches to pray, thinking that their piety would move God to take pity on them; in fact, the crowds in ill-ventilated buildings provided ideal conditions for the spread of the infection. If your means are to be adequate to your ends, you must have knowledge, not merely superstition or prejudice.

3 A third reason is that truth is better than falsehood. There is something ignominious in going about sustained by comfortable lies. The deceived

husband is traditionally ludicrous, and there is something of the same laughable or pitiable quality about all happiness that depends upon being deceived or deluded.

VOCABULARY

philosophy (title)	superstition (2)
irrational (1)	ignominious (3)
proportionate (1)	ludicrous (3)
monopoly (1)	pitiable (3)
amicably (1)	deluded (3)
piety (2)	

QUESTIONS ON CONTENT

1. Philosophy is the love and pursuit of wisdom by intellectual means and moral self-discipline. Why do you suppose that anyone needs to defend philosophy?
2. In paragraph 1 Russell suggests the first good of philosophy. What is it?
3. What is the second good of philosophy? Of what use might this be in the present-day world?
4. What is the third good of philosophy? Even if this involves a goal impossible to attain, can you supply convincing evidence that it is worthwhile trying?
5. What is the difference between science and philosophy?

QUESTIONS ON FORM

1. How is the organization of Russell's article made clear? Point to specific indicators.
2. In paragraph 1 the phrase "power of neutrals" is a paradox. What does Russell mean by it?
3. By what method is paragraph 2 developed? Why does this paragraph focus on the Middle Ages?
4. Paragraph 3 is developed through an analogy. Explain this analogy in relation to the study of philosophy.

SUGGESTIONS FOR WRITING

1. The third paragraph in Russell's essay is the shortest. Develop it into a three-hundred-word essay using any method of development that suits your purpose.
2. Write a brief essay in which you expose the dangers of philosophy.

ALAN SIMPSON

from THE MARKS OF AN EDUCATED MAN

Alan Simpson's description of an educated man goes back to the Renaissance ideal that placed equal stress on the mental, moral, and physical excellence of human beings.

1 Any education that matters is *liberal*. All the saving truths and healing

graces that distinguish a good education from a bad one or a full education from a half-empty one are contained in that word. Whatever ups and downs the term "liberal" suffers in the political vocabulary, it soars above all controversy in the educational world. In the blackest pits of pedagogy the squirming victim has only to ask, "What's liberal about this?" to shame his persecutors. In times past a liberal education set off a free man from a slave or a gentleman from laborers and artisans. It now distinguishes whatever nourishes the mind and spirit from the training which is merely practical or professional or from the trivialities which are no training at all. Such an education involves a combination of knowledge, skills, and standards.

2 So far as knowledge is concerned, the record is ambiguous. It is sufficiently confused for the fact-filled freak who excels in quiz shows to have passed himself off in some company as an educated man. More respectable is the notion that there are some things which every educated man ought to know; but many highly educated men would cheerfully admit to a vast ignorance, and the framers of curriculums have differed greatly in the knowledge they prescribe. If there have been times when all the students at school or college studied the same things, as if it were obvious that without exposure to a common body of knowledge they would not be educated at all, there have been other times when specialization ran so wild that it might almost seem as if educated men had abandoned the thought of ever talking to each other once their education was completed.

3 If knowledge is one of our marks, we can hardly be dogmatic about the kind or the amount. A single fertile field tilled with care and imagination can probably develop all the instincts of an educated man. However, if the framer of a curriculum wants to minimize his risks, he can invoke an ancient doctrine which holds that an educated man ought to know a little about everything and a lot about something.

4 The "little about everything" is best interpreted these days by those who have given most thought to the sort of general education an informed individual ought to have. More is required than a sampling of the introductory courses which specialists offer in their own disciplines. Courses are needed in each of the major divisions of knowledge—the humanities, the natural sciences, and social sciences—which are organized with the breadth of view and the imaginative power of competent staffs who understand the needs of interested amateurs. But, over and above this exciting smattering of knowledge, students should bite deeply into at least one subject and taste its full flavor. It is not enough to be dilettantes in everything without striving also to be craftsmen in something.

5 If there is some ambiguity about the knowledge an educated man should have, there is none at all about the skills. The first is simply the training of the mind in the capacity to think clearly. This has always been the business of education, but the way it is done varies enormously. Marshalling the notes of a lecture is one experience; the opportunity to argue with a teacher is another. Thinking within an accepted tradition is one thing; to challenge the tradition

itself is another. The best results are achieved when the idea of the examined life is held firmly before the mind and when the examination is conducted with the zest, rigor, and freedom which really stretches everyone's capacities.

6 The vital aid to clear thought is the habit of approaching everything we hear and everything we are taught to believe with a certain skepticism. The method of using doubt as an examiner is a familiar one among scholars and scientists, but it is also the best protection which a citizen has against the cant and humbug that surround us.

7 To be able to listen to a phony argument and to see its dishonesty is surely one of the marks of an educated man. We may not need to be educated to possess some of this quality. A shrewd peasant was always well enough protected against impostors in the market place, and we have all sorts of businessmen who have made themselves excellent judges of phoniness without the benefit of a high-school diploma; but this kind of shrewdness goes along with a great deal of credulity. Outside the limited field within which experience has taught the peasant or the illiterate businessman his lessons, he is often hopelessly gullible. The educated man, by contrast, has tried to develop a critical faculty for general use, and he likes to think that he is fortified against imposture in all its forms.

8 It does not matter for our purposes whether the impostor is a deliberate liar or not. Some are, but the commonest enemies of mankind are the unconscious frauds. Most salesmen under the intoxication of their own exuberance seem to believe in what they say. Most experts whose *expertise* is only a pretentious sham behave as if they had been solemnly inducted into some kind of priesthood. Very few demagogues are so cynical as to remain undeceived by their own rhetoric, and some of the worst tyrants in history have been fatally sincere. We can leave the disentanglement of motives to the students of fraud and error, but we cannot afford to be taken in by the shams.

9 We are, of course, surrounded by shams. Until recently the schools were full of them—the notion that education can be had without tears, that puffed rice is a better intellectual diet than oatmeal, that adjustment to the group is more important than knowing where the group is going, and that democracy has made it a sin to separate the sheep from the goats. Mercifully, these are much less evident now than they were before Sputnik startled us into our wits.

10 In front of the professor are the shams of the learned fraternity. There is the sham science of the social scientist who first invented a speech for fuddling thought and then proceeded to tell us in his lockjawed way what we already knew. There is the sham humanism of the humanist who wonders why civilization that once feasted at his table is repelled by the shredded and desiccated dishes that often lie on it today. There is the sham message of the physical scientist who feels that his mastery of nature has made him an expert in politics and morals, and there are all the other brands of hokum which have furnished material for satire since the first quacks established themselves in the first cloisters.

11 If this is true of universities with their solemn vows and limited tempta-

tions, how much truer is it of the naughty world outside, where the prizes are far more dazzling and the only protection against humbug is the skepticism of the ordinary voter, customer, reader, listener, and viewer? Of course, the follies of human nature are not going to be exorcised by anything that the educator can do, and I am not sure that he would want to exorcise them if he could. There is something irresistibly funny about the old Adam, and life would be duller without his antics. But they ought to be kept within bounds. We are none the better for not recognizing a clown when we see one.

12 The other basic skill is simply the art of self-expression in speech and on paper. A man is uneducated who has not mastered the elements of clean forcible prose and picked up some relish for style.

13 It is a curious fact that we style everything in this country—our cars, our homes, our clothes—except our minds. They still chug along like a Model T—rugged, persevering, but far from graceful.

14 No doubt this appeal for style, like the appeal for clear thinking, can be carried too far. There was once an American who said that the only important thing in life was "to set a chime of words ringing in a few fastidious minds." As far as can be learned, he left this country in a huff to tinkle his little bell in a foreign land. Most of us would think that he lacked a sense of proportion. After all, the political history of this country is full of good judgment expressed in bad prose, and the business history has smashed through to some of its grandest triumphs across acres of broken syntax. But we can discard some of these frontier manners without becoming absurdly precious.

15 The road ahead bristles with obstacles. There is the reluctance of many people to use one word where they can get away with a half-dozen or a word of one syllable if they can find a longer one. No one has ever told them about the first rule in English composition: every slaughtered syllable is a good deed. The most persuasive teachers of this maxim are undoubtedly the commercial firms that offer a thousand dollars for the completion of a slogan in twenty-five words. They are the only people who are putting a handsome premium on economy of statement.

16 There is the decay of the habit of memorizing good prose and good poetry in the years when tastes are being formed. It is very difficult to write a bad sentence if the Bible has been a steady companion and very easy to imagine a well-turned phrase if the ear has been tuned on enough poetry.

17 There is the monstrous proliferation of gobbledy-gook in government, business, and the professions. Take this horrible example of verbal smog.

> It is inherent to motivational phenomena that there is a drive for more gratification than is realistically possible, on any level or in any type of personality organization. Likewise it is inherent to the world of objects that not all potentially desirable opportunities can be realized within a human life span. Therefore, any personality must involve an organization that allocates opportunities for gratification, that systematizes precedence relative to the limited possibilities. The possibilities of gratification, simultaneously or sequentially, of all need-dispositions are

severely limited by the structure of the object system and by the intra-systemic incompatibility of the consequences of gratifying them all.

What this smothered soul is trying to say is simply, "We must pick and choose, because we cannot have everything we want."

18 Finally, there is the universal employment of the objective test as part of the price which has to be paid for mass education. Nothing but the difficulty of finding enough readers to mark essays can condone a system which reduces a literate student to the ignoble necessity of "blackening the answer space" when he might be giving his mind and pen free play. Though we have managed to get some benefits from these examinations, the simple fact remains that the shapely prose of the Declaration of Independence or the "Gettysburg Address" was never learned under an educational system which employed objective tests. It was mastered by people who took writing seriously, who had good models in front of them, good critics to judge them, and an endless capacity for taking pains. Without that sort of discipline, the arts of self-expression will remain as mutilated as they are now.

19 The standards which mark an educated man can be expressed in terms of three tests.

20 The first is a matter of sophistication. Emerson put it nicely when he talked about getting rid of "the nonsense of our wigwams." The wigwam may be an uncultivated home, a suburban conformity, a crass patriotism, or a cramped dogma. Some of this nonsense withers in the classroom. More of it rubs off by simply mixing with people, provided they are drawn from a wide range of backgrounds and exposed within a good college to a civilized tradition. An educated man can be judged by the quality of his prejudices. There is a refined nonsense which survives the raw nonsense which Emerson was talking about.

21 The second test is a matter of moral values. Though we all know individuals who have contrived to be both highly educated and highly immoral, and though we have all heard of periods in history when the subtlest resources of wit and sophistication were employed to make a mockery of simple values, we do not really believe that a college is doing its job when it is simply multiplying the number of educated scoundrels, hucksters, and triflers.

22 The health of society depends on simple virtues like honesty, decency, courage, and public spirit. There are forces in human nature which constantly tend to corrupt them, and every age has its own vices. The worst feature of ours is probably the obsession with violence. Up to some such time as 1914, it was possible to believe in a kind of moral progress. The quality which distinguished the Victorian from the Elizabethan was a sensitivity to suffering and a revulsion from cruelty which greatly enlarged the idea of human dignity. Since 1914 we have steadily brutalized ourselves. The horrors of modern war, the bestialities of modern political creeds, the uncontrollable vices of modern cities, the favorite themes of modern novelists—all have conspired to degrade us. Some of the corruption is blatant. The authors of the best sellers, after

exhausting all the possibilities of sex in its normal and abnormal forms and all the variations of alcoholism and drug addiction, are about to invade the recesses of the hospitals. A clinical study of a hero undergoing the irrigation of his colon is about all there is left to gratify a morbid appetite.

23 Some of the corruption is insidious. A national columnist recently wrote an article in praise of cockfighting. He had visited a cockfight in the company of Ernest Hemingway. After pointing out that Hemingway had made bull-fighting respectable, he proceeded to describe the terrible beauty of fierce indomitable birds trained to kill each other for the excitement of the specta-tors. Needless to say, there used to be a terrible beauty about Christians defending themselves against lions or about heretics being burned at the stake, and there are still parts of the world where a public execution is regarded as a richly satisfying feast. But for three or four centuries the West taught itself to resist these excitements in the interest of a moral idea.

24 Educators are needlessly squeamish about their duty to uphold moral values and needlessly perplexed about how to implant them. The corruptions of our times are a sufficient warning that we cannot afford to abandon the duty to the homes and the churches, and the capacity which many institutions have shown to do their duty in a liberal spirit is a sufficient guaranty against bigotry.

25 Finally, there is the test imposed by the unique challenge of our own times. We are not unique in suffering from moral confusion—these crises are a familiar story—but we are unique in the tremendous acceleration of the rate of social change and in the tremendous risk of a catastrophic end to all our hopes. We cannot afford educated men who have every grace except the gift for survival. An indispensable mark of the modern educated man is the kind of versatile, flexible mind that can deal with new and explosive conditions.

26 With this reserve, there is little in this profile which has not been familiar for centuries. Unfortunately, the description which once sufficed to suggest its personality has been debased in journalistic currency. The "well-rounded man" has become the organization man, or the man who is so well rounded that he rolls wherever he is pushed. The humanists who invented the idea and preached it for centuries would recoil in contempt from any such notion. They understood the possibilities of the whole man and wanted an educational system which would give the many sides of his nature some chance to develop in harmony. They thought it a good idea to mix the wisdom of the world with the learning of the cloister, to develop the body as well as the mind, to pay a great deal of attention to character, and to neglect no art which could add to the enjoyment of living. It was a spacious idea which offered every hospitality to creative energy. Anyone who is seriously interested in a liberal education must begin by rediscovering it.

VOCABULARY

pedagogy (1)	dogmatic (3)
artisans (1)	amateurs (4)
ambiguous (2)	humbug (6)

credulity (7)	proliferation (17)
demagogues (8)	gobbledy-gook (17)
humanism (10)	sophistication (20)
desiccated (10)	blatant (22)
hokum (10)	squeamish (24)
exorcisè (11)	unique (25)
fastidious (14)	versatile (25)
precious (14)	cloister (26)

QUESTIONS ON CONTENT

1. How does Alan Simpson define liberal education at the start of his essay? Why is this definition important to the remainder of the essay?
2. From the courses offered at your college, name two considered liberal and two that can be classified as training.
3. In which paragraph is the first skill of the educated person discussed? What is this skill and what does it enable one to do?
4. At what point does Simpson introduce the second skill of the educated man? What is it?
5. What tests of an educated man does Simpson propose? Make an outline of his discussion of these tests.
6. List the obstacles to proper written and spoken communications that Simpson cites. In which paragraphs are they described?
7. In paragraph 25 Simpson says that the modern educated man must have a versatile, flexible mind that can deal with "new and explosive conditions." Name at least three potentially explosive conditions in our society.
8. In his final paragraph whom does Simpson hold up as an example of truly educated men? What virtues did they exhibit?

QUESTIONS ON FORM

1. What contrast is developed in paragraph 1? Find other contrasts in different paragraphs.
2. By what means are the beautiful balance and coherence of paragraphs 9 and 10 achieved?
3. In what way do the opening sentences of paragraphs 4, 9, and 10 provide transitions from the preceding paragraphs?
4. Simpson makes free use of metaphors in his essay. How effective are the following? Comment on each.
   (a) sheep and goats (paragraph 9)
   (b) feast and dishes (paragraph 10)
   (c) to smash across acres of broken syntax (paragraph 14)
   (d) a road bristling with obstacles (paragraph 15)
   (e) journalistic currency (paragraph 26)

SUGGESTIONS FOR WRITING

1. Write an essay describing a person whom you consider truly educated. Be specific about his characteristics.
2. What pitfalls attend the lack of a liberal education? Write an essay enumerating

these pitfalls. Organize your essay around two or three major points that are in turn subdivided.

3. Write a sentence outline delineating your college curriculum and what educational values you expect to get out of it.

TERM PAPER SUGGESTION

Write a research paper based on the unique contribution to education made by one of the following Renaissance humanists: Desiderius Erasmus, Thomas More, John Colet, John Milton.

EDWARD VERRAL LUCAS

A FUNERAL

In this brief, wistful essay Edward Verral Lucas (1868–1938), essayist and publisher, recounts the funeral of a close friend. It illustrates the impact and force of a well-organized essay.

1 It was in a Surrey churchyard on a grey, damp afternoon—all very solitary and quiet, with no alien spectators and only a very few mourners; and no desolating sense of loss, although a very true and kindly friend was passing from us. A football match was in progress in a field adjoining the churchyard, and I wondered, as I stood by the grave, if, were I the schoolmaster, I would stop the game just for the few minutes during which a body was committed to the earth; and I decided that I would not. In the midst of death we are in life, just as in the midst of life we are in death; it is all as it should be in this bizarre, jostling world. And he whom we had come to bury would have been the first to wish the boys to go on with their sport.

2 He was an old scholar—not so very old, either—whom I had known for some five years, and had many a long walk with: a short and sturdy Irish gentleman, with a large, genial grey head stored with odd lore and the best literature; and the heart of a child. I never knew a man of so transparent a character. He showed you all his thoughts: as some one once said, his brain was like a beehive under glass—you could watch all its workings. And the honey in it! To walk with him at any season of the year was to be reminded or newly told of the best that the English poets have said on all the phenomena of wood and hedgerow, meadow and sky. He had the more lyrical passages of Shakespeare at his tongue's end, and all Wordsworth and Keats. These were his favourites; but he had read everything that has the true rapturous note, and had forgotten none of its spirit.

3 His life was divided between his books, his friends, and long walks. A solitary man, he worked at all hours without much method, and probably courted his fatal illness in this way. To his own name there is not much to show; but such was his liberality that he was continually helping others, and the fruits of his erudition are widely scattered, and have gone to increase many

a comparative stranger's reputation. His own *magnum opus* he left unfinished; he had worked at it for years, until to his friends it had come to be something of a joke. But though still shapeless, it was a great feast, as the world, I hope, will one day know. If, however, this treasure does not reach the world, it will not be because its worth was insufficient, but because no one can be found to decipher the manuscript; for I may say incidentally that our old friend wrote the worst hand in London, and it was not an uncommon experience of his correspondents to carry his missives from one pair of eyes to another, seeking a clue; and I remember on one occasion two such inquirers meeting unexpectedly, and each simultaneously drawing a letter from his pocket and uttering the request that the other should put everything else on one side in order to solve the enigma.

4 Lack of method and a haphazard and unlimited generosity were not his only Irish qualities. He had a quick, chivalrous temper, too, and I remember the difficulty I once had in restraining him from leaping the counter of a small tobacconist's in Great Portland Street, to give the man a good dressing for an imagined rudeness—not to himself, but to me. And there is more than one bus conductor in London who has cause to remember this sturdy Quixotic passenger's championship of a poor woman to whom insufficient courtesy seemed to him to have been shown. Normally kindly and tolerant, his indignation on hearing of injustice was red hot. He burned at a story of meanness. It would haunt him all the evening. "Can it really be true?" he would ask, and burst forth again to flame.

5 Abstemious himself in all things, save reading and writing and helping his friends and correspondents, he mixed excellent whisky punch, as he called it. He brought to this office all the concentration which he lacked in his literary labours. It was a ritual with him; nothing might be hurried or left undone, and the result, I might say, justified the means. His death reduces the number of such convivial alchemists to one only, and he is in Tasmania, and, so far as I am concerned, useless.

6 His avidity as a reader—his desire to master his subject led to some charming eccentricities, as when, for a daily journey between Earl's Court Road and Addison Road stations, he would carry a heavy hand-bag filled with books, "to read in the train." This was no satire on the railway system, but pure zeal. He had indeed no satire in him; he spoke his mind and it was over.

7 It was a curious little company that assembled to do honour to this old kindly bachelor—the two or three relatives that he possessed, and eight of his literary friends, most of them of a good age, and for the most part men of intellect, and in one or two cases of world-wide reputation, and all a little uncomfortable in unwonted formal black. We were very grave and thoughtful, but it was not exactly a sad funeral, for we knew that had he lived longer—he was sixty-three—he would certainly have been an invalid, which would have irked his active, restless mind and body almost unbearably; and we knew, also, that he had died in his first real illness after a very happy life. Since we knew this, and also that he was a bachelor and almost alone, those of us who were not his kin were not melted and unstrung by that poignant sense of

untimely loss and irreparable removal that makes some funerals so tragic; but death, however it come, is a mystery before which one cannot stand unmoved and unregretful; and I, for one, as I stood there, remembered how easy it would have been oftener to have ascended to his eyrie and lured him out into Hertfordshire or his beloved Epping, or even have dragged him away to dinner and whisky punch; and I found myself meditating, too, as the profoundly impressive service rolled on, how melancholy it was that all that storied brain, with its thousands of exquisite phrases and its perhaps unrivalled knowledge of Shakespearean philology, should have ceased to be. For such a cessation, at any rate, say what one will of immortality, is part of the sting of death, part of the victory of the grave, which St. Paul denied with such magnificent irony.

8 And then we filed out into the churchyard, which is a new and very large one, although the church is old, and at a snail's pace, led by the clergyman, we crept along, a little black company, for, I suppose, nearly a quarter of a mile, under the cold grey sky. As I said, many of us were old, and most of us were indoor men, and I was amused to see how close to the head some of us held our hats—the merest barleycorn of interval being maintained for reverence' sake; whereas the sexton and the clergyman had slipped on those black velvet skull-caps which God, in His infinite mercy, either completely overlooks, or seeing, smiles at. And there our old friend was committed to the earth, amid the contending shouts of the football players, and then we all clapped our hats on our heads with firmness (as he would have wished us to do long before), and returned to the town to drink tea in an ancient hostelry, and exchange memories, quaint, and humorous, and touching, and beautiful, of the dead.

VOCABULARY

desolating (1)	alchemists (5)
rapturous (2)	avidity (6)
erudition (3)ʳ	unwonted (7)
magnum opus (3)	poignant (7)
enigma (3)	eyrie (7)
chivalrous (4)	philology (7)
Quixotic (4)	cessation (7)
abstemious (5)	hostelry (8)
convivial (5)	

QUESTIONS ON CONTENT

1. Whose funeral does this describe? What was the relationship of the deceased to the narrator?
2. Which poets had been the dead man's favorites?
3. Why is his *magnum opus* unlikely to be published?
4. What were some of the dead man's characteristics?

5. The narrator says that "we were very grave and thoughtful, but it was not exactly a sad funeral" (paragraph 7). Why not?

QUESTIONS ON FORM

1. Paragraphs 1, 7, and 8 use a common organizing focus. What is it?
2. What is the organizing focus of paragraphs 2, 3, 4, 5, and 6?
3. The narrator writes: "He showed you all his thoughts: as some one once said, his brain was like a beehive under glass—you could watch all its workings." What figure of speech is this?
4. Paragraph 4 begins: "Lack of method and a haphazard and unlimited generosity were not his only Irish qualities." What is the purpose of this sentence in the paragraph?
5. A well-organized essay frequently leaves the reader with a sense of completeness or closure. How does the writer achieve closure here?

SUGGESTIONS FOR WRITING

1. Write a chronologically organized essay describing any ceremony such as a funeral or a wedding you have attended.
2. Write an essay titled, "We Are Too Solemn at Funerals."

JAMES THURBER

THE CATBIRD SEAT

A conventional, well-behaved office clerk suddenly finds his job threatened by an aggressive, loud-mouthed "special adviser to the president." To protect his job, this unobtrusive little man resorts to a most unusual crime.

1 Mr. Martin bought the pack of Camels on Monday night in the most crowded cigar store on Broadway. It was theatre time and seven or eight men were buying cigarettes. The clerk didn't even glance at Mr. Martin, who put the pack in his overcoat pocket and went out. If any of the staff at F & S had seen him buy the cigarettes, they would have been astonished, for it was generally known that Mr. Martin did not smoke, and never had. No one saw him.

2 It was just a week to the day since Mr. Martin had decided to rub out Mrs. Ulgine Barrows. The term "rub out" pleased him because it suggested nothing more than the correction of an error—in this case an error of Mr. Fitweiler. Mr. Martin had spent each night of the past week working out his plan and examining it. As he walked home now he went over it again. For the hundredth time he resented the element of imprecision, the margin of guess-work that entered into the business. The project as he had worked it out was casual and bold, the risks were considerable. Something might go wrong anywhere along the line. And therein lay the cunning of his scheme. No one

would ever see in it the cautious, painstaking hand of Erwin Martin, head of the filing department at F & S, of whom Mr. Fitweiler had once said, "Man is fallible but Martin isn't." No one would see his hand, that is, unless it were caught in the act.

3 Sitting in his apartment, drinking a glass of milk, Mr. Martin reviewed his case against Mrs. Ulgine Barrows, as he had every night for seven nights. He began at the beginning. Her quacking voice and braying laugh had first profaned the halls of F & S on March 7, 1941 (Mr. Martin had a head for dates). Old Roberts, the personnel chief, had introduced her as the newly appointed special adviser to the president of the firm, Mr. Fitweiler. The woman had appalled Mr. Martin instantly, but he hadn't shown it. He had given her his dry hand, a look of studious concentration, and a faint smile. "Well," she had said, looking at the papers on his desk, "are you lifting the oxcart out of the ditch?" As Mr. Martin recalled that moment, over his milk, he squirmed slightly. He must keep his mind on her crimes as a special adviser, not on her peccadillos as a personality. This he found difficult to do, in spite of entering an objection and sustaining it. The faults of the woman as a woman kept chattering on in his mind like an unruly witness. She had, for almost two years now, baited him. In the halls, in the elevator, even in his own office, into which she romped now and then like a circus horse, she was constantly shouting these silly questions at him. "Are you lifting the oxcart out of the ditch? Are you tearing up the pea patch? Are you hollering down the rain barrel? Are you scraping around the bottom of the pickle barrel? Are you sitting in the catbird seat?"

4 It was Joey Hart, one of Mr. Martin's two assistants, who had explained what the gibberish meant. "She must be a Dodger fan," he had said. "Red Barber announces the Dodger games over the radio and he uses those expressions—picked 'em up down South." Joey had gone on to explain one or two. "Tearing up the pea patch" meant going on a rampage; "sitting in the catbird seat" meant sitting pretty, like a batter with three balls and no strikes on him. Mr. Martin dismissed all this with an effort. It had been annoying, it had driven him near to distraction, but he was too solid a man to be moved to murder by anything so childish. It was fortunate, he reflected as he passed on to the important charges against Mrs. Barrows, that he had stood up under it so well. He had maintained always an outward appearance of polite tolerance. "Why, I even believe you like the woman," Miss Paird, his other assistant, had once said to him. He had simply smiled.

5 A gavel rapped in Mr. Martin's mind and the case proper was resumed. Mrs. Ulgine Barrows stood charged with willful, blatant, and persistent attempts to destroy the efficiency and system of F & S. It was competent, material, and relevant to review her advent and rise to power. Mr. Martin had got the story from Miss Paird, who seemed always able to find things out. According to her, Mrs. Barrows had met Mr. Fitweiler at a party, where she had rescued him from the embraces of a powerfully built drunken man who had mistaken the president of F & S for a famous retired Middle Western

football coach. She had led him to a sofa and somehow worked upon him a monstrous magic. The aging gentleman had jumped to the conclusion there and then that this was a woman of singular attainments, equipped to bring out the best in him and in the firm. A week later he had introduced her into F & S as his special adviser. On that day confusion got its foot in the door. After Miss Tyson, Mr. Brundage, and Mr. Bartlett had been fired and Mr. Munson had taken his hat and stalked out, mailing in his resignation later, old Roberts had been emboldened to speak to Mr. Fitweiler. He mentioned that Mr. Munson's department had been "a little disrupted" and hadn't they perhaps better resume the old system there? Mr. Fitweiler had said certainly not. He had the greatest faith in Mrs. Barrows' ideas. "They require a little seasoning, a little seasoning, is all," he had added. Mr. Roberts had given it up. Mr. Martin reviewed in detail all the changes wrought by Mrs. Barrows. She had begun chipping at the cornices of the firm's edifice and now she was swinging at the foundation stones with a pickaxe.

6 Mr. Martin came now, in his summing up, to the afternoon of Monday, November 2, 1942—just one week ago. On that day, at 3 P.M., Mrs. Barrows had bounced into his office. "Boo!" she had yelled. "Are you scraping around the bottom of the pickle barrel?" Mr. Martin had looked at her from under his green eyeshade, saying nothing. She had begun to wander about the office, taking it in with her great, popping eyes. "Do you really need *all* these filing cabinets?" she had demanded suddenly. Mr. Martin's heart had jumped. "Each of these files," he had said, keeping his voice even, "plays an indispensable part in the system of F & S." She had brayed at him, "Well, don't tear up the pea patch!" and gone to the door. From there she had bawled, "But you sure have got a lot of fine scrap in here!" Mr. Martin could no longer doubt that the finger was on his beloved department. Her pickaxe was on the upswing, poised for the first blow. It had not come yet; he had received no blue memo from the enchanted Mr. Fitweiler bearing nonsensical instructions deriving from the obscene woman. But there was no doubt in Mr. Martin's mind that one would be forthcoming. He must act quickly. Already a precious week had gone by. Mr. Martin stood up in his living room, still holding his milk glass. "Gentlemen of the jury" he said to himself, "I demand the death penalty for this horrible person."

7 The next day Mr. Martin followed his routine, as usual. He polished his glasses more often and once sharpened an already sharp pencil, but not even Miss Paird noticed. Only once did he catch sight of his victim; she swept past him in the hall with a patronizing "Hi!" At five-thirty he walked home, as usual, and had a glass of milk, as usual. He had never drunk anything stronger in his life—unless you could count ginger ale. The late Sam Schlosser, the S of F & S, had praised Mr. Martin at a staff meeting several years before for his temperate habits. "Our most efficient worker neither drinks nor smokes," he had said. "The results speak for themselves." Mr. Fitweiler had sat by, nodding approval.

8 Mr. Martin was still thinking about that red-letter day as he walked over

to the Schrafft's on Fifth Avenue near Forty-sixth Street. He got there, as he always did, at eight o'clock. He finished his dinner and the financial page of the *Sun* at a quarter to nine, as he always did. It was his custom after dinner to take a walk. This time he walked down Fifth Avenue at a casual pace. His gloved hands felt moist and warm, his forehead cold. He transferred the Camels from his overcoat to a jacket pocket. He wondered, as he did so, if they did not represent an unnecessary note of strain. Mrs. Barrows smoked only Luckies. It was his idea to puff a few puffs on a Camel (after the rubbing-out), stub it out in the ashtray holding her lipstick-stained Luckies, and thus drag a small red herring across the trail. Perhaps it was not a good idea. It would take time. He might even choke, too loudly.

9   Mr. Martin had never seen the house on West Twelfth Street where Mrs. Barrows lived, but he had a clear enough picture of it. Fortunately, she had bragged to everybody about her ducky first-floor apartment in the perfectly darling three-story red-brick. There would be no doorman or other attendants; just the tenants of the second and third floors. As he walked along, Mr. Martin realized that he would get there before nine-thirty. He had considered walking north on Fifth Avenue from Schrafft's to a point from which it would take him until ten o'clock to reach the house. At that hour people were less likely to be coming in or going out. But the procedure would have made an awkward loop in the straight thread of his casualness, and he had abandoned it. It was impossible to figure when people would be entering or leaving the house, anyway. There was a great risk at any hour. If he ran into anybody, he would simply have to place the rubbing-out of Ulgine Barrows in the inactive file forever. The same thing would hold true if there were someone in her apartment. In that case he would just say that he had been passing by, recognized her charming house, and thought to drop in.

10   It was eighteen minutes after nine when Mr. Martin turned into Twelfth Street. A man passed him, and a man and a woman, talking. There was no one within fifty paces when he came to the house, halfway down the block. He was up the steps and in the small vestibule in no time, pressing the bell under the card that said "Mrs. Ulgine Barrows." When the clicking in the lock started, he jumped forward against the door. He got inside fast, closing the door behind him. A bulb in a lantern hung from the hall ceiling on a chain seemed to give a monstrously bright light. There was nobody on the stair, which went up ahead of him along the left wall. A door opened down the hall in the wall on the right. He went toward it swiftly, on tiptoe.

11   "Well, for God's sake, look who's here!" bawled Mrs. Barrows, and her braying laugh rang out like the report of a shotgun. He rushed past her like a football tackle, bumping her. "Hey, quit shoving!" she said, closing the door behind them. They were in her living room, which seemed to Mr. Martin to be lighted by a hundred lamps. "What's after you?" she said. "You're as jumpy as a goat." He found he was unable to speak. His heart was wheezing in his throat. "I—yes," he finally brought out. She was jabbering and laughing as she started to help him off with his coat. "No, no," he said. "I'll put it here."

He took it off and put it on a chair near the door. "Your hat and gloves, too," she said. "You're in a lady's house." He put his hat on top of the coat. Mrs. Barrows seemed larger than he had thought. He kept his gloves on. "I was passing by," he said. "I recognized—is there anyone here?" She laughed louder than ever. "No," she said, "we're all alone. You're as white as a sheet, you funny man. Whatever *has* come over you? I'll mix you a toddy." She started toward a door across the room. "Scotch-and-soda be all right? But say, you don't drink, do you?" She turned and gave him her amused look. Mr. Martin pulled himself together. "Scotch-and-soda will be all right," he heard himself say. He could hear her laughing in the kitchen.

12 Mr. Martin looked quickly around the living room for the weapon. He had counted on finding one there. There were andirons and a poker and something in a corner that looked like an Indian club. None of them would do. It couldn't be that way. He began to pace around. He came to a desk. On it lay a metal paper knife with an ornate handle. Would it be sharp enough? He reached for it and knocked over a small brass jar. Stamps spilled out of it and it fell to the floor with a clatter. "Hey," Mrs. Barrows yelled from the kitchen, "are you tearing up the pea patch?" Mr. Martin gave a strange laugh. Picking up the knife, he tried its point against his left wrist. It was blunt. It wouldn't do.

13 When Mrs. Barrows reappeared, carrying two highballs, Mr. Martin, standing there with his gloves on, became acutely conscious of the fantasy he had wrought. Cigarettes in his pocket, a drink prepared for him—it was all too grossly improbable. It was more than that; it was impossible. Somewhere in the back of his mind a vague idea stirred, sprouted. "For heaven's sake, take off those gloves," said Mrs. Barrows. "I always wear them in the house," said Mr. Martin. The idea began to bloom, strange and wonderful. She put the glasses on a coffee table in front of a sofa and sat on the sofa. "Come over here, you odd little man," she said. Mr. Martin went over and sat beside her. It was difficult getting a cigarette out of the pack of Camels, but he managed it. She held a match for him, laughing. "Well," she said, handing him his drink, "this is perfectly marvellous. You with a drink and a cigarette."

14 Mr. Martin puffed, not too awkwardly, and took a gulp of the highball. "I drink and smoke all the time," he said. He clinked his glass against hers. "Here's nuts to that old windbag, Fitweiler," he said, and gulped again. The stuff tasted awful, but he made no grimace. "Really, Mr. Martin," she said, her voice and posture changing, "you are insulting our employer." Mrs. Barrows was now all special adviser to the president. "I am preparing a bomb," said Mr. Martin, "which will blow the old goat higher than hell." He had only had a little of the drink, which was not strong. It couldn't be that. "Do you take dope or something?" Mrs. Barrows asked coldly. "Heroin," said Mr. Martin. "I'll be coked to the gills when I bump that old buzzard off." "Mr. Martin!" she shouted, getting to her feet. "That will be all of that. You must go at once." Mr. Martin took another swallow of his drink. He tapped his cigarette out in the ashtray and put the pack of Camels on the coffee table.

Then he got up. She stood glaring at him. He walked over and put on his hat and coat. "Not a word about this," he said, and laid an index finger against his lips. All Mrs. Barrows could bring out was "Really!" Mr. Martin put his hand on the doorknob. "I'm sitting in the catbird seat," he said. He stuck his tongue out at her and left. Nobody saw him go.

15 Mr. Martin got to his apartment, walking, well before eleven. No one saw him go in. He had two glasses of milk after brushing his teeth, and he felt elated. It wasn't tipsiness, because he hadn't been tipsy. Anyway, the walk had worn off all effects of the whiskey. He got in bed and read a magazine for a while. He was asleep before midnight.

16 Mr. Martin got to the office at eight-thirty the next morning, as usual. At a quarter to nine, Ulgine Barrows, who had never before arrived at work before ten, swept into his office. "I'm reporting to Mr. Fitweiler now!" she shouted. "If he turns you over to the police, it's no more than you deserve!" Mr. Martin gave her a look of shocked surprise. "I beg your pardon?" he said. Mrs. Barrows snorted and bounced out of the room, leaving Miss Paird and Joey Hart staring after her. "What's the matter with that old devil now?" asked Miss Paird. "I have no idea," said Mr. Martin, resuming his work. The other two looked at him and then at each other. Miss Paird got up and went out. She walked slowly past the closed door of Mr. Fitweiler's office. Mrs. Barrows was yelling inside, but she was not braying. Miss Paird could not hear what the woman was saying. She went back to her desk.

17 Forty-five minutes later, Mrs. Barrows left the president's office and went into her own, shutting the door. It wasn't until half an hour later that Mr. Fitweiler sent for Mr. Martin. The head of the filing department, neat, quiet, attentive, stood in front of the old man's desk. Mr. Fitweiler was pale and nervous. He took his glasses off and twiddled them. He made a small, bruffing sound in his throat. "Martin," he said, "you have been with us more than twenty years." "Twenty-two, sir," said Mr. Martin. "In that time," pursued the president, "your work and your—uh—manner have been exemplary." "I trust so, sir," said Mr. Martin. "I have understood, Martin," said Mr. Fitweiler, "that you have never taken a drink or smoked." "That is correct, sir," said Mr. Martin. "Ah, yes." Mr. Fitweiler polished his glasses. "You may describe what you did after leaving the office yesterday, Martin," he said. Mr. Martin allowed less than a second for his bewildered pause. "Certainly, sir," he said. "I walked home. Then I went to Schrafft's for dinner. Afterward I walked home again. I went to bed early, sir, and read a magazine for a while. I was asleep before eleven." "Ah, yes," said Mr. Fitweiler again. He was silent for a moment, searching for the proper words to say to the head of the filing department. "Mrs. Barrows," he said finally, "Mrs. Barrows has worked hard, Martin, very hard. It grieves me to report that she has suffered a severe breakdown. It has taken the form of a persecution complex accompanied by distressing hallucinations." "I am very sorry, sir," said Mr. Martin. "Mrs. Barrows is under the delusion," continued Mr. Fitweiler, "that you visited her last evening and behaved yourself in an—uh—unseemly manner."

He raised his hand to silence Mr. Martin's little pained outcry. "It is the nature of these psychological diseases," Mr. Fitweiler said, "to fix upon the least likely and most innocent party as the—uh—source of persecution. These matters are not for the lay mind to grasp, Martin. I've just had my psychiatrist, Dr. Fitch, on the phone. He would not, of course, commit himself, but he made enough generalizations to substantiate my suspicions. I suggested to Mrs. Barrows, when she had completed her—uh—story to me this morning, that she visit Dr. Fitch, for I suspected a condition at once. She flew, I regret to say, into a rage, and demanded—uh—requested that I call you on the carpet. You may not know, Martin, but Mrs. Barrows had planned a reorganization of your department—subject to my approval, of course, subject to my approval. This brought you, rather than anyone else, to her mind—but again that is a phenomenon for Dr. Fitch and not for us. So, Martin, I am afraid Mrs. Barrows' usefulness here is at an end." "I am dreadfully sorry, sir," said Mr. Martin.

18 It was at this point that the door to the office blew open with the suddenness of a gas-main explosion and Mrs. Barrows catapulted through it. "Is the little rat denying it?" she screamed. "He can't get away with that!" Mr. Martin got up and moved discreetly to a point beside Mr. Fitweiler's chair. "You drank and smoked at my apartment," she bawled at Mr. Martin, "and you know it! You called Mr. Fitweiler an old windbag and said you were going to blow him up when you got coked to the gills on your heroin!" She stopped yelling to catch her breath and a new glint came into her popping eyes. "If you weren't such a drab, ordinary little man," she said, "I'd think you'd planned it all. Sticking your tongue out, saying you were sitting in the catbird seat, because you thought no one would believe me when I told it! My God, it's really too perfect!" She brayed loudly and hysterically, and the fury was on her again. She glared at Mr. Fitweiler. "Can't you see how he has tricked us, you old fool? Can't you see his little game?" But Mr. Fitweiler had been surreptitiously pressing all the buttons under the top of his desk and employees of F & S began pouring into the room. "Stockton," said Mr. Fitweiler, "you and Fishbein will take Mrs. Barrows to her home. Mrs. Powell, you will go with them." Stockton, who had played a little football in high school, blocked Mrs. Barrows as she made for Mr. Martin. It took him and Fishbein together to force her out of the door into the hall, crowded with stenographers and office boys. She was still screaming imprecations at Mr. Martin, tangled and contradictory imprecations. The hubbub finally died out down the corridor.

19 "I regret that this has happened," said Mr. Fitweiler. "I shall ask you to dismiss it from your mind, Martin." "Yes, sir," said Mr. Martin, anticipating his chief's "That will be all" by moving to the door. "I will dismiss it." He went out and shut the door, and his step was light and quick in the hall. When he entered his department he had slowed down to his customary gait, and he walked quietly across the room to the W20 file, wearing a look of studious concentration.

VOCABULARY

fallible (2)	ducky (9)
appalled (3)	monstrously (10)
peccadillos (3)	wheezing (11)
romped (3)	grossly (13)
gibberish (4)	bruffing (17)
edifice (5)	exemplary (17)
indispensable (6)	hallucinations (17)
obscene (6)	unseemly (17)
patronizing (7)	catapulted (18)
temperate (7)	surreptitiously (18)
red herring (8)	imprecations (18)

QUESTIONS ON CONTENT

1. Part of the humor and interest in this story hinges on the contrast between Mr. Martin and Mrs. Barrows. Describe the contrast in their natures and methods of operating.
2. Both Mr. Martin and Mrs. Barrows are portrayed as caricatures; that is, their traits are exaggerated. Cite specific examples of caricature in each.
3. What are the reasons for Mr. Martin's decision to "rub out" Mrs. Barrows?
4. Why does Mr. Martin change his plan, and why does the new plan work?
5. The author makes no explicit value judgment on Mr. Martin's revenge. Each reader is expected to do that for himself. What is your judgment of Mr. Martin's action? Was he justified or not? Explain your answer.

QUESTIONS ON FORM

1. The organization of the story falls naturally into four divisions: (a) the trial and verdict of Mrs. Barrows, (b) preparation for the crime, (c) change of plan and perpetration of the crime, (d) result of the crime. Summarize what happens in each of these segments.
2. Early in the story the author tells us that Mr. Martin plans to kill Mrs. Barrows. Why does this announcement not eliminate suspense from the story?
3. What is the emotional climax of the story?
4. What role does Fitweiler play in the plot?

SUGGESTIONS FOR WRITING

1. Choose one of your close friends and write a short caricature of him by exaggerating his traits.
2. Write an essay analyzing the humorous devices used by Thurber in the story "The Catbird Seat." Pay attention to such factors as character, plot reversal, and style.

WILLIAM SHAKESPEARE

THAT TIME OF YEAR (SONNET 73)

The English or Shakespearean sonnet is composed of three quatrains of four lines each and a concluding couplet of two, rhyming *abab cdcd efef gg*. There is usually a correspondence between the units marked off by the rhymes and the development of the thought. The three quatrains, for instance, may represent three different images or three questions from which a conclusion is drawn in the final couplet. As a result, the sonnet is one of the most tightly organized poetic forms used.

That time of year thou mayst in me behold
When yellow leaves, or none, or few, do hang
Upon those boughs which shake against the cold,
Bare ruined choirs where late the sweet birds sang.
In me thou see'st the twilight of such day
As after sunset fadeth in the west,
Which by and by black night doth take away,
Death's second self, that seals up all in rest.
In me thou see'st the glowing of such fire,
That on the ashes of his youth doth lie
As the deathbed whereon it must expire,
Consumed with that which it was nourished by.
   This thou perceivest, which makes thy love more strong,
   To love that well which thou must leave ere long.

QUESTIONS ON CONTENT

1. After reading the poem, what can you say about the speaker? What kind of person is he? What seems to have provoked his thoughts?
2. In the first quatrain what image does the poet focus on? What relationship does this image have to the speaker?
3. In the second quatrain the speaker shifts to another image. What is it and what relationship does it bear to him?
4. In the third quatrain yet another image is introduced. What is the image and how does it relate to the speaker? Analyze the rather complex philosophical paradox involved.
5. The final couplet states the poet's thesis (or theme). What is that theme? State it in your own words.
6. What importance does the speaker attach to love? State how you arrived at your answer.

QUESTIONS ON FORM

1. The entire poem is organized around three analogies. State them in three succinct sentences.

2. The three images in the poem are presented in a particular order. Do you see any reason for this order?
3. In lines 3 and 4, what effect on the rhythm and meter do the words "cold,/Bare ruined choirs" have?
4. In line 2, what would be the result of substituting "hang" for "do hang"?
5. What is the antecedent of "this" in line 13?

SUGGESTIONS FOR WRITING

1. In two or three well-developed paragraphs, answer the question, "What is the single worst aspect about old age?"
2. Write an essay in which you outline a plan to make your own old age as pleasant and fulfilling as possible.

part 2

Writing

How Do I Get from Outline to Paragraph?
Paragraph Writing

model

STEPHEN LEACOCK

from AMERICANS

Americans are queer people. they can't play. Americans rush to work as soon as they grow up. They want their work as soon as they wake. It is a stimulant—the only one they're not afraid of. They used to open their offices at ten o'clock; then at nine; then at eight; then at seven. Now they never shut them. Every business in America is turning into an open-all-day-and-night business. They eat all night, dance all night, build buildings all night, make a noise all night. They *can't play.* They try to, but they can't. They turn football into a fight, baseball into a lawsuit, and yachting into machinery. They *can't play.* The little children *can't play;* they use mechanical toys instead—toy cranes, hoisting toy loads, toy machinery spreading a toy industrial depression of infantile dullness. The grownup people *can't play;* they use a mechanical gymnasium and a clockwork horse. They can't swim; they use a float. They can't run; they use a car. They can't laugh; they hire a comedian and watch him laugh.

The characteristics of a good paragraph are: unity, coherence, and completeness. Consider the above paragraph with these characteristics in mind:

1. Unity

Unity in a paragraph is developed when one general idea governs the entire paragraph. This general idea, commonly called the topic sentence, is usually found at the beginning of the paragraph, but it also can be found at the end or in the middle, and may be implied rather than stated. Regardless of where it is situated, all other sentences and details must support this topic sentence.

In our model, the topic sentence opens the paragraph: "Americans are queer people: they can't play." Every detail that follows supports this sentence; nothing irrelevant is introduced. The paragraph has unity.

2. Coherence

Coherence in a paragraph means that one sentence follows another in clear, logical sequence. Coherence allows the reader to move from one idea to the next, seeing the connection between ideas, and the connection of the ideas with the topic sentence.

In our model, coherence is gained through the repetition of "they" (see circles), standing for various kinds of Americans, and by the repetition of the key phrase "can't play" (see italics). Other devices often used to assure coherence are parallel grammatical structures and signals such as "first," "second," "third," and so on.

3. Completeness

Completeness in a paragraph occurs when enough is said in support of the topic sentence to make it convincing.

In our model, completeness is achieved because the author piles up enough details to make us believe that Americans cannot play. The following diagram will illustrate this point:

Americans can't play TOPIC SENTENCE	Americans rush to work and stay there They never shut their offices Businesses go day and night Even football, baseball, and yachting are turned into work Children's toys represent work The play of grownups is passive, not active	SUPPORTING DETAILS

advice

A. M. TIBBETTS AND CHARLENE TIBBETTS

WRITING SUCCESSFUL PARAGRAPHS

This selection offers four specific suggestions for writing good paragraphs.

1 A paragraph is a collection of sentences that helps you fulfill your thesis (theme promise). Itself a small "theme," a paragraph should be clearly written

and specific; and it should not wander or make irrelevant remarks. Each paragraph should be related in some way to the theme promise. Here are suggestions for writing successful paragraphs:

1 *Get to the point of your paragraph quickly and specifically.*

2 Don't waste time or words in stating your paragraph promise. Consider this good example of getting to the point—the writer is explaining the ancient Romans' technique for conquering their world:

> The technique of expansion was simple. *Divide et impera* [divide and conquer]: enter into solemn treaty with a neighbouring country, foment internal disorder, intervene in support of the weaker side on the pretense that Roman honour was involved, replace the legitimate ruler with a puppet, giving him the status of a subject ally; later, goad him into rebellion, seize and sack the country, burn down the temples, and carry off the captive gods to adorn a triumph. Conquered territories were placed under the control of a provincial governor-general, an ex-commander-in-chief who garrisoned it, levied taxes, set up courts of summary justice, and linked the new frontiers with the old by so-called Roman roads—usually built by Greek engineers and native forced labour. Established social and religious practices were permitted so long as they did not threaten Roman administration or offend against the broad-minded Roman standards of good taste. The new province presently became a springboard for further aggression.—Robert Graves, "It Was a Stable World"

3 Graves makes his promise in the first nine words, in which he mentions the "simple" technique the Romans had for "dividing" and "conquering" in order to expand their empire. Suppose Graves had started his paragraph with these words:

> The technique of expansion was interesting. It was based upon a theory about human nature that the Romans practically invented. This theory had to do with how people reacted to certain political and military devices which . . .

4 Do you see what is wrong? Since the beginning sentences are so vague, the paragraph never gets going. The writer can't fulfill a promise because he hasn't made one. Another example of a poor paragraph beginning:

> The first step involves part of the golf club head. The club head has removable parts, some of which are metal. You must consider these parts when deciding how to repair the club.

5 Specify the beginning of this paragraph and get to the point quicker:

> Your first step in repairing the club head is to remove the metal plate held on by Phillips Screws.

6 This solid, specific paragraph beginning gives your reader a clear promise which you can fulfill easily without wasting words. (Observe, by the way, that specifying a writer's stance—as we did in the last example—can help you write clearer paragraph beginnings.)

2 *Fulfill your reader's expectation established by the paragraph promise.*

7 Do this with specific details and examples—explain as fully as you can. Example:

> The next thing is to devise a form for your essay. This, which ought to be obvious, is not. I learned it for the first time from an experienced newspaperman. When I was at college I earned extra pocket- and book-money by writing several weekly columns for a newspaper. They were usually topical, they were always carefully varied, they tried hard to be witty, and (an essential) they never missed a deadline. But once, when I brought in the product, a copy editor stopped me. He said, "Our readers seem to like your stuff all right; but we think it's a bit amateurish." With due humility I replied, "Well, I am an amateur. What should I do with it?" He said, "Your pieces are not coherent; they are only sentences and epigrams strung together; they look like a heap of clothespins in a basket. Every article ought to have a shape. Like this" (and he drew a big letter S on his pad) "or this" (he drew a descending line which turned abruptly upward again) "or this" (and he sketched a solid central core with five or six lines pushing outward from it) "or even this" (and he outlined two big arrows coming into collision). I never saw the man again, but I have never ceased to be grateful to him for his wisdom and for his kindness. Every essay must have a shape. You can ask a question in the first paragraph, discussing several different answers to it till you reach one you think is convincing. You can give a curious fact and offer an explanation of it. You can take a topic that interests you and do a descriptive analysis of it: a man's character (as Hazlitt did with his fives champion), a building, a book, a striking adventure, a peculiar custom. There are many other shapes which essays can take; but the principle laid down by the copy editor was right. Before you start you must have a form in your mind; and it ought to be a form felt in paragraphs or sections, not in words or sentences—so that, if necessary, you could summarize each paragraph in a single line and put the entire essay on a postcard.—Gilbert Highet, "How to Write an Essay"

Highet makes a promise in the first three sentences, and in the remaining sentences he specifically fulfills it.

3 *Avoid fragmentary paragraphs.*

8 A fragmentary paragraph does not develop its topic or fulfill its promise. A series of fragmentary paragraphs jumps from idea to idea in a jerky and unconvincing fashion:

> [1]My freshman rhetoric class is similar in some ways to my senior English class in high school, but it is also very different.
> [2]In my English class we usually had daily homework assignments that were discussed during the class period. If we were studying grammar, the assignments were to correct grammatical errors in the text. If we were studying literature, we were supposed to read the material and understand its ideas.
> [3]In rhetoric class, we do basically the same things, except that in the readings we are assigned, we look much deeper into the purpose of the author.
> [4]In my English class . . .

Fragmentary paragraphs are often the result of a weak writer's stance.

4 *Avoid irrelevancies in your paragraphs.*

9 The italicized sentence does not fit the development of this paragraph:

We need a better working atmosphere at Restik Tool Company. The workers must feel that they are a working team instead of just individuals. If the men felt they were part of a team, they would not misuse the special machine tools, which now need to be resharpened twice as often as they used to be. *Management's attitude toward the union could be improved too.* The team effort is also being damaged by introduction of new products before their bugs have been worked out. Just when the men are getting used to one routine, a new one is installed, and their carefully created team effort is seriously damaged.

As with the fragmentary paragraph, the problem of irrelevancies in a paragraph is often the result of a vague writer's stance. The paragraph above does not seem to be written for any particular reader.

VOCABULARY

foment (2)   epigrams (7)
topical (7)   peculiar (7)

discussion

RICHARD M. WEAVER

THE FUNCTION OF THE PARAGRAPH

What follows gives a brief history of the paragraph and explains its function
as a visual aid that signals the beginning of a new thought.

1 The mind naturally looks for lines of division in anything it is considering. By these it is enabled to take in, or understand, because understanding is largely a matter of perceiving parts and their relationships. The paragraph is a kind of division, and paragraphing is a way of separating out the parts of a composition. Standing between the sentence as a unit at one end of the scale and the section or chapter at the other, the paragraph has the useful role of organizing our thoughts into groups of intermediate size.

2 The usefulness of a visual aid to division was recognized long before paragraphs were set off as they are today. In medieval manuscripts, which do not have the sort of indentation that we employ now, a symbol was written in the margin to mark a turn in the thought; and the word "paragraph" means "something written beside." Where the medieval scribe used a symbol, we use indentation. But the purpose served is the same, and that is to advise the reader that a new set of thoughts is beginning.

3 A paragraph may therefore be understood as a visible division of the

subject matter. The division is initially a convenience to the reader, as it prepares him to turn his attention to something new. But beyond this, most paragraphs have an internal unity, and they can be analyzed as compositions in miniature.

4 Occasionally one finds paragraphs which are compositions in the sense that they are not parts of a larger piece of writing. These occur in the form of single-paragraph statements, themes, and even stories, which are complete and which are not related to anything outside themselves. They will naturally reflect the rules of good composition if they are successful writing. They will have unity, coherence, and emphasis. They will be about something; they will make a progression, and they will have a major point.

5 Substantially the same may be said about paragraphs which are parts of a composition. They will have a relative self-containment, or basic unity and coherence, and they will emphasize some point or idea. Therefore what we have said about the composition in its entirety may be said with almost equal application of single paragraphs within the larger piece. Especially is it true that the subject must be reasonably definite and that the development must follow some plan, although the possible plans of development are various.

6 The point to be carried in mind is that the relative independence of the paragraph rests upon something. The paragraph is not a device marked off at mechanical intervals simply because it is felt that the reader needs a change. He does need a change, but the place of the change must be related to the course of the thought. Where that changes significantly, a new paragraph begins. It is a signal that something else is starting. This may be a different phase of the subject, an illustration, a qualification, a change of scale, or any one of a large number of things which can mark the course of systematic thinking about a subject.

VOCABULARY

intermediate (1) self-containment (5)
scribe (2) systematic (6)
miniature (3)

QUESTIONS ON CONTENT

1. Weaver describes the paragraph as an intermediary. Between what two ends does it stand?
2. What is the root meaning of the word "paragraph"? Explain its relevance.
3. Weaver calls the paragraph a composition in miniature. What does he mean?
4. The paragraph does not occur at regular intervals. When only does it occur?
5. What does Weaver consider the requirements for a good paragraph?

QUESTIONS ON FORM

1. Does Weaver follow his own rule about when paragraphs should occur? See the last half of paragraph 6.

2. In paragraph 4, through what means is coherence achieved?
3. What is the topic sentence for paragraph 6?

SUGGESTIONS FOR WRITING

In the essay that follows—a provocative statement from one of the first black students admitted to Exeter Academy in New Hampshire—we have purposely left out all paragraph indentations. After carefully reading the essay, supply appropriate paragraph signals.

THEE SMITH

I AM THE NEW BLACK

First of all, you should realize that you are white, and that I am black. . . . By and large, when I say that I am black, you picture one of two types of black men. But I refuse to be either; and if you listen as if I were one of them, you will never realize who and what I actually represent, and you will leave this place just as your fathers left it. *I am the New Black.* I will neither babble about how much I love Jesus, nor entertain you with sparkling racial comedy. I will not eat with my fingers nor go out of my way to sit down at a dining hall table with you. I will not flunk out of this place, but neither will I participate in the childish fanaticism of raving with you about your math test, or your Phy Sci lab, or your grade in English. I want neither to be your enemy, nor your friend. I don't want your love, or your pity, or your guilt, or your fear. I demand only that you respect me. . . . I, the New Black, am not exactly sure why I am here. . . . Last year I *did* know, without being told. Last year I was to eventually become a responsible American citizen. I felt that an investment had been made in me—not merely by this school but by your whole society— to provide a "safe," well-balanced, and responsible leadership for the black revolution. . . . The fact that I once accepted your definition of my role as a black nauseates me. I see in your definition, and in my agreement, a continuation of what blacks in this country have been trying to do since the Civil War; a continuation of the efforts to teach blacks how to act "white," and at the same time teach them to deny the legitimacy of their own culture. As the New Black, I shall not tolerate the teaching of other blacks to be industrious, puritanical, and relatively unemotional—as you are; for I feel that we, as human beings, have much more to lose by becoming white than by remaining true to ourselves, true to our culture, and true to our blackness. . . . The problem, again, is you people. Our minority black middle class is willing and ready to prostitute itself before you, and you still cannot see *your* sickness inside them. The problem *is* racial. All men are *not* born equal. White *is* right. In a riot, *all* blacks are suspected of theft, and rape, and murder. . . . I, the New Black, acknowledge my blackness, and the improbability of my ever becoming respected in your society by getting white. I, the New Black, not only accept but agree with your classification of all of us, regardless of class, as blacks. We have our blackness in common and we are united by your definition of what blacks in America are. . . . I am a black first, and an American when I can afford to be. I am at Exeter, not to be like you, nor to prepare myself to enter your society as a Roy Wilkins or a James Meredith. This school's efforts to prepare me for that type of role in tomorrow's world are futile. That role no longer offers effective leadership for change, because it is based on the theory that a black leader should strive for assimilation of the black masses. Assimilation is no longer the solution, though. Civil rights, as a movement, is dying. My most effective role in tomorrow's society will be to lead the advancement of Black Power; and I, the New Black, dedicate my life to that role. . . . We are at Exeter to obtain knowledge of ourselves, and when we become leaders, we will derive our strength not from your friendship, or your brains, or your money, but from ourselves.

examples

J. I. SIMMONS AND BARRY WINOGRAD

from THE HANG-LOOSE ETHIC

One of the fundamental characteristics of the hang-loose ethic is that it is *irreverent*. It repudiates, or at least questions, such cornerstones of conventional society as Christianity, "my country right or wrong," the sanctity of marriage and premarital chastity, civil obedience, the accumulation of wealth, the right and even competence of parents, the schools, and the government to head and make decisions for everyone—in sum, the Establishment. This irreverence is probably what most arouses the ire and condemnation of the populace. Not only are the mainstream institutions and values violated, but their very legitimacy is challenged and this has heaped insult upon moral injury in the eyes of the rank and file.

VOCABULARY

repudiates	legitimacy
Establishment	rank and file
populace	

QUESTIONS ON CONTENT

1. Obviously this paragraph is a general introduction to the irreverence of the hang-loose ethic. Can you infer what kind of people follow the hang-loose ethic?

2. Which is the "insult" and which is the "injury" caused by the hang-loose ethic? Supply some examples of both.

QUESTIONS ON FORM

1. What is the topic sentence of the paragraph?
2. By what means does the paragraph achieve coherence?

EDITH HAMILTON

from THE LESSONS OF THE PAST

Basic to all the Greek achievement was freedom. The Athenians were the only free people in the world. In the great empires of antiquity—Egypt, Babylon, Assyria, Persia—splendid though they were, with riches beyond reckoning and immense power, freedom was unknown. The idea of it never dawned in any of them. It was born in Greece, a poor little country, but with it able to remain unconquered no matter what manpower and what wealth were arrayed against her. At Marathon and at Salamis overwhelming numbers of Persians had been defeated by small Greek forces. It had been proved that one free man was superior to many submissively obedient subjects of a tyrant. Athens was the leader in that amazing victory, and to the Athenians freedom was their dearest possession. Demosthenes said that they would not think it worth their while to live if they could not do so as free men, and years later a great teacher said, "Athenians, if you deprive them of their liberty, will die."

VOCABULARY

arrayed	tyrant
Marathon	Demosthenes
Salamis	

QUESTIONS ON CONTENT

1. Were you convinced of the truth of the topic sentence after reading the paragraph? If so, what convinced you?
2. In what way are free men superior to those who are submissively obedient to a tyrant?

QUESTIONS ON FORM

1. What is the topic sentence of the paragraph?
2. Who is the "great teacher" alluded to?

DAVID L. ROSENHAN

from ON BEING SANE IN INSANE PLACES

If sanity and insanity exist, how shall we know them?

The question is neither capricious nor itself insane. However much we may be personally convinced that we can tell the normal from the abnormal, the evidence is simply not compelling. It is commonplace, for example, to read about murder trials wherein eminent psychiatrists for the defense are contradicted by equally eminent psychiatrists for the prosecution on the matter of the defendant's sanity. More generally, there is a large and conflicting literature on the reliability, utility and meaning of such terms as "sanity," "insanity," "mental illness," and "schizophrenia." Finally, as early as 1934, Benedict suggested that normality and abnormality are not universal. What is viewed as normal in one culture may be seen as quite aberrant in another. Thus, notions of normality and abnormality may not be quite as accurate as people believe they are.

VOCABULARY

capricious	schizophrenia
compelling	aberrant
eminent	

QUESTIONS ON CONTENT

1. As applied to the word "sane," what is the difference between "reliability," "utility," and "meaning"?
2. Why does the author use the example of psychiatrists contradicting each other in murder trials?

QUESTIONS ON FORM

1. In the case of this paragraph, there is no topic sentence as such, only a controlling question. How is the question answered, either directly or by implication?
2. What signal words help the coherence of the paragraph?

W. H. HUDSON

MY FRIEND THE PIG

This humorous paragraph illustrates the skillful use of specific, supporting detail.

I have a friendly feeling towards pigs generally, and consider them the most intelligent of beasts, not excepting the elephant and the anthropoid ape—the dog is not to be mentioned in this connection. I also like his disposition and attitude towards all other creatures, especially man. He is not suspicious, or shrinkingly submissive, like horses, cattle and sheep; nor an impudent devil-may-care like the goat; nor hostile like the goose; nor condescending like the cat; nor a flattering parasite like the dog. He views us from a totally different, a sort of democratic, standpoint as fellow-citizens and brothers, and takes it for granted, or grunted, that we understand his language, and without servility or insolence he has a natural, pleasant, camerados-all or hail-fellow-well-met air with us.

VOCABULARY

anthropoid   camerados
servility

QUESTIONS ON CONTENT

1. How does the writer feel about pigs?
2. What does he like about the pig's disposition?
3. What does he think of the goat?
4. Which animals does he consider suspicious and submissive?

QUESTIONS ON FORM

1. What is the topic sentence of this paragraph? Where is it stated?
2. The writer says that he likes the pig's attitude toward all other creatures. What technique does he then use to characterize the attitude of the pig?
3. What is accomplished by the writer's cataloguing the dispositions of other animals?
4. What term is given to the practice of imputing human characteristics to animals or inanimate objects?

E. B. WHITE

NEW YORK

This descriptive paragraph on New York exemplifies a topic sentence developed through the use of concrete examples.

It is a miracle that New York works at all. The whole thing is implausible. Every time the residents brush their teeth, millions of gallons of water must be drawn from the Catskills and the hills of Westchester. When a young man in Manhattan writes a letter to his girl in Brooklyn, the love message gets blown to her through a pneumatic tube—*pfft*—just like that. The subterranean system of telephone cables, power lines, steam pipes, gas mains and sewer pipes is reason enough to abandon the island to the gods and the weevils. Every time an incision is made in the pavement, the noisy surgeons expose ganglia that are tangled beyond belief. By rights New York should have destroyed itself long ago, from panic or fire or rioting or failure of some vital supply line in its circulatory system or from some deep labyrinthine short circuit. Long ago the city should have experienced an insoluble traffic snarl at some impossible bottleneck. It should have perished of hunger when food lines failed for a few days. It should have been wiped out by a plague starting in its slums or carried in by ships' rats. It should have been overwhelmed by the sea that licks at it on every side. The workers in its myriad cells should have succumbed to nerves, from the fearful pall of smoke-fog that drifts over every few days from Jersey, blotting out all light at noon and leaving the high offices suspended, men groping and depressed, and the sense of world's end. It should have been touched in the head by the August heat and gone off its rocker.

VOCABULARY

implausible	ganglia
pneumatic	labyrinthine
subterranean	myriad

QUESTIONS ON CONTENT

1. Why does the author say that New York is implausible?
2. What does he think should have happened to the workers of New York?

QUESTIONS ON FORM

1. What is the topic sentence of this paragraph?
2. How is the topic sentence in the paragraph developed?
3. The author writes, "It should have been touched in the head by the August heat and gone off its rocker." What technique is he using here in characterizing the city?

WILL DURANT

THE POLITICAL CAUSES OF THE DECAY OF ROME

In this tightly organized, detailed paragraph, American historian Will Durant discusses some of the reasons for the fall of Rome.

The political causes of decay were rooted in one fact—that increasing despotism destroyed the citizen's civic sense and dried up statesmanship at its source. Powerless to express his political will except by violence, the Roman lost interest in government and became absorbed in his business, his amusements, his legion, or his individual salvation. Patriotism and the pagan religion had been bound together, and now together decayed. The Senate, losing ever more of its power and prestige after Pertinax, relapsed into indolence, subservience, or venality; and the last barrier fell that might have saved the state from militarism and anarchy. Local governments, overrun by imperial *correctores,*[1] and *exactores,*[2] no longer attracted first-rate men. The responsibility of municipal officials for the tax quotas of their areas, the rising expense of their unpaid honors, the fees, liturgies, benefactions, and games expected of them, the dangers incident to invasion and class war, led to a flight from office corresponding to the flight from taxes, factories, and farms. Men deliberately made themselves ineligible by debasing their social category; some fled to other towns, some became farmers, some monks. In 313 Constantine extended to the Christian clergy that exemption from municipal office, and from several taxes, which pagan priests had traditionally enjoyed; the Church was soon swamped with candidates for ordination, and cities complained of losses in revenue and senators; in the end Constantine was compelled to rule that no man eligible for municipal position should be admitted to the priesthood. The imperial police pursued fugitives from political honors as it hunted evaders of taxes or conscription; it brought them back to the cities and forced them to serve; finally it decreed that a son must inherit the social status of his father, and must accept election if eligible to it by his rank. A serfdom of office rounded out the prison of economic caste.

VOCABULARY

despotism	liturgies
indolence	benefactions
subservience	debasing
venality	conscription
anarchy	serfdom

QUESTIONS ON CONTENT

1. The author writes that the political causes of decay were rooted in one fact. What fact was this?
2. Why did local governments no longer attract first-rate men?
3. What exemption did Constantine grant in 313?

QUESTIONS ON FORM

1. What is the topic sentence of this paragraph?
2. What purpose does the final sentence in the paragraph serve?

[1]Improvers (bureaucrats).—Ed.
[2]Tax collectors, superintendents.—Ed.

RALPH WALDO EMERSON

from SELF-RELIANCE

Let him not peep or steal, or skulk up and down with the air of a charity-boy, a bastard, or an interloper in the world which exists for him. But the man in the street, finding no worth in himself which corresponds to the force which built a tower or sculptured a marble god, feels poor when he looks on these. To him a palace, a statue, or a costly book have an alien and forbidding air, much like a gay equipage, and seem to say like that, "Who are you, sir?" Yet they all are his, suitors for his notice, petitioners to his faculties that they will come out and take possession. The picture waits for my verdict; it is not to command me, but I am to settle its claim to praise. That popular fable of the sot who was picked up dead drunk in the street, carried to the duke's house, washed and dressed and laid in the duke's bed, and, on his waking, treated with all obsequious ceremony like the duke, and assured that he had been insane—owes its popularity to the fact that it symbolizes so well the state of man, who is in the world a sort of sot, but now and then wakes up, exercises his reason and finds himself a true prince.

VOCABULARY

skulk	petitioners
interloper	sot
equipage	obsequious
suitors	

QUESTIONS ON CONTENT

1. What is the meaning of "peep or steal" in the first line?
2. Why would a "gay equipage" have a forbidding air?
3. What famous author wrote a book based on the fable mentioned?

QUESTIONS ON FORM

1. In this paragraph, the opening sentence is an exhortation for man to be self-reliant. Can you word this topic sentence in more direct language?
2. Why does the author shift from "you" to "I" in the middle of the paragraph?

W. SOMERSET MAUGHAM

from THE SUMMING UP

At first sight it is curious that our own offenses should seem to us so much less heinous than the offenses of others. I suppose the reason is that we know all the circumstances that have occasioned them and so manage to excuse in ourselves what we cannot excuse in others. We turn our attention away from our own defects, and when we are forced by untoward events to consider them, find it easy to condone them. For all I know we are right to do this; they are part of us and we must accept the good and the bad in ourselves together. But when we come to judge others it is not by ourselves as we really are that we judge them, but by an image that we have formed of ourselves from which we have left out everything that offends our vanity or would discredit us in the eyes of the world. To take a trivial instance: how scornful we are when we catch someone out telling a lie; but who can say that he has never told not one, but a hundred? We are shocked when we discover that great men were weak and petty, dishonest or selfish . . . vain or intemperate; and many people think it disgraceful to disclose to the public its heroes' failings. There is not much to choose between men. They are all a hotchpotch of greatness and littleness, of virtue and vice, of nobility and baseness. Some have more strength of character, or more opportunity, and so in one direction or another give their instincts freer play, but potentially they are the same. For my part I do not think I am better or any worse than most people, but I know that if I set down every action in my life and every thought that has crossed my mind the world would consider me a monster of depravity.

VOCABULARY

heinous	condone
untoward	depravity

QUESTIONS ON CONTENT

1. What difference does Maugham see between the way we judge ourselves and the way we judge others? To what extent does he view this inconsistency as blameworthy?
2. How much variety does Maugham find in human nature generally, and how does this affect his view of himself and of others?
3. Does Maugham seem to advocate total self-revelation on the part of anyone? Explain your answer.

QUESTIONS ON FORM

1. Where is the topic sentence of this paragraph? Is there an advantage in placing it there? If so, what?
2. Point out at least one instance of parallelism in the paragraph.

MARK TWAIN

THE PILGRIM BIRD

Part of Twain's novel *Innocents Abroad,* this passage relates a visit to one of Europe's zoological gardens. The "we" referred to are Twain's travel companions.

In the great Zoölogical Gardens, we found specimens of all the animals the world produces, I think, including a dromedary, a monkey ornamented with tufts of brilliant blue and carmine hair—a very gorgeous monkey he was—a hippopotamus from the Nile, and a sort of tall, long-legged bird with a beak like a powder-horn, and close-fitting wings like the tails of a dress coat. This fellow stood up with his eyes shut and his shoulders stooped forward a little, and looked as if he had his hands under his coat tails. Such tranquil stupidity, such supernatural gravity, such self-righteousness, and such ineffable self-complacency as were in the countenance and attitude of that gray-bodied, dark-winged, bald-headed, and preposterously uncomely bird! He was so ungainly, so pimply about the head, so scaly about the legs; yet so serene, so unspeakably satisfied! He was the most comical looking creature that can be imagined. It was good to hear Dan and the doctor laugh—such natural and such enjoyable laughter had not been heard among our excursionists since our ship sailed away from America. This bird was a god-send to us, and I should be an ingrate if I forgot to make honorable mention of him in these pages. Ours was a pleasure excursion; therefore we stayed with that bird an hour, and made the most of him. We stirred him up occasionally, but he only unclosed an eye and slowly closed it again, abating no jot of his stately piety of demeanor or his tremendous seriousness. He only seemed to say, "Defile not Heaven's anointed with unsanctified hands." We did not know his name, and so we called him "The Pilgrim." Dan said:

"All he wants now is a Plymouth Collection."[1]

VOCABULARY

dromedary	ungainly
carmine	ingrate
powder-horn	abating
ineffable	demeanor
preposterously	anointed
uncomely	unsanctified

QUESTIONS ON CONTENT

1. This humorous description of a bird does not contain a conventional topic sentence, but is nonetheless governed by a unifying impression. What is this impression?
2. Why is this portrait of a bird looking like a pilgrim not offensive? Is Twain making fun of the pilgrims? What is his purpose?

QUESTIONS ON FORM

1. The literary device of attributing human characteristics to animals or inanimate objects is called "personification." Point out specific words that personify this bird.
2. How is the unity of the paragraph maintained?

[1]A hymn book published for the use of Henry Ward Beecher's Plymouth Church in Brooklyn, of which many tourists in the group were members.—Ed.

ROBERT FROST

THE FLOOD

Blood has been harder to dam back than water.
Just when we think we have it impounded safe
Behind new barrier walls (and let it chafe!),
It breaks away in some new kind of slaughter.
We choose to say it is let loose by the devil;
But power of blood itself releases blood.
It goes by might of being such a flood
Held high at so unnatural a level.
It will have outlet, brave and not so brave.
Weapons of war and implements of peace
Are but the points at which it finds release.
And now it is once more the tidal wave
That when it has swept by leaves summits stained.
Oh, blood will out. It cannot be contained.

VOCABULARY

impounded
chafe

QUESTIONS ON CONTENT

1. What interpretation can be given to Frost's mention of a flood of blood?
2. What is meant by the statement "power of blood itself releases blood"?
3. What is the "tidal wave" Frost refers to? Why does it leave summits stained?
4. What is the theme of the poem?

QUESTIONS ON FORM

1. In poetry the stanza serves a similar purpose as the paragraph. That being the case, what do you consider the topic sentence of this poem? Is it stated more than once?
2. Both water and blood are mentioned in this poem. Which of these words is used literally and which symbolically?

CHAPTER WRITING ASSIGNMENTS

1. Select one of the following topic sentences and develop it into a unified, coherent, and complete paragraph.
   (a) Carelessness can do more harm than lack of knowledge.
   (b) Today the prevailing fashion in campus clothes is not to care about style.
   (c) Cars are not designed for safety.
   (d) A kiss is a beautiful symbol.
   (e) A plagiarized paper has several bad effects.

2. List the particular details that you would use to write a convincing paragraph for the following topic sentences:
   (a) I dislike sarcastic people.
   (b) Ecology is compelling people to buy small cars.
   (c) I like the security of dating the same person "steady" (or, I like the freedom of dating different persons).
   (d) Children and fools speak the truth.
   (e) Common sense is . . . (Define it.)

SIX

What's the Best Way of Following Through?
Development

model

ANN C. BRIEGEL

PATTERNS OF DEVELOPMENT FOR THE SUBJECT "REVERENCE"

This selection has been adapted by the editors.

1. Definition

Reverence is a feeling which evidences respect along with mild fear and affection. There is no terror in the fear which is present in a state of reverence because of the quality of esteem present. The esteem is of the highest quality; this is the evidence of respect. Coupling the esteem with mild fear does not imply a terror-like fear; rather, it is the fear of not measuring up to the ideals and qualifications of that which is regarded with reverence. Influence by beings or places held in reverence produces a kindly feeling or affection; this is not necessarily a sensual love, but in some instances it can border on it. The church is our most common example of a place held in reverence. It is hallowed or respected as a hall of worship. The fear of it is not because of the harm it can cause, but because of apprehension over not measuring up to its high standards. The affection for it stems from its eternal and sheltering nature.

2. Description

James Boswell's *Life of Johnson* clearly reveals the reverence of its author for Samuel Johnson's impact on eighteenth-century England. Every aspect of the man depicted exhibits the vitality of Johnson. Boswell por-

149

trays the role of Johnson in a largely male society as a sage, a moralist, a scholar, and a critic. Boswell's biography gives Johnson the role of the dominant conversationalist in all the episodes included in his chronicle. In these conversations Johnson looms as a wide traveler, a voracious reader, a profound philosopher, and a social mentor of enviable prestige.

3. Division

There are three kinds of reverence. First, there is the reverence which is a feeling. The nun has the utmost reverence for the Church. Second, there is the actual deed of reverence. In reverence, the Marine kneels before the grave of the Unknown Soldier. Third, there is the quality which commands respect. The reverence of the crowd listening to the President take his oath of office has humbled television viewers throughout the world.

4. Comparison and Contrast

Reverence and respect are alike in that they both involve the feeling of admiration for something. However, reverence pushes this feeling further than does respect, into the realm of worshipful awe. Respect is barren compared with reverence. One respects what he fully understands, but one reverses what remains partially mysterious. Thus acts of respect tend to be plain and direct whereas acts of reverence tend to be ritualistic and ceremonial.

5. Causal Analysis

The computer is rapidly stripping the elements of kindness and tolerance from almost all areas of human endeavor because of the reverence the business world has for its operational efficiency. The computer has a mechanical brain which is controlled by a system of devices as intricate as the human body's. However, there is no element of emotion embedded in this closely interwoven mesh of controls. The computer does not care if man despairs at having his personal accounts laid bare to its greedy claws. Deaf to human excuses for delay and tardiness because of reasons beyond control, it flings out barbed, terse reminders of the penalties for such. Because of this monstrous, all-enveloping machine's irruption into the lives of mankind, an erosion of frustration, impatience, and rebellion may result, giving way to that worst of all emotional responses, vacuous acceptance. The business world's reverence for the computer may reduce life to an arid emotional desert.

6. Example

When a dog moves on signal from his master only, he has reverence for the master. Such a dog was Pitt. Burke, his master, could lay the most succulent bone on earth before Pitt; but if Burke told him to "stay," Pitt would remain quivering and stationary before the tempting morsel. Not even the appearance of a canine intruder would deter Pitt from his reverence for the command of his master. All other commands of "go," "sit," "guard," and "fetch" elicited the same obedience from Pitt. His regard for Burke was indeed one of awe mingled with deep affection.

advice

AURELIA TOLDE

A NOTE ON PATTERN WRITING

What follows is a condensed prescription of six ways in which to develop a paragraph.

Because of the uses it serves, factual prose is frequently written in patterns. It is mainly used to say what a thing is (definition), to describe a thing (description), to divide a thing into types (division and classification), to compare or contrast one thing with another (comparison and contrast), to say why a thing performs as it does (causal analysis), or to give examples of how a thing functions (example). These same patterns apply to all factual prose, whether it is written on the bumblebee, history, automobile mechanics, or pot making. The young writer who drills himself in these patterns will find them useful in most of the factual prose he will be required to write.

1. First Pattern: The Definition

The definition says what a thing is, and what it is not. First, it shows the category into which the thing falls; then it shows how that thing differs from all others in the same category. The typical definition will therefore begin with the wording, "This is a that," and then go on to say how "this" is different from all other things in "that," i.e. "love is a feeling," or "history is a social science which," and so on. Here is a complete example:

> Chemistry is that branch of science which has the task of investigating the materials out of which the universe is made. It is not concerned with the forms into which they may be fashioned. Such objects as chairs, tables, vases, bottles, or wires are of no significance in chemistry; but such substances as glass, wool, iron, sulfur, and clay, as the materials out of which they are made, are what it studies. Chemistry is concerned not only with the composition of such substances, but also with their inner structure.
>
> —John Arrend Timm, *General Chemistry*

A clear definition is the hub of an argumentative essay. There can be no argument if the writer has failed to commit himself to a single meaning for each of his argued terms. For example, an essay attempting to argue the premise, "love is a bad habit," had better make immediately clear what the writer means by "love" and what he means by "habit."

2. Second Pattern: The Description

The description tells what a thing looks like. Vivid descriptions do not merely catalogue adjectives: they enumerate characteristics under a specific theme or dominant impression. The writer must search out the thing for the dominant impression it has on him and then use this impression as the focus of his description. Here is an example:

> Now, how am I going to describe and explain about that time when that time's gone? The white folks lived in the Big House and they had many to tend on them. Old Marster, he lived there like Pharaoh and Solomon, mighty splendid and fine. He had his flocks and his herds, his butler and his baker; his fields ran from the river to the woods and back again. He'd ride around the fields each day on his big horse, Black Billy, just like thunder and lightning, and evenings he'd sit at his table and drink his wine. Man, that was a sight to see, with all the silver knives and the silver forks, the glass decanters, and the gentlemen and ladies from all over. It was a sight to see. When Cue was young, it seemed to him that Old Marster must own the whole world, right up to the edge of the sky. You can't blame him for thinking that.
>
> —Stephen Vincent Benét

Bad description enumerates detail with no focus: worse description merely joins metaphor to metaphor in the name of whim.

3. Third Pattern: Division and Classification

We grasp finiteness more easily than bulk, the parts more readily than the whole. To slake our addiction to particulars, we have divided all of nature and hold the following dossier on the honeybee:

Order:	Hymenoptera
Superfamily:	Apoidea
Family:	Apidae
Genus:	Apis
Species:	Mellifera

This is an example of division and classification.

To divide and to classify means to break a thing down into its parts to show how these parts relate to the whole. Factual prose resorts to this device as a means of explaining. Here is an example:

> A few words about the world's reaction to the concentration camps: the terrors committed in them were experienced as uncanny by most civilized persons. It came as a shock to their pride that supposedly civilized nations could stoop to

such inhuman acts. The implication that modern man has such inadequate control over his cruelty was felt as a threat. Three different psychological mechanisms were most frequently used for dealing with the phenomenon of the concentration camp: (a) its applicability to man in general was denied by asserting (contrary to available evidence) that the acts of torture were committed by a small group of insane or perverted persons; (b) the truth of the reports were denied by ascribing them to deliberate propaganda. This method was favored by the German government which called all reports on terror in the camps horror propaganda. (Greuelpropaganda); (c) the reports were believed, but the knowledge of the terror was repressed as soon as possible.

—Bruno Bettelheim

To be useful, a division must be based on a single principle, must account for the whole, and must have mutually exclusive types.

4. Fourth Pattern: Comparison and Contrast

A thing by itself is an unknown: to be known, it must be shown in relation to other things. Writers are therefore often called on to compare or contrast one thing with another. The writing pattern for the comparison is the same as for the contrast, with this difference: a comparison stresses how two things are alike, a contrast stresses how two things are unlike. The comparison paragraph is stocked with phrases which emphasize similarities, i.e. "likewise," "in the same way," "similarly," "as with the," while the contrast paragraph is stocked with phrases which emphasize dissimilarities, i.e. "on the other hand," "unlike this," "in contrast with," and so on.

To be useful, the comparison/contrast must match the two things to be compared/contrasted on the same point. If one thing is examined for color, the other must also be examined for color; if one is examined for length, the other must also be examined for length.

Two patterns have evolved for the comparison/contrast. The first, the inter paragraph pattern, is used for lengthy comparisons/contrasts: one thing is examined on one point in a single paragraph, and the next thing is compared/contrasted on that same point in a separate paragraph. The second, the intra paragraph pattern, is for more succinct comparisons/contrasts; each thing is successively measured up against the same points and within a single paragraph. Here is an example of the intra paragraph comparison/contrast:

Thanks to this universality of athletic sports, English training is briefer and less severe. The American makes, and is forced to make, a long and tedious business of getting fit, whereas an Englishman has merely to exercise and sleep a trifle more than usual, and this only for a brief period. Our oarsmen work daily from January to July, about six months, or did so before Mr. Lehmann brought English ideas among us; the English varsity crew rows together nine or ten weeks. Our football players slog daily for six or seven weeks; English teams seldom or never "practice" and play at most two matches a week. Our track athletes are in training at frequent intervals throughout the college year and are often at the training table six weeks; in England six weeks is the maximum period of training, and the men as a rule are given only three days a week on the cinder track. To an American training is an abnormal condition; to an Englishman it is the consummation of the normal.

—John Corbin

5. Fifth Pattern: Causal Analysis

We are wedded to the belief that nothing occurs without cause. Some even maintain that there is an infinite series of causes for every effect, and likewise an infinite consequence to every action—we cannot pluck a flower without disturbing a star, wrote the poet Thompson. A paragraph or composition analyzing cause must focus only on proximate cause, and studiously ignore the call of the infinite. A writer asked to analyze why a business is failing should deal only with immediate causes, lack of advertising, poor management, low employee morale, and ignore the remote, invasion of Rome by the Visigoths, Saturn in the eighth house, poor grunion run last summer. Here is an example of a causal analysis:

> Yet actually, as a matter of historical fact, there is a much stronger foundation for the great constitutional right of freedom of speech, and as a matter of practical human experience there is a much more compelling reason for cultivating the habits of free men. We take, it seems to me, a naively self-righteous view when we argue as if the right of our opponents to speak were something that we protect because we are magnanimous, noble, and unselfish. The compelling reason why, if liberty of opinion did not exist, we should have to invent it, why it will eventually have to be restored in all civilized countries where it is now suppressed, is that we must protect the right of our opponents to speak because we must hear what they have to say.
>
> —Walter Lippmann

Analysis of cause, whether in a paragraph or a page, must make clear to the reader the connection between the imputed cause and its effect. If this connection is blurred or unclear, the reader will have difficulty following the reasoning.

6. Sixth Pattern: The Example

Nature abhors a vacuum; prose abhors a generality. The writer, if he means to sound convincing, must support his generalities with examples. Here is an example:

> Tolerance to the amphetamines develops rapidly and increasingly large amounts must be used to achieve the same results. When large amounts are used, blood-pressure may be raised sufficiently high to blow out a blood vessel in the brain, thus causing a stroke.

> True addiction, as well, seems to occur. Recently, a patient in a drug-abuse clinic stated that it was harder for him to kick the "meth" habit than it was to get off heroin. At the time he was shooting up two hundred milligrams of "crystals"

every two hours. He was found dead a few weeks later, apparently from an overdose.

—Eugene Schoenfeld, M.D.

This example is grim, but it convinces. Generalities without examples sound pious and vapid: with examples, they sound real. Of all six patterns, this is the least difficult to master. If the writer has even a sickly grasp of his subject matter, he must at least have examples of what he means.

The paragraph is the smallest unit of these patterns and it is at this level that the beginning writer should attempt to master them. All essays are made up of one of these patterns, or of a combination of them. An essay comparing Roman art with Grecian art will draw heavily on the comparison/contrast pattern while the encyclopedia entry on the bee will draw on all six patterns: one or more paragraphs will define the bee, describe the bee, divide the bee kingdom into its types, compare and contrast the bee with other insects, analyze the causes of bee migration, and give examples of how bees mate.

An essay may have paragraphs written in different patterns, but within the paragraphs themselves the patterns must not be mixed. A paragraph which begins with a comparison/contrast pattern must end as a comparison/contrast pattern. Since the paragraph is the building block of the essay, for the sake of clarity and structure of thought its pattern must be pure. This convention consigns all changes in thought pattern to the paragraph level and is the basic assumption behind all factual prose essays.

DESCRIPTION

ADVICE: HOW TO WRITE A DESCRIPTION

1. *Create a dominant impression.*

Good descriptions have two ingredients: a dominant impression and apt details. The dominant impression must hit your reader first, so don't dilute it or make it fuzzy. Don't write, "The student lounge is a place where students congregate in a leisurely fashion and as a consequence it is not always attractive and neat." Distill your meaning into one single impression: "The student lounge is a messy room." Focusing on the word *messy* creates a focal point to which the reader's attention is immediately drawn. He now expects you to prove in the words that follow how messy the lounge is. Don't disappoint him by tucking in irrelevant details about lonely students or colorful wall paper. Just stick to *messy*. Describe chewing gum stuck to the shag carpet, eggshells lying in crumpled sandwich bags on deserted tables, and Coke cans covered by cigarette ashes that got lost as they were flicked into the can opening.

Among the selections that follow, notice how clearly the dominant impression emerges from H. L. Mencken's essay, "The Libido for the Ugly." No sensitive reader can miss the point that certain houses in Westmoreland County, Pennsylvania, are hideously ugly. Nor can anyone doubt that the dominant impression of James Joyce's hell is that it is a place of unrelieved terror.

2. *Observe details.*

The details of a good description must be carefully chosen. In observing an object, a person, an action, or a scene, set yourself the task of watching for hidden details, not just obvious generalizations. For example, in observing a man who is obviously fat, don't simply write, "The man was terribly fat." Go further; add, "Two buttons on his vest had popped off, his cheeks rolled over his collar, and his belly jiggled with every step he took." Dickens's excerpt concerning Miss Havisham serves as a good example. The dominant impression of decayed elegance is supported by details such as the yellowed wedding garment, the withered flowers, and the woman who looked like a piece of ghastly waxwork.

3. *Use fresh similes and metaphors.*

An additional effective technique is to use similes; that is, to compare a feature of your subject with something else. Poets do this all the time. For example, you might write, "He removed his scuba diving suit as easily as he would peel a banana." Or, "The room was as silent as a medieval cathedral." Or, "Her sunglasses sat on the bridge of her nose like two glossy black golf balls." If the comparison is not actually stated by the use of such words such as "like" or "as," then the comparison is implicit and it is called a metaphor. May Swenson uses metaphors throughout her description of the pigeon woman. An example is the last stanza, when the purling pigeons form "a lake of love" and the retreating pigeons are "flints of love." One word of caution in using similes or metaphors: avoid comparisons that have been worn out through use. To state that "Tom Higgins turned as white as snow" is trite. Why not be different and say, "Tom Higgins turned as pale as a scoop of vanilla ice cream"?

In short, you must make a constant effort to perceive experiences in specific terms.

examples

CHARLES DICKENS

from GREAT EXPECTATIONS

In this excerpt from the novel *Great Expectations,* Pip, the adopted son of a blacksmith, is being introduced to a strange, rich lady who is neurotically fixated on the past.

1 This was very uncomfortable, and I was half afraid. However, the only thing to be done being to knock at the door, I knocked, and was told from within to enter. I entered, therefore, and found myself in a pretty large room, well lighted with wax candles. No glimpse of daylight was to be seen in it. It was a dressing-room, as I supposed from the furniture, though much of it was of forms and uses then quite unknown to me. But prominent in it was a draped table with a gilded looking-glass, and that I made out at first sight to be a fine lady's dressing-table.

Whether I should have made out this object so soon, if there had been no fine lady sitting at it, I cannot say. In an arm-chair, with an elbow resting on the table and her head leaning on that hand, sat the strangest lady I have ever seen, or shall ever see.

2 She was dressed in rich materials—satins, and lace, and silks—all of white. Her shoes were white. And she had a long white veil dependent from her hair, and she had bridal flowers in her hair, but her hair was white. Some bright jewels sparkled on her neck and on her hands, and some other jewels lay sparkling on the table. Dresses, less splendid than the dress she wore, and half-packed trunks, were scattered about. She had not quite finished dressing, for she had but one shoe on—the other was on the table near her hand—her veil was but half arranged, her watch and chain were not put on, and some lace for her bosom lay with those trinkets, and with her handkerchief, and gloves, and some flowers, and a Prayer-Book, all confusedly heaped about the looking-glass.

3 It was not in the first few moments that I saw all these things, though I saw more of them in the first moments than might be supposed. But, I saw that everything within my view which ought to be white, had been white long ago, and had lost its lustre, and was faded and yellow. I saw that the bride within the bridal dress had withered like the dress, and like the flowers, and had no brightness left but the brightness of her sunken eyes. I saw that the dress had been put upon the rounded figure of a young woman, and that the figure upon which it now hung loose, had shrunk to skin and bone. Once, I had been taken to see some ghastly waxwork at the Fair, representing I know not what impossible personage lying in state. Once, I had been taken to one of our old marsh churches to see a skeleton in the ashes of a rich dress, that had been dug out of a vault under the church pavement. Now, waxwork and skeleton seemed to have dark eyes that moved and looked at me. I should have cried out, if I could.

"Who is it?" said the lady at the table.

"Pip, ma'am."

"Pip?"

"Mr. Pumblechook's boy, ma'am. Come—to play."

"Come nearer; let me look at you. Come close."

4 It was when I stood before her, avoiding her eyes, that I took note of the surrounding objects in detail, and saw that her watch had stopped at twenty minutes to nine, and that a clock in the room had stopped at twenty minutes to nine.

"Look at me," said Miss Havisham. "You are not afraid of a woman who has never seen the sun since you were born?"

5 I regret to state that I was not afraid of telling the enormous lie comprehended in the answer "No."

"Do you know what I touch here?" she said, laying her hands, one upon the other, on her left side.

"Yes, ma'am." (It made me think of the young man.)

"What do I touch?"

"Your heart."

"Broken!"

6 She uttered the word with an eager look, and with strong emphasis, and with a weird smile that had a kind of boast in it. Afterwards, she kept her hands there for a little while, and slowly took them away as if they were heavy.

"I am tired," said Miss Havisham. "I want diversion, and I have done with men and women. Play."

7 I think it will be conceded by my most disputatious reader, that she could hardly have directed an unfortunate boy to do anything in the wide world more difficult to be done under the circumstances.

"I sometimes have sick fancies," she went on, "and I have a sick fancy that I want to see some play. There, there!" with an impatient movement of the fingers of her right hand; "play, play, play!"

8 For a moment, with the fear of my sister's working me before my eyes, I had a desperate idea of starting round the room in the assumed character of Mr. Pumblechook's chaise-cart. But, I felt myself so unequal to the performance that I gave it up, and stood looking at Miss Havisham in what I suppose she took for a dogged manner, inasmuch as she said, when we had taken a good look at each other,

"Are you sullen and obstinate?"

"No, ma'am, I am very sorry for you, and very sorry I can't play just now. If you complain of me I shall get into trouble with my sister, so I would do it if I could; but it's so new here, and so strange, and so fine—and melancholy—" I stopped, fearing I might say too much, or had already said it, and we took another look at each other.

9 Before she spoke again, she turned her eyes from me, and I looked at the dress she wore, and at the dressing-table, and finally at herself in the looking-glass.

"So new to him," she muttered, "so old to me; so strange to him, so familiar to me; so melancholy to both of us! Call Estella."

10 As she was still looking at the reflection of herself, I thought she was still talking to herself, and kept quiet.

"Call Estella," she repeated, flashing a look at me. "You can do that. Call Estella. At the door."

11 To stand in the dark in a mysterious passage of an unknown house, bawling Estella to a scornful young lady neither visible nor responsive, and feeling it a dreadful liberty so to roar out her name, was almost as bad as

playing to order. But, she answered at last, and her light came along the dark passage like a star.

12 Miss Havisham beckoned her to come close, and took up a jewel from the table, and tried its effect upon her fair young bosom and against her pretty brown hair. "Your own, one day, my dear, and you will use it well. Let me see you play cards with this boy."

"With this boy! Why, he is a common labouring-boy!"

13 I thought I overheard Miss Havisham answer—only it seemed so unlikely—"Well? You can break his heart."

"What do you play, boy?" asked Estella of myself, with the greatest disdain.

"Nothing but beggar my neighbour, miss."

"Beggar him," said Miss Havisham to Estella. So we sat down to cards.

14 It was then I began to understand that everything in the room had stopped, like the watch and the clock, a long time ago. I noticed that Miss Havisham put down the jewel exactly on the spot from which she had taken it up. As Estella dealt the cards, I glanced at the dressing-table again, and saw that the shoe upon it, once white, now yellow, had never been worn. I glanced down at the foot from which the shoe was absent, and saw that the silk stocking on it, once white, now yellow, had been trodden ragged. Without this arrest of everything, this standing still of all the pale decayed objects, not even the withered bridal dress on the collapsed form could have looked so like grave-clothes, or the long veil so like a shroud.

VOCABULARY

gilded (1)	diversion (6)
dependent (2)	disputatious (7)
ghastly (3)	dogged (8)
vault (3)	sullen (8)
comprehended (5)	shroud (14)

QUESTIONS ON CONTENT

1. What is the dominant impression in this description? List the details that convey this impression.
2. From whose point of view is the scene described? How is the point of view clarified?
3. Can you suggest why time has been arrested by the strange inmate of this huge house?
4. Why does Miss Havisham tell Estella in paragraph 13 to break the speaker's heart?

QUESTIONS ON FORM

1. What is the advantage of narrating a description from the "I" point of view, as Dickens does in this selection?

2. At one point in the description, the narrator steps in not as a boy but as a mature writer. Where is the intrusion and what is the purpose of it?
3. What hints are supplied to suggest the time period during which this story takes place?
4. Suggest an enlarged meaning for the following passage: "I saw that the bride within the bridal dress had withered like the dress, and like the flowers, and had no brightness left but the brightness of her sunken eyes."

SUGGESTIONS FOR WRITING

1. Write a one-paragraph description of the narrator in the Dickens story. Give a dominant impression and support that impression with appropriate details.
2. Write a one-paragraph description of Estella. Give a dominant impression and support that impression with appropriate details.

H. L. MENCKEN

THE LIBIDO FOR THE UGLY

In this colorful essay H. L. Mencken (1880–1956), an American editor who was one of the most forceful writers of his day, describes some of the "unlovely" cities of America.

1 On a Winter day some years ago, coming out of Pittsburgh on one of the expresses of the Pennsylvania Railroad, I rolled eastward for an hour through the coal and steel towns of Westmoreland county. It was familiar ground; boy and man, I had been through it often before. But somehow I had never quite sensed its appalling desolation. Here was the very heart of industrial America, the center of its most lucrative and characteristic activity, the boast and pride of the richest and grandest nation ever seen on earth—and here was a scene so dreadfully hideous, so intolerably bleak and forlorn that it reduced the whole aspiration of man to a macabre and depressing joke. Here was wealth beyond computation, almost beyond imagination—and here were human habitations so abominable that they would have disgraced a race of alley cats.

2 I am not speaking of mere filth. One expects steel towns to be dirty. What I allude to is the unbroken and agonizing ugliness, the sheer revolting mon-strousness, of every house in sight. From East Liberty to Greensburg, a distance of twenty-five miles, there was not one in sight from the train that did not insult and lacerate the eye. Some were so bad, and they were among the most pretentious—churches, stores, warehouses, and the like—that they were downright startling; one blinked before them as one blinks before a man with his face shot away. A few linger in memory, horrible even there: a crazy little church just west of Jeannette, set like a dormer-window on the side of a bare, leprous hill; the headquarters of the Veterans of Foreign Wars at another forlorn town, a steel stadium like a huge rat-trap somewhere further down the

line. But most of all I recall the general effect—of hideousness without a break. There was not a single decent house within eye-range from the Pittsburgh suburbs to the Greensburg yards. There was not one that was not misshapen, and there was not one that was not shabby.

3 The country itself is not uncomely, despite the grime of the endless mills. It is, in form, a narrow river valley, with deep gullies running up into the hills. It is thickly settled, but not noticeably overcrowded. There is still plenty of room for building, even in the larger towns, and there are very few solid blocks. Nearly every house, big and little, has space on all four sides. Obviously, if there were architects of any professional sense or dignity in the region, they would have perfected a chalet to hug the hillsides—a chalet with a high-pitched roof, to throw off the heavy Winter snows, but still essentially a low and clinging building, wider than it was tall. But what have they done? They have taken as their model a brick set on end. This they have converted into a thing of dingy clapboards, with a narrow, low-pitched roof. And the whole they have set upon thin, preposterous brick piers. By the hundreds and thousands these abominable houses cover the bare hillsides, like gravestones in some gigantic and decaying cemetery. On their deep sides they are three, four and even five stories high; on their low sides they bury themselves swinishly in the mud. Not a fifth of them are perpendicular. They lean this way and that, hanging on to their bases precariously. And one and all they are streaked in grime, with dead and eczematous patches of paint peeping through the streaks.

4 Now and then there is a house of brick. But what brick! When it is new it is the color of a fried egg. When it has taken on the patina of the mills it is the color of an egg long past all hope or caring. Was it necessary to adopt that shocking color? No more than it was necessary to set all of the houses on end. Red brick, even in a steel town, ages with some dignity. Let it become downright black, and it is still sightly, especially if its trimmings are of white stone, with soot in the depths and the high spots washed by the rain. But in Westmoreland they prefer that uremic yellow, and so they have the most loathsome towns and villages ever seen by mortal eye.

5 I award this championship only after laborious research and incessant prayer. I have seen, I believe, all of the most unlovely towns of the world; they are all to be found in the United States. I have seen the mill towns of decomposing New England and the desert towns of Utah, Arizona and Texas. I am familiar with the back streets of Newark, Brooklyn and Chicago, and have made scientific explorations to Camden, N.J. and Newport News, Va. Safe in a Pullman, I have whirled through the gloomy, God-forsaken villages of Iowa and Kansas, and the malarious tide-water hamlets of Georgia. I have been to Bridgeport, Conn., and to Los Angeles. But nowhere on this earth, at home or abroad, have I seen anything to compare to the villages that huddle along the line of the Pennsylvania from the Pittsburgh yards to Greensburg. They are incomparable in color, and they are incomparable in design. It is as if some titanic and aberrant genius, uncompromisingly inimical to man, had

devoted all the ingenuity of Hell to the making of them. They show grotesqueries of ugliness that, in retrospect, become almost diabolical. One cannot
imagine mere human beings concocting such dreadful things, and one can
scarcely imagine human beings bearing life in them.

6 Are they so frightful because the valley is full of foreigners—dull, insen-
sate brutes, with no love of beauty in them? Then why didn't these foreigners
set up similar abominations in the countries that they came from? You will, in
fact, find nothing of the sort in Europe—save perhaps in the more putrid parts
of England. There is scarcely an ugly village on the whole Continent. The
peasants, however poor, somehow manage to make themselves graceful and
charming habitations, even in Spain. But in the American village and small
town the pull is always toward ugliness, and in that Westmoreland valley it has
been yielded to with an eagerness bordering upon passion. It is incredible that
mere ignorance should have achieved such masterpieces of horror.

7 On certain levels of the American race, indeed, there seems to be a
positive libido for the ugly, as on other and less Christian levels there is a
libido for the beautiful. It is impossible to put down the wallpaper that defaces
the average American home of the lower middle class to mere inadvertence,
or to the obscene humor of the manufacturers. Such ghastly designs, it must
be obvious, give a genuine delight to a certain type of mind. They meet, in
some unfathomable way, its obscure and unintelligible demands. They caress
it as "The Palms" caresses it, or the art of the movie, or jazz. The taste for
them is as enigmatical and yet as common as the taste for dogmatic theology
and the poetry of Edgar A. Guest.

8 Thus I suspect (though confessedly without knowing) that the vast majority of the honest folk of Westmoreland county, and especially the 100%
Americans among them, actually admire the houses they live in, and are proud
of them. For the same money they could get vastly better ones, but they prefer
what they have got. Certainly there was no pressure upon the Veterans of
Foreign Wars to choose the dreadful edifice that bears their banner, for there
are plenty of vacant buildings along the track-side, and some of them are
appreciably better. They might, indeed, have built a better one of their own.
But they chose that clapboarded horror with their eyes open, and having
chosen it, they let it mellow into its present shocking depravity. They like it as
it is: beside it, the Parthenon would no doubt offend them. In precisely the
same way the authors of the rat-trap stadium that I have mentioned made a
deliberate choice. After painfully designing and erecting it, they made it
perfect in their own sight by putting a completely impossible pent-house,
painted a staring yellow, on top of it. The effect is that of a fat woman with a
black eye. It is that of a Presbyterian grinning. But they like it.

9 Here is something that the psychologists have so far neglected: the love of
ugliness for its own sake, the lust to make the world intolerable. Its habitat is
the United States. Out of the melting pot emerges a race which hates beauty as
it hates truth. The etiology of this madness deserves a great deal more study
than it has got. There must be causes behind it; it arises and flourishes in

obedience to biological laws, and not as a mere act of God. What, precisely, are the terms of those laws? And why do they run stronger in America than elsewhere? Let some honest *Privat Dozent* in pathological sociology apply himself to the problem.

VOCABULARY

lucrative (1)	inimical (5)
aspiration (1)	grotesqueries (5)
macabre (1)	insensate (6)
lacerate (2)	libido (7)
dormer-window (2)	inadvertence (7)
clapboards (3)	enigmatical (7)
eczematous (3)	dogmatic (7)
patina (4)	Parthenon (8)
uremic (4)	etiology (9)
malarious (5)	Privat Dozent (9)
aberrant (5)	pathological (9)

QUESTIONS ON CONTENT

1. What area of the country does this essay describe?
2. What is the principal occupation of the region?
3. Mencken not only criticizes the architecture of the region, he suggests an alternative. What sort of architecture does he think suited to this region?
4. On what does Mencken blame the ugliness he describes?
5. What are Mencken's views of the villages in Europe? In his view, how do they compare with American towns?

QUESTIONS ON FORM

1. A good description focuses on a dominant impression, and develops it. Examine the second paragraph. What is the dominant impression here?
2. Examine the third paragraph. What dominant impression does Mencken focus on in his description of the buildings?
3. What aspect of the ugliness does paragraph 4 deal with?
4. "I have seen, I believe, all of the most unlovely towns of the world; they are all to be found in the United States." Why does he say "unlovely" rather than "ugly"? Which is more effective? Why?
5. "And one and all they are streaked in grime, with dead and eczematous patches of paint peeping through the streaks." What comparison is implied in this metaphor?

SUGGESTIONS FOR WRITING

1. Write an essay describing the town or city you live in.
2. Write an analysis of Mencken's diction in this essay, paying particular attention to his use of adjectives.

JAMES JOYCE

HELL

This selection is taken from a Jesuit sermon in *A Portrait of the Artist As a Young Man,* a novel by James Joyce (1882–1941). It is a vivid description of hell as a place of fiendish torture.

1 Hell is a strait and dark and foulsmelling prison, an abode of demons and lost souls, filled with fire and smoke. The straitness of this prisonhouse is expressly designed by God to punish those who refused to be bound by His laws. In earthly prisons the poor captive has at least some liberty of movement, were it only within the four walls of his cell or in the gloomy yard of his prison. Not so in hell. There, by reason of the great number of the damned, the prisoners are heaped together in their awful prison, the walls of which are said to be four thousand miles thick: and the damned are so utterly bound and helpless that, as a blessed saint, saint Anselm, writes in his book on similitudes, they are not even able to remove from the eye a worm that gnaws it.

2 —They lie in exterior darkness. For, remember, the fire of hell gives forth no light. As, at the command of God, the fire of the Babylonian furnace lost its heat but not its light so, at the command of God, the fire of hell, while retaining the intensity of its heat, burns eternally in darkness. It is a never-ending storm of darkness, dark flames and dark smoke of burning brimstone, amid which the bodies are heaped one upon another without even a glimpse of air. Of all the plagues with which the land of the Pharaohs was smitten one plague alone, that of darkness, was called horrible. What name, then, shall we give to the darkness of hell which is to last not for three days alone but for all eternity?

3 —The horror of this strait and dark prison is increased by its awful stench. All the filth of the world, all the offal and scum of the world, we are told, shall run there as to a vast reeking sewer when the terrible conflagration of the last day has purged the world. The brimstone too which burns there in such prodigious quantity fills all hell with its intolerable stench; and the bodies of the damned themselves exhale such a pestilential odour that as saint Bonaventure says, one of them alone would suffice to infect the whole world. The very air of this world, that pure element, becomes foul and unbreathable when it has been long enclosed. Consider then what must be the foulness of the air of hell. Imagine some foul and putrid corpse that has lain rotting and decomposing in the grave, a jellylike mass of liquid corruption. Imagine such a corpse a prey to flames, devoured by the fire of burning brimstone and giving off dense choking fumes of nauseous loathsome decomposition. And then imagine this sickening stench, multiplied a millionfold and a millionfold again from the millions upon millions of fetid carcasses massed together in the reeking darkness, a huge and rotting human fungus. Imagine all this and you will have some idea of the horror of the stench of hell.

4 —But this stench is not, horrible though it is, the greatest physical torment to which the damned are subjected. The torment of fire is the greatest

torment to which the tyrant has ever subjected his fellowcreatures. Place your finger for a moment in the flame of a candle and you will feel the pain of fire. But our earthly fire was created by God for the benefit of man, to maintain in him the spark of life and to help him in the useful arts whereas the fire of hell is of another quality and was created by God to torture and punish the unrepentant sinner. Our earthly fire also consumes more or less rapidly according as the object which it attacks is more or less combustible so that human ingenuity has even succeeded in inventing chemical preparations to check or frustrate its action. But the sulphurous brimstone which burns in hell is a substance which is specially designed to burn for ever and for ever with unspeakable fury. Moreover our earthly fire destroys at the same time as it burns so that the more intense it is the shorter is its duration: but the fire of hell has this property that it preserves that which it burns and though it rages with incredible intensity it rages for ever.

5 —Our earthly fire again, no matter how fierce or widespread it may be, is always of a limited extent: but the lake of fire in hell is boundless, shoreless and bottomless. It is on record that the devil himself, when asked the question by a certain soldier, was obliged to confess that if a whole mountain were thrown into the burning ocean of hell it would be burned up in an instant like a piece of wax. And this terrible fire will not afflict the bodies of the damned only from without but each lost soul will be a hell unto itself, the boundless fire raging in its very vitals. O, how terrible is the lot of those wretched beings! The blood seethes and boils in the veins, the brains are boiling in the skull, the heart in the breast glowing and bursting, the bowels a redhot mass of burning pulp, the tender eyes flaming like molten balls.

6 —And yet what I have said as to the strength and quality and boundlessness of this fire is as nothing when compared to its intensity, an intensity which it has as being the instrument chosen by divine design for the punishment of soul and body alike. It is a fire which proceeds directly from the ire of God, working not of its own activity but as an instrument of divine vengeance. As the waters of baptism cleanse the soul with the body so do the fires of punishment torture the spirit with the flesh. Every sense of the flesh is tortured and every faculty of the soul therewith: the eyes with impenetrable utter darkness, the nose with noisome odours, the ears with yells and howls and execrations, the taste with foul matter, leprous corruption, nameless suffocating filth, the touch with redhot goads and spikes, with cruel tongues of flame. And through the several torments of the senses the immortal soul is tortured eternally in its very essence amid the leagues upon leagues of glowing fires kindled in the abyss by the offended majesty of the Omnipotent God and fanned into everlasting and ever increasing fury by the breath of the anger of the Godhead.

7 —Consider finally that the torment of this infernal prison is increased by the company of the damned themselves. Evil company on earth is so noxious that even the plants, as if by instinct, withdraw from the company of whatsoever is deadly or hurtful to them. In hell all laws are overturned: there is no thought of family or country, of ties, of relationships. The damned howl and

scream at one another, their torture and rage intensified by the presence of beings tortured and raging like themselves. All sense of humanity is forgotten. The yells of the suffering sinners fill the remotest corners of the vast abyss. The mouths of the damned are full of blasphemies against God and of hatred for their fellowsufferers and of curses against those souls which were their accomplices in sin. In olden times it was the custom to punish the parricide, the man who had raised his murderous hand against his father, by casting him into the depths of the sea in a sack in which were placed a cock, a monkey and a serpent. The intention of those lawgivers who framed such a law, which seems cruel in our times, was to punish the criminal by the company of hateful and hurtful beasts. But what is the fury of those dumb beasts compared with the fury of execration which bursts from the parched lips and aching throats of the damned in hell when they behold in their companions in misery those who aided and abetted them in sin, those whose words sowed the first seeds of evil thinking and evil living in their minds, those whose immodest suggestions led them on to sin, those whose eyes tempted and allured them from the path of virtue. They turn upon those accomplices and upbraid them and curse them. But they are helpless and hopeless: it is too late now for repentance.

VOCABULARY

strait (1)	fetid (3)
similitudes (1)	noisome (6)
offal (3)	parricide (7)
conflagration (3)	execration (7)
prodigious (3)	allured (7)
pestilential (3)	upbraid (7)

QUESTIONS ON CONTENT

1. How thick are the walls of hell?
2. What peculiar characteristic does the fire of hell have?
3. What is the greatest physical torment which the damned of hell suffer?
4. What is the source of the fire in hell?
5. How were parricides punished in olden times?

QUESTIONS ON FORM

1. Examine carefully this description of hell. What is its overall structure? How are its paragraphs deployed?
2. Examine paragraph 4. How is it developed? What is its purpose?
3. What is the purpose of mentioning the "earthly prisons" in paragraph 1?
4. Examine paragraph 5. How is this paragraph structured? What technique does the writer use to make his description so vivid?
5. In the novel *A Portrait of the Artist As a Young Man*, this description of hell is delivered in a sermon. Identify at least one technique that the preacher uses to involve his listeners in the description.

SUGGESTIONS FOR WRITING

1. Write an essay on hell as it is described here, arguing for or against a belief in its existence.
2. Following the example of this selection, write a brief description of heaven.

EUDORA WELTY

A WORN PATH

A woman, undaunted by age and hardships, presses on toward her goal—to get the medicine her sick grandchildren must have in order to survive.

1 It was December—a bright frozen day in the early morning. Far out in the country there was an old Negro woman with her head tied in a red rag, coming along a path through the pinewoods. Her name was Phoenix Jackson. She was very old and small and she walked slowly in the dark pine shadows, moving a little from side to side in her steps, with the balanced heaviness and lightness of a pendulum in a grandfather clock. She carried a thin, small cane made from an umbrella, and with this she kept tapping the frozen earth in front of her. This made a grave and persistent noise in the still air, that seemed meditative, like the chirping of a solitary little bird.

2 She wore a dark striped dress reaching down to her shoetops, and an equally long apron of bleached sugar sacks, with a full pocket; all neat and tidy, but every time she took a step she might have fallen over her shoe-laces, which dragged from her unlaced shoes. She looked straight ahead. Her eyes were blue with age. Her skin had a pattern all its own of numberless branching wrinkles and as though a whole little tree stood in the middle of her forehead, but a golden color ran underneath, and the two knobs of her cheeks were illuminated by a yellow burning under the dark. Under the red rag her hair came down on her neck in the frailest of ringlets, still black, and with an odor like copper.

3 Now and then there was a quivering in the thicket. Old Phoenix said, "Out of my way, all you foxes, owls, beetles, jack rabbits, coons, and wild animals! . . . Keep out from under these feet, little bobwhites. . . . Keep the big wild hogs out of my path. Don't let none of those come running my direction. I got a long way." Under her small black-freckled hand her cane, limber as a buggy whip, would switch at the brush as if to rouse up any hiding things.

4 On she went. The woods were deep and still. The sun made the pine needles almost too bright to look at, up where the wind rocked. The cones dropped as light as feathers. Down in the hollow was the mourning dove—it was not too late for him.

5 The path ran up a hill. "Seem like there is chains about my feet, time I get this far," she said, in the voice of argument old people keep to use with

themselves. "Something always take a hold on this hill—pleads I should stay."

6 After she got to the top she turned and gave a full, severe look behind her where she had come. "Up through pines," she said at length. "Now down through oaks."

7 Her eyes opened their widest and she started down gently. But before she got to the bottom of the hill a bush caught her dress.

8 Her fingers were busy and intent, but her skirts were full and long, so that before she could pull them free in one place they were caught in another. It was not possible to allow the dress to tear. "I in the thorny bush," she said. "Thorns, you doing your appointed work. Never want to let folks past—no sir. Old eyes thought you was a pretty little *green* bush."

9 Finally, trembling all over, she stood free, and after a moment dared to stoop for her cane.

"Sun so high!" she cried, leaning back and looking, while the thick tears went over her eyes. "The time getting all gone here."

10 At the foot of this hill was a place where a log was laid across the creek.

"Now comes the trial," said Phoenix.

11 Putting her right foot out, she mounted the log and shut her eyes. Lifting her skirt, leveling her cane fiercely before her, like a festival figure in some parade, she began to march across. Then she opened her eyes and she was safe on the other side.

"I wasn't as old as I thought," she said.

12 But she sat down to rest. She spread her skirts on the bank around her and folded her hands over her knees. Up above her was a tree in a pearly cloud of mistletoe. She did not dare to close her eyes, and when a little boy brought her a little plate with a slice of marble-cake on it she spoke to him. "That would be acceptable," she said. But when she went to take it there was just her own hand in the air.

13 So she left that tree, and had to go through a barbed-wire fence. There she had to creep and crawl, spreading her knees and stretching her fingers like a baby trying to climb the steps. But she talked loudly to herself: she could not let her dress be torn now, so late in the day, and she could not pay for having her arm or her leg sawed off if she got caught fast where she was.

14 At last she was safe through the fence and risen up out in the clearing. Big dead trees, like black men with one arm, were standing in the purple stalks of the withered cotton field. There sat a buzzard.

"Who you watching?"

15 In the furrow she made her way along.

"Glad this not the season for bulls," she said, looking sideways, "and the good Lord made his snakes to curl up and sleep in the winter. A pleasure I don't see no two-headed snake coming around that tree, where it come once. It took a while to get by him, back in the summer."

16 She passed through the old cotton and went into a field of dead corn. It whispered and shook, and was taller than her head. "Through the maze now," she said, for there was no path.

17 Then there was something tall, black, and skinny there, moving before her.

18 At first she took it for a man. It could have been a man dancing in the field. But she stood still and listened, and it did not make a sound. It was as silent as a ghost.

19 "Ghost," she said sharply, "who be you the ghost of? For I have heard of nary death close by."

But there was no answer, only the ragged dancing in the wind.

20 She shut her eyes, reached out her hand, and touched a sleeve. She found a coat and inside that an emptiness, cold as ice.

"You scarecrow," she said. Her face lighted. "I ought to be shut up for good," she said with laughter. "My senses is gone. I too old. I the oldest people I ever know. Dance, old scarecrow," she said, "while I dancing with you."

21 She kicked her foot over the furrow, and with mouth drawn down shook her head once or twice in a little strutting way. Some husks blew down and whirled in streamers about her skirts.

22 Then she went on, parting her way from side to side with the cane, through the whispering field. At last she came to the end, to a wagon track, where the silver grass blew between the red ruts. The quail were walking around like pullets, seeming all dainty and unseen.

"Walk pretty," she said. "This is the easy place. This is the easy going."

23 She followed the track, swaying through the quiet bare fields, through the little strings of trees silver in their dead leaves, past cabins silver from weather, with the doors and windows boarded shut, all like old women under a spell sitting there. "I walking in their sleep," she said, nodding her head vigorously.

24 In a ravine she went where a spring was silently flowing through a hollow log. Old Phoenix bent and drank. "Sweetgum makes the water sweet," she said, and drank more. "Nobody knows who made this well, for it was here when I was born."

25 The track crossed a swampy part where the moss hung as white as lace from every limb. "Sleep on, alligators, and blow your bubbles." Then the track went into the road.

26 Deep, deep the road went down between the high green-colored banks. Overhead the live-oaks met, and it was as dark as a cave.

27 A black dog with a lolling tongue came up out of the weeds by the ditch. She was meditating, and not ready, and when he came at her she only hit him a little with her cane. Over she went in the ditch, like a little puff of milk-weed.

28 Down there, her senses drifted away. A dream visited her, and she reached her hand up, but nothing reached down and gave her a pull. So she lay there and presently went to talking. "Old woman," she said to herself, "that black dog come up out of the weeds to stall you off, and now there he sitting on his fine tail, smiling at you."

29 A white man finally came along and found her—a hunter, a young man, with his dog on a chain.

"Well, Granny!" he laughed. "What are you doing there?"

"Lying on my back like a June-bug waiting to be turned over, mister," she said, reaching up her hand.

30 He lifted her up, gave her a swing in the air, and set her down, "Anything broken, Granny?"

"No sir, them old dead weeds is springy enough," said Phoenix, when she had got her breath. "I thank you for your trouble."

"Where do you live, Granny?" he asked, while the two dogs were growling at each other.

"Away back yonder, sir, behind the ridge. You can't even see it from here."

"On your way home?"

"No sir, I going to town."

"Why, that's too far! That's as far as I walk when I come out myself, and I get something for my trouble." He patted the stuffed bag he carried, and there hung down a little closed claw. It was one of the bobwhites, with its beak hooked bitterly to show it was dead. "Now you go on home, Granny!"

"I bound to go to town, mister," said Phoenix. "The time come around."

31 He gave another laugh, filling the whole landscape. "I know you colored people! Wouldn't miss going to town to see Santa Claus!"

32 But something held Old Phoenix very still. The deep lines in her face went into a fierce and different radiation. Without warning she had seen with her own eyes a flashing nickel fall out of the man's pocket on to the ground.

"How old are you, Granny?" he was saying.

"There is no telling, mister," she said, "no telling."

33 Then she gave a little cry and clapped her hands, and said, "Git on away from here, dog! Look! Look at that dog!" She laughed as if in admiration. "He ain't scared of nobody. He a big black dog." She whispered, "Sick him!"

"Watch me get rid of that cur," said the man. "Sick him, Pete! Sick him!"

34 Phoenix heard the dogs fighting and heard the man running and throwing sticks. She even heard a gunshot. But she was slowly bending forward by that time, further and further forward, the lids stretched down over her eyes, as if she were doing this in her sleep. Her chin was lowered almost to her knees. The yellow palm of her hand came out from the fold of her apron. Her fingers slid down and along the ground under the piece of money with the grace and care they would have in lifting an egg from under a sitting hen. Then she slowly straightened up, she stood erect, and the nickel was in her apron pocket. A bird flew by. Her lips moved. "God watching me the whole time. I come to stealing."

35 The man came back, and his own dog panted about them. "Well, I scared him off that time," he said, and then he laughed and lifted his gun and pointed it at Phoenix.

She stood straight and faced him.

"Doesn't the gun scare you?" he said, still pointing it.

"No sir, I seen plenty go off closer by, in my day, and for less than what I done," she said, holding utterly still.

36 He smiled, and shouldered the gun. "Well, Granny," he said, "you must be a hundred years old, and scared of nothing. I'd give you a dime if I had any money with me. But you take my advice and stay home, and nothing will happen to you."

"I bound to go on my way, mister," said Phoenix. She inclined her head in the red rag. Then they went in different directions, but she could hear the gun shooting again and again over the hill.

37 She walked on. The shadows hung from the oak trees to the road like curtains. Then she smelled wood-smoke, and smelled the river, and she saw a steeple and the cabins on their steep steps. Dozens of little black children whirled around her. There ahead was Natchez shining. Bells were ringing. She walked on.

38 In the paved city it was Christmas time. There were red and green electric lights strung and crisscrossed everywhere, and all turned on in the daytime. Old Phoenix would have been lost if she had not distrusted her eyesight and depended on her feet to know where to take her.

39 She paused quietly on the sidewalk, where people were passing by. A lady came along in the crowd, carrying an armful of red-, green-, and silver-wrapped presents; she gave off perfume like the red roses in hot summer, and Phoenix stopped her.

"Please, missy, will you lace up my shoe?" She held up her foot.

"What do you want, Grandma?"

"See my shoe," said Phoenix. "Do all right for out in the country, but wouldn't look right to go in a big building."

"Stand still then, Grandma," said the lady. She put her packages down carefully on the sidewalk beside her and laced and tied both shoes tightly.

"Can't lace 'em with a cane," said Phoenix. "Thank you, missy. I doesn't mind asking a nice lady to tie up my shoes when I gets out on the street."

40 Moving slowly and from side to side, she went into the stone building and into a tower of steps, where she walked up and around and around until her feet knew to stop.

41 She entered a door, and there she saw nailed up on the wall the document that had been stamped with the gold seal and framed in the gold frame which matched the dream that was hung up in her head.

"Here I be," she said. There was a fixed and ceremonial stiffness over her body.

"A charity case, I suppose," said an attendant who sat at the desk before her.

42 But Phoenix only looked above her head. There was sweat on her face; the wrinkles shone like a bright net.

"Speak up, Grandma," the woman said. "What's your name? We must have your history, you know. Have you been here before? What seems to be the trouble with you?"

43 Old Phoenix only gave a twitch to her face as if a fly were bothering her.

"Are you deaf?" cried the attendant.

44 But then the nurse came in.

"Oh, that's just old Aunt Phoenix," she said. "She doesn't come for herself—she has a little grandson. She makes these trips just as regular as clockwork. She lives away back off the Old Natchez Trace." She bent down. "Well, Aunt Phoenix, why don't you just take a seat? We won't keep you standing after your long trip." She pointed.

45 The old woman sat down, bolt upright in the chair.

"Now how is the boy?" asked the nurse.

Old Phoenix did not speak.

"I said, how is the boy?"

But Phoenix only waited and stared straight ahead, her face very solemn and withdrawn into rigidity.

"Is his throat any better?" asked the nurse. "Aunt Phoenix, don't you hear me? Is your grandson's throat any better since the last time you came for the medicine?"

46 With her hand on her knees, the old woman waited, silent, erect and motionless, just as if she were in armor.

"You mustn't take up our time this way, Aunt Phoenix," the nurse said. "Tell us quickly about your grandson, and get it over. He isn't dead, is he?"

47 At last there came a flicker and then a flame of comprehension across her face, and she spoke.

"My grandson. It was my memory had left me. There I sat and forgot why I made my long trip."

"Forgot?" The nurse frowned. "After you came so far?"

48 Then Phoenix was like an old woman begging a dignified forgiveness for waking up frightened in the night. "I never did go to school—I was too old at the Surrender," she said in a soft voice. "I'm an old woman without an education. It was my memory fail me. My little grandson, he is just the same, and I forgot it in the coming."

"Throat never heals, does it?" said the nurse, speaking in a loud, sure voice to Old Phoenix. By now she had a card with something written on it, a little list. "Yes. Swallowed lye. When was it—January—two—three years ago—"

49 Phoenix spoke unasked now. "No, missy, he not dead, he just the same. Every little while his throat begin to close up again, and he not able to swallow. He not get his breath. He not able to help himself. So the time come around, and I go on another trip for the soothing medicine."

"All right. The doctor said as long as you came to get it you could have it," said the nurse. "But it's an obstinate case."

"My little grandson, he sit up there in the house all wrapped up, waiting by himself," Phoenix went on. "We is the only two left in the world. He suffer and it don't seem to put him back at all. He got a sweet look. He going to last. He wear a little patch quilt and peep out, holding his mouth open like a little bird. I remembers so plain now. I not going to forget him again, no, the whole enduring time. I could tell him from all the others in creation."

"All right." The nurse was trying to hush her now. She brought her a bottle of medicine. "Charity," she said, making a check mark in a book.

50 Old Phoenix held the bottle close to her eyes and then carefully put it into her pocket.

"I thank you," she said.

"It's Christmas time, Grandma," said the attendant. "Could I give you a few pennies out of my purse?"

"Five pennies is a nickel," said Phoenix stiffly.

"Here's a nickel," said the attendant.

51 Phoenix rose carefully and held out her hand. She received the nickel and then fished the other nickel out of her pocket and laid it beside the new one. She stared at her palm closely, with her head on one side.

52 Then she gave a tap with her cane on the floor.

"This is what come to me to do," she said. "I going to the store and buy my child a little windmill they sells, made out of paper. He going to find it hard to believe there such a thing in the world. I'll march myself back where he waiting, holding it straight up in this hand."

53 She lifted her free hand, gave a little nod, turned round, and walked out of the doctor's office. Then her slow step began on the stairs, going down.

VOCABULARY

meditative (1)	strutting (21)
illuminated (2)	husks (21)
bobwhites (3)	pullets (22)
limber (3)	sweetgum (24)
appointed (8)	lolling (27)
furrow (15)	radiation (32)
maze (16)	ceremonial (41)
nary (19)	lye (48)

QUESTIONS ON CONTENT

1. In Egyptian mythology the phoenix was a bird of great splendor. Every five hundred years it consumed itself by fire and rose renewed from its own ashes. In what way is Phoenix Jackson like this bird?
2. The narrative abounds in descriptive passages. What is the dominant impression in paragraph 2? Are any details included that do not support this impression? What other descriptive passages can you single out?
3. Why does Phoenix keep talking to herself? What do her monologues add to the total portrait of her?
4. What is the meaning of the episode in which Phoenix steals the nickel? Does the act offend our sense of honesty? Explain your answer.
5. What significance can you attach to the fact that the journey takes place at Christmas time?

QUESTIONS ON FORM

1. What kind of plot structure is the story based on? What is the conflict in the plot? When is the conflict resolved?

2. Analyze Phoenix's language. What is conveyed through her speech?
3. Point out some specific instances of humor. What kind of humor is it?
4. During what decade would you judge this story to have taken place? What clues to your answer are given in the story?
5. In paragraph 46 we read: "With her hand on her knees, the old woman waited, silent, erect and motionless, just as if she were in armor." What meaning do you attribute to this passage?

SUGGESTIONS FOR WRITING

1. Using your imagination, describe Phoenix's journey home. Make your scenes descriptive by selecting details that support a dominant impression.
2. Describe your home town at Christmas time. Center your description on one dominant impression.

MAY SWENSON

PIGEON WOMAN

The meaning of "Pigeon Woman" emerges from the irony contained in a strange old lady's fantasy.

Slate, or dirty-marble-colored,
or rusty-iron-colored, the pigeons
on the flagstones in front of the
Public Library make a sharp lake

into which the pigeon woman wades
at exactly 1:30. She wears a
plastic pink raincoat with a round
collar (looking like a little

girl, so gay) and flat gym shoes,
her hair square-cut, orange.
Wide-apart feet carefully enter
the spinning, crooning waves

(as if she'd just learned how
to walk, each step conscious,
an accomplishment); blue knots in the
calves of her bare legs (uglied marble),

age in angled cords of jaw
and neck, her pimento-colored hair,
hanging in thin tassles, is gray
around a balding crown.

The day-old bread drops down
from her veined hand dipping out
of a paper sack. Choppy, shadowy ripples,
the pigeons strike around her legs.

Sack empty, she squats and seems to rinse
her hands in them—the rainy greens and
oily purples of their necks. Almost
they let her wet her thirsty fingertips—

but drain away in an untouchable tide.
A make-believe trade
she has come to, in her lostness
or illness or age—to treat the motley

city pigeons at 1:30 every day, in all
weathers. It is for them she colors
her own feathers. Ruddy-footed
on the lime-stained paving,

purling to meet her when she comes,
they are a lake of love. Retreating
from her hands as soon as empty,
they are the flints of love.

VOCABULARY

crooning	purling
pimento	flints
motley	

QUESTIONS ON CONTENT

1. What is the dominant impression conveyed by this "pigeon woman"? In terms of her looks, what role could she play in a fairy tale?
2. As the poem develops, how do our feelings change about the woman?
3. What is the fantasy that gives purpose to the woman's life? Describe it.
4. What is the meaning of the final stanza?
5. Is this woman an impossible figment of the poet's imagination, or does she represent a kind of reality? Comment.

QUESTIONS ON FORM

1. How does the level of language used contribute to the description of the woman?
2. How do you explain the image of the pigeons as a lake?
3. What are the "blue knots in the/calves of her bare legs" (lines 15–16)? Comment on the effectiveness of this image.

4. What is the meaning of the metaphor "her own feathers" in the next-to-last stanza?
5. Interpret the metaphor "the flints of love" in the final line.

SUGGESTIONS FOR WRITING

1. As vividly as possible, describe the relationship between a human being and an animal.
2. Imagine the loneliness that comes from being old and alone. Describe this loneliness in terms of specific, concrete details.

EXAMPLE

ADVICE: HOW TO WRITE WITH EXAMPLES

A writer is under an obligation to support his or her generalizations with examples. Prose which generalizes without exampling is tedious and vague. For instance, consider this snippet from an essay in which the writer is trying to define courage.

> Courage is the willingness to take risk when the outcome is uncertain, and when the risk taken may involve harm, loss, or danger to the one taking it. The courageous person fears no one and no thing. He or she is undaunted by danger or peril. He or she will venture boldly into an uncertain situation, hardly giving a thought to the harm or consequences which may result to his or her person.

The writer generalizes throughout the paragraph; one assertion about courage merely sums up and restates another. The paragraph is cloyed with vague, stultifying writing about courage. Without specific examples, twenty volumes of this sort of writing will still not convey to the reader what the writer means by courage. Compare this rewritten version:

> Courage is the willingness to take risk when the outcome is uncertain, and when the risk taken may involve harm, loss or danger to the one taking it. For example, in a Los Angeles suburb, a twelve-year-old girl ran into a burning house to rescue her baby brother, pulled him unconscious out of the burning bedroom, and dragged him down the stairs and outside to safety. This was a rousing display of courage. The girl was safe outside the flaming house when she remembered her sleeping brother. Disregarding her personal safety, she plunged into the flaming house for her sleeping brother.

It is easier to understand here what the writer means by courage. First, she generalizes about courage; then she gives an example. The definition of courage is still incomplete—more examples are needed—but at least the writer's meaning is clearer.

The use of examples in writing is necessary because language is ambiguous and circular. Words are defined by other words. The dictionary, for instance, defines courage as "the quality of being fearless or brave; spirit; temper"—in effect, it refers the reader from the one word "courage" to several words:

fearless, brave, spirit, temper. By giving an example, the writer creates a context specifying more exactly what is meant by "courage" and avoids the circularity inherent in language.

As an instance of how examples are used, consider one of the selections that follows, "Getting at the Truth." The writer, explaining the difficulties of biographical research and the slippery nature of historical facts, begins with a generalization:

> A biographer needs to be both humble and cautious when he remembers the nature of the material he is working with, for a historical fact is rather like the flamingo that Alice in Wonderland tried to use as a croquet mallet.

She immediately supports this generalization with the example of Sir Philip Sidney's leg wound, and the three different contemporary accounts of his failure to wear his leg armor into battle. Later, in paragraph 8, she considers the possibility of prejudice in historical accounts. Again she generalizes, then gives examples:

> The only safe way to study contemporary testimony is to bear constantly in mind this possibility of prejudice and to put almost as much attention on the writer himself as on what he has written. *For instance,* Sir Anthony Weldon's description of the Court of King James is lively enough and often used as source material; but a note from the publisher admits that the pamphlet was issued as a warning to anyone who wished to "side with this bloody house" of Stuart. The publisher, at any rate, did not consider Weldon an impartial witness.

We now have a distinct and clear idea of what she means by "prejudice." It means that people lie about one another, even in historical documents. But no amount of generalizing about this would have convinced as lucidly as her example does.

The commonest accusation made against freshman writing is this: students generalize without exampling. Movies, a student will write, are wretched things: they distort, they warp, they impose improbable endings on their material. Fine and good. The instructor waits for the examples. Instead, he or she is barraged by more generalities: movies are not only wretched, they are also horrid; they are dishonest; how they end is dictated more by box office probabilities than by dramatic necessities. The result is inconclusive and vague. Only an example could have demonstrated to the instructor what the student meant.

> For instance, in the *Sands of Iwo Jima* John Wayne . . .

or:

> The movie *Straw Dogs* furnishes an example of this . . .

Each should be followed by a discussion of the example.

Our advice therefore is to give many examples of what you mean when you write. Bear in mind that the best writing is specific and concrete; the worst is general and vague.

1. *Select appropriate examples.*

The example you cite must appropriately support your generalization. If you are writing an essay about the dangers of having a handgun in the house, your example must representatively specify this danger. One danger certainly is that someone will accidentally shoot someone else. A more remote danger is that the gun owner's pet orangutan will find the gun and deliberately shoot its master. Since most people do not own pet orangutans, this doleful story would be an unrepresentative example of the typical dangers of owning a handgun. Far better to cite the typical case of a man whose son thought the gun was unloaded, and accidentally shot his friend.

2. *Make it clear what you are exampling.*

Having generalized, most writers will introduce the example with a phrase such as "for example." Other phrases commonly used to introduce examples are:

As an example, consider
For instance
To illustrate
A case in point is
Thus
Hence
An illustration of this

Sometimes, if it is clear from the context what the example is intended to illustrate, a writer will omit the introductory phrase.

3. *Do not overexample.*

Overexampling can be interpreted as padding. Examples are used to support generalizations. If, for instance, a writer declaims against immorality in movies in two sentences, then lists one hundred immoral movies, the instructor will justifiably feel shortchanged. Examples are, after all, subsidiary to generalizations. Essay assignments are intended to give a student practice in original thinking and writing, not in cataloguing. Use examples; but use them judiciously to support a generalization, not to usurp it.

examples

BRUNO BETTELHEIM

A VICTIM

Bruno Bettelheim's personal prison experience in a Nazi camp taught him a lesson about how victims should react to their persecutors. Bettelheim is a noted psychiatrist. (From *Informed Heart*.)

1 Many students of discrimination are aware that the victim often reacts in ways as undesirable as the action of the aggressor. Less attention is paid to this because it is easier to excuse a defendant than an offender, and because they assume that once the aggression stops the victim's reactions will stop too. But I doubt if this is of real service to the persecuted. His main interest is that the persecution cease. But that is less apt to happen if he lacks a real understanding of the phenomenon of persecution, in which victim and persecutor are inseparably interlocked.

2 Let me illustrate with the following example: in the winter of 1938 a Polish Jew murdered the German attaché in Paris, vom Rath. The Gestapo used the event to step up anti-Semitic actions, and in the camp new hardships were inflicted on Jewish prisoners. One of these was an order barring them from the medical clinic unless the need for treatment had originated in a work accident.

3 Nearly all prisoners suffered from frostbite which often led to gangrene and then amputation. Whether or not a Jewish prisoner was admitted to the clinic to prevent such a fate depended on the whim of an SS[1] private. On reaching the clinic entrance, the prisoner explained the nature of his ailment to the SS man, who then decided if he should get treatment or not.

4 I too suffered from frostbite. At first I was discouraged from trying to get medical care by the fate of Jewish prisoners whose attempts had ended up in no treatment, only abuse. Finally things got worse and I was afraid that waiting longer would mean amputation. So I decided to make the effort.

5 When I got to the clinic, there were many prisoners lined up as usual, a score of them Jews suffering from severe frostbite. The main topic of discussion was one's chances of being admitted to the clinic. Most Jews had planned their procedure in detail. Some thought it best to stress their service in the German army during World War I: wounds received or decorations won. Others planned to stress the severity of their frostbite. A few decided it was best to tell some "tall story," such as that an SS officer had ordered them to report at the clinic.

6 Most of them seemed convinced that the SS man on duty would not see through their schemes. Eventually they asked me about my plans. Having no definite ones, I said I would go by the way the SS man dealt with other Jewish prisoners who had frostbite like me, and proceed accordingly. I doubted how wise it was to follow a preconceived plan, because it was hard to anticipate the reactions of a person you didn't know.

7 The prisoners reacted as they had at other times when I had voiced similar ideas on how to deal with the SS. They insisted that one SS man was like another, all equally vicious and stupid. As usual, any frustration was immediately discharged against the person who caused it, or was nearest at hand. So in abusive terms they accused me of not wanting to share my plan with them, or of intending to use one of theirs; it angered them that I was ready to meet the enemy unprepared.

[1]Abbreviation for *Schutzstaffel,* the elite military and police unit of the Nazi party.—Ed.

8 No Jewish prisoner ahead of me in the line was admitted to the clinic. The more a prisoner pleaded, the more annoyed and violent the SS became. Expressions of pain amused him; stories of previous services rendered to Germany outraged him. He proudly remarked that *he* could not be taken in by Jews, that fortunately the time had passed when Jews could reach their goal by lamentations.

9 When my turn came he asked me in a screeching voice if I knew that work accidents were the only reason for admitting Jews to the clinic, and if I came because of such an accident. I replied that I knew the rules, but that I couldn't work unless my hands were freed of the dead flesh. Since prisoners were not allowed to have knives, I asked to have the dead flesh cut away. I tried to be matter-of-fact, avoiding pleading, deference, or arrogance. He replied: "If that's all you want, I'll tear the flesh off myself." And he started to pull at the festering skin. Because it did not come off as easily as he may have expected, or for some other reason, he waved me into the clinic.

10 Inside, he gave me a malevolent look and pushed me into the treatment room. There he told the prisoner orderly to attend to the wound. While this was being done, the guard watched me closely for signs of pain but I was able to suppress them. As soon as the cutting was over, I started to leave. He showed surprise and asked why I didn't wait for further treatment. I said I had gotten the service I asked for, at which he told the orderly to make an exception and treat my hand. After I had left the room, he called me back and gave me a card entitling me to further treatment, and admittance to the clinic without inspection at the entrance.

11 Because my behavior did not correspond to what he expected of Jewish prisoners on the basis of his projection, he could not use his prepared defenses against being touched by the prisoner's plight. Since I did not act as the dangerous Jew was expected to, I did not activate the anxieties that went with his stereotype. Still he did not altogether trust me, so he continued to watch while I received treatment.

12 Throughout these dealings, the SS felt uneasy with me, though he did not unload on me the annoyance his uneasiness aroused. Perhaps he watched me closely because he expected that sooner or later I would slip up and behave the way his projected image of the Jew was expected to act. This would have meant that his delusional creation had become real.

VOCABULARY

discrimination (1)	lamentations (8)
aggressor (1)	deference (9)
phenomenon (1)	malevolent (10)
attaché (2)	projection (11)
Gestapo (2)	stereotype (11)
Semitic (2)	anxieties (11)
preconceived (6)	delusional (12)
abusive (7)	

QUESTIONS ON CONTENT

1. What was the author's purpose in telling his prison camp experience?
2. How did the SS expect the author to react? How was the author's behavior different from this expectation?
3. What was the effect of the author's behavior on the SS man?
4. From the point of view of the SS, what was the Jewish stereotype? What other stereotype is involved?
5. What general prescription for a victim's behavior toward his persecutor can you draw from this example?

QUESTIONS ON FORM

1. What advantage does Bettelheim derive from relating a personal example to support his thesis?
2. How does the author make the transition from thesis to example? Comment on the clarity of his approach.
3. How is coherence achieved in paragraph 8?
4. What effect does the brief quotation in paragraph 9 have?
5. Express the final sentence ("This would have meant that his delusional creation had become real") in more concrete terms.

SUGGESTIONS FOR WRITING

1. Pretend that you are an officer in the army and giving advice to your men on how they are to behave if caught by the enemy. Be as specific as possible.
2. Write a paragraph in which you describe any group whom you consider a victim in our society. Describe the victim and describe the persecutor.

LINCOLN STEFFENS

I BECOME A STUDENT

The American editor and author Lincoln Steffens (1866–1936) tells in his autobiography how his university experiences led him to view true education as the act of seeking answers to questions.

1 It is possible to get an education at a university. It has been done; not often, but the fact that a proportion, however small, of college students do get a start in interested, methodical study, proves my thesis, and the two personal experiences I have to offer illustrate it and show how to circumvent the faculty, the other students, and the whole college system of mind-fixing. My method might lose a boy his degree, but a degree is not worth so much as the capacity and the drive to learn, and the undergraduate desire for any empty baccalaureate is one of the holds the educational system has on students. Wise students some day will refuse to take degrees, as the best men (in England, for instance) give, but do not themselves accept, titles.

2 My method was hit on by accident and some instinct. I specialized. With several courses prescribed, I concentrated on the one or two that interested me most, and letting the others go, I worked intensively on my favorites. In my first two years, for example, I worked at English and political economy and read philosophy. At the beginning of my junior year I had several cinches in history. Now I liked history; I had neglected it partly because I rebelled at the way it was taught, as positive knowledge unrelated to politics, art, life, or anything else. The professors gave us chapters out of a few books to read, con, and be quizzed on. Blessed as I was with a "bad memory," I could not commit to it anything that I did not understand and intellectually need. The bare record of the story of man, with names, dates, and irrelative events, bored me. But I had discovered in my readings of literature, philosophy, and political economy that history had light to throw upon unhistorical questions. So I proposed in my junior and senior years to specialize in history, taking all the courses required and those also that I had flunked in. With this in mind I listened attentively to the first introductory talk of Professor William Cary Jones on American constitutional history. He was a dull lecturer, but I noticed that, after telling us what pages of what books we must be prepared in, he mumbled off some other references "for those that may care to dig deeper."

3 When the rest of the class rushed out into the sunshine, I went up to the professor and, to his surprise, asked for this memorandum. He gave it to me. Up in the library I ran through the required chapters in the two different books, and they differed on several points. Turning to the other authorities, I saw that they disagreed on the same facts and also on others. The librarian, appealed to, helped me search the book-shelves till the library closed, and then I called on Professor Jones for more references. He was astonished, invited me in, and began to approve my industry, which astonished me. I was not trying to be a good boy; I was better than that: I was a curious boy. He lent me a couple of his books, and I went off to my club to read them. They only deepened the mystery, clearing up the historical question, but leaving the answer to be dug for and written.

4 The historians did not know! History was not a science, but a field for research, a field for me, for any young man, to explore, to make discoveries in and write a scientific report about. I was fascinated. As I went on from chapter to chapter, day after day, finding frequently essential differences of opinion and of fact, I saw more and more work to do. In this course, American constitutional history, I hunted far enough to suspect that the Fathers of the Republic who wrote our sacred Constitution of the United States not only did not, but did not want to, establish a democratic government, and I dreamed for a while—as I used as a child to play I was Napoleon or a trapper—I promised myself to write a true history of the making of the American Constitution. I did not do it; that chapter has been done or well begun since by two men: Smith of the University of Washington and Beard (then) of Columbia (afterward forced out, perhaps for this very work). I found other events, men, and epochs waiting for students. In all my other courses, in ancient, in

European, and in modern history, the disagreeing authorities carried me back to the need of a fresh search for (or of) the original documents or other clinching testimony. Of course I did well in my classes. The history professors soon knew me as a student and seldom put a question to me except when the class had flunked it. Then Professor Jones would say, "Well, Steffens, tell them about it."

5 Fine. But vanity wasn't my ruling passion then. What I had was a quickening sense that I was learning a method of studying history and that every chapter of it, from the beginning of the world to the end, is crying out to be rewritten. There was something for Youth to do; these superior old men had not done anything, finally.

6 Years afterward I came out of the graft prosecution office in San Francisco with Rudolph Spreckels, the banker and backer of the investigation. We were to go somewhere, quick, in his car, and we couldn't. The chauffeur was trying to repair something wrong. Mr. Spreckels smiled; he looked closely at the defective part, and to my silent, wondering inquiry he answered: "Always, when I see something badly done or not done at all, I see an opportunity to make a fortune. I never kick at bad work by my class: there's lots of it and we suffer from it. But our failures and neglects are chances for the young fellows coming along and looking for work."

7 Nothing is done. Everything in the world remains to be done or done over. "The greatest picture is not yet painted, the greatest play isn't written (not even by Shakespeare), the greatest poem is unsung. There isn't in all the world a perfect railroad, nor a good government, nor a sound law." Physics, mathematics, and especially the most advanced and exact of the sciences, are being fundamentally revised. Chemistry is just becoming a science; psychology, economics, and sociology are awaiting a Darwin, whose work in turn is awaiting an Einstein. If the rah-rah boys in our colleges could be told this, they might not all be such specialists in football, petting parties, and unearned degrees. They are not told it, however; they are told to learn what is known. This is nothing, philosophically speaking.

8 Somehow or other in my later years at Berkeley, two professors, Moses and Howison, representing opposite schools of thought, got into a controversy, probably about their classes. They brought together in the house of one of them a few of their picked students, with the evident intention of letting us show in conversation how much or how little we had understood of their respective teachings. I don't remember just what the subject was that they threw into the ring, but we wrestled with it till the professors could stand it no longer. Then they broke in, and while we sat silent and highly entertained, they went at each other hard and fast and long. It was after midnight when, the debate over, we went home. I asked the other fellows what they had got out of it, and their answers showed that they had seen nothing but a fine, fair fight. When I laughed, they asked me what I, the D.S., had seen that was so much more profound.

9 I said that I had seen two highly-trained, well-educated Masters of Arts

and Doctors of Philosophy disagreeing upon every essential point of thought and knowledge. They had all there was of the sciences; and yet they could not find any knowledge upon which they could base an acceptable conclusion. They had no test of knowledge; they didn't know what is and what is not. And they have no test of right and wrong; they have no basis for even an ethics.

10 Well, and what of it? They asked me that, and that I did not answer. I was stunned by the discovery that it was philosophically true, in a most literal sense, that nothing is known; that it is precisely the foundation that is lacking for science; that all we call knowledge rested upon assumptions which the scientists did not all accept; and that, likewise, there is no scientific reason for saying, for example, that stealing is wrong. In brief: there was no scientific basis for an ethics. No wonder men said one thing and did another; no wonder they could settle nothing either in life or in the academies.

11 I could hardly believe this. Maybe these professors, whom I greatly respected, did not know it all. I read the books over again with a fresh eye, with a real interest, and I could see that, as in history, so in other branches of knowledge, everything was in the air. And I was glad of it. Rebel though I was, I had got the religion of scholarship and science; I was in awe of the authorities in the academic world. It was a release to feel my worship cool and pass. But I could not be sure. I must go elsewhere, see and hear other professors, men these California professors quoted and looked up to as their high priests. I decided to go as a student to Europe when I was through Berkeley, and I would start with the German universities.

12 My father listened to my plan, and he was disappointed. He had hoped I would succeed him in his business; it was for that that he was staying in it. When I said that, whatever I might do, I would never go into business, he said rather sadly, that he would sell out his interest and retire. And he did soon after our talk. But he wanted me to stay home and, to keep me, offered to buy an interest in a certain San Francisco daily paper. He had evidently had this in mind for some time. I had always done some writing, verse at the poetical age of puberty, then a novel which my mother alone treasured. Journalism was the business for a boy who liked to write, he thought, and he said I had often spoken of a newspaper as my ambition. No doubt I had in the intervals between my campaigns as Napoleon. But no more. I was now going to be a scientist, a philosopher. He sighed: he thought it over, and with the approval of my mother, who was for every sort of education, he gave his consent.

VOCABULARY

circumvent (1)	clinching (4)
prescribed (2)	graft (6)
con (2)	defective (6)
irrelative (2)	respective (8)
memorandum (3)	

QUESTIONS ON CONTENT

1. Steffens opens his essay by stating, "It is possible to get an education at a university." This statement entails a special understanding of the word "education." How does Steffens define education? What is it? What is it not?
2. Why is it better to be a "curious" student than a "good" one?
3. Through his studies the author discovered a definition of history. What is this definition? What is history *not?*
4. What is the lesson learned from the author's encounter with Rudolph Spreckels (paragraph 6)? How can this lesson be applied to all students?
5. What is the stunning discovery made by the author following the debate by his two professors? How does the discovery relate to his view of education?

QUESTIONS ON FORM

1. What is the purpose of the forward flash in time? (See paragraph 6.)
2. Both examples used serve the same purpose—to prove that scholars don't know everything. What then is the point in using two separate examples?
3. What do the "Napoleon" and "trapper" fantasies (paragraph 4) have in common? Why do they seem appropriate?
4. What is meant by the metaphor "the religion of scholarship and science" (paragraph 11)? What connotation does the metaphor carry?
5. What is the topic sentence of paragraph 7? By what method is the paragraph developed?

SUGGESTIONS FOR WRITING

1. Write a five-hundred-word essay in which you expose the single worst aspect of today's educational system. Support your criticism through the use of personal examples.
2. Write a five-hundred-word essay in which you defend the pursuit of a prescribed college course. Defend your position through the use of examples.
3. Write a paragraph in which you describe what might have happened if the author had gone into his father's business.

MARCHETTE CHUTE

GETTING AT THE TRUTH

This essay by biographer Marchette Chute gives some examples illustrating how variable and slippery a "fact" may be.

1 This is a rather presumptuous title for a biographer to use, since truth is a very large word. In the sense that it means the reality about a human being it is probably impossible for a biographer to achieve. In the sense that it means a reasonable presentation of all the available facts it is more nearly possible, but even this limited goal is harder to reach than it appears to be. A biographer

needs to be both humble and cautious when he remembers the nature of the material he is working with, for a historical fact is rather like the flamingo that Alice in Wonderland tried to use as a croquet mallet. As soon as she got its neck nicely straightened out and was ready to hit the ball, it would turn and look at her with a puzzled expression, and any biographer knows that what is called a "fact" has a way of doing the same.

2 Here is a small example. When I was writing my forthcoming biography, *Ben Jonson of Westminster*, I wanted to give a paragraph or two to Sir Philip Sidney, who had a great influence on Jonson. No one thinks of Sidney without thinking of chivalry, and to underline the point I intended to use a story that Sir Fulke Greville told of him. Sidney died of gangrene, from a musket shot that shattered his thigh, and Greville says that Sidney failed to put on his leg armor while preparing for battle because the marshal of the camp was not wearing leg armor and Sidney was unwilling to do anything that would give him a special advantage.

3 The story is so characteristic both of Sidney himself and of the misplaced high-mindedness of late Renaissance chivalry that I wanted to use it, and since Sir Fulke Greville was one of Sidney's closest friends the information seemed to be reliable enough. But it is always well to check each piece of information as thoroughly as possible and so I consulted another account of Sidney written by a contemporary, this time a doctor who knew the family fairly well. The doctor, Thomas Moffet, mentioned the episode but he said that Sidney left off his leg armor because he was in a hurry.

4 The information was beginning to twist in my hand and could no longer be trusted. So I consulted still another contemporary who had mentioned the episode, to see which of the two he agreed with. This was Sir John Smythe, a military expert who brought out his book a few years after Sidney's death. Sir John was an old-fashioned conservative who advocated the use of heavy armor even on horseback, and he deplored the current craze for leaving off leg protection, "the imitating of which . . . cost that noble and worthy gentleman Sir Philip Sidney his life."

5 So here I was with three entirely different reasons why Sidney left off his leg armor, all advanced by careful writers who were contemporaries of his. The flamingo had a legitimate reason for looking around with a puzzled expression.

6 The only thing to do in a case like this is to examine the point of view of the three men who are supplying the conflicting evidence. Sir Fulke Greville was trying to prove a thesis: that his beloved friend had an extremely chivalric nature, Sir John Smythe also was trying to prove a thesis: that the advocates of light arming followed a theory that could lead to disaster. Only the doctor, Thomas Moffet, was not trying to prove a thesis. He was not using his own explanation to reinforce some point he wanted to make. He did not want anything except to set down on paper what he believed to be the facts; and since we do not have Sidney's own explanation of why he did not put on leg armor, the chances are that Dr. Moffet is the safest man to trust.

7 For Moffet was without desire. Nothing can so quickly blur and distort

the facts as desire—the wish to use the facts for some purpose of your own—and nothing can so surely destroy the truth. As soon as the witness wants to prove something he is no longer impartial and his evidence is no longer to be trusted.

8 The only safe way to study contemporary testimony is to bear constantly in mind this possibility of prejudice and to put almost as much attention on the writer himself as on what he has written. For instance, Sir Anthony Weldon's description of the Court of King James is lively enough and often used as source material; but a note from the publisher admits that the pamphlet was issued as a warning to anyone who wished to "side with this bloody house" of Stuart. The publisher, at any rate, did not consider Weldon an impartial witness. At about the same time Arthur Wilson published his history of Great Britain, which contained an irresistibly vivid account of the agonized death of the Countess of Somerset. Wilson sounds reasonably impartial; but his patron was the Earl of Essex, who had good reason to hate that particular countess, and there is evidence that he invented the whole scene to gratify his patron.

9 Sometimes a writer will contradict what he has already written, and in that case the only thing to do is to investigate what has changed his point of view. For instance, in 1608 Captain John Smith issued a description of his capture by Powhatan, and he made it clear that the Indian chief had treated him with unwavering courtesy and hospitality. In 1624 the story was repeated in Smith's *General History of Virginia,* but the writer's circumstances had changed. Smith needed money, "having a prince's mind imprisoned in a poor man's purse," and he wanted the book to be profitable. Powhatan's daughter, the princess Pocahontas, had recently been in the news, for her visit to England had aroused a great deal of interest among the sort of people that Smith hoped would buy his book. So Smith supplied a new version of the story, in which the once-hospitable Powhatan would have permitted the hero's brains to be dashed out if Pocahontas had not saved his life. It was the second story that achieved fame, and of course it may have been true. But it is impossible to trust it because the desire of the writer is so obviously involved; as Smith said in his prospectus, he needed money and hoped that the book would give "satisfaction."

10 It might seem that there was an easy way for a biographer to avoid the use of this kind of prejudiced testimony. All he has to do is to construct his biography from evidence that cannot be tampered with—from parish records, legal documents, bills, accounts, court records, and so on. Out of these solid gray blocks of impersonal evidence it should surely be possible to construct a road that will lead straight to the truth and that will never bend itself to the misleading curve of personal desire.

11 This might be so if the only problem involved were the reliability of the material. But there is another kind of desire that is much more subtle, much more pervasive, and much more dangerous than the occasional distortions of fact that contemporary writers may have permitted themselves to make; and this kind of desire can destroy the truth of a biography even if every individual fact in it is as solid and as uncompromising as rock. Even if the road is built of

the best and most reliable materials it can still curve away from the truth because of this other desire that threatens it: the desire of the biographer himself.

12 A biographer is not a court record or a legal document. He is a human being, writing about another human being, and his own temperament, his own point of view, and his own frame of reference are unconsciously imposed upon the man he is writing about. Even if the biographer is free from Captain Smith's temptation—the need for making money—and wants to write nothing but the literal truth, he is still handicapped by the fact that there is no such thing as a completely objective human being.

13 An illustration of what can happen if the point of view is sufficiently strong is the curious conclusion that the nineteenth-century biographers reached about William Shakespeare. Shakespeare joined a company of London actors in 1594, was listed as an actor in 1598 and 1603, and was still listed as one of the "men actors" in the company in 1609. Shortly before he joined this company Shakespeare dedicated two narrative poems to the Earl of Southampton, and several years after Shakespeare died his collected plays were dedicated to the Earl of Pembroke. This was his only relationship with either of the two noblemen, and there is nothing to connect him with them during the fifteen years in which he belonged to the same acting company and during which he wrote nearly all his plays.

14 But here the desire of the biographers entered in. They had been reared in the strict code of nineteenth-century gentility and they accepted two ideas without question. One was that there are few things more important than an English lord; the other was that there were few things less important than a mere actor. They already knew the undeniable fact that Shakespeare was one of the greatest men who ever lived; and while they could not go quite so far as to claim him as an actual member of the nobility, it was clear to them that he must have been the treasured friend of both the Earl of Southampton and the Earl of Pembroke and that he must have written his plays either while basking in their exalted company or while he was roaming the green countryside by the waters of the river Avon. (It is another basic conviction of the English gentleman that there is nothing so inspiring as nature.) The notion that Shakespeare had spent all these years as the working member of a company of London actors was so abhorrent that it was never seriously considered. It could not be so; therefore it was not.

15 These biographers did their work well. When New South Wales built its beautiful memorial library to Shakespeare, it was the coat of arms of the Earl of Southampton that alternated with that of royalty in dignified splendor over the bookshelves. Shakespeare had been recreated in the image of desire, and desire will always ignore whatever is not relevant to its purpose. Because the English gentlemen did not like Shakespeare's background it was explained away as though it had never existed, and Shakespeare ceased to be an actor because so lowly a trade was not suited to so great a man.

16 All this is not to say that a biography should be lacking in a point of view.

If it does not have a point of view it will be nothing more than a kind of expanded article for an encyclopedia—a string of facts arranged in chronological order with no claim to being a real biography at all. A biography must have a point of view and it must have a frame of reference. But it should be a point of view and a frame of reference implicit in the material itself and not imposed upon it.

17 It might seem that the ideal biographical system, if it could be achieved, would be to go through the years of research without feeling any kind of emotion. The biographer would be a kind of fact-finding machine and then suddenly, after his years of research, a kind of total vision would fall upon him and he would transcribe it in his best and most persuasive English for a waiting public. But research is fortunately not done by machinery, nor are visions likely to descend in that helpful manner. They are the product not only of many facts but also of much thinking, and it is only when the biographer begins to get emotional in his thinking that he ought to beware.

18 It is easy enough to make good resolutions in advance, but a biographer cannot altogether control his sense of excitement when the climax of his years of research draws near and he begins to see the pieces fall into place. Almost without his volition, A, B, and D fit together and start to form a pattern, and it is almost impossible for the biographer not to start searching for C. Something turns up that looks remarkably like C, and with a little trimming of the edges and the ignoring of one very slight discrepancy it will fit the place allotted for C magnificently.

19 It is at this point that the biographer ought to take a deep breath and sit on his hands until he has had time to calm down. He has no real, fundamental reason to believe that his discovery is C, except for the fact that he wants it to be. He is like a man looking for a missing piece in a difficult jigsaw puzzle, who has found one so nearly the right shape that he cannot resist the desire to jam it into place.

20 If the biographer had refused to be tempted by his supposed discovery of C and had gone on with his research, he might have found not only the connecting, illuminating fact he needed but much more besides. He is not going to look for it now. Desire has blocked the way. And by so much his biography will fall short of what might have been the truth.

21 It would not be accurate to say that a biographer should be wholly lacking in desire. Curiosity is a form of desire. So is the final wish to get the material down on paper in a form that will be fair to the reader's interest and worthy of the subject. But a subconscious desire to push the facts around is one of the most dangerous things a biographer can encounter, and all the more dangerous because it is so difficult to know when he is encountering it.

22 The reason Alice had so much trouble with her flamingo is that the average flamingo does not wish to be used as a croquet mallet. It has other purposes in view. The same thing is true of a fact, which can be just as self-willed as a flamingo and has its own kind of stubborn integrity. To try to force a series of facts into a previously desired arrangement is a form of misuse to

which no self-respecting fact will willingly submit itself. The best and only way to treat it is to leave it alone and be willing to follow where it leads, rather than to press your own wishes upon it.

23 To put the whole thing into a single sentence: you will never succeed in getting at the truth if you think you know, ahead of time, what the truth ought to be.

VOCABULARY

chivalry (2) volition (18)
pervasive (11) discrepancy (18)
abhorrent (14)

QUESTIONS ON CONTENT

1. What are the two senses in which the writer understands the word "truth"?
2. What three reasons did the author find for Sidney's leaving off his leg armor?
3. According to the author, what most quickly destroys truth?
4. Why is there reason to doubt the story told by John Smith about Pocahontas and Powhatan?
5. According to the author, where should the biographer get his or her point of view and frame of reference?

QUESTIONS ON FORM

1. What function does the analogy between a fact and Alice's croquet mallet serve in this essay?
2. The author frequently gives examples of what she means. When does she introduce an example? What are the circumstances leading up to the introduction of an example?
3. How are the examples introduced? What prefatory remarks does the author use in introducing her examples?
4. The second example in paragraph 8 is introduced without a prefatory remark. Why?
5. Examine paragraph 15. What is the example here intended to illustrate?

SUGGESTIONS FOR WRITING

1. Write an essay giving examples of the eccentricities of a friend or relative.
2. Write an essay defining truth, and supplying examples of it.

EMILY DICKINSON

SUCCESS IS COUNTED SWEETEST

In her quaint but delicate style, the poet makes an observation about success and failure.

Success is counted sweetest
By those who ne'er succeed.
To comprehend a nectar
Requires sorest need.

Not one of all the purple Host
Who took the Flag today
Can tell the definition
So clear of Victory

As he defeated—dying—
On whose forbidden ear
The distant strains of triumph
Burst agonized and clear!

VOCABULARY

nectar
host

QUESTIONS ON CONTENT

1. What is the theme of the poem? How many examples does the poet use to support her main idea? Point out the line where each example begins.
2. What clue in the first stanza suggests why the poet chose "nectar" as a subject?
3. What is the setting described in the last two stanzas?
4. What point is made in the last two stanzas? State it in your own words. How does this point relate to the theme of the poem?

QUESTIONS ON FORM

1. In few words the poet makes a philosophic statement about life. How is she able to make this statement so concisely?
2. Suggest a reason for the choice of the color purple in line 5.
3. Can you identify a symbol in the poem? What does it stand for?
4. What is the meaning of "forbidden ear" in line 10?

SUGGESTIONS FOR WRITING

1. Using the opening two lines of Emily Dickinson's poem as your thesis, develop a three-hundred-word essay in which you use examples from your own experience to make your point.
2. Write an essay in which you prove that failure can be a strong motivation toward eventual success. Use examples from your own experience.

DEFINITION

ADVICE: HOW TO WRITE A DEFINITION

1. *Begin with a dictionary definition.*

A definition answers the question, "What is it?" Thus the best way to start a definition is by giving the term in question a concise dictionary definition. For example, an essay defining *gullibility* could well start as follows: "Gullibility is the quality of easily being duped." Do not, however, define a word by using another form of that same word: "Gullibility is the quality of being gullible." This kind of definition is circular and adds nothing to the reader's understanding.

2. *Expand your definition to answer the question, "What is it?"*

In developing an essay by definition, any approach that clearly answers the question, "What is it?" can be useful. Notice that the article "Kitsch" by Gilbert Highet first defines *kitsch* as anything that is "vulgar showoff." Then it goes on to supply numerous examples of kitsch in art and literature.

One effective way to define is to state what a term is not. For example, you might expand a definition of gullibility by stating that it is not a conviction founded on incontrovertible evidence or fact. Part of John Henry Newman's definition of "liberal education" is to tell us what a liberal education is not: it is not education that leads to "useful or mechanical arts," such as architecture, medicine, or business.

Another way to extend a definition is by contrast. You might, for instance, contrast gullibility with firmly based belief. No one approach is best because only that approach is best that most clearly answers the question, "What is it?"

examples

JOHN HENRY NEWMAN

ON LIBERAL KNOWLEDGE

The noted leader of conservative Anglicanism gives a definition of liberal knowledge that has influenced modern liberal education. The excerpt below is part of a series of lectures delivered at the Catholic University of Dublin in 1852.

1 Now bear with me, Gentlemen, if what I am about to say, has at first sight a fanciful appearance. Philosophy, then, or Science, is related to Knowledge in this way:—Knowledge is called by the name of Science or Philosophy,

when it is acted upon, informed, or if I may use a strong figure, impregnated by Reason. Reason is the principle of that intrinsic fecundity of Knowledge, which, to those who possess it, is its especial value, and which dispenses with the necessity of their looking abroad for any end to rest upon external to itself. Knowledge, indeed, when thus exalted into a scientific form, is also power; not only is it excellent in itself, but whatever such excellence may be, it is something more, it has a result beyond itself. Doubtless; but that is a further consideration, with which I am not concerned. I only say that, prior to its being a power, it is a good; that it is, not only an instrument, but an end. I know well it may resolve itself into an art, and terminate in a mechanical process, and in tangible fruit; but it also may fall back upon that Reason which informs it, and resolve itself into Philosophy. In one case it is called Useful Knowledge, in the other Liberal. The same person may cultivate it in both ways at once; but this again is a matter foreign to my subject; here I do but say that there are two ways of using Knowledge, and in matter of fact those who use it in one way are not likely to use it in the other, or at least in a very limited measure. You see, then, here are two methods of Education; the end of the one is to be philosophical, of the other to be mechanical; the one rises towards general ideas, the other is exhausted upon what is particular and external. Let me not be thought to deny the necessity, or to decry the benefit, of such attention to what is particular and practical, as belongs to the useful or mechanical arts; life could not go on without them; we owe our daily welfare to them; their exercise is the duty of the many, and we owe to the many a debt of gratitude for fulfilling that duty. I only say that Knowledge, in proportion as it tends more and more to be particular, ceases to be Knowledge. It is a question whether Knowledge can in any proper sense be predicated of the brute creation; without pretending to metaphysical exactness of phraseology, which would be unsuitable to an occasion like this, I say, it seems to me improper to call that passive sensation, or perception of things, which brutes seem to possess, by the name of Knowledge. When I speak of Knowledge, I mean something intellectual, something which grasps what it perceives through the senses; something which takes a view of things; which sees more than the senses convey; which reasons upon what it sees, and while it sees; which invests it with an idea. It expresses itself, not in a mere enunciation, but by an enthymeme:[1] it is of the nature of science from the first, and in this consists its dignity. The principle of real dignity in Knowledge, its worth, its desirableness, considered irrespectively of its results, is this germ within it of a scientific or a philosophical process. This is how it comes to be an end in itself; this is why it admits of being called Liberal. Not to know the relative disposition of things is the state of slaves or children; to have mapped out the Universe is the boast, or at least the ambition, of Philosophy.

2 Moreover, such knowledge is not a mere extrinsic or accidental advantage, which is ours to-day and another's to-morrow, which may be got up from

---

[1]Truncated syllogism in which one of the premises is understood but not stated.—Ed.

a book, and easily forgotten again, which we can command or communicate at our pleasure, which we can borrow for the occasion, carry about in our hand, and take into the market; it is an acquired illumination, it is a habit, a personal possession, and an inward endowment. And this is the reason, why it is more correct, as well as more usual, to speak of a University as a place of education, than of instruction, though, when knowledge is concerned, instruction would at first sight have seemed the more appropriate word. We are instructed, for instance, in manual exercises, in the fine and useful arts, in trades, and in ways of business; for these are methods, which have little or no effect upon the mind itself, are contained in rules committed to memory, to tradition, or to use, and bear upon an end external to themselves. But education is a higher word; it implies an action upon our mental nature, and the formation of a character; it is something individual and permanent, and is commonly spoken of in connexion with religion and virtue. When, then, we speak of the communication of Knowledge as being Education, we thereby really imply that that Knowledge is a state or condition of mind; and since cultivation of mind is surely worth seeking for its own sake, we are thus brought once more to the conclusion, which the word "Liberal" and the word "Philosophy" have already suggested, that there is a Knowledge, which is desirable, though nothing come of it, as being of itself a treasure, and a sufficient remuneration of years of labour.

VOCABULARY

fanciful (1)	phraseology (1)
impregnated (1)	enunciation (1)
intrinsic (1)	irrespectively (1)
fecundity (1)	extrinsic (2)
instrument (1)	illumination (2)
decry (1)	endowment (2)
predicated (1)	remuneration (2)
metaphysical (1)	

QUESTIONS ON CONTENT

1. Newman begins his definition of liberal knowledge (or philosophy) by stating that this kind of knowledge must be impregnated. By what must it be impregnated? Explain this metaphor.
2. Newman helps to define liberal knowledge by stating what it is not. What knowledge does he exclude from liberal knowledge?
3. What is Newman's definition of liberal knowledge? In what way does it differ from the other kind of knowledge described?
4. Name three or four courses offered at your college and classify them under one or the other kind of knowledge.
5. According to Newman, why is it more proper to refer to a university as a place of education than of instruction? Do you agree with his view? Comment.

QUESTIONS ON FORM

1. Most students consider Newman's style of writing difficult to follow. Can you offer any reasons for their view?
2. What techniques, if any, allow you to follow Newman's train of argument? Point out specific ones if they exist.
3. What is Newman's purpose in alluding to the way animals perceive? Does this allusion break the unity of the paragraph? Explain why or why not.
4. Can you point out parallelism and balance in paragraph 1?

SUGGESTIONS FOR WRITING

1. Write a paragraph in which you define "Useful Knowledge" according to your own understanding.
2. Write a five-hundred-word essay in which you argue the advantages of a "useful" education over a "liberal" one.

GILBERT HIGHET

KITSCH

Although Highet's piece on "kitsch" concerns itself mostly with literature, the concept of "kitsch" can be applied to all matters of taste.

1 If you have ever passed an hour wandering through an antique shop (not looking for anything exactly, but simply looking), you must have noticed how your taste gradually grows numb, and then—if you stay—becomes perverted. You begin to see unsuspected charm in those hideous pictures of plump girls fondling pigeons, you develop a psychopathic desire for spinning wheels and cobblers' benches, you are apt to pay out good money for a bronze statuette of Otto von Bismarck, with a metal hand inside a metal frock coat and metal pouches under his metallic eyes. As soon as you take the things home, you realize that they are revolting. And yet they have a sort of horrible authority; you don't like them; you know how awful they are; but it is a tremendous effort to drop them in the garbage, where they belong.

2 To walk along a whole street of antique shops—that is an experience which shakes the very soul. Here is a window full of bulbous Chinese deities; here is another littered with Zulu assagais, Indian canoe paddles, and horse pistols which won't fire; the next shopfront is stuffed with gaudy Italian majolica vases, and the next, even worse, with Austrian pottery—tiny ladies and gentlemen sitting on lace cushions and wearing lace ruffles, with every frill, every wrinkle and reticulation translated into porcelain: pink; stiff; but fortunately not unbreakable. The nineteenth century produced an appalling amount of junky art like this, and sometimes I imagine that clandestine underground factories are continuing to pour it out like illicit drugs.

3 There is a name for such stuff in the trade, a word apparently of Russian origin, kitsch:* it means vulgar showoff, and it is applied to anything that took a lot of trouble to make and is quite hideous.

4 It is paradoxical stuff, kitsch. It is obviously bad: so bad that you can scarcely understand how any human being would spend days and weeks making it, and how anybody else would buy it and take it home and keep it and dust it and leave it to her heirs. It is terribly ingenious, and terribly ugly, and utterly useless; and yet it has one of the qualities of good art—which is that, once seen, it is not easily forgotten. Of course it is found in all the arts: think of Milan Cathedral, or the statues in Westminster Abbey, or Liszt's settings of Schubert songs. There is a lot of it in the United States—for instance, the architecture of Miami, Florida, and Forest Lawn Cemetery in Los Angeles. Many of Hollywood's most ambitious historical films are superb kitsch. Most Tin Pan Alley love songs are perfect 100 per cent kitsch.

5 There is kitsch in the world of books also. I collect it. It is horrible, but I enjoy it.

6 The gem of my collection is the work of the Irish novelist Mrs. Amanda McKittrick Ros, whose masterpiece, *Delina Delaney,* was published about 1900. It is a stirringly romantic tale, telling how Delina, a fisherman's daughter from Erin Cottage, was beloved by Lord Gifford, the heir of Columbia Castle, and—after many trials and even imprisonment—married him. The story is dramatic, not to say impossible; but it is almost lost to view under the luxuriant style. Here, for example, is a sentence in which Mrs. Ros explains that her heroine used to earn extra cash by doing needlework.

> She tried hard to assist in keeping herself a stranger to her poor old father's slight income by the use of the finest production of steel, whose blunt edge eyed the reely covering with marked greed, and offered its sharp dart to faultless fabrics of flaxen fineness.

Revolting, but distinctive: what Mr. Polly called 'rockockyo' in manner. For the baroque vein, here is Lord Gifford saying goodby to his sweetheart:

> My darling virgin! my queen! my Delina! I am just in time to hear the toll of a parting bell strike its heavy weight of appalling softness against the weakest fibers of a heart of love, arousing and tickling its dormant action, thrusting the dart of evident separation deeper into its tubes of tenderness, and fanning the flame, already unextinguishable, into volumes of blaze.

Mrs. Ros had a remarkable command of rhetoric, and could coin an unforgettable phrase. She described her hero's black eyes as 'glittering jet revolvers.' When he became ill, she said he fell 'into a state of lofty fever'— doubtless because commoners have high fever, but lords have lofty fever. And her reflections on the moral degeneracy of society have rarely been equaled, in power and penetration:

> Days of humanity, whither hast thou fled? When bows of compulsion, smiles for

*The Russian verb *keetcheetsya* means 'to be haughty and puffed up.'

the deceitful, handshakes for the dogmatic, and welcome for the tool of power live under your objectionable, unambitious beat, not daring to be checked by the tongue of candour because the selfish world refuses to dispense with her rotten policies. The legacy of your forefathers, which involved equity, charity, reason, and godliness, is beyond the reach of their frivolous, mushroom offspring— deceit, injustice, malice, and unkindness—and is not likely to be codiciled with traits of harmony so long as these degrading vices of mock ambition fester the human heart.

Perhaps one reason I enjoy this stuff is because it so closely resembles a typical undergraduate translation of one of Cicero's finest perorations: sound and fury, signifying nothing. I regret only that I have never seen Mrs. Ros's poetry. One volume was called *Poems of Puncture* and another *Bayonets of Bastard Sheen:* alas, jewels now almost unprocurable. But at least I know the opening of her lyric written on first visiting St. Paul's Cathedral:

> Holy Moses, take a look,
> Brain and brawn in every nook!

Such genius is indestructible. Soon, soon now, some earnest researcher will be writing a Ph.D. thesis on Mrs. Amanda McKittrick Ros, and thus (as she herself might put it) conferring upon her dewy brow the laurels of concrete immortality.

7 Next to Mrs. Ros in my collection of kitsch is the work of the Scottish poet William McGonagall. This genius was born in 1830, but did not find his vocation until 1877. Poor and inadequate poets pullulate in every tongue, but (as the *Times Literary Supplement* observes) McGonagall's 'is the only truly memorable bad poet in our language.' In his command of platitude and his disregard of melody, he was the true heir of William Wordsworth as a descriptive poet.

8 In one way his talents, or at least his aspirations, exceeded those of Wordsworth. He was at his best in describing events he had never witnessed, such as train disasters, shipwrecks, and sanguinary battles, and in picturing magnificent scenery he had never beheld except with the eye of the imagination. Here is his unforgettable Arctic landscape:

> Greenland's icy mountains are fascinating and grand,
> And wondrously created by the Almighty's command;
> And the works of the Almighty there's few can understand:
> Who knows but it might be a part of Fairyland?

> Because there are churches of ice, and houses glittering like glass,
> And for scenic grandeur there's nothing can it surpass,
> Besides there's monuments and spires, also ruins,
> Which serve for a safe retreat from the wild bruins.

> The icy mountains they're higher than a brig's topmast,
> And the stranger in amazement stands aghast
> As he beholds the water flowing off the melted ice
> Adown the mountain sides, that he cries out, Oh! how nice!

9 McGonagall also had a strong dramatic sense. He loved to tell of agonizing adventures, more drastic perhaps but not less moving than that related in Wordsworth's 'Vaudracour and Julia.' The happy ending of one of his 'Gothic' ballads is surely unforgettable:

> So thus ends the story of Hanchen, a heroine brave,
> That tried hard her master's gold to save,
> And for her bravery she got married to the miller's eldest son,
> And Hanchen on her marriage night cried Heaven's will be done.

10 These scanty selections do not do justice to McGonagall's ingenuity as a rhymester. His sound effects show unusual talent. Most poets would be baffled by the problem of producing rhymes for the proper names *General Graham* and *Osman Digna,* but McGonagall gets them into a single stanza, with dazzling effect:

> Ye sons of Great Britain, I think no shame
> To write in praise of brave General Graham!
> Whose name will be handed down to posterity without any stigma,
> Because, at the battle of El-Tab, he defeated Osman Digna.

11 One of McGonagall's most intense personal experiences was his visit to New York. Financially, it was not a success. In one of his vivid autobiographical sketches, he says, 'I tried occasionally to get an engagement from theatrical proprietors and music-hall proprietors, but alas! 'twas all in vain, for they all told me they didn't encourage rivalry.' However, he was deeply impressed by the architecture of Manhattan. In eloquent verses he expressed what many others have felt, although without adequate words to voice their emotion:

> Oh! Mighty City of New York, you are wonderful to behold,
> Your buildings are magnificent, the truth be it told;
> They were the only thing that seemed to arrest my eye,
> Because many of them are thirteen stories high.
>
> And the tops of the houses are all flat,
> And in the warm weather the people gather to chat;
> Besides on the house-tops they dry their clothes,
> And also many people all night on the house-tops repose.

Yet McGonagall felt himself a stranger in the United States. And here again his close kinship with Wordsworth appears. The Poet Laureate, in a powerful sonnet written at Calais, once reproached the English Channel for delaying his return by one of those too frequent storms in which (reckless tyrant!) it will indulge itself:

> Why cast ye back upon the Gallic shore,
> Ye furious waves! a patriotic Son
> Of England?

In the same vein McGonagall sings with rapture of his return to his 'ain countree':

> And with regard to New York, and the sights I did see,
> One street in Dundee is more worth to me,
> And, believe me, the morning I sailed from New York,
> For bonnie Dundee—my heart it felt as light as a cork.

12 Indeed, New York is a challenging subject for ambitious poets. Here, from the same shelf, is a delicious poem on the same theme, by Ezra Pound:

> My City, my beloved,
> Thou art a maid with no breasts
> Thou art slender as a silver reed.
> Listen to me, attend me!
> And I will breathe into thee a soul,
> And thou shalt live for ever.

13 The essence of this kind of trash is incongruity. The kitsch writer is always sincere. He really means to say something important. He feels he has a lofty spiritual message to bring to an unawakened world, or else he has had a powerful experience which he must communicate to the public. But either his message turns out to be a majestic platitude, or else he chooses the wrong form in which to convey it—or, most delightful of all, there is a fundamental discrepancy between the writer and his subject, as when Ezra Pound, born in Idaho, addresses the largest city in the world as a maid with no breasts, and enjoins it to achieve inspiration and immortality by listening to him. This is like climbing Mount Everest in order to carve a head of Mickey Mouse in the east face.

14 Bad love poetry, bad religious poetry, bad mystical prose, bad novels both autobiographical and historical—one can form a superb collection of kitsch simply by reading with a lively and awakened eye. College songs bristle with it. The works of Father Divine[1] are full of it—all the more delightful because in him it is usually incomprehensible. One of the Indian mystics, Sri Ramakrishna, charmed connoisseurs by describing the Indian scriptures (in a phrase which almost sets itself to kitsch-music) as

> fried in the butter of knowledge and steeped in the honey of love.

Bad funeral poetry is a rich mine of the stuff. Here, for example, is the opening of a jolly little lament, 'The Funeral' by Stephen Spender, apparently written during his pink period:

> Death is another milestone on their way.
> With laughter on their lips and with winds blowing round them
> They record simply
> How this one excelled all others in making driving belts.

Observe the change from humanism to communism. Spender simply took Browning's 'Grammarian's Funeral,' threw away the humor and the marching

---

[1] A black evangelist of New York.—Ed.

rhythm, and substituted wind and the Stakhanovist[2] speed-up. Such also is a delicious couplet from Archibald MacLeish's elegy on the late Harry Crosby:

> He walks with Ernest in the streets in Saragossa
> They are drunk their mouths are hard they say *qué cosa.*

15 From an earlier romantic period, here is a splendid specimen. Coleridge attempted to express the profound truth that men and animals are neighbors in a hard world; but he made the fundamental mistake of putting it into a monologue address to a donkey:

> Poor Ass! Thy master should have learnt to show
> Pity—best taught by fellowship of Woe!
> Innocent foal! thou poor despised forlorn!
> I hail thee brother. . . .

16 Once you get the taste for this kind of thing it is possible to find pleasure in hundreds of experiences which you might otherwise have thought either anesthetic or tedious: bad translations, abstract painting, grand opera . . . Dr. Johnson, with his strong sense of humor, had a fancy for kitsch, and used to repeat a poem in celebration of the marriage of the Duke of Leeds, composed by 'an inferiour domestick . . . in such homely rhimes as he could make':

> When the Duke of Leeds shall married be
> To a fine young lady of high quality,
> How happy will that gentlewoman be
> In his Grace of Leed's good company.
>
> She shall have all that's fine and fair,
> And the best of silk and sattin shall wear;
> And ride in a coach to take the air,
> And have a house in St. James's Square.

Folk poetry is full of such jewels. Here is the epitaph on an old gentleman from Vermont who died in a sawmill accident:

> How shocking to the human mind
> The log did him to powder grind.
> God did command his soul away
> His summings we must all obey.

Kitsch is well known in drama, although (except for motion pictures) it does not usually last long. One palmary instance was a play extolling the virtues of the Boy Scout movement, called *Young England.* It ran for a matter of years during the 1930's, to audiences almost wholly composed of kitsch-fanciers, who eventually came to know the text quite as well as the unfortunate actors. I can still remember the opening of one magnificent episode. Scene: a woodland glade. Enter the hero, a Scoutmaster, riding a bicycle, and followed by

---

[2]Alexei Stakhanov, a Russian miner who devised a worker incentive system.—Ed.

the youthful members of his troop. They pile bicycles in silence. Then the Scoutmaster raises his finger, and says (accompanied fortissimo by most of the members of the audience):

Fresh water must be our first consideration!

17 In the decorative arts kitsch flourishes, and is particularly widespread in sculpture. One of my favorite pieces of bad art is a statue in Rockefeller Center, New York. It is supposed to represent Atlas, the Titan condemned to carry the sky on his shoulders. That is an ideal of somber, massive tragedy: greatness and suffering combined as in Hercules or Prometheus. But this version displays Atlas as a powerful moron, with a tiny little head, rather like the pan-fried young men who appear in the health magazines. Instead of supporting the heavens, he is lifting a spherical metal balloon: it is transparent, and quite empty; yet he is balancing insecurely on one foot like a furniture mover walking upstairs with a beach ball; and he is scowling like a mad baboon. If he ever gets the thing up, he will drop it; or else heave it onto a Fifth Avenue bus. It is a supremely ridiculous statue, and delights me every time I see it.

18 Perhaps you think this is a depraved taste. But really it is an extension of experience. At one end, Homer. At the other, Amanda McKittrick Ros. At one end, *Hamlet*. At the other, McGonagall, who is best praised in his own inimitable words:

The poetry is moral and sublime
And in my opinion nothing could be more fine.
True genius there does shine so bright
Like unto the stars of night.

VOCABULARY

psychopathic (1)	platitude (7)
frock coat (1)	sanguinary (8)
bulbous (2)	rapture (11)
Zulu (2)	incongruity (13)
assagais (2)	enjoins (13)
majolica (2)	mystical (14)
reticulation (2)	incomprehensible (14)
appalling (2)	connoisseurs (14)
illicit (2)	anesthetic (16)
paradoxical (4)	palmary (16)
ingenious (4)	extolling (16)
luxuriant (6)	fortissimo (16)
perorations (6)	spherical (17)
unprocurable (6)	depraved (18)
pullulate (7)	inimitable (18)

QUESTIONS ON CONTENT

1. Where in his essay does Highet give a succinct definition of "kitsch"? After reading the essay, how would you explain this word to a friend who has never heard it?
2. Can you think of some well-known examples of kitsch in America not cited by Highet? What makes them kitsch?
3. Highet admits that certain kitsch items delight him. Explain how a person of taste might feel such delight.
4. How do you explain the overwhelming popularity of kitsch?
5. According to Highet, what quality lies at the heart of all kitsch? In what paragraph is this stated?

QUESTIONS ON FORM

1. What is the predominant tone of the essay? Supply appropriate examples of this tone.
2. Point out some examples of striking figurative language in the essay. Are they serious or humorous?
3. What mode of development does Highet use more than any other? How does this method help in his definition?
4. In the final paragraph, what is the irony of using McGonagall's own words to praise him?

SUGGESTIONS FOR WRITING

1. Using Gilbert Highet's definition of "kitsch," choose one area of popular taste today and show how it fits the definition.
2. Write a paragraph in which you compare or contrast the meaning of "camp" with "kitsch."

RALPH NADER

WE NEED A NEW KIND OF PATRIOTISM

Originally written for *Life* magazine, this article defines and analyzes the various meanings attached to "patriotism," and then proposes a new, more inclusive definition of the word.

1 At a recent meeting of the national PTA, the idealism and commitment of many young people to environmental and civil rights causes were being discussed. A middle-aged woman, who was listening closely, stood up and asked: "But what can we do to make young people today patriotic?"

2 In a very direct way, she illuminated the tensions contained in the idea of patriotism. These tensions, which peak at moments of public contempt or respect for patriotic symbols such as the flag, have in the past few years divided the generations and pitted children against parents. Highly charged

exchanges take place between those who believe that patriotism is automatically possessed by those in authority and those who assert that patriotism is not a pattern imposed but a condition earned by the quality of an individual's, or a people's, behavior. The struggle over symbols, epithets and generalities impedes a clearer understanding of the meaning and value of patriotism. It is time to talk of patriotism, not as an abstraction steeped in nostalgia, but as behavior that can be judged by the standard of "liberty and justice for all."

3 Patriotism can be a great asset for any organized society, but it can also be a tool manipulated by unscrupulous or cowardly leaders and elites. The development of a sense of patriotism was a strong unifying force during our Revolution and its insecure aftermath. Defined then and now as "love of country," patriotism was an extremely important motivating force with which to confront foreign threats to the young nation. It was no happenstance that *The Star Spangled Banner* was composed during the War of 1812 when the Redcoats were not only coming but already here. For a weak frontier country beset by the competitions and aggressions of European powers in the New World, the martial virtues were those of sheer survival. America produced patriots who never moved beyond the borders of their country. They were literally defenders of their home.

4 As the United States moved into the 20th century and became a world power, far-flung alliances and wars fought thousands of miles away stretched the boundaries of patriotism. "Making the world safe for democracy" was the grandiose way Woodrow Wilson put it. At other times and places (such as Latin America) it became distorted into "jingoism." World War II was the last war that all Americans fought with conviction. Thereafter, when "bombs bursting in air" would be atomic bombs, world war became a suicidal risk. Wars that could be so final and swift lost their glamour even for the most militaristically minded. When we became the most powerful nation on earth, the old insecurity that made patriotism into a conditioned reflex of "my country right or wrong" should have given way to a thinking process; as expressed by Carl Schurz: "Our country . . . when right, to be kept right. When wrong, to be put right." It was not until the Indochina war that we began the search for a new kind of patriotism.

5 If we are to find true and concrete meaning in patriotism, I suggest these starting points. First, in order that a free and just consensus be formed, patriotism must once again be rooted in the individual's own conscience and beliefs. Love is conceived by the giver (citizens) when merited by the receiver (the governmental authorities). If "consent of the governed" is to have any meaning, the abstract ideal of country has to be separated from those who direct it; otherwise the government cannot be evaluated by its citizens. The authorities in the State Department, the Pentagon, or the White House are not infallible; they have been and often are wrong, vain, misleading, shortsighted or authoritarian. When they are, leaders like these are shortchanging, not representing, America. To identify America with them is to abandon hope and settle for tragedy. Americans who consider themselves patriotic in the tradi-

tional sense do not usually hesitate to heap criticism in domestic matters over what they believe is oppressive or wasteful or unresponsive government handling of their rights and dignity. They should be just as vigilant in weighing similar government action which harnesses domestic resources for foreign involvements. Citizenship has an obligation to cleanse patriotism of the misdeeds done in its name abroad.

6 The flag, as the Pledge of Allegiance makes clear, takes its meaning from that "for which it stands"; it should not and cannot stand for shame, injustice and tyranny. It must not be used as a bandanna or a fig leaf by those unworthy of this country's leadership.

7 Second, patriotism begins at home. Love of country in fact is inseparable from citizen action to make the country more lovable. This means working to end poverty, discrimination, corruption, greed and other conditions that weaken the promise and potential of America.

8 Third, if it is unpatriotic to tear down the flag (which is a symbol of the country), why isn't it more unpatriotic to desecrate the country itself—to pollute, despoil and ravage the air, land and water? Such environmental degradation makes the "pursuit of happiness" ragged indeed. Why isn't it unpatriotic to engage in the colossal waste that characterizes so many defense contracts? Why isn't it unpatriotic to draw our country into a mistaken war and then keep extending the involvement, with untold casualties to soldiers and innocents, while not telling Americans the truth? Why isn't the deplorable treatment of returning veterans by government and industry evaluated by the same standards as is their dispatch to war? Why isn't the systematic contravention of the U.S. Constitution and the Declaration of Independence in our treatment of minority groups, the poor, the young, the old and other disadvantaged or helpless people crassly unpatriotic? Isn't all such behavior contradicting the innate worth and the dignity of the individual in America? Is it not time to end the tragic twisting of patriotism whereby those who work to expose and correct deep injustices, and who take intolerable risks while doing it, are accused of running down America by the very forces doing just that? Our country and its ideals are something for us to uphold as individuals and together, not something to drape, as a deceptive cloak, around activities that mar or destroy these ideals.

9 Fourth, there is no reason why patriotism has to be so heavily associated, in the minds of the young as well as adults, with military exploits, jets and missiles. Citizenship must include the duty to advance our ideals actively into practice for a better community, country and world, if peace is to prevail over war. And this obligation stems not just from a secular concern for humanity but from a belief in the brotherhood of man—"I am my brother's keeper"— that is common to all major religions. It is the classic confrontation—barbarism *vs.* the holy ones. If patriotism has no room for deliberation, for acknowledging an individual's sense of justice and his religious principles, it will continue to close minds, stifle the dissent that has made us strong, and deter the participation of Americans who challenge in order to correct, and

who question in order to answer. We need only to recall recent history in other countries where patriotism was converted into an epidemic of collective madness and destruction. A patriotism manipulated by the government asks only for a servile nod from its subjects. A new patriotism requires a thinking assent from its citizens. If patriotism is to have any "manifest destiny," it is in building a world where all mankind is our bond in peace.

VOCABULARY

epithets (2)	conditioned reflex (4)
steeped (2)	authoritarian (5)
nostalgia (2)	despoil (8)
unscrupulous (3)	degradation (8)
happenstance (3)	contravention (8)
grandiose (4)	innate (8)
jingoism (4)	secular (9)

QUESTIONS ON CONTENT

1. What standard does Nader propose to judge patriotism by?
2. Why were the martial values important to early America?
3. What, according to Nader, makes the search for a new kind of patriotism necessary?
4. What is the obligation of citizenship?
5. What does a patriotism manipulated by the government ask of its citizens?

QUESTIONS ON FORM

1. What is the function of paragraph 2? How does it contribute to the definition of patriotism?
2. What kind of definition does paragraph 3 give for patriotism? How is it developed within the paragraph?
3. Nader says that patriotism has been defined as "love of country." How does he then extend this definition?
4. What function does paragraph 4 have? What does he mean by "wars fought thousands of miles away stretched the boundaries of patriotism"? How can the "boundaries of patriotism" be stretched?
5. In paragraph 9 Nader uses two quotations. What is the purpose of these quotations?

SUGGESTIONS FOR WRITING

1. Write an essay defining happiness.
2. Write an essay arguing for or against Nader's assertion that we need a new kind of patriotism.

ARCHIBALD MAC LEISH

ARS POETICA

With a poet's instinct and intuition Archibald MacLeish defines poetry.

A poem should be palpable and mute
As a globed fruit,

Dumb
As old medallions to the thumb,

Silent as the sleeve-worn stone
Of casement ledges where the moss has grown—

A poem should be wordless
As the flight of birds.

A poem should be motionless in time
As the moon climbs,

Leaving, as the moon releases
Twig by twig the night-entangled trees,

Leaving, as the moon behind the winter leaves,
Memory by memory the mind—

A poem should be motionless in time
As the moon climbs.

A poem should be equal to:
Not true.

For all the history of grief
An empty doorway and a maple leaf.

For love
The leaning grasses and two lights above the sea—

A poem should not mean
But be.

VOCABULARY

palpable   casement
medallions

QUESTIONS ON CONTENT

1. Translated, the poem's Latin title means "the art of poetry." Why is the title in Latin? How does the title relate to the poem?
2. Where does MacLeish give an explicit definition of poetry? How does he convey to the reader what poetry is?
3. In lines 17–18, what does the poet mean by the words "equal to:/Not true"?
4. The final stanza contains MacLeish's summarized view of poetry. What is your interpretation of the stanza?
5. What is your own definition of poetry? How does it compare or contrast with that of MacLeish?

QUESTIONS ON FORM

1. "Ars Poetica" is developed through a series of paradoxes. Analyze and interpret each.
2. MacLeish suggests that all the history of grief could be summarized by "an empty doorway and a maple leaf." Do you consider this an appropriate image? Can you suggest another equally appropriate?
3. What image does the poet suggest for love? Do you find this appropriate? Explain.
4. What synonyms for "mute" does the poet use? Cite them all.
5. What is the significance of repeating the fifth stanza in the eighth?

SUGGESTIONS FOR WRITING

1. Consulting a collection of their works, find a definition of poetry by either Wordsworth, Coleridge, Keats, or Shelley and contrast that definition with "Ars Poetica." State which definition is more suitable and why.
2. Write a paragraph in which you give a definition of love, and support that definition with appropriate images. Then write another paragraph in which you do the same thing for hate.

COMPARISON/CONTRAST

ADVICE: HOW TO WRITE A COMPARISON OR CONTRAST

Comparisons and contrasts clarify a situation by pointing out similarities and differences. Comparing means to point out similarities; contrasting means to point out differences. Students today are often compared or contrasted with students of yesterday. A Cadillac is contrasted with a Rolls Royce, or détente with peaceful coexistence. The effects of marijuana are compared with the effects of alcohol. And in a special kind of comparison called "analogy," conditions are compared that on surface view seem completely unlike: for instance, giving aid to Third World nations is compared to helping shipwrecked persons into a lifeboat, or the functions of the brain are compared to the functions of an IBM computer. Analogies are useful for illustration but rarely for proving an argument, because sooner or later the analogy breaks down and becomes illogical.

1. *Clarify the bases of your comparison or contrast.*

Regardless of whether you compare or contrast, your first step is to identify the bases of your comparison or contrast. Notice, for example, how Emerson's essay "Conservatism and Liberalism" contrasts on the basis of people's attitudes toward change and reform. Robert Pirsig's excerpt contrasts the romantic and classical modes according to how people view the world, how they feel, and how they understand.

2. *Organize your comparison or contrast.*

Let us assume that you wish to contrast the usefulness of a motorcycle with that of an automobile. First, you must establish the bases on which your contrast will rest—perhaps expense, upkeep, and safety. Once these have been established, you can develop your paragraphs in two ways. One approach is to write about the difference between a motorcycle and a car insofar as expense is concerned, then move to the difference as far as upkeep is concerned, and finally to the difference as far as safety is concerned. This system would yield the following outline:

I. Expense
   A. Motorcycle
   B. Automobile
II. Upkeep
   A. Motorcycle
   B. Automobile
III. Safety
   A. Motorcycle
   B. Automobile

Another approach is to divide the essay into two parts, one dealing with the motorcycle and its expense, upkeep, and safety, the other dealing similarly with the automobile. This system would be outlined as follows:

I. Motorcycle
   A. Expense
   B. Upkeep
   C. Safety
II. Automobile
   A. Expense
   B. Upkeep
   C. Safety

The second system has the advantage of allowing you to deal with one item at a time (the motorcycle, without mentioning the automobile), but has the disadvantage of forcing your reader to wait until the end of the essay to draw a conclusive contrast between the two sides. The first system is more clearly a contrast because it requires the reader to move back and forth between the motorcycle and the automobile, continuously contrasting the two.

3. *Use verbal indicators to maintain coherence.*

A good writer will sprinkle his contrast paragraphs with indicators such as "on the other hand," "whereas," "but," "in contrast to," "unlike." If he is comparing, he will use indicators such as "like," "as," "likewise," "similarly," "also." These indicators help the coherence of the development.

examples

RALPH WALDO EMERSON

from CONSERVATISM AND LIBERALISM

This selection, on the contrast between conservatism and liberalism, exemplifies the intra paragraph development of a comparison/contrast.

1 The two parties which divide the state, the party of Conservatism and that of Innovation, are very old, and have disputed the possession of the world ever since it was made. This quarrel is the subject of civil history. The conservative party established the reverend hierarchies and monarchies of the most ancient world. The battle of patrician and plebeian, of parent state and colony, of old usage and accommodation to new facts, of the rich and the poor, reappears in all countries and times. The war rages not only in battlefields, in national councils, and ecclesiastical synods, but agitates every man's bosom with opposing advantages every hour. On rolls the old world meantime, and now one, now the other gets the day, and still the fight renews itself as if for the first time, under new names and hot personalities.

2 Such an irreconcilable antagonism, of course, must have a correspondent depth of seat in the human constitution. It is the opposition of Past and Future, of Memory and Hope, of the Understanding and the Reason. It is the primal antagonism, the appearance in trifles of the two poles of nature. . . .

3 There is always a certain meanness in the agrument of conservatism, joined with a certain superiority in its fact. It affirms because it holds. Its fingers clutch the fact, and it will not open its eyes to see a better fact. The castle, which conservatism is set to defend, is the actual state of things, good and bad. The project of innovation is the best possible state of things. Of course, conservatism always has the worst of the argument, is always apologizing, pleading a necessity, pleading that to change would be to deteriorate; it must saddle itself with the mountainous load of the violence and vice of society, must deny the possibility of good, deny ideas, and suspect and stone the prophet; whilst innovation is always in the right, triumphant, attacking,

and sure of final success. Conservatism stands on man's confessed limitations; reform, on his indisputable infinitude; conservatism, on circumstance; liberalism, on power; one goes to make an adroit member of the social frame; the other to postpone all things to the man himself; conservatism is debonair and social; reform is individual and imperious. We are reformers in spring and summer; in autumn and winter we stand by the old; reformers in the morning, conservers at night. Reform is affirmative, conservatism negative; conservatism goes for comfort, reform for truth. Conservatism is more candid to behold another's worth; reform more disposed to maintain and increase its own. Conservatism makes no poetry, breathes no prayer, has no invention; it is all memory. Reform has no gratitude, no prudence, no husbandry. It makes a great difference to your figure and to your thought, whether your foot is advancing or receding. Conservatism never puts the foot forward; in the hour when it does that, it is not establishment, but reform. Conservatism tends to universal seeming and treachery, believes in a negative fate; believes that men's temper governs them; that for me, it avails not to trust in principles; they will fail me; I must bend a little; it distrusts nature; it thinks there is a general law without a particular application,—law for all that does not include any one. Reform in its antagonism inclines to asinine resistance, to kick with hoofs; it runs to egotism and bloated self-conceit; it runs to a bodiless pretension, to unnatural refining and elevation, which ends in hypocrisy and sensual reaction.

4 And so whilst we do not go beyond general statements, it may be safely affirmed of these two metaphysical antagonists, that each is a good half, but an impossible whole. Each exposes the abuses of the other, but in a true society, in a true man, both must combine. Nature does not give the crown of its approbation, namely, beauty, to any action or emblem or actor, but to one which combines both these elements; not to the rock which resists the waves from age to age, nor to the wave which lashes incessantly the rock, but the superior beauty is with the oak which stands with its hundred arms against the storms of a century, and grows every year like a sapling; or the river which ever flowing, yet is found in the same bed from age to age; or, greatest of all, the man who has subsisted for years amid the changes of nature, yet has distanced himself, so that when you remember what he was, and see what he is, you say, what strides! what a disparity is here!

VOCABULARY

hierarchies (1)	infinitude (3)
patrician (1)	debonair (3)
plebeian (1)	imperious (3)
ecclesiastical (1)	asinine (3)
synods (1)	sensual (3)
agitates (1)	approbation (4)
primal (2)	disparity (4)

QUESTIONS ON CONTENT

1. Emerson writes: "Such an irreconcilable antagonism, of course, must have a correspondent depth of seat in the human constitution" (paragraph 2). What does he mean by that?
2. Which of the two attitudes contrasted has the worst of the argument? Why is the other sure of final success?
3. Emerson says that conservatism is "all memory." What does he mean by that?
4. What are the weaknesses of conservatism? What are the weaknesses of liberalism? Why is it necessary that they be combined in a person?
5. Emerson says that either conservatism or liberalism makes a "good half, but an impossible whole." What does he mean by that?

QUESTIONS ON FORM

1. Reread the final sentence in the first paragraph. Is this the natural wording of this sentence? Why is the sentence worded this way?
2. "The battle of patrician and plebeian, of parent state and colony, of old usage and accommodation to new facts, of the rich and the poor, reappears in all countries and times."—What characteristic of style marks the sentence? Which sentences in paragraph 3 show similar construction?
3. "The castle, which conservatism is set to defend, is the actual state of things, good and bad."—Does Emerson mean "castle" literally or figuratively? If the latter, what figure of speech is this, and what does "castle" mean?
4. "It makes a great difference to your figure and to your thought, whether your foot is advancing or receding."—What figure of speech is this?
5. The contrast between liberalism and conservatism is developed within paragraphs. What technique of sentence construction makes this possible?

SUGGESTIONS FOR WRITING

1. Contrast your own political beliefs with those of a conservative or a liberal.
2. Analyze and discuss Emerson's characterization of conservatism.

BRUCE CATTON

GRANT AND LEE: A STUDY IN CONTRASTS

This article by a noted American historian exemplifies the development of a comparison/contrast between, rather than within, separate paragraphs.

1 When Ulysses S. Grant and Robert E. Lee met in the parlor of a modest house at Appomattox Court House, Virginia, on April 9, 1865, to work out the terms for the surrender of Lee's Army of Northern Virginia, a great chapter in American life came to a close, and a great new chapter began.

2 These men were bringing the Civil War to its virtual finish. To be sure, other armies had yet to surrender, and for a few days the fugitive Confederate

government would struggle desperately and vainly, trying to find some way to go on living now that its chief support was gone. But in effect it was all over when Grant and Lee signed the papers. And the little room where they wrote out the terms was the scene of one of the poignant, dramatic contrasts in American history.

3 They were two strong men, these oddly different generals, and they represented the strengths of two conflicting currents that, through them, had come into final collision.

4 Back of Robert E. Lee was the notion that the old aristocratic concept might somehow survive and be dominant in American life.

5 Lee was tidewater Virginia, and in his background were family, culture, and tradition . . . the age of chivalry transplanted to a New World which was making its own legends and its own myths. He embodied a way of life that had come down through the age of knighthood and the English country squire. America was a land that was beginning all over again, dedicated to nothing much more complicated than the rather hazy belief that all men had equal rights and should have an equal chance in the world. In such a land Lee stood for the feeling that it was somehow of advantage to human society to have a pronounced inequality in the social structure. There should be a leisure class, backed by ownership of land; in turn, society itself should be keyed to the land as the chief source of wealth and influence. It would bring forth (according to this ideal) a class of men with a strong sense of obligation to the community; men who lived not to gain advantage for themselves, but to meet the solemn obligations which had been laid on them by the very fact that they were privileged. From them the country would get its leadership; to them it could look for the higher values—of thought, of conduct, of personal deportment— to give it strength and virtue.

6 Lee embodied the noblest elements of this aristocratic ideal. Through him, the landed nobility justified itself. For four years, the Southern states had fought a desperate war to uphold the ideals for which Lee stood. In the end, it almost seemed as if the Confederacy fought for Lee; as if he himself was the Confederacy . . . the best thing that the way of life for which the Confederacy stood could ever have to offer. He had passed into legend before Appomattox. Thousands of tired, underfed, poorly clothed Confederate soldiers, long since past the simple enthusiasm of the early days of the struggle, somehow considered Lee the symbol of everything for which they had been willing to die. But they could not quite put this feeling into words. If the Lost Cause, sanctified by so much heroism and so many deaths, had a living justification, its justification was General Lee.

7 Grant, the son of a tanner on the Western frontier, was everything Lee was not. He had come up the hard way and embodied nothing in particular except the eternal toughness and sinewy fiber of the men who grew up beyond the mountains. He was one of a body of men who owed reverence and obeisance to no one, who were self-reliant to a fault, who cared hardly anything for the past but who had a sharp eye for the future.

8 These frontier men were the precise opposites of the tidewater aristo-

crats. Back of them, in the great surge that had taken people over the Alleghenies and into the opening Western country, there was a deep, implicit dissatisfaction with a past that had settled into grooves. They stood for democracy, not from any reasoned conclusion about the proper ordering of human society, but simply because they had grown up in the middle of democracy and knew how it worked. Their society might have privileges, but they would be privileges each man had won for himself. Forms and patterns meant nothing. No man was born to anything, except perhaps to a chance to show how far he could rise. Life was competition.

9 Yet along with this feeling had come a deep sense of belonging to a national community. The Westerner who developed a farm, opened a shop, or set up in business as a trader, could hope to prosper only as his own community prospered—and his community ran from the Atlantic to the Pacific and from Canada down to Mexico. If the land was settled, with towns and highways and accessible markets, he could better himself. He saw his fate in terms of the nation's own destiny. As its horizons expanded, so did his. He had, in other words, an acute dollars-and-cents stake in the continued growth and development of his country.

10 And that, perhaps, is where the contrast between Grant and Lee becomes most striking. The Virginia aristocrat, inevitably, saw himself in relation to his own region. He lived in a static society which could endure almost anything except change. Instinctively, his first loyalty would go to the locality in which that society existed. He would fight to the limit of endurance to defend it, because in defending it he was defending everything that gave his own life its deepest meaning.

11 The Westerner, on the other hand, would fight with an equal tenacity for the broader concept of society. He fought so because everything he lived by was tied to growth, expansion, and a constantly widening horizon. What he lived by would survive or fall with the nation itself. He could not possibly stand by unmoved in the face of an attempt to destroy the Union. He would combat it with everything he had, because he could only see it as an effort to cut the ground out from under his feet.

12 So Grant and Lee were in complete contrast, representing two diametrically opposed elements in American life. Grant was the modern man emerging; beyond him, ready to come on the stage, was the great age of steel and machinery, of crowded cities and a restless, burgeoning vitality. Lee might have ridden down from the old age of chivalry, lance in hand, silken banner fluttering over his head. Each man was the perfect champion of his cause, drawing both his strengths and his weaknesses from the people he led.

13 Yet it was not all contrast, after all. Different as they were—in background, in personality, in underlying aspiration—these two great soldiers had much in common. Under everything else, they were marvelous fighters. Furthermore, their fighting qualities were really very much alike.

14 Each man had, to begin with, the great virtue of utter tenacity and fidelity. Grant fought his way down the Mississippi Valley in spite of acute personal discouragement and profound military handicaps. Lee hung on in the

trenches at Petersburg after hope itself had died. In each man there was an indomitable quality . . . the born fighter's refusal to give up as long as he can still remain on his feet and lift his two fists.

15 Daring and resourcefulness they had, too; the ability to think faster and move faster than the enemy. These were the qualities which gave Lee the dazzling campaigns of Second Manassas and Chancellorsville and won Vicksburg for Grant.

16 Lastly, and perhaps greatest of all, there was the ability, at the end, to turn quickly from war to peace once the fighting was over. Out of the way these two men behaved at Appomattox came the possibility of a peace of reconciliation. It was a possibility not wholly realized, in the years to come, but which did, in the end, help the two sections to become one nation again . . . after a war whose bitterness might have seemed to make such a reunion wholly impossible. No part of either man's life became him more than the part he played in their brief meeting in the McLean house at Appomattox. Their behavior there put all succeeding generations of Americans in their debt. Two great Americans, Grant and Lee—very different, yet under everything very much alike. Their encounter at Appomattox was one of the great moments of American history.

VOCABULARY

poignant (2)	obeisance (7)
deportment (5)	tenacity (11)
embodied (6)	diametrically (12)
sanctified (6)	burgeoning (12)

QUESTIONS ON CONTENT

1. What was Lee's background? What ideal did he represent?
2. What was Grant's background? What did he represent?
3. What was Grant's view of the past? What was his attitude toward society and democracy?
4. What was the most striking contrast between Grant and Lee?
5. The author writes that the behavior of Grant and Lee at Appomattox "put all succeeding generations of Americans in their debt." Why?

QUESTIONS ON FORM

1. Although the article is entitled "Grant and Lee: A Study in Contrasts," the author begins by examining what Lee represented. Why? What logic is there to his order?
2. What function does paragraph 4 serve? Why is this one sentence set off by itself in a separate paragraph?
3. What common contrast phrase does paragraph 11 use?
4. In paragraph 8 the author writes: "These frontier men were the precise opposites of the tidewater aristocrats." What do these types have to do with a contrast between Grant and Lee?
5. What function does paragraph 8 serve?

SUGGESTIONS FOR WRITING

1. Examine and analyze the organization of the contrast in this essay. In what various respects are Grant and Lee contrasted? How does the author order and structure his contrast?
2. Discuss the idea that a society can benefit from the presence of a privileged class.

MATTHEW ARNOLD

HEBRAISM AND HELLENISM

In this selection Matthew Arnold (1822–88), the English poet, essayist, and critic, compares and contrasts Hebraism with Hellenism.

1 Hebraism and Hellenism,—between these two points of influence moves our world. At one time it feels more powerfully the attraction of one of them, at another time of the other; and it ought to be, though it never is, evenly and happily balanced between them.

2 The final aim of both Hellenism and Hebraism, as of all great spiritual disciplines, is no doubt the same: man's perfection or salvation. The very language which they both of them use in schooling us to reach this aim is often identical. Even when their language indicates by variation,—sometimes a broad variation, often a but slight and subtle variation,—the different courses of thought which are uppermost in each discipline, even then the unity of the final end and aim is still apparent. To employ the actual words of that discipline with which we ourselves are all of us most familiar, and the words of which, therefore, come most home to us, that final end and aim is "that we might be partakers of the divine nature." These are the words of a Hebrew apostle, but of Hellenism and Hebraism alike this is, I say, the aim. When the two are confronted, as they very often are confronted, it is nearly always with what I may call a rhetorical purpose; the speaker's whole design is to exalt and enthrone one of the two, and he uses the other only as a foil and to enable him the better to give effect to his purpose. Obviously, with us, it is usually Hellenism which is thus reduced to minister to the triumph of Hebraism. There is a sermon on Greece and the Greek spirit by a man never to be mentioned without interest and respect, Frederick Robertson,[1] in which this rhetorical use of Greece and the Greek spirit, and the inadequate exhibition of them necessarily consequent upon this, is almost ludicrous, and would be censurable if it were not to be explained by the exigencies of a sermon. On the other hand, Heinrich Heine,[2] and other writers of his sort, give us the spectacle of the table completely turned, and of Hebraism brought in just as a foil and contrast to Hellenism, and to make the superiority of Hellenism more manifest. In both these cases there is injustice and misrepresentation. The aim

[1]Frederick Robertson (1816–53), author and well-known clergyman.—Ed.
[2]Heinrich Heine (1797–1856), German poet and critic. Arnold probably got the terms "Hebraism" and "Hellenism" from Heine's writing.—Ed.

and end of both Hebraism and Hellenism is, as I have said, one and the same, and this aim and end is august and admirable.

3 Still, they pursue this aim by very different courses. The uppermost idea with Hellenism is to see things as they really are; the uppermost idea with Hebraism is conduct and obedience. Nothing can do away with this ineffaceable difference. The Greek quarrel with the body and its desires is, that they hinder right thinking; the Hebrew quarrel with them is, that they hinder right acting. "He that keepeth the law, happy is he";[3] "Blessed is the man that feareth the Eternal, that delighteth greatly in his commandments";[4] that is the Hebrew notion of felicity; and, pursued with passion and tenacity, this notion would not let the Hebrew rest till, as is well known, he had at last got out of the law a network of prescriptions to enwrap his whole life, to govern every moment of it, every impulse, every action. The Greek notion of felicity, on the other hand, is perfectly conveyed in these words of a great French moralist: *"C'est le bonheur des hommes,"*[5]—when? when they abhor that which is evil?—no; when they exercise themselves in the law of the Lord day and night?—no; when they die daily?—no; when they walk about the New Jerusalem with palms in their hands?—no; but when they think aright, when their thought hits: *"quand ils pensent juste."* At the bottom of both the Greek and the Hebrew notion is the desire, native in man, for reason and the will of God, the feeling after the universal order,—in a word, the love of God. But, while Hebraism seizes upon certain plain, capital intimations of the universal order, and rivets itself, one may say, with unequalled grandeur of earnestness and intensity on the study and observance of them, the bent of Hellenism is to follow, with flexible activity, the whole play of the universal order, to be apprehensive of missing any part of it, of sacrificing one part to another, to slip away from resting in this or that intimation of it, however capital. An unclouded clearness of mind, an unimpeded play of thought, is what this bent drives at. The governing idea of Hellenism is *spontaneity of consciousness;* that of Hebraism, *strictness of conscience.*

VOCABULARY

Hebraism (title)	exigencies (2)
Hellenism (title)	ineffaceable (3)
foil (2)	felicity (3)
ludicrous (2)	prescriptions (3)
censurable (2)	intimations (3)

QUESTIONS ON CONTENT

1. What is the final aim of both Hebraism and Hellenism?

---

[3]He that . . . he: Proverbs 29:18—Ed.
[4]Blessed . . . commandments: Psalms 112:1.—Ed.
[5]"C'est le bonheur des hommes quand ils pensent juste": It is happiness for men when they think right. Michel Eyquem de Montaigne (1533–92).—Ed.

2. According to Arnold, how do speakers generally use the concepts of Hebraism and Hellenism?
3. What is the uppermost idea of Hebraism? What is the uppermost idea of Hellenism?
4. What is the Greek quarrel with the body? What is the Hebrew quarrel with it? State the answer in your own words.
5. What is the Hebrew notion of felicity? What is the Greek notion?

QUESTIONS ON FORM

1. "The Greek quarrel with the body and its desires is, that they hinder right thinking; the Hebrew quarrel with them is, that they hinder right acting."— What characteristic does this sentence possess?
2. Where does Arnold use a sentence similar to the one quoted in the preceding question? What does this kind of sentence contribute to the essay?
3. "The Greek notion of felicity, on the other hand, is perfectly conveyed in these words of a great French moralist: *'C'est le bonheur des hommes,'*—when? when they abhor that which is evil?—no; when they exercise themselves in the law of the Lord day and night?—no; when they die daily?—no; when they walk about the New Jerusalem with palms in their hands?—no; but when they think aright, when their thought hits: *'quand ils pensent juste.'*"—What is the purpose of the questions interposed in this sentence?
4. What is the purpose of the French quotation?
5. Elsewhere Arnold quotes the Bible. Why? What is achieved by these quotations, French and Biblical alike?

SUGGESTIONS FOR WRITING

1. Arnold says that "at the bottom of both the Greek and the Hebrew notion is the desire, native in man, for reason and the will of God, the feeling after the universal order." Analyze and discuss the presence of this desire in yourself, and say whether you draw upon Hebraism or upon Hellenism in fulfilling it.
2. Do you incline more toward Hebraism or toward Hellenism? Discuss the influence of either force upon your own life.

ROBERT M. PIRSIG

CLASSICAL UNDERSTANDING AND ROMANTIC UNDERSTANDING

This selection is taken from the best-selling book *Zen and the Art of Motorcycle Maintenance*. It contrasts two common and usually opposing modes of understanding, the classical and the romantic.

1 I want to divide human understanding into two kinds—classical understanding and romantic understanding. In terms of ultimate truth a dichotomy of this sort has little meaning but it is quite legitimate when one is operating

within the classic mode used to discover or create a world of underlying form. The terms *classic* and *romantic,* as Phaedrus[1] used them, mean the following:

2 A classical understanding sees the world primarily as underlying form itself. A romantic understanding sees it primarily in terms of immediate appearance. If you were to show an engine or a mechanical drawing or electronic schematic to a romantic it is unlikely he would see much of interest in it. It has no appeal because the reality he sees is its surface. Dull, complex lists of names, lines and numbers. Nothing interesting. But if you were to show the same blueprint or schematic or give the same description to a classical person he might look at it and then become fascinated by it because he sees that within the lines and shapes and symbols is a tremendous richness of underlying form.

3 The romantic mode is primarily inspirational, imaginative, creative, intuitive. Feelings rather than facts predominate. "Art" when it is opposed to "Science" is often romantic. It does not proceed by reason or by laws. It proceeds by feeling, intuition and esthetic conscience. In the northern European cultures the romantic mode is usually associated with femininity, but this is certainly not a necessary association.

4 The classic mode, by contrast, proceeds by reason and by laws—which are themselves underlying forms of thought and behavior. In the European cultures it is primarily a masculine mode and the fields of science, law and medicine are unattractive to women largely for this reason. Although motorcycle riding is romantic, motorcycle maintenance is purely classic. The dirt, the grease, the mastery of underlying form required all give it such a negative romantic appeal that women never go near it.

5 Although surface ugliness is often found in the classic mode of understanding it is not inherent in it. There is a classic esthetic which romantics often miss because of its subtlety. The classic style is straightforward, unadorned, unemotional, economical and carefully proportioned. Its purpose is not to inspire emotionally, but to bring order out of chaos and make the unknown known. It is not an esthetically free and natural style. It is esthetically restrained. Everything is under control. Its value is measured in terms of the skill with which this control is maintained.

6 To a romantic this classic mode often appears dull, awkward and ugly, like mechanical maintenance itself. Everything is in terms of pieces and parts and components and relationships. Nothing is figured out until it's run through the computer a dozen times. Everything's got to be measured and proved. Oppressive. Heavy. Endlessly grey. The death force.

7 Within the classic mode, however, the romantic has some appearances of his own. Frivolous, irrational, erratic, untrustworthy, interested primarily in pleasure-seeking. Shallow. Of no substance. Often a parasite who cannot or will not carry his own weight. A real drag on society. By now these battle lines should sound a little familiar.

[1]The name Pirsig uses to refer to his former personality. This alter ego suffered a psychotic breakdown as he sought to reconcile romanticism and classicism in a new understanding.—Ed.

8 This is the source of the trouble. Persons tend to think and feel exclusively in one mode or the other and in doing so tend to misunderstand and underestimate what the other mode is all about. But no one is willing to give up the truth as he sees it, and as far as I know, no one now living has any real reconciliation of these truths or modes. There is no point at which these visions of reality are unified.

9 And so in recent times we have seen a huge split develop between a classic culture and a romantic counterculture—two worlds growingly alienated and hateful toward each other with everyone wondering if it will always be this way, a house divided against itself. No one wants it really—despite what his antagonists in the other dimension might think.

VOCABULARY

dichotomy (1)   intuitive (3)
schematic (2)   esthetic (3)

QUESTIONS ON CONTENT

1. How does a classical understanding see the world? How does a romantic understanding see it?
2. What characteristics does a romantic mode have?
3. What characteristics does the classic mode proceed by?
4. What is the purpose of the classic mode?
5. How does the romantic appear within the classic mode?

QUESTIONS ON FORM

1. In doing a comparison/contrast, items must be compared/contrasted on the same points. On what point is the contrast in paragraph 2 based?
2. A comparison/contrast may be drawn within a single paragraph, or between paragraphs. Which of these organizations is evident in paragraph 2? In paragraphs 3 and 4?
3. What contrast expression does the author use in paragraph 4?
4. The comparison/contrast in paragraphs 6 and 7 is expressed in a similar manner. How is this similarity of expression achieved? What does this similar phrasing accomplish?
5. What transition word or expression does the author use in paragraph 7?

SUGGESTIONS FOR WRITING

1. Which mode of understanding do you live by, the classical or the romantic? Write an essay describing the mode you favor in your own life. Give examples of it.
2. Write an essay comparing/contrasting the way you see the world with the way your nearest friend or relative sees it.

LOREN C. EISELEY

THE BIRD AND THE MACHINE

A professor of anthropology writes in a lyrical style about the essential difference between machines and living beings.

1 I suppose their little bones have years ago been lost among the stones and winds of those high glacial pastures. I suppose their feathers blew eventually into the piles of tumbleweed beneath the straggling cattle fences and rotted there in the mountain snows, along with dead steers and all the other things that drift to an end in the corners of the wire. I do not quite know why I should be thinking of birds over the *New York Times* at breakfast, particularly the birds of my youth half a continent away. It is a funny thing what the brain will do with memories and how it will treasure them and finally bring them into odd juxtapositions with other things, as though it wanted to make a design, or get some meaning out of them, whether you want it or not, or even see it.

2 It used to seem marvelous to me, but I read now that there are machines that can do these things in a small way, machines that can crawl about like animals, and that it may not be long now until they do more things—maybe even make themselves—I saw that piece in the *Times* just now. And then they will, maybe—well, who knows—but you read about it more and more with no one making any protest, and already they can add better than we and reach up and hear things through the dark and finger the guns over the night sky.

3 This is the new world that I read about at breakfast. This is the world that confronts me in my biological books and journals, until there are times when I sit quietly in my chair and try to hear the little purr of the cogs in my head and the tubes flaring and dying as the messages go through them and the circuits snap shut or open. This is the great age, make no mistake about it; the robot has been born somewhat appropriately along with the atom bomb, and the brain they say now is just another type of more complicated feedback system. The engineers have its basic principles worked out; it's mechanical, you know; nothing to get superstitious about; and man can always improve on nature once he gets the idea. Well, he's got it all right and that's why, I guess, that I sit here in my chair, with the article crunched in my hand, remembering those two birds and that blue mountain sunlight. There is another magazine article on my desk that reads "Machines Are Getting Smarter Every Day." I don't deny it, but I'll still stick with the birds. It's life I believe in, not machines.

4 Maybe you don't believe there is any difference. A skeleton is all joints and pulleys, I'll admit. And when man was in his simpler stages of machine building in the eighteenth century, he quickly saw the resemblances. "What," wrote Hobbes,[1] "is the heart but a spring, and the nerves but so many strings,

---

[1]The English philosopher Thomas Hobbes (1588–1679).—Ed.

and the joints but so many wheels, giving motion to the whole body?'' Tinkering about in their shops, it was inevitable in the end that men would see the world as a huge machine "subdivided into an infinite number of lesser machines.''

5 The idea took on with a vengeance. Little automatons toured the country—dolls controlled by clockwork. Clocks described as little worlds were taken on tours by their designers. They were made up of moving figures, shifting scenes and other remarkable devices. The life of the cell was unknown. Man, whether he was conceived as possessing a soul or not, moved and jerked about like these tiny puppets. A human being thought of himself in terms of his own tools and implements. He had been fashioned like the puppets he produced and was only a more clever model make by a greater designer.

6 Then in the nineteenth century, the cell was discovered, and the single machine in its turn was found to be the product of millions of infinitesimal machines—the cells. Now, finally, the cell itself dissolves away into an abstract chemical machine—and that into some intangible, inexpressible flow of energy. The secret seems to lurk all about, the wheels get smaller and smaller, and they turn more rapidly, but when you try to seize it the life is gone—and so, by popular definition, some would say that life was never there in the first place. The wheels and the cogs are the secret and we can make them better in time—machines that will run faster and more accurately than real mice to real cheese.

7 I have no doubt it can be done, though a mouse harvesting seeds on an autumn thistle is to me a fine sight and more complicated, I think, in his multiform activity, than a machine "mouse" running a maze. Also, I like to think of the possible shape of the future brooding in mice, just as it brooded once in a rather ordinary mousy insectivore who became a man. It leaves a nice fine indeterminate sense of wonder that even an electronic brain hasn't got, because you know perfectly well that if the electronic brain changes, it will be because of something man has done to it. But what man will do to himself he doesn't really know. A certain scale of time and a ghostly intangible thing called change are ticking in him. Powers and potentialities like the oak in the seed, or a red and awful ruin. Either way, it's impressive; and the mouse has it, too. Or those birds, I'll never forget those birds—yet before I measured their significance, I learned the lesson of time first of all. I was young then and left alone in a great desert—part of an expedition that had scattered its men over several hundred miles in order to carry on research more effectively. I learned there that time is a series of planes existing superficially in the same universe. The tempo is a human illusion, a subjective clock ticking in our own kind of protoplasm.

8 As the long months passed, I began to live on the slower planes and to observe more readily what passed for life there. I sauntered, I passed more and more slowly up and down the canyons in the dry baking heat of midsummer. I slumbered for long hours in the shade of huge brown boulders that had gathered in tilted companies out on the flats. I had forgotten the world of men

and the world had forgotten me. Now and then I found a skull in the canyons, and these justified my remaining there. I took a serene cold interest in these discoveries. I had come, like many a naturalist before me, to view life with a wary and subdued attention. I had grown to take pleasure in the divested bone.

9 I sat once on a high ridge that fell away before me into a waste of sand dunes. I sat through hours of a long afternoon. Finally, as I glanced beside my boot an indistinct configuration caught my eye. It was a coiled rattlesnake, a big one. How long he had sat with me I do not know. I had not frightened him. We were both locked in the sleepwalking tempo of the earlier world, baking in the same high air and sunshine. Perhaps he had been there when I came. He slept on as I left, his coils, so ill discerned by me, dissolving once more among the stones and gravel from which I had barely made him out.

10 Another time I got on a higher ridge, among some tough little wind-warped pines half covered over with sand in a basin-like depression that caught everything carried by the air up to those heights. There were a few thin bones of birds, some cracked shells of indeterminable age, and the knotty fingers of pine roots bulged out of shape from their long and agonizing grasp upon the crevices of the rock. I lay under the pines in the sparse shade and went to sleep once more.

11 It grew cold finally, for autumn was in the air by then, and the few things that lived thereabouts were sinking down into an even chillier scale of time. In the moments between sleeping and waking I saw the roots about me and slowly, slowly, a foot in what seemed many centuries, I moved my sleep-stiffened hands over the scaling bark and lifted my numbed face after the vanishing sun. I was a great awkward thing of knots and aching limbs, trapped up there in some long, patient endurance that involved the necessity of putting living fingers into rock and by slow, aching expansion bursting those rocks asunder. I suppose, so thin and slow was the time of my pulse by then, that I might have stayed on to drift still deeper into the lower cadences of the frost, or the crystalline life that glistens pebbles, or shines in a snowflake, or dreams in the meteoric iron between the worlds.

12 It was a dim descent, but time was present in it. Somewhere far down in that scale the notion struck me that one might come the other way. Not many months thereafter I joined some colleagues heading higher into a remote windy tableland where huge bones were reputed to protrude like boulders from the turf. I had drowsed with reptiles and moved with the century-long pulse of trees; now, lethargically, I was climbing back up some invisible ladder of quickening hours. There had been talk of birds in connection with my duties. Birds are intense, fast-living creatures—reptiles, I suppose one might say, that have escaped out of the heavy sleep of time, transformed fairy creatures dancing over sunlit meadows. It is a youthful fancy, no doubt, but because of something that happened up there among the escarpments of that range, it remains with me a lifelong impression. I can never bear to see a bird imprisoned.

13 We came into that valley through the trailing mists of a spring night. It

was a place that looked as though it might never have known the foot of man, but our scouts had been ahead of us and we knew all about the abandoned cabin of stone that lay far up on one hillside. It had been built in the land rush of the last century and then lost to the cattlemen again as the marginal soils failed to take to the plow.

14 There were spots like this all over that country. Lost graves marked by unlettered stones and old corroding rim-fire cartridge cases lying where somebody had made a stand among the boulders that rimmed the valley. They are all that remain of the range wars; the men are under the stones now. I could see our cavalcade winding in and out through the mist below us: torches, the reflection of the truck lights on our collecting tins, and the far-off bumping of a loose dinosaur thigh bone in the bottom of a trailer. I stood on a rock a moment looking down and thinking what it cost in money and equipment to capture the past.

15 We had, in addition, instructions to lay hands on the present. The word had come through to get them alive—birds, reptiles, anything. A zoo somewhere abroad needed restocking. It was one of those reciprocal matters in which science involves itself. Maybe our museum needed a stray ostrich egg and this was the payoff. Anyhow, my job was to help capture some birds and that was why I was there before the trucks.

16 The cabin had not been occupied for years. We intended to clean it out and live in it, but there were holes in the roof and the birds had come in and were roosting in the rafters. You could depend on it in a place like this where everything blew away, and even a bird needed some place out of the weather and away from coyotes. A cabin going back to nature in a wild place draws them till they come in, listening at the eaves, I imagine, pecking softly among the shingles till they find a hole and then suddenly the place is theirs and man is forgotten.

17 Sometimes of late years I find myself thinking the most beautiful sight in the world might be the birds taking over New York after the last man has run away to the hills. I will never live to see it, of course, but I know just how it will sound because I've lived up high and I know the sort of watch birds keep on us. I've listened to sparrows tapping tentatively on the outside of air conditioners when they thought no one was listening, and I know how other birds test the vibrations that come up to them through the television aerials.

18 "Is he gone?" they ask, and the vibrations come up from below, "Not yet, not yet."

19 Well, to come back, I got the door open softly and I had the spotlight all ready to turn on and blind whatever birds there were so they couldn't see to get out through the roof. I had a short piece of ladder to put against the far wall where there was a shelf on which I expected to make the biggest haul. I had all the information I needed just like any skilled assassin. I pushed the door open, the hinges squeaking only a little. A bird or two stirred—I could hear them— but nothing flew and there was a faint starlight through the holes in the roof.

20 I padded across the floor, got the ladder up and the light ready, and slithered up the ladder till my head and arms were over the shelf. Everything

was dark as pitch except for the starlight at the little place back of the shelf near the eaves. With the light to blind them, they'd never make it. I had them. I reached my arm carefully over in order to be ready to seize whatever was there and I put the flash on the edge of the shelf where it would stand by itself when I turned it on. That way I'd be able to use both hands.

21 Everything worked perfectly except for one detail—I didn't know what kind of birds were there. I never thought about it at all, and it wouldn't have mattered if I had. My orders were to get something interesting. I snapped on the flash and sure enough there was a great beating and feathers flying, but instead of my having them, they, or rather he, had me. He had my hand, that is, and for a small hawk not much bigger than my fist he was doing all right. I heard him give one short metallic cry when the light went on and my hand descended on the bird beside him; after that he was busy with his claws and his beak was sunk in my thumb. In the struggle I knocked the lamp over on the shelf, and his mate got her sight back and whisked neatly through the hole in the roof and off among the stars outside. It all happened in fifteen seconds and you might think I would have fallen down the ladder, but no, I had a professional assassin's reputation to keep up, and the bird, of course, made the mistake of thinking the hand was the enemy and not the eyes behind it. He chewed my thumb up pretty effectively and lacerated my hand with his claws, but in the end I got him, having two hands to work with.

22 He was a sparrow hawk and a fine young male in the prime of life. I was sorry not to catch the pair of them, but as I dripped blood and folded his wings carefully, holding him by the back so that he couldn't strike again, I had to admit the two of them might have been more than I could have handled under the circumstances. The little fellow had saved his mate by diverting me, and that was that. He was born to it, and made no outcry now, resting in my hand hopelessly, but peering toward me in the shadows behind the lamp with a fierce, almost indifferent glance. He neither gave nor expected mercy and something out of the high air passed from him to me, stirring a faint embarrassment.

23 I quit looking into that eye and managed to get my huge carcass with its fist full of prey back down the ladder. I put the bird in a box too small to allow him to injure himself by struggle and walked out to welcome the arriving trucks. It had been a long day, and camp still to make in the darkness. In the morning that bird would be just another episode. He would go back with the bones in the truck to a small cage in a city where he would spend the rest of his life. And a good thing, too. I sucked my aching thumb and spat out some blood. An assassin has to get used to these things. I had a professional reputation to keep up.

24 In the morning, with the change that comes on suddenly in that high country, the mist that had hovered below us in the valley was gone. The sky was a deep blue, and one could see for miles over the high outcroppings of stone. I was up early and brought the box in which the little hawk was imprisoned out onto the grass where I was building a cage. A wind as cool as a mountain spring ran over the grass and stirred my hair. It was a fine day to be

alive. I looked up and all around and at the hole in the cabin roof out of which the other little hawk had fled. There was no sign of her anywhere that I could see.

25 "Probably in the next county by now," I thought cynically, but before beginning work I decided I'd have a look at my last night's capture.

26 Secretively, I looked again all around the camp and up and down and opened the box. I got him right out in my hand with his wings folded properly and I was careful not to startle him. He lay limp in my grasp and I could feel his heart pound under the feathers but he only looked beyond me and up.

27 I saw him look that last look away beyond me into a sky so full of light that I could not follow his gaze. The little breeze flowed over me again, and nearby a mountain aspen shook all its tiny leaves. I suppose I must have had an idea then of what I was going to do, but I never let it come up into consciousness. I just reached over and laid the hawk on the grass.

28 He lay there a long minute without hope, unmoving, his eyes still fixed on that blue vault above him. It must have been that he was already so far away in heart that he never felt the release from my hand. He never even stood. He just lay with his breast against the grass.

29 In the next second after that long minute he was gone. Like a flicker of light, he had vanished with my eyes full on him, but without actually seeing even a premonitory wing beat. He was gone straight into that towering emptiness of light and crystal that my eyes could scarcely bear to penetrate. For another long moment there was silence. I could not see. The light was too intense. Then from far up somewhere a cry came ringing down.

30 I was young then and had seen little of the world, but when I heard that cry my heart turned over. It was not the cry of the hawk I had captured; for, by shifting my position against the sun, I was now seeing further up. Straight out of the sun's eye, where she must have been soaring restlessly above us for untold hours, hurtled his mate. And from far up, ringing from peak to peak of the summits over us, came a cry of such unutterable and ecstatic joy that it sounds down across the years and tingles among the cups on my quiet breakfast table.

31 I saw them both now. He was rising fast to meet her. They met in a great soaring gyre that turned to a whirling circle and a dance of wings. Once more, just once, their two voices, joined in a harsh wild medley of question and response, struck and echoed against the pinnacles of the valley. Then they were gone forever somewhere into those upper regions beyond the eyes of men.

32 I am older now, and sleep less, and have seen most of what there is to see and am not very much impressed any more, I suppose, by anything. "What Next in the Attributes of Machines?" my morning headline runs. "It Might Be the Power to Reproduce Themselves."

33 I lay the paper down and across my mind a phrase floats insinuatingly: "It does not seem that there is anything in the construction, constituents, or behavior of the human being which it is essentially impossible for science to duplicate and synthesize. On the other hand . . ."

34 All over the city the cogs in the hard, bright mechanisms have begun to turn. Figures move through computers, names are spelled out, a thoughtful machine selects the fingerprints of a wanted criminal from an array of thousands. In the laboratory an electronic mouse runs swiftly through a maze toward the cheese it can neither taste nor enjoy. On the second run it does better than a living mouse.

35 "On the other hand . . ." Ah, my mind takes up, on the other hand the machine does not bleed, ache, hang for hours in the empty sky in a torment of hope to learn the fate of another machine, nor does it cry out with joy nor dance in the air with the fierce passion of a bird. Far off, over a distance greater than space, that remote cry from the heart of heaven makes a faint buzzing among my breakfast dishes and passes on and away.

VOCABULARY

juxtapositions (1)	marginal (13)
insectivore (7)	cavalcade (14)
protoplasm (7)	lacerated (21)
cadences (11)	premonitory (29)
protrude (12)	gyre (31)
escarpments (12)	insinuatingly (33)

QUESTIONS ON CONTENT

1. How does the title of this selection relate to the content of the essay?
2. In paragraph 3 the author refers to "the new world that I read about at breakfast." What is this new world? Describe it in your own words.
3. What does Eiseley mean when he says, in paragraph 8, "I had come, like many a naturalist before me, to view life with a wary and subdued attention"?
4. What is the author describing in paragraph 11?
5. The author tells us that, because of something that happened up in the mountains, he can never bear to see a bird imprisoned. What happened? Recount the entire incident in your own words.
6. According to paragraph 17, what does the author think might be the most beautiful sight in the world? Why?
7. According to paragraph 22, a faint embarrassment passes between the captured hawk and the author. How do you account for this embarrassment?

QUESTIONS ON FORM

1. Is the comparison between the bird and the machine explicit or implicit? Support your answer with evidence from the text.
2. The author makes his readers feel the passage of time as the story proceeds. What are some of the transitions used to achieve this movement?
3. In the passage where the male hawk joins his mate, the birds seem human. How does Eiseley achieve this personification?
4. In paragraph 4 Eiseley compares the human body to a machine. What are the specific similarities?

5. In paragraph 7, what simile does Eiseley use to illustrate man's power and potential?

SUGGESTIONS FOR WRITING

1. Using one of the following pairs of symbols, write a five-hundred-word essay contrasting the symbols and what they represent:
   (a) a white rose and a red rose
   (b) a dove and a hawk
   (c) folded hands and a clenched fist
   (d) a green bud and a brown leaf
2. Write a five-hundred-word essay in which you contrast our modern technological society with an earlier agrarian society. Limit your contrast to one of the following areas:
   (a) mass communication or transportation
   (b) health
   (c) education
   (d) sanitation
   (e) art

GILBERT HIGHET

DIOGENES AND ALEXANDER

Author of the popular teaching guide, *The Art of Teaching,* and a noted authority in the classics, Professor Highet draws a clearly-etched portrait of two famous Greeks. (From *Great Confrontations,* I.)

1 Lying on the bare earth, shoeless, bearded, half-naked, he looked like a beggar or a lunatic. He was one, but not the other. He had opened his eyes with the sun at dawn, scratched, done his business like a dog at the roadside, washed at the public fountain, begged a piece of breakfast bread and a few olives, eaten them squatting on the ground, and washed them down with a few handfuls of water scooped from the spring. (Long ago he had owned a rough wooden cup, but he threw it away when he saw a boy drinking out of his hollowed hands.) Having no work to go to and no family to provide for, he was free. As the market place filled up with shoppers and merchants and gossipers and sharpers and slaves and foreigners, he had strolled through it for an hour or two. Everybody knew him, or knew of him. They would throw sharp questions at him and get sharper answers. Sometimes they threw jeers, and got jibes; sometimes bits of food, and got scant thanks; sometimes a mischievous pebble, and got a shower of stones and abuse. They were not quite sure whether he was mad or not. He knew they were mad, all mad, each in a different way; they amused him. Now he was back at his home.

2 It was not a house, not even a squatter's hut. He thought everybody lived far too elaborately, expensively, anxiously. What good is a house? No one needs privacy: natural acts are not shameful; we all do the same things,

and need not hide them. No one needs beds and chairs and such furniture: the animals live healthy lives and sleep on the ground. All we require, since nature did not dress us properly, is one garment to keep us warm, and some shelter from rain and wind. So he had one blanket—to dress him in the daytime and cover him at night—and he slept in a cask. His name was Diogenes. He was the founder of the creed called Cynicism (the word means "doggishness"); he spent much of his life in the rich, lazy, corrupt Greek city of Corinth, mocking and satirizing its people, and occasionally converting one of them.

3 His home was not a barrel made of wood: too expensive. It was a storage jar made of earthenware, something like a modern fuel tank—no doubt discarded because a break had made it useless. He was not the first to inhabit such a thing: the refugees driven into Athens by the Spartan invasion had been forced to sleep in casks. But he was the first who ever did so by choice, out of principle.

4 Diogenes was not a degenerate or a maniac. He was a philosopher who wrote plays and poems and essays expounding his doctrine; he talked to those who cared to listen; he had pupils who admired him. But he taught chiefly by example. All should live naturally, he said, for what is natural is normal and cannot possibly be evil or shameful. Live without conventions, which are artificial and false; escape complexities and superfluities and extravagances: only so can you live a free life. The rich man believes he possesses his big house with its many rooms and its elaborate furniture, his pictures and his expensive clothes, his horses and his servants and his bank accounts. He does not. He depends on them, he worries about them, he spends most of his life's energy looking after them; the thought of losing them makes him sick with anxiety. They possess him. He is their slave. In order to procure a quantity of false, perishable goods he has sold the only true, lasting good, his own independence.

5 There have been many men who grew tired of human society with its complications, and went away to live simply—on a small farm, in a quiet village, in a hermit's cave, or in the darkness of anonymity. Not so Diogenes. He was not a recluse, or a stylite, or a beatnik. He was a missionary. His life's aim was clear to him: it was "to restamp the currency." (He and his father had once been convicted for counterfeiting, long before he turned to philosophy, and this phrase was Diogenes' bold, unembarrassed joke on the subject.) To restamp the currency: to take the clean metal of human life, to erase the old false conventional markings, and to imprint it with its true values.

6 The other great philosophers of the fourth century before Christ taught mainly their own private pupils. In the shady groves and cool sanctuaries of the Academy, Plato discoursed to a chosen few on the unreality of this contingent existence. Aristotle, among the books and instruments and specimens and archives and research-workers of his Lyceum, pursued investigations and gave lectures that were rightly named *esoteric* "for those within the walls." But for Diogenes, laboratory and specimens and lecture halls and pupils were all to be found in a crowd of ordinary people. Therefore he chose to live in Athens or in the rich city of Corinth, where travelers from all over

the Mediterranean world constantly came and went. And, by design, he publicly behaved in such ways as to show people what real life was. He would constantly take up their spiritual coin, ring it on a stone, and laugh at its false superscription.

7 He thought most people were only half-alive, most men only half-men. At bright noonday he walked through the market place carrying a lighted lamp and inspecting the face of everyone he met. They asked him why. Diogenes answered, "I am trying to find a *man*."

8 To a gentleman whose servant was putting on his shoes for him, Diogenes said, "You won't be really happy until he wipes your nose for you: that will come after you lose the use of your hands."

9 Once there was a war scare so serious that it stirred even the lazy, profit-happy Corinthians. They began to drill, clean their weapons, and rebuild their neglected fortifications. Diogenes took his old cask and began to roll it up and down, back and forward. "When you are all so busy," he said, "I felt I ought to do *something!*"

10 And so he lived—like a dog, some said, because he cared nothing for privacy and other human conventions, and because he showed his teeth and barked at those whom he disliked. Now he was lying in the sunlight, as contented as a dog on the warm ground, happier (he himself used to boast) than the Shah of Persia. Although he knew he was going to have an important visitor, he would not move.

11 The little square began to fill with people. Page boys elegantly dressed, spearmen speaking a rough foreign dialect, discreet secretaries, hard-browed officers, suave diplomats, they all gradually formed a circle centered on Diogenes. He looked them over, as a sober man looks at a crowd of tottering drunks, and shook his head. He knew who they were. They were the attendants of the conqueror of Greece, the servants of Alexander, the Macedonian king, who was visiting his newly subdued realm.

12 Only twenty, Alexander was far older and wiser than his years. Like all Macedonians he loved drinking, but he could usually handle it; and toward women he was nobly restrained and chivalrous. Like all Macedonians he loved fighting; he was a magnificent commander, but he was not merely a military automaton. He could think. At thirteen he had become a pupil of the greatest mind in Greece, Aristotle. No exact record of his schooling survives. It is clear, though, that Aristotle took the passionate, half-barbarous boy and gave him the best of Greek culture. He taught Alexander poetry: the young prince slept with the *Iliad* under his pillow and longed to emulate Achilles, who brought the mighty power of Asia to ruin. He taught him philosophy, in particular the shapes and uses of political power: a few years later Alexander was to create a supranational empire that was not merely a power system but a vehicle for the exchange of Greek and Middle Eastern cultures.

13 Aristotle taught him the principles of scientific research: during his invasion of the Persian domains Alexander took with him a large corps of scientists, and shipped hundreds of zoological specimens back to Greece for study. Indeed, it was from Aristotle that Alexander learned to seek out

everything strange which might be instructive. Jugglers and stunt artists and virtuosos of the absurd he dismissed with a shrug; but on reaching India he was to spend hours discussing the problems of life and death with naked Hindu mystics, and later to see one demonstrate Yoga self-command by burning himself impassively to death.

14 Now, Alexander was in Corinth to take command of the League of Greek States which, after conquering them, his father Philip had created as a disguise for the New Macedonian Order. He was welcomed and honored and flattered. He was the man of the hour, of the century: he was unanimously appointed commander-in-chief of a new expedition against old, rich, corrupt Asia. Nearly everyone crowded to Corinth in order to congratulate him, to seek employment with him, even simply to see him: soldiers and statesmen, artists and merchants, poets and philosophers. He received their compliments graciously. Only Diogenes, although he lived in Corinth, did not visit the new monarch. With that generosity which Aristotle had taught him was a quality of the truly magnanimous man, Alexander determined to call upon Diogenes. Surely Dio-genes, the God-born, would acknowledge the conqueror's power by some gift of hoarded wisdom.

15 With his handsome face, his fiery glance, his strong supple body, his purple and gold cloak, and his air of destiny, he moved through the parting crowd, toward the Dog's kennel. When a king approaches, all rise in respect. Diogenes did not rise, he merely sat up on one elbow. When a monarch enters a precinct, all greet him with a bow or an acclamation. Diogenes said nothing.

16 There was a silence. Some years later Alexander speared his best friend to the wall, for objecting to the exaggerated honors paid to His Majesty; but now he was still young and civil. He spoke first, with a kindly greeting. Looking at the poor broken cask, the single ragged garment, and the rough figure lying on the ground, he said: "Is there anything I can do for you, Diogenes?"

17 "Yes," said the Dog, "Stand to one side. You're blocking the sunlight."

18 There was silence, not the ominous silence preceding a burst of fury, but a hush of amazement. Slowly, Alexander turned away. A titter broke out from the elegant Greeks, who were already beginning to make jokes about the Cur that looked at the King. The Macedonian officers, after deciding that Diogenes was not worth the trouble of kicking, were starting to guffaw and nudge one another. Alexander was still silent. To those nearest him he said quietly, "If I were not Alexander, I should be Diogenes." They took it as a paradox, designed to close the awkward little scene with a polite curtain line. But Alexander meant it. He understood Cynicism as the others could not. Later he took one of Diogenes' pupils with him to India as a philosophical interpreter (it was he who spoke to the naked *saddhus*). He was what Diogenes called himself, a *cosmopolitēs*, "citizen of the world." Like Diogenes, he admired the heroic figure of Hercules, the mighty conqueror who labors to help mankind while all others toil and sweat only for themselves. He knew that of all men then alive in the world only Alexander the conqueror and Diogenes the beggar were truly free.

VOCABULARY

expounding (4)	archives (6)
conventions (4)	superscription (6)
superfluities (4)	suave (11)
stylite (5)	supranational (12)
discoursed (6)	virtuosos (13)
contingent (6)	

Professor Highet explains the meaning of several words used in the essay. How does he interpret the following:

Cynicism (2)	Dio-genes (14)
esoteric (6)	cosmopolites (18)

QUESTIONS ON CONTENT

1. What characteristics do Diogenes and Alexander share?
2. In what ways are Diogenes and Alexander different?
3. What is Diogenes' rationale for living so humbly?
4. According to Diogenes, the richer a man is, the more enslaved he becomes. How does he explain this statement?
5. How did the teaching method of Diogenes differ from that of Plato or Aristotle?
6. Paragraph 12 states that Alexander was far older and wiser than his twenty years. How is this maturity indicated?
7. According to the essay, Alexander "understood Cynicism as the others could not." What is Cynicism? Why did Alexander understand it better than others?

QUESTIONS ON FORM

1. In what paragraph does the focus shift from Diogenes to Alexander?
2. Does the author draw his contrast by alternating back and forth between Diogenes and Alexander, or does he first draw a full portrait of Diogenes and then a full portrait of Alexander? What does the author's method require of the reader?
3. How do you explain the paradox, "If I were not Alexander, I should be Diogenes"?
4. The opening paragraph contains a sentence characterized by balance and parallelism. What are the opening words of the sentence?
5. What is the literary term for the phrase "to restamp the currency"? What is the meaning?
6. What is the topic sentence for paragraphs 7, 8, and 9? How is it developed?

SUGGESTIONS FOR WRITING

1. Write a five-hundred-word essay in which you state why you admire Alexander more than Diogenes, or vice versa.
2. Choosing one of the pairs listed below, write an essay developed by contrast. Begin with a thesis that summarizes the contrast. Keep in mind the basis of your contrast.
   (a) jealousy/envy
   (b) Thoreau/Gandhi
   (c) wisdom/knowledge
   (d) statesman/politician
   (e) old age/youth

CHARLES BUKOWSKI

THE TWINS

While the comparison/contrast is usually a pattern found in prose, it is also
occasionally used in poetry, as this poem illustrates.

he hinted at times that I was a bastard and I told him to listen to Brahms,
and I told him to learn to paint and drink and not be dominated by
          women and dollars
but he screamed at me, For Christ's sake remember your mother,
remember your country,
you'll kill us all! . . .

I move through my father's house (on which he owes $8,000 after 20
years on the same job) and look at his dead shoes
the way his feet curled the leather as if he were angry planting roses,
and he was, and I look at his dead cigarette, his last cigarette
and the last bed he slept in that night, and I feel I should remake it
but I can't, for a father is always your master even when he's gone;
I guess these things have happened time and again but I can't help
thinking
          to die on a kitchen floor at 7 o'clock in the morning
          while other people are frying eggs
          is not so rough
          unless it happens to you.

I go outside and pick an orange and peel back the bright skin;
things are still living: the grass is growing quite well,
the sun sends down its rays circled by a Russian satellite;
a dog barks senselessly somewhere, the neighbors peek behind blinds:
I am a stranger here, and have been (I suppose) somewhat the rogue,
and I have no doubt he painted me quite well (the old boy and I
fought like mountain lions) and they say he left it all to some woman
in Duarte but I don't give a damn—she can have it: he was my old
man
          and he died.

inside, I try on a light blue suit
much better than anything I have ever worn
and I flap the arms like a scarecrow in the wind
but it's no good:
I can't keep him alive
no matter how much we hated each other.

we looked exactly alike, we could have been twins
the old man and I: that's what they
said. he had his bulbs on the screen
ready for planting
while I was laying with a whore from 3rd street.

very well. grant us this moment: standing before a mirror
in my dead father's suit
waiting also
to die.

QUESTIONS ON CONTENT

1. Where is the speaker at the beginning of the poem? Why is he there?
2. The speaker says: "I look at his dead cigarette, his last cigarette/and the last bed he slept in that night, and I feel I should remake it/but I can't, for a father is always your master even when he's gone." What does he mean by that? What is the significance of the bed?
3. How does the poet characterize his father? By implication, how does he characterize himself?
4. What contrasts exist between the speaker and his father? How are they brought out in the poem?
5. What is the significance of the ending of the poem?

QUESTIONS ON FORM

1. What is the effect of the language of the poem? How would you characterize the diction of the poem?
2. The caesura is a break within a line of poetry. What does the use of the ceasura contribute to this poem?
3. Why does the poet include some of his remarks in parentheses? What effect does this have on the poem?
4. "we looked exactly alike, we could have been twins/the old man and I: that's what they/said. he had his bulbs on the screen/ready for planting/while I was laying with a whore from 3rd street."—What tone is the poet using here?
5. "to die on a kitchen floor at 7 o'clock in the morning/while other people are frying eggs/is not so rough/unless it happens to you."—What is the effect of setting these lines off by themselves in a separate stanza?

SUGGESTIONS FOR WRITING

1. Compare and contrast yourself with your father if you are a man, or with your mother if you are a woman.
2. The poet says, "a father is always your master even when he's gone." Analyze and discuss this statement as it applies to your own relationship with your father.

DIVISION AND CLASSIFICATION

ADVICE: HOW TO WRITE A DIVISION AND CLASSIFICATION

The term "division" refers to any piece of writing that intends to break a subject down into smaller units. For instance, an essay on types of automobiles which analyzes and classifies automobiles according to their sizes, is developed by division; similarly, an essay on American types, such as the one anthologized below, is also developed by division.

Division and classification are common to the way we think. We divide and classify the plant and animal kingdoms into phyla, genera, families, and species; we divide the military into the Army, Navy, Air Force, Marines, and Coast Guard. We divide and classify people into kinds and types. When we ask, "What kind of person is he?" we are asking for information developed by division and classification. An assignment asking for an essay developed by division is therefore an exercise in this common mode of thinking.

In developing an essay by division, it is useful to make this intent immediately clear. For instance, the essay "Thinking as a Hobby," which is anthologized in this section, makes it clear in the first paragraph what the writer intends to do.

> While I was still a boy, I came to the conclusion that there were three grades of thinking; and since I was later to claim thinking as my hobby, I came to an even stranger conclusion—namely, that I myself could not think at all.

We are therefore prepared for his division of thinking into three types, and for his anecdotes about why he has decided that he cannot think. Likewise, in the essay "Some American Types," the first paragraph (as well as the title) announces the author's intent to divide and classify American personalities.

> Anyone familiar with American literature will know that it contains stock portraits of its own which express social types. I want to use these traditional types as backdrops and stress some of the social roles that are new and still in process of formation.

Having promised a division, both essays deliver it.

1. *Divide your subject by a single principle.*

Once the division is made, stick to it. In the example below, the writer has violated this:

> Mating between man and woman takes place in four stages: the courtship, commitment, marriage, and deciding who will be responsible for household chores.

Courtship, commitment, and marriage are all part of mating; assigning responsibilities for household chores is not. Even if well executed, this essay contains a gross flaw by failing to subdivide its subjects according to the promised single principle—stages of mating.

2. *Make your categories mutually exclusive.*

Obviously, if you are dividing a subject into smaller categories, these must mutually exclude each other. This proposed division fails to develop mutually exclusive categories:

> College students may be divided into three groups: the so-called athletic "jock"; the scholarly "egghead"; and the student working his way through.

Both the "jock" and the "egghead" could also be working his or her way through. The categories are therefore not mutually exclusive.

3. *Make the division complete.*

A division is useless if its categories are incomplete. For instance:

> The dialogue and the recitation are the primary ways in which information can be passed from teacher to student.

This division omits the lecture method and is therefore faulty.

Students sometimes wonder why essays are assigned to conform to specific types of development such as division and classification—why a student is not allowed to simply meander over a subject freely. The answer is that writing by strict means of development also trains the student to think. A pattern such as division forces the student to submit his meanderings to the discipline of structure. Moreover, the pattern itself is not only a writing pattern but a thought pattern. Division and classification are a necessary part of logical thinking; assignments on them force a student to think on paper.

examples

MAX LERNER

SOME AMERICAN TYPES

As its title indicates, this essay comments on our society not by describing individual Americans, but by dividing Americans into certain distinguishable classes or categories.

1 Seventeenth-century England produced a number of books on *Characters* depicting English society through the typical personality patterns of the era. Trying something of the same sort for contemporary America, the first fact one encounters is the slighter emphasis on a number of character types than stand out elsewhere in Western society: to be sure, they are to be found in America as well, but they are not characteristically American. One thinks of the scholar, the aesthete, the priest or "parson," the "aristocratic" Army officer, the revolutionary student, the civil servant, the male schoolteacher, the marriage broker, the courtesan, the mystic, the saint. Anyone familiar

with European literature will recognize these characters as stock literary types and therefore as social types. Each of them represents a point of convergence for character and society. Anyone familiar with American literature will know that it contains stock portraits of its own which express social types. I want to use these traditional types as backdrops and stress some of the social roles that are new and still in process of formation.

2 Thus there is the *fixer,* who seems an organic product of a society in which the middleman function eats away the productive one. He may be public-relations man or influence peddler; he may get your traffic fine settled, or he may be able—whatever the commodity—to "get it for you wholesale." He is contemptuous of those who take the formal rules seriously; he knows how to cut corners—financial, political, administrative, or moral. At best there is something of the iconoclast in him, an unfooled quality far removed from the European personality types that always obey authority. At worst he becomes what the English call a "spiv" or cultural procurer.

3 Related to the fixer is the *inside dopester,* as Riesman[1] has termed him. He is oriented not so much toward getting things fixed as toward being "in the know" and "wised up" about things that innocents take at face value. He is not disillusioned because he has never allowed himself the luxury of illusions. In the 1920s and 1930s he consumed the literature of "debunking"; in the current era he knows everything that takes place in the financial centers of Wall Street, the political centers of Capitol Hill, and the communications centers of Madison Avenue—yet among all the things he knows there is little he believes in. His skepticism is not the wisdom which deflates pretentious-ness but that of the rejecting man who knows ahead of time that there is "nothing in it" whatever the "it" may be. In short, he is "hep."

4 Another link leads to the *neutral* man. He expresses the devaluing tendency in a culture that tries to avoid commitments. Fearful of being caught in the crosscurrents of conflict that may endanger his safety or status, he has a horror of what he calls "controversial figures"—and anyone becomes "con-troversial" if he is attacked. As the fixer and the inside dopester are the products of a middleman's society, so the neutral man is the product of a technological one. The technician's detachment from everything except effec-tive results becomes—in the realm of character—an ethical vacuum that strips the results of much of their meaning.

5 From the neutral man to the *conformist* is a short step. Although he is not neutral—in fact, he may be militantly partisan—his partisanship is on the side of the big battalions. He lives in terror of being caught in a minority where his insecurity will be conspicuous. He gains a sense of stature by joining the dominant group, as he gains security by making himself indistinguishable from that group. Anxious to efface any unique traits of his own, he exacts confor-mity from others. He fears ideas whose newness means they are not yet accepted, but once they are firmly established he fights for them with a courage born of the knowledge that there is no danger in championing them.

[1]David Riesman wrote *The Lonely Crowd, Faces in the Crowd,* and other works.—Ed.

He hates foreigners and immigrants. When he talks of the "American way," he sees a world in which other cultures have become replicas of his own.

6 It is often hard to distinguish the conformist from the *routineer*. Essentially he is a man in uniform, sometimes literally, always symbolically. The big public-service corporations—railroads, air lines, public utilities—require their employees to wear uniforms that will imprint a common image of the enterprise as a whole. City employees, such as policemen and firemen, wear uniforms. Gas-station attendants, hotel clerks, bellhops, must similarly keep their appearance within prescribed limits. Even the sales force in big department stores or the typists and stenographers in big corporations tend toward the same uniformity. There are very few young Americans who are likely to escape the uniform of the Armed Services. With the uniform goes an urge toward pride of status and a routineering habit of mind. There is the confidence that comes of belonging to a large organization and sharing symbolically in its bigness and power. There is a sense of security in having grooves with which to move. This is true on every level of corporate business enterprise, from the white-collar employee to "the man in the gray flannel suit," although it stops short of the top executives who create the uniforms instead of wearing them. Even outside the government and corporate bureaus there are signs of American life becoming bureaucratized, in a stress on forms and routines, on "going through channels."

7 Unlike the conformist or routineer, the *status seeker* may possess a resourceful energy and even originality, but he directs these qualities toward gaining status. What he wants is a secure niche in a society whose men are constantly being pulled upward or trodden down. Scott Fitzgerald has portrayed a heartbreaking case history of this character type in *The Great Gatsby,* whose charm and energy are invested fruitlessly in an effort to achieve social position. The novels of J. P. Marquand are embroideries of a similar theme, narrated through the mind of one who already has status and is confronted by the risk of losing it. At various social levels the status seeker becomes a "joiner" of associations which give him symbolic standing.

VOCABULARY

aesthete (1)	pretentiousness (3)
courtesan (1)	hep (3)
mystic (1)	devaluing (4)
convergence (1)	militantly (5)
organic (2)	battalions (5)
contemptuous (2)	replicas (5)
iconoclast (2)	bureaucratized (6)
procurer (2)	niche (7)

QUESTIONS ON CONTENT

1. Max Lerner describes six types of Americans. What other categories has he deliberately left out?

2. In listing his six types, what basic criticism is Lerner leveling at America?
3. Have you had any personal dealings with either a fixer, an inside dopester, a neutral man, a conformist, a routineer, or a status seeker? Describe this experience in detail.
4. Which of the types described do you consider the most harmful to our society? Which is the least harmful? Give reasons for your views.

QUESTIONS ON FORM

1. What is the purpose of Lerner's introductory paragraph?
2. How does Lerner keep his essay organized and coherent? Point to the specific words or passages that help achieve coherence and organization.
3. A good division must divide up an entire group. What entire group does Lerner's essay subdivide?
4. Lerner describes his types by supplying details that bring each type to life. Are some descriptions better than others? Why?

SUGGESTIONS FOR WRITING

1. Divide Americans into recognizable types, using categories which you have created.
2. In paragraph 2, Lerner subdivides the fixer into four more categories: financial, political, administrative, moral. Develop an essay in which these subdivisions are portrayed vividly.

WILLIAM GOLDING

THINKING AS A HOBBY

William Golding, best known for his novel *Lord of the Flies* (1954), once described his hobbies as "thinking, classical Greek, sailing, and archaeology." In the essay that follows, he divides thinking into three recognizable types.

1 While I was still a boy, I came to the conclusion that there were three grades of thinking; and since I was later to claim thinking as my hobby, I came to an even stranger conclusion—namely, that I myself could not think at all.

2 I must have been an unsatisfactory child for grownups to deal with. I remember how incomprehensible they appeared to me at first, but not, of course, how I appeared to them. It was the headmaster of my grammar school who first brought the subject of thinking before me—though neither in the way, nor with the result he intended. He had some statuettes in his study. They stood on a high cupboard behind his desk. One was a lady wearing nothing but a bath towel. She seemed frozen in an eternal panic lest the bath towel slip down any farther; and since she had no arms, she was in an unfortunate position to pull the towel up again. Next to her, crouched the statuette of a leopard, ready to spring down at the top drawer of a filing cabinet labeled A–AH. My innocence interpreted this as the victim's last, despairing

cry. Beyond the leopard was a naked, muscular gentleman, who sat, looking down, with his chin on his fist and his elbow on his knee. He seemed utterly miserable.

3 Some time later, I learned about these statuettes. The headmaster had placed them where they would face delinquent children, because they symbolized to him the whole of life. The naked lady was the Venus of Milo. She was Love. She was not worried about the towel. She was just busy being beautiful. The leopard was Nature, and he was being natural. The naked, muscular gentleman was not miserable. He was Rodin's Thinker, an image of pure thought. It is easy to buy small plaster models of what you think life is like.

4 I had better explain that I was a frequent visitor to the headmaster's study, because of the latest thing I had done or left undone. As we now say, I was not integrated. I was, if anything, disintegrated; and I was puzzled. Grownups never made sense. Whenever I found myself in a penal position before the headmaster's desk, with the statuettes glimmering whitely above him, I would sink my head, clasp my hands behind my back and writhe one shoe over the other.

5 The headmaster would look opaquely at me through flashing spectacles.

"What are we going to do with you?"

Well, what *were* they going to do with me? I would writhe my shoe some more and stare down at the worn rug.

"Look up, boy! Can't you look up?"

6 Then I would look up at the cupboard, where the naked lady was frozen in her panic and the muscular gentleman contemplated the hindquarters of the leopard in endless gloom. I had nothing to say to the headmaster. His spectacles caught the light so that you could see nothing human behind them. There was no possibility of communication.

"Don't you ever think at all?"

No, I didn't think, wasn't thinking, couldn't think—I was simply waiting in anguish for the interview to stop.

"Then you'd better learn—hadn't you?"

7 On one occasion the headmaster leaped to his feet, reached up and plonked Rodin's masterpiece on the desk before me.

"That's what a man looks like when he's really thinking."

I surveyed the gentleman without interest or comprehension.

"Go back to your class."

8 Clearly there was something missing in me. Nature had endowed the rest of the human race with a sixth sense and left me out. This must be so, I mused, on my way back to the class, since whether I had broken a window, or failed to remember Boyle's Law, or been late for school, my teachers produced me one, adult answer: "Why can't you think?"

9 As I saw the case, I had broken the window because I had tried to hit Jack Arney with a cricket ball and missed him; I could not remember Boyle's Law because I had never bothered to learn it; and I was late for school because I preferred looking over the bridge into the river. In fact, I was wicked. Were my teachers, perhaps, so good that they could not understand

the depths of my depravity? Were they clear, untormented people who could direct their every action by this mysterious business of thinking? The whole thing was incomprehensible. In my earlier years, I found even the statuette of the Thinker confusing. I did not believe any of my teachers were naked, ever. Like someone born deaf, but bitterly determined to find out about sound, I watched my teachers to find out about thought.

10 There was Mr. Houghton. He was always telling me to think. With a modest satisfaction, he would tell me that he had thought a bit himself. Then why did he spend so much time drinking? Or was there more sense in drinking than there appeared to be? But if not, and if drinking were in fact ruinous to health—and Mr. Houghton was ruined, there was no doubt about that—why was he always talking about the clean life and the virtues of fresh air? He would spread his arms wide with the action of man who habitually spent his time striding along mountain ridges.

"Open air does me good, boys—I know it!"

11 Sometimes, exalted by his own oratory, he would leap from his desk and hustle us outside into a hideous wind.

"Now, boys! Deep breaths! Feel it right down inside you—huge draughts of God's good air!"

12 He would stand before us, rejoicing in his perfect health, an open-air man. He would put his hands on his waist and take a tremendous breath. You could hear the wind, trapped in the cavern of his chest and struggling with all the unnatural impediments. His body would reel with shock and his ruined face go white at the unaccustomed visitation. He would stagger back to his desk and collapse there, useless for the rest of the morning.

13 Mr. Houghton was given to high-minded monologues about the good life, sexless and full of duty. Yet in the middle of one of these monologues, if a girl passed the window, tapping along on her neat little feet, he would interrupt his discourse, his neck would turn of itself and he would watch her out of sight. In this instance, he seemed to me ruled not by thought but by an invisible and irresistible spring in his nape.

14 His neck was an object of great interest to me. Normally it bulged a bit over his collar. But Mr. Houghton had fought in the First World War alongside both Americans and French, and had come—by who knows what illogic?—to a settled detestation of both countries. If either country happened to be prominent in current affairs, no argument could make Mr. Houghton think well of it. He would bang the desk, his neck would bulge still further and go red. "You can say what you like," he would cry, "but I've thought about this—and I know what I think!"

15 Mr. Houghton thought with his neck.

16 There was Miss Parsons. She assured us that her dearest wish was our welfare, but I knew even then, with the mysterious clairvoyance of childhood, that what she wanted most was the husband she never got. There was Mr. Hands—and so on.

17 I have dealt at length with my teachers because this was my introduction to the nature of what is commonly called thought. Through them I discovered

that thought is often full of unconscious prejudice, ignorance and hypocrisy. It will lecture on disinterested purity while its neck is being remorselessly twisted toward a skirt. Technically, it is about as proficient as most businessmen's golf, as honest as most politicians' intentions, or—to come near my own preoccupation—as coherent as most books that get written. It is what I came to call grade-three thinking, though more properly, it is feeling, rather than thought.

18 True, often there is a kind of innocence in prejudices, but in those days I viewed grade-three thinking with an intolerant contempt and an incautious mockery. I delighted to confront a pious lady who hated the Germans with the proposition that we should love our enemies. She taught me a great truth in dealing with grade-three thinkers; because of her, I no longer dismiss lightly a mental process which for nine-tenths of the population is the nearest they will ever get to thought. They have immense solidarity. We had better respect them, for we are outnumbered and surrounded. A crowd of grade-three thinkers, all shouting the same thing, all warming their hands at the fire of their own prejudices, will not thank you for pointing out the contradictions in their beliefs. Man is a gregarious animal, and enjoys agreement as cows will graze all the same way on the side of a hill.

19 Grade-two thinking is the detection of contradictions. I reached grade two when I trapped the poor, pious lady. Grade-two thinkers do not stampede easily, though often they fall into the other fault and lag behind. Grade-two thinking is a withdrawal, with eyes and ears open. It became my hobby and brought satisfaction and loneliness in either hand. For grade-two thinking destroys without having the power to create. It set me watching the crowds cheering His Majesty the King and asking myself what all the fuss was about, without giving me anything positive to put in the place of that heady patriotism. But there were compensations. To hear people justify their habit of hunting foxes and tearing them to pieces by claiming that the foxes liked it. To hear our Prime Minister talk about the great benefit we conferred on India by jailing people like Pandit Nehru and Gandhi. To hear American politicians talk about peace in one sentence and refuse to join the League of Nations in the next. Yes, there were moments of delight.

20 But I was growing toward adolescence and had to admit that Mr. Houghton was not the only one with an irresistible spring in his neck. I, too, felt the compulsive hand of nature and began to find that pointing out contradiction could be costly as well as fun. There was Ruth, for example, a serious and attractive girl. I was an atheist at the time. Grade-two thinking is a menace to religion and knocks down sects like skittles. I put myself in a position to be converted by her with an hypocrisy worthy of grade three. She was a Methodist—or at least, her parents were, and Ruth had to follow suit. But, alas, instead of relying on the Holy Spirit to convert me, Ruth was foolish enough to open her pretty mouth in argument. She claimed that the Bible (King James Version) was literally inspired. I countered by saying that the Catholics believed in the literal inspiration of Saint Jerome's *Vulgate,* and the two books were different. Argument flagged.

21 At last she remarked that there were an awful lot of Methodists, and they couldn't be wrong, could they—not all those millions? That was too easy, said I restively (for the nearer you were to Ruth, the nicer she was to be near to) since there were more Roman Catholics than Methodists anyway; and they couldn't be wrong, could they—not all those hundreds of millions? An awful flicker of doubt appeared in her eyes. I slid my arm round her waist and murmured breathlessly that if we were counting heads, the Buddhists were the boys for my money. But Ruth had *really* wanted to do me good, because I was so nice. She fled. The combination of my arm and those countless Buddhists was too much for her.

22 That night her father visited my father and left, red-cheeked and indignant. I was given the third degree to find out what had happened. It was lucky we were both of us only fourteen. I lost Ruth and gained an undeserved reputation as a potential libertine.

23 So grade-two thinking could be dangerous. It was in this knowledge, at the age of fifteen, that I remember making a comment from the heights of grade two, on the limitations of grade three. One evening I found myself alone in the school hall, preparing it for a party. The door of the headmaster's study was open. I went in. The headmaster had ceased to thump Rodin's Thinker down on the desk as an example to the young. Perhaps he had not found any more candidates, but the statuettes were still there, glimmering and gathering dust on top of the cupboard. I stood on a chair and rearranged them. I stood Venus in her bath towel on the filing cabinet, so that now the top drawer caught its breath in a gasp of sexy excitement. "A-ah!" The portentous Thinker I placed on the edge of the cupboard so that he looked down at the bath towel and waited for it to slip.

24 Grade-two thinking, though it filled life with fun and excitement, did not make for content. To find out the deficiencies of our elders bolsters the young ego but does not make for personal security. I found that grade two was not only the power to point out contradictions. It took the swimmer some distance from the shore and left him there, out of his depth. I decided that Pontius Pilate was a typical grade-two thinker. "What is truth?" he said, a very common grade-two thought, but one that is used always as the end of an argument instead of the beginning. There is a still higher grade of thought which says, "What is truth?" and sets out to find it.

25 But these grade-one thinkers were few and far between. They did not visit my grammar school in the flesh though they were there in books. I aspired to them, partly because I was ambitious and partly because I now saw my hobby as an unsatisfactory thing if it went no further. If you set out to climb a mountain, however high you climb, you have failed if you cannot reach the top.

26 I *did* meet an undeniably grade-one thinker in my first year at Oxford. I was looking over a small bridge in Magdalen Deer Park, and a tiny mustached and hatted figure came and stood by my side. He was a German who had just fled from the Nazis to Oxford as a temporary refuge. His name was Einstein.

27 But Professor Einstein knew no English at that time and I knew only two

words of German. I beamed at him, trying wordlessly to convey by my bearing all the affection and respect that the English felt for him. It is possible—and I have to make the admission—that I felt here were two grade-one thinkers standing side by side; yet I doubt if my face conveyed more than a formless awe. I would have given my Greek and Latin and French and a good slice of my English for enough German to communicate. But we were divided; he was as inscrutable as my headmaster. For perhaps five minutes we stood together on the bridge, undeniable grade-one thinker and breathless aspirant. With true greatness, Professor Einstein realized that any contact was better than none. He pointed to a trout wavering in midstream.

28 He spoke: *"Fisch."*

29 My brain reeled. Here I was, mingling with the great, and yet helpless as the veriest grade-three thinker. Desperately I sought for some sign by which I might convey that I, too, revered pure reason. I nodded vehemently. In a brilliant flash I used up half of my German vocabulary. *"Fisch. Ja. Ja."*

30 For perhaps another five minutes we stood side by side. Then Professor Einstein, his whole figure still conveying good will and amiability, drifted away out of sight.

31 I, too, would be a grade-one thinker. I was irreverent at the best of times. Political and religious systems, social customs, loyalties and traditions, they all came tumbling down like so many rotten apples off a tree. This was a fine hobby and a sensible substitute for cricket, since you could play it all the year round. I came up in the end with what must always remain the justification for grade-one thinking, its sign, seal and charter. I devised a coherent system for living. It was a moral system, which was wholly logical. Of course, as I readily admitted, conversion of the world to my way of thinking might be difficult, since my system did away with a number of trifles, such as big business, centralized government, armies, marriage . . .

32 It was Ruth all over again. I had some very good friends who stood by me, and still do. But my acquaintances vanished, taking the girls with them. Young women seemed oddly contented with the world as it was. They valued the meaningless ceremony with a ring. Young men, while willing to concede the chaining sordidness of marriage, were hesitant about abandoning the organizations which they hoped would give them a career. A young man on the first rung of the Royal Navy, while perfectly agreeable to doing away with big business and marriage, got as red-necked as Mr. Houghton when I proposed a world without any battleships in it.

33 Had the game gone too far? Was it a game any longer? In those prewar days, I stood to lose a great deal, for the sake of a hobby.

34 Now you are expecting me to describe how I saw the folly of my ways and came back to the warm nest, where prejudices are so often called loyalties, where pointless actions are hallowed into custom by repetition, where we are content to say we think when all we do is feel.

35 But you would be wrong. I dropped my hobby and turned professional.

36 If I were to go back to the headmaster's study and find the dusty statuettes still there, I would arrange them differently. I would dust Venus and

put her aside, for I have come to love her and know her for the fair thing she is. But I would put the Thinker, sunk in his desperate thought, where there were shadows before him—and at his back, I would put the leopard, crouched and ready to spring.

VOCABULARY

incomprehensible (2)	proposition (18)
statuettes (2)	solidarity (18)
integrated (4)	Pandit (19)
penal (4)	skittles (20)
opaquely (5)	flagged (20)
ruinous (10)	restively (21)
draughts (11)	libertine (22)
impediments (12)	inscrutable (27)
monologues (13)	veriest (29)
detestation (14)	revered (29)
clairvoyance (16)	amiability (30)
disinterested (17)	coherent (31)
proficient (17)	

QUESTIONS ON CONTENT

1. Into what three types does Golding divide all thinking? Describe each type in your own words. Is there a value judgment implied in the division?
2. Why does Golding take up so much time describing some of his grade-school teachers? How are they related to the purpose of the essay?
3. Why is it so difficult to find grade-one thinkers? Describe someone whom you consider a grade-one thinker.
4. How do you interpret Golding's last two paragraphs? Has the author reverted to grade-three or grade-two thinking, or has he become a grade-one thinker? Comment.
5. To be a grade-one thinker, must one do away with big business, centralized government, armies, marriages, etc.? How could one be a grade-one thinker without wanting to destroy these?

QUESTIONS ON FORM

1. In paragraph 2, the author describes three statuettes on a cupboard behind the headmaster's desk. In what paragraph is each of the statuettes explained? Why is the explanation necessary?
2. Much of the article reflects a young boy's point of view. How is this point of view achieved? Point to some specific passages.
3. Paragraphs 14, 15, and 17 allude to the word "neck" repeatedly. What has the *neck* come to symbolize in this context?
4. What is the analogy used in paragraph 18 to describe grade-three thinkers? Is the analogy effective? Explain.
5. What is Golding's purpose in alluding to the jailing of Nehru and Gandhi, and to the Americans' refusal to join the League of Nations?

SUGGESTIONS FOR WRITING

1. Write an essay in which you answer the question, "Does a college education help to get rid of prejudice and hypocrisy?" Support your answer with examples from your own experience.
2. Write an essay in which you divide your acquaintances into types according to the kinds of behavior they project. Be sure that your categories are mutually exclusive and that they take in all your acquaintances.

JOHN HOLT

KINDS OF DISCIPLINE

Because "discipline" is an ambiguous word and often misunderstood, the author attempts to give it a clearer meaning by focusing on three specific kinds of discipline.

1 The word "discipline" has more and more important meanings than just this. A child, in growing up, may meet and learn from three different kinds of disciplines. The first and most important is what we might call the Discipline of Nature or of Reality. When he is trying to do something real, if he does the wrong thing or doesn't do the right one, he doesn't get the result he wants. If he doesn't pile one block right on top of another, or tries to build on a slanting surface, his tower falls down. If he hits the wrong key, he hears the wrong note. If he doesn't hit the nail squarely on the head, it bends, and he has to pull it out and start with another. If he doesn't measure properly what he is trying to build, it won't open, close, fit, stand up, fly, float, whistle, or do whatever he wants it to do. If he closes his eyes when he swings, he doesn't hit the ball. A child meets this kind of discipline every time he tries to *do* something, which is why it is so important in school to give children more chances to do things, instead of just reading or listening to someone talk (or pretending to). This discipline is a great teacher. The learner never has to wait long for his answer; it usually comes quickly, often instantly. Also it is clear, and very often points toward the needed correction; from what happened he can not only see that what he did was wrong, but also why, and what he needs to do instead. Finally, and most important, the giver of the answer, call it Nature, is impersonal, impartial, and indifferent. She does not give opinions, or make judgments; she cannot be wheedled, bullied, or fooled; she does not get angry or disappointed; she does not praise or blame; she does not remember past failures or hold grudges; with her one always gets a fresh start, this time is the one that counts.

2 The next discipline we might call the Discipline of Culture, of Society, of What People Really Do. Man is a social, a cultural animal. Children sense around them this culture, this network of agreements, customs, habits, and rules binding the adults together. They want to understand it and be a part of it. They watch very carefully what people around them are doing and want to

do the same. They want to do right, unless they become convinced they can't do right. Thus children rarely misbehave seriously in church, but sit as quietly as they can. The example of all those grownups is contagious. Some mysterious ritual is going on, and children, who like rituals, want to be part of it. In the same way, the little children that I see at concerts or operas, though they may fidget a little, or perhaps take a nap now and then, rarely make any disturbance. With all those grownups sitting there, neither moving nor talking, it is the most natural thing in the world to imitate them. Children who live among adults who are habitually courteous to each other, and to them, will soon learn to be courteous. Children who live surrounded by people who speak a certain way will speak that way, however much we may try to tell them that speaking that way is bad or wrong.

3 The third discipline is the one most people mean when they speak of discipline—the Discipline of Superior Force, of sergeant to private, of "you do what I tell you or I'll make you wish you had." There is bound to be some of this in a child's life. Living as we do surrounded by things that can hurt children, or that children can hurt, we cannot avoid it. We can't afford to let a small child find out from experience the danger of playing in a busy street, or of fooling with the pots on the top of a stove, or of eating up the pills in the medicine cabinet. So, along with other precautions, we say to him, "Don't play in the street, or touch things on the stove, or go into the medicine cabinet, or I'll punish you." Between him and the danger too great for him to imagine we put a lesser danger, but one he can imagine and maybe therefore wants to avoid. He can have no idea of what it would be like to be hit by a car, but he can imagine being shouted at, or spanked, or sent to his room. He avoids these substitutes for the greater danger until he can understand it and avoid it for its own sake. But we ought to use this discipline only when it is necessary to protect the life, health, safety, or well-being of people or other living creatures, or to prevent destruction of things that people care about. We ought not to assume too long, as we usually do, that a child cannot understand the real nature of the danger from which we want to protect him. The sooner he avoids the danger, not to escape our punishment, but as a matter of good sense, the better. He can learn that faster than we think. In Mexico, for example, where people drive their cars with a good deal of spirit, I saw many children no older than five or four walking unattended on the streets. They understood about cars, they knew what to do. A child whose life is full of the threat and fear of punishment is locked into babyhood. There is no way for him to grow up, to learn to take responsibility for his life and acts. Most important of all, we should not assume that having to yield to the threat of our superior force is good for the child's character. It is never good for *anyone's* character. To bow to superior force makes us feel impotent and cowardly for not having had the strength or courage to resist. Worse, it makes us resentful and vengeful. We can hardly wait to make someone pay for our humiliation, yield to us as we were once made to yield. No, if we cannot always avoid using the Discipline of Superior Force, we should at least use it as seldom as we can.

4 There are places where all three disciplines overlap. Any very demanding

human activity combines in it the disciplines of Superior Force, of Culture, and of Nature. The novice will be told, "Do it this way, never mind asking why, just do it that way, that is the way we always do it." But it probably *is* just the way they always do it, and usually for the very good reason that it is a way that has been found to work. Think, for example, of ballet training. The student in a class is told to do this exercise, or that; to stand so; to do this or that with his head, arms, shoulders, abdomen, hips, legs, feet. He is constantly corrected. There is no argument. But behind these seemingly autocratic demands by the teacher lie many decades of custom and tradition, and behind that, the necessities of dancing itself. You cannot make the moves of classical ballet unless over many years you have acquired, and renewed every day, the needed strength and suppleness in scores of muscles and joints. Nor can you do the difficult motions, making them look easy, unless you have learned hundreds of easier ones first. Dance teachers may not always agree on all the details of teaching these strengths and skills. But no novice could learn them all by himself. You could not go for a night or two to watch the ballet and then, without any other knowledge at all, teach yourself how to do it. In the same way, you would be unlikely to learn any complicated and difficult human activity without drawing heavily on the experience of those who know it better. But the point is that the authority of these experts or teachers stems from, grows out of their greater competence and experience, the fact that what they do *works,* not the fact that they happen to be the teacher and as such have the power to kick a student out of the class. And the further point is that children are always and everywhere attracted to that competence, and ready and eager to submit themselves to a discipline that grows out of it. We hear constantly that children will never do anything unless compelled to by bribes or threats. But in their private lives, or in extracurricular activities in school, in sports, music, drama, art, running a newspaper, and so on, they often submit themselves willingly and wholeheartedly to very intense disciplines, simply because they want to learn to do a given thing well. Our Little-Napoleon football coaches, of whom we have too many and hear far too much, blind us to the fact that millions of children work hard every year getting better at sports and games without coaches barking and yelling at them.

VOCABULARY

wheeled (1)   novice (4)
ritual (2)   autocratic (4)
impotent (3)

QUESTIONS ON CONTENT

1. What principle or basis of division does Holt use?
2. How does Holt clarify for the reader what he means by "Discipline of Nature or of Reality"? Is this method effective? Why?

3. What are the advantages of learning from nature or reality?
4. What additional examples can you supply for how children submit to the discipline of culture or society?
5. According to the author, when only should the discipline of superior force be used? Do you agree?
6. At the end of his essay Holt identifies the most successful motivation for discipline. What is it?

QUESTIONS ON FORM

1. In the last sentence of paragraph 1, the author uses the feminine pronouns "she" and "her" in referring to nature. What is his purpose?
2. What transitional guideposts does the author use in order to gain coherence and organization?
3. What is the effect of labeling certain football coaches "Little Napoleons"?

SUGGESTIONS FOR WRITING

1. Write a five-hundred-word essay in which you divide discipline according to the kinds of effects it produces. Example: discipline that results in strong study habits.
2. Develop the following topic sentence into a three-paragraph essay: "To be successful, a person must have three kinds of discipline: of the intellect, of the emotions, and of the body."

ELISABETH KUBLER ROSS, M.D.

STAGES OF DYING

Dr. Kubler Ross does something few people would dare to do: she shares the result of a study of approximately five hundred terminally ill patients in order to find out what they could teach us about dying. The result is an honest but sensitive study of what dying is and how people who are dying can be helped by others.

1 People used to be born at home and die at home. In the old days, children were familiar with birth and death as part of life. This is perhaps the first generation of American youngsters who have never been close by during the birth of a baby and have never experienced the death of a beloved family member.

2 Nowadays when people grow old, we often send them to nursing homes. When they get sick, we transfer them to a hospital, where children are usually unwelcome and are forbidden to visit terminally ill patients—even when those patients are their parents. This deprives the dying patient of significant family members during the last few days of his life and it deprives the children of an experience of death, which is an important learning experience.

3 At the University of Chicago's Billings Hospital, some of my colleagues and I interviewed and followed approximately 500 terminally ill patients in

order to find out what they could teach us and how we could be of more benefit, not just to them but to the members of their families as well. We were most impressed by the fact that even those patients who were not told of their serious illness were quite aware of its potential outcome. They were not only able to say that they were close to dying, but many were able to predict the approximate time of their death.

4 It is important for next of kin and members of the helping professions to understand these patients' communications in order to truly understand their needs, fears, and fantasies. Most of our patients welcomed another human being with whom they could talk openly, honestly, and frankly about their predicament. Many of them shared with us their tremendous need to be informed, to be kept up-to-date on their medical condition, and to be told when the end was near. We found out that patients who had been dealt with openly and frankly were better able to cope with the imminence of death and finally to reach a true stage of acceptance prior to death.

5 Two things seem to determine the ultimate adjustment to a terminal illness. When patients were allowed hope at the beginning of a fatal illness and when they were informed that they would not be deserted "no matter what," they were able to drop their initial shock and denial rather quickly and could arrive at a peaceful acceptance of their finiteness.

6 Most patients respond to the awareness that they have a terminal illness with the statement, "Oh no, this can't happen to me." After the first shock, numbness, and need to deny the reality of the situation, the patient begins to send out cues that he is ready to "talk about it." If *we,* at that point, need to deny the reality of the situation, the patient will often feel deserted, isolated, and lonely and unable to communicate with another human being what he needs so desperately to share.

7 When, on the other hand, the patient has one person with whom he can talk freely, he will be able to talk (often for only a few minutes at a time) about his illness and about the consequences of his deteriorating health, and he will be able to ask for help. Sometimes, he'll need to talk about financial matters; and, toward the end of the life, he will frequently ask for some spiritual help.

8 Most patients who have passed the stage of denial will become angry as they ask the question, "Why me?" Many look at others in their environment and express envy, jealousy, anger, and rage toward those who are young, healthy, and full of life. These are the patients who make life difficult for nurses, physicians, social workers, clergymen, and members of their families. Without justification they criticize everyone.

9 What we have to learn is that the stage of anger in terminal illness is a blessing, not a curse. These patients are not angry at their families or at the members of the helping professions. Rather, they are angry at what these people represent: health, pep, energy.

10 Without being judgmental, we must allow these patients to express their anger and dismay. We must try to understand that the patients have to ask, "Why me?" and that there is no need on our part to answer this question concretely. Once a patient has ventilated his rage and his envy, then he can

arrive at the bargaining stage. During this time, he's usually able to say, "Yes, it is happening to me—*but*." The *but* usually includes a prayer to God: "If you give me one more year to live, I will be a good Christian (or I'll go to the synagogue every day)."

11 Most patients promise something in exchange for prolongation of life. Many a patient wants to live just long enough for the children to get out of school. The moment they have completed high school, he may ask to live until the son gets married. And the moment the wedding is over, he hopes to live until the grandchild arrives. These kinds of bargains are compromises, the patient's beginning acknowledgement that his time is limited, and an expression of finiteness, all necessary in reaching a stage of acceptance. When a patient drops the *but,* then he is able to say, "Yes, me." At this point, he usually becomes very depressed. And here again we have to allow him to express his grief and his mourning.

12 If we stop and think how much we would grieve if we lost a beloved spouse, it will make us realize what courage it takes for a man to face his own impending death, which involves the loss of everyone and everything he has ever loved. This is a thousand times more crushing than to become a widow or a widower.

13 To such patients, we should never say, "Come on now, cheer up." We should allow them to grieve, to cry. And we should even convey to them that "it takes a brave person to cry," meaning that it takes courage to face death. If the patient expresses his grief, he will feel more comfortable, and he will usually go through the stage of depression much more rapidly than he will if he has to suppress it or hide his tears.

14 Only through this kind of behavior on our part are our patients able to reach the stage of acceptance. Here, they begin to separate themselves from the interpersonal relationships in their environment. Here, they begin to ask for fewer and fewer visitors. Finally, they will require only one beloved person who can sit quietly and comfortably near.

15 This is the time when a touch becomes more important than words, the time when a patient may simply say one day, "My time is very close now, and it's all right." It is not necessarily a happy stage, but the patient now shows no more fear, bitterness, anguish, or concern over unfinished business. People who have been able to sit through this stage with patients and who have experienced the beautiful feeling of inner and outer peace that they show will soon appreciate that working with terminally ill patients is not a morbid, depressing job but can be an inspiring experience.

16 The tragedy is that in our death-denying society, people grow up uncomfortable in the presence of a dying patient, unable to talk to the terminally ill and lost for words when they face a grieving person.

17 We tried to use dying patients as teachers. We talked with these patients so they could teach our young medical students, social work students, nurses, and members of the clergy about one part of life that all of us eventually have to face. When we interviewed them, we had a screened window setup in which we were able to talk with them in privacy while our students observed

and listened. Needless to say this observation was done with the knowledge and agreement of our patients.

18 This teaching by dying patients who volunteered this service to us enabled them to share some of their turmoil and some of their needs with us. But perhaps more important than that, they were able to help our own young students to face the reality of death, to identify at times with our dying patients, and to become aware of their own finiteness.

19 Many of our young students who originally were petrified at the thought of facing dying patients were eventually able to express to us their own concerns, their own fears, and their own fantasies about dying. Most of our students who have been able to attend one quarter or perhaps a semester of these weekly death-and-dying seminars have learned to come to grips with their own fears of death and have ultimately become good counselors to terminally ill patients.

20 One thing this teaches us is that it would be helpful if we could rear our children with the awareness of death and of their own finiteness. Even in a death-denying society, this can be and has been done.

21 In our hospital we saw a small child with acute leukemia. She made the rounds and asked the adults, "What is it going to be like when I die?" The grown-ups responded in a variety of ways, most of them unhelpful or even harmful for this little girl who was searching for an answer. The only message she really received through the grown-ups' response was that they had a lot of fear when it came to talking about dying.

22 When the child confronted the hospital chaplain with the same question, he turned to her and asked, "What do you think it's going to be like?" She looked at him and said, "One of these days I'm going to fall asleep and when I wake up I'm going to be with Jesus and my little sister." He then said something like "That should be very beautiful." The child nodded and happily returned to play. Perhaps this is an exaggerated example, but I think it conveys how children face the reality even of their own death if the adults in their environment don't make it a frightening, horrible experience to be avoided at all costs.

23 The most forgotten people in the environment of the dying patient are the brothers and sisters of dying children. We have seen rather tragic examples of siblings who were terribly neglected during the terminal illness of a brother or a sister. Very often those children are left alone with many unanswered questions while the mother attends the dying child in the hospital and the father doesn't come home from work because he wants to visit the hospital in the evening.

24 The tragedy is that these children at home not only are anxious, lonely, and frightened at the thought of their sibling's death, but they also feel that somehow their wish for a sibling to "drop dead" (which all children have at times) is being fulfilled. When such a sibling actually dies, they feel responsible for the death, just as they do when they lose a parent during the preschool years. If these children receive no help prior to, and especially immediately after, the death of a parent or a sibling, they are likely to grow up with

abnormal fears of death and a lot of unresolved conflicts that often result in emotional illness later on in life.

25 We hope that teachers are aware of the needs of these children and can make themselves available to them in order to elicit expression of their fears, their fantasies, their needs. If they're allowed to express their anger for being neglected and their shame for having "committed a crime," then these children can be helped before they develop permanent emotional conflict.

26 A beautiful example of death education in an indirect way is expressed in a letter I received from a man who became aware of my work and felt the need to convey some of his life experiences to me. I will quote his letter verbatim because it shows what an early childhood memory can do for a man when he's faced with the imminent death of his own father.

27   Dear Dr. Ross: May I commend you and your colleagues who took part in the Conference on "death. . . ."

I am a production-line brewery worker here in Milwaukee who feels strongly on this subject. Because of your efforts, maybe one day we can all look death in the eye. . . . In reading and rereading the enclosed account of your meeting, I found myself with the urge to relate to you a personal experience of my own.

28   About six years ago, my dad was a victim of terminal cancer. He was a tough, life-loving 73-year-old father of 10 with 10 grandchildren who kept him aglow and always on the go. It just couldn't be that his time had come. The last time I saw him alive was the result of an urgent phone call from my sister. "You'd better come home as soon as possible; it's Pa."

29   The 500-mile drive to northern Minnesota wasn't the enjoyable trip that so many others had been. I learned after I arrived that he wasn't in the hospital, but at home. I also learned that "he didn't know." The doctor told the family that it was up to us to tell him or not tell him. My brother and sisters who live in the area thought it best "not to" and so advised me.

30   When I walked in on him, we embraced as we always did when we'd visit about twice or so each year. But this time it was different—sort of restrained and lacking the spirit of earlier get-togethers; and each of us, I know, sensed this difference.

31   Then, some hours later, after the usual kinds of questions and answers and talk, it was plain to me that he appeared so alone and withdrawn, almost moody or sulking. It was scary to see him just sitting there, head in hand, covering his eyes. I didn't know what to say or do. I asked if he'd care for a drink—no response. Something had to give. It all seemed so cruel. So I stepped into the kitchen and poured me a good one—and another. This was it, and if he didn't "know," he would now.

32   I went over and sat down beside and sort of facing him, and I was scared. I was always scared of my father, but it was a good kind of fear, the respectful kind. I put one hand on his shoulder and the other on his knee. I said, "Pa, you know why I came home, don't you? This is the last time we will be together." The dam burst. He threw his arms around me, and just hung on.

33   And here's the part I'll never forget and yet always cherish. I remember when our tears met, I recalled, in a sort of vivid flashback, a time 30 years before when I was five or six and he took me out into the woods to pick

hazelnuts. My very first big adventure! I remembered being afraid of the woods. Afraid of bears or monsters or something that would eat me up. But even though I was afraid, I at the same time was brave, because my big strong daddy was with me.

34   Needless to say, thanks to that hazelnut hunt, I knew how my dad was feeling at that moment. And I could only hope that I gave him some small measure of courage; the kind he had given me. I do know he was grateful and appreciated my understanding. As I remember, he regained his composure and authority enough to scold *me* for crying. It was at the kitchen table, after a couple or three fingers of brandy, that we talked and reminisced and planned. I would even guess he was eager to start a long search for his wife, who also had known how to die. . . .

35 What I am trying to convey is that everything depends on the way we rear our children. If we help them to face fear and show them that through strength and sharing we can overcome even the fear of dying, then they will be better prepared to face any kind of crisis that might confront them, including the ultimate reality of death.

VOCABULARY

terminally (2)	convey (13)
finiteness (5)	morbid (15)
impending (12)	elicit (25)

QUESTIONS ON CONTENT

1. What is the ultimate purpose of Dr. Kubler Ross's essay? In which paragraph is that purpose stated?
2. How many stages does a terminally ill person go through? What are these stages?
3. What do the dying patients of Dr. Kubler Ross's study teach the medical students, social work students, nurses, and members of the clergy?
4. What is the purpose of relating the story about the little girl who is dying of leukemia?
5. According to Dr. Kubler Ross, who are often the most neglected people during a terminal illness? Why?
6. What is the purpose of including the letter from a man whose father had died?

QUESTIONS ON FORM

1. Dr. Kubler Ross's essay is more than a division of dying; it contains four segments. What is the topic of each segment?
2. Throughout the essay, snatches of personal conversation are re-created. What is the effect?

SUGGESTIONS FOR WRITING

1. Write a five-hundred-word essay describing one of the following:
   (a) the stages of falling asleep

(b) the stages a child goes through to reach maturity

(c) the stages of a love affair until marriage

2. Write an essay identifying the major stages in your personality development.

FRANCIS BACON

THE IDOLS

In his work the *Novum Organum* Francis Bacon (1561–1626), the inventor of the scientific method in England, points out four false gods that need to be eliminated from human thought habits.

1 The *Idols* and false notions which have already preoccupied the human understanding, and are deeply rooted in it, not only so beset men's minds, that they become difficult to access, but even when access is obtained, will again meet and trouble us in the instauration of the sciences, unless mankind, when forewarned, guard themselves with all possible care against them.

2 Four species of *Idols* beset the human mind: to which (for distinction's sake) we have assigned names: calling the first *Idols of the Tribe;* the second *Idols of the Den;* the third *Idols of the Market;* the fourth *Idols of the Theater.*

3 The formation of notions and axioms on the foundations of true *induction,* is the only fitting remedy, by which we can ward off and expel these *Idols.* It is however of great service to point them out. For the doctrine of *Idols* bears the same relation to the *interpretation of nature,* as that of the confutation of sophisms does to common logic.

4 The *Idols of the Tribe* are inherent in human nature, and the very tribe or race of man. For man's sense is falsely asserted to be the standard of things. On the contrary, all the perceptions, both of the senses and the mind, bear reference to man, and not to the universe, and the human mind resembles those uneven mirrors, which impart their own properties to different objects, from which rays are emitted, and distort and disfigure them.

5 The *Idols of the Den* are those of each individual. For every body (in addition to the errors common to the race of man) has his own individual den or cavern, which intercepts and corrupts the light of nature; either from his own peculiar and singular disposition, or from his education and intercourse with others, or from his reading, and the authority acquired by those whom he reverences and admires, or from a different impression produced on the mind, as it happens to be preoccupied and predisposed, or equable and tranquil, and the like: so that the spirit of man (according to its several dispositions) is variable, confused, and as it were actuated by chance; and Heraclitus[1] said well that men search for knowledge in lesser worlds and not in the greater or common world.

6 There are also *Idols* formed by the reciprocal intercourse and society of

---

[1]Greek philosopher of the sixth century B.C.—Ed.

man with man, which we call *Idols of the Market,* from the commerce and association of men with each other. For men converse by means of language; but words are formed at the will of the generality; and there arises from a bad and unapt formation of words a wonderful obstruction to the mind. Nor can the definitions and explanations, with which learned men are wont to guard and protect themselves in some instances, afford a complete remedy: words still manifestly force the understanding, throw everything into confusion, and lead mankind into vain and innumerable controversies and fallacies.

7 Lastly there are *Idols* which have crept into men's minds from the various dogmas of peculiar systems of philosophy, and also from the perverted rules of demonstration, and these we denominate *Idols of the Theater.* For we regard all the systems of philosophy hitherto received or imagined, as so many plays brought out and performed, creating fictitious and theatrical worlds. Nor do we speak only of the present systems, or of the philosophy and sects of the ancients, since numerous other plays of a similar nature can be still composed and made to agree with each other, the causes of the most opposite errors being generally the same. Nor, again, do we allude merely to the general systems, but also to many elements and axioms of sciences, which have become inveterate by tradition, implicit credence and neglect. We must, however, discuss each species of *Idols* more fully and distinctly in order to guard the human understanding against them.

VOCABULARY

beset (1)	reciprocal (6)
instauration (1)	wont (6)
axioms (3)	dogmas (7)
induction (3)	denominate (7)
confutation (3)	sects (7)
sophisms (3)	inveterate (7)
inherent (4)	implicit (7)
predisposed (5)	credence (7)
equable (5)	

QUESTIONS ON CONTENT

1. Exactly what is being divided in this essay? Why does Bacon use the term "idols"?
2. Using your own words, describe each idol in the order listed by Bacon. Supply an example for each from your own experience.
3. According to Bacon, what is the remedy for all these idols? How will this remedy work?
4. Compare Bacon's division with some more contemporary ideas on the same subject. Is his essay still valid or is it out of date? Give reasons for your answer.

QUESTIONS ON FORM

1. What connection is there between Bacon's thought and his style?
2. Point out specific words or phrases to show that Bacon's style is archaic.

3. What method of thinking does Bacon use in order to conclude that "idols" preoccupy the human understanding? Trace his use of the method in the essay.
4. What is the analogy used to illustrate the last idol? Explain how this analogy helps clarify the idol.

SUGGESTIONS FOR WRITING

1. Write an essay in which you divide your bad habits into three or four categories. Make sure that these categories are mutually exclusive and that they include the entire range of bad habits.
2. Write a brief report on Francis Bacon's major contributions to society. In the report, organize these contributions into separate divisions.

SYLVIA PLATH

DEATH & CO.

This poem by the American poet Sylvia Plath (1932–63) exposes the personal fears and horrors haunting a human being.

Two, of course there are two.
It seems perfectly natural now—
The one who never looks up, whose eyes are lidded
And balled, like Blake's,[1]
Who exhibits

The birthmarks that are his trademark—
The scald scar of water,
The nude
Verdigris of the condor.
I am red meat. His beak

Claps sidewise: I am not his yet.
He tells me how badly I photograph.
He tells me how sweet
The babies look in their hospital
Icebox, a simple

Frill at the neck,
Then the flutings of their Ionian[2]
Death-gowns,
Then two little feet.
He does not smile or smoke.

[1]William Blake (1757–1827), English poet of the pre-Romantic period.—Ed.
[2]Anything pertaining to the Ionians, a Hellenic people who settled in Attica about 1100 B.C.—Ed.

The other does that,
His hair long and plausive.
Bastard
Masturbating a glitter,
He wants to be loved.

I do not stir.
The frost makes a flower,
The dew makes a star,
The dead bell,
The dead bell.

Somebody's done for.

VOCABULARY

verdigris   plausive
condor

QUESTIONS ON CONTENT

1. What is the meaning of the title and how does it relate to the purpose of the poem?
2. Who are the "two" mentioned in the opening line of the poem? Who is the speaker? What is the context of the words spoken?
3. What are the characteristics of "the one who never looks up"? Support your answer with examples from the poem.
4. What are the characteristics of "the other"? Support your answer with examples from the poem.
5. What is the speaker's reaction to "Death & Co."? How do you interpret the reaction?

QUESTIONS ON FORM

1. Where does the first description end and the second begin? What word forms the connecting link between the two?
2. What is the cumulative effect of "balled" eyes, "scald scar," "verdigris of the condor," "his beak claps sidewise"?
3. How do you interpret the lines "The frost makes a flower" and "The dew makes a star"?

SUGGESTIONS FOR WRITING

1. Write a paragraph in which you describe the kind of person who writes "Death & Co." Do not judge her, but try to express how she feels.
2. In concrete prose, describe the two subjects presented by Sylvia Plath. Use imagery of your own choice to make your subjects come to life.

CAUSAL ANALYSIS

ADVICE: HOW TO WRITE A CAUSAL ANALYSIS

Some essays have as their dominant purpose the analysis of cause or effect. "Cause" refers to events that have occurred in the past; "effect" refers to consequences that will occur in the future. An essay on why some students get poor grades, which points to the failure to study, is analyzing cause. However, an essay on the consequences of failing to study for a test is analyzing effect. Both essays are said to be rhetorically developed by causal analysis, even though one focuses on cause and the other on effect. Generally, the essay asking for the analysis of cause or for the prediction of effect requires the most abstract thinking and gives students the most trouble. Causes do not parade around wearing identity tags. Moreover, even simple effects can be said to be produced by a complex of multiple causes, which the student must sift out and analyze.

Take, for instance, the straightforward enough incident of a student getting a poor grade on a test. Why did the student get a poor grade? Possibly, because he failed to study. On the other hand, perhaps the student failed to study because he thought he was doomed to failure anyway, and didn't see any point in a meaningless exertion. Why did he feel that way? Possibly, because the instructor impressed upon the class how high his standards were, and how impossible it was for anyone to pass. The instructor, in turn, may have been reacting to pressure brought by the Regents against him and his department, for having in the past given out too many high grades. The Regents, on the other hand, may have been set upon by the community because of a newspaper article that accused the University of wasting taxpayers' money by giving out cheap grades. The possibilities are virtually endless. Every cause, if traced back fanatically enough, will lead through infinite regression to the Creator himself (or herself).

It is useful, therefore, to bear in mind that there are three kinds of causes: necessary, contributory, and sufficient. A necessary cause is one that *must* be present for an effect to occur, but by itself cannot cause the occurrence of the effect. For instance, irrigation is necessary for a good crop of corn, but irrigation alone will not cause a good crop. Other factors such as adequate sunshine, good soil, and correct planting must also be present.

A contributory cause is one that *may* produce an effect, but cannot produce the effect by itself. For instance, good training may help a fighter win a bout, but that alone is not enough. The fighter also has to have sharper reflexes, more skill, and be stronger than his opponent.

A sufficient cause is one that *can* produce an effect by itself. For instance, a heart attack alone can kill, even though the person may have other problems such as an ulcer, a toothache, or a weak back.

Most causes are not sufficient; they are either contributory or necessary. Bearing this in mind will restrain you from dogmatizing about cause. For instance, the following assertions mistake a contributory cause for a sufficient one:

> Crime in America is caused by a breakdown of discipline in the family structure. In the farming days, both the father and the mother were around to supervise the upbringing and disciplining of the children. Nowadays, however, the father is away working, as is the mother, and the children are left to the schools for rearing. This breakdown of the family structure is the cause of crime.

The fragmentation of the family is probably a contributory cause of crime, but it is hardly a sufficient one. Many children reared in families where both parents work have not succumbed to crime. Simplistic thinking and writing about cause usually comes from mistaking a contributory for a sufficient cause.

1. *Make your purpose initially clear.*

For instance, the article by Bertrand Russell, "The Unhappy American Way," begins with a clear enunciation of what it intends to do.

> When I try to understand what it is that prevents so many Americans from being as happy as one might expect, it seems to me that there are two causes, of which one goes much deeper than the other.

This sort of definiteness in the opening paragraph adds a guiding focus to your essay.

2. *Be modest in your choice of a subject.*

It is difficult enough to analyze the causes of simple effects without compounding your problem through the choice of a monstrously large subject. The student, for instance, who takes it upon himself or herself to write an essay on the causes of war is already in deep trouble. Such a complex phenomenon bristles with billions of causes. Selecting a more manageable subject for causal analysis will make your task a lot easier.

3. *Concentrate on proximate, as opposed to remote, causes.*

As we pointed out earlier, it is easy in analysis of cause to become entangled in the infinite. In a series of causations, the proximate cause is the nearest cause. For instance, in the case of the student who received poor grades, the proximate cause for the poor grade was his failure to study. The remote cause was the dissatisfaction of the community with the University. Common sense should guide you in this sort of analysis; but since infinity can be unraveled out of the reason why someone purchases a popsicle, it is, as a rule of thumb, safer to stay with the proximate cause and ignore the remote.

4. *Do not dogmatize about cause.*

Institutions of learning rigorously demand that students analyze cause with caution and prudence. The reasoning is simple enough: colleges and universities are quite determined to impress their students with the complexity of the world. It is advisable, therefore, that you be modest in your claims of causation. A dogmatic statement is easy enough to dilute by interjecting qualifiers into your claims. Instead of

> The divorce rate in America is caused by the sexual revolution, with its promiscuity and ideas on free love.

you could more prudently write:

> The divorce rate in America is probably influenced by the sexual revolution, with its promiscuity and ideas on free love.

This paragraph, for instance, had it been written by a student, would no doubt draw the ire of the instructor:

> This brings me to the major cause of unhappiness, which is that most people in America act not on impulse but on some principle, and that principles upon which people act are usually based upon a false psychology and a false ethic. There is a general theory as to what makes for happiness and this theory is false. Life is conceived as a competitive struggle in which felicity consists in getting ahead of your neighbor. The joys which are not competitive are forgotten.

Yet this paragraph is from Bertrand Russell's article, "The Unhappy American Way," anthologized here, which we will read with much sagacious head nodding. Bertrand Russell was a Nobel Laureate, a mathematician, and a philosopher when he wrote this. No doubt it is unfair, but his obvious accomplishments gain for him a temporary suspension of the rules against dogmatizing. Students, however, are not readily granted such license. For the time being, anyway, we advise that you generalize about cause prudently.

examples

BERTRAND RUSSELL

from THE UNHAPPY AMERICAN WAY

In this article the British philosopher and mathematician, Bertrand Russell (1872–1970), gives two causes for the unhappiness of Americans.

1 When I try to understand what it is that prevents so many Americans from being as happy as one might expect, it seems to me that there are two causes, of which one goes much deeper than the other. The one that goes least deep is the necessity for subservience in some large organization. If you are an energetic man with strong views as to the right way of doing the job with which you are concerned, you find yourself invariably under the orders of some big man at the top who is elderly, weary and cynical. Whenever you have a bright idea, the boss puts a stopper on it. The more energetic you are and the more vision you have, the more you will suffer from the impossibility

of doing any of the things that you feel ought to be done. When you go home and moan to your wife, she tells you that you are a silly fellow and that if you became the proper sort of yes-man your income would soon be doubled. If you try divorce and remarriage it is very unlikely that there will be any change in this respect. And so you are condemned to gastric ulcers and premature old age.

2 It was not always so. When Dr. Johnson compiled his dictionary, he compiled it as he thought fit. When he felt like saying that oats is food for men in Scotland and horses in England, he said so. When he defined a fishing-rod as a stick with a fish at one end and a fool at the other, there was nobody to point out to him that a remark of this sort would damage the sale of his great work among fishermen. But if, in the present day, you are (let us say) a contributor to an encyclopedia, there is an editorial policy which is solemn, wise and prudent, which allows no room for jokes, no place for personal preferences and no tolerance for idiosyncrasies. Everything has to be flattened out except where the prejudices of the editor are concerned. To these you must conform, however little you may share them. And so you have to be content with dollars instead of creative satisfaction. And the dollars, alas, leave you sad.

3 This brings me to the major cause of unhappiness, which is that most people in America act not on impulse but on some principle, and that principles upon which people act are usually based upon a false psychology and a false ethic. There is a general theory as to what makes for happiness and this theory is false. Life is conceived as a competitive struggle in which felicity consists in getting ahead of your neighbor. The joys which are not competitive are forgotten.

4 Now, I will not for a moment deny that getting ahead of your neighbor is delightful, but it is not the only delight of which human beings are capable. There are innumerable things which are not competitive. It is possible to enjoy food and drink without having to reflect that you have a better cook and a better wine merchant than your former friends whom you are learning to cold-shoulder. It is possible to be fond of your wife and your children without reflecting how much better she dresses than Mrs. So-and-So and how much better they are at athletics than the children of that old stick-in-the-mud Mr. Such-and-Such. There are those who can enjoy music without thinking how cultured the other ladies in their women's club will be thinking them. There are even people who can enjoy a fine day in spite of the fact that the sun shines on everybody. All these simple pleasures are destroyed as soon as competitiveness gets the upper hand.

5 But it is not only competitiveness that is the trouble. I could imagine a person who has turned against competitiveness and can only enjoy after conscious rejection of the competitive element. Such a person, seeing the sunshine in the morning, says to himself, "Yes, I may enjoy this and indeed I must, for it is a joy open to all." And however bored he may become with the sunshine he goes on persuading himself that he is enjoying it because he thinks he ought to.

6 "But," you will say, "are you maintaining that our actions ought not to be governed by moral principles? Are you suggesting that every whim and every impulse should be given free rein? Do you consider that if So-and-So's nose annoys you by being too long that gives you a right to tweak it? Sir," you will continue with indignation, "your doctrine is one which would uproot all the sources of morality and loosen all the bonds which hold society together. Only self-restraint, self-repression, iron self-control make it possible to endure the abominable beings among whom we have to live. No, sir! Better misery and gastric ulcers than such chaos as your doctrine would produce!"

7 I will admit at once that there is force in this objection. I have seen many noses that I should have liked to tweak, but never once have I yielded to the impulse. But this, like everything else, is a matter of degree. If you always yield to impulse, you are mad. If you never yield to impulse, you gradually dry up and very likely become mad to boot. In a life which is to be healthy and happy, impulse, though not allowed to run riot, must have sufficient scope to remain alive and to preserve that variety and diversity of interest which is natural to a human being. A life lived on a principle, no matter what, is too narrowly determined, too systematic and uniform, to be happy. However much you care about success, you should have times when you are merely enjoying life without a thought of subsequent gain. However proud you may be, as president of a women's club, of your impeccable culture, you should not be ashamed of reading a lowbrow book if you want to. A life which is all principle is a life on rails. The rails may help toward rapid locomotion, but preclude the joy of wandering. Man spent some million years wandering before he invented rails, and his happiness still demands some reminiscence of the earlier ages of freedom.

VOCABULARY

subservience (1)	impeccable (7)
cynical (1)	locomotion (7)
idiosyncrasies (2)	preclude (7)
whim (6)	reminiscence (7)
self-repression (6)	

QUESTIONS ON CONTENT

1. What is the first cause of the unhappiness of Americans?
2. What is the second cause?
3. Russell writes: "A life which is all principle is a life on rails." How is this related to the second cause of unhappiness?
4. What is Russell's implied solution for the causes of American unhappiness?

QUESTIONS ON FORM

1. Russell states the first cause in paragraph 1. How does paragraph 2 add to the development of this first cause?

2. Russell writes: "There are even people who can enjoy a fine day in spite of the fact that the sun shines on everybody." What tone is the author using here?
3. How does Russell develop his discussion of the second cause in paragraph 4?
4. What point does paragraph 5 make? How is this point made?
5. What assumption is Russell's causal analysis of American unhappiness based on?

SUGGESTIONS FOR WRITING

1. Are Americans unhappy? Discuss this idea either pro or con and state the causes of their happiness or unhappiness.
2. Have you ever had to stifle an opinion because of possible financial repercussions? Recount the incident in an essay and relate it to Russell's first cause of American unhappiness.

JULIAN HUXLEY

WAR AS A BIOLOGICAL PHENOMENON

In this selection the English biologist Julian Huxley analyzes war and its causes from a biological perspective.

1 Whenever we tend to become completely absorbed in an enterprise or an idea, it is a good thing to stand off from it now and again and look at it from the most dispassionate point of view possible. War is no exception. Quite rightly, all our major efforts must to-day be devoted to the urgent business of making sure that we win the war[1] and win it as quickly as possible. We are for most purposes immersed in the war; however, it will not merely do no harm, but will actually be of service, if now and again we try to get outside it and to look at it as objectively as we can in long perspective.

2 The longest possible perspective is that of the biologist, to whom man is a single animal species among hundreds of thousands of others, merely one of the products (albeit the latest and the most successful) of millions of years of evolution.

3 How does war look when pinned out in the biologist's collection? In the first place, he is able to say with assurance that war is not a general law of life, but an exceedingly rare biological phenomenon. War is not the same thing as conflict or bloodshed. It means something quite definite: an organized physical conflict between groups of one and the same species. Individual disputes between members of the same species are not war, even if they involve bloodshed and death. Two stags fighting for a harem of hinds, or a man murdering another man, or a dozen dogs fighting over a bone, are not engaged in war. Competition between two different species, even if it involves physical conflict, is not war. When the brown rat was accidentally brought to Europe and proceeded to oust the black rat from most of its haunts, that was not war

[1]The war referred to is the Second World War.—Ed.

between the two species of rat; nor it is war in any but a purely metaphorical sense when we speak of making war on the malaria mosquito or the boll-weevil. Still less is it war when one species preys upon another, even when the preying is done by an organized group. A pack of wolves attacking a flock of sheep or deer, or a peregrine killing a duck, is not war. Much of nature, as Tennyson correctly said, is "red in tooth and claw"; but this only means what it says, that there is a great deal of killing in the animal world, not that war is the rule of life.

4 In point of fact, there are only two kinds of animals that habitually make war—man and ants. Even among ants war is mainly practised by one group, comprising only a few species among the tens of thousands that are known to science. They are the harvester ants, inhabitants of arid regions where there is little to pick up during the dry months. Accordingly they collect the seeds of various grasses at the end of the growing season and store them in special underground granaries in their nests. It is these reserve supplies which are the object of ant warfare. The inhabitants of one nest set out deliberately to raid the supplies of another group. According to Forel and other students of ant life, they may employ quite elaborate military tactics, and the battles generally result in heavy casualties. If the attackers win, they remove the stores grain by grain to their own nest. Ant wars never last nearly so long as human wars. One campaign observed by the American myrmecologist McCook in Penn Square in the centre of Philadelphia, lasted almost 3 weeks. The longest on record is 6½ weeks.

5 Harvesters are the only kind of ants to go in for accumulating property, as well as the chief kind to practise war. This association of property with war is interesting, as various anthropologists believe that in the human species war, or at any rate habitual and organized war, did not arise in human evolution until man had reached the stage of settled civilization, when he began to accumulate stores of grain and other forms of wealth.

6 Less deliberate wars may also occur in some other species, between communities whose nests are so close that they compete for the same food-territory. When similarly provoked conflicts occur between closely related species, the term war may perhaps be extended to them. On the other hand, the raids of the slave-making ants are not true war, but a curious combination of predation and parasitism.

7 There is another group of ants called army ants, which suggests military activity; but the phrase is really a misnomer, for these army ants are in reality simply predatory species which happen to hunt in packs: they are the wolves of the insect world, not the war-mongers.

8 So much then for war as a biological phenomenon. The facts speak for themselves. War, far from being a universal law of nature, or even a common occurrence, is a very rare exception among living creatures; and where it occurs, it is either associated with another phenomenon, almost equally rare, the amassing of property, or with territorial rights.

9 Biology can help put war in its proper perspective in another way. War has often been justified on biological grounds. The program of life, say war's

apologists, depends on the struggle for existence. This struggle is universal and results in what Darwin called "Natural Selection," and this in its turn results in the "Survival of the Fittest." Natural Selection, of course, works only in a mass way, so that those which survive in the struggle will merely have an average of fitness a little above those which perish or fail to reproduce themselves. But some of the qualities which make for success in the struggle, and so for a greater chance of survival, will certainly be inherited; and since the process continues generation after generation not merely for thousands but for millions of years, the average fitness and efficiency of the race will steadily and continuously be raised until it can be pushed no higher. In any case, say the believers in this doctrine, struggle is necessary to maintain fitness; if the pressure of competition and conflict is removed, biological efficiency will suffer, and degeneration will set in.

10 Darwin's principle of Natural Selection, based as it is on constant pressure of competition or struggle, has been invoked to justify various policies in human affairs. For instance, it was used, especially by politicians in late Victorian England, to justify the principles of *laissez-faire* and free competition in business and economic affairs. And it was used, especially by German writers and politicians from the late nineteenth century onwards, to justify militarism. War, so ran this particular version of the argument, is the form which is taken by Natural Selection and the Struggle for Existence in the affairs of the nations. Without war, the heroic virtues degenerate; without war, no nation can possibly become great or successful.

11 It turns out, however, that both the *laissez-faire* economists and the militarists were wrong in appealing to biology for justification of their policies. War is a rather special aspect of competition between members of the same species—what biologists call "intra-specific competition." It is a special case because it involves physical conflict and often the death of those who undertake it, and also because it is physical conflict not between individuals but between organized groups; yet it shares certain properties in common with all other forms of intra-specific struggle or competition. And recent studies of the way in which Natural Selection works and how the Struggle for Existence operates in different conditions have resulted in this rather surprising but very important conclusion—that intra-specific competition need not, and usually does not, produce results of any advantage to the species as a whole.

12 A couple of examples will show what I mean. In birds like the peacock or the argus pheasant, the males are polygamous—if they can secure a harem. They show off their gorgeous plumage before the hen birds in an elaborate and very striking display, at definite assembly grounds where males and females go for the purpose of finding mates. The old idea that the hen deliberately selects the male she thinks the most beautiful is putting the matter in human terms which certainly do not apply to a bird's mind; but it seems certain that the brilliant and exciting display does have an effect on the hen bird, stimulating her to greater readiness to mate. Individual male birds meet with different degrees of success in this polygamous love business: some secure quite a number of mates, others only one or a few, and some get none at all. This puts

an enormous biological premium on success: the really successful male leaves many times more descendants than the unsuccessful. Here, then, is Natural Selection working at an exceedingly high pitch of intensity to make their display plumage and display actions more effective in their business of stimulating the hens. Accordingly, in polygamous birds of this kind, we often find the display plumage developed to a fantastic extent, even so far as to be a handicap to the species as a whole. Thus the display organ of the peacock, his train of enormously over-grown tail-covert feathers, is so long and cumbersome that it is a real handicap in flight. In the argus pheasant the chief display organs are the beautifully adorned wings which the male throws up and forward in display so that he looks like a gigantic bell-shaped flower. The business of display has been so important that it has overridden the business of flying, and now the male argus pheasant can fly only with difficulty, a few feet at a time.

13 Here are two good examples of how a purely intra-specific struggle, in this case between individual rival males, can produce results which are not merely useless, but harmful to the species as a whole in its struggle for existence against its enemies and the forces of nature. In general, selection for success in reproduction reaches greater intensities than selection for individual survival, for the simple reason that reproduction implies multiplication: the individual is a single unit, but, as we have just seen for polygamous birds, success in reproduction may give the individual's characteristics a multiple representation in later generations.

14 In flowering plants, the intra-specific struggle for reproduction between different individuals often produces results which, if not directly harmful to the species, are at least incredibly wasteful. We need only think of the fantastic profusion of bloom on flowering trees like dogwood or hawthorn or catalpa, or the still more fantastic profusion of pollen in trees which rely on fertilization by the wind, like pine and fir. The individual trees are competing for the privilege of surviving in their descendants; the species could certainly perpetuate itself with a much more modest expenditure of living material.

15 One final example. Naturalists have often noted the almost unbelievable perfection of the protective resemblance of certain insects to their surroundings. The most extraordinary cases are the resemblances of various butterflies, like the Kallima, to dead leaves. Not only do the folded wings perfectly resemble a dead life in shape and colour, not only do they have a projection to imitate the stalk, and dark lines which perfectly simulate the veins, but some even go so far as to be marked with imitation mould-spots and holes!

16 Now, in all butterflies the survival of the species depends to a preponderant degree on the capacity of the defenceless and juicy caterpillar and chrysalis to survive. Selection presses with much greater intensity on the larval and pupal stages than on the adult. Furthermore, there is some sort of balance between the number of adults which survive to reproduce themselves and the intensity of selection which presses on the next generation of caterpillars. If more adults reproduce, there will be many more caterpillars, and they will be more easily found by their enemies, especially the tiny parasitic wasps which

lay eggs inside the caterpillars, the eggs growing into grubs which devour the unfortunate animals from within. Conversely, if fewer adults reproduce, there are many fewer caterpillars, but each of them has a better chance of surviving to the butterfly stage. Accordingly, the protection of the adults is, from the point of view of the species, a secondary matter. Of course they must be protected sufficiently well for a reasonable number to survive and reproduce, but after this it is quite unimportant—for the species—if a slightly higher or a slightly lower proportion survives.

17 It is unimportant for the species but it remains important for the individual. If one kind of adult is better protected than another, it will automatically leave a higher average number of offspring; and so the intra-specific struggle for reproduction among the individual adult butterflies will continue to push any protective devices they possess on toward ever greater efficiency, even though this may be quite immaterial to the survival of the species. The perfection of the Kallima's resemblance to a dead leaf is one of the marvels of nature; not the least marvelous part of it is that it is of no value to the species as a whole.

18 On the other hand, intra-specific competition and struggle need not always lead to results which are useless to the species. The competition between individuals may concern qualities which are also useful in the struggle of the species against its enemies, as in deer or zebra or antelope—the same extra turn of speed which gives one individual an advantage over another in escaping from wolf or lion or cheetah will also stand the whole species in good stead. Or it may concern qualities which help the species in surviving in a difficult environment; an extra capacity for resisting drought in an individual cactus or yucca will help the species in colonizing new and more arid regions. It will not be useless or harmful to the species unless the competition is directed solely or mainly against other individuals like itself.

19 Furthermore, the results will differ according to conditions. When there is competition for mates among male birds, it will become really intense only when polygamy prevails and the advantage of success is therefore multiplied. Monogamous birds also stimulate their mates with a display of bright plummage, but in this case the display plumage is never developed to a pitch at which it is actually harmful in the general struggle for existence; the balance is struck at a different level.

20 All these considerations apply to war. In the first place it is obvious that war is an example of intra-specific competition—it is a physical conflict between groups within the same species. As such, it might be not merely useless but harmful to the species as a whole—a drag on the evolutionary progress of humanity. But, further, it might turn out to be harmful in some conditions and not in others. This indeed seems to be the truth. Those who say that war is always and inevitably harmful to humanity are indulging in an unjustified generalization (though not nearly so unjustified as the opposite generalization of the militarists who say that war is both necessary and beneficial to humanity). Warfare between peoples living on the tribal level of early barbarism may quite possibly have been on balance a good thing for the

species—by encouraging the manly virtues, by mixing the heritage of otherwise closed communities through the capture of women, by keeping down excessive population-pressure, and in other ways. War waged by small professional armies according to a professional code was at least not a serious handicap to general progress. But long-continued war in which the civilian population is starved, oppressed, and murdered and whole countries are laid waste, as in the Thirty Years War—that is harmful to the species; and so is total war in the modern German sense in which entire populations may be enslaved and brutalized, as with Poland or Greece to-day, whole cities smashed, like Rotterdam, the resources of large regions deliberately destroyed, as in the Ukraine. The more total war becomes, both intensively, as diverting more of the energies of the population from construction to destruction, and extensively, as involving more and more of the countries of the globe, the more of a threat does it become to the progress of the human species. As H. G. Wells and many others have urged, it might even turn back the clock of civilization and force the world into another Dark Age. War of this type is an intra-specific struggle from which nobody, neither humanity at large nor any of the groups engaged in the conflict, can really reap any balance of advantage, though of course we may snatch particular advantages out of the results of war.

21 But it is one thing to demonstrate that modern war is harmful to the species, another thing to do something about abolishing it. What has the biologist to say to those who assert that war is inevitable, since, they say, it is a natural outcome of human nature and human nature cannot possibly be changed?

22 To this the biologist can give a reassuring answer. War is not an inevitable phenomenon of human life; and when objectors of this type talk of human nature they really mean the expression of human nature, and this can be most thoroughly changed.

23 As a matter of observable fact, war occurs in certain conditions, not in others. There is no evidence of prehistoric man's having made war, for all his flint implements seem to have been designed for hunting, for digging, or for scraping hides; and we can be pretty sure that even if he did, any wars between groups in the hunting stage of human life would have been both rare and mild. Organized warfare is most unlikely to have begun before the stage of settled civilization. In man, as in ants, war in any serious sense is bound up with the existence of accumulations of property to fight about.

24 However, even after man had learned to live in cities and amass property, war does not seem to have been inevitable. The early Indus civilization, dating from about 3000 B.C, reveals no traces of war. There seem to have been periods in early Chinese history, as well as in the Inca civilization in Peru, in which war was quite or almost absent.

25 As for human nature, it contains no specific war instinct, as does the nature of harvester ants. There is in man's make-up a general aggressive tendency, but this, like all other human urges, is not a specific and unvarying

instinct; it can be moulded into the most varied forms. It can be canalized into competitive sport, as in our own society, or as when certain Filipino tribes were induced to substitute football for head-hunting. It can be sublimated into non-competitive sport, like mountain-climbing, or into higher types of activity altogether, like exploration or research or social crusades.

26 There is no theoretical obstacle to the abolition of war. But do not let us delude ourselves with the idea that this will be easy. The first step needed is the right kind of international machinery. To invent that will not be particularly simple: sanctions against aggressors, the peaceful reconciliation of national interests in a co-operative international system, an international police force—we can see in principle that these and other necessary bits of anti-war machinery are possible, but it will take a great deal of hard thinking to design them so that they will really work.

27 The second step is a good deal more difficult. It is to find what William James called a "moral equivalent for war," while at the same time reducing the reservoir of potential aggressiveness which now exists in every powerful nation. This is a psychological problem. Thanks to Freud and modern psychology in general, we are now beginning to understand how the self-assertive impulses of the child may be frustrated and repressed in such a way as to drive them underground. There in the subconscious they may persist in the form of crude urges to aggression and cruelty, which are all the more dangerous for not being consciously recognized.

28 To prevent the accumulation of this store of psychological dynamite and to find ways in which our self-assertive impulses can issue along conscious and constructive channels is a big job. It means a better structure of social and family life, one which does not inflict such frustration on the growing human personality; it means a new approach to education; it means providing outlets in the form of physical or mental adventure for the impulses which would otherwise be unused even if not repressed. It is a difficult task; but by no means an impossible one.

29 Thus in the perspective of biology war first dwindles to the status of a rare curiosity. Further probing, however, makes it loom larger again. For one thing, it is a form of intra-specific struggle, and as such may be useless or even harmful to the species as a whole. Then we find that one of the very few animal species which make war is man; and man is to-day not merely the highest product of evolution, but the only type still capable of real evolutionary progress. And war, though it need not always be harmful to the human species and its progress, indubitably is so when conducted in the total fashion which is necessary in this technological age. Thus war is not merely a human problem; it is a biological problem of the broadest scope, for on its abolition may depend life's ability to continue the progress which it has slowly but steadily achieved through more than a thousand million years.

30 But the biologist can end on a note of tempered hope. War is not inevitable for man. His aggressive impulses *can* be canalized into other outlets; his political machinery *can* be designed to make war less likely. These

things *can* be done: but to do them will require a great deal of hard thinking and hard work. While waging this particular war with all our might, we have a duty to keep a corner of our minds open, engaged on the job of thinking out ways and means of preventing war in general in the future.

VOCABULARY

myrmecologist (4)	preponderant (16)
predation (6)	chrysalis (16)
parasitism (6)	conversely (16)
misnomer (7)	immaterial (17)
degeneration (9)	monogamous (19)
laissez-faire (10)	sanctions (26)
polygamous (12)	tempered (30)

QUESTIONS ON CONTENT

1. How does war differ from conflict or bloodshed? What is the definition of war used by the author?
2. Which are the only two animals that make war?
3. What is the association between war and property? What other characteristic is also associated with war?
4. What argument is frequently used to justify war? How is this argument refuted?
5. According to the author, what two steps are needed to abolish war?

QUESTIONS ON FORM

1. What is the purpose of paragraph 3?
2. What function do both paragraphs 8 and 21 serve in this analysis?
3. In paragraph 10 the author points out that natural selection has been used by Victorian politicians to justify *laissez-faire* and by German writers to justify militarism. What is the point of this observation? How does it relate to his analysis?
4. The author writes in paragraph 11 that intra-specific competition "need not, and usually does not, produce results of any advantage to the species as a whole." How does he prove this point? What value does it have for his analysis?
5. Paragraph 15 begins: "One final example." Is this a sentence? What function does it have in the paragraph?

SUGGESTIONS FOR WRITING

1. The author writes: "The business of display has been so important that it has overridden the business of flying, and now the male argus pheasant can fly only with difficulty, a few feet at a time." Discuss this as a metaphor that might apply to the effects of war on man.
2. Discuss the author's analysis of war, breaking his argument down into its various parts. Analyze his use of examples and comment on their effectiveness.

MERVYN CADWALLADER

MARRIAGE AS A WRETCHED INSTITUTION

Taking the position that the marriage contract, as originally conceived in Western Europe, was never meant to carry the lifelong load of highly emotional romantic freight that we pile on it, the author suggests that marriage as an institution is doomed to wretchedness unless we find new alternatives to the present mode of marriage alliances.

1 Our society expects us all to get married. With only rare exceptions we all do just that. Getting married is a rather complicated business. It involves mastering certain complex hustling and courtship games, the rituals and the ceremonies that celebrate the act of marriage, and finally the difficult requirements of domestic life with a husband or wife. It is an enormously elaborate round of activity, much more so than finding a job, and yet while many resolutely remain unemployed, few remain unmarried.

2 Now all this would not be particularly remarkable if there were no question about the advantages, the joys, and the rewards of married life, but most Americans, even young Americans, know or have heard that marriage is a hazardous affair. Of course, for all the increase in divorce, there are still young marriages that work, unions made by young men and women intelligent or fortunate enough to find the kind of mates they want, who know that they want children and how to love them when they come, or who find the artful blend between giving and receiving. It is not these marriages that concern us here, and that is not the trend in America today. We are concerned with the increasing number of others who, with mixed intentions and varied illusions, grope or fling themselves into married disaster. They talk solemnly and sincerely about working to make their marriage succeed, but they are very aware of the countless marriages they have seen fail. But young people in particular do not seem to be able to relate the awesome divorce statistics to the probability of failure of their own marriage. And they rush into it, in increasing numbers, without any clear idea of the reality that underlies the myth.

3 Parents, teachers, and concerned adults all counsel against premature marriage. But they rarely speak the truth about marriage as it really is in modern middle-class America. The truth as I see it is that contemporary marriage is a wretched institution. It spells the end of voluntary affection, of love freely given and joyously received. Beautiful romances are transmuted into dull marriages, and eventually the relationship becomes constricting, corrosive, grinding, and destructive. The beautiful love affair becomes a bitter contract.

4 The basic reason for this sad state of affairs is that marriage was not designed to bear the burdens now being asked of it by the urban American middle class. It is an institution that evolved over centuries to meet some very

specific functional needs of a nonindustrial society. Romantic love was viewed as tragic, or merely irrelevant. Today it is the titillating prelude to domestic tragedy, or, perhaps more frequently, to domestic grotesqueries that are only pathetic.

5 Marriage was not designed as a mechanism for providing friendship, erotic experience, romantic love, personal fulfillment, continuous lay psychotherapy, or recreation. The Western European family was not designed to carry a lifelong load of highly emotional romantic freight. Given its present structure, it simply has to fail when asked to do so. The very idea of an irrevocable contract obligating the parties concerned to a lifetime of romantic effort is utterly absurd.

6 Other pressures of the present era have tended to overburden marriage with expectations it cannot fulfill. Industrialized, urbanized America is a society which has lost the sense of community. Our ties to our society, to the bustling multitudes that make up this dazzling kaleidoscope of contemporary America, are as formal and as superficial as they are numerous. We all search for community, and yet we know that the search is futile. Cut off from the support and satisfactions that flow from community, the confused and searching young American can do little but place all of his bets on creating a community in microcosm, his own marriage.

7 And so the ideal we struggle to reach in our love relationship is that of complete candor, total honesty. Out there all is phony, but within the romantic family there are to be no dishonest games, no hypocrisy, no misunderstanding. Here we have a painful paradox, for I submit that total exposure is probably always mutually destructive in the long run. What starts out as a tender coming together to share one's whole person with the beloved is transmuted by too much togetherness into attack and counterattack, doubt, disillusionment, and ambivalence. The moment the once-upon-a-time lover catches a glimpse of his own hatred, something precious and fragile is shattered. And soon another brave marriage will end.

8 The purposes of marriage have changed radically, yet we cling desperately to the outmoded structures of the past. Adult Americans behave as though the more obvious the contradiction between the old and the new, the more sentimental and irrational should be their advice to young people who are going steady or are engaged. Our schools, both high schools and colleges, teach sentimental rubbish in their marriage and family courses. The texts make much of a posture of hard-nosed objectivity that is neither objective nor hard-nosed. The basic structure of Western marriage is never questioned, alternatives are not proposed or discussed. Instead, the prospective young bride and bridegroom are offered housekeeping advice and told to work hard at making their marriage succeed. The chapter on sex, complete with ugly diagrams of the male and female genitals, is probably wedged in between a chapter on budgets and life insurance. The message is that if your marriage fails, you have been weighed in the domestic balance and found wanting. Perhaps you did not master the fifth position for sexual intercourse, or maybe you bought cheap term life rather than a preferred policy with income

protection and retirement benefits. If taught honestly, these courses would alert the teenager and young adult to the realities of matrimonial life in the United States and try to advise them on how to survive marriage if they insist on that hazardous venture.

9 But teen-agers and young adults do insist upon it in greater and greater numbers with each passing year. And one of the reasons they do get married with such astonishing certainty is because they find themselves immersed in a culture that is preoccupied with and schizophrenic about sex. Advertising, entertainment, and fashion are all designed to produce and then to exploit sexual tension. Sexually aroused at an early age and asked to postpone marriage until they become adults, they have no recourse but to fill the intervening years with courtship rituals and games that are supposed to be sexy but sexless. Dating is expected to culminate in going steady, and that is the beginning of the end. The dating game hinges on an important exchange. The male wants sexual intimacy, and the female wants social commitment. The game involves bartering sex for security amid the sweet and heady agitations of a romantic entanglement. Once the game reaches the going-steady stage, marriage is virtually inevitable. The teen-ager finds himself driven into a corner, and the one way to legitimize his sex play and assuage the guilt is to plan marriage.

10 Another reason for the upsurge in young marriages is the real cultural break between teen-agers and adults in our society. This is a recent phenomenon. In my generation there was no teen culture. Adolescents wanted to become adults as soon as possible. The teen-age years were a time of impatient waiting, as teen-age boys tried to dress and act like little men. Adolescents sang the adults' songs ("South of the Border," "The Music Goes Round and Round," "Mairzy Doats"—notice I didn't say anything about the quality of the music), saw their movies, listened to their radios, and waited confidently to be allowed in. We had no money, and so there was no teen-age market. There was nothing to do then but get it over with. The boundary line was sharp, and you crossed it when you took your first serious job, when you passed the employment test.

11 Now there is a very definite adolescent culture, which is in many ways hostile to the dreary culture of the adult world. In its most extreme form it borrows from the beats and turns the middle-class value system inside out. The hip teen-ager on Macdougal Street or Telegraph Avenue can buy a costume and go to a freak show. It's fun to be an Indian, a prankster, a beat, or a swinging troubadour. He can get stoned. That particular trip leads to instant mysticism.

12 Even in less extreme form, teen culture is weighted against the adult world of responsibility. I recently asked a roomful of eighteen-year-olds to tell me what an adult is. Their deliberate answer, after hours of discussion, was that an adult is someone who no longer plays, who is no longer playful. Is Bob Dylan an adult? No, never! Of course they did not want to remain children, or teens, or adolescents; but they did want to remain youthful, playful, free of squares, and free of responsibility. The teen-ager wants to be old enough to

drive, drink, fornicate, and travel. He does not want to get pushed into square maturity. He wants to drag the main, be a surf bum, a ski bum, or dream of being a bum. He doesn't want to go to Vietnam, or to IBM, or to buy a split-level house in Knotty Pines Estates.

13 This swing away from responsibility quite predictably produces friction between the adolescent and his parents. The clash of cultures is likely to drive the adolescent from the home, to persuade him to leave the dead world of his parents and strike out on his own. And here we find the central paradox of young marriages. For the only way the young person can escape from his parents is to assume many of the responsibilities that he so reviles in the lifestyle of his parents. He needs a job and an apartment. And he needs some kind of emotional substitute, some means of filling the emotional vacuum that leaving home has caused. And so he goes steady, and sooner rather than later, gets married to a girl with similar inclinations.

14 When he does this, he crosses the dividing line between the cultures. Though he seldom realizes it at the time, he has taken the first step to adulthood. Our society does not have a conventional "rite of passage." In Africa the Masai adolescent takes a lion test. He becomes an adult the first time he kills a lion with a spear. Our adolescents take the domesticity test. When they get married they have to come to terms with the system in one way or another. Some brave individuals continue to fight it. But most simply capitulate.

15 The cool adolescent finishing school or starting college has a skeptical view of virtually every institutional sector of his society. He knows that government is corrupt, the military dehumanizing, the corporations rapacious, the churches organized hypocrisy, and the schools dishonest. But the one area that seems to be exempt from his cynicism is romantic love and marriage. When I talk to teen-agers about marriage, that cool skepticism turns to sentimental dreams right out of *Ladies' Home Journal* or the hard-hitting pages of *Readers' Digest*. They all mouth the same vapid platitudes about finding happiness through sharing and personal fulfillment through giving (each is to give 51 percent). They have all heard about divorce, and most of them have been touched by it in some way or another. Yet they insist that their marriage will be different.

16 So, clutching their illusions, young girls with ecstatic screams of joy lead their awkward brooding boys through the portals of the church into the land of the Mustang, Apartment 24, Macy's, Sears, and the ubiquitous drive-in. They have become members in good standing of the adult world.

17 The end of most of these sentimental marriages is quite predictable. They progress, in most cases, to varying stages of marital ennui, depending on the ability of the couple to adjust to reality; most common are (1) a lackluster standoff, (2) a bitter business carried on for the children, church, or neighbors, or (3) separation and divorce, followed by another search to find the right person.

18 Divorce rates have been rising in all Western countries. In many countries the rates are rising even faster than in the United States. In 1910 the

divorce rate for the United States was 87 per 1000 marriages. In 1965 the rate had risen to an estimated figure of well over 300 per 1000 in many parts of the country. At the present time some 40 percent of all brides are between the ages of fifteen and eighteen; half of these marriages break up within five years. As our population becomes younger and the age of marriage continues to drop, the divorce rate will rise to significantly higher levels.

19 What do we do, what can we do, about this wretched and disappointing institution? In terms of the immediate generation, the answer probably is, not much. Even when subjected to the enormous strains I have described, the habits, customs, traditions, and taboos that make up our courtship and marriage cycle are uncommonly resistant to change. Here and there creative and courageous individuals can and do work out their own unique solutions to the problem of marriage. Most of us simply suffer without understanding and thrash around blindly in an attempt to reduce the acute pain of a romance gone sour. In times, all of these individual actions will show up as a trend away from the old and toward the new, and the bulk of sluggish moderates in the population will slowly come to accept this trend as part of social evolution. Clearly, in middle-class America, the trend is ever toward more romantic courtship and marriage, earlier premarital sexual intercourse, earlier first marriages, more extramarital affairs, earlier first divorces, more frequent divorces and remarriages. The trend is away from stable lifelong monogamous relationships toward some form of polygamous male-female relationship. Perhaps we should identify it as serial or consecutive polygamy, simply because Americans in significant numbers are going to have more than one husband or more than one wife. Attitudes and laws that make multiple marriages (in sequence, of course) difficult for the romantic and sentimental among us are archaic obstacles that one learns to circumvent with the aid of weary judges and clever attorneys.

20 Now, the absurdity of much of this lies in the fact that we pretend that marriages of short duration must be contracted for life. Why not permit a flexible contract perhaps for one to two or more years, with periodic options to renew? If a couple grew disenchanted with their life together, they would not feel trapped for life. They would not have to carry about the stigma of marital failure, like the mark of Cain on their foreheads. Instead of a declaration of war, they could simply let their contract lapse, and while still friendly, be free to continue their romantic quest. Sexualized romanticism is now so fundamental to American life—and is bound to become even more so—that marriage will simply have to accommodate itself to it in one way or another. For a great proportion of us it already has.

21 What of the children in a society that is moving inexorably toward consecutive plural marriages? Under present arrangements in which marriages are ostensibly lifetime contracts and then are dissolved through hypocritical collusions or messy battles in court, the children do suffer. Marriage and divorce turn lovers into enemies, and the child is left to thread his way through the emotional wreckage of his parents' lives. Financial support of the children, mere subsistence, is not really a problem in a society as affluent as

ours. Enduring emotional support of children by loving, healthy, and friendly adults is a serious problem in America, and it is a desperately urgent problem in many families where divorce is unthinkable. If the bitter and poisonous denouement of divorce could be avoided by a frank acceptance of short-term marriages, both adults and children would benefit. Any time husbands and wives and ex-husbands and ex-wives treat each other decently, generously, and respectfully, their children will benefit.

22 The braver and more critical among our teen-agers and youthful adults will still ask, But if the institution is so bad, why get married at all? This is a tough one to deal with. The social pressures pushing any couple who live together into marriage are difficult to ignore even by the most resolute rebel. It can be done, and many should be encouraged to carry out their own creative experiments in living together in a relationship that is wholly voluntary. If the demands of society to conform seem overwhelming, the couple should know that simply to be defined by others as married will elicit married-like behavior in themselves, and that is precisely what they want to avoid.

23 How do you marry and yet live like gentle lovers, or at least like friendly roommates? Quite frankly, I do not know the answer to that question.

VOCABULARY

titillating (4)	platitudes (15)
grotesqueries (4)	ubiquitous (16)
kaleidoscope (6)	ennui (17)
microcosm (6)	taboos (19)
ambivalence (7)	stigma (20)
schizophrenic (9)	inexorably (21)
reviles (13)	collusions (21)
rapacious (15)	affluent (21)
cynicism (15)	denouement (21)
vapid (15)	elicit (22)

QUESTIONS ON CONTENT

1. The author labels contemporary marriage "a wretched institution." What evidence does he provide in support of such a label? Do you agree? If so, can you add further evidence?
2. In what paragraph does the author start giving reasons for the wretchedness of marriage? How would you summarize these reasons?
3. According to Cadwallader, marriage is "an institution that evolved over centuries to meet some very specific functional needs of a nonindustrial society." Since the author does not mention any of these needs, can you supply some from your knowledge of history?
4. What are the reasons given for the fact that, despite the failure of so many marriages, teen-agers and young adults continue to get married?
5. Does Cadwallader offer some solutions to the problem of the wretchedness of marriage? What are his solutions? Do you agree with him? What alternatives do you suggest?

QUESTIONS ON FORM

1. The author often provides verbal links as he moves from one idea to the next. What are some of these links?
2. What are the connotations of the allusions in paragraph 12 to Bob Dylan, IBM, and Knotty Pines?
3. Explain the paradox in paragraph 13.
4. In paragraph 15, what point of view does the author communicate?
5. What is the effect of ending the essay with an unanswered question?

SUGGESTIONS FOR WRITING

1. Write a five-hundred-word essay entitled, "Marriage as a Blessed Institution." Provide evidence that contradicts Cadwallader's view.
2. In five hundred words state the major causes for the excess of unsuccessful marriages today. Begin with a thesis, as for instance: "Marriages today fail because society has failed."

JOHN M. DARLEY AND BIBB LATANÉ

WHY PEOPLE DON'T HELP IN A CRISIS

This essay examines the apparent indifference of passers-by to individuals who are being mugged, murdered, or otherwise endangered. John M. Darley and Bibb Latané are university psychologists, the former at Princeton and the latter at Ohio State. Their joint study, "The Unresponsive Bystander: Why Doesn't He Help?," won the thousand-dollar Socio-Psychological Prize awarded by the American Association for the Advancement of Science in 1968. This essay resulted from their study.

1 Kitty Genovese is set upon by a maniac as she returns home from work at 3 A.M. Thirty-eight of her neighbors in Kew Gardens, N.Y., come to their windows when she cries out in terror; not one comes to her assistance, even though her assailant takes half an hour to murder her. No one so much as calls the police. She dies.

2 Andrew Mormille is stabbed in the head and neck as he rides in a New York City subway train. Eleven other riders flee to another car as the 17-year-old boy bleeds to death; not one comes to his assistance, even though his attackers have left the car. He dies.

3 Eleanor Bradley trips and breaks her leg while shopping on New York City's Fifth Avenue. Dazed and in shock, she calls for help, but the hurrying stream of people simply parts and flows past. Finally, after 40 minutes, a taxi driver stops and helps her to a doctor.

4 How can so many people watch another human being in distress and do nothing? Why don't they help?

5 Since we started research on bystander responses to emergencies, we have heard many explanations for the lack of intervention in such cases. "The

megalopolis in which we live makes closeness difficult and leads to the alienation of the individual from the group," says the psychoanalyst. "This sort of disaster," says the sociologist, "shakes the sense of safety and sureness of the individuals involved and causes psychological withdrawal." "Apathy," say others. "Indifference."

6 All of these analyses share one characteristic: they set the indifferent witness apart from the rest of us. Certainly not one of us who reads about these incidents in horror is apathetic, alienated or depersonalized. Certainly these terrifying cases have no personal implications for us. We needn't feel guilty, or re-examine ourselves, or anything like that. Or should we?

7 If we look closely at the behavior of witnesses to these incidents, the people involved begin to seem a little less inhuman and a lot more like the rest of us. They were not indifferent. The 38 witnesses of Kitty Genovese's murder, for example, did not merely look at the scene once and then ignore it. They continued to stare out of their windows, caught, fascinated, distressed, unwilling to act but unable to turn away.

8 Why, then, didn't they act?

There are three things the bystander must do if he is to intervene in an emergency: *notice* that something is happening; *interpret* that event as an emergency; and decide that he has *personal responsibility* for intervention. As we shall show, the presence of other bystanders may at each stage inhibit his action.

The Unseeing Eye

9 Suppose that a man has a heart attack. He clutches his chest, staggers to the nearest building and slumps sitting to the sidewalk. Will a passerby come to his assistance? First, the bystander has to notice that something is happening. He must tear himself away from his private thoughts and pay attention. But Americans consider it bad manners to look closely at other people in public. We are taught to respect the privacy of others, and when among strangers we close our ears and avoid staring. In a crowd, then, each person is less likely to notice a potential emergency than when alone.

10 Experimental evidence corroborates this. We asked college students to an interview about their reactions to urban living. As the students waited to see the interviewer, either by themselves or with two other students, they filled out a questionnaire. Solitary students often glanced idly about while filling out their questionnaires; those in groups kept their eyes on their own papers.

11 As part of the study, we staged an emergency: smoke was released into the waiting room through a vent. Two thirds of the subjects who were alone noticed the smoke immediately, but only 25 percent of those waiting in groups saw it as quickly. Although eventually all the subjects did become aware of the smoke—when the atmosphere grew so smoky as to make them cough and rub their eyes—this study indicates that the more people present, the slower an

individual may be to perceive an emergency and the more likely he is not to see it at all.

Seeing Is Not Necessarily Believing

12 Once an event is noticed, an onlooker must decide if it is truly an emergency. Emergencies are not always clearly labeled as such; "smoke" pouring into a waiting room may be caused by fire, or it may merely indicate a leak in a steam pipe. Screams in the street may signal an assault or a family quarrel. A man lying in a doorway may be having a coronary—or he may simply be sleeping off a drunk.

13 A person trying to interpret a situation often looks at those around him to see how he should react. If everyone else is calm and indifferent, he will tend to remain so; if everyone else is reacting strongly, he is likely to become aroused. This tendency is not merely slavish conformity; ordinarily we derive much valuable information about new situations from how others around us behave. It's a rare traveler who, in picking a roadside restaurant, chooses to stop at one where no other cars appear in the parking lot.

14 But occasionally the reactions of others provide false information. The studied nonchalance of patients in a dentist's waiting room is a poor indication of their inner anxiety. It is considered embarrassing to "lose your cool" in public. In a potentially acute situation, then, everyone present will appear more unconcerned than he is in fact. A crowd can thus force inaction on its members by implying, through its passivity, that an event is not an emergency. Any individual in such a crowd fears that he may appear a fool if he behaves as though it were.

15 To determine how the presence of other people affects a person's interpretation of an emergency, Latané and Judith Rodin set up another experiment. Subjects were paid $2 to participate in a survey of game and puzzle preferences conducted at Columbia University by the Consumer Testing Bureau. An attractive young market researcher met them at the door and took them to the testing room, where they were given questionnaires to fill out. Before leaving, she told them that she would be working next door in her office, which was separated from the room by a folding room-divider. She then entered her office, where she shuffled papers, opened drawers and made enough noise to remind the subjects of her presence. After four minutes she turned on a high-fidelity tape recorder.

16 On it, the subjects heard the researcher climb up on a chair, perhaps to reach for a stack of papers on the bookcase. They heard a loud crash and a scream as the chair collapsed and she fell, and they heard her moan, "Oh, my foot . . . I . . . I . . . can't move it. Oh, I . . . can't get this . . . thing . . . off me." Her cries gradually got more subdued and controlled.

17 Twenty-six people were alone in the waiting room when the "accident" occurred. Seventy percent of them offered to help the victim. Many pushed back the divider to offer their assistance; others called out to offer their help.

18 Among those waiting in pairs, only 20 percent—8 out of 40—offered to help. The other 32 remained unresponsive. In defining the situation as a non-emergency, they explained to themselves why the other member of the pair did not leave the room; they also removed any reason for action themselves. Whatever had happened, it was believed to be not serious. "A mild sprain," some said. "I didn't want to embarrass her." In a "real" emergency, they assured us, they would be among the first to help.

The Lonely Crowd

19 Even if a person defines an event as an emergency, the presence of other bystanders may still make him less likely to intervene. He feels that his responsibility is diffused and diluted. Thus, if your car breaks down on a busy highway, hundreds of drivers whiz by without anyone's stopping to help—but if you are stuck on a nearly deserted country road, whoever passes you first is likely to stop.

20 To test this diffusion-of-responsibility theory, we simulated an emergency in which people overheard a victim calling for help. Some thought they were the only person to hear the cries; the rest believed that others heard them, too. As with the witnesses to Kitty Genovese's murder, the subjects could not *see* one another or know what others were doing. The kind of direct group inhibition found in the other two studies could not operate.

21 For the simulation, we recruited 72 students at New York University to participate in what was referred to as a "group discussion" of personal problems in an urban university. Each student was put in an individual room equipped with a set of headphones and a microphone. It was explained that this precaution had been taken because participants might feel embarrassed about discussing their problems publicly. Also, the experimenter said that he would not listen to the initial discussion, but would only ask for reactions later. Each person was to talk in turn.

22 The first to talk reported that he found it difficult to adjust to New York and his studies. Then, hesitantly and with obvious embarrassment, he mentioned that he was prone to nervous seizures when he was under stress. Other students then talked about their own problems in turn. The number of people in the "discussion" varied. But whatever the apparent size of the group—two, three or six people—only the subject was actually present; the others, as well as the instructions and the speeches of the victim-to-be, were present only on a pre-recorded tape.

23 When it was the first person's turn to talk again, he launched into the following performance, becoming louder and having increasing speech difficulties: "I can see a lot of er of er how other people's problems are similar to mine because er I mean er they're not er e-easy to handle sometimes and er I er um I think I I need er if if could er er somebody er er er give me give me a little er give me a little help here because er I er *uh* I've got a a one of the er seiz-er er things coming *on* and and er uh uh (choking sounds) . . ."

24 Eighty-five percent of the people who believed themselves to be alone

with the victim came out of their room to help. Sixty-two percent of the people who believed there was *one* other bystander did so. Of those who believed there were four other bystanders, only 31 percent reported the fit. The responsibility-diluting effect of other people was so strong that single individuals were more than twice as likely to report the emergency as those who thought other people also knew about it.

The Lesson Learned

25 People who failed to report the emergency showed few signs of the apathy and indifference thought to characterize "unresponsive bystanders." When the experimenter entered the room to end the situation, the subject often asked if the victim was "all right." Many of them showed physical signs of nervousness; they often had trembling hands and sweating palms. If anything, they seemed more emotionally aroused than did those who reported the emergency. Their emotional behavior was a sign of their continuing conflict concerning whether to respond or not.

26 Thus, the stereotype of the unconcerned, depersonalized *homo urbanus,*[1] blandly watching the misfortunes of others, proves inaccurate. Instead, we find that a bystander to an emergency is an anguished individual in genuine doubt, wanting to do the right thing but compelled to make complex decisions under pressure of stress and fear. His reactions are shaped by the actions of others—and all too frequently by their inaction.

27 And we are that bystander. Caught up by the apparent indifference of others, we may pass by an emergency without helping or even realizing that help is needed. Once we are aware of the influence of those around us, however, we can resist it. We can choose to see distress and step forward to relieve it.

VOCABULARY

assailant (1)	nonchalance (14)
megalopolis (5)	diffused (19)
alienation (5)	recruited (21)
depersonalized (6)	stereotype (26)
corroborates (10)	

QUESTIONS ON CONTENT

1. According to the authors, what are the popular reasons given for people's refusal to help in an emergency situation? Who are the sources for these views?
2. What three stages must an observer of an accident pass through before he will take the responsibility of seeking help? Do you agree that these stages are necessary? If not, what is *your* analysis of the average person's response? What other motivating factors could play a part?

[1]Latin, "man of the city."—Ed.

3. A large portion of the essay is used to prove that the presence of other people has an important bearing on an observer's reaction to an emergency. How do the authors make this view convincing?
4. What hope for all of us do the authors express in the final paragraph of the essay?

QUESTIONS ON FORM

1. What technique is used to start the essay? What are the advantages of this technique?
2. What are two examples of sentence balance in paragraph 7?
3. How many times in the essay do the authors ask a direct question? What is the purpose of this?
4. What is the general tone of the essay? What different tone might some readers expect?
5. What are the connotations of the adverb "blandly" in paragraph 26?

SUGGESTIONS FOR WRITING

1. Do a five-hundred-word causal analysis of why accidents usually attract crowds of staring people.
2. Describe an incident when you watched a person in trouble but refused to help. Analyze the reasons for your detachment.

KATHERINE ANNE PORTER

FLOWERING JUDAS

Fiction often focuses on the causes for a character's behavior. This story draws heavily on symbolism to explain the behavior of its main character, Laura.

1 Braggioni sits heaped upon the edge of a straight-backed chair much too small for him, and sings to Laura in a furry, mournful voice. Laura has begun to find reasons for avoiding her own house until the latest possible moment, for Braggioni is there almost every night. No matter how late she is, he will be sitting there with a surly, waiting expression, pulling at his kinky yellow hair, thumbing the strings of his guitar, snarling a tune under his breath. Lupe the Indian maid meets Laura at the door, and says with a flicker of a glance towards the upper room, "He waits."

2 Laura wishes to lie down, she is tired of her hairpins and the feel of her long tight sleeves, but she says to him, "Have you a new song for me this evening?" If he says yes, she asks him to sing it. If he says no, she remembers his favorite one, and asks him to sing it again. Lupe brings her a cup of chocolate and plate of rice, and Laura eats at the small table under the lamp, first inviting Braggioni, whose answer is always the same: "I have eaten, and besides, chocolate thickens the voice."

3 Laura says, "Sing, then," and Braggioni heaves himself into song. He

scratches the guitar familiarly as though it were a pet animal, and sings passionately off key, taking the high notes in a prolonged painful squeal. Laura, who haunts the markets listening to the ballad singers, and stops every day to hear the blind boy playing his reed-flute in Sixteenth of September Street, listens to Braggioni with pitiless courtesy, because she dares not smile at his miserable performance. Nobody dares to smile at him. Braggioni is cruel to everyone, with a kind of specialized insolence, but he is so vain of his talents, and so sensitive to slights, it would require a cruelty and vanity greater than his own to lay a finger on the vast cureless wound of his self-esteem. It would require courage, too, for it is dangerous to offend him, and nobody has this courage.

4 Braggioni loves himself with such tenderness and amplitude and eternal charity that his followers—for he is a leader of men, a skilled revolutionist, and his skin has been punctured in honorable warfare—warm themselves in the reflected glow, and say to each other: "He has a real nobility, a love of humanity raised above mere personal affections." The excess of this self-love has flowed out, inconveniently for her, over Laura, who, with so many others, owes her comfortable situation and her salary to him. When he is in a very good humor, he tells her, "I am tempted to forgive you for being a *gringa. Gringita!*"[1] and Laura, burning, imagines herself leaning forward suddenly, and with a sound back-handed slap wiping the suety smile from his face. If he notices her eyes at these moments he gives no sign.

5 She knows what Braggioni would offer her, and she must resist tenaciously without appearing to resist, and if she could avoid it she would not admit even to herself the slow drift of his intention. During these long evenings which have spoiled a long month for her, she sits in her deep chair with an open book on her knees, resting her eyes on the consoling rigidity of the printed page when the sight and sound of Braggioni singing threaten to identify themselves with all her remembered afflictions and to add their weight to her uneasy premonitions of the future. The gluttonous bulk of Braggioni has become a symbol of her many disillusions, for a revolutionist should be lean, animated by heroic faith, a vessel of abstract virtues. This is nonsense, she knows it now and is ashamed of it. Revolution must have leaders, and leadership is a career for energetic men. She is, her comrades tell her, full of romantic error, for what she defines as cynicism in them is merely "a developed sense of reality." She is almost too willing to say, "I am wrong, I suppose I don't really understand the principles," and afterward she makes a secret truce with herself, determined not to surrender her will to such expedient logic. But she cannot help feeling that she has been betrayed irreparably by the disunion between her way of living and her feeling of what life should be, and at times she is almost contented to rest in this sense of grievance as a private store of consolation. Sometimes she wishes to run away, but she stays. Now she longs to fly out of this room, down the narrow stairs, and into the

---

[1]*Gringa:* the feminine of *gringo,* a disparaging term used by Spanish Americans in referring to foreigners, especially Americans and English.—Ed.

street where the houses lean together like conspirators under a single mottled lamp, and leave Braggioni singing to himself.

6 Instead she looks at Braggioni, frankly and clearly, like a good child who understands the rules of behavior. Her knees cling together under sound blue serge, and her round white collar is not purposely nun-like. She wears the uniform of an idea, and has renounced vanities. She was born Roman Catholic, and in spite of her fear of being seen by someone who might make a scandal of it, she slips now and again into some crumbling little church, kneels on the chilly stone, and says a Hail Mary on the gold rosary she bought in Tehuantepec. It is no good and she ends by examining the altar with its tinsel flowers and ragged brocades, and feels tender about the battered doll-shape of some male saint whose white, lace-trimmed drawers hang limply around his ankles below the hieratic dignity of his velvet robe. She has encased herself in a set of principles derived from her early training, leaving no detail of gesture or of personal taste untouched, and for this reason she will not wear lace made on machines. This is her private heresy, for in her special group the machine is sacred, and will be the salvation of the workers. She loves fine lace, and there is a tiny edge of fluted cobweb on this collar, which is one of twenty precisely alike, folded in blue tissue paper in the upper drawer of her clothes chest.

7 Braggioni catches her glance solidly as if he had been waiting for it, leans forward, balancing his paunch between his spread knees, and sings with tremendous emphasis, weighing his words. He has, the song relates, no father and no mother, nor even a friend to console him; lonely as a wave of the sea he comes and goes, lonely as a wave. His mouth opens round and yearns sideways, his balloon cheeks grow oily with the labor of song. He bulges marvelously in his expensive garments. Over his lavender collar, crushed upon a purple necktie, held by a diamond hoop: over his ammunition belt of tooled leather worked in silver, buckled cruelly around his gasping middle: over the tops of his glossy yellow shoes Braggioni swells with ominous ripeness, his mauve silk hose stretched taut, his ankles bound with the stout leather thongs of his shoes.

8 When he stretches his eyelids at Laura she notes that his eyes are the true tawny yellow cat's eyes. He is rich, not in money, he tells her, but in power, and his power brings with it the blameless ownership of things, and the right to indulge his love of small luxuries. "I have a taste for the elegant refinements," he said once, flourishing a yellow handkerchief before her nose. "Smell that? It is Jockey Club, imported from New York." Nonetheless he is wounded by life. He will say so presently. "It is true everything turns to dust in the hand, to gall on the tongue." He sighs and his leather belt creaks like a saddle girth. "I am disappointed in everything as it comes. Everything." He shakes his head. "You, poor thing, you will be disappointed too. You are born for it. We are more alike than you realize in some things. Wait and see. Some day you will remember what I have told you, you will know that Braggioni was your friend."

9 Laura feels a slow chill, a purely physical sense of danger, a warning in

her blood that violence, mutilation, a shocking death, waits for her with lessening patience. She has translated this fear into something homely, immediate, and sometimes hesitates before crossing the street. "My personal fate is nothing, except as the testimony of a mental attitude," she reminds herself, quoting from some forgotten philosophic primer, and is sensible enough to add, "Anyhow, I shall not be killed by an automobile if I can help it."

10 "It may be true I am as corrupt, in another way, as Braggioni," she thinks in spite of herself, "as callous, as incomplete," and if this is so, any kind of death seems preferable. Still she sits quietly, she does not run. Where could she go? Uninvited she has promised herself to this place; she can no longer imagine herself as living in another country, and there is no pleasure in remembering her life before she came here.

11 Precisely what is the nature of this devotion, its true motives, and what are its obligations? Laura cannot say. She spends part of her days in Xochimilco, near by, teaching Indian children to say in English, "The cat on the mat." When she appears in the classroom they crowd about her with smiles on their wise, innocent, clay-colored faces, crying, "Good morning, my titcher!" in immaculate voices, and they make of her desk a fresh garden of flowers every day.

12 During her leisure she goes to union meetings and listens to busy important voices quarreling over tactics, methods, internal politics. She visits prisoners of her own political faith in their cells, where they entertain themselves with counting cockroaches, repenting of their indiscretions, composing their memoirs, writing out manifestoes and plans for their comrades who are still walking about free, hands in pockets, sniffing fresh air. Laura brings them food and cigarettes and a little money, and she brings messages disguised in equivocal phrases from the men outside who dare not set foot in the prison for fear of disappearing into the cells kept empty for them. If the prisoners confuse night and day, and complain, "Dear little Laura, time doesn't pass in this infernal hole, and I won't know when it is time to sleep unless I have a reminder," she brings them their favorite narcotics, and says in a tone that does not wound them with pity, "Tonight will really be night for you," and though her Spanish amuses them, they find her comforting, useful. If they lose patience and all faith, and curse the slowness of their friends in coming to their rescue with money and influence, they trust her not to repeat everything, and if she inquires, "Where do you think we can find money, or influence?" they are certain to answer, "Well, there is Braggioni, why doesn't he do something?"

13 She smuggles letters from headquarters to men hiding from firing squads in back streets in mildewed houses, where they sit in tumbled beds and talk bitterly as if all Mexico were at their heels, when Laura knows positively they might appear at the band concert in the Alameda on Sunday morning, and no one would notice them. But Braggioni says, "Let them sweat a little. The next time they may be careful. It is very restful to have them out of the way for a while." She is not afraid to knock on any door in any street after midnight, and

enter in the darkness, and say to one of these men who is really in danger: "They will be looking for you—seriously—tomorrow morning after six. Here is some money from Vicente. Go to Vera Cruz and wait."

14 She borrows money from the Roumanian agitator to give to his bitter enemy the Polish agitator. The favor of Braggioni is their disputed territory, and Braggioni holds the balance nicely, for he can use them both. The Polish agitator talks love to her over café tables, hoping to exploit what he believes is her secret sentimental preference for him, and he gives her misinformation which he begs her to repeat as the solemn truth to certain persons. The Roumanian is more adroit. He is generous with his money in all good causes, and lies to her with an air of ingenuous candor, as if he were her good friend and confidant. She never repeats anything they may say. Braggioni never asks questions. He has other ways to discover all that he wishes to know about them.

15 Nobody touches her, but all praise her gray eyes, and the soft, round under lip which promises gayety, yet is always grave, nearly always firmly closed: and they cannot understand why she is in Mexico. She walks back and forth on her errands, with puzzled eyebrows, carrying her little folder of drawings and music and school papers. No dancer dances more beautifully than Laura walks, and she inspires some amusing, unexpected ardors, which cause little gossip, because nothing comes of them. A young captain who had been a soldier in Zapata's army attempted, during a horseback ride near Cuernavaca, to express his desire for her with the noble simplicity befitting a rude folk-hero: but gently, because he was gentle. This gentleness was his defeat, for when he alighted, and removed her foot from the stirrup, and essayed to draw her down into his arms, her horse, ordinarily a tame one, shied fiercely, reared and plunged away. The young hero's horse careered blindly after his stable-mate, and the hero did not return to the hotel until rather late that evening. At breakfast he came to her table in full charro dress, gray buckskin jacket and trousers with strings of silver buttons down the legs, and he was in a humorous, careless mood. "May I sit with you?" and "You are a wonderful rider. I was terrified that you might be thrown and dragged. I should never have forgiven myself. But I cannot admire you enough for your riding!"

16 "I learned to ride in Arizona," said Laura.

17 "If you will ride with me again this morning, I promise you a horse that will not shy with you," he said. But Laura remembered that she must return to Mexico City at noon.

18 Next morning the children made a celebration and spent their playtime writing on the blackboard, "We lov ar ticher," and with tinted chalks they drew wreaths of flowers around the words. The young hero wrote her a letter: "I am a very foolish, wasteful, impulsive man. I should have first said I love you, and then you would not have run away. But you shall see me again." Laura thought, "I must send him a box of colored crayons," but she was trying to forgive herself for having spurred her horse at the wrong moment.

19 A brown, shock-haired youth came and stood in her patio one night and sang like a lost soul for two hours, but Laura could think of nothing to do about it. The moonlight spread a wash of gauzy silver over the clear spaces of the garden, and the shadows were cobalt blue. The scarlet blossoms of the Judas tree were dull purple, and the names of the colors repeated themselves automatically in her mind, while she watched not the boy, but his shadow, fallen like a dark garment across the fountain rim, trailing in the water. Lupe came silently and whispered expert counsel in her ear: "If you throw him one little flower, he will sing another song or two and go away." Laura threw the flower, and he sang a last song and went away with the flower tucked in the band of his hat. Lupe said, "He is one of the organizers of the Typographers Union, and before that he sold corridos in the Merced market, and before that, he came from Guanajuato, where I was born. I would not trust any man, but I trust least those from Guanajuato."

20 She did not tell Laura that he would be back again the next night, and the next, nor that he would follow her at a certain fixed distance around the Merced market, through the Zócolo, up Francisco I. Madero Avenue, and so along the Paseo de la Reforma to Chapultepec Park, and into the Philosopher's Footpath, still with that flower withering in his hat, and an indivisible attention in his eyes.

21 Now Laura is accustomed to him, it means nothing except that he is nineteen years old and is observing a convention with all propriety, as though it were founded on a law of nature, which in the end it might well prove to be. He is beginning to write poems which he prints on a wooden press, and he leaves them stuck like handbills in her door. She is pleasantly disturbed by the abstract, unhurried watchfulness of his black eyes which will in time turn easily towards another object. She tells herself that throwing the flower was a mistake, for she is twenty-two years old and knows better; but she refuses to regret it, and persuades herself that her negation of all external events as they occur is a sign that she is gradually perfecting herself in the stoicism she strives to cultivate against that disaster she fears, though she cannot name it.

22 She is not at home in the world. Every day she teaches children who remain strangers to her, though she loves their tender round hands and their charming opportunist savagery. She knocks at unfamiliar doors not knowing whether a friend or a stranger shall answer, and even if a known face emerges from the sour gloom of that unknown interior, still it is the face of a stranger. No matter what this stranger says to her, nor what her message to him, the very cells of her flesh reject knowledge and kinship in one monotonous word. No. No. No. She draws her strength from this one holy talismanic word which does not suffer her to be led into evil. Denying everything, she may walk anywhere in safety, she looks at everything without amazement.

23 No, repeats this firm unchanging voice of her blood; and she looks at Braggioni without amazement. He is a great man, he wishes to impress this simple girl who covers her great round breasts with thick dark cloth, and who hides long, invaluably beautiful legs under a heavy skirt. She is almost thin except for the incomprehensible fullness of her breasts, like a nursing

mother's, and Braggioni, who considers himself a judge of women, speculates again on the puzzle of her notorious virginity, and takes the liberty of speech which she permits without a sign of modesty, indeed, without any sort of sign, which is disconcerting.

24 "You think you are so cold, *gringita!* Wait and see. You will surprise yourself some day! May I be there to advise you!" He stretches his eyelids at her, and his ill-humored cat's eyes waver in a separate glance for the two points of light marking the opposite ends of a smoothly drawn path between the swollen curve of her breasts. He is not put off by that blue serge, nor by her resolutely fixed gaze. There is all the time in the world. His cheeks are bellying with the wind of song. "O girl with the dark eyes," he sings, and reconsiders. "But yours are not dark. I can change all that. O girl with the green eyes, you have stolen my heart away!" then his mind wanders to the song, and Laura feels the weight of his attention being shifted elsewhere. Singing thus, he seems harmless, he is quite harmless, there is nothing to do but sit patiently and say "No," when the moment comes. She draws a full breath, and her mind wanders also, but not far. She dares not wander too far.

25 Not for nothing has Braggioni taken pains to be a good revolutionist and a professional lover of humanity. He will never die of it. He has the malice, the cleverness, the wickedness, the sharpness of wit, the hardness of heart, stipulated for loving the world profitably. *He will never die of it.* He will live to see himself kicked out from his feeding trough by other hungry world-saviors. Traditionally he must sing in spite of his life which drives him to bloodshed, he tells Laura, for his father was a Tuscany peasant who drifted to Yucatan and married a Maya woman: a woman of race, an aristocrat. They gave him the love and knowledge of music, thus: and under the rip of his thumbnail, the strings of the instrument complain like exposed nerves.

26 Once he was called Delgadito by all the girls and married women who ran after him; he was so scrawny all his bones showed under his thin cotton clothing, and he could squeeze his emptiness to the very backbone with his two hands. He was a poet and the revolution was only a dream then; too many women loved him and sapped away his youth, and he could never find enough to eat anywhere, anywhere! Now he is a leader of men, crafty men who whisper in his ear, hungry men who wait for hours outside his office for a word with him, emaciated men with wild faces who waylay him at the street gate with a timid, "Comrade, let me tell you . . ." and they blow the foul breath from their empty stomachs in his face.

27 He is always sympathetic. He gives them handfuls of small coins from his own pocket, he promises them work, there will be demonstrations, they must join the unions and attend meetings, above all they must be on the watch for spies. They are closer to him than his own brothers, without them he can do nothing—until tomorrow, comrade!

28 Until tomorrow. "They are stupid, they are lazy, they are treacherous, they would cut my throat for nothing," he says to Laura. He has good food and abundant drink, he hires an automobile and drives in the Paseo on Sunday morning, and enjoys plenty of sleep in a soft bed beside a wife who dares not

disturb him; and he sits pampering his bones in easy billows of fat, singing to Laura, who knows and thinks these things about him. When he was fifteen, he tried to drown himself because he loved a girl, his first love, and she laughed at him. "A thousand women have paid for that," and his tight little mouth turns down at the corners. Now he perfumes his hair with Jockey Club, and confides to Laura: "One woman is really as good as another for me, in the dark. I prefer them all."

29 His wife organizes unions among the girls in the cigarette factories, and walks in picket lines, and even speaks at meetings in the evening. But she cannot be brought to acknowledge the benefits of true liberty. "I tell her I must have my freedom, net. She does not understand my point of view." Laura has heard this many times. Braggioni scratches the guitar and meditates. "She is an instinctively virtuous woman, pure gold, no doubt of that. If she were not, I should lock her up, and she knows it."

30 His wife, who works so hard for the good of the factory girls, employs part of her leisure lying on the floor weeping because there are so many women in the world, and only one husband for her, and she never knows where nor when to look for him. He told her: "Unless you can learn to cry when I am not here, I must go away for good." That day he went away and took a room at the Hotel Madrid.

31 It is this month of separation for the sake of higher principles that has been spoiled not only for Mrs. Braggioni, whose sense of reality is beyond criticism, but for Laura, who feels herself bogged in a nightmare. Tonight Laura envies Mrs. Braggioni, who is alone, and free to weep as much as she pleases about a concrete wrong. Laura has just come from a visit to the prison, and she is waiting for tomorrow with a bitter anxiety as if tomorrow may not come, but time may be caught immovably in this hour, with herself transfixed, Braggioni singing on forever, and Eugenio's body not yet discovered by the guard.

32 Braggioni says: "Are you going to sleep?" Almost before she can shake her head, he begins telling her about the May-day disturbances coming on in Morelia, for the Catholics hold a festival in honor of the Blessed Virgin, and the Socialists celebrate their martyrs on that day. "There will be two independent processions, starting from either end of town, and they will march until they meet, and the rest depends . . ." He asks her to oil and load his pistols. Standing up, he unbuckles his ammunition belt, and spreads it laden across her knees. Laura sits with the shells slipping through the cleaning cloth dipped in oil, and he says again he cannot understand why she works so hard for the revolutionary idea unless she loves some man who is in it. "Are you not in love with someone?" "No," says Laura. "And no one is in love with you?" "No." "Then it is your own fault. No woman need go begging. Why, what is the matter with you? The legless beggar woman in the Alameda has a perfectly faithful lover. Did you know that?"

33 Laura peers down the pistol barrel and says nothing, but a long, slow faintness rises and subsides in her; Braggioni curves his swollen fingers around the throat of the guitar and softly smothers the music out of it, and

when she hears him again he seems to have forgotten her, and is speaking in the hypnotic voice he uses when talking in small rooms to a listening, close-gathered crowd. Some day this world, now seemingly so composed and eternal, to the edges of every sea shall be merely a tangle of gaping trenches, or crashing walls and broken bodies. Everything must be torn from its accustomed place where it has rotted for centuries, hurled skyward and distributed, cast down again clean as rain, without separate identity. Nothing shall survive that the stiffened hands of poverty have created for the rich and no one shall be left alive except the elect spirits destined to procreate a new world cleansed of cruelty and injustice, ruled by benevolent anarchy: "Pistols are good, I love them, cannon are even better, but in the end I pin my faith to good dynamite," he concludes, and strokes the pistol lying in her hands. "Once I dreamed of destroying this city, in case it offered resistance to General Ortíz, but it fell into his hands like an overripe pear."

34 He is made restless by his own words, rises and stands waiting. Laura holds up the belt to him: "Put that on and go kill somebody in Morelia, and you will be happier," she says softly. The presence of death in the room makes her bold. "Today, I found Eugenio going into a stupor. He refused to allow me to call the prison doctor. He had taken all the tablets I brought him yesterday. He said he took them because he was bored."

35 "He is a fool, and his death is his own business," says Braggioni, fastening his belt carefully.

36 "I told him if he had waited only a little while longer, you would have got him set free," said Laura. "He said he did not want to wait."

37 "He is a fool and we are well rid of him," says Braggioni, reaching for his hat.

38 He goes away. Laura knows his mood has changed, she will not see him any more for a while. He will send word when he needs her to go on errands into strange streets, to speak to the strange faces that will appear, like clay masks with the power of human speech, to mutter their thanks to Braggioni for his help. Now she is free, and she thinks, I must run while there is time. But she does not go.

39 Braggioni enters his own house where for a month his wife has spent many hours every night weeping and tangling her hair upon her pillow. She is weeping now, and she weeps more at the sight of him, the cause of all her sorrows. He looks about the room. Nothing is changed, the smells are good and familiar, he is well acquainted with the woman who comes toward him with no reproach except grief on her face. He says to her tenderly: "You are so good, please don't cry any more, you dear good creature." She says, "Are you tired, my angel? Sit here and I will wash your feet." She brings a bowl of water, and kneeling, unlaces his shoes, and when from her knees she raises her sad eyes under her blackened lids, he is sorry for everything, and bursts into tears. "Ah, yes, I am hungry, I am tired, let us eat something together," he says, between sobs. His wife leans her head on his arm and says, "Forgive me!" and this time he is refreshed by the solemn, endless rain of her tears.

40 Laura takes off her serge dress and puts on a white linen nightgown and

goes to bed. She turns her head a little to one side, and lying still, reminds herself that it is time to sleep. Numbers tick in her brain like little clocks, soundless doors close of themselves around her. If you would sleep, you must not remember anything, the children will say tomorrow, good morning, my teacher, the poor prisoners who come every day bringing flowers to their jailor. 1–2–3–4–5—it is monstrous to confuse love with revolution, night with day, life with death—ah, Eugenio!

41 The tolling of the midnight bell is a signal, but what does it mean? Get up, Laura, and follow me: come out of your sleep, out of your bed, out of this strange house. What are you doing in this house? Without a word, without fear she rose and reached for Eugenio's hand, but he eluded her with a sharp, sly smile and drifted away. This is not all, you shall see—Murderer, he said, follow me, I will show you a new country, but it is far away and we must hurry. No, said Laura, not unless you take my hand, no; and she clung first to the stair rail, and then to the topmost branch of the Judas tree that bent down slowly and set her upon the earth, and then to the rocky ledge of a cliff, and then to the jagged wave of a sea that was not water but a desert of crumbling stone. Where are you taking me, she asked in wonder but without fear. To death, and it is a long way off, and we must hurry, said Eugenio. No, said Laura, not unless you take my hand. Then eat these flowers, poor prisoner, said Eugenio in a voice of pity, take and eat: and from the Judas tree he stripped the warm bleeding flowers, and held them to her lips. She saw that his hand was fleshless, a cluster of small white petrified branches, and his eye sockets were without light, but she ate the flowers greedily for they satisfied both hunger and thirst. Murderer! said Eugenio, and Cannibal! This is my body and my blood. Laura cried No! and at the sound of her own voice, she awoke trembling, and was afraid to sleep again.

VOCABULARY

suety (4)	stoicism (21)
premonitions (5)	opportunist (22)
vessel (5)	talismanic (22)
mottled (5)	disconcerting (23)
hieratic (6)	emaciated (26)
equivocal (12)	transfixed (31)
adroit (14)	procreate (33) ·
ingenuous (14)	anarchy (33)

QUESTIONS ON CONTENT

1. What is Laura like? Why is she in Mexico?
2. What is Braggioni like? How does he feel about the revolution?
3. The author writes: "The gluttonous bulk of Braggioni has become a symbol of her many disillusions, for a revolutionist should be lean, animated by heroic faith, a vessel of abstract virtues." What does this reveal about Laura? What does it reveal about Braggioni?

4. What is Laura's attitude toward men? What is Braggioni's attitude toward women?
5. What is the significance of the dream at the end of the story? Notice certain images related to Christ's Last Supper. Remember also that dreams can reveal a person's unconscious feelings.

QUESTIONS ON FORM

1. Examine the descriptions of Braggioni (paragraphs 1, 3, 7, 8). What animal is he associated with in these descriptions? What is the significance of this association?
2. "Braggioni loves himself with such tenderness and amplitude and eternal charity that his followers—for he is a leader of men, a skilled revolutionist, and his skin has been punctured in honorable warfare—warm themselves in the reflected glow, and say to each other: 'He has a real nobility, a love of humanity raised above mere personal affections.'"—What tone is the author using here? Explain.
3. Reread paragraph 20. Why does the author use so many place names in it? What do they contribute to the story?
4. Braggioni's wife washes his feet with water. What is the significance of this act? How does it relate to the rest of the story?
5. How is the Judas tree in the dream related to Catholic ritual?

SUGGESTIONS FOR WRITING

1. Analyze and discuss the use of religious symbolism in this story.
2. Analyze and discuss Laura's motive for living in Mexico and associating herself with the revolution.

CHAPTER WRITING ASSIGNMENTS

1. Choose one of the following terms and write an essay in which you first define the term as a dictionary would define it. Then give an extended definition, using the development most suitable for answering the question, "What is it?"
   (a) romance   (d) education
   (b) tyranny   (e) humility
   (c) adolescence (f) prejudice
2. Write an essay in which you contrast one of the following pairs of words.
   (a) jealousy—envy
   (b) liberty—license
   (c) servant—slave
   (d) democracy—demagoguery
   (e) art—craft
3. Choose one of the following subjects and develop an essay by dividing the subject into categories.
   (a) anxieties   (f) fashions
   (b) colleges   (g) children
   (c) humor   (h) books
   (d) values   (i) movies
   (e) violence
4. Write a causal analysis for one of the following conditions.
   (a) poor writing habits of today's students
   (b) lack of discipline in high schools

    (c) popularity of pack trips

    (d) growing interest in church attendance

    (e) need for prison reform

    (f) failure of rapid transit systems in major cities

    (g) need to conserve our beaches

    (h) increased rate of abortions

    (i) tendency to buy throwaway items

5. Use a personal example to support or negate one of the following theses.

    (a) People in positions that command respect can act dishonorably.

    (b) To follow your conscience is a good rule.

    (c) Money does not guarantee happiness.

    (d) Quiet moments in nature can bring extraordinary rewards.

    (e) To be alive means to be curious.

    (f) We have become a plastic nation.

6. Write a vivid description by observing the following procedure:

    (a) With notebook in hand, go to the scene of some activity. (Examples: an airport, restaurant, park, supermarket, employment office.)

    (b) Observe until you can formulate a general impression of the place.

    (c) Take notes that support your general impression (leave out the details that do not support the general impression).

    (d) Organize your notes and write the description.

What's the Right Word?
Semantics

model

KENNETH BURKE

THE SEMANTIC IDEAL ILLUSTRATED

The following is an excerpt from *The Philosophy of Literary Form*.

For our point of departure, let us take the address on an envelope:

> M........ (name)
> .... (street and number)
> .... (city or town)
> .... (state)
> .... (nation)

By filling out those few lines, you can effectively isolate one man among two billion, quite as though each individual were identified by an automobile license, with a record kept in some central bureau, like the Bertillon measurements of known criminals.

Perhaps we have exaggerated the case. The formula wouldn't work for getting an advertisement to a mid-African chieftain. Yet it can effectively isolate one of the two billion, if he happens to be among the hundreds of millions available through postal organization. The matter to be emphasized is this: In whatever areas the postal organization prevails, this brief formula generally serves to isolate the desired individual.

The formula has no orientative value in itself. It depends for its significance upon the establishment of a postal structure, as a going concern. It is like the coin in a slot machine. Given the machine, in good order, the coin will "work." The address, as a counter, works insofar as it indicates to the postal authorities what kind of operation should be undertaken. But it *assumes* an organization. Its *meaning,* then, involves the established procedures of the mails, and is in the instructions it gives for the performance of desired operations within this going concern.

The man who writes the address on an envelope may know very little about the concreteness of these operations. Likewise, the sorter who first tosses the letter into the "state" or "nation" bin will not concretely envision the act of final delivery, after the letter has been sifted down through various subclassifications, until it reaches the pouch of the mailman on his route. Any single worker, handling the letter in its various stages of transit, interprets the address as instructions for a different kind of operation. Its "totality" is in the organized interlocking of these operations themselves, whereby each "specialist," performing a "partial" act, yet contributes to the performing of a "total" act, the entire arc of the letter's transit, from insertion in the mailbox at the corner to delivery at the door.

This kind of meaning I should call a *semantic* meaning. And extending from that I should state, as the semantic ideal, the aim *to evolve a vocabulary that gives the name and address of every event in the universe.*

The above illustration suggests that ideally the semantic meaning of a word simply points to what that word is in the most precise way possible. It clarifies what a word is, but it does not take into account the subjective feelings (connotations) that the word can evoke.

advice

RICHARD K. REDFERN

A BRIEF LEXICON OF JARGON

FOR THOSE WHO WANT TO SPEAK AND WRITE VERBOSELY AND VAGUELY

Through verbal irony this "Lexicon" tells how to avoid the hideous vagueness and verbosity in much of today's bureaucratic language.

Area

1 The first rule about using *area* is simple. Put *area* at the start or end of hundreds of words and phrases. *The area of* is often useful when you want to add three words to a sentence without changing its meaning.

2 *Instead of*

civil rights
in spelling and pronunciation

problems, topics
major subjects

Say or write

the area of civil rights
in the area of spelling and pronunciation
problem areas, topic areas
major subject (*or* subject-matter)
areas

3 Second, particularly in speech, use *area* as an all-purpose synonym. After mentioning scheduled improvements in classrooms and offices, use *area* for later references to this idea. A few minutes later, in talking about the courses to be offered next term, use *area* to refer to required courses, to electives, and to both required and elective courses. Soon you can keep three or four *area*'s going and thus keep your audience alert by making them guess which idea you have in mind, especially if you insert, once or twice, a neatly disguised geographical use of *area:* "Graduate student response in this area is gratifying."

Field

4 If the temptation arises to say "clothing executive," "publishing executive," and the like, resist it firmly. Say and write "executive in the clothing field" and "executive in the field of publishing." Note that *the field of* (like *the area of*) qualifies as jargon because it adds length, usually without changing the meaning, as in "from the field of literature as a whole" and "prowess in the field of academic achievement" (which is five words longer than the "academic prowess" of plain English). With practice you can combine *field* with *area, level,* and other standbys:

5 In the sportswear field, this is one area which is growing. (Translation from context: Ski sweaters are selling well.)
[The magazine is] a valuable source of continuing information for educa-
tors at all levels and for everyone concerned with this field. (Plain English: The magazine is a valuable source of information for anyone interested in education.)

6 A master of jargon can produce a sentence so vague that it can be dropped into dozens of other articles and books: "At what levels is coverage of the field important?" Even in context (a scholarly book about the teaching of English), it is hard to attach meaning to *that* sentence!

In Terms of

7 A sure sign of the ability to speak and write jargon is the redundant use of *in terms of*. If you are a beginner, use the phrase instead of prepositions such as *in* ("The faculty has been divided in terms of opinions and attitudes") and

of ("We think in terms of elementary, secondary, and higher education"). Then move on to sentences in which you waste more than two words:

8 *Instead of* — *Say or write*

Instead of	Say or write
The Campus School expects to have three fourth grades.	In terms of the future, the Campus School expects to have three fourth grades. (5 extra words)
I'm glad that we got the response we wanted.	I'm glad that there was a response to that in terms of what we wanted. (6 extra words)

9 Emulate the masters of jargon. They have the courage to abandon the effort to shape a thought clearly:

A field trip should be defined in terms of where you are.
They are trying to get under way some small and large construction in terms of unemployment.
When we think in terms of muscles, we don't always think in terms of eyes.

Level

10 Although *level* should be well known through overuse, unobservant young instructors may need a review of some of its uses, especially if they are anxious to speak and write *on the level of* jargon. (Note the redundancy of the italicized words.)

11 *Instead of* — *Say or write*

Instead of	Say or write
She teaches fifth grade.	She teaches on the fifth grade level. (3 extra words)
Readers will find more than one meaning.	It can be read on more than one level of meaning. (4 extra words)
My students	The writers on my level of concern (5 extra words)

Long Forms

12 When the shorter of two similar forms is adequate, choose the longer; e.g., say *analyzation* (for *analysis*), *orientate* (for *orient*), *origination* (for *origin*), *summarization* (for *summary*). Besides using an unnecessary syllable or two, the long form can make your audience peevish when they know the word has not won acceptance or, at least, uneasy ("Is that a new word that I ought to know?"). If someone asks why you use *notate* instead of *note* (as in "Please notate in the space below your preference . . ."), fabricate an elaborate distinction. Not having a dictionary in his pocket, your questioner will be too polite to argue.

13 With practice, you will have the confidence to enter unfamiliar territory. Instead of the standard forms (*confirm, interpret, penalty, register,* and *scrutiny*), try *confirmate, interpretate, penalization, registrate,* and *scrutinization.*

14 You have little chance of making a name for yourself as a user of jargon unless you sprinkle your speech and writing with vogue words and phrases, both the older fashions (e.g., *aspect, background, field, level, situation*) and the newer (e.g., *escalate, relate to, share with; facility, involvement; limited, minimal*). An old favorite adds the aroma of the cliché, while a newly fashionable term proves that you are up-to-date. Another advantage of vogue words is that some of them are euphemisms. By using *limited,* for example, you show your disdain for the directness and clarity of *small,* as in "a man with a limited education" and "a limited enrollment in a very large room."

Unfortunately, some vogue expressions are shorter than standard English, but their obscurity does much to offset the defect of brevity.

15 *Instead of*

Say or write

The children live in a camp and have both classes and recreation outdoors.

The children live in a camp-type situation.

She reads, writes, and speaks German and has had four years of Latin.

She has a good foreign-language background.

Many hospitals now let a man stay with his wife during labor.

The trend is to let the father have more involvement.

16 A final word to novices: dozens of words and phrases have been omitted from this brief lexicon, but try to spot them yourselves. Practice steadily, always keeping in mind that the fundamentals of jargon—verbosity and needless vagueness—are best adorned by pretentiousness. Soon, if you feel the impulse to say, for example, that an office has one secretary and some part-time help, you will write "Administrative clerical aids implement the organizational function." Eventually you can produce sentences which mean anything or possibly nothing: "We should leave this aspect of the definition relatively operational" or "This condition is similar in regard to other instances also."

VOCABULARY

lexicon (title)	escalate (14)
jargon (title)	cliché (14)
redundant (7)	euphemism (14)
emulate (9)	novices (16)
peevish (12)	verbosity (16)

discussion

GEORGE ORWELL

POLITICS AND THE ENGLISH LANGUAGE

In the following essay the English novelist and essayist George Orwell (1903–50) attacks what he considers the worst aspects of our present use of language. Warning that a decadent written language leads to a decadent society, he asks that we renew our efforts to write good English.

1 Most people who bother with the matter at all would admit that the English language is in a bad way, but it is generally assumed that we cannot by conscious action do anything about it. Our civilization is decadent and our language—so the argument runs—must inevitably share in the general collapse. It follows that any struggle against the abuse of language is a sentimental archaism, like preferring candles to electric light or hansom cabs to aeroplanes. Underneath this lies the half-conscious belief that language is a natural growth and not an instrument which we shape for our own purposes.

2 Now, it is clear that the decline of a language must ultimately have political and economic causes: it is not due simply to the bad influence of this or that individual writer. But an effect can become a cause, reinforcing the original cause and producing the same effect in an intensified form, and so on indefinitely. A man may take to drink because he feels himself to be a failure, and then fail all the more completely because he drinks. It is rather the same thing that is happening to the English language. It becomes ugly and inaccurate because our thoughts are foolish, but the slovenliness of our language makes it easier for us to have foolish thoughts. The point is that the process is reversible. Modern English, especially written English, is full of bad habits which spread by imitation and which can be avoided if one is willing to take the necessary trouble. If one gets rid of these habits one can think more clearly, and to think clearly is a necessary first step towards political regeneration: so that the fight against bad English is not frivolous and is not the exclusive concern of professional writers. I will come back to this presently, and I hope that by that time the meaning of what I have said here will have become clearer. Meanwhile, here are five specimens of the English language as it is now habitually written.

3 These five passages have not been picked out because they are especially bad—I could have quoted far worse if I had chosen—but because they illustrate various of the mental vices from which we now suffer. They are a little below the average, but are fairly representative samples. I number them so that I can refer back to them when necessary:

(1) I am not, indeed, sure whether it is not true to say that the Milton who once seemed not unlike a seventeenth-century Shelley had not become, out of an

experience ever more bitter in each year, more alien [*sic*] to the founder of that Jesuit sect which nothing could induce him to tolerate.

Professor Harold Laski
(Essay in *Freedom of Expression*)

(2) Above all, we cannot play ducks and drakes with a native battery of idioms which prescribes such egregious collocations of vocables as the Basic *put up with* for *tolerate* or *put at a loss* for *bewilder*.

Professor Lancelot Hogben *(Interglossa)*

(3) On the one side we have the free personality: by definition it is not neurotic, for it has neither conflict nor dream. Its desires, such as they are, are transparent, for they are just what institutional approval keeps in the forefront of consciousness; another institutional pattern would alter their number and intensity; there is little in them that is natural, irreducible, or culturally dangerous. But *on the other side,* the social bond itself is nothing but the mutual reflection of these self-secure integrities. Recall the definition of love. Is not this the very picture of a small academic? Where is there a place in this hall of mirrors for either personality or fraternity?

Essay on psychology in *Politics* (New York)

(4) All the "best people" from the gentlemen's clubs, and all the frantic fascist captains, united in common hatred of Socialism and bestial horror of the rising tide of the mass revolutionary movement, have turned to acts of provocation, to foul incendiarism, to medieval legends of poisoned wells, to legalize their own destruction of proletarian organizations, and rouse the agitated petty-bourgeoisie to chauvinistic fervour on behalf of the fight against the revolutionary way out of the crisis.

Communist pamphlet

(5) If a new spirit *is* to be infused into this old country, there is one thorny and contentious reform which must be tackled, and that is the humanization and galvanization of the B.B.C. Timidity here will bespeak canker and atrophy of the soul. The heart of Britain may be sound and of strong beat, for instance, but the British lion's roar at present is like that of Bottom in Shakespeare's *Midsummer Night's Dream*—as gentle as any sucking dove. A virile new Britain cannot continue indefinitely to be traduced in the eyes or rather ears, of the world by the effete languors of Langham Place, brazenly masquerading as "standard English." When the Voice of Britain is heard at nine o'clock, better far and infinitely less ludicrous to hear aitches honestly dropped than the present priggish, inflated, inhibited, school-ma'amish arch braying of blameless bashful mewing maidens!

Letter in *Tribune*

4 Each of these passages has faults of its own, but, quite apart from avoidable ugliness, two qualities are common to all of them. The first is staleness of imagery; the other is lack of precision. The writer either has a meaning and cannot express it, or he inadvertently says something else, or he is almost indifferent as to whether his words mean anything or not. This mixture of vagueness and sheer incompetence is the most marked characteris-

tic of modern English prose, and especially of any kind of political writing. As soon as certain topics are raised, the concrete melts into the abstract and no one seems able to think of turns of speech that are not hackneyed: prose consists less and less of *words* chosen for the sake of their meaning, and more and more of *phrases* tacked together like the sections of a prefabricated hen-house. I list below, with notes and examples, various of the tricks by means of which the work of prose-construction is habitually dodged:

5 *Dying metaphors.* A newly invented metaphor assists thought by evoking a visual image, while on the other hand a metaphor which is technically "dead" (e.g. *iron resolution*) has in effect reverted to being an ordinary word and can generally be used without loss of vividness. But in between these two classes there is a huge dump of worn-out metaphors which have lost all evocative power and are merely used because they save people the trouble of inventing phrases for themselves. Examples are: *Ring the changes on, take up the cudgels for, toe the line, ride roughshod over, stand shoulder to shoulder with, play into the hands of, no axe to grind, grist to the mill, fishing in troubled waters, on the order of the day, Achilles' heel, swan song, hotbed.* Many of these are used without knowledge of their meaning (what is a "rift," for instance?), and incompatible metaphors are frequently mixed, a sure sign that the writer is not interested in what he is saying. Some metaphors now current have been twisted out of their original meaning without those who use them even being aware of the fact. For example, *toe the line* is sometimes written *tow the line.* Another example is *the hammer and the anvil,* now always used with the implication that the anvil gets the worst of it. In real life it is always the anvil that breaks the hammer, never the other way about: a writer who stopped to think what he was saying would be aware of this, and would avoid perverting the original phrase.

6 *Operators* or *verbal false limbs.* These save the trouble of picking out appropriate verbs and nouns, and at the same time pad each sentence with extra syllables which give it an appearance of symmetry. Characteristic phrases are *render, inoperative, militate against, make contact with, be subjected to, give rise to, give grounds for, have the effect of, play a leading part (role) in, make itself felt, take effect, exhibit a tendency to, serve the purpose of,* etc., etc. The keynote is the elimination of simple verbs. Instead of being a single word, such as *break, stop, spoil, mend, kill,* a verb becomes a *phrase,* made up of a noun or adjective tacked on to some general-purposes verb such as *prove, serve, form, play, render.* In addition, the passive voice is wherever possible used in preference to the active, and noun constructions are used instead of gerunds (*by examination of* instead of *by examining*). The range of verbs is further cut down by means of the *-ize* and *de-* formations, and the banal statements are given an appearance of profundity by means of the *not un-* formation. Simple conjunctions and prepositions are replaced by such phrases as *with respect to, having regard to, the fact that, by dint of, in view of, in the interests of, on the hypothesis that;* and the ends of sentences are saved from anticlimax by such resounding common-places as *greatly to be*

desired, cannot be left out of account, a development to be expected in the near future, deserving of serious consideration, brought to a satisfactory conclusion, and so on and so forth.

7 *Pretentious diction*. Words like *phenomenon, element, individual* (as noun), *objective, categorical, effective, virtual, basic, primary, promote, constitute, exhibit, exploit, utilize, eliminate, liquidate*, are used to dress up simple statements and give an air of scientific impartiality to biased judgments. Adjectives like *epoch-making, epic, historic, unforgettable, triumphant, age-old, inevitable, inexorable, veritable*, are used to dignify the sordid processes of international politics, while writing that aims at glorifying war usually takes on an archaic colour, its characteristic words being: *realm, throne, chariot, mailed fist, trident, sword, shield, buckler, banner, jackboot, clarion*. Foreign words and expressions such as *cul de sac, ancien régime, deus ex machina, mutatis mutandis, status quo, gleichschaltung, weltanschauung*, are used to given an air of culture and elegance. Except for the useful abbreviations *i.e., e.g.,* and *etc.,* there is no real need for any of the hundreds of foreign phrases now current in English. Bad writers, and especially scientific, political and sociological writers, are nearly always haunted by the notion that Latin or Greek words are grander than Saxon ones, and unnecessary words like *expedite, ameliorate, predict, extraneous, deracinated, clandestine, subaqueous* and hundreds of others constantly gain ground from their Anglo-Saxon opposite numbers.[1] The jargon peculiar to Marxist writing (*hyena, hangman, cannibal, petty bourgeois, these gentry, lacquey, flunkey, mad dog, White Guard*, etc.) consists largely of words and phrases translated from Russian, German or French; but the normal way of coining a new word is to use a Latin or Greek root with the appropriate affix and, where necessary, the size formation. It is often easier to make up words of this kind (*deregionalize, impermissible, extramarital, non-fragmentary*, and so forth) than to think up the English words that will cover one's meaning. The result, in general, is an increase in slovenliness and vagueness.

8 *Meaningless words*. In certain kinds of writing, particularly in art criticism and literary criticism, it is normal to come across long passages which are almost completely lacking in meaning.[2] Words like *romantic, plastic, values, human, dead, sentimental, natural, vitality*, as used in art criticism, are strictly meaningless, in the sense that they not only do not point to any discoverable object, but are hardly ever expected to do so by the reader. When one critic writes, "The outstanding feature of Mr. X's work is its living

---

[1]An interesting illustration of this is the way in which the English flower names which were in use till very recently are being ousted by Greek ones, *snapdragon* becoming *antirrhinum, forget-me-not* becoming *myosotis*, etc. It is hard to see any practical reason for this change of fashion: it is probably due to an instinctive turning-away from the more homely word and a vague feeling that the Greek word is scientific.

[2]Example: "Comfort's catholicity of perception and image, strangely Whitmanesque in range, almost the exact opposite in aesthetic compulsion, continues to evoke that trembling atmospheric accumulative hinting at a cruel, an inexorably serene timelessness. . . . Wrey Gardiner scores by aiming at simple bull's-eyes with precision. Only they are not so simple, and through this contented sadness runs more than the surface bitter-sweet of resignation." (*Poetry Quarterly*.)

quality," while another writes, "The immediately striking thing about Mr. X's work is its peculiar deadness," the reader accepts this as a simple difference of opinion. If words like *black* and *white* were involved, instead of the jargon words *dead* and *living,* he would see at once that language was being used in an improper way. Many political words are similarly abused. The word *Fascism* has now no meaning except in so far as it signifies "something not desirable." The words *democracy, socialism, freedom, patriotic, realistic, justice,* have each of them several different meanings which cannot be reconciled with one another. In the case of a word like *democracy,* not only is there no agreed definition, but the attempt to make one is resisted from all sides. It is almost universally felt that when we call a country democratic we are praising it: consequently the defenders of every kind of régime claim that it is a democracy, and fear that they might have to stop using the word if it were tied down to any one meaning. Words of this kind are often used in a consciously dishonest way. That is, the person who uses them has his own private definition, but allows his hearer to think he means something quite different. Statements like *Marshal Pétain was a true patriot, The Soviet Press is the freest in the world, The Catholic Church is opposed to persecution,* are almost always made with intent to deceive. Other words used in variable meanings, in most cases more or less dishonestly, are: *class, totalitarian, science, progressive, reactionary, bourgeois, equality.*

9 Now that I have made this catalogue of swindles and perversions, let me give another example of the kind of writing that they lead to. This time it must of its nature be an imaginary one. I am going to translate a passage of good English into modern English of the worst sort. Here is a well-known verse from *Ecclesiastes:*

> I returned and saw under the sun, that the race is not to the swift, nor the battle to the strong, neither yet bread to the wise, nor yet riches to men of understanding, nor yet favor to men of skill; but time and chance happeneth to them all.

10 Here it is in modern English:

> Objective consideration of contemporary phenomena compels the conclusion that success or failure in competitive activities exhibits no tendency to be commensurate with innate capacity, but that a considerable element of the unpredictable must invariably be taken into account.

11 This is a parody, but not a very gross one. Exhibit (3), above, for instance, contains several patches of the same kind of English. It will be seen that I have not made a full translation. The beginning and ending of the sentence follow the original meaning fairly closely, but in the middle the concrete illustrations—race, battle, bread—dissolve into the vague phrase "success or failure in competitive activities." This had to be so, because no modern writer of the kind I am discussing—no one capable of using phrases like "objective consideration of contemporary phenomena"—would ever tabulate his thoughts in that precise and detailed way. The whole tendency of modern prose is away from concreteness. Now analyse these two sentences

a little more closely. The first contains forty-nine words but only sixty syllables, and all its words are those of everyday life. The second contains thirty-eight words of ninety syllables: eighteen of its words are from Latin roots, and one from Greek. The first sentence contains six vivid images, and only one phrase ("time and chance") that could be called vague. The second contains not a single fresh, arresting phrase, and in spite of its ninety syllables it gives only a shortened version of the meaning contained in the first. Yet without a doubt it is the second kind of sentence that is gaining ground in modern English. I do not want to exaggerate. This kind of writing is not yet universal, and outcrops of simplicity will occur here and there in the worst-written page. Still, if you or I were told to write a few lines on the uncertainty of human fortunes, we should probably come much nearer to my imaginary sentence than to the one from *Ecclesiastes*.

12 As I have tried to show, modern writing at its worst does not consist in picking out words for the sake of their meaning and inventing images in order to make the meaning clearer. It consists in gumming together long strips of words which have already been set in order by someone else, and making the results presentable by sheer humbug. The attraction of this way of writing is that it is easy. It is easier—even quicker, once you have the habit—to say *In my opinion it is not an unjustifiable assumption that* than to say *I think*. If you use ready-made phrases, you not only don't have to hunt for words; you also don't have to bother with the rhythms of your sentences, since these phrases are generally so arranged as to be more or less euphonious. When you are composing in a hurry—when you are dictating to a stenographer, for instance, or making a public speech—it is natural to fall into a pretentious, Latinized style. Tags like *a consideration which we should do well to bear in mind* or *a conclusion to which all of us would readily assent* will save many a sentence from coming down with a bump. By using stale metaphors, similes and idioms, you save much mental effort, at the cost of leaving your meaning vague, not only for your reader but for yourself. This is the significance of mixed metaphors. The sole aim of a metaphor is to call up a visual image. When these images clash—as in *The Fascist octopus has sung its swan song, the jackboot is thrown into the melting pot*—it can be taken as certain that the writer is not seeing a mental image of the objects he is naming; in other words he is not really thinking. Look again at the examples I gave at the beginning of this essay. Professor Laski (1) uses five negatives in fifty-three words. One of these is superfluous, making nonsense of the whole passage, and in addition there is the slip *alien* for akin, making further nonsense, and several avoidable pieces of clumsiness which increase the general vagueness. Professor Hogben (2) plays ducks and drakes with a battery which is able to write prescriptions, and, while disapproving of the every day phrase *put up with,* is unwilling to look *egregious* up in the dictionary and see what it means; (3), if one takes an uncharitable attitude towards it, is simply meaningless: probably one could work out its intended meaning by reading the whole of the article in which it occurs. In (4), the writer knows more or less what he wants to say, but an accumulation of stale phrases chokes him like tea leaves blocking a sink. In

(5), words and meaning have almost parted company. People who write in this manner usually have a general emotional meaning—they dislike one thing and want to express solidarity with another—but they are not interested in the detail of what they are saying. A scrupulous writer, in every sentence that he writes, will ask himself at least four questions, thus: What am I trying to say? What words will express it? What image or idiom will make it clearer? Is this image fresh enough to have an effect? And he will probably ask himself two more: Could I put it more shortly? Have I said anything that is avoidably ugly? But you are not obliged to go to all this trouble. You can shirk it by simply throwing your mind open and letting the ready-made phrases come crowding in. They will construct your sentences for you—even think your thoughts for you, to a certain extent—and at need they will perform the important service of partially concealing your meaning even from yourself. It is at this point that the special connection between politics and the debasement of language becomes clear.

13 In our time it is broadly true that political writing is bad writing. Where it is not true, it will generally be found that the writer is some kind of rebel, expressing his private opinions and not a "party line." Orthodoxy, of whatever colour, seems to demand a lifeless, imitative style. The political dialects to be found in pamphlets, leading articles, manifestos, White Papers and the speeches of under-secretaries do, of course, vary from party to party, but they are all alike in that one almost never finds in them a fresh, vivid, home-made turn of speech. When one watches some tired hack on the platform mechanically repeating the familiar phrase—*bestial atrocities, iron heel, bloodstained tyranny, free peoples of the world, stand shoulder to shoulder*—one often has a curious feeling that one is not watching a live human being but some kind of dummy: a feeling which suddenly becomes stronger at moments when the light catches the speaker's spectacles and turns them into blank discs which seem to have no eyes behind them. And this is not altogether fanciful. A speaker who uses that kind of phraseology has gone some distance towards turning himself into a machine. The appropriate noises are coming out of his larynx, but his brain is not involved as it would be if he were choosing his words for himself. If the speech he is making is one that he is accustomed to make over and over again, he may be almost unconscious of what he is saying, as one is when one utters the responses in church. And this reduced state of consciousness, if not indispensable, is at any rate favorable to political conformity.

14 In our time, political speech and writing are largely the defence of the indefensible. Things like the continuance of British rule in India, the Russian purges and deportations, the dropping of the atom bombs on Japan, can indeed be defended, but only by arguments which are too brutal for most people to face, and which do not square with the professed aims of political parties. Thus political language has to consist largely of euphemism, question-begging and sheer cloudy vagueness. Defenceless villages are bombarded from the air, the inhabitants driven out into the countryside, the cattle machine-gunned, the huts set on fire with incendiary bullets: this is called

pacification. Missions of peasants are robbed of their farms and set trudging along the roads with no more than they can carry: this is called *transfer of population* or *rectification of frontiers.* People are imprisoned for years without trial, or shot in the back of the neck or sent to die of scurvy in Arctic lumber camps: this is called *elimination of unreliable elements.* Such phraseology is needed if one wants to name things without calling up mental pictures of them. Consider for instance some comfortable English professor defending Russian totalitarianism. He cannot say outright, "I believe in killing off your opponents when you can get good results by doing so." Probably, therefore, he will say something like this:

> While freely conceding that the Soviet régime exhibits certain features which the humanitarian may be inclined to deplore, we must, I think, agree that a certain curtailment of the right to political opposition is an unavoidable concomitant of transitional periods, and that the rigours which the Russian people have been called upon to undergo have been amply justified in the sphere of concrete achievement.

15 The inflated style is itself a kind of euphemism. A mass of Latin words falls upon the facts like soft snow, blurring the outlines and covering up all the details. The great enemy of clear language is insincerity. When there is a gap between one's real and one's declared aims, one turns as it were instinctively to long words and exhausted idioms, like a cuttlefish squirting out ink. In our age there is no such thing as "keeping out of politics." All issues are political issues, and politics itself is a mass of lies, evasions, folly, hatred and schizophrenia. When the general atmosphere is bad, language must suffer. I should expect to find—this is a guess which I have not sufficient knowledge to verify—that the German, Russian and Italian languages have all deteriorated in the last ten or fifteen years, as a result of dictatorship.

16 But if thought corrupts language, language can also corrupt thought. A bad usage can spread by tradition and imitation, even among people who should and do know better. The debased language that I have been discussing is in some ways very convenient. Phrases like *a not unjustifiable assumption, leaves much to be desired, would serve no good purpose, a consideration which we should do well to bear in mind,* are a continuous temptation, a packet of aspirins always at one's elbow. Look back through this essay, and for certain you will find that I have again and again committed the very faults I am protesting against. By this morning's post I have received a phamphlet dealing with conditions in Germany. The author tells me that he "felt impelled" to write it. I open it at random, and here is almost the first sentence that I see: "[The Allies] have an opportunity not only of achieving a radical transformation of Germany's social and political structure in such a way as to avoid a nationalistic reaction in Germany itself, but at the same time of laying the foundations of a co-operative and unified Europe." You see, he "feels impelled" to write—feels, presumably, that he has something new to say—and yet his words, like cavalry horses answering the bugle, group themselves automatically into the familiar dreary pattern. This invasion of one's mind by

ready-made phrases *(lay the foundations, achieve a radical transformation)* can only be prevented if one is constantly on guard against them, and every such phrase anaesthetizes a portion of one's brain.

17 I said earlier that the decadence of our language is probably curable. Those who deny this would argue, if they produced an argument at all, that language merely reflects existing social conditions, and that we cannot influence its development by any direct tinkering with words and constructions. So far as the general tone or spirit of a language goes, this may be true, but it is not true in detail. Silly words and expressions have often disappeared, not through any evolutionary process but owing to the conscious action of a minority. Two recent examples were *explore every avenue* and *leave no stone unturned,* which were killed by the jeers of a few journalists. There is a long list of flyblown metaphors which could similarly be got rid of if enough people would interest themselves in the job; and it should also be possible to laugh the *not un-* formation out of existence,[3] to reduce the amount of Latin and Greek in the average sentence, to drive out foreign phrases and strayed scientific words, and, in general, to make pretentiousness unfashionable. But all these are minor points. The defence of the English language implies more than this, and perhaps it is best to start by saying what it does *not* imply.

18 To begin with it has nothing to do with archaism, with the salvaging of obsolete words and turns of speech, or with the setting up of a "standard English" which must never be departed from. On the contrary, it is especially concerned with the scrapping of every word or idiom which has outworn its usefulness. It has nothing to do with correct grammar and syntax, which are of no importance so long as one makes one's meaning clear, or with the avoidance of Americanisms, or with having what is called a "good prose style." On the other hand it is not concerned with fake simplicity and the attempt to make written English colloquial. Nor does it even imply in every case preferring the Saxon word to the Latin one, though it does imply using the fewest and shortest words that will cover one's meaning. What is above all needed is to let the meaning choose the word, and not the other way about. In prose, the worst thing one can do with words is to surrender to them. When you think of a concrete object, you think wordlessly, and then, if you want to describe the thing you have been visualizing you probably hunt about till you find the exact words that seem to fit it. When you think of something abstract you are more inclined to use words from the start, and unless you make a conscious effort to prevent it, the existing dialect will come rushing in and do the job for you, at the expense of blurring or even changing your meaning. Probably it is better to put off using words as long as possible and get one's meaning as clear as one can through pictures or sensations. Afterwards one can choose—not simply *accept*—the phrase that will best cover the meaning, and then switch round and decide what impression one's words are likely to make on another person. This last effort of the mind cuts out all stale or mixed images, all prefabricated

---

[3]One can cure oneself of the *not un-* formation by memorizing this sentence: *A not unblack dog was chasing a not unsmall rabbit across a not ungreen field.*

phrases, needless repetitions, and humbug and vagueness generally. But one can often be in doubt about the effect of a word or a phrase, and one needs rules that one can rely on when instinct fails. I think the following rules will cover most cases:

(i) Never use a metaphor, simile or other figure of speech which you are used to seeing in print.

(ii) Never use a long word where a short one will do.

(iii) If it is possible to cut a word out, always cut it out.

(iv) Never use the passive when you can use the active.

(v) Never use a foreign phrase, a scientific word or a jargon word if you can think of an everyday English equivalent.

(vi) Break any of these rules sooner than say anything outright barbarous.

These rules sound elementary, and so they are, but they demand a deep change of attitude in anyone who has grown used to writing in the style now fashionable. One could keep all of them and still write bad English, but one could not write the kind of stuff that I quoted in those five specimens at the beginning of this article.

19 I have not here been considering the literary use of language, but merely language as an instrument for expressing and not for concealing or preventing thought. Stuart Chase and others have come near to claiming that all abstract words are meaningless, and have used this as a pretext for advocating a kind of political quietism. Since you don't know what Fascism is, how can you struggle against Fascism? One need not swallow such absurdities as this, but one ought to recognize that the present political chaos is connected with the decay of language, and that one can probably bring about some improvement by starting at the verbal end. If you simplify your English, you are freed from the worst follies of orthodoxy. You cannot speak any of the necessary dialects, and when you make a stupid remark its stupidity will be obvious, even to yourself. Political language—and with variations this is true of all political parties, from Conservatives to Anarchists—is designed to make lies sound truthful and murder respectable, and to give an appearance of solidity to pure wind. One cannot change this all in a moment, but one can at least change one's own habits, and from time to time one can even, if one jeers loudly enough, send some worn-out and useless phrase—some *jackboot, Achilles' heel, hotbed, melting pot, acid test, veritable inferno* or other lump of verbal refuse—into the dustbin where it belongs.

VOCABULARY

decadent (1)	hackneyed (4)
archaism (1)	metaphor (5)
slovenliness (2)	evocative (5)
inadvertently (4)	banal (6)

pretentious (7)   debasement (12)
régime (8)   orthodoxy (13)
parody (11)   incendiary (14)
arresting (11)   schizophrenia (15)
euphonious (12)   barbarous (18)
solidarity (12)   quietism (19)
scrupulous (12)

QUESTIONS ON CONTENT

1. What connections does the author make between politics and the English language?
2. In paragraph 3 Orwell cites five examples of bad writing. What two faults do all of them commit?
3. According to Orwell, why do people use hackneyed imagery and prefabricated phrases?
4. Many people use big words and foreign words in order to sound educated. According to Orwell, what do such words do to a piece of writing?
5. What does Orwell mean when he states that "in our time, political speech and writing are largely the defence of the indefensible" (paragraph 14)?
6. Orwell states, "In prose, the worst thing one can do with words is to surrender to them" (paragraph 18). Give an example of what is meant by this surrender.
7. Enumerate Orwell's six elementary rules concerning the choice of words and phrases. If in your opinion he has left out any major rule, state it.

QUESTIONS ON FORM

1. Orwell deplores the use of stale imagery. Identify at least three examples of fresh imagery used in his essay.
2. What is the analogy used for illustration in paragraph 2?
3. Which paragraph is developed first by contrast and then by example?
4. In what paragraph does Orwell make the transition from poor writing in general to poor writing in politics? Point out the transitional sentence.
5. What is the topic sentence for paragraph 14? What is the chief method of development?

SUGGESTIONS FOR WRITING

1. Using Orwell's standards, analyze a speech or written article by some contemporary politician.
2. In a brief essay, attack or defend Orwell's statement: "If you simplify your English, you are freed from the worst follies of orthodoxy."

THE FINE PRINT TRANSLATED

Numerous companies are following the example of New York's First National City Bank by rewriting their loan contracts or other business documents so that the average reader can understand them. They are avoiding long-winded, confusing legalese. Compare the original on the left with the new version on the right. (From *Time* magazine, September 12, 1975.)

From the old and new personal-loan notes of the First National City Bank:

In the event of default in the payment of this or any other Obligation or the performance of observance of any term or covenant contained herein or in any note or other contract or agreement evidencing or relating to any Obligation or any Collateral on the Borrower's part to be performed or observed; or the undersigned Borrower shall die; or any of the undersigned become insolvent or make an assignment for the benefit of creditors; or a petition shall be filed by or against any of the undersigned under any provision of the Bankruptcy Act; or any money, securities or property of the undersigned now or hereafter on deposit with or in the possession or under the control of the Bank shall be attached or become subject to distraint proceedings or any order or process of any court . . .

I'll be in default:
1. If I don't pay an installment on time; or
2. If any other creditor tries by legal process to take any money of mine in your possession.

From the old and new Sentry auto-insurance policies:

If the company revises this policy form with respect to policy provisions, endorsements or rules by which the insurance hereunder could be extended or broadened without additional premium charge, such insurance as is afforded hereunder shall be so extended or broadened effective immediately upon approval or acceptance of such revision during the policy period by the appropriate insurance supervisory authority.

We'll automatically give you the benefits of any extension or broadening of this policy if the change doesn't require additional premium.

From the old and new Master Charge agreements of the First National Bank of Boston:

Cardholder and any other person applying for, using or signing the Card promise, jointly and severally, to pay to Bank the principal of all loans plus, as provided in paragraph 4, FINANCE CHARGES. Payments shall be made each month at Bank or as Bank may direct, on or before the Payment Due Date, in the amount of (a) the greater of $10 or an amount equal to ⅟₃₆th of the Total Debit Balance not in excess of the Maximum Credit on the related Statement Date plus (b) any amounts owing and delinquent plus (c) any excess of the Total Debit Balance over the Maximum Credit.

You must pay us a monthly minimum payment. This monthly minimum payment will be ⅟₃₆ of the balance plus, of course, any amounts which are past due, but at least $10. If the balance is less than $10, the minimum payment will be the entire balance. The balance will include the outstanding amount that you have borrowed plus a finance charge.

BAFFLE-GAB THESAURUS

> We present the "Baffle-Gab Thesaurus" as an amusing exercise. Try writing a letter of complaint to an imaginary firm, flooding your content with combinations from this "obfuscating" word guide. (And if you do not already know the word "obfuscating," look it up.) (From *Time* magazine, September 13, 1968.)

As any self-respecting bureaucrat knows, it is bad form indeed to use a single, simple word when six or seven obfuscating ones will do.

But where is the Washington phrasemaker to turn if he is hung up for what Horace called "words a foot and a half long"? Simple. Just glance at the Systematic Buzz Phrase Projector, or S.B.P.P.

The S.B.P.P. has aptly obscure origins but appears to come from a Royal Canadian Air Force listing of fuzzy phrases. It was popularized in Washington by Philip Broughton, a U.S. Public Health Service official, who circulated it among civil servants and businessmen. A sort of mini-thesaurus of baffle-gab, it consists of a three-column list of 30 overused but appropriately portentous words. Whenever a GS-14 or deputy assistant secretary needs an opaque phrase, he need only think of a three-digit number—any one will do as well as the next—and select the corresponding "buzz words" from the three columns. For example, 257 produces "systematized logistical projection," which has the ring of absolute authority and means absolutely nothing.

Broughton's baffle-gab guide:

A	B	C
0) Integrated	Management	Options
1) Total	Organizational	Flexibility
2) Systematized	Monitored	Capability
3) Parallel	Reciprocal	Mobility
4) Functional	Digital	Programming
5) Responsive	Logistical	Concept
6) Optional	Transitional	Time-Phase
7) Synchronized	Incremental	Projection
8) Compatible	Third-Generation	Hardware
9) Balanced	Policy	Contingency

JONATHAN SWIFT

A SCHEME FOR ABOLISHING WORDS

This outrageous scheme for abolishing words is part of Jonathan Swift's satirical portrayal of the Grand Academy of Lagado in the famous book *Gulliver's Travels,* published in 1726. It is from the third part of this work, "A Voyage to Laputa, Balnibarbi, Luggnagg, Glubbdubdrib, and Japan," that the following account (Chapter 5) is taken. Some of the specific details in the description would have been recognized by Swift's contemporaries as comic versions of actual experiments reported in the *Transactions of the Royal Society,* the organ of the leading scientific group in England. The suggestion for the abolition of words probably refers to Thomas Sprat's ideal of an economical scientific prose that would express "so many 'Things,' almost in an equal number of 'Words.'"

1 We next went to the school of languages, where three professors sat in consultation upon improving that of their own country.

2 The first project was to shorten discourse by cutting polysyllables into one, and leaving out verbs and participles; because in reality, all things imagined are but nouns.

3 The other was a scheme for entirely abolishing all words whatsoever and this was urged as a great advantage in point of health as well as brevity; for, it is plain, that every word we speak is in some degree a diminution of our lungs by corrosion, and consequently contributes to the shortening of our lives. An expedient was therefore offered, that since words are only names for things, it would be more convenient for all men to carry about them such things as were necessary to express the particular business they are to discourse on. And this invention would certainly have taken place, to the great ease as well as health of the subject, if the women, in conjunction with the vulgar and illiterate, had

not threatened to raise a rebellion, unless they might be allowed the liberty to speak with their tongues, after the manner of their forefathers; such constant irreconcilable enemies to science are the common people. However, many of the most learned and wise adhere to the new scheme of expressing themselves by things; which hath only this inconvenience attending it, that if a man's business be very great, and of various kinds, he must be obliged in proportion to carry a greater bundle of things upon his back, unless he can afford one or two strong servants to attend him. I have often beheld two of those sages almost sinking under the weight of their packs, like pedlers among us, who, when they met in the streets, would lay down their loads, open their sacks, and hold conversation for an hour together; then put up their implements, help each other to resume their burdens, and take their leave. But for short conversation a man may carry implements in his pockets and under his arms, enough to supply him, and in his house he cannot be at a loss; therefore the room where company meet to practise this art is full of all things ready at hand, requisite to furnish matter for this kind of artificial converse.

VOCABULARY

polysyllables (2)	irreconcilable (3)
diminution (3)	requisite (3)
corrosion (3)	converse (noun) (3)
expedient (3)	

QUESTIONS ON CONTENT

1. Before you can gain the full impact of this passage, you must be sensitive to tone. What tone is used?
2. In paragraph 3 Swift creates a topsy-turvy world in which the "learned" are acting foolish and the "illiterate" are acting with practical insight. What might Swift be implying by making such a reversal?
3. Why does Swift lump the women with the "vulgar and illiterate"?
4. What do you consider the point of the entire excerpt? If you think there is more than one, state them.

QUESTIONS ON FORM

1. Since *Gulliver's Travels* was published in 1726, Swift's manner of writing is different from ours today. Can you point to specific examples of an archaic style?
2. How does Swift manage to sound "scientific"?

SUGGESTIONS FOR WRITING

1. Read Swift's "A Modest Proposal" (p. 364) and write a brief essay comparing it with the scheme for abolishing words.
2. In straightforward prose, write an essay advocating the same ideas that Jonathan Swift seems to propose.

examples

S. I. HAYAKAWA

A SEMANTIC PARABLE

"A Semantic Parable" is about language habits. In it the American semanticist S. I. Hayakawa suggests what can result when people feel labeled. He also shows how words inevitably lead to quarrels when each of the arguing parties bestows a different meaning on the words used in the argument. (From *Language in Thought and Action*.)

1 Once upon a time (said the Professor), there were two small communities, spiritually as well as geographically situated at a considerable distance from each other. They had, however, these problems in common: Both were hard hit by a depression, so that in each of the towns there were about one hundred heads of families unemployed. There was, to be sure, enough food, enough clothing, enough materials for housing, but these families simply did not have money to procure these necessities.

2 The city fathers of A-town, the first community, were substantial businessmen, moderately well educated, good to their families, kindhearted, and sound-thinking. The unemployed tried hard, as unemployed people usually do, to find jobs; but the situation did not improve. The city fathers, as well as the unemployed themselves, had been brought up to believe that there is always enough work for everyone, if you only look for it hard enough. Comforting themselves with this doctrine, the city fathers could have shrugged their shoulders and turned their backs on the problem, except for the fact that they were genuinely kindhearted men. They could not bear to see the unemployed men and their wives and children starving. In order to prevent starvation, they felt that they had to provide these people with some means of sustenance. Their principles told them, nevertheless, that if people were given something for nothing, it would demoralize their character. Naturally this made the city fathers even more unhappy, because they were faced with the horrible choice of (1) letting the unemployed starve, or (2) destroying their moral character.

3 The solution they finally hit upon, after much debate and soul-searching, was this. They decided to give the unemployed families relief of fifty dollars a month; but to insure against the pauperization of the recipients, they decided that this fifty dollars was to be accompanied by a moral lesson, to wit: the obtaining of the assistance would be made so difficult, humiliating, and disagreeable that there would be no temptation for anyone to go through the process unless it was absolutely necessary; the moral disapproval of the community would be turned upon the recipients of the money at all times in such a way that they would try hard to get off relief and regain their self-respect. Some even proposed that people on relief be denied the vote, so that the moral lesson would be more deeply impressed upon them. Others sug-

gested that their names be published at regular intervals in the newspapers, so that there would be a strong incentive to get off relief. The city fathers had enough faith in the goodness of human nature to expect that the recipients would be grateful, since they were getting something for nothing, something which they hadn't worked for.

4 When the plan was put into operation, however, the recipients of the relief checks proved to be an ungrateful, ugly bunch. They seemed to resent the cross-examinations and inspections at the hands of the relief investigators, who, they said, took advantage of a man's misery to snoop into every detail of his private life. In spite of uplifting editorials in A-town *Tribune* telling how grateful they ought to be, the recipients of the relief refused to learn any moral lessons, declaring that they were "just as good as anybody else." When, for example, they permitted themselves the rare luxury of a movie or an evening of bingo, their neighbors looked at them sourly as if to say, "I work hard and pay my taxes just in order to support loafers like you in idleness and pleasure." This attitude, which was fairly characteristic of those members of the community who still had jobs, further embittered the relief recipients, so that they showed even less gratitude as time went on and were constantly on the lookout for insults, real or imaginary, from people who might think that they weren't as good as anybody else. A number of them took to moping all day long, to thinking that their lives had been failures; one or two even committed suicide. Others found that it was hard to look their wives and kiddies in the face, because they had failed to provide. They all found it difficult to maintain their club and fraternal relationships, since they could not help feeling that their fellow citizens despised them for having sunk so low. Their wives, too, were unhappy for the same reasons and gave up their social activities. Children whose parents were on relief felt inferior to classmates whose parents were not public charges. Some of these children developed inferiority complexes which affected not only their grades at school, but their careers after graduation. Several other relief recipients, finally, felt they could stand their loss of self-respect no longer and decided, after many efforts to gain honest jobs, to earn money by their own efforts, even if they had to go in for robbery. They did so and were caught and sent to the state penitentiary.

5 The depression, therefore, hit A-town very hard. The relief policy had averted starvation, no doubt, but suicide, personal quarrels, unhappy homes, the weakening of social organizations, the maladjustment of children, and, finally, crime, had resulted. The town was divided in two, the "haves" and the "have-nots," so that there was class hatred. People shook their heads sadly and declared that it all went to prove over again what they had known from the beginning, that giving people something for nothing inevitably demoralizes their character. The citizens of A-town gloomily waited for prosperity to return, with less and less hope as time went on.

6 The story of the other community, B-ville, was entirely different. B-ville was a relatively isolated town, too far out of the way to be reached by Rotary Club speakers and university extension services. One of the aldermen, however, who was something of an economist, explained to his fellow aldermen

that unemployment, like sickness, accident, fire, tornado, or death, hits unexpectedly in modern society, irrespective of the victim's merits or deserts. He went on to say that B-ville's homes, parks, streets, industries, and everything else B-ville was proud of had been built in part by the work of these same people who were now unemployed. He then proposed to apply a principle of insurance: If the work these unemployed people had previously done for the community could be regarded as a form of premium paid to the community against a time of misfortune, payments now made to them to prevent their starvation could be regarded as insurance claims. He therefore proposed that all men of good repute who had worked in the community in whatever line of useful endeavor, whether as machinists, clerks, or bank managers, be regarded as citizen policyholders, having claims against the city in the case of unemployment for fifty dollars a month until such time as they might again be employed. Naturally, he had to talk very slowly and patiently, since the idea was entirely new to his fellow aldermen. But he described his plan as a "straight business proposition," and finally they were persuaded. They worked out the details as to the conditions under which citizens should be regarded as policyholders in the city's social insurance plan to everybody's satisfaction and decided to give checks for fifty dollars a month to the heads of each of B-ville's indigent families.

7 B-ville's claim adjusters, whose duty it was to investigate the claims of the citizen policyholders, had a much better time than A-town's relief investigators. While the latter had been resentfully regarded as snoopers, the former, having no moral lesson to teach but simply a business transaction to carry out, treated their clients with businesslike courtesy and got the same amount of information as the relief investigators with considerably less difficulty. There were no hard feelings. It further happened, fortunately, that news of B-ville's plans reached a liberal newspaper editor in the big city at the other end of the state. This writer described the plan in a leading feature story headed "B-VILLE LOOKS AHEAD. Great Adventure in Social Pioneering Launched by Upper Valley Community." As a result of this publicity, inquiries about the plan began to come to the city hall even before the first checks were mailed out. This led, naturally, to a considerable feeling of pride on the part of the aldermen, who, being boosters, felt that this was a wonderful opportunity to put B-ville on the map.

8 Accordingly, the aldermen decided that instead of simply mailing out the checks as they had originally intended, they would publicly present the first checks at a monster civic ceremony. They invited the governor of the state, who was glad to come to bolster his none-too-enthusiastic support in that locality, the president of the state university, the senator from their district, and other functionaries. They decorated the National Guard armory with flags and got out the American Legion Fife and Drum Corps, the Boy Scouts, and other civic organizations. At the big celebration, each family to receive a social insurance check was marched up to the platform to receive it, and the governor and the mayor shook hands with each of them as they came trooping

up in their best clothes. Fine speeches were made; there was much cheering and shouting; pictures of the event showing the recipients of the checks shaking hands with the mayor, and the governor patting the heads of the children, were published not only in the local papers but also in several metropolitan picture sections.

9 Every recipient of these insurance checks had a feeling, therefore, that he had been personally honored, that he lived in a wonderful little town, and that he could face his unemployment with greater courage and assurance, since his community was back of him. The men and women found themselves being kidded in a friendly way by their acquaintances for having been "up there with the big shots," shaking hands with the governor, and so on. The children at school found themselves envied for having had their pictures in the papers. All in all, B-ville's unemployed did not commit suicide, were not haunted by a sense of failure, did not turn to crime, did not get personal maladjustments, did not develop class hatred, as the result of their fifty dollars a month. . . .

10 At the conclusion of the Professor's story, the discussion began:

"That just goes to show," said the Advertising Man, who was known among his friends as a realistic thinker, "what good promotional work can do. B-ville's city council had real advertising sense, and that civic ceremony was a masterpiece . . . made everyone happy . . . put over the scheme in a big way. Reminds me of the way we do things in our business: as soon as we called horse-mackerel tuna-fish, we developed a big market for it. I suppose if you called relief 'insurance,' you could actually get people to like it, couldn't you?"

11 "What do you mean, 'calling' it insurance?" asked the Social Worker. "B-ville's scheme wasn't relief at all. It *was* insurance. That's what all such payments should be. What gets me is the stupidity of A-town's city council and all people like them in not realizing that what they call 'relief' is simply the payment of just claims which those unemployed have on a community in a complex interdependent industrial society."

12 "Good grief, man! Do you realize what you're saying?" cried the Advertising Man in surprise. "Are you implying that those people had any *right* to that money? All I said was that it's a good idea to *disguise* relief as insurance if it's going to make people any happier. But it's still relief, no matter what you *call* it. It's all right to kid the public along to reduce discontent, but we don't need to kid ourselves as well!"

13 "But they *do* have a right to that money! They're not getting something for nothing. It's insurance. They did something for the community, and that's their prem—"

"Say, are you crazy?"

"Who's crazy?"

"You're crazy. Relief is relief, isn't it? If you'd only call things by their right names . . ."

"But, confound it, insurance is insurance, isn't it?"

(Since the gentlemen are obviously losing their tempers, it will be best to leave them. The Professor has already sneaked out. When last heard of, not only had the quarrelers stopped speaking to each other, but so had their wives—and the Advertising Man was threatening to disinherit his son if he didn't break off his engagement with the Social Worker's daughter.)

14 This story has been told not to advance arguments in favor of "social insurance" or "relief" or for any other political and economic arrangement, but simply to show a fairly characteristic sample of language in action. Do the words we use make as much difference in our lives as the story of A-town and B-ville seems to indicate? We often talk about "choosing the right words to express our thoughts," as if thinking were a process entirely independent of the words we think in. But is thinking such an independent process? Do the words we utter arise as a result of the thoughts we have, or are the thoughts we have determined by the linguistic systems we happen to have been taught? The Advertising Man and the Social Worker seem to be agreed that the results of B-ville's program were good, so that we can assume that their notions of what is socially desirable are similar. Nevertheless, they *cannot agree.*

15 Alfred Korzybski, in his preface to *Science and Sanity* (which discusses many problems similar to those discussed in this book), asks the reader to imagine what the state of technology would be if all lubricants contained emery dust, the presence of which had never been detected. Machines would be short-lived and expensive; the machine age would be a dream of the distant future. If, however, someone were to discover the presence of the emery, we should at once know *in what direction to proceed* in order to release the potentialities of machine power.

16 Why do people disagree? It isn't a matter of education or intelligence, because quarreling, bitterness, conflict, and breakdown are just as common among the educated as the uneducated, among the clever as the stupid. Human relations are no better among the privileged than the underprivileged. Indeed, well-educated people are often the cleverest in proving that insurance is *really* insurance and that relief is *really* relief—and being well educated they often have such high principles that nothing will make them modify their position in the slightest. Are disagreements then the inevitable results of the nature of human problems and the nature of man? Possibly so—but if we give this answer, we are confessing to being licked before we have even started our investigations.

17 The student of language observes, however, that it is an extremely rare quarrel that does not involve some kind of *talking.* Almost invariably, before noses are punched or shooting begins, *words are exchanged*—sometimes only a few, sometimes millions. We shall, therefore, look for the "previously undetected emery dust" (or whatever it is that heats up and stops our intellectual machinery) in *language*—that is to say, *our linguistic habits* (how we talk and think and listen) and *our unconscious attitudes toward language.* If we are even partially successful in our search, we may get an inkling of the *direction in which to proceed* in order to release the now imperfectly realized potentialities of human co-operation.

18 P.S. Those who have concluded that the point of the story is that the Social Worker and the Advertising Man were "only arguing about different names for the same thing," are asked to reread the story and explain what they mean by (1) "only" and (2) "the same thing."

VOCABULARY

semantic (title)	aldermen (6)
parable (title)	indigent (6)
procure (1)	functionaries (8)
demoralize (2)	interdependent (11)
incentive (3)	lubricants (15)
averted (5)	

QUESTIONS ON CONTENT

1. The story is called a "parable." What specifically makes it such?
2. What is the dilemma of A-town? Can you suggest any group or groups in our society today who might have suffered a similar experience?
3. With which paragraph does the crux of the story begin?
4. According to Hayakawa, what is the reason for disagreements? To what extent do education and intelligence prevent them? Explain.
5. Where, according to Hayakawa, shall we find the answer to the problem of proper communication?
6. What does Hayakawa mean by "our linguistic habits"?

QUESTIONS ON FORM

1. Why does Hayakawa use a professor to tell the story of A-town and B-ville?
2. What is the purpose of the direct quotations in paragraph 4?
3. What kind of image does B-ville reflect? Cite the details that create this image.
4. In paragraph 15 Hayakawa alludes to an analogy drawn by Alfred Korzybski. How would you explain this analogy in your own words?
5. What is the function of the "P.S." in the story? What is the implied expectancy on the part of the author?

SUGGESTIONS FOR WRITING

1. From our society choose a group which you consider to have been labeled in some way. Describe the results of this labeling. Be specific in your use of examples and details. Here are some possibilities: policemen, migrant workers, garbage collectors.
2. Look through some recent newspapers to find words which have the potential for being misunderstood unless they are given a specific meaning. Explain why you think these words are potentially dangerous.

LAURA BOHANNAN

SHAKESPEARE IN THE BUSH

Cultural anthropologists are all concerned with *meaning,* with the difficult task of translation from one language to another. In this classic of anthropology, Laura Bohannan shows the difficulty of translating the meaning of *Hamlet* to the Tiv in West Africa. The article forcefully demonstrates the way in which different cultures provide distinct and separate worlds of meaning for those who have learned to live by them.

1 Just before I left Oxford for the Tiv in West Africa, conversation turned to the season at Stratford. "You Americans," said a friend, "often have difficulty with Shakespeare. He was, after all, a very English poet, and one can easily misinterpret the universal by misunderstanding the particular."

2 I protested that human nature is pretty much the same the whole world over; at least the general plot and motivation of the greater tragedies would always be clear—everywhere—although some details of custom might have to be explained and difficulties of translation might produce other slight changes. To end an argument we could not conclude, my friend gave me a copy of *Hamlet* to study in the African bush: it would, he hoped, lift my mind above its primitive surroundings, and possibly I might, by prolonged meditation, achieve the grace of correct interpretation.

3 It was my second field trip to that African tribe, and I thought myself ready to live in one of its remote sections—an area difficult to cross even on foot. I eventually settled on the hillock of a very knowledgeable old man, the head of a homestead of some hundred and forty people, all of whom were either his close relatives or his wives and children. Like the other elders of the vicinity, the old man spent most of his time performing ceremonies seldom seen these days in the more accessible parts of the tribe. I was delighted. Soon there would be three months of enforced isolation and leisure, between the harvest that takes place just before the rising of the swamps and the clearing of new farms when the water goes down. Then, I thought, they would have even more time to perform ceremonies and explain them to me.

4 I was quite mistaken. Most of the ceremonies demanded the presence of elders from several homesteads. As the swamps rose, the old men found it too difficult to walk from one homestead to the next, and the ceremonies gradually ceased. As the swamps rose even higher, all activities but one came to an end. The women brewed beer from maize and millet. Men, women, and children sat on their hillocks and drank it.

5 People began to drink by dawn. By midmorning the whole homestead was singing, dancing, and drumming. When it rained, people had to sit inside their huts: there they drank and sang or they drank and told stories. In any case, by noon or before, I either had to join the party or retire to my own hut and my books. "One does not discuss serious matters when there is beer.

Come drink with us." Since I lacked their capacity for the thick native beer, I spent more and more time with *Hamlet*. Before the end of the second month, grace descended on me. I was quite sure that *Hamlet* had only one possible interpretation, and that one universally obvious.

6 Early every morning, in the hope of having some serious talk before the beer party, I used to call on the old man at his reception hut—a circle of posts supporting a thatched roof above a low mud wall to keep out wind and rain. One day I crawled through the low doorway and found most of the men of the homestead sitting huddled in their ragged cloths on stools, low plank beds, and reclining chairs, warming themselves against the chill of the rain around a smoky fire. In the center were three pots of beer. The party had started.

7 The old man greeted me cordially. "Sit down and drink." I accepted a large calabash full of beer, poured some into a small drinking gourd, and tossed it down. Then I poured some more into the same gourd for the man second in seniority to my host before I handed my calabash over to a young man for further distribution. Important people shouldn't ladle beer themselves.

8 "It is better like this," the old man said, looking at me approvingly and plucking at the thatch that had caught in my hair. "You should sit and drink with us more often. Your servants tell me that when you are not with us, you sit inside your hut looking at a paper."

9 The old man was acquainted with four kinds of "papers": tax receipts, bride price receipts, court fee receipts, and letters. The messenger who brought him letters from the chief used them mainly as a badge of office, for he always knew what was in them and told the old man. Personal letters from the few who had relatives in the government or mission stations were kept until someone went to a large market where there was a letter writer and reader. Since my arrival, letters were brought to me to be read. A few men also brought me bride price receipts, privately, with requests to change the figures to a higher sum. I found moral arguments were of no avail, since in-laws are fair game, and the technical hazards of forgery difficult to explain to an illiterate people. I did not wish them to think me silly enough to look at any such papers for days on end, and I hastily explained that my "paper" was one of the "things of long ago" of my country.

"Ah," said the old man. "Tell us."

10 I protested that I was not a storyteller. Storytelling is a skilled art among them; their standards are high, and the audiences critical—and vocal in their criticism. I protested in vain. This morning they wanted to hear a story while they drank. They threatened to tell me no more stories until I told them one of mine. Finally, the old man promised that no one would criticize my style "for we know you are struggling with our language." "But," put in one of the elders, "you must explain what we do not understand, as we do when we tell you our stories." Realizing that here was my chance to prove *Hamlet* universally intelligible, I agreed.

11 The old man handed me some more beer to help me on with my

storytelling. Men filled their long wooden pipes and knocked coals from the fire to place in the pipe bowls; then, puffing contentedly, they sat back to listen. I began in the proper style, "Not yesterday, not yesterday, but long ago, a thing occurred. One night three men were keeping watch outside the homestead of the great chief, when suddenly they saw the former chief approach them."

"Why was he no longer their chief?"

"He was dead," I explained. "That is why they were troubled and afraid when they saw him."

"Impossible," began one of the elders, handing his pipe on to his neighbor, who interrupted, "Of course it wasn't the dead chief. It was an omen sent by a witch. Go on."

12 Slightly shaken, I continued. "One of these three was a man who knew things"—the closest translation of scholar, but unfortunately it also meant witch. The second elder looked triumphantly at the first. "So he spoke to the dead chief saying, 'Tell us what we must do so you may rest in your grave,' but the dead chief did not answer. He vanished, and they could see him no more. Then the man who knew things—his name was Horatio—said this event was the affair of the dead chief's son, Hamlet."

13 There was a general shaking of heads round the circle. "Had the dead chief no living brothers? Or was this son the chief?"

"No," I replied, "That is, he had one living brother who became the chief when the elder brother died."

The old men muttered: such omens were matters for chiefs and elders, not for youngsters; no good could come of going behind a chief's back; clearly Horatio was not a man who knew things.

"Yes, he was," I insisted, shooing a chicken away from my beer. "In our country the son is next to the father. The dead chief's younger brother had become the great chief. He had also married his elder brother's widow only about a month after the funeral."

"He did well," the old man beamed and announced to the others, "I told you that if we knew more about Europeans, we would find they really were very like us. In our country also," he added to me, "the younger brother marries the elder brother's widow and becomes the father of his children. Now, if your uncle, who married your widowed mother, is your father's full brother, then he will be a real father to you. Did Hamlet's father and uncle have one mother?"

14 His question barely penetrated my mind; I was too upset and thrown too far off balance by having one of the most important elements of *Hamlet* knocked straight out of the picture. Rather uncertainly I said that I thought they had the same mother, but I wasn't sure—the story didn't say. The old man told me severely that these genealogical details made all the difference and that when I got home I must ask the elders about it. He shouted out the door to one of his younger wives to bring his goatskin bag.

15 Determined to save what I could of the mother motif, I took a deep

breath and began again. "The son Hamlet was very sad because his mother had married again so quickly. There was no need for her to do so, and it is our custom for a widow not to go to her next husband until she has mourned for two years."

"Two years is too long," objected the wife, who had appeared with the old man's battered goatskin bag. "Who will hoe your farms for you while you have no husband?"

"Hamlet," I retorted without thinking, "was old enough to hoe his mother's farms himself. There was no need for her to remarry." No one looked convinced. I gave up. "His mother and the great chief told Hamlet not to be sad, for the great chief himself would be a father to Hamlet. Furthermore, Hamlet would be the next chief: therefore he must stay to learn the things of a chief. Hamlet agreed to remain, and all the rest went off to drink beer."

16 While I paused, perplexed at how to render Hamlet's disgusted soliloquy to an audience convinced that Claudius and Gertrude had behaved in the best possible manner, one of the younger men asked me who had married the other wives of the dead chief.

"He had no other wives," I told him.

"But a chief must have many wives! How else can he brew beer and prepare food for all his guests?"

17 I said firmly that in our country even chiefs had only one wife, that they had servants to do their work, and that they paid them from tax money.

It was better, they returned, for a chief to have many wives and sons who would help him hoe his farms and feed his people; then everyone loved the chief who gave much and took nothing—taxes were a bad thing.

I agreed with the last comment, but for the rest fell back on their favorite way of fobbing off my questions: "That is the way it is done, so that is how we do it."

18 I decided to skip the soliloquy. Even if Claudius was here thought quite right to marry his brother's widow, there remained the poison motif, and I knew they would disapprove of fratricide. More hopefully I resumed, "That night Hamlet kept watch with the three who had seen his dead father. The dead chief again appeared, and although the others were afraid, Hamlet followed his dead father off to one side. When they were alone, Hamlet's dead father spoke."

"Omens can't talk!" The old man was emphatic.

19 "Hamlet's dead father wasn't an omen. Seeing him might have been an omen, but he was not." My audience looked as confused as I sounded. "It *was* Hamlet's dead father. It was a thing we call a 'ghost.'" I had to use the English word, for unlike many of the neighboring tribes, these people didn't believe in the survival after death of any individuating part of the personality.

"What is a 'ghost'? An omen?"

"No, a 'ghost' is someone who is dead but who walks around and can talk, and people can hear him and see him but not touch him."

They objected. "One can touch zombis."

"No, no! It was not a dead body the witches had animated to sacrifice and eat. No one else made Hamlet's dead father walk. He did it himself."

"Dead men can't walk," protested my audience as one man.

20 I was quite willing to compromise. "A 'ghost' is the dead man's shadow."

But again they objected. "Dead men cast no shadows."

"They do in my country," I snapped.

The old man quelled the babble of disbelief that arose immediately and told me with that insincere, but courteous, agreement one extends to the fancies of the young, ignorant, and superstitious, "No doubt in your country the dead can also walk without being zombis." From the depths of his bag he produced a withered fragment of kola nut, bit off one end to show it wasn't poisoned, and handed me the rest as a peace offering.

21 "Anyhow," I resumed, "Hamlet's dead father said that his own brother, the one who became chief, had poisoned him. He wanted Hamlet to avenge him. Hamlet believed this in his heart, for he did not like his father's brother." I took another swallow of beer. "In the country of the great chief, living in the same homestead, for it was a very large one, was an important elder who was often with the chief to advise and help him. His name was Polonius. Hamlet was courting his daughter, but her father and her brother . . . [I cast hastily about for some tribal analogy] warned her not to let Hamlet visit her when she was alone on her farm, for he would be a great chief and so could not marry her."

"Why not?" asked the wife, who had settled down on the edge of the old man's chair. He frowned at her for asking stupid questions and growled, "They lived in the same homestead."

22 "That was not the reason," I informed them. "Polonius was a stranger who lived in the homestead because he helped the chief, not because he was a relative."

"Then why couldn't Hamlet marry her?"

"He could have," I explained, "but Polonius didn't think he would. After all, Hamlet was a man of great importance who ought to marry a chief's daughter, for in his country a man could have only one wife. Polonius was afraid that if Hamlet made love to his daughter, then no one else would give a high price for her."

"That might be true," remarked one of the shrewder elders, "but a chief's son would give his mistress's father enough presents and patronage to more than make up the difference. Polonius sounds like a fool to me."

23 "Many people think he was," I agreed. "Meanwhile Polonius sent his son Laertes off to Paris to learn the things of that country, for it was the homestead of a very great chief indeed. Because he was afraid that Laertes might waste a lot of money on beer and women and gambling, or get into trouble by fighting, he sent one of his servants to Paris secretly, to spy out what Laertes was doing. One day Hamlet came upon Polonius's daughter

Ophelia. He behaved so oddly he frightened her. Indeed"—I was fumbling for words to express the dubious quality of Hamlet's madness—"the chief and many others had also noticed that when Hamlet talked one could understand the words but not what they meant. Many people thought that he had become mad." My audience suddenly became much more attentive. "The great chief wanted to know what was wrong with Hamlet, so he sent for two of Hamlet's age mates [school friends would have taken long explanation] to talk to Hamlet and find out what troubled his heart. Hamlet, seeing that they had been bribed by the chief to betray him, told them nothing. Polonius, however, insisted that Hamlet was mad because he had been forbidden to see Ophelia, whom he loved."

24 "Why," inquired a bewildered voice, "should anyone bewitch Hamlet on that account?"

"Bewitch him?"

"Yes, only witchcraft can make anyone mad, unless, of course, one sees the beings that lurk in the forest."

25 I stopped being a storyteller, took out my notebook and demanded to be told more about these two causes of madness. Even while they spoke and I jotted notes, I tried to calculate the effect of this new factor on the plot. Hamlet had not been exposed to the beings that lurk in the forest. Only his relatives in the male line could bewitch him. Barring relatives not mentioned by Shakespeare, it had to be Claudius who was attempting to harm him. And, of course, it was.

26 For the moment I staved off questions by saying that the great chief also refused to believe that Hamlet was mad for the love of Ophelia and nothing else. "He was sure that something much more important was troubling Hamlet's heart."

"Now Hamlet's age mates," I continued, "had brought with them a famous storyteller. Hamlet decided to have this man tell the chief and all his homestead a story about a man who had poisoned his brother because he desired his brother's wife and wished to be chief himself. Hamlet was sure the great chief could not hear the story without making a sign if he was indeed guilty, and then he would discover whether his dead father had told him the truth."

27 The old man interrupted, with deep cunning, "Why should a father lie to his son?" he asked.

I hedged: "Hamlet wasn't sure that it really was his dead father." It was impossible to say anything, in that language, about devil-inspired visions.

"You mean," he said, "it actually was an omen, and he knew witches sometimes send false ones. Hamlet was a fool not to go to one skilled in reading omens and divining the truth in the first place. A man-who-sees-the-truth could have told him how his father died, if he really had been poisoned, and if there was witchcraft in it; then Hamlet could have called the elders to settle the matter."

28 The shrewd elder ventured to disagree. "Because his father's brother was a great chief, one-who-sees-the-truth might therefore have been afraid to

tell it. I think it was for that reason that a friend of Hamlet's father—a witch and an elder—sent an omen so his friend's son would know. Was the omen true?''

"Yes," I said, abandoning ghosts and the devil; a witch-sent omen it would have to be. "It was true, for when the storyteller was telling his tale before all the homestead, the great chief rose in fear. Afraid that Hamlet knew his secret, he planned to have him killed."

29 The stage set of the next bit presented some difficulties of translation. I began cautiously. "The great chief told Hamlet's mother to find out from her son what he knew. But because a woman's children are always first in her heart, he had the important elder Polonius hide behind a cloth that hung against the wall of Hamlet's mother's sleeping hut. Hamlet started to scold his mother for what she had done."

There was a shocked murmur from everyone. A man should never scold his mother.

"She called out in fear, and Polonius moved behind the cloth. Shouting, 'A rat!' Hamlet took his machete and slashed through the cloth." I paused for dramatic effect. "He had killed Polonius!"

30 The old men looked at each other in surpreme disgust. "That Polonius truly was a fool and a man who knew nothing! What child would not know enough to shout, 'It's me!'" With a pang, I remembered that these people are ardent hunters, always armed with bow, arrow, and machete; at the first rustle in the grass an arrow is aimed and ready, and the hunter shouts "Game!" If no human voice answers immediately, the arrow speeds on its way. Like a good hunter Hamlet had shouted, "A rat!"

31 I rushed in to save Polonius's reputation. "Polonius did speak. Hamlet heard him. But he thought it was the chief and wished to kill him to avenge his father. He had meant to kill him earlier that evening . . ." I broke down, unable to describe to these pagans, who had no belief in individual afterlife, the difference between dying at one's prayers and dying "unhousell'd, disappointed, unaneled."

This time I had shocked my audience seriously. "For a man to raise his hand against his father's brother and the one who has become his father—that is a terrible thing. The elders ought to let such a man be bewitched."

I nibbled at my kola nut in some perplexity, then pointed out that after all the man had killed Hamlet's father.

32 "No," pronounced the old man, speaking less to me than to the young men sitting behing the elders. "If your father's brother has killed your father, you must appeal to your father's age mates; *they* may avenge him. No man may use violence against his senior relatives." Another thought struck him. "But if his father's brother had indeed been wicked enough to bewitch Hamlet and make him mad that would be a good story indeed, for it would be his fault that Hamlet, being mad, no longer had any sense and thus was ready to kill his father's brother."

33 There was a murmur of applause. *Hamlet* was again a good story to them, but it no longer seemed quite the same story to me. As I thought over

the coming complications of plot and motive, I lost courage and decided to skim over dangerous ground quickly.

"The great chief," I went on, "was not sorry that Hamlet had killed Polonius. It gave him a reason to send Hamlet away, with his two treacherous age mates, with letters to a chief of a far country, saying that Hamlet should be killed. But Hamlet changed the writing on their papers, so that the chief killed his age mates instead." I encountered a reproachful glare from one of the men whom I had told undetectable forgery was not merely immoral but beyond human skill. I looked the other way.

34 "Before Hamlet could return, Laertes came back for his father's funeral. The great chief told him Hamlet had killed Polonius. Laertes swore to kill Hamlet because of this, and because his sister, Ophelia, hearing her father had been killed by the man she loved, went mad and drowned in the river."

"Have you already forgotten what we told you?" The old man was reproachful. "One cannot take vengeance on a madman; Hamlet killed Polonius in his madness. As for the girl, she not only went mad, she was drowned. Only witches can make people drown. Water itself can't hurt anything. It is merely something one drinks and bathes in."

I began to get cross. "If you don't like the story, I'll stop."

35 The old man made soothing noises and himself poured me some more beer. "You tell the story well, and we are listening. But it is clear that the elders of your country have never told you what the story really means. No, don't interrupt! We believe you when you say your marriage customs are different, or your clothes and weapons. But people are the same everywhere; therefore, there are always witches and it is we, the elders, who know how witches work. We told you it was the great chief who wished to kill Hamlet, and now your own words have proved us right. Who were Ophelia's male relatives?"

36 "There were only her father and her brother." Hamlet was clearly out of my hands.

"There must have been many more; this also you must ask of your elders when you get back to your country. From what you tell us, since Polonius was dead, it must have been Laertes who killed Ophelia, although I do not see the reason for it."

We had emptied one pot of beer, and the old men argued the point with slightly tipsy interest. Finally one of them demanded of me, "What did the servant of Polonius say on his return?"

With difficulty I recollected Reynaldo and his mission. "I don't think he did return before Polonius was killed."

37 "Listen," said the elder, "and I will tell you how it was and how your story will go, then you may tell me if I am right. Polonius knew his son would get into trouble, and so he did. He had many fines to pay for fighting, and debts from gambling. But he had only two ways of getting money quickly. One was to marry off his sister at once, but it is difficult to find a man who will marry a woman desired by the son of a chief. For if the chief's heir commits adultery with your wife, what can you do? Only a fool calls a case against a

man who will someday be his judge. Therefore Laertes had to take the second way: he killed his sister by witchcraft, drowning her so he could secretly sell her body to the witches."

38 I raised an objection. "They found her body and buried it. Indeed Laertes jumped into the grave to see his sister once more—so, you see, the body was truly there. Hamlet, who had just come back, jumped in after him."

"What did I tell you?" The elder appealed to the others. "Laertes was up to no good with his sister's body. Hamlet prevented him, because the chief's heir, like a chief, does not wish any other man to grow rich and powerful. Laertes would be angry, because he would have killed his sister without benefit to himself. In our country he would try to kill Hamlet for that reason. Is this not what happened?"

39 "More or less," I admitted. "When the great chief found Hamlet was still alive, he encouraged Laertes to try to kill Hamlet and arranged a fight with machetes between them. In the fight both the young men were wounded to death. Hamlet's mother drank the poisoned beer that the chief meant for Hamlet in case he won the fight. When he saw his mother die of poison, Hamlet, dying, managed to kill his father's brother with his machete."

"You see, I was right!" exclaimed the elder.

40 "That was a very good story," added the old man, "and you told it with very few mistakes. There was just one more error, at the very end. The poison Hamlet's mother drank was obviously meant for the survivor of the fight, whichever it was. If Laertes had won, the great chief would have poisoned him, for no one would know that he arranged Hamlet's death. Then, too, he need not fear Laertes' witchcraft; it takes a strong heart to kill one's only sister by witchcraft.

41 "Sometime," concluded the old man, gathering his ragged toga about him, "you must tell us some more stories of your country. We, who are elders, will instruct you in their true meaning, so that when you return to your own land your elders will see that you have not been sitting in the bush, but among those who know things and who have taught you wisdom."

VOCABULARY

hillock (3)	soliloquy (16)
accessible (3)	fratricide (18)
calabash (7)	zombis (19)
hazards (9)	patronage (22)
genealogical (14)	unhousell'd (31)
motif (15)	unaneled (31)
retorted (15)	toga (41)

QUESTIONS ON CONTENT

1. In relating her experience with a primitive tribe in West Africa, what point about language and culture does Laura Bohannan make?

2. While the author tells her story, we learn a great deal about the customs and beliefs of the Tiv. What are some of them?
3. What is the proper style of beginning a story among the Tiv? What is our equivalent?
4. What causes the repeated breakdown in communicating the Hamlet story?
5. How could the Hamlet story be made comprehensible to a tribe like the Tiv?

QUESTIONS ON FORM

1. What is the purpose for such a long introductory description of the homestead where the Hamlet story is told?
2. The story consists largely of narrative development. What other technique is used? What is the purpose of it?
3. Why is there no accurate Tiv translation for the word "scholar"?
4. If you had to translate the word "restaurant" for primitive people, what might you say?
5. What is the implied meaning of the final sentence in the selection?
6. Laura Bohannan is an anthropologist. At what level of education in her audience does she aim?

SUGGESTIONS FOR WRITING

1. Summarize the plot of *Othello* or some other famous story so that someone who does not understand English well can understand it.
2. Using all the details gathered from your reading of this essay, write a vivid description of the Tiv tribe.

CARL SANDBURG

THREES

I was a boy when I heard three red words
a thousand Frenchmen died in the streets
for: Liberty, Equality, Fraternity—I asked
why men die for words.

I was older; men with mustaches, sideburns,
lilacs, told me the high golden words are:
Mother, Home, and Heaven—other older men with
face decorations said: God, Duty, Immortality
—they sang these threes slow from deep lungs.

Years ticked off their say-so on the great clocks
of doom and damnation, soup and nuts: meteors flashed
their say-so: and out of great Russia came three
dusky syllables workmen took guns and went out to die
for: Bread, Peace, Land.

> And I met a marine of the U.S.A., a leatherneck with
> a girl on his knee for a memory in ports circling the
> earth and he said: Tell me how to say three things
> and I always get by—gimme a plate of ham and eggs—
> how much?—and, do you love me, kid?

QUESTIONS ON CONTENT

1. What is the theme of this poem?
2. At this stage in your life, on which of the word clusters mentioned do you place highest value? Why?
3. What values are implied by each word cluster?
4. What kind of person does the marine of the last stanza appear to be?

QUESTIONS ON FORM

1. Who is the speaker in the poem? What does he represent?
2. What is the connotation of "mustaches, sideburns,/lilacs" in the second stanza?
3. What is the effect of juxtaposing such words as "doom and damnation" with "soup and nuts"?
4. Why does the poet allude to Russia in the third stanza?
5. How does the poet indicate the passing of time?

ANTON CHEKHOV

Translated by Constance Garnett

THE NEW VILLA

This story by Russian author Anton Chekhov (1860–1904) points up the tragedy that can ensue when people from different cultures have not learned to communicate with each other. The clash between the engineer and the peasants of Obrutchanovo is a working out of Hayakawa's parable. What could have been a happy, progressive community is paralyzed because of poor language habits.

1

1 Two miles from the village of Obrutchanovo a huge bridge was being built. From the village, which stood up high on the steep river-bank, its trellis-like skeleton could be seen, and in foggy weather and on still winter days, when its delicate iron girders and all the scaffolding around was covered with hoar frost, it presented a picturesque and even fantastic spectacle. Kutcherov, the engineer who was building the bridge, a stout, broad-shouldered, bearded man in a soft crumpled cap, drove through the village in his racing droshky or his open carriage. Now and then on holidays navvies working on the bridge would come to the village; they begged for alms, laughed at the women, and

sometimes carried off something. But that was rare; as a rule the days passed quietly and peacefully as though no bridge-building were going on, and only in the evening, when camp fires gleamed near the bridge, the wind faintly wafted the songs of the navvies. And by day there was sometimes the mournful clang of metal, don-don-don.

2 It happened that the engineer's wife came to see him. She was pleased with the riverbanks and the gorgeous view over the green valley with trees, churches, flocks, and she began begging her husband to buy a small piece of ground and to build them a cottage on it. Her husband agreed. They bought sixty acres of land, and on the high bank in a field, where in earlier days the cows of Obrutchanovo used to wander, they built a pretty house of two storeys with a terrace and a verandah, with a tower and a flagstaff on which a flag fluttered on Sundays—they built it in about three months, and then all the winter they were planting big trees, and when spring came and everything began to be green there were already avenues to the new house, a gardener and two labourers in white aprons were digging near it, there was a little fountain, and a globe of looking-glass flashed so brilliantly that it was painful to look at. The house had already been named the New Villa.

3 On a bright, warm morning at the end of May two horses were brought to Obrutchanovo to the village blacksmith, Rodion Petrov. They came from the New Villa. The horses were sleek, graceful beasts, as white as snow, and strikingly alike.

"Perfect swans!" said Rodion, gazing at them with reverent admiration.

4 His wife Stepanida, his children and grandchildren came out into the street to look at them. By degrees a crowd collected. The Lytchkovs, father and son, both men with swollen faces and entirely beardless, came up bareheaded. Kozov, a tall, thin old man with a long, narrow beard, came up leaning on a stick with a crook handle: he kept winking with his crafty eyes and smiling ironically as though he knew something.

"It's only that they are white; what is there in them?" he said. "Put mine on oats, and they will be just as sleek. They ought to be in a plough and with a whip, too. . . ."

5 The coachman simply looked at him with disdain, but did not utter a word. And afterwards, while they were blowing up the fire at the forge, the coachman talked while he smoked cigarettes. The peasants learned from him various details: his employers were wealthy people; his mistress, Elena Ivanovna, had till her marriage lived in Moscow in a poor way as a governess; she was kindhearted, compassionate, and fond of helping the poor. On the new estate, he told them, they were not going to plough or to sow, but simply to live for their pleasure, live only to breathe the fresh air. When he had finished and led the horses back a crowd of boys followed him, the dogs barked, and Kozov, looking after him, winked sarcastically.

"Landowners, too-oo!" he said. "They have built a house and set up horses, but I bet they are nobodies—landowners, too-oo."

6 Kozov for some reason took a dislike from the first to the new house, to the white horses, and to the handsome, well-fed coachman. Kozov was a

solitary man, a widower; he had a dreary life (he was prevented from working by a disease which he sometimes called a rupture and sometimes worms); he was maintained by his son, who worked at a confectioner's in Harkov and sent him money; and from early morning till evening he sauntered at leisure about the river or about the village; if he saw, for instance, a peasant carting a log, or fishing, he would say: "That log's dry wood—it is rotten," or, "They won't bite in weather like this." In times of drought he would declare that there would not be a drop of rain till the frost came; and when the rains came he would say that everything would rot in the fields, that everything was ruined. And as he said these things he would wink as though he knew something.

7 At the New Villa they burned Bengal lights and sent up fireworks in the evenings, and a sailing-boat with red lanterns floated by Obrutchanovo. One morning the engineer's wife, Elèna Ivanovna, and her little daughter drove to the village in a carriage with yellow wheels and a pair of dark bay ponies; both mother and daughter were wearing broadbrimmed straw hats, bent down over their ears.

8 This was exactly at the time when they were carting manure, and the blacksmith Rodion, a tall, gaunt old man, bareheaded and barefooted, was standing near his dirty and repulsive-looking cart and, flustered, looked at the ponies, and it was evident by his face that he had never seen such little horses before.

"The Kutcherov lady has come!" was whispered around. "Look, the Kutcherov lady has come!"

9 Elena Ivanovna looked at the huts as though she were selecting one, and then stopped at the very poorest, at the windows of which there were so many children's heads—flaxen, red, and dark. Stepanida, Rodion's wife, a stout woman, came running out of the hut; her kerchief slipped off her grey head; she looked at the carriage facing the sun, and her face smiled and wrinkled up as though she were blind.

"This is for your children," said Elena Ivanovna, and she gave her three roubles.

10 Stepanida suddenly burst into tears and bowed down to the ground. Rodion, too, flopped to the ground, displaying his brownish bald head, and as he did so he almost caught his wife in the ribs with the fork. Elena Ivanovna was overcome with confusion and drove back.

2

11 The Lytchkovs, father and son, caught in their meadows two carthorses, a pony, and a broad-faced Aalhaus bull-calf, and with the help of redheaded Volodka, son of the blacksmith Rodion, drove them to the village. They called the village elder, collected witnesses, and went to look at the damage.

"All right, let 'em!" said Kozov, winking, "le-et 'em! Let them get out of it if they can, the engineers! Do you think there is no such thing as law? All right! Send for the police inspector, draw up a statement! . . .''

"Draw up a statement," repeated Volodka.

"I don't want to let this pass!" shouted the younger Lytchkov. He shouted louder and louder, and his beardless face seemed to be more and more swollen. "They've set up a nice fashion! Leave them free, and they will ruin all the meadows! You've no sort of right to ill-treat people! We are not serfs now!"

12 "We are not serfs now!" repeated Volodka.

"We got on all right without a bridge," said the elder Lytchkov gloomily; "we did not ask for it. What do we want a bridge for? We don't want it!"

"Brothers, good Christians, we cannot leave it like this!"

"All right, let 'em!" said Kozov, winking. "Let them get out of it if they can! Landowners, indeed!"

13 They went back to the village, and as they walked the younger Lytchkov beat himself on the breast with his fist and shouted all the way, and Volodka shouted, too, repeating his words. And meanwhile quite a crowd had gathered in the village round the thoroughbred bull-calf and the horses. The bull-calf was embarrassed and looked up from under his brows, but suddenly lowered his muzzle to the ground and took to his heels, kicking up his hind legs; Kozov was frightened and waved his stick at him, and they all burst out laughing. Then they locked up the beasts and waited.

14 In the evening the engineer sent five roubles for the damage, and the two horses, the pony and the bull-calf, without being fed or given water, returned home, their heads hanging with a guilty air as though they were convicted criminals.

On getting the five roubles the Lytchkovs, father and son, the village elder and Volodka, punted over the river in a boat and went to a hamlet on the other side where there was a tavern, and there had a long carousal. Their singing and the shouting of the younger Lytchkov could be heard from the village. Their women were uneasy and did not sleep all night. Rodion did not sleep either.

15 "It's bad business," he said, sighing and turning from side to side. "The gentleman will be angry, and then there will be trouble. . . . They have insulted the gentleman. . . . Oh, they've insulted him. It's a bad business. . . .''

It happened that the peasants, Rodion amongst them, went into their forest to divide the clearings for mowing, and as they were returning home they were met by the engineer. He was wearing a red cotton shirt and high boots; a setter dog with its long tongue hanging out, followed behind him.

"Good-day, brothers," he said.

16 The peasants stopped and took off their hats.

"I have long wanted to have a talk with you, friends," he went on. "This is what it is. Ever since the early spring your cattle have been in my copse and garden every day. Everything is trampled down; the pigs have rooted up the meadow, are ruining everything in the kitchen garden, and all the undergrowth in the copse is destroyed. There is no getting on with your herdsmen; one asks them civilly, and they are rude. Damage is done on my estate every day and I do nothing—I don't fine you or make a complaint; meanwhile you impounded my horses and my bull-calf and exacted five roubles. Was that right? Is that neighbourly?'' he went on, and his face was so soft and persuasive, and his expression was not forbidding. "Is that the way decent people behave? A week ago one of your people cut down two oak saplings in my copse. You have dug up the road to Eresnevo, and now I have to go two miles round. Why do you injure me at every step? What harm have I done you? For God's sake, tell me! My wife and I do our utmost to live with you in peace and harmony; we help the peasants as we can. My wife is a kind, warm-hearted woman; she never refuses you help. That is her dream—to be of use to you and your children. You reward us with evil for our good. You are unjust, my friends. Think of that. I ask you earnestly to think it over. We treat you humanely; repay us in the same coin.''

17 He turned and went away. The peasants stood a little longer, put on their caps and walked away. Rodion, who always understood everything that was said to him in some peculiar way of his own, heaved a sigh and said:

"We must pay. 'Repay in coin, my friends' . . . he said.''

18 They walked to the village in silence. On reaching home Rodion said his prayer, took off his boots, and sat down on the bench beside his wife. Stepanida and he always sat side by side when they were at home, and always walked side by side in the street; they ate and they drank and they slept always together, and the older they grew the more they loved one another. It was hot and crowded in their hut, and there were children everywhere—on the floors, in the windows, on the stove. . . . In spite of her advanced years Stepanida was still bearing children, and now, looking at the crowd of children, it was hard to distinguish which were Rodion's and which were Volodka's, Volodka's wife, Lukerya, a plain young woman with prominent eyes and a nose like the beak of a bird, was kneading dough in a tub; Volodka was sitting on the stove with his legs hanging.

19 "On the road near Nikita's buckwheat . . . the engineer with his dog . . .'' Rodion began, after a rest, scratching his ribs and his elbow. "'You must pay,' says he . . . 'coin,' says he. . . . Coin or no coin, we shall have to collect ten kopecks from every hut. We've offended the gentleman very much. I am sorry for him. . . .''

"We've lived without a bridge,'' said Volodka, not looking at anyone, "and we don't want one.''

"What next; the bridge is a government business.''

"We don't want it.''

"Your opinion is not asked. What is it to you?''

"'Your opinion is not asked,''' Volodka mimicked him. "We don't want to drive anywhere; what do we want with a bridge? If we have to, we can cross by the boat.''

20 Someone from the yard outside knocked at the window so violently that it seemed to shake the whole hut.

"Is Volodka at home?" he heard the voice of the younger Lytchkov. "Volodka, come out, come along."

Volodka jumped down off the stove and began looking for his cap. "Don't go, Volodka," said Rodion diffidently. "Don't go with them, son. You are foolish, like a little child; they will teach you no good; don't go!"

21 "Don't go, son," said Stepanida, and she blinked as though about to shed tears. "I bet they are calling you to the tavern."

"'To the tavern,'" Volodka mimicked.

"You'll come back drunk again, you currish Herod," said Lukerya, looking at him angrily. "Go along, go along, and may you burn up with vodka, you tailless Satan!"

"You hold your tongue," shouted Volodka.

"They've married me to a fool, they've ruined me, a luckless orphan, you redheaded drunkard . . ." wailed Lukerya, wiping her face with a hand covered with dough. "I wish I had never set eyes on you."

Volodka gave her a blow on the ear and went off.

3

22 Elena Ivanovna and her little daughter visited the village on foot. They were out for a walk. It was a Sunday, and the peasant women and girls were walking up and down the street in their brightly-coloured dresses. Rodion and Stepanida, sitting side by side at their door, bowed and smiled to Elena Ivanovna and her little daughter as to acquaintances. From the windows more than a dozen children stared at them; their faces expressed amazement and curiosity, and they could be heard whispering:

23 "The Kutcherov lady has come! The Kutcherov lady!"

"Good-morning," said Elena Ivanova, and she stopped; she paused, and then asked: "Well, how are you getting on?"

"We get along all right, thank God," answered Rodion, speaking rapidly. "To be sure we get along."

"The life we lead!" smiled Stepanida. "You can see our poverty yourself, dear lady! The family is fourteen souls in all, and only two breadwinners. We are supposed to be blacksmiths, but when they bring us a horse to shoe we have no coal, nothing to buy it with. We are worried to death, lady," she went on, and laughed. "Oh, oh, we are worried to death."

24 Elena Ivanovna sat down at the entrance and, putting her arm round her little girl, pondered something, and judging from the little girl's expression, melancholy thoughts were straying through her mind, too; as she brooded she played with the sumptuous lace on the parasol she had taken out of her mother's hands.

"Poverty," said Rodion, "a great deal of anxiety—you see no end to it. Here, God sends no rain . . . our life is not easy, there is no denying it."

"You have a hard time in this life," said Elena Ivanovna, "but in the other world you will be happy."

25 Rodion did not understand her, and simply coughed into his clenched hand by way of reply. Stepanida said:

"Dear lady, the rich men will be all right in the next world, too. The rich put up candles, pay for services; the rich give to beggars, but what can the poor man do? He has no time to make the sign of the cross. He is the beggar of beggars himself; how can he think of his soul? And many sins come from poverty; from trouble we snarl at one another like dogs, we haven't a good word to say to one another, and all sorts of things happen, dear lady—God forbid! It seems we have no luck in this world nor the next. All the luck has fallen to the rich."

26 She spoke gaily; she was evidently used to talking of her hard life. And Rodion smiled, too; he was pleased that his old woman was so clever, so ready of speech.

"It is only on the surface that the rich seem to be happy," said Elena Ivanova. "Every man has his sorrow. Here my husband and I do not live poorly, we have means, but are we happy? I am young, but I have had four children; my children are always being ill. I am ill, too, and constantly being doctored."

"And what is your illness?" asked Rodion.

27 "A woman's complaint. I get no sleep; a continual headache gives me no peace. Here I am sitting and talking, but my head is bad, I am weak all over, and I should prefer the hardest labour to such a condition. My soul, too, is troubled; I am in continual fear for my children, my husband. Every family has its own trouble of some sort; we have ours. I am not of noble birth. My grandfather was a simple peasant, my father was a tradesman in Moscow; he was a plain, uneducated man, too, while my husband's parents were wealthy and distinguished. They did not want him to marry me, but he disobeyed them, quarrelled with them, and they have not forgiven us to this day. That worries my husband; it troubles him and keeps him in constant agitation; he loves his mother, loves her dearly. So I am uneasy, too, my soul is in pain."

28 Peasants, men and women, were by now standing round Rodion's hut and listening. Kozov came up, too, and stood twitching his long, narrow beard. The Lytchkovs, father and son, drew near.

"And say what you like, one cannot be happy and satisfied if one does not feel in one's proper place," Elena Ivanovna went on. "Each of you has his strip of land, each of you works and knows what he is working for; my husband builds bridges—in short, everyone has his place, while I, I simply walk about. I have not my bit to work. I don't work, and feel as though I were an outsider. I am saying all this that you may not judge from outward appearances; if a man is expensively dressed and has means it does not prove that he is satisfied with his life."

29 She got up to go away and took her daughter by the hand.

"I like your place here very much," she said, and smiled, and from that faint, diffident smile one could tell how unwell she really was, how young and how pretty; she had a pale, thinnish face with dark eyebrows and fair hair. And the little girl was just such another as her mother: thin, fair, and slender. There was a fragrance of scent about them.

30 "I like the river and the forest and the village," Elena Ivanovna went on; "I could live here all my life, and I feel as though here I should get strong and find my place. I want to help you—I want to dreadfully—to be of use, to be a real friend to you. I know your need, and what I don't know I feel, my heart guesses. I am sick, feeble, and for me perhaps it is not possible to change my life as I would. But I have children. I will try to bring them up that they may be of use to you, may love you. I shall impress upon them continually that their life does not belong to them, but to you. Only I beg you earnestly, I beseech you, trust us, live in friendship with us. My husband is a kind, good man. Don't worry him, don't irritate him. He is sensitive to every trifle, and yesterday, for instance, your cattle were in our vegetable garden, and one of your people broke down the fence to the bee-hives, and such an attitude to us drives my husband to despair. I beg you," she went on in an imploring voice, and she clasped her hands on her bosom—"I beg you to treat us as good neighbours; let us live in peace! There is a saying, you know, that even a bad peace is better than a good quarrel, and, 'Don't buy property, but buy neighbours.' I repeat my husband is a kind man and good; if all goes well we promise to do everything in our power for you; we will mend the roads, we will build a school for your children. I promise you."

31 "Of course we thank you humbly, lady," said Lytchkov the father, looking at the ground; "you are educated people; it is for you to know best. Only, you see, Voronov, a rich peasant at Eresnevo, promised to build a school; he, too, said, 'I will do this for you,' 'I will do that for you,' and he only put up the framework and refused to go on. And then they made the peasants put the roof on and finish it; it cost them a thousand roubles. Voronov did not care; he only stroked his beard, but the peasants felt it a bit hard."

32 "That was a crow, but now there's a rook, too," said Kozov, and he winked.

There was the sound of laughter.

"We don't want a school," said Volodka sullenly. "Our children go to Petrovskoe, and they can go on going there; we don't want it."

Elena Ivanovna seemed suddenly intimidated; her face looked paler and thinner, she shrank into herself as though she had been touched with something coarse, and walked away without uttering another word. And she walked more and more quickly, without looking round.

33 "Lady," said Rodion, walking after her, "lady, wait a bit; hear what I would say to you."

He followed her without his cap, and spoke softly as though begging.

"Lady, wait and hear what I will say to you."

They had walked out of the village, and Elena Ivanovna stopped beside a cart in the shade of an old mountain ash.

34 "Don't be offended, lady," said Rodion. "What does it mean? Have

patience. Have patience for a couple of years. You will live here, you will have patience, and it will all come round. Our folks are good and peaceable; there's no harm in them; it's God's truth I'm telling you. Don't mind Kozov and the Lytchkovs, and don't mind Volodka. He's a fool; he listens to the first that speaks. The others are quiet folks; they are silent. Some would be glad, you know, to say a word from the heart and to stand up for themselves, but cannot. They have a heart and a conscience, but no tongue. Don't be offended . . . have patience. . . . What does it matter?''

35 Elena Ivanovna looked at the broad, tranquil river, pondering, and tears flowed down her cheeks. And Rodion was troubled by those tears; he almost cried himself.

"Never mind . . ." he muttered. "Have patience for a couple of years. You can have the school, you can have the roads, only not all at once. If you went, let us say, to sow corn on that mound you would first have to weed it out, to pick out all the stones, and then to plough, and work and work . . . and with the people, you see, it is the same . . . you must work and work until you overcome them.''

36 The crowd had moved away from Rodion's hut, and was coming along the street towards the mountain ash. They began singing songs and playing the concertina, and they kept coming closer and closer. . . .

"Mamma, let us go away from here," said the little girl, huddling up to her mother, pale and shaking all over; "let us go away, mamma!"

"Where?''

"To Moscow. . . . Let us go, mamma.''

The child began crying.

37 Rodion was utterly overcome; his face broke into profuse perspiration; he took out of his pocket a little crooked cucumber, like a half-moon, covered with crumbs of rye bread, and began thrusting it into the little girl's hands.

"Come, come," he muttered, scowling severely; "take the little cucumber, eat it up. . . . You mustn't cry. Mamma will whip you. . . . She'll tell your father of you when you get home. Come, come. . . .''

They walked on, and he still followed behind them, wanting to say something friendly and persuasive to them. And seeing that they were both absorbed in their own thoughts and their own griefs, and not noticing him, he stopped and, shading his eyes from the sun, looked after them for a long time till they disappeared into their copse.

4

38 The engineer seemed to grow irritable and petty, and in every trivial incident saw an act of robbery or outrage. His gate was kept bolted even by day, and at night two watchmen walked up and down the garden beating a board; and they gave up employing anyone from Obrutchanovo as a labourer. As ill-luck would have it someone (either a peasant or one of the workmen) took the new wheels off the cart and replaced them by old ones, then soon

afterwards two bridles and a pair of pincers were carried off, and murmurs arose even in the village. People began to say that a search should be made at the Lytchkovs' and at Volodka's, and then the bridles and the pincers were found under the hedge in the engineer's garden; someone had thrown them down there.

39 It happened that the peasants were coming in a crowd out of the forest, and again they met the engineer on the road. He stopped, and without wishing them good-day he began, looking angrily first at one, then at another:

"I have begged you not to gather mushrooms in the park and near the yard, but to leave them for my wife and children, but your girls come before daybreak and there is not a mushroom left. . . . Whether one asks you or not it makes no difference. Entreaties, and friendliness, and persuasion I see are all useless."

40 He fixed his indignant eyes on Rodion and went on:

"My wife and I behaved to you as human beings, as to our equals, and you? But what's the use of talking! It will end by our looking down upon you. There is nothing left!"

And making an effort to restrain his anger, not to say too much, he turned and went on.

On getting home, Rodion said his prayer, took off his boots, and sat down beside his wife.

41 "Yes . . ." he began with a sigh. "We were walking along just now, and Mr. Kutcherov met us. . . . Yes. . . . He saw the girls at daybreak. . . . 'Why don't they bring mushrooms,' he said . . . 'to my wife and children?' he said. . . . And then he looked at me and he said: 'I and my wife will look after you,' he said. I wanted to fall down at his feet, but I hadn't the courage. . . . God give him health. . . . God bless him! . . ."

Stepanida crossed herself and sighed.

"They are kind, simple-hearted people," Rodion went on. " 'We shall look after you.' . . . He promised me that before everyone. In our old age . . . it wouldn't be a bad thing. . . . I should always pray for them. . . . Holy Mother, bless them. . . ."

42 The Feast of the Exaltation of the Cross, the fourteenth of September, was the festival of the village church. The Lytchkovs, father and son, went across the river early in the morning and returned to dinner drunk; they spent a long time going about the village, alternately singing and swearing; then they had a fight and went to the New Villa to complain. First Lytchkov the father went into the yard with a long ashen stick in his hands. He stopped irresolutely and took off his hat. Just at that moment the engineer and his family were sitting on the verandah, drinking tea.

"What do you want?" shouted the engineer.

"Your honour . . ." Lytchkov began, and burst into tears. "Show the Divine mercy, protect me . . . my son makes my life a misery . . . your honour . . ."

43 Lytchkov the son walked up, too; he, too, was bareheaded and had a

stick in his hand; he stopped and fixed his drunken senseless eyes on the verandah.

"It is not my business to settle your affairs," said the engineer. "Go to the rural captain or the police officer."

"I have been everywhere. . . . I have lodged a petition . . ." said Lytchkov the father, and he sobbed. "Where can I go now? He can kill me now, it seems. He can do anything. Is that the way to treat a father? A father?"

44 He raised his stick and hit his son on the head; the son raised his stick and struck his father just on his bald patch such a blow that the stick bounced back. The father did not even flinch, but hit his son again and again on the head. And so they stood and kept hitting one another on the head, and it looked not so much like a fight as some sort of a game. And peasants, men and women, stood in a crowd at the gate and looked into the garden, and the faces of all were grave. They were the peasants who had come to greet them for the holiday, but seeing the Lytchkovs, they were ashamed and did not go in.

The next morning Elena Ivanovna went with the children to Moscow. And there was a rumour that the engineer was selling his house. . . .

5

45 The peasants had long ago grown used to the sight of the bridge, and it was difficult to imagine the river at that place without a bridge. The heap of rubble left from the building of it had long been overgrown with grass, the navvies were forgotten, and instead of the strains of the "Dubinushka" that they used to sing, the peasants heard almost every hour the sounds of a passing train.

The New Villa has long ago been sold; now it belongs to a government clerk who comes here from the town for the holidays with his family, drinks tea on the terrace, and then goes back to the town again. He wears a cockade on his cap; he talks and clears his throat as though he were a very important official, though he is only of the rank of a collegiate secretary, and when the peasants bow he makes no response.

46 In Obrutchanovo everyone has grown older; Kozov is dead. In Rodion's hut there are even more children. Volodka has grown a long red beard. They are still as poor as ever.

In the early spring the Obrutchanovo peasants were sawing wood near the station. And after work they were going home; they walked without haste one after the other. Broad saws curved over their shoulders; the sun was reflected in them. The nightingales were singing in the bushes on the bank, larks were trilling in the heavens. It was quiet at the New Villa; there was not a soul there, and only golden pigeons—golden because the sunlight was streaming upon them—were flying over the house. All of them—Rodion, the two Lytchkovs, and Volodka—thought of the white horses, the little ponies, the fireworks, the boat with the lanterns; they remembered how the engineer's wife, so beautiful and so grandly dressed, had come into the village and talked to them in such a friendly way. And it seemed as though all that had never been; it was like a dream or a fairy-tale.

47 They trudged along, tired out, and mused as they went. . . . In their village, they mused, the people were good, quiet, sensible, fearing God, and Elena Ivanova, too, was quiet, kind, and gentle; it made one sad to look at her but why had they not got on together? Why had they parted like enemies? How was it that some mist had shrouded from their eyes what mattered most, and had let them see nothing but damage done by cattle, bridles, pincers, and all those trivial things which now, as they remembered them, seemed so nonsensical? How was it that with the new owner they lived in peace, and yet had been on bad terms with the engineer?

48 And not knowing what answer to make to these questions they were all silent except Volodka, who muttered something.

"What is it?" Rodion asked.

"We lived without a bridge . . ." said Volodka gloomily. "We lived without a bridge, and did not ask for one . . . and we don't want it. . . ."

No one answered him and they walked on in silence with drooping heads.

VOCABULARY

navvies (1)	copse (16)
confectioner (6)	concertina (36)
Bengal lights (7)	pincers (38)
serfs (11)	

QUESTIONS ON CONTENT

1. The story is partly a conflict in values. How do you perceive this conflict?
2. On three different occasions semantic confusion causes one of the peasants to misunderstand the engineer. Describe these misunderstandings.
3. Of all the peasants described in the story, which are the most dangerous? Why?
4. If you had been Kutcherov, how would you have handled the communication problem with the peasants?
5. In the end, what happens to the bridge and to the community?

QUESTIONS ON FORM

1. How does Chekhov use words to convey atmosphere? Give two examples.
2. The story contains a number of symbols. Name at least three and identify what they stand for.

SUGGESTIONS FOR WRITING

1. Using the story "The New Villa" as your basis, develop an essay contrasting the problems of the rich with those of the poor.
2. Write an essay exposing the problems that keep privileged classes from communicating with deprived classes.

CHAPTER WRITING ASSIGNMENTS

1. Using any of the selections in this chapter, write a five-hundred-word essay delineating the major aspects of semantics.
2. Write a five-hundred-word essay indicating how a study of semantics can prevent quarrels between persons as well as governments. Use specific examples to strengthen your points.

Why Doesn't It Make Sense?
Logic

advice

RICHARD D. ALTICK

OBSTACLES TO CLEAR THINKING

This article spells out some of the common pitfalls in reasoning and offers the reader advice on how to avoid them. (From *Preface to Critical Reading*.)

1 In addition to the many pitfalls awaiting the unwary in formal inductive and deductive thinking, there are a number of common errors which perhaps can be called "abuses of logic" only by courtesy; some of them, at least, may best be described as sheer avoidances of logic.

2 1. Among them, an important class involves the *introduction of irrelevant and irrational evidence*. In the chapter on connotation, we have met a number of examples of such errors. There they were termed "name-calling" and "glittering generalities." Here we shall give them the labels they have in the books on clear thinking. But it is far less important to remember their names than it is to be able to recognize instances of them when we meet them—and to react to them as intelligent readers should react.

3 (a) The *argumentum ad hominem*. Here the writer or speaker departs from his task of proving the point at issue to prejudice his audience against his opponent. In American politics, this argument (which is too dignified a word for it!) is called "mud slinging." If, for example, in attacking his opponent's position on the reduction of the national debt, a candidate refers to Mr. X's intimate connection with certain well-known gamblers, he ceases to argue his case on its objective merits and casts doubt upon his opponent's personal character. His object is not primarily to hurt Mr. X's feelings, but to arouse bias against Mr. X in his hearer's mind. Every critical reader or listener must

343

train himself to detect and reject these irrelevant aspersions. It may be, indeed, that Mr. X *has* shady connections with the underworld. But that has nothing to do with the abstract rights or wrongs of his position on a national issue. Although, as the history of American politics shows, it is a hard thing to do, issues should be discussed apart from character and motives. The latter are also important, since obviously they bear upon a candidate's fitness for public office, but they call for a separate discussion.

4 (b) The *argumentum ad populum*. This too involves an appeal to the feelings, passions, and prejudices, rather than the reason, of the group addressed; but whereas the preceding argument is directed specifically against one's opponent, the *ad populum* argument has a wider range. The writer uses emotionally weighted words to bias his audience in favor of or against a person (not necessarily his opponent), an idea, a political party, a class, a nation. The monotonously repeated phrases of Communist propaganda against Americans—"Wall Street monopolists," "rich gangsters," "capitalistic warmongers"—are the most familiar recent examples of the negative, or name-calling, aspect of this argument. But just as common is the other aspect—that of the glittering generality, by which a writer attempts to sway his readers to enthusiasm for something or someone. The twin language-devices of the *argumentum ad populum,* then, are the stenchbomb and the perfume atomizer. The constant task of the critical reader is to ignore the odor with which an idea has been sprayed and to concentrate on the idea itself.

5 The "transfer" device is a particular favorite of those who find it to their advantage to use the *argumentum ad populum*. Like the use of name-calling and the glittering generality, it depends for its effectiveness upon the reader's or hearer's willingness to associate one idea with another, even though the two are not logically connected. Essentially, it represents an attempt to clothe one's pet policy or principle in borrowed raiment which will lend it a strength and dignity it does not possess by itself.

6 A common example of transfer is the habit which political orators have of working into their speeches quotations from Scripture or from the secular "sacred writings" (the Declaration of Independence, the Preamble to the Constitution, the Gettysburg Address). Such quotations are depended upon to arouse favorable emotions in the breasts of the auditors, emotions which are then transferred to the orator's pet policy. Much of William Jennings Bryan's success as a public figure was due to the way in which he transformed an ordinary political campaign into a quasi-religious crusade by his "Cross of Gold" speech: "You shall not press down upon the brow of labor this crown of thorns; you shall not crucify mankind upon a cross of gold!" Actually, although the underlying idea, that the national monetary policy at the end of the nineteenth century worked to the serious disadvantage of the "common man," was entirely valid, the metaphor in which it was expressed was not. There is no connection between economics and the passion and crucifixion of Jesus. But the metaphor succeeded admirably in rallying to Bryan's ranks millions of Americans to whom Biblical quotation and allusion had the most powerful of connotations. It is noteworthy that as the influence of the Bible

upon men's emotional habits declines, knowing politicians make less use of Biblical references; but such standard emotion-rousers as mention of Valley Forge, the Founding Fathers, and Abraham Lincoln are still found sprinkled through much propaganda. Whether they have any logical connection with the issues discussed is, to the speaker and (he hopes) to his audience, irrelevant; what they do is shed their own emotional effulgence upon ideas and pleas which might not otherwise be so acceptable.

7 The advertiser employs the transfer device just as commonly. Perhaps the most familiar instance of it is the use of the picture of a beautiful girl, not merely to attract attention to the advertisement but also to place the reader in a receptive frame of mind. Whether the girl has anything to do with the subject of the advertisement does not matter—so long as the reader is pleasantly affected. At certain periods when patriotic sentiment runs high, as during a war, commercial advertisers use the emotional symbols of patriotism for their own needs. Not only do they use the national colors and pictures of, or references to, the fighting men; their text often is designed to arouse fervent patriotic emotions which can then be transferred to a particular product. The following advertisement, dominated by a large drawing of the eagle on the United States seal, once appeared in eastern newspapers:

PRIDE IN THE AMERICAN WAY

8   The way of life that is American, that expounds democracy, is a proud way of life. It is a manner of living so fine, so high in ideals and purpose that it stands over and above all others. The Grabosky Family, makers of Royalist cigars, are proud to be members of The American Family, proud to present a cigar so fine in quality that it stands above all others. Over 50 years of superb cigar-making experience lie behind Royalist . . . a proud name in a proud America![1]

9 (c) The *argumentum ad verecundiam*. This is a special instance of the more general "transfer" device. Here it is not a matter of borrowing prestige from one institution, such as religion or a nation, to adorn something else; instead, the prestige is specifically that of a great name, an "authority," which is expected to have weight with the public. On the general matter of authority we shall have more to say in a little while. At this point, we need only stress the importance of critically analyzing any appeal which uses quotations from men and women who have achieved fame in one field or another. One crucial question is: Is the quotation appropriate here? Does it have real relevance to the point at issue? It is all very well to quote Jefferson or Lincoln or Franklin Roosevelt in support of one's political stand—but it must be remembered that circumstances have changed immensely since these quotations were first uttered, and their applicability to a new situation is open to question. The implication is, This man, who we all agree *was* great and wise, said certain things which prove the justice of my own stand; therefore it behooves you to

---

[1]Note that the brand name of the cigar is not conspicuously in harmony with the sentiments expressed in the advertisement itself; yet it probably sells cigars. Why?

believe I am right. But to have a valid argument, the writer must prove that the word of the authorities whom he cites has a logical bearing on the present issue. If that is true, then he is borrowing not so much their popular prestige as their wisdom—which is perfectly permissible.

10 In essence, what the writer who invokes august authority for his point of view does is to imply that if the great men of the past were living today, they would write testimonials in behalf of his position. The familiar testimonials of present-day advertising are another instance of the transfer device. In some cases, the authority who testifies has some connection with the type of product advertised. The problem to settle here is, When we decide which brand of cigarette is best, how much weight may we reasonably attach to the enthusiastic statements of tobacco buyers, warehousemen, and auctioneers? In other cases, the testifying authority may have no formal, professional connection with the product advertised. An actor, who may very well be a master of his particular art, praises a whiskey, an after-shaving lotion, or a new convertible. He likes it, he says: but, we may ask, does the fact that he is a successful actor make him any better qualified than anyone who is *not* an actor to judge a whiskey, a lotion, or a car? Competence in one field does not necessarily imply competence in another.

11 Furthermore, in recent times it has been increasingly the custom for advertisers to borrow the prestige of science and medicine to enhance the reputation of their products. The American people have come to feel for the laboratory scientist and the physician an awe once reserved for bishops and statesmen. The alleged approval of such men thus carries great weight when it is a question of selling something, or (which is the same thing) inducing someone to believe something. Phrases such as "leading medical authorities say . . ." or "independent laboratory tests show . . ." are designed simply to transfer the prestige of science, which presumably is incapable of either error or corruption, to a toothpaste or a cereal. Seldom if ever are the precise "medical authorities" or "independent laboratories" named. But the mere phrases have vast weight with the uncritical. Similarly too the honorific "Dr." or "professor" implies that the person quoted speaks with all the authority of which learned men are capable—when as a matter of fact "doctorates" can be bought from mail-order colleges. Whenever, therefore, an attempt is made to convince by appeal to the prestige that surrounds the learned, the reader should demand full credentials. Just *what* medical authorities say this? Can they be trusted? *What* independent laboratories made the test—and what, actually, did the tests reveal? Who is this man that speaks as a qualified educator or psychologist or economist? Regardless of the fact that he is called "doctor," does he know what he is talking about?

12 In all cases where the persuasive power of reputation and authority is invoked in behalf of a policy or a product, it is profitable to remember that before he can testify in a court of law, a man about to provide specialized evidence, which may have an important bearing on the jury's decision, must establish his competence in his field. A pathologist, a psychiatrist, an engi- neer, is asked briefly to outline the nature of his special training and experi-

ence. It would not hurt if, when we encounter the appeal to authority in any type of persuasive writing, we adopted the strategy of the opposing lawyer and probed more deeply into the witness' genuine competence to speak on the particular issue that is before us. A few pages later on, we shall suggest some pertinent questions in this respect.

13 2. *Begging the question.* Here the statement which is ostensibly offered as a proposition to be proved actually assumes the proposition as already proven. "This ordinance will certainly reduce juvenile delinquency, because it provides for steps which will prevent crimes on the part of teen-agers." In other words, A is good because A is good. "The reason why Sally is so mischievous is that she has just a little of the devil in her." "I would trust him with any of my personal affairs because he is certainly a reliable lawyer."

14 Every instance of name-calling or of the glittering generality involves question-begging. When a writer or speaker brands someone a "dangerous radical" or acclaims a policy as "the only way to escape national disaster" he is using words the truth of which he never questions—nor expects his audience to question. Yet all such words and phrases, weighted as they are with emotion and charged with controversy, stand very much in need of proof. And even if, when stripped of their irrelevant emotional wording, the ideas can be established as true, the argument remains sterile. Since its premise is identical with its conclusion, nobody who does not already accept the conclusion will accept the premise, and hence it convinces nobody.

15 3. *False analogy.* This fallacy consists of presenting a situation which is acknowledged to be true, and then, on the basis of it, commenting on another situation which is said to be similar. It is usually employed in an attempt to simplify and make more vivid a complex issue. Newspaper political cartoons are often nothing more than pictorial analogies. Often, of course, such analogies serve admirably to point up, dramatically and colorfully, the crux of a problem. The analogy of a governmental agency in the role of the legendary Dutch boy, trying desperately to stop a leak in the dike ("national economy") while the waves of the sea ("inflation") are already spilling over the top of the dike, is plainly very useful. But the ever-present danger is that the analogy will assume a vital resemblance between the two objects of comparison, where none really exists. "Don't change horses in the middle of a stream" is a familiar cry in political campaigns when, pleading a national emergency, the partisans of the incumbent in office declare he cannot be superseded without grave danger to the country. There is, of course, a superficial similarity between the two situations: changing horses in the middle of a swift stream is dangerous, and so too may be changing public officials at certain junctures in national affairs. But riding horseback is not much like being president of the United States, and while there may be only one or two reasons why one should or should not change horses, there may be very many reasons, none of them having anything to do with horseback riding, why one man should be elected president and not another. Equally dangerous is any attempt to prove a point which is based on the fancy that the nations of the world are like school children, and that when one nation does not have its way it goes into a corner

and sulks; or that two opponents, labor and capital, for example, may be likened to two prize-fighters squaring off in the ring, with some government official or agency as referee. Such analogies are, we repeat, useful in dramatizing a situation; but it is always perilous to maintain that because two situations are "alike" in one or two respects, what is true of one is necessarily true of the other.

16 4. *Oversimplification*. False analogy may well be considered a particular type of oversimplification—than which there is no more common error. When we discussed in the beginning of this chapter the method of reasoning by hypothesis, we stressed the fact that no hypothesis can be considered sound unless we have taken into account all the factors that are related to it. Unfortunately, with our natural human indolence, to say nothing of our intellectual limitations, we are always eager to view questions in their simplest terms and to make our decisions on the basis of only a few of the many aspects which the problem involves. If that is true of problems of a practical nature, such as those we used to illustrate the use of the hypothesis, how much more true it is of those involving a problem of human conduct, or a grave decision facing the voters or the statesmen of a nation! Few of the decisions which we are called upon to make are so simple that we can say with confidence that one choice is completely right and the other is completely wrong. The problem of the so-called minority groups in America, for instance, is not simply one of abstract justice, as many would like to think it; it involves deeply complex questions of economics, sociology, and politics. Nor can one say with easy assurance: "The federal government should guarantee every farmer a decent income, even if the money comes from the pocketbooks of the citizens who are the farmer's own customers"—or "It is the obligation of every educational institution to purge its faculty of everyone who holds leftist sympathies." Perhaps each of these propositions is sound, perhaps neither is; but before he adopts it as a settled conviction, the intelligent man or woman must canvass its full implications, just as he should do with any hypothesis. After the implications have been explored, it may be found that there is more evidence telling against the proposition than there is supporting it; in which case it should be abandoned. In any event, no one can call himself a conscientious citizen who fails to explore, so far as he is humanly able, the honest pros and cons of any issue he is called upon to help decide—and then to adopt the position he feels is best justified by the evidence he has surveyed.

17 Countless false generalizations concerning parties, races, religions, and nations—to say nothing of individuals—are the result of the deep-seated human desire to reduce a complex idea to its simplest terms. Democrats tend naturally to think of all Republicans as progress-obstructing conservatives, when in fact many Republicans are more "liberal" than many Democrats. Many Protestants regard Catholics as bigoted and superstitious, even though the views they regard as "bigoted" and the practices they regard as "superstitious" may have their roots deep in the philosophical grounds of the Catholic religion. Similarly many Catholics regard Protestants as infidels or atheists, although there may be as much philosophical justification for Protestant

doctrine as there is for Catholic. It is easier to condemn than to understand. But every man and woman has a pressing moral, as well as intellectual, obligation to examine the basis of every judgment he or she makes: "Am I examining every aspect of the issue that needs to be examined—do I understand the pros and cons of the problem sufficiently to be able to make a fair decision—or am I taking the easiest way out?"

18 5. The innate intellectual laziness of human beings invites one further, crowning device of deception: the *distortion or the actual suppression of the truth*. If men will not actively demand the truth, why should persuaders provide them with it, when doing so would hurt their chances of success? And so it is usual in all forms of persuasion to prevent considerations which would damage the cause from reaching the minds of those who are to be persuaded.

19 (a) One such device—there are many—is *card stacking* (also called "smoke screen"[2]), which is used by a group, a political party for instance, to divert attention from certain issues which it does not care to have discussed. Card stacking consists of laying heavy and insistent emphasis upon certain selected topics, discussion of which can probably do the party no harm. The party then hopes that the public, its attention centered on these topics, will not bother about the less attractive side of the party's record or program. A state administration, running for re-election, may devote all its propaganda to boasting about the reduction in taxes which it has effected in an "economy program"—and it will assiduously fail to mention the way in which state services have deteriorated as a result of the "slashed budget." This same practice is evident in virtually every advertisement one reads. The attractive points of a product are dwelt upon unceasingly; the less attractive ones, never. An automobile may be streamlined and easy-riding, it may have fast pickup in traffic, it may have a wealth of gadgets—these facts will be proclaimed from every newspaper, magazine, and billboard; but that the car eats up gasoline and oil, has a poorly made engine block, and costs $200 more than other cars in the same price-class—these facts are religiously suppressed. But, as you will no doubt agree, they are worth knowing about.

20 (b) Another closely related means by which attention is drawn from the whole truth is one dear to every practical politician: the *red herring*. The red herring is an irrelevant issue which is drawn across the path of an argument when one side or the other is becoming embarrassed and wishes to change the subject. In a campaign for the mayoralty of a large city, for example, Party A (which is in office) may find itself in serious trouble because Party B has successfully given evidence of its waste of public funds. Four days before the election, therefore, Party A suddenly "discovers" that Party B's candidate has been seen in night clubs with a lady who is not his wife. Party A hopes that the injection into the contest of another, more appealing, topic of discussion will allow the public to forget the serious accusations that have been leveled against it. Whether or not Party A is able to prove that the B candidate's

[2]Although their purposes are the same, card stacking and the smoke screen have slightly different techniques. The first is usually prepared in advance; the second is impromptu, being devised to meet exigencies as they occur in the course of an argument.

private frailties (if they do exist) disqualify him from holding public office, the red herring will have served its purpose if it ends the embarrassing talk about Party A's own shortcomings.

21 (c) A third such device is that of *wrenching from context*. A sentence or a phrase can easily mean one thing when it is quoted alone, and a quite different thing if it is read against the background of the whole discussion to which it belongs. An extreme example is a sentence from a newspaper review of a new movie: "For about five minutes 'Fruits of Desire' is a top-notch show, brilliantly acted and magnificently photographed. After that it degenerates into a dismal spectacle of Hollywood hokum." It would not be surprising to see the subsequent advertisements of the movie flaunting this headline: "'A top-notch show, brilliantly acted and magnificently photographed . . . a spectacle'—Smith, *Daily News*." The familiar "avoid foreign entanglements" advice in Washington's farewell address, when read in full context, means something very different from what it means when quoted separately. And probably no public figure whose statements are quoted in the newspapers or on the radio has ever escaped the chagrin that comes from seeing prominence given to one or two paragraphs of his latest speech which, thus isolated, completely distort his total argument. Such quotations must always be read with the greatest caution. The only way to be sure that they fairly represent the author's viewpoint is to read the complete text of his speech as printed in, for instance, *The New York Times*.

VOCABULARY

aspersions (3)	fallacy (15)
raiment (5)	partisans (15)
effulgence (6)	superseded (15)
behooves (9)	junctures (15)
august (10)	indolence (16)
invoked (12)	impromptu (footnote 2)
ostensibly (13)	assiduously (19)
acclaims (14)	chagrin (21)

discussion

JOHN C. SHERWOOD

INTRODUCTION TO LOGIC

This selection discusses the relationship between belief, values, and logic. It defines the difference between induction and deduction, between generalizations and judgments, and discusses the use of each in everyday reasoning. (From *Discourse of Reason*.)

1 Even for the most skeptical, belief is an absolute necessity for practical experience. At the very least, we have to have faith that the material world will continue in its accustomed ways, that tomorrow as today iron will be hard and clay soft, that objects will continue to fall toward the earth instead of flying off into the sky. Even in the less certain and less easily analyzed realm of human character, we constantly act on beliefs—that a soft answer turneth away wrath, that a veteran soldier will fight bravely, that a mother will love and protect her children, that the mailman will deliver the mail instead of stealing it. Without belief, action would be paralyzed; we should never know what to do in a given situation. What really distinguishes the rational from the irrational thinker is not the presence or absence of belief, but the grounds on which belief is accepted.

2 There are some sources of belief which are either absolutely unsound or to be resorted to only when all other methods fail. A "hunch" is not an absolutely useless guide, because it may be based on knowledge which has temporarily slipped our minds, but we would be foolish to trust a hunch when objective evidence was available. Our casual impression of a prospective employee may be useful, but full knowledge of his previous record is more valuable. Tradition may be a proper guide in some areas of life, but we cannot accept witchcraft or even the Newtonian physics because our forefathers did. All too often we believe simply because we want to believe. It is comforting to think that "there is always room at the top" or that "there are no atheists in foxholes" or that "football makes good citizens." But such beliefs are the most treacherous of all beliefs, because we tend to protect them by ignoring contrary evidence until at some crisis the brute facts force themselves on our attention. An unfounded belief is not merely wrong morally; it is an unsafe guide to conduct.

3 What then are the legitimate sources of belief? In a scientific age we instinctively answer, evidence or investigation. We believe that a worker is reliable because we have seen him at work frequently over a considerable period of time; we believe that a certain remedy will cure a certain disease because trained observers have watched its operation in a large number of cases (here, as often, we have to trust the reports of others' investigations); we believe that haste makes waste because we have seen it happen so many times. In effect, we infer from a certain number of instances of a thing that a characteristic of the thing we have observed in these instances will also appear in other instances. This is the process of *induction*. Somewhat less often (unless we are very much given to theoretical reasoning) we use *deduction*. Where induction puts facts together to get ideas or *generalizations,* deduction puts ideas together to discover what other ideas can be inferred from them. If John is the son of David who is the son of William, then John must be the grandson of William—we know this without asking. If a student must pass composition to graduate, and Mr. X has not yet passed it, then Mr. X cannot yet graduate. In each case, given the first two ideas or *premises,* we know that the third—the *conclusion*—must be true: no further investigation is needed.

(If the conclusion proved not to be true, then we would assume that one of the premises was wrong; perhaps a student must take composition unless excused.)

4 In every mind there will be a few beliefs which cannot be proved either by induction or deduction: basic standards of value, ultimate articles of faith, matters of inner conviction which we would be hard put to prove but without which we could scarcely think or act. Religious principles might be thought of as the most obvious example, but philosophy and even science illustrate the same necessity. In plane geometry we must begin with axioms and postulates from which the rest of the system is deduced. It is an article of faith that "things equal to the same thing are equal to each other"; we must believe it or give up plane geometry. Virtually all induction, and hence all scientific conclusions and practically all action depend on a faith in the uniformity of nature—that the laws of matter will be the same tomorrow as today. It seems only common sense to assume that water will continue to freeze at 32° Fahrenheit hereafter, but there is no way of proving the assumption theoretically.

5 Induction and deduction are not merely the tools of the philosopher and the scientist, but in rough-and-ready half-conscious forms are part of the everyday thought processes of all sane human beings, however limited their education. It is not infrequently argued that logic in the more formal sense is neither necessary nor useful for human life, since "common" or "horse" sense can serve us far better in practical affairs. All this involves a half truth. In the first place, we might question whether logic and common sense are really so opposed. If common sense has any value, it is because it is based on "experience"; in other words, having generalized from a series of seemingly like instances observed in the past, we apply the generalization to a further instance that has just come to our attention. What really distinguishes common sense from logic is that it tends to take shortcuts: it seldom bothers to work out all the steps in the argument. Certain processes work in our brains, and we acquire a sudden conviction that something is true. It is fortunate that we have common sense and "intuition" to depend on, for time does not always allow us to work things out logically or go hunting for evidence. It is certainly better to investigate a prospective employee thoroughly, but if we have to fill the job on the spot, we shall have to trust our impressions of his character. Very rarely (if we are wise) we may even trust our common sense in preference to what seems to be scientific evidence. Many a parent or teacher has finally nerved himself to go against the "scientific findings" of a child psychologist or educator. (But perhaps here what is wrong is not really science but its interpretation by self-appointed prophets.) Whole areas of human decision lie outside of the range of logic and sometimes even of common sense. One may be able to prove by critical principle that a book has every virtue that belongs to a masterpiece, and the book may in fact be quite unreadable. Science has not conquered all areas of human life. It is useless to tell a young man that a certain girl has all the qualifications of an ideal wife if he happens to hate her. Nevertheless, to scorn logic and hold to "horse

sense" is a dangerous business. An appeal to common sense—or worst yet, intuition—all too often represents an attempt to evade the responsibility of looking at evidence or working out the problem rationally. Common sense sometimes tells people peculiar things about such matters as family life and racial and economic problems. If by common sense we mean a kind of informal, everyday logic, then it is an absolute necessity of rational existence; but if by it we mean a defiance of logic, it ought not to exist at all, and it is unhappily true that most of us use logic too little rather than too much.[1] To come down to the practical problem of communication—which after all is our basic concern here—our personal intuitions are probably of very little interest to our readers or listeners, who may even not be much impressed by our common sense, however much they may value their own. What they expect from us is logic and evidence.

6 By its very nature, logic deals in statements or *propositions;* they are the materials of deductive reasoning and the products of inductive reasoning. By a proposition we mean a group of words which can be affirmed or denied—of which it can be said it is either true or false. (Even if it is false, it is still a proposition.) Not all sentences are propositions. A question or command is not a proposition; we cannot say that "Who is there?" is true or that "Do your homework!" is false. A proposition is roughly equivalent to the grammarian's *declarative sentence,* though not exactly equivalent, since a declarative sentence might contain several different propositions ("The sky is blue, and the grass is green") or express what is really a question or command ("The audience will leave quietly").

7 Another important distinction is that between a proposition which is merely factual and one which implies a *judgment.* "He served at Valley Forge" and "He was a loyal soldier" are both statements, but not of the same kind. The first is a matter of fact: either he served or he did not, and there is the possibility at least of proving the matter one way or another to the satisfaction of all. The second is a little different; it passes a judgment since the word "loyal" implies praise for something the speaker approves of or judges good. Another speaker, fully apprised of the same facts, might differ because of a differing conception of what constitutes loyalty, and absolute proof one way or another is impossible, since an element of personal feeling will always enter in. We should not confuse this distinction between *fact* and *judgment* with the distinction between *established truth* and *mere opinion.* Fact here means "piece of verifiable information"; what makes it a fact is the concrete quality which makes conclusive proof at least theoretically possible. "Columbus died in 1491" and "Martians have six legs" are in this sense factual, though the one statement is known to be false and the other is at present impossible of verification. "George Washington was loyal" still involves a

---

[1]Perhaps we should distinguish common sense, which does involve some conscious reasoning on evidence, from intuition, which involves no reasoning at all, but only a "feeling" that something is so. Intuition certainly ought to be a last resort, but sometimes there is nothing else to follow. Often, if the intuition is sound, one can find evidence or construct an argument to confirm it. One ought to be able to defend it rationally, however irrational its origins.

judgment, however much the statement is confirmed by evidence and however universally it is believed. A British writer in 1776 might plausibly have called Washington disloyal, and while we could find plenty of arguments to challenge the writer with, it is very possible that we should never come to an agreement with him. Unhappily for logic, the distinction between fact and judgment is far from clear-cut. The statement "He is intelligent" certainly contains an element of judgment; yet it is susceptible of confirmation by means of standard tests and might approach the status of a fact. It may be especially hard to distinguish between judgments and generalizations derived from a number of facts. Generalizations, like statements of single facts, differ from judgments in not necessarily implying any approval or disapproval. "A 1.5 concentration of alcohol in the blood usually impairs reactions" is a generalization; "It is wrong to drive in such a state" is a judgment.

8 Needless to say, judgments are not to be condemned; they are merely to be recognized for what they are. It may not always be easy to do this. When the educator says "The learner cannot be considered aside from his environment," he seems to be stating a generalization. But a little reflection reminds us that, rightly or wrongly, pupils are often judged without reference to their environment, and that to make sense the sentence must read "The learner *ought not* to be considered aside from his environment"—a form which clearly identifies it as a judgment. "Good children brush their teeth" has the form of a generalization and might actually represent the result of investigation on the dental habits of children known to be "good." Probably, however, it is a judgment, telling how the speaker thinks children ought to behave, and in a certain context the sentence might amount to a command. What is important is to make our meaning clear in the first place, and to show our readers that our evaluations have been rational. Judgments may be supported by evidence and argument; they need not be mere emotional reactions. The statement "He was loyal" can be supported by a definition of loyalty and instances of loyal conduct.

9 It goes without saying that one cannot work logically with a statement which does not have a clear-cut, ascertainable meaning. Puritanical logicians sometimes deny cognitive meaning to any statement which cannot be proved true or false (or at least shown to be probable or improbable) by reference to material facts. Since such an assumption would throw out much philosophy and theology, we should hardly wish to go so far, but we should at least try to avoid those statements, all too common in controversy, which do nothing more than express feeling or prejudice. The following is technically a valid argument: X is a no-good rat; No-good rats should be hung; X should be hung. But we should hope that no jury would follow such reasoning. . . . One cannot deduce anything from a feeling.

VOCABULARY

prospective (2)	deduction (3)
infer (3)	premises (3)
induction (3)	axioms (4)

postulates (4)	susceptible (7)
intuition (5)	impairs (7)
propositions (6)	ascertainable (9)
apprised (7)	puritanical (9)
plausibly (7)	cognitive (9)

QUESTIONS ON CONTENT

1. What is the difference between a rational and an irrational thinker?
2. What are legitimate sources of belief?
3. What is induction? What is deduction? How do they differ?
4. The author says scientific induction depends on an act of faith. Faith in what?
5. What is the difference between "common sense" and "logic"?
6. What is a proposition? Where do propositions come from? What is the difference between a proposition and an axiom?
7. What is the difference between a fact and a judgment? Between a generalization and a judgment?

QUESTIONS ON FORM

1. Examine the opening sentences of the first four paragraphs. What key word is repeated in each sentence? What effect does this repetition have on these paragraphs?
2. The author readily supports his generalizations with examples. What does this contribute to the selection?
3. What method of logic does this article most heavily rely on—induction or deduction?
4. In paragraph 3 the author uses the pronoun "we." Whom does this "we" refer to? What effect does its use have on the examples?
5. In paragraph 2 the author gives three examples of unfounded beliefs: (a) "there is always room at the top"; (b) "there are no atheists in foxholes"; (c) "football makes good citizens." By what other name are these and similar beliefs known?

SUGGESTIONS FOR WRITING

1. List five statements of fact that apply to your own life, then relist them as statements of judgment. How do they differ?
2. Discuss at least one instance in your life where you either abandoned a belief because of contrary logic or abandoned logic because of a contrary belief.

examples

W. E. B. DU BOIS

ON BEING CRAZY

In this selection the black historian and educator W. E. B. Du Bois (1868–1963) relates his ironic encounters with the illogicality of prejudice.

It was one o'clock and I was hungry. I walked into a restaurant, seated myself, and reached for the bill of fare. My table companion rose.

"Sir," said he, "do you wish to force your company on those who do not want you?"

No, said I, I wish to eat.

"Are you aware, sir, that this is social equality?"

Nothing of the sort, sir, it is hunger—and I ate.

The day's work done, I sought the theatre. As I sank into my seat, the lady shrank and squirmed.

I beg pardon, I said.

"Do you enjoy being where you are not wanted?" she asked coldly.

Oh no, I said.

"Well you are not wanted here."

I was surprised. I fear you are mistaken, I said, I certainly want the music, and I like to think the music wants me to listen to it.

"Usher," said the lady, "this is social equality."

"No, madame," said the usher, "it is the second movement of Beethoven's Fifth Symphony."

After the theatre, I sought the hotel where I had sent my baggage. The clerk scowled.

"What do you want?"

Rest, I said.

"This is a white hotel," he said.

I looked around. Such a color scheme requires a great deal of cleaning, I said, but I don't know that I object.

"We object," said he.

Then why, I began, but he interrupted.

"We don't keep niggers," he said, "we don't want social equality."

Neither do I, I replied gently, I want a bed.

I walked thoughtfully to the train. I'll take a sleeper through Texas. I'm a little bit dissatisfied with this town.

"Can't sell you one."

I only want to hire it, said I, for a couple of nights.

"Can't sell you a sleeper in Texas," he maintained. "They consider that social equality."

I consider it barbarism, I said, and I think I'll walk.

Walking, I met another wayfarer, who immediately walked to the other side of the road, where it was muddy. I asked his reason.

"Niggers is dirty," he said.

So is mud, said I. Moreover, I am not as dirty as you—yet.

"But you're a nigger, ain't you?" he asked.

My grandfather was so called.

"Well then!" he answered triumphantly.

Do you live in the South? I persisted, pleasantly.

"Sure," he growled, "and starve there."

I should think you and the Negroes should get together and vote out starvation.

"We don't let them vote."

We? Why not? I said in surprise.

"Niggers is too ignorant to vote."

But, I said, I am not so ignorant as you.

"But you're a nigger."

Yes, I'm certainly what you mean by that.

"Well then!" he returned, with that curiously inconsequential note of triumph. "Moreover," he said, "I don't want my sister to marry a nigger."

I had not seen his sister, so I merely murmured, let her say no.

"By God, you shan't marry her, even if she said yes."

But—but I don't want to marry her, I answered, a little perturbed at the personal turn.

"Why not," he yelled, angrier than ever.

Because I'm already married and I rather like my wife.

"Is she a nigger?" he asked suspiciously.

Well, I said again, her grandmother was called that.

"Well then!" he shouted in that oddly illogical way.

I gave up.

Go on, I said, either you are crazy or I am.

"We both are," he said as he trotted along in the mud.

QUESTIONS ON CONTENT

1. What term, borrowed from logic, could be used to characterize the responses of the white people to the narrator?
2. The narrator and the people who rebuff him are obviously thinking on different levels. How would you characterize these two levels?
3. What is the central illogicality to emerge from the narrator's meeting with the other wayfarer?

QUESTIONS ON FORM

1. Is the title serious? How does it fit in with the rest of the story?
2. The narrator responds, but not in dialogue. Why does the author use this technique? What effect does it have on the story?

SUGGESTIONS FOR WRITING

1. Analyze the logic, or lack of it, in this selection.
2. Write an essay describing an experience with prejudice.

CLARENCE DARROW

WHY I AM AN AGNOSTIC

In 1929 Clarence Darrow, the famous trial lawyer, took part in a symposium on religion along with a rabbi, a Protestant bishop, and a Catholic judge. The following argument in favor of scepticism was presented by Darrow at that symposium.

1 An agnostic is a doubter. The word is generally applied to those who doubt the verity of accepted religious creeds of faiths. Everyone is an agnostic as to the beliefs or creeds they do not accept. Catholics are agnostic to the Protestant creeds, and the Protestants are agnostic to the Catholic creed. Anyone who thinks is an agnostic about something, otherwise he must believe that he is possessed of all knowledge. And the proper place for such a person is in the madhouse or the home for the feeble-minded. In a popular way, in the western world, an agnostic is one who doubts or disbelieves the main tenets of the Christian faith.

2 I would say that belief in at least three tenets is necessary to the faith of a Christian: a belief in God, a belief in immortality, and a belief in a supernatural book. Various Christian sects require much more, but it is difficult to imagine that one could be a Christian, under any intelligent meaning of the word, with less. Yet there are some people who claim to be Christians who do not accept the literal interpretation of all the Bible, and who give more credence to some portions of the book than to others.

3 I am an agnostic as to the question of God. I think that it is impossible for the human mind to believe in an object or thing unless it can form a mental picture of such object or thing. Since man ceased to worship openly an anthropomorphic God and talked vaguely and not intelligently about some force in the universe, higher than man, that is responsible for the existence of man and the universe, he cannot be said to believe in God. One cannot believe in a force excepting as a force that pervades matter and is not an individual entity. To believe in a thing, an image of the thing must be stamped on the mind. If one is asked if he believes in such an animal as a camel, there immediately arises in his mind an image of the camel. This image has come from experience or knowledge of the animal gathered in some way or other. No such image comes, or can come, with the idea of a God who is described as a force.

4 Man has always speculated upon the origin of the universe, including himself. I feel, with Herbert Spencer, that whether the universe had an origin—and if it had—what the origin is will never be known by man. The Christian says that the universe could not make itself; that there must have been some higher power to call it into being. Christians have been obsessed for many years by Paley's argument that if a person passing through a desert should find a watch and examine its spring, its hands, its case and its crystal, he would at once be satisfied that some intelligent being capable of design had

made the watch. No doubt this is true. No civilized man would question that someone made the watch. The reason he would not doubt it is because he is familiar with watches and other appliances made by man. The savage was once unfamiliar with a watch and would have had no idea upon the subject. There are plenty of crystals and rocks of natural formation that are as intricate as a watch, but even to intelligent man they carry no implication that some intelligent power must have made them. They carry no such implication because no one has any knowledge or experience of someone having made these natural objects which everywhere abound.

5 To say that God made the universe gives us no explanation of the beginning of things. If we are told that God made the universe, the question immediately arises: Who made God? Did he always exist, or was there some power back of that? Did he create matter out of nothing, or is his existence co-extensive with matter? The problem is still there. What is the origin of it all? If, on the other hand, one says that the universe was not made by God, that it always existed, he has the same difficulty to confront. To say that the universe was here last year, or millions of years ago, does not explain its origin. This is still a mystery. As to the question of the origin of things, man can only wonder and doubt and guess.

6 As to the existence of the soul, all people may either believe or disbelieve. Everyone knows the origin of the human being. They know that it came from a single cell in the body of the mother, and that the cell was one out of ten thousand in the mother's body. Before gestation the cell must have been fertilized by a spermatozoön from the body of the father. This was one out of perhaps a billion spermatozoa that was the capacity of the father. When the cell is fertilized a chemical process begins. The cell divides and multiplies and increases into millions of cells, and finally a child is born. Cells die and are born during the life of the individual until they finally drop apart, and this is death.

7 If there is a soul, what is it, and where did it come from, and where does it go? Can anyone who is guided by his reason possibly imagine a soul independent of a body, or the place of its residence, or the character of it, or anything concerning it? If man is justified in any belief or disbelief on any subject, he is warranted in the disbelief in a soul. Not one scrap of evidence exists to prove any such impossible thing.

8 Many Christians base the belief of a soul and God upon the Bible. Strictly speaking, there is no such book. To make the Bible, sixty-six books are bound into one volume. These books are written by many people at different times, and no one knows the time or the identity of any author. Some of the books were written by several authors at various times. These books contain all sorts of contradictory concepts of life and morals and the origin of things. Between the first and the last nearly a thousand years intervened, a longer time than has passed since the discovery of America by Columbus.

9 When I was a boy the theologians used to assert that the proof of the divine inspiration of the Bible rested on miracles and prophecies. But a miracle means a violation of a natural law, and there can be no proof imagined

that could be sufficient to show the violation of a natural law; even though proof seemed to show violation, it would only show that we were not acquainted with all natural laws. One believes in the truthfulness of a man because of his long experience with the man, and because the man has always told a consistent story. But no man has told so consistent a story as nature.

10 If one should say that the sun did not rise, to use the ordinary expression, on the day before, his hearer would not believe it, even though he had slept all day and knew that his informant was a man of the strictest veracity. He would not believe it because the story is inconsistent with the conduct of the sun in all the ages past.

11 Primitive and even civilized people have grown so accustomed to believing in miracles that they often attribute the simplest manifestations of nature to agencies of which they know nothing. They do this when the belief is utterly inconsistent with knowledge and logic. They believe in old miracles and new ones. Preachers pray for rain, knowing full well that no such prayer was ever answered. When a politician is sick, they pray for God to cure him, and the politician almost invariably dies. The modern clergyman who prays for rain and for the health of the politician is no more intelligent in this matter than the primitive man who saw a separate miracle in the rising and setting of the sun, in the birth of an individual, in the growth of a plant, in the stroke of lightning, in the flood, in every manifestation of nature and life.

12 As to prophecies, intelligent writers gave them up long ago. In all prophecies facts are made to suit the prophecy, or the prophecy was made after the facts, or the events have no relation to the prophecy. Weird and strange and unreasonable interpretations are used to explain simple statements, that a prophecy may be claimed.

13 Can any rational person believe that the Bible is anything but a human document? We now know pretty well where the various books came from, and about when they were written. We know that they were written by human beings who had no knowledge of science, little knowledge of life, and were influenced by the barbarous morality of primitive times, and were grossly ignorant of most things that men know today. For instance, Genesis says that God made the earth, and he made the sun to light the day and the moon to light the night, and in one clause disposes of the stars by saying that "he made the stars also." This was plainly written by someone who had no conception of the stars. Man, by the aid of his telescope, has looked out into the heavens and found stars whose diameter is as great as the distance between the earth and the sun. We know that the universe is filled with stars and suns and planets and systems. Every new telescope looking further into the heavens only discovers more and more worlds and suns and systems in the endless reaches of space. The men who wrote Genesis believed, of course, that this tiny speck of mud that we call the earth was the center of the universe, the only world in space, and made for man, who was the only being worth considering. These men believed that the stars were only a little way above the earth, and were set in the firmament for man to look at, and for nothing else. Everyone today knows that this conception is not true.

14 The origin of the human race is not as blind a subject as it once was. Let alone God creating Adam out of hand, from the dust of the earth, does anyone believe that Eve was made from Adam's rib—that the snake walked and spoke in the Garden of Eden—that he tempted Eve to persuade Adam to eat an apple, and that it is on that account that the whole human race was doomed to hell—that for four thousand years there was no chance for any human to be saved, though none of them had anything whatever to do with the temptation; and that finally men were saved only through God's son dying for them, and that unless human beings believed this silly, impossible and wicked story they were doomed to hell? Can anyone with intelligence really believe that a child born today should be doomed because the snake tempted Eve and Eve tempted Adam? To believe that is not God-worship; it is devil-worship.

15 Can anyone call this scheme of creation and damnation moral? It defies every principle of morality, as man conceives morality. Can anyone believe today that the whole world was destroyed by flood, save only Noah and his family and a male and female of each species of animal that entered the Ark? There are almost a million species of insects alone. How did Noah match these up and make sure of getting male and female to reproduce life in the world after the flood had spent its force? And why should all the lower animals have been destroyed? Were they included in the sinning of man? This is a story which could not beguile a fairly bright child of five years of age today.

16 Do intelligent people believe that the various languages spoken by man on earth came from the confusion of tongues at the Tower of Babel, some four thousand years ago? Human languages were dispersed all over the face of the earth long before that time. Evidences of civilizations are in existence now that were old long before the date that romancers fix for the building of the Tower, and even before the date claimed for the flood.

17 Do Christians believe that Joshua made the sun stand still, so that the day could be lengthened, that a battle might be finished? What kind of person wrote that story, and what did he know about astronomy? It is perfectly plain that the author thought that the earth was the center of the universe and stood still in the heavens, and that the sun either went around it or was pulled across its path each day, and that the stopping of the sun would lengthen the day. We know now that had the sun stopped when Joshua commanded it, and had it stood still until now, it would not have lengthened the day. We know that the day is determined by the rotation of the earth upon its axis, and not by the movement of the sun. Everyone knows that this story simply is not true, and not many even pretend to believe the childish fable.

18 What of the tale of Balaam's ass speaking to him, probably in Hebrew? Is it true, or is it a fable? Many asses have spoken, and doubtless some in Hebrew, but they have not been that breed of asses. Is salvation to depend on a belief in a monstrosity like this?

19 Above all the rest, would any human being today believe that a child was born without a father? Yet this story was not at all unreasonable in the ancient world; at least three or four miraculous births are recorded in the Bible, including John the Baptist and Samson. Immaculate conceptions were com-

mon in the Roman world at the time and at the place where Christianity really had its nativity. Women were taken to the temples to be inoculated of God so that their sons might be heroes, which meant, generally, wholesale butchers. Julius Caesar was a miraculous conception—indeed, they were common all over the world. How many miraculous-birth stories is a Christian now expected to believe?

20 In the days of the formation of the Christian religion, disease meant the possession of human beings by devils. Christ cured a sick man by casting out the devils, who ran into the swine, and the swine ran into the sea. Is there any question but what that was simply the attitude and belief of a primitive people? Does anyone believe that sickness means the possession of the body by devils, and that the devils must be cast out of the human being that he may be cured? Does anyone believe that a dead person can come to life? The miracles recorded in the Bible are not the only instances of dead men coming to life. All over the world one finds testimony of such miracles; miracles which no person is expected to believe, unless it is his kind of a miracle. Still at Lourdes today, and all over the present world, from New York to Los Angeles and up and down the lands, people believe in miraculous occurrences, and even in the return of the dead. Superstition is everywhere prevalent in the world. It has been so from the beginning, and most likely will be so unto the end.

21 The reasons for agnosticism are abundant and compelling. Fantastic and foolish and impossible consequences are freely claimed for the belief in religion. All the civilization of any period is put down as a result of religion. All the cruelty and error and ignorance of the period has no relation to religion. The truth is that the origin of what we call civilization is not due to religion but to skepticism. So long as men accepted miracles without question, so long as they believed in original sin and the road to salvation, so long as they believed in a hell where man would be kept for eternity on account of Eve, there was no reason whatever for civilization: life was short, and eternity was long, and the business of life was preparation for eternity.

22 When every event was a miracle, when there was no order or system or law, there was no occasion for studying any subject, or being interested in anything excepting a religion which took care of the soul. As man doubted the primitive conceptions about religion, and no longer accepted the literal, miraculous teachings of ancient books, he set himself to understand nature. We no longer cure disease by casting out devils. Since that time, men have studied the human body, have built hospitals and treated illness in a scientific way. Science is responsible for the building of railroads and bridges, of steamships, of telegraph lines, of cities, towns, large buildings and small, plumbing and sanitation, of the food supply, and the countless thousands of useful things that we now deem necessary to life. Without skepticism and doubt, none of these things could have been given to the world.

23 The fear of God is not the beginning of wisdom. The fear of God is the death of wisdom. Skepticism and doubt lead to study and investigation, and investigation is the beginning of wisdom.

24 The modern world is the child of doubt and inquiry, as the ancient world was the child of fear and faith.

VOCABULARY

agnostic (1)	pervades (3)
verity (1)	co-extensive (5)
tenets (1)	veracity (10)
credence (2)	beguile (15)
anthropomorphic (3)	skepticism (21)

QUESTIONS ON CONTENT

1. What three minimum beliefs of Christianity does Darrow cite?
2. Darrow rejects the idea of miracles. What is the basis of his argument? Is it logical?
3. The author writes: "As to prophecies, intelligent writers gave them up long ago." How would you characterize that statement? Is it logical? Illogical? Alogical?
4. According to Darrow, what has been religion's influence on civilization?
5. How does Darrow characterize the thinking behind religion? By implication, what kind of thinking does he suggest in its place?

QUESTIONS ON FORM

1. How does the author marshal his argument against religion? Does he rely heavily on a single technique?
2. What evidence does the author present to support his argument?
3. Is this argument primarily inductive or deductive?
4. Reread paragraph 10. What technique is the author using to present his argument?
5. In paragraph 18 the author writes: "Many asses have spoken, and doubtless some in Hebrew, but they have not been that breed of asses." How would you characterize his tone?
6. The author writes: "When I was a boy the theologians used to assert that the proof of the divine inspiration of the Bible rested on miracles and prophecies. But a miracle means a violation of a natural law, and there can be no proof imagined that could be sufficient to show the violation of a natural law; even though the proof seemed to show violation, it would only show that we were not acquainted with all natural laws." How would you characterize this reasoning?

SUGGESTIONS FOR WRITING

1. Write an essay supporting or refuting the arguments in "Why I Am an Agnostic."
2. State your own religious beliefs and attempt to justify them logically.

TERM PAPER SUGGESTION

Investigate the major proofs of the existence of God and examine their logic.

JONATHAN SWIFT

A MODEST PROPOSAL

FOR PREVENTING THE CHILDREN OF POOR PEOPLE FROM BEING A BURTHEN TO THEIR PARENTS OR THE COUNTRY AND FOR MAKING THEM BENEFICIAL TO THE PUBLIC

In this famous satire Jonathan Swift (1667–1745), assuming the role of a concerned and logical citizen, turns society's indifference to the value of human life into an outraged attack against poverty in Ireland.

1 It is a melancholy object to those who walk through this great town, or travel in the country, when they see the streets, the roads, and cabin doors crowded with beggars of the female sex followed by three, four, or six children, all in rags and importuning every passenger for an alms. These mothers, instead of being able to work for their honest livelihood, are forced to employ all their time in strolling, to beg sustenance for their helpless infants, who, as they grow up, either turn thieves for want of work or leave their dear native country to fight for the Pretender in Spain or sell themselves to the Barbadoes.[1]

2 I think it is agreed by all parties that this prodigious number of children, in the arms or on the backs or at the heels of their mothers and frequently of their fathers, is in the present deplorable state of the kingdom a very great additional grievance, and therefore whoever could find out a fair, cheap, and easy method of making these children sound and useful members of the commonwealth would deserve so well of the public as to have his statue set up for a preserver of the nation.

3 But my intention is very far from being confined to provide only for the children of professed beggars; it is of a much greater extent, and shall take in the whole number of infants at a certain age who are born of parents in effect as little able to support them as those who demand our charity in the streets.

4 As to my own part, having turned my thoughts for many years upon this important subject and maturely weighed the several schemes of other projectors, I have always found them grossly mistaken in their computation. It is true, a child just dropped from its dam may be supported by her milk for a solar year, with little other nourishment, at the most not above the value of two shillings, which the mother may certainly get, or the value in scraps, by her lawful occupation of begging; and it is exactly at one year old that I propose to provide for them in such a manner as, instead of being a charge upon their parents or the parish or wanting food and raiment for the rest of their lives, they shall on the contrary contribute to the feeding, and partly to the clothing, of many thousands.

---

[1]Swift refers to the exiled Stuart claimant of the English throne, and to the custom of poor emigrants to commit themselves to work for a number of years to pay off their transportation to a colony.—Ed.

5 There is likewise another great advantage in my scheme, that it· will prevent those voluntary abortions and that horrid practice of women murdering their bastard children, alas! too frequent among us, sacrificing the poor innocent babes, I doubt more to avoid the expense than the shame, which would move tears and pity in the most savage and inhuman breast.

6 The number of souls in this kingdom being usually reckoned one million and a half, of these I calculate there may be about two hundred thousand couple whose wives are breeders, from which number I subtract thirty thousand couple who are able to maintain their own children (although I apprehend there cannot be so many, under the present distresses of the kingdom); but this being granted, there will remain a hundred and seventy thousand breeders. I again subtract fifty thousand for those women who miscarry or whose children die by accident or disease within the year. There only remain a hundred and twenty thousand children of poor parents annually born. The question therefore is how this number shall be reared and provided for, which, as I have already said, under the present situation of affairs is utterly impossible by all the methods hitherto proposed. For we can neither employ them in handicraft or agriculture; we neither build houses (I mean in the country) nor cultivate land; they can very seldom pick up a livelihood by stealing, till they arrive at six years old, except where they are of towardly parts, although I confess they learn the rudiments much earlier, during which time they can, however, be properly looked upon only as *probationers;* as I have been informed by a principal gentleman in the County of Cavan who protested to me that he never knew above one or two instances under the age of six, even in a part of the kingdom so renowned for the quickest proficiency in that art.

7 I am assured by our merchants that a boy or a girl before twelve years old is no saleable commodity, and even when they come to this age they will not yield above three pounds or three pounds and half a crown at most on the exchange, which cannot turn to account either to the parents or the kingdom, the charge of nutriment and rags having been at least four times that value.

8 I shall now, therefore, humbly propose my own thoughts, which I hope will not be liable to the least objection.

9 I have been assured by a very knowing American of my acquaintance in London that a young, healthy child well nursed is, at a year old, a most delicious, nourishing, and wholesome food, whether stewed, roasted, baked, or boiled; and I make no doubt that it will equally serve in a fricassee or a ragout.

10 I do therefore humbly offer it to public consideration that of the hundred and twenty thousand children already computed, twenty thousand may be reserved for breed, whereof only one fourth part to be males, which is more than we allow to sheep, black cattle, or swine; and my reason is that these children are seldom the fruits of marriage, a circumstance not much regarded by our savages; therefore one male will be sufficient to serve four females. That the remaining hundred thousand may, at a year old, be offered in sale to the persons of quality and fortune through the kingdom, always advising the

mother to let them suck plentifully in the last month, so as to render them plump and fat for a good table. A child will make two dishes at an entertainment for friends; and when the family dines alone, the fore- or hind-quarter will make a reasonable dish, and seasoned with a little pepper or salt, will be very good boiled on the fourth day, especially in winter. I have reckoned, upon a medium, that a child just born will weigh twelve pounds, and in a solar year, if tolerably nursed, will increase to twenty-eight pounds.

11 I grant this food will be somewhat dear, and therefore very proper for the landlords, who, as they have already devoured most of the parents, seem to have the best title to the children.

12 Infant's flesh will be in season throughout the year, but more plentifully in March and a little before and after; for we are told by a grave author, an eminent French physician, that fish being a prolific diet, there are more children born in Roman Catholic countries about nine months after Lent than at any other season; therefore, reckoning a year after Lent, the markets will be more glutted than usual, because the number of Popish infants is at least three to one in this kingdom; and therefore it will have one other collateral advantage, by lessening the number of Papists among us. I have already computed the charge of nursing a beggar's child (in which list I reckon all cottagers, laborers, and four fifths of the farmers) to be about two shillings per annum, rags included; and I believe no gentleman would repine to give ten shillings for the carcass of a good fat child, which, as I have said, will make four dishes of excellent nutritive meat, when he has only some particular friend or his own family to dine with him. Thus the squire will learn to be a good landlord and grow popular among his tenants; the mother will have eight shillings net profit and be fit for work till she produces another child.

13 Those who are more thrifty (as I must confess the times require) may flay the carcass, the skin of which, artificially dressed, will make admirable gloves for ladies and summer boots for fine gentlemen.

14 As to our city of Dublin, shambles[2] may be appointed for this purpose in the most convenient parts of it; and butchers, we may be assured, will not be wanting, although I rather recommend buying the children alive than dressing them hot from the knife as we do roasting pigs.

15 A very worthy person, a true lover of his country, and whose virtues I highly esteem, was lately pleased in discoursing on this matter to offer a refinement upon my scheme. He said that many gentlemen of this kingdom having of late destroyed their deer, he conceived that the want of venison might be well supplied by the bodies of young lads and maidens, not exceeding fourteen years of age nor under twelve, so great a number of both sexes in every country being now ready to starve for want of work and service; and these to be disposed of by their parents if alive, or otherwise by their nearest relations. But with due deference to so excellent a friend and so deserving a patriot, I cannot be altogether in his sentiments; for as to the males, my American acquaintance assured me, from frequent experience, that their flesh

---

[2]Slaughterhouses.—Ed.

was generally tough and lean, like that of our school-boys, by continual exercise, and their taste disagreeable; and to fatten them would not answer the charge. Then as to the females, it would, I think, with humble submission, be a loss to the public, because they would soon become breeders themselves: and besides, it is not improbable that some scrupulous people might be apt to censure such a practice (although indeed very unjustly) as a little bordering upon cruelty, which, I confess, has always been with me the strongest objection against any project, however so well intended.

16 But in order to justify my friend, he confessed that this expedient was put into his head by the famous Psalmanazar, a native of the island Formosa, who came from thence to London above twenty years ago and in conversation told my friend that in his country, when any young person happened to be put to death, the executioner sold the carcass to persons of quality as a prime dainty and that in his time the body of a plump girl of fifteen, who was crucified for an attempt to poison the emperor, was sold to his imperial Majesty's prime minister of state and other great mandarins of the court in joints from the gibbet at four hundred crowns. Neither, indeed, can I deny that if the same use were made of several plump young girls in this town who, without one single groat to their fortunes, cannot stir abroad without a chair, and appear at playhouse and assemblies in foreign fineries which they never will pay for, the kingdom would not be the worse.

17 Some persons of a desponding spirit are in great concern about that vast number of poor people who are aged, diseased, or maimed, and I have been desired to employ my thoughts what course may be taken to ease the nation of so grievous an encumbrance. But I am not in the least pain upon the matter, because it is very well known that they are every day dying and rotting by cold, and famine, and filth, and vermin, as fast as can be reasonably expected. And as to the young laborers, they are now in almost as hopeful a condition; they cannot get work and consequently pine away for want of nourishment to a degree that if at any time they are accidentally hired to common labor, they have not strength to perform it; and thus the country and themselves are happily delivered from the evils to come.

18 I have too long digressed and therefore shall return to my subject. I think the advantages by the proposal which I have made are obvious and many, as well as of the highest importance.

19 For first, as I have already observed, it would greatly lessen the number of Papists, with whom we are yearly overrun, being the principal breeders of the nation as well as our most dangerous enemies, and who stay at home on purpose to deliver the kingdom to the Pretender, hoping to take their advantage by the absence of so many good Protestants, who have chosen rather to leave their country than stay at home and pay tithes, against their conscience, to an Episcopal curate.

20 Secondly, the poorer tenants will have something valuable of their own which by law may be made liable to distress and help to pay their landlord's rent, their corn and cattle being already seized and money a thing unknown.

21 Thirdly, whereas the maintenance of a hundred thousand children from

two years old and upward cannot be computed at less than ten shillings apiece per annum, the nation's stock will thereby be increased fifty thousand pounds per annum, beside the profit of a new dish introduced to the tables of all gentlemen of fortune in the kingdom who have any refinement in taste. And the money will circulate among ourselves, the goods being entirely of our own growth and manufacture.

22 Fourthly, the constant breeders, beside the gain of eight shillings sterling per annum by the sale of their children, will be rid of the charge of maintaining them after the first year.

23 Fifthly, this food would likewise bring great custom to taverns, where the vintners will certainly be so prudent as to procure the best receipts for dressing it to perfection and consequently have their houses frequented by all the fine gentlemen who justly value themselves upon their knowledge in good eating; and a skillful cook who understands how to oblige his guests will contrive to make it as expensive as they please.

24 Sixthly, this would be a great inducement to marriage, which all wise nations have either encouraged by rewards or enforced by laws and penalties. It would increase the care and tenderness of mothers toward their children when they were sure of a settlement for life to the poor babes, provided in some sort by the public, to their annual profit or expense. We would see an honest emulation among the married women, which of them could bring the fattest child to the market. Men would become as fond of their wives during the time of their pregnancy as they are now of their mares in foal, their cows in calf, or sows when they are ready to farrow, nor offer to beat or kick them (as is too frequent a practice) for fear of a miscarriage.

25 Many other advantages might be enumerated. For instance, the addition of some thousand carcasses in our exportation of barreled beef; the propagation of swine's flesh and improvement in the art of making good bacon, so much wanted among us by the great destruction of pigs, too frequent at our table, which are no way comparable in taste or magnificence to a well-grown, fat yearling child, which, roasted whole, will make a considerable figure at a lord mayor's feast or any other public entertainment. But this and many others I omit, being studious of brevity.

26 Supposing that one thousand families in this city would be constant customers for infant's flesh, beside others who might have it at merry-meetings, particularly at weddings and christenings, I compute that Dublin would take off annually about twenty thousand carcasses and the rest of the kingdom (where probably they will be sold somewhat cheaper) the remaining eighty thousand.

27 I can think of no one objection that will possibly be raised against this proposal unless it should be urged that the number of people will be thereby much lessened in the kingdom. This I freely own, and it was indeed one principal design in offering it to the world. I desire the reader will observe that I calculate my remedy for this one individual kingdom of Ireland and for no other that ever was, is, or I think ever can be, upon earth. Therefore let no

man talk to me of other expedients: of taxing our absentees at five shillings a pound; of using neither clothes nor household furniture except what is of our own growth and manufacture; of utterly rejecting the materials and instruments that promote foreign luxury; of curing the expensiveness of pride, vanity, idleness, and gaming in our women; of introducing a vein of parsimony, prudence, and temperance; of learning to love our country, in the want of which we differ even from Laplanders and the inhabitants of Tupinamba; of quitting our animosities and factions, nor acting any longer like the Jews, who were murdering one another at the very moment their city was taken; of being a little cautious not to sell our country and conscience for nothing; of teaching landlords to have at least one degree of mercy toward their tenants; lastly, of putting a spirit of honesty, industry, and skill into our shop-keepers, who, if a resolution could now be taken to buy only our native goods, would immediately unite to cheat and exact upon us in the price, the measure, and the goodness, nor could ever yet be brought to make one fair proposal of just dealing, though often and earnestly invited to it.

28 Therefore, I repeat, let no man talk to me of these and the like expedients till he has at least some glimpse of hope that there will be ever some hearty and sincere attempt to put them in practice.

29 But as to myself, having been wearied out for many years with offering vain, idle, visionary thoughts and at length utterly despairing of success, I fortunately fell upon this proposal, which, as it is wholly new, so it has something solid and real, of no expense and little trouble, full in our own power, and whereby we can incur no danger in disobliging England. For this kind of commodity will not bear exportation, the flesh being of too tender a consistence to admit a long continuance in salt, although perhaps I could name a country which would be glad to eat up our whole nation without it.

30 After all, I am not so violently bent upon my own opinion as to reject any offer proposed by wise men which shall be found equally innocent, cheap, easy, and effectual. But before something of that kind shall be advanced in contradiction to my scheme and offering a better, I desire the author or authors will be pleased maturely to consider two points: first, as things now stand, how they will be able to find food and raiment for a hundred thousand useless mouths and backs; and secondly, there being a round million of creatures in human figure throughout this kingdom whose whole subsistence, put into a common stock, would leave them in debt two millions of pounds sterling, adding those who are beggars by profession to the bulk of farmers, cottagers, and laborers, with the wives and children who are beggars in effect, I desire those politicians who dislike my overture, and may perhaps be so bold as to attempt an answer, that they will first ask the parents of these mortals whether they would not at this day think it a great happiness to have been sold for food at a year old in the manner I prescribe, and thereby have avoided such a perpetual scene of misfortunes as they have since gone through by the oppression of landlords, the impossibility of paying rent without money or trade, the want of common sustenance, with neither house nor clothes to

cover them from the inclemencies of the weather, and the most inevitable prospect of entailing the like of greater miseries upon their breed forever.

31 I profess in the sincerity of my heart that I have not the least personal interest in endeavoring to promote this necessary work, having no other motive than the public good of my country, by advancing our trade, providing for infants, relieving the poor, and giving some pleasure to the rich. I have no children by which I can propose to get a single penny, the youngest being nine years old and my wife past childbearing.

VOCABULARY

importuning (1)	encumbrance (17)
sustenance (1)	digressed (18)
prodigious (2)	propagation (25)
proficiency (6)	parsimony (27)
collateral (12)	overture (30)
censure (15)	inclemencies (30)
gibbet (16)	

QUESTIONS ON CONTENT

1. What premise is "A Modest Proposal" based on? What is the chief assumption of its argument?
2. Reread paragraph 11. Why do the landlords have "the best title to the children"?
3. Swift's satire redefines children in economic terms. What does this imply about his view of the society he lived in?
4. What does the satire imply about the religious feelings in Ireland during Swift's time?
5. Given the state of affairs as the author describes them, is his argument logical? Explain.

QUESTIONS ON FORM

1. What is the effect of the word "modest" in the title?
2. Swift describes people with words like "breeder," "dam," "carcass," "yearling child." What effect do these words have?
3. Satire usually hints at the true state of things as it proposes its own alternatives. How does Swift hint at the true state of things? Give examples.
4. How would you characterize the tone of this piece?
5. Reread the final paragraph. What is its purpose?

SUGGESTIONS FOR WRITING

1. Infer from "A Modest Proposal" the state of life in Ireland during Swift's time. Make specific references to the article to justify your inferences.
2. Discuss the relationship implied in "A Modest Proposal" between society and the individual.

SIMONE DE BEAUVOIR

Translated by Patrick O'Brian

ON AGING

Logic is not only reckoned as the dispassionate linking of one fact to another; it also includes the art of persuasion. In this article the well-known French writer and feminist Simone de Beauvoir mounts a vivid and persuasive argument against our treatment of the elderly. (From *The Coming of Age*.)

1 Old age is not the necessary conclusion of human existence. Unlike the human body, old age does not even represent what Sartre has called "the necessity of our contingency." Many animals die after reproducing themselves, without going through a degenerative stage. However, it is an empirical, universal truth that after a certain number of years the human organism submits to degeneration. The process is inexorable. After a time the individual's activities are reduced; very often his mental faculties diminish and his attitude toward the world is altered.

2 Sometimes old age has been valued for political or social reasons. Certain individuals—for example the women in Old China—could find refuge in it from the harshness of the adult condition. Others accept old age with a deep pessimism: when the will to live seems a source of unhappiness, it is logical to prefer a half-death. But the vast majority approach old age either with sorrow or rebellion. It inspires more repugnance than death itself.

3 In fact it is old age, more than death, that is the negation of life. It parodies life. Death transforms life with destiny; in a way, it saves life by conferring on it an absolute dimension, "so that finally eternity itself changes it." It abolishes time. The man who is buried—his last days on earth have no more validity than the rest; his existence has become a totality, all of whose parts are equally present in the grasp of nothingness. Victor Hugo is at the same time and never both 30 and 80 years old. But when he was 80 his present life obliterated his past. This supersedence is saddening when, as is almost always the case, the present is a degradation or even a denial of what was. Past events, acquired knowledge, retain their place when life is extinguished: they have been. But when memory crumbles they are engulfed in a mocking darkness: life is unraveled thread by thread like a tattered sweater, leaving nothing in the hands of the aged but the formless shreds. Even worse, the indifference which has overcome him challenges his own passions, his convictions and his activities. That was the case when de Charlus ruined the aristocratic pride which had been his raison d'être with a gesture of his hat. Or when Arina Pavlovki reconciled herself with a son she had always hated. What good is it to have worked so hard—"wasting your trouble," as Rousseau put it—if you no longer value the results you have achieved? Michelangelo's disdain for his "puppets" is heartbreaking—if we consider with him his

old age we also feel sadly the vanity of his efforts. But with death these moments of discouragement can do nothing against the grandeur of his work.

4 Not all old people are resigned. On the contrary, many are distinguished by their stubbornness. Often, however, they become caricatures of themselves. Their will power perseveres out of a kind of inertia, without reason or even against all reason. At the beginning they were strong-willed because they had a certain goal in view. Now they remain strong-willed because they were strong-willed before. What happens on the whole with old people is that they substitute habits, reflexes, rigidity, for innovation. There is truth in an angry essay written by Faguet called "The Ten Commandments of Old Age" when he says: Old age is a continual comedy that people act out to create an illusion for themselves and others, and it is comical above all when it is badly acted.

5 Morality preaches the serene acceptance of those evils which science and technology are powerless to eliminate: pain, sickness, age. To bear bravely the very state which diminishes us will, it is claimed, help us grow. For lack of anything else to do, an aging person might become involved in this project. But here we are just playing with words. Projects only concern our activities. Growing old isn't an activity. Growing up, maturing, aging, dying: the passage of time is a fatality.

6 If old age is not to be a derisive parody of our past existence there is only one solution: to continue to pursue the goals which give meaning to our lives—devotion to individuals, to collectivities, to causes, to social or political work which is intellectual and creative. Contrary to what the moralists advise, we should wish to retain in our old age passions which are strong enough to prevent us from withdrawing into ourselves. Life keeps its rewards as long as people give of it to others, through love, friendship, indignation, compassion. Then there are still reasons to act or to speak. People are often advised to "prepare" for their old age. But if that simply means putting money aside, choosing a place for retirement or planning hobbies, one won't be any more ready when the day arrives. Instead of thinking about it too much, people would be better off if they lived lives of involvement and purpose to sustain them after all illusions have been lost and passions cooled.

7 However, these options are only granted to a handful of the privileged: it is during old age that the gap between the privileged and the vast majority of men is widest. In comparing the two groups we can answer the question: what is there that is inevitable in the decline of the individual? To what extent is it society that is responsible?

8 It is clear that the age at which decline begins has always depended on the class one belongs to. Today a miner is finished at 50, whereas among the privileged, many carry their 80 years with ease. Drained of his forces sooner, the worker also suffers a much more rapid decline. His exhausted body is prey to injuries and sickness even in his prime, whereas an old person who has been able to take care of his body can keep it more or less intact until the day he dies.

9 The exploited are condemned in old age to squalor or, at the very least,

to severe poverty, oppressive living conditions and solitude, which lead to a sense of failing and a generalized anxiety. They sink into a stunned numbness which is reflected in their bodies: even the diseases which affect them are to a large extent the product of the system.

10 Even if a person in retirement preserves his health and his mental faculties he is still prey to the terrible blight of boredom. Deprived of his grip on the world, he is unable to regain it because apart from his work his leisure was alienated. The manual laborer isn't even able to kill time. His morose idleness turns into apathy which compromises what remains to him of his physical and moral balance.

11 But the injury that is done to him in the course of his existence is even more basic. If a retired person feels desperate about the meaninglessness of his present life it is because his life has been robbed of meaning throughout. A law implacable as the "Iron Law" has permitted him only to reproduce his life, denying him the opportunity of creating justifications for it. Outside the limits of his profession, he sees around him nothing but a wasteland: he was never given the chance to involve himself in projects which would have contributed to world aims, values, raisons d'être.

12 This is the crime of our society. Its "politics of old age" is scandalous. But even more scandalous is the treatment the society inflicts on the majority of people during their youth and their maturity. Society "prefabricates" the mutilated, miserable condition which is their lot in old age. It is the fault of society that the decline of age begins prematurely and is precipitous, physically painful and morally terrifying—because people come to it with empty hands. When their strength deserts them, the exploited and alienated are fatally transformed into discarded rubbish.

13 That is why all the remedies that are proposed to alleviate the distress of old people are so ludicrous: none is capable of repairing the systematic destruction that has victimized them throughout their entire existence. Even if they are cared for, no one can give them back their health. Even if one builds for them decent places to live, one will not have created the culture, interests and responsibilities which would give meaning to their lives. I am not saying that it is entirely vain to try to improve their condition at this time. But that won't offer any solution to the real problem of old age, which is: What should a society be like so that in his old age a man can remain a man?

14 The answer is simple: he must always have been treated like a man. Society reveals itself in the fate it assigns to its inactive members: society has always considered them merely idle equipment. Society admits that only profit counts, that its "humanism" is purely facade. In the 19th century the ruling classes explicitly categorized the proletariat as barbarians. Workers' struggles have succeeded in integrating the proletariat into humanity, but only insofar as they are productive. The old workers' society turns it back on them as if they were a strange species.

15 This is precisely why the question has been buried in concerted silence. Old age denounces the failure of our whole civilization. It is the whole man

that must be remade, and all relations among people recreated, if we want the condition of the old to be acceptable. A man shouldn't come to the end of his life alone and empty-handed. If culture were life and practice—and not inert knowledge, acquired once and then ignored—if the individual had, through culture, a grasp on his environment which fulfilled and renewed itself over the years, he would be an active, useful citizen at any age. If the individual from childhood on were not atomized, shut off and isolated among other atoms, if he participated in life, he would never know exile. Nowhere have such conditions ever been achieved. The socialist countries, if they approach this condition a little more closely than the capitalist countries, remain very distant from it.

16 In the ideal society I am picturing we could dream that old age, so to speak, would not exist. Just as with certain privileged cases now, the individual, privately weakened by age but not visibly diminished, would one day fall victim to a fatal illness: he would die without suffering degradation. Old age would conform in reality to the definition that certain bourgeois theorists give to it: that is, a moment in existence which is different from youth and maturity, but possessing its own balance, and leaving open to the individual a wide range of possibilities.

17 We are far from that. Society concerns itself with the individual only insofar as he is productive. Young people know all about this. Their anxiety on entering social life is the counterpart of the agony of old people on being excluded from it. In the intervening time, daily routine masks these problems. A young person fears this machine which will use him up; sometimes he tries to fight back by throwing paving stones; the old man, rejected by it, used up, exposed, has nothing left but his eyes to cry with. Between the two the machine turns, crusher of men who let themselves be crushed because they cannot even imagine escaping from it. Once one has understood what the condition of old people is, one cannot be content to demand more generous "politics of old age," higher pensions, decent housing, organized leisure activities. It is the whole system which is at stake, and the demand can only be radical: to change life.

VOCABULARY

contingency (1)	morose (10)
empirical (1)	apathy (10)
degeneration (1)	prefabricates (12)
inexorable (1)	precipitous (12)
repugnance (2)	alleviate (13)
supersedence (3)	proletariat (14)
caricatures (4)	concerted (15)
innovation (4)	atomized (15)
derisive (6)	bourgeois (16)
squalor (9)	

QUESTIONS ON CONTENT

1. The author writes: "It is old age, more than death, that is the negation of life." What does she mean by that? What does she mean by "old age"?
2. What, according to the author, is the solution of old age?
3. Why is the gap between the privileged and the poor widest in old age?
4. What is the "politics of old age"?
5. Why does the author say that society is to blame for old age?
6. What parallel does the author see between the old and the young?

QUESTIONS ON FORM

1. The author begins by claiming that "old age is not the necessary conclusion of human existence." How does she prove this thesis? What are the stages in her argument?
2. Paragraph 7 ends by posing two questions that the rest of the essay attempts to answer. What function is therefore served by the first six paragraphs?
3. The argument in paragraph 3 is summed up in a central simile. What is this simile? How does it relate to the rest of the paragraph?

SUGGESTIONS FOR WRITING

1. Write an essay contesting or supporting the author's argument that society is to blame for old age.
2. Imagine that you are eighty-five years old. Write an essay describing how people treat you, how you live your life from day to day, and what you would like done to improve your lot.

BENJAMIN FRANKLIN

AN ARGUMENT AGAINST PAYMENT OF SALARIES TO EXECUTIVE OFFICERS OF THE FEDERAL GOVERNMENT

This speech, delivered at the Constitutional Convention on June 2, 1787, is a brief argument of the classical type. In studying the argument, it is important to bear in mind that Franklin did not foresee how big the American government would become, and that in Franklin's day leading men could be expected to serve in public office without financial compensation.

1 Sir, it is with reluctance that I rise to express a disapprobation of any one article of the plan, for which we are so much obliged to the honorable gentleman who laid it before us. From its first reading, I have borne a good will to it, and in general, wished it success. In this particular of salaries to the executive branch, I happen to differ; and, as my opinion may appear new and chimerical, it is only from a persuasion that it is right, and from a sense of duty, that I hazard it. The Committee will judge of my reasons when they have heard them, and their judgment may possibly change mine. I think I see

inconveniences in the appointment of salaries; I see none in refusing them, but on the contrary great advantages.

2 Sir, there are two passions which have a powerful influence in the affairs of men. These are *ambition* and *avarice:* the love of power and the love of money. Separately, each of these has great force in prompting men to action; but when united in view of the same object, they have in many minds the most violent effects. Place before the eyes of such men a post of *honor,* that shall at the same time be a place of *profit,* and they will move heaven and earth to obtain it. The vast number of such places it is that renders the British government so tempestuous. The struggles for them are the true source of all those factions which are perpetually dividing the nation, distracting its councils, hurrying it sometimes into fruitless and mischievous wars, and often compelling a submission to dishonorable terms of peace.

3 And of what kind are the men that will strive for this profitable preeminence, through all the bustle of cabal, the heat of contention, the infinite mutual abuse of parties, tearing to pieces the best of characters? It will not be the wise and moderate, the lovers of peace and good order, the men fittest for the trust. It will be the bold and violent, the men of strong passions and indefatigable activity in their selfish pursuits. These will thrust themselves into your government, and be your rulers. And these, too, will be mistaken in the expected happiness of their situation; for their vanquished competitors, of the same spirit, and from the same motives, will perpetually be endeavoring to distress their administration, thwart their measures, and render them odious to the people.

4 Besides these evils, sir, though we may set out in the beginning with moderate salaries, we shall find that such will not be of long continuance. Reasons will never be wanting for proposed augmentations, and there will always be a party for giving more to the rulers, that the rulers may be able to return to give more to them. Hence, as all history informs us, there has been in every state and kingdom a constant kind of warfare between the governing and the governed; the one striving to obtain more for its support, and the other to pay less. And this alone has occasioned great convulsions, actual civil wars, ending either in dethroning of the princes or enslaving of the people.

5 Generally, indeed, the ruling power carries its point, and we see the revenues of princes constantly increasing, and we see that they are never satisfied, but always in want of more. The more the people are discontented with the oppression of taxes, the greater need the prince has of money to distribute among his partisans, and pay the troops that are to suppress all resistance and enable him to plunder at pleasure. There is scarce a king in a hundred, who would not, if he could, follow the example of Pharaoh—get first all the people's money, then all their lands, and then make them and their children servants forever.

6 It will be said that we do not propose to establish kings. I know it. But there is a natural inclination in mankind to kingly government. It sometimes relieves them from aristocratic domination. They had rather have one tyrant than five hundred. It gives more of the appearance of equality among citizens;

and that they like. I am apprehensive, therefore—perhaps too apprehensive—that the government of these States may in future times end in a monarchy. But this catastrophe, I think, may be long delayed, if in our proposed system we do not sow the seeds of contention, faction, and tumult, by making our posts of honor places of profit. If we do, I fear that, though we employ at first a number and not a single person, the number will in time be set aside; it will only nourish the foetus of a king (as the honorable gentleman from Virginia very aptly expressed it), and a king will the sooner be set over us.

7 It may be imagined by some that this is an utopian idea, and that we can never find men to serve us in the executive department, without paying them well for their services. I conceive this to be a mistake. Some existing facts present themselves to me, which incline me to a contrary opinion. The High Sheriff of a county in England is an honorable office, but it is not a profitable one. It is rather expensive, and therefore not sought for. But yet it is executed, and well executed, and usually by some of the principal gentlemen of the county. In France, the office of Counsellor, or member of their judiciary parliaments, is more honorable. It is therefore purchased at a high price; there are indeed fees on the law proceedings, which are divided among them, but these fees do not amount to more than three per cent on the sum paid for the place. Therefore, as legal interest is there at five per cent, they in fact pay two per cent for being allowed to do the judiciary business of the nation, which is at the same time entirely exempt from the burden of paying them any salaries for their services. I do not, however, mean to recommend this as an eligible mode for our judiciary department. I only bring the instance to show that the pleasure of doing good and serving their country, and the respect such conduct entitles them to, are sufficient motives with some minds to give up a great portion of their time to the public, without the mean inducement of pecuniary satisfaction.

8 Another instance is that of a respectable society, who have made the experiment, and practiced it with success, now more than a hundred years. I mean the Quakers. It is an established rule with them that they are not to go to law, but in their controversies they must apply to their monthly, quarterly, and yearly meetings. Committees of these sit with patience to hear the parties, and spend much time in composing their differences. In doing this, they are supported by a sense of duty and the respect paid to usefulness. It is honorable to be so employed, but it was never made profitable by salaries, fees, or perquisites. And indeed, in all cases of public service, the less the profit the greater the honor.

9 To bring the matter nearer home, have we not seen the greatest and most important of our offices, that of General of our Armies, executed for eight years together, without the smallest salary, by a patriot whom I will not now offend by any other praise; and this, through fatigues and distresses, in common with the other brave men, his military friends and companions, and the constant anxieties peculiar to his station? And shall we doubt finding three or four men in all the United States, with public spirit enough to bear sitting in peaceful council, for perhaps an equal term, merely to preside over our civil

concerns, and see that our laws are duly executed? Sir, I have a better opinion of our country. I think we shall never be without a sufficient number of wise and good men to undertake, and execute well and faithfully, the office in question.

10 Sir, the saving of the salaries, that may at first be proposed, is not an object with me. The subsequent mischiefs of proposing them are what I apprehend. And therefore it is that I move the amendment. If it is not seconded or accepted, I must be contented with the satisfaction of having delivered my opinion frankly, and done my duty.

VOCABULARY

disapprobation (1)	apprehensive (6)
chimerical (1)	contention (6)
tempestuous (2)	faction (6)
pre-eminence (3)	tumult (6)
cabal (3)	foetus (6)
indefatigable (3)	utopian (7)
vanquished (3)	conceive (7)
odious (3)	pecuniary (7)
augmentations (4)	Quakers (8)
convulsions (4)	perquisites (8)
revenues (5)	fatigues (9)
partisans (5)	amendment (10)

QUESTIONS ON CONTENT

1. What is the main contention of Franklin's argument and where is it stated?
2. A solid argument must be supported by convincing evidence. What evidence does Franklin offer?
3. In paragraph 9, who is the "General of our Armies" who executed his duties without pay for eight years? Why does Franklin allude to him?
4. In his final argument, why does Franklin reject the idea that "the saving of the salaries" is not part of his objective?
5. Why does Franklin offer no specific examples for his generalization that history informs us that the more money rulers are paid, the more they will want?
6. What are the specific examples Franklin uses to argue that his proposal is not utopian?

QUESTIONS ON FORM

1. How would you chart the progress of Franklin's speech?
2. What is the importance of the allusion to "Pharaoh" in paragraph 5?
3. Franklin's argument is sprinkled with the words "hence" and "therefore." What purpose do they serve?
4. What is the tone of Franklin's address?

SUGGESTIONS FOR WRITING

1. Write a five-hundred-word essay refuting Franklin's argument. Use the same basic structure that he did.
2. In five hundred words, write a convincing article reasserting Lord Acton's saying that power corrupts and that absolute power corrupts absolutely. Supply examples and testimony.

JAMES MICHIE

DOOLEY IS A TRAITOR

In this humorous poem a murderer makes a spirited defense against being compelled to fight a war not of his own making.

"So then you won't fight?"
"Yes, your Honour," I said, "that's right."
"Now is it that you simply aren't willing,
Or have you a fundamental moral objection to killing?"
Says the judge, blowing his nose
And making his words stand to attention in long rows.
I stand to attention too, but with half a grin
(In my time I've done a good many in).
"No objection at all, sir," I said.
"There's a deal of the world I'd rather see dead—
Such as Johnny Stubbs or Fred Settle or my last landlord, Mr. Syme.
Give me a gun and your blessing, your Honour, and I'll be killing them
          all the time.
But my conscience says a clear no
To killing a crowd of gentlemen I don't know.
Why, I'd as soon think of killing a worshipful judge,
High-court, like yourself (against whom, God knows, I've got no
          grudge—
So far), as murder a heap of foreign folk.
If you've got no grudge, you've got no joke
To laugh at after."
                    Now the words never come flowing
Proper for me till I get the old pipe going.
And just as I was poking
Down baccy, the judge looks up sharp with "No smoking,
Mr. Dooley. We're not fighting this war for fun.
And we want a clearer reason why you refuse to carry a gun.
This war is not a personal feud, it's a fight
Against wrong ideas on behalf of the Right.
Mr. Dooley, won't you help to destroy evil ideas?"

"Ah, your Honour, here's
The tragedy," I said. "I'm not a man of the mind.
I couldn't find it in my heart to be unkind
To an idea. I wouldn't know one if I saw one. I haven't one of my own.
So I'd best be leaving other people's alone."
"Indeed," he sneers at me, "this defence is
Curious for someone with convictions in two senses.
A criminal invokes conscience to his aid
To support an individual withdrawal from a communal crusade
Sanctioned by God, led by the Church, against a godless, churchless
       nation!"
I asked his Honour for a translation.
"You talk of conscience," he said. "What do you know of the Christian
       creed?"
"Nothing, sir, except what I can read,
That's the most you can hope for from us jail-birds.
I just open the Book here and there and look at the words.
And I find when the Lord himself misliked an evil notion
He turned it into a pig and drove it squealing over a cliff into the ocean,
And the loony ran away
And lived to think another day.
There was a clean job done and no blood shed!
Everybody happy and forty wicked thoughts drowned dead.
A neat and Christian murder. None of your mad slaughter
Throwing away the brains with the blood and the baby with the
       bathwater.
Now I look at the war as a sportsman. It's a matter of choosing
The decentest way of losing.
Heads or tails, losers or winners,
We all lose, we're all damned sinners.
And I'd rather be with the poor cold people at the wall that's shot
Than the bloody guilty devils in the firing-line, in Hell and keeping hot."
"But what right, Dooley, what right," he cried,
"Have you to say the Lord is on your side?"
"That's a dirty crooked question," back I roared.
"I said not the Lord was on my side, but I was on the side of the Lord."
Then he was up at me and shouting,
But by and by he calms: "Now we're not doubting
Your sincerity, Dooley, only your arguments,
Which don't make sense."
('Hullo,' I thought, 'that's the wrong way round.
I may be skylarking a bit, but my brainpan's sound.')
Then biting his nail and sugaring his words sweet:
"Keep your head, Mr. Dooley. Religion is clearly not up your street.
But let me ask you as a plain patriotic fellow
Whether you'd stand there so smug and yellow

If the foe were attacking your own dear sister.''
"I'd knock their brains out, mister,
On the floor," I said. "There," he says kindly, "I knew you were no
      pacifist.
It's your straight duty as a man to enlist.
The enemy is at the door." You could have downed
Me with a feather. "Where?" I gasp, looking round.
"Not this door," he says angered. "Don't play the clown.
But they're two thousand miles away planning to do us down.
Why, the news is full of the deeds of those murderers and rapers.''
"Your Eminence," I said, "my father told me never to believe the
      papers
But to go by my eyes,
And at two thousand miles the poor things can't tell truth from lies.''
His fearful spectacles glittered like the moon: "For the last time what
      right
Has a man like you to refuse to fight?''
"More right," I said, "than you.
You've never murdered a man, so you don't know what it is I won't do.
I've done it in good hot blood, so haven't I the right to make bold
To declare that I shan't do it in cold?''
Then the judge rises in a great rage
And writes DOOLEY IS A TRAITOR in black upon a page
And tells me I must die.
"What, me?" says I.
"If you still won't fight."
"Well, yes, your Honour," I said, "that's right.''

QUESTIONS ON CONTENT

1. Dooley is an admitted murderer, yet he still refuses to fight. Why? What is his primary objection to war?
2. How many arguments does the judge use in trying to persuade Dooley? What are these and in what order are they used?
3. Are the judge's arguments logical? Do they appeal to reason and evidence, or to emotion?

QUESTIONS ON FORM

1. The poem is written in rhyming couplets. What does the rhyme contribute to the poem's tone?
2. How is Dooley characterized? What techniques are used?
3. How is the judge characterized? What techniques are used?

SUGGESTIONS FOR WRITING

1. Analyze the logic in the exchanges between Dooley and the judge. Pinpoint the difference between their respective ways of thinking.

2. Assume that you are in Dooley's position and must argue against your participation in a war. Formulate an argument in your defense.

CHAPTER WRITING ASSIGNMENTS

1. Analyze and discuss the views on society in "On Aging" and "A Modest Proposal." Say what these views have in common.
2. Discuss the idea that religion is a "conditioned reflex."
3. Analyze and compare the generalizations of the judge in "Dooley Is a Traitor" with the generalizations of the bigots in "On Being Crazy."
4. Discuss the place of logic and belief in your own life.
5. Construct an argument for or against competitiveness in business.

How Do I Polish the Finish?
Style

model

With few exceptions, most good style is the result of revision. The surface of the writer's work must be scratched clean of deadwood, crabbed phrases, and jarring rhythms. He must strop his sentences until they glint cleanly with his meaning. This entails work and drudgery, but most writers go through this labor of revision, of dickering with their better judgment over apt words and phrases. W. Somerset Maugham, considered among the best prose stylists of the language, admitted that when he wrote well it was only "with strenuous effort," because the first words that occurred to him were usually "far-fetched or commonplace." His case is not the exception among writers: it is the norm.

In the model we see an example of the revising that Lincoln did on his First Inaugural Address. Secretary of State designate William Seward thought that the speech ended too abruptly, and that it should conclude with a final appeal for unity. He submitted a draft of this ending, which Lincoln then edited.

LINCOLN'S REVISION OF HIS FIRST INAUGURAL ADDRESS

Seward	Lincoln
I close.	I am loth to close.
We are not, we must not be, aliens or enemies, but fellow-countrymen and brethren.	We are not enemies, but friends. We must not be enemies.
Although passion has strained our bonds of affection too hardly, they must not, I am sure they will not, be broken.	Though passion may have strained, it must not break our bonds of affection.

Seward	Lincoln
The mystic chords which, proceeding from so many battlefields and so many patriot graves, pass through all the hearts and all the hearths in this broad continent of ours, will yet again harmonize in their ancient music when breathed upon by the guardian angel of the nation.	The mystic chords of memory, stretching from every battlefield, and patriot grave, to every living heart and hearth-stone, all over this broad land, will yet swell the chorus of the Union, when again touched, as surely they will be, by the better angels of our nature.

Altogether, Lincoln's editing added intensity and tightness to Seward's draft. "We are not enemies, but friends" is more emphatic and intense than "We are not, we must not be, aliens or enemies, but fellow-countrymen and brethren." The model illustrates what every writer who wants to write well must do: he must examine his work as with a microscope and make excisions as with a scalpel.

Students sometimes overlook this aspect of writing and assume that the original version must be the more inspired and therefore closer to what they really meant to write. We have collected in this chapter a number of differing opinions addressed to this and other fallacies. Most of the selections urge a style founded on directness and clarity; some attempt a definition of style; a few make suggestions for improving it; all exemplify it at its best.

advice

F. L. LUCAS

WHAT IS STYLE?

In this article F. L. Lucas, the distinguished scholar and lecturer of King's College, Cambridge, discusses the problem of style and gives some advice on improving it.

1 When it was suggested to Walt Whitman that one of his works should be bound in vellum, he was outraged—"Pshaw!" he snorted, "—hangings, curtains, finger bowls, chinaware, Matthew Arnold!" And he might have been equally irritated by talk of style; for he boasted of "my barbaric yawp"—he would *not* be literary; his readers should touch not a book but a man. Yet Whitman took the pains to rewrite *Leaves of Grass* four times, and his style is unmistakable. Samuel Butler maintained that writers who bothered about their style became unreadable but he bothered about his own. "Style" has got a bad name by growing associated with precious and superior persons who, like Oscar Wilde, spend a morning putting in a comma, and the afternoon (so

he said) taking it out again. But such abuse of "style" is misuse of English. For the word means merely "a way of expressing oneself, in language, manner, or appearance"; or, secondly, "a *good* way of so expressing oneself"—as when one says, "Her behavior never lacked style."

2 Now there is no crime in expressing oneself (though to try to impress oneself on others easily grows revolting or ridiculous). Indeed one cannot help expressing oneself, unless one passes one's life in a cupboard. Even the most rigid Communist, or Organization-man, is compelled by Nature to have a unique voice, unique fingerprints, unique handwriting. Even the signatures of the letters on your breakfast table may reveal more than their writers guess. There are blustering signatures that swish across the page like cornstalks bowed before a tempest. There are cryptic signatures, like a scrabble of lightning across a cloud, suggesting that behind is a lofty divinity whom all must know, or an aloof divinity whom none is worthy to know (though, as this might be highly inconvenient, a docile typist sometimes interprets the mystery in a bracket underneath). There are impetuous squiggles implying that the author is a sort of strenuous Sputnik streaking around the globe every eighty minutes. There are florid signatures, all curlicues and danglements and flamboyance, like the youthful Disraeli (though these seem rather out of fashion). There are humble, humdrum signatures. And there are also, sometimes, signatures that are courteously clear, yet mindful of a certain simple grace and artistic economy—in short, of style.

3 Since, then, not one of us can put pen to paper, or even open his mouth, without giving something of himself away to shrewd observers, it seems mere common sense to give the matter a little thought. Yet it does not seem very common. Ladies may take infinite pains about having style in their clothes, but many of us remain curiously indifferent about having it in our words. How many women would dream of polishing not only their nails but also their tongues? They may play freely on that perilous little organ, but they cannot often be bothered to tune it. And how many men think of improving their talk as well as their golf handicap?

4 No doubt strong silent men, speaking only in gruff monosyllables, may despise "mere words." No doubt the world does suffer from an endemic plague of verbal dysentery. But that, precisely, is bad style. And consider the amazing power of mere words. Adolf Hitler was a bad artist, bad statesman, bad general, and bad man. But largely because he could tune his rant, with psychological nicety, to the exact wave length of his audiences and make millions quarrelsome-drunk all at the same time by his command of windy nonsense, skilled statesmen, soldiers, scientists were blown away like chaff, and he came near to rule the world. If Sir Winston Churchill had been a mere speechifier, we might well have lost the war; yet his speeches did quite a lot to win it.

5 No man was less of a literary aesthete than Benjamin Franklin; yet this tallow-chandler's son, who changed world history, regarded as "a principal means of my advancement" that pungent style which he acquired partly by working in youth over old *Spectators;* but mainly by being Benjamin Franklin.

The squinting demagogue, John Wilkes, as ugly as his many sins, had yet a tongue so winning that he asked only half an hour's start (to counteract his face) against any rival for a woman's favor. "Vote for you!" growled a surly elector in his constituency. "I'd sooner vote for the devil!" "But in case your friend should not stand . . .?" Cleopatra, the ensnarer of world conquerors, owed less to the shape of her nose than to the charm of her tongue. Shakespeare himself has often poor plots and thin ideas; even his mastery of character has been questioned; what does remain unchallenged is his verbal magic. Men are often taken, like rabbits, by the ears. And though the tongue has no bones, it can sometimes break millions of them.

6 "But," the reader may grumble, "I am neither Hitler, Cleopatra, nor Shakespeare. What is all this to me?" Yet we all talk—often too much; we all have to write letters—often too many. We live not by bread alone but also by words. And not always with remarkable efficiency. Strikes, lawsuits, divorces, all sorts of public nuisance and private misery, often come just from the gaggling incompetence with which we express ourselves. Americans and British get at cross-purposes because they use the same words with different meanings. Men have been hanged on a comma in a statute. And in the valley of Balaclava a mere verbal ambiguity, about *which* guns were to be captured, sent the whole Light Brigade to futile annihilation.

7 Words can be more powerful, and more treacherous, than we sometimes suspect; communication more difficult than we may think. We are all serving life sentences of solitary confinement within our own bodies; like prisoners, we have, as it were, to tap in awkward code to our fellow men in their neighboring cells. Further, when A and B converse, there take part in their dialogue not two characters, as they suppose, but six. For there is A's real self—call it A_1; there is also A's picture of himself—A_2; there is also B's picture of A—A_3. And there are three corresponding personalities of B. With six characters involved even in a simple tête-à-tête, no wonder we fall into muddles and misunderstandings.

8 Perhaps, then, there are five main reasons for trying to gain some mastery of language:

We have no other way of understanding, informing, misinforming, or persuading one another.

Even alone, we think mainly in words; if our language is muddy, so will our thinking be.

By our handling of words we are often revealed and judged. "Has he written anything?" said Napoleon of a candidate for an appointment. "Let me see his *style.*"

Without a feeling for language one remains half-blind and deaf to literature.

Our mother tongue is bettered or worsened by the way each generation uses it. Languages evolve like species. They can degenerate; just as oysters and barnacles have lost their heads. Compare ancient Greek with modern. A heavy responsibility, though often forgotten.

9 Why and how did I become interested in style? The main answer, I suppose, is that I was born that way. Then I was, till ten, an only child running loose in a house packed with books, and in a world (thank goodness) still undistracted by radio and television. So at three I groaned to my mother, "Oh, I *wish* I could read," and at four I read. Now travel among books is the best travel of all, and the easiest, and the cheapest. (Not that I belittle ordinary travel—which I regard as one of the three main pleasures in life.) One learns to write by reading good books, as one learns to talk by hearing good talkers. And if I have learned anything in writing, it is largely from writers like Montaigne, Dorothy Osborne, Horace Walpole, Johnson, Goldsmith, Montesquieu, Voltaire, Flaubert and Anatole France. Again, I was reared on Greek and Latin, and one can learn much from translating Homer or the Greek Anthology, Horace or Tacitus, if one is thrilled by the originals and tries, however vainly, to recapture some of that thrill in English.

10 But at Rugby I could *not* write English essays. I believe it stupid to torment boys to write on topics that they know and care nothing about. I used to rush to the school library and cram the subject, like a python swallowing rabbits; then, still replete as a postprandial python, I would tie myself in clumsy knots to embrace those accursed themes. Bacon was wise in saying that reading makes a full man; talking, a ready one; writing, an exact one. But writing from an empty head is futile anguish.

11 At Cambridge, my head having grown a little fuller, I suddenly found I *could* write—not with enjoyment (it is always tearing oneself in pieces)—but fairly fluently. Then came the War of 1914–18; and though soldiers have other things than pens to handle, they learn painfully to be clear and brief. Then the late Sir Desmond MacCarthy invited me to review for the *New Statesman;* it was a useful apprenticeship, and he was delightful to work for. But I think it was well after a few years to stop; reviewers remain essential, but there are too many books one *cannot* praise, and only the pugnacious enjoy amassing enemies. By then I was an ink-addict—not because writing is much pleasure, but because not to write is pain; just as some smokers do not so much enjoy tobacco as suffer without it. The positive happiness of writing comes, I think, from work when done—decently, one hopes, and not without use—and from the letters of readers which help to reassure, or delude, one that so it is.

12 But one of my most vivid lessons came, I think, from service in a war department during the Second World War. Then, if the matter one sent out was too wordy, the communication channels might choke; yet if it was not absolutely clear, the results might be serious. So I emerged, after six years of it, with more passion than ever for clarity and brevity, more loathing than ever for the obscure and the verbose.

13 For forty years at Cambridge I have tried to teach young men to write well, and have come to think it impossible. To write really well is a gift inborn; those who have it teach themselves; one can only try to help and hasten the process. After all, the uneducated sometimes express themselves far better than their "betters." In language, as in life, it is possible to be perfectly

correct—and yet perfectly tedious, or odious. The illiterate last letter of the doomed Vanzetti[1] was more moving than most professional orators; 18th Century ladies, who should have been spanked for their spelling, could yet write far better letters than most professors of English; and the talk of Synge's Irish peasants seems to me vastly more vivid than the latter styles of Henry James. Yet Synge averred that his characters owed far less of their eloquence to what he invented for them than to what he had overheard in the cottages of Wicklow and Kerry:

> CHRISTY. It's little you'll think if my love's a poacher's, or an earl's itself, when you'll feel my two hands stretched around you, and I squeezing kisses on your puckered lips, till I'd feel a kind of pity for the Lord God in all ages sitting lonesome in His golden chair.
>
> PEGEEN. That'll be right fun, Christy Mahon, and any girl would walk her heart out before she'd meet a young man was your like for eloquence, or talk at all.

14 Well she might! It's not like that they talk in universities—more's the pity.

15 But though one cannot teach people to write well, one can sometimes teach them to write rather better. One can give a certain number of hints, which often seem boringly obvious—only experience shows they are not.

16 One can say: Beware of pronouns—they are devils. Look at even Addison, describing the type of pedant who chatters of style without having any:

> Upon enquiry I found my learned friend had dined that day with Mr. Swan, the famous punster; and desiring *him* to give me some account of Mr. Swan's conversation, *he* told me that *he* generally talked in the Paronomasia, that *he* sometimes gave it to the Plocé, but that in *his* humble opinion *he* shone most in the Antanaclasis.

What a sluttish muddle of *he* and *him* and *his!* It all needs rewording. Far better repeat a noun, or a name, than puzzle the reader, even for a moment, with ambiguous pronouns. Thou shalt not puzzle thy reader.

17 Or one can say: Avoid jingles. The B.B.C. news bulletins seem compiled by earless persons, capable of crying around the globe: "The enemy is re*port*ed to have seized this im*port*ant *port,* and reinforcements are hurrying up in sup*port.*" Any fool, once told, can hear such things to be insupportable.

18 Or one can say: Be sparing with relative clauses. Don't string them together like sausages, or jam them inside one another like Chinese boxes or the receptacles of Buddha's tooth. Or one can say: Don't flaunt jargon, like Addison's Mr. Swan, or the type of modern critic who gurgles more technical terms in a page than Johnson used in all his *Lives* or Sainte-Beuve in thirty volumes. But dozens of such snippety precepts, though they may sometimes save people from writing badly, will help them little toward writing well. Are there no general rules of a more positive kind, and of more positive use?

19 Perhaps. There *are* certain basic principles which seem to me observed

[1] See p. 39.—Ed.

by many authors I admire, which I think have served me and which may serve others. I am not talking of geniuses, who are a law to themselves (and do not always write a very good style, either); nor of poetry, which has different laws from prose; nor of poetic prose, like Sir Thomas Browne's or De Quincey's, which is often more akin to poetry; but of the plain prose of ordinary books and documents, letters and talk.

20 The writer should respect truth and himself; therefore honesty. He should respect his readers; therefore courtesy. These are two of the cornerstones of style. Confucius saw it, twenty-five centuries ago: "The Master said, The gentleman is courteous, but not pliable: common men are pliable, but not courteous."

21 First, honesty. In literature, as in life, one of the fundamentals is to find, and be, one's true self. One's true self may indeed be unpleasant (though one can try to better it); but a false self, sooner or later, becomes disgusting—just as a nice plain woman, painted to the eyebrows, can become horrid. In writing, in the long run, pretense does not work. As the police put it, anything you say may be used as evidence against you. If handwriting reveals character, writing reveals it still more. You cannot fool *all* your judges *all* the time.

22 Most style is not honest enough. Easy to say, but hard to practice. A writer may take to long words, as young men to beards—to impress. But long words, like beards, are often the badge of charlatans. Or a writer may cultivate the obscure, to seem profound. But even carefully muddied puddles are soon fathomed. Or he may cultivate eccentricity, to seem original. But really original people do not have to think about being original—they can no more help it than they can help breathing. They do not need to dye their hair green. The fame of Meredith, Wilde or Bernard Shaw might now shine brighter, had they struggled less to be brilliant; whereas Johnson remains great, not merely because his gifts were formidable but also because, with all his prejudice and passion, he fought no less passionately to "clear his mind of cant."

23 Secondly, courtesy—respect for the reader. From this follow several other basic principles of style. Clarity is one. For it is boorish to make your reader rack his brains to understand. One should aim at being impossible to misunderstand—though men's capacity for misunderstanding approaches infinity. Hence Molière and Po Chu-i tried their work on their cooks; and Swift his on his men-servants—"which, if they did not comprehend, he would alter and amend, until they understood it perfectly." Our bureaucrats and pundits, unfortunately, are less considerate.

24 Brevity is another basic principle. For it is boorish, also, to waste your reader's time. People who would not dream of stealing a penny of one's money turn not a hair at stealing hours of one's life. But that does not make them less exasperating. Therefore there is no excuse for the sort of writer who takes as long as a marching army corps to pass a given point. Besides, brevity is often more effective; the half can say more than the whole, and to imply things may strike far deeper than to state them at length. And because one is particularly apt to waste words on preambles before coming to the substance,

there was sense in the Scots professor who always asked his pupils—"Did ye remember to tear up that fir-r-st page?"

25 Here are some instances that would only lose by lengthening.

It is useless to go to bed to save the light, if the result is twins. (Chinese proverb.)

My barn is burnt down—
Nothing hides the moon. (Complete Japanese poem.)

Je me regrette.[2] (Dying words of the gay Vicomtesse d'Houdetot.)

I have seen their backs before. (Wellington, when French marshals turned their backs on him at a reception.)

Continue until the tanks stop, then get out and walk. (Patton to the Twelfth Corps, halted for fuel supplies at St. Dizier, 8/30/44.)

26 Or there is the most laconic diplomatic note on record: when Philip of Macedon wrote to the Spartans that, if he came within their borders, he would leave not one stone of their city, they wrote back the one word—"If."

27 Clarity comes before even brevity. But it is a fallacy that wordiness is necessarily clearer. Metternich when he thought something he had written was obscure would simply go through it crossing out everything irrelevant. What remained, he found, often became clear. Wellington, asked to recommend three names for the post of Commander-in-Chief, India, took a piece of paper and wrote three times—"Napier." Pages could not have been clearer— or as forcible. On the other hand the lectures, and the sentences, of Coleridge became at times bewildering because his mind was often "wiggle-waggle"; just as he could not even walk straight on a path.

28 But clarity and brevity, though a good beginning, are only a beginning. By themselves, they may remain bare and bleak. When Calvin Coolidge, asked by his wife what the preacher had preached on, replied "Sin," and, asked what the preacher had said, replied, "He was against it," he was brief enough. But one hardly envies Mrs. Coolidge.

29 An attractive style requires, of course, all kinds of further gifts—such as variety, good humor, good sense, vitality, imagination. Variety means avoiding monotony of rhythm, of language, of mood. One needs to vary one's sentence length (this present article has too many short sentences; but so vast a subject grows here as cramped as a djin in a bottle); to amplify one's vocabulary; to diversify one's tone. There are books that petrify one throughout, with the rigidly pompous solemnity of an owl perched on a leafless tree. But ceaseless facetiousness can be as bad; or perpetual irony. Even the smile of Voltaire can seem at times a fixed grin, a disagreeable wrinkle. Constant peevishness is far worse, as often in Swift; even on the stage too much irritable dialogue may irritate an audience, without its knowing why.

30 Still more are vitality, energy, imagination gifts that must be inborn before they can be cultivated. But under the head of imagination two common devices may be mentioned that have been the making of many a style—

[2]"I shall miss myself."—Ed.

metaphor and simile. Why such magic power should reside in simply saying, or implying, that A is like B remains a little mysterious. But even our unconscious seems to love symbols; again, language often tends to lose itself in clouds of vaporous abstraction, and simile or metaphor can bring it back to concrete solidity; and, again, such imagery can gild the gray flats of prose with sudden sun-glints of poetry.

31 If a foreigner may for a moment be impertinent, I admire the native gift of Americans for imagery as much as I wince at their fondness for slang. (Slang seems to me a kind of linguistic fungus; as poisonous, and as short-lived, as toadstools.) When Matthew Arnold lectured in the United States, he was likened by one newspaper to "an elderly macaw pecking at a trellis of grapes"; he observed, very justly, "How lively journalistic fancy is among the Americans!" General Grant, again, unable to hear him, remarked: "Well, wife, we've paid to see the British lion, but as we can't hear him roar, we'd better go home." By simile and metaphor, these two quotations bring before us the slightly pompous, fastidious, inaudible Arnold as no direct description could have done.

32 Or consider how language comes alive in the Chinese saying that lending to the feckless is "like pelting a stray dog with dumplings," or in the Arab proverb: "They came to shoe the pasha's horse, and the beetle stretched forth his leg"; in the Greek phrase for a perilous cape—"stepmother of ships"; or the Hebrew adage that "as the climbing up a sandy way is to the feet of the aged, so is a wife full of words to a quiet man"; in Shakespeare's phrase for a little England lost in the world's vastness—"in a great Poole, a Swan's nest"; or Fuller's libel on tall men—"Ofttimes such who are built four stories high are observed to have little in their cockloft"; in Chateaubriand's "I go yawning my life"; or in Jules Renard's portrait of a cat, "well buttoned in her fur." Or, to take a modern instance, there is Churchill on dealing with Russia:

> Trying to maintain good relations with a Communist is like wooing a crocodile. You do not know whether to tickle it under the chin or beat it over the head. When it opens its mouth, you cannot tell whether it is trying to smile or preparing to eat you up.

What a miracle human speech can be, and how dull is most that one hears! Would one hold one's hearers, it is far less help, I suspect, to read manuals on style than to cultivate one's own imagination and imagery.

33 I will end with two remarks by two wise old women of the civilized 18th Century.

34 The first is from the blind Mme. du Deffand (the friend of Horace Walpole) to that Mlle. de Lespinasse with whom, alas, she was to quarrel so unwisely: "You must make up your mind, my queen, to live with me in the greatest truth and sincerity. You will be charming so long as you let yourself be natural, and remain without pretension and without artifice." The second is from Mme. de Charrière, the Zélide whom Boswell had once loved at Utrecht in vain, to a Swiss girl friend: "Lucinde, my clever Lucinde, while you wait for the Romeos to arrive, you have nothing better to do than become perfect.

Have ideas that are clear, and expressions that are simple." (*"Ayez des idées nettes et des expressions simples."*) More than half the bad writing in the world, I believe, comes from neglecting those two very simple pieces of advice.

35 In many ways, no doubt, our world grows more and more complex; sputniks cannot be simple; yet how many of our complexities remain futile, how many of our artificialities false. Simplicity too can be subtle—as the straight lines of a Greek temple, like the Parthenon at Athens, are delicately curved, in order to look straighter still.

VOCABULARY

curlicues (2)	degenerate (8)
endemic (4)	replete (10)
aesthete (5)	postprandial (10)
tallow-chandler (5)	pugnacious (11)
demagogue (5)	verbose (12)
gaggling (6)	odious (13)
annihilation (6)	averred (13)
tête-à-tête (7)	pedant (16)

discussion

W. SOMERSET MAUGHAM

LUCIDITY, SIMPLICITY, EUPHONY

In this selection from *The Summing Up*, the English novelist and playwright W. Somerset Maugham (1874–1965) discusses three characteristics of a good style.

1 I have never had much patience with the writers who claim from the reader an effort to understand their meaning. You have only to go to the great philosophers to see that it is possible to express with lucidity the most subtle reflections. You may find it difficult to understand the thought of Hume, and if you have no philosophical training its implications will doubtless escape you; but no one with any education at all can fail to understand exactly what the meaning of each sentence is. Few people have written English with more grace than Berkeley. There are two sorts of obscurity that you find in writers. One is due to negligence and the other to willfulness. People often write obscurely because they have never taken the trouble to learn to write clearly. This sort of obscurity you find too often in modern philosophers, in men of science, and even in literary critics. Here it is indeed strange. You would have thought that men who passed their lives in the study of the great masters of literature would be sufficiently sensitive to the beauty of language to write if

not beautifully at least with perspicuity. Yet you will find in their works sentence after sentence that you must read twice to discover the sense. Often you can only guess at it, for the writers have evidently not said what they intended.

2 Another cause of obscurity is that the writer is himself not quite sure of his meaning. He has a vague impression of what he wants to say, but has not, either from lack of mental power or from laziness, exactly formulated it in his mind and it is natural enough that he should not find a precise expression for a confused idea. This is due largely to the fact that many writers think, not before, but as they write. The pen originates the thought. The disadvantage of this, and indeed it is a danger against which the author must be always on his guard, is that there is a sort of magic in the written word. The idea acquires substance by taking on a visible nature, and then stands in the way of its own clarification. But this sort of obscurity merges very easily into the willful. Some writers who do not think clearly are inclined to suppose that their thoughts have a significance greater than at first sight appears. It is flattering to believe that they are too profound to be expressed so clearly that all who run may read, and very naturally it does not occur to such writers that the fault is with their own minds which have not the faculty of precise reflection. Here again the magic of the written word obtains. It is very easy to persuade oneself that a phrase that one does not quite understand may mean a great deal more than one realizes. From this there is only a little way to go to fall into the habit of setting down one's impressions in all their original vagueness. Fools can always be found to discover a hidden sense in them. There is another form of willful obscurity that masquerades as aristocratic exclusiveness. The author wraps his meaning in mystery so that the vulgar shall not participate in it. His soul is a secret garden into which the elect may penetrate only after overcoming a number of perilous obstacles. But this kind of obscurity is not only pretentious; it is short-sighted. For time plays it an odd trick. If the sense is meagre time reduces it to a meaningless verbiage that no one thinks of reading. This is the fate that has befallen the lucubrations of those French writers who were seduced by the example of Guillaume Apollonaire. But occasionally it throws a sharp cold light on what had seemed profound and thus discloses the fact that these contortions of language disguised very commonplace notions. There are few of Mallarmé's poems now that are not clear; one cannot fail to notice that his thought singularly lacked originality. Some of his phrases were beautiful; the materials of his verse were the poetic platitudes of his day.

3 Simplicity is not such an obvious merit as lucidity. I have aimed at it because I have no gift for richness. Within limits I admire richness in others, though I find it difficult to digest in quantity. I can read one page of Ruskin with delight, but twenty only with weariness. The rolling period, the stately epithet, the noun rich in poetic associations, the subordinate clauses that give the sentence weight and magnificence, the grandeur like that of wave following wave in the open sea; there is no doubt that in all this there is something inspiring. Words thus strung together fall on the ear like music. The appeal is sensuous rather than intellectual, and the beauty of the sound leads you easily

to conclude that you need not bother about the meaning. But words are tyrannical things, they exist for their meanings, and if you will not pay attention to these, you cannot pay attention at all. Your mind wanders. This kind of writing demands a subject that will suit it. It is surely out of place to write in the grand style of inconsiderable things. No one wrote in this manner with greater success than Sir Thomas Browne, but even he did not always escape this pitfall. In the last chapter of *Hydriotaphia* the matter, which is the destiny of man, wonderfully fits the baroque splendor of the language, and here the Norwich doctor produced a piece of prose that has never been surpassed in our literature; but when he describes the finding of his urns in the same splendid manner the effect (at least to my taste) is less happy. When a modern writer is grandiloquent to tell you whether or no a little trollop shall hop into bed with a commonplace young man you are right to be disgusted.

4 But if richness needs gifts with which everyone is not endowed, simplicity by no means comes by nature. To achieve it needs rigid discipline. So far as I know ours is the only language in which it has been found necessary to give a name to the piece of prose which is described as the purple patch; it would not have been necessary to do so unless it were characteristic. English prose is elaborate rather than simple. It was not always so. Nothing could be more racy, straightforward and alive than the prose of Shakespeare; but it must be remembered that this was dialogue written to be spoken. We do not know how he would have written if like Corneille he had composed prefaces to his plays. It may be that they would have been as euphuistic as the letters of Queen Elizabeth. But earlier prose, the prose of Sir Thomas More, for instance, is neither ponderous, flowery nor oratorical. It smacks of the English soil. To my mind King James's Bible has been a very harmful influence on English prose. I am not so stupid as to deny its great beauty. It is majestical. But the Bible is an oriental book. Its alien imagery has nothing to do with us. Those hyperboles, those luscious metaphors, are foreign to our genius. I cannot but think that not the least of the misfortunes that the Secession from Rome brought upon the spiritual life of our country is that this work for so long a period became the daily, and with many the only, reading of our people. Those rhythms, that powerful vocabulary, that grandiloquence, became part and parcel of the national sensibility. The plain, honest English speech was overwhelmed with ornament. Blunt Englishmen twisted their tongues to speak like Hebrew prophets. There was evidently something in the English temper to which this was congenial, perhaps a native lack of precision in thought, perhaps a naïve delight in fine words for their own sake, an innate eccentricity and love of embroidery, I do not know; but the fact remains that ever since, English prose has had to struggle against the tendency to luxuriance. When from time to time the spirit of the language has reasserted itself, as it did with Dryden and the writers of Queen Anne, it was only to be submerged once more by the pomposities of Gibbon and Dr. Johnson. When English prose recovered simplicity with Hazlitt, the Shelley of the letters and Charles Lamb at his best, it lost it again with De Quincey, Carlyle, Meredith and Walter Pater. It is obvious that the grand style is more striking than the plain.

Indeed many people think that a style that does not attract notice is not style. They will admire Walter Pater's, but will read an essay by Matthew Arnold without giving a moment's attention to the elegance, distinction and sobriety with which he set down what he had to say.

5 The dictum that the style is the man is well known. It is one of those aphorisms that say too much to mean a great deal. Where is the man in Goethe, in his birdlike lyrics or in his clumsy prose? And Hazlitt? But I suppose that if a man has a confused mind he will write in a confused way, if his temper is capricious his prose will be fantastical, and if he has a quick, darting intelligence that is reminded by the matter in hand of a hundred things, he will, unless he has great self-control, load his pages with metaphor and simile. There is a great difference between the magniloquence of the Jacobean writers, who were intoxicated with the new wealth that had lately been brought into the language, and the turgidity of Gibbon and Dr. Johnson, who were the victims of bad theories. I can read every word that Dr. Johnson wrote with delight, for he had good sense, charm and wit. No one could have written better if he had not willfully set himself to write in the grand style. He knew good English when he saw it. No critic has praised Dryden's prose more aptly. He said of him that he appeared to have no art other than that of expressing with clearness what he thought with vigor. And one of his Lives he finished with the words: "Whoever wishes to attain an English style, familiar but not coarse, and elegant but not ostentatious, must give his days and nights to the volumes of Addison." But when he himself sat down to write it was with a very different aim. He mistook the orotund for the dignified. He had not the good breeding to see that simplicity and naturalness are the truest marks of distinction.

6 For to write good prose is an affair of good manners. It is, unlike verse, a civil art. Poetry is baroque. Baroque is tragic, massive and mystical. It is elemental. It demands depth and insight. I cannot but feel that the prose writers of the baroque period, the authors of King James's Bible, Sir Thomas Browne, Glanville, were poets who had lost their way. Prose is a rococo art. It needs taste rather than power, decorum rather than inspiration and vigor rather than grandeur. Form for the poet is the bit and the bridle without which (unless you are an acrobat) you cannot ride your horse; but for the writer of prose it is the chassis without which your car does not exist. It is not an accident that the best prose was written when rococo, with its elegance and moderation, at its birth attained its greatest excellence. For rococo was evolved when baroque had become declamatory and the world, tired of the stupendous, asked for restraint. It was the natural expression of persons who valued a civilized life. Humor, tolerance and horse sense made the great tragic issues that had preoccupied the first half of the seventeenth century seem excessive. The world was a more comfortable place to live in and perhaps for the first time in centuries the cultivated classes could sit back and enjoy their leisure. It has been said that good prose should resemble the conversation of a well-bred man. Conversation is only possible when men's minds are free from pressing anxieties. Their lives must be reasonably secure and they must have

no grave concern about their souls. They must attach importance to the refinements of civilization. They must value courtesy, they must pay attention to their persons (and have we not also been told that good prose should be like the clothes of a well-dressed man, appropriate but unobtrusive?), they must fear to bore, they must be neither flippant nor solemn, but always apt; and they must look upon "enthusiasm" with a critical glance. This is a soil very suitable for prose. It is not to be wondered at that it gave a fitting opportunity for the appearance of the best writer of prose that our modern world has seen, Voltaire. The writers of English, perhaps owing to the poetic nature of the language, have seldom reached the excellence that seems to have come so naturally to him. It is in so far as they have approached the ease, sobriety and precision of the great French masters that they are admirable.

7 Whether you ascribe importance to euphony, the last of the three characteristics that I mentioned, must depend on the sensitiveness of your ear. A great many readers, and many admirable writers, are devoid of this quality. Poets as we know have always made a great use of alliteration. They are persuaded that the repetition of a sound gives an effect of beauty. I do not think it does so in prose. It seems to me that in prose alliteration should be used only for a special reason; when used by accident it falls on the ear very disagreeably. But its accidental use is so common that one can only suppose that the sound of it is not universally offensive. Many writers without distress will put two rhyming words together, join a monstrous long adjective to a monstrous long noun, or between the end of one word and the beginning of another have a conjunction of consonants that almost breaks your jaw. These are trivial and obvious instances. I mention them only to prove that if careful writers can do such things it is only because they have no ear. Words have weight, sound and appearance; it is only by considering these that you can write a sentence that is good to look at and good to listen to.

8 I have read many books on English prose, but have found it hard to profit by them; for the most part they are vague, unduly theoretical, and often scolding. But you cannot say this of Fowler's *Dictionary of Modern English Usage*. It is a valuable work. I do not think anyone writes so well that he cannot learn much from it. It is lively reading. Fowler liked simplicity, straightforwardness and common sense. He had no patience with pretentiousness. He had a sound feeling that idiom was the backbone of a language and he was all for the racy phrase. He was no slavish admirer of logic and was willing enough to give usage right of way through the exact demesnes of grammar. English grammar is very difficult and few writers have avoided making mistakes in it. So heedful a writer as Henry James, for instance, on occasion wrote so ungrammatically that a schoolmaster, finding such errors in a schoolboy's essay, would be justly indignant. It is necessary to know grammar, and it is better to write grammatically than not, but it is well to remember that grammar is common speech formulated. Usage is the only test. I would prefer a phrase that was easy and unaffected to a phrase that was grammatical. One of the differences between French and English is that in French you can be grammatical with complete naturalness, but in English not invariably. It is a

difficulty in writing English that the sound of the living voice dominates the look of the printed word. I have given the matter of style a great deal of thought and have taken great pains. I have written few pages that I feel I could not improve and far too many that I have left with dissatisfaction because, try as I would, I could do no better. I cannot say of myself what Johnson said of Pope: "He never passed a fault unamended by indifference, nor quitted it by despair." I do not write as I want to; I write as I can.

9 But Fowler had no ear. He did not see that simplicity may sometimes make concessions to euphony. I do not think a far-fetched, an archaic or even an affected word is out of place when it sounds better than the blunt, obvious one or when it gives a sentence a better balance. But, I hasten to add, though I think you may without misgiving make this concession to pleasant sound, I think you should make none to what may obscure your meaning. Anything is better than not to write clearly. There is nothing to be said against lucidity, and against simplicity only the possibility of dryness. This is a risk that is well worth taking when you reflect how much better it is to be bald than to wear a curly wig. But there is in euphony a danger that must be considered. It is very likely to be monotonous. When George Moore began to write, his style was poor; it gave you the impression that he wrote on wrapping paper with a blunt pencil. But he developed gradually a very musical English. He learnt to write sentences that fall away on the ear with a misty languor and it delighted him so much that he could never have enough of it. He did not escape monotony. It is like the sound of water lapping a shingly beach, so soothing that you presently cease to be sensible of it. It is so mellifluous that you hanker for some harshness, for an abrupt dissonance, that will interrupt the silky concord. I do not know how one can guard against this. I suppose the best chance is to have a more lively faculty of boredom than one's readers so that one is wearied before they are. One must always be on the watch for mannerisms and when certain cadences come too easily to the pen ask oneself whether they have not become mechanical. It is very hard to discover the exact point where the idiom one has formed to express oneself has lost its tang. As Dr. Johnson said: "He that has once studiously formed a style, rarely writes afterwards with complete ease." Admirably as I think Matthew Arnold's style was suited to his particular purposes, I must admit that his mannerisms are often irritating. His style was an instrument that he had forged once for all; it was not like the human hand capable of performing a variety of actions.

10 If you could write lucidly, simply, euphoniously and yet with liveliness you would write perfectly: you would write like Voltaire. And yet we know how fatal the pursuit of liveliness may be: it may result in the tiresome acrobatics of Meredith. Macaulay and Carlyle were in their different ways arresting; but at the heavy cost of naturalness. Their flashy effects distract the mind. They destroy their persuasiveness; you would not believe a man was very intent on ploughing a furrow if he carried a hoop with him and jumped through it at every other step. A good style should show no sign of effort. What is written should seem a happy accident. I think no one in France now writes more admirably than Colette, and such is the ease of her expression

that you cannot bring yourself to believe that she takes any trouble over it. I am told that there are pianists who have a natural technique so that they can play in a manner that most executants can achieve only as the result of unremitting toil, and I am willing to believe that there are writers who are equally fortunate. Among them I was much inclined to place Colette. I asked her. I was exceedingly surprised to hear that she wrote everything over and over again. She told me that she would often spend a whole morning working upon a single page. But it does not matter how one gets the effect of ease. For my part, if I get it at all, it is only by strenuous effort. Nature seldom provides me with the word, the turn of phrase, that is appropriate without being far-fetched or commonplace.

VOCABULARY

perspicuity (1)	magniloquence (5)
verbiage (2)	turgidity (5)
lucubrations (2)	ostentatious (5)
platitudes (2)	orotund (5)
sensuous (3)	rococo (6)
baroque (3)	decorum (6)
grandiloquent (3)	declamatory (6)
trollop (3)	unobtrusive (6)
euphuistic (4)	euphony (7)
hyperboles (4)	demesnes (8)
luxuriance (4)	archaic (9)
dictum (5)	mellifluous (9)
aphorisms (5)	dissonance (9)
capricious (5)	concord (9)

QUESTIONS ON CONTENT

1. According to Maugham, what are the two cases of obscurity?
2. What kind of subject is a grand style most suited to? What is it least suited to?
3. What influence does the author believe the King James version of the Bible has had on English prose?
4. Why does Maugham see good prose as an affair of good manners?
5. What does he take to be the only test of grammar?
6. According to the author, why is it more difficult to write good English prose than good French prose?
7. What is the danger of euphony in writing?
8. What characterizes a good style?

QUESTIONS ON FORM

1. What method of development does Maugham use to discuss obscurity?
2. "The pen originates the thought."—What figure of speech is this? What does it contribute to Maugham's style?

3. Maugham writes: "But earlier prose, the prose of Sir Thomas More, for instance, is neither ponderous, flowery nor oratorical. It smacks of the English soil."
   (a) "Ponderous," "flowery," and "oratorical" are close in meaning. What effect does the use of all three have on the sentence?
   (b) What figure of speech is used in the second sentence?
4. "Form for the poet is the bit and bridle without which (unless you are an acrobat) you cannot ride your horse; but for the writer of prose it is the chassis without which your car does not exist."—What figure of speech is this? Is it appropriate to Maugham's argument? Explain.
5. How does Maugham manage to develop his discussion of style without actually quoting?

SUGGESTIONS FOR WRITING

1. Maugham writes that "good prose is an affair of good manners." Discuss this idea.
2. Analyze and discuss the statement "Style is the man" as it applies to writing.

examples

DAN GREENBURG

THREE BEARS IN SEARCH OF AN AUTHOR

What is style? How do we recognize the differences between two styles? In "Three Bears in Search of an Author" Dan Greenburg presents two versions of the Goldilocks story, one written in the style of *The Catcher in the Rye* by J. D. Salinger, and the other in the style of *A Farewell to Arms* by Ernest Hemingway.

1. Catch Her in the Oatmeal

If you actually want to hear about it, what I'd better do is I'd better warn you right now that you aren't going to believe it. I mean it's a true *story* and all, but it still sounds sort of phony.

Anyway, my name is Goldie Lox. It's sort of a boring name, but my parents said that when I was born I had this very blonde hair and all. Actually I was born bald. I mean how many babies get born with blonde hair? None. I mean I've *seen* them and they're all wrinkled and red and slimy and everything. And bald. And then all the phonies have to come around and tell you he's as cute as a bug's ear. A bug's ear, boy, that really kills me. You ever *seen* a bug's ear? What's cute about a bug's *ear,* for Chrissake! Nothing, that's what.

So, like I was saying, I always seem to be getting into these very stupid situations. Like this time I was telling you about. Anyway, I was walking through the forest and all when I see this very interesting house. A *house.* You wouldn't think anybody would be living way the hell out in the goddam *forest,* but they were. No one was home or anything and the door was open, so I walked in. I figured what I'd do is I'd probably horse around until the guys that lived there came home and maybe asked me to stay for dinner or something. Some people think they *have* to ask you to stay for dinner even if they *hate* you. Also I didn't exactly feel like going home and getting asked a lot of lousy questions. I mean that's *all* I ever seem to do.

Anyway, while I was waiting I sort of sampled some of this stuff they had on the table that tasted like oatmeal. *Oatmeal.* It would have made you puke, I mean it. Then something very spooky started happening. I started getting dizzier than hell. I figured I'd feel better if I could just rest for a while. Sometimes if you eat something like lousy oatmeal you can feel better if you just rest for awhile, so I sat down. That's when the goddam *chair* breaks in half. No kidding, you start feeling lousy and some stupid *chair* is going to break on you every time. I'm not kidding. Anyway I finally found the crummy bedroom and I lay down on this very tiny bed. I was really depressed.

I don't know how long I was asleep or anything but all of a sudden I hear this very strange voice say, "Someone's been sleeping in *my* sack, for Chrissake, and there she is!" So I open my eyes and here at the foot of the bed are these three crummy *bears. Bears!* I swear to God. By that time I was *really* feeling depressed. There's nothing more depressing than waking up and finding three *bears* talking about you, I mean.

So I didn't stay around and shoot the breeze with them or anything. If you want to know the truth, I sort of ran out of there like a madman or something. I do that quite a little when I'm depressed like that.

On the way home, though, I got to figuring. What probably happened is these bears wandered in when they smelled this oatmeal and all. Probably bears *like* oatmeal, I don't know. And the voice I heard when I woke up was probably something I dreamt.

So that's the story.

I wrote it all up once as a theme in school, but my crummy teacher said it was too *whimsical.* Whimsical. That killed me. You got to meet her sometime, boy. She's a real queen.

2. A Farewell to Porridge

In the late autumn of that year we lived in a house in the forest that looked across the river to the mountains, but we always thought we lived on the plain because we couldn't see the forest for the trees.

Sometimes people would come to the door and ask if we would like to subscribe to *The Saturday Evening Post* or buy Fuller brushes, but when we would answer the bell they would see we were only bears and go away.

Sometimes we would go for long walks along the river and you could almost forget for a little while that you were a bear and not people.

Once when we were out strolling for a very long time we came home and you could see that someone had broken in and the door was open.

"*La porte est ouverte!*" said Mama Bear. "The door should not be open." Mama Bear had French blood on her father's side.

"It is all right," I said. "We will close it."

"It should not have been left open," she said.

"It is all right," I said. "We will close it. Then it will be good like in the old days."

"*Bien,*" she said. "It is well."

We walked in and closed the door. There were dishes and bowls and all manner of eating utensils on the table and you could tell that someone had been eating porridge. We did not say anything for a long while.

"It is lovely here," I said finally. "But someone has been eating my porridge."

"Mine as well," said Mama Bear.

"It is all right," I said, "It is nothing."

"Darling," said Mama Bear, "do you love me?"

"Yes I love you."

"You really love me?"

"I really love you. I'm crazy in love with you."

"And the porridge? How about the porridge?"

"That too. I really love the porridge too."

"It was supposed to be a surprise. I made it as a surprise for you, but someone has eaten it all up."

"You sweet. You made it as a surprise. Oh, you're lovely," I said.

"But it is gone."

"It is all right," I said. "It will be all right."

Then I looked at my chair and you could see someone had been sitting in it and Mama Bear looked at her chair and someone had been sitting in that too and Baby Bear's chair is broken.

"We will go upstairs," I said and we went upstairs to the bedroom but you could see that someone had been sleeping in my bed and in Mama Bear's too although that was the same bed but you have to mention it that way because that is the story. Truly. And then we looked in Baby Bear's bed and there she was.

"I ate your porridge and sat in your chairs and I broke one of them," she said.

"It is all right," I said. "It will be all right."

"And now I am lying in Baby Bear's bed."

"Baby Bear can take care of himself."

"I mean that I am sorry. I have behaved badly and I am sorry for all of this."

"*Ça ne fait rien,*" said Mama Bear, "It is nothing." Outside it had started to rain again.

"I will go now," she said. "I am sorry." She walked slowly down the stairs.

I tried to think of something to tell her but it wasn't any good. "Good-by," she said.

Then she opened the door and went outside and walked all the way back to her hotel in the rain.

QUESTIONS ON FORM

1. Are the two stories the same in substance?
2. How do the stories' points of view differ?
3. Compare the dictions of the two stories. How do they differ?
4. How do the two stories differ in sentence structure? Do they use similar kinds of sentences?
5. Does each story tell anything about the personality of its narrator? If so, how is this effect achieved?

SUGGESTIONS FOR WRITING

1. Write a "third bear" story in the style of your favorite author. Specify whose style you are imitating.
2. Analyze and discuss the differences in style of each story.

GEORGE ORWELL

SHOOTING AN ELEPHANT

George Orwell (1903–50), the English novelist and essayist, writes in a style which has been described as having "singular directness and honesty." In this selection he relates an incident that occurred while he was with the Imperial Police in Burma.

1 In Moulmein, in Lower Burma, I was hated by large numbers of people—the only time in my life that I have been important enough for this to happen to me. I was sub-divisional police officer of the town, and in an aimless, petty kind of way anti-European feeling was very bitter. No one had the guts to raise a riot, but if a European woman went through the bazaars alone somebody would probably spit betel juice over her dress. As a police officer I was an obvious target and was baited whenever it seemed safe to do so. When a nimble Burman tripped me up on the football field and the referee (another Burman) looked the other way, the crowd yelled with hideous laughter. This happened more than once. In the end the sneering yellow faces of young men that met me everywhere, the insults hooted after me when I was at a safe distance, got badly on my nerves. The young Buddhist priests were the worst of all. There were several thousand of them in the town and none of them seemed to have anything to do except stand on street corners and jeer at Europeans.

2 All this was perplexing and upsetting. For at that time I had already made up my mind that imperialism was an evil thing and the sooner I chucked up my job and got out of it the better. Theoretically—and secretly, of course—I was all for the Burmese and all against their oppressors, the British. As for the job I was doing, I hated it more bitterly than I can perhaps make clear. In a job like that you see the dirty work of Empire at close quarters. The

wretched prisoners huddling in the stinking cages of the lock-ups, the grey, cowed faces of the long-term convicts, the scarred buttocks of the men who had been flogged with bamboos—all these oppressed me with an intolerable sense of guilt. But I could get nothing into perspective. I was young and ill-educated and I had had to think out my problems in the utter silence that is imposed on every Englishman in the East. I did not even know that the British Empire is dying, still less did I know that it is a great deal better than the younger empires that are going to supplant it. All I knew was that I was stuck between my hatred of the empire I served and my rage against the evil-spirited little beasts who tried to make my job impossible. With one part of my mind I thought of the British Raj as an unbreakable tyranny, as something clamped down, in *saecula saeculorum*,[1] upon the will of prostrate peoples; with another part I thought that the greatest joy in the world would be to drive a bayonet into a Buddhist priest's guts. Feelings like these are the normal by-products of imperialism; ask any Anglo-Indian official, if you can catch him off duty.

3 One day something happened which in a roundabout way was enlightening. It was a tiny incident in itself, but it gave me a better glimpse than I had had before of the real nature of imperialism—the real motives for which despotic governments act. Early one morning the sub-inspector at a police station the other end of the town rang me up on the 'phone and said that an elephant was ravaging the bazaar. Would I please come and do something about it? I did not know what I could do, but I wanted to see what was happening and I got on to a pony and started out. I took my rifle, an old .44 Winchester and much too small to kill an elephant, but I thought the noise might be useful *in terrorem*.[2] Various Burmans stopped me on the way and told me about the elephant's doings. It was not, of course, a wild elephant, but a tame one which had gone "must." It had been chained up, as tame elephants always are when their attack of "must" is due, but on the previous night it had broken its chain and escaped. Its mahout, the only person who could manage it when it was in that state, had set out in pursuit, but had taken the wrong direction and was now twelve hours' journey away, and in the morning the elephant had suddenly reappeared in the town. The Burmese population had no weapons and were quite helpless against it. It had already destroyed somebody's bamboo hut, killed a cow and raided some fruit-stalls and devoured the stock; also it had met the municipal rubbish van and, when the driver jumped out and took to his heels, had turned the van over and inflicted violences upon it.

4 The Burmese sub-inspector and some Indian constables were waiting for me in the quarter where the elephant had been seen. It was a very poor quarter, a labyrinth of squalid bamboo huts, thatched with palm-leaf, winding all over a steep hillside. I remember that it was a cloudy, stuffy morning at the beginning of the rains. We began questioning the people as to where the

[1]Latin, "forever and ever."—Ed.
[2]Latin, "as a warning."—Ed.

elephant had gone and, as usual, failed to get any definite information. That is invariably the case in the East; a story always sounds clear enough at a distance, but the nearer you get to the scene of events the vaguer it becomes. Some of the people said that the elephant had gone in one direction, some said that he had gone in another, some professed not even to have heard of any elephant. I had almost made up my mind that the whole story was a pack of lies, when we heard yells a little distance away. There was a loud, scandalized cry of "Go away, child! Go away this instant!" and an old woman with a switch in her hand came round the corner of a hut, violently shooing away a crowd of naked children. Some more women followed, clicking their tongues and exclaiming; evidently there was something that the children ought not to have seen. I rounded the hut and saw a man's dead body sprawling in the mud. He was an Indian, a black Dravidian coolie, almost naked, and he could not have been dead many minutes. The people said that the elephant had come suddenly upon him round the corner of the hut, caught him with its trunk, put its foot on his back and ground him into the earth. This was the rainy season and the ground was soft, and his face had scored a trench a foot deep and a couple of yards long. He was lying on his belly with arms crucified and head sharply twisted to one side. His face was coated with mud, the eyes wide open, the teeth bared and grinning with an expression of unendurable agony. (Never tell me, by the way, that the dead look peaceful. Most of the corpses I have seen looked devilish.) The friction of the great beast's foot had stripped the skin from his back as neatly as one skins a rabbit. As soon as I saw the dead man I sent an orderly to a friend's house nearby to borrow an elephant rifle. I had already sent back the pony, not wanting it to go mad with fright and throw me if it smelt the elephant.

5 The orderly came back in a few minutes with a rifle and five cartridges, and meanwhile some Burmans had arrived and told us that the elephant was in the paddy fields below, only a few hundred yards away. As I started forward practically the whole population of the quarter flocked out of the houses and followed me. They had seen the rifle and were all shouting excitedly that I was going to shoot the elephant. They had not shown much interest in the elephant when he was merely ravaging their homes, but it was different now that he was going to be shot. It was a bit of fun to them, as it would be to an English crowd; besides they wanted the meat. It made me vaguely uneasy. I had no intention of shooting the elephant—I had merely sent for the rifle to defend myself if necessary—and it is always unnerving to have a crowd following you. I marched down the hill, looking and feeling a fool, with the rifle over my shoulder and an ever-growing army of people jostling at my heels. At the bottom, when you got away from the huts, there was a metalled road and beyond that a miry waste of paddy fields a thousand yards across, not yet ploughed but soggy from the first rains and dotted with coarse grass. The elephant was standing eight yards from the road, his left side towards us. He took not the slightest notice of the crowd's approach. He was tearing up bunches of grass, beating them against his knees to clean them and stuffing them into his mouth.

6 I had halted on the road. As soon as I saw the elephant I knew with perfect certainty that I ought not to shoot him. It is a serious matter to shoot a working elephant—it is comparable to destroying a huge and costly piece of machinery—and obviously one ought not to do it if it can possibly be avoided. And at that distance, peacefully eating, the elephant looked no more danger-ous than a cow. I thought then and I think now that his attack of "must" was already passing off; in which case he would merely wander harmlessly about until the mahout came back and caught him. Moreover, I did not in the least want to shoot him. I decided that I would watch him for a little while to make sure that he did not turn savage again, and then go home.

7 But at that moment I glanced round at the crowd that had followed me. It was an immense crowd, two thousand at the least and growing every minute. It blocked the road for a long distance on either side. I looked at the sea of yellow faces above the garish clothes—faces all happy and excited over this bit of fun, all certain that the elephant was going to be shot. They were watching me as they would watch a conjurer about to perform a trick. They did not like me, but with the magical rifle in my hands I was momentarily worth watching. And suddenly I realized that I should have to shoot the elephant after all. The people expected it of me and I had got to do it; I could feel their two thousand wills pressing me forward, irresistibly. And it was at this moment, as I stood there with the rifle in my hands, that I first grasped the hollowness, the futility of the white man's dominion in the East. Here was I, the white man with his gun, standing in front of the unarmed native crowd—seemingly the leading actor of the piece; but in reality I was only an absurd puppet pushed to and fro by the will of those yellow faces behind. I perceived in this moment that when the white man turns tyrant it is his own freedom that he destroys. He becomes a sort of hollow, posing dummy, the conventional-ized figure of a sahib. For it is the condition of his rule that he shall spend his life in trying to impress the "natives," and so in every crisis he had got to do what the "natives" expect of him. He wears a mask, and his face grows to fit it. I had got to shoot the elephant. I had committed myself to doing it when I sent for the rifle. A sahib has got to act like a sahib; he has got to appear resolute, to know his own mind and do definite things. To come all that way, rifle in hand, with two thousand people marching at my heels, and then to trail feebly away, having done nothing—no, that was impossible. The crowd would laugh at me. And my whole life, every white man's life in the East, was one long struggle not to be laughed at.

8 But I did not want to shoot the elephant. I watched him beating his bunch of grass against his knees, with that preoccupied grandmotherly air that elephants have. It seemed to me that it would be murder to shoot him. At that age I was not squeamish about killing animals, but I had never shot an elephant and never wanted to. (Somehow it always seems worse to kill a *large* animal.) Besides, there was the beast's owner to be considered. Alive, the elephant was worth at least a hundred pounds; dead, he would only be worth the value of his tusks, five pounds, possibly. But I had got to act quickly. I turned to some experienced-looking Burmans who had been there when we

arrived, and asked them how the elephant had been behaving. The all said the same thing: he took no notice of you if you left him alone, but he might charge if you went too close to him.

9 It was perfectly clear to me what I ought to do. I ought to walk up to within, say, twenty-five yards of the elephant and test his behavior. If he charged, I could shoot; if he took no notice of me, it would be safe to leave him until the mahout came back. But also I knew that I was going to do no such thing. I was a poor shot with a rifle and the ground was soft mud into which one would sink at every step. If the elephant charged and I missed him, I should have about as much chance as a toad under a steam-roller. But even then I was not thinking particularly of my own skin, only of the watchful yellow faces behind. For at that moment, with the crowd watching me, I was not afraid in the ordinary sense, as I would have been if I had been alone. A white man mustn't be frightened in front of "natives"; and so, in general, he isn't frightened. The sole thought in my mind was that if anything went wrong those two thousand Burmans would see me pursued, caught, trampled on and reduced to a grinning corpse like that Indian up the hill. And if that happened it was quite probable that some of them would laugh. That would never do. There was only one alternative. I shoved the cartridges into the magazine and lay down on the road to get a better aim.

10 The crowd grew very still, and a deep, low, happy sigh, as of people who see the theatre curtain go up at last, breathed from innumerable throats. They were going to have their bit of fun after all. The rifle was a beautiful German thing with cross-hair sights. I did not then know that in shooting an elephant one would shoot to cut an imaginary bar running from ear-hole to ear-hole. I ought, therefore, as the elephant was sideway on, to have aimed straight at his ear-hole; actually I aimed several inches in front of this, thinking the brain would be further forward.

11 When I pulled the trigger I did not hear the bang or feel the kick—one never does when a shot goes home—but I heard the devilish roar of glee that went up from the crowd. In that instant, in too short a time, one would have thought, even for the bullet to get there, a mysterious, terrible change had come over the elephant. He neither stirred nor fell, but every line of his body had altered. He looked suddenly stricken, shrunken, immensely old, as though the frightful impact of the bullet had paralyzed him without knocking him down. At last, after what seemed a long time—it might have been five seconds, I dare say—he sagged flabbily to his knees. His mouth slobbered. An enormous senility seemed to have settled upon him. One could have imagined him thousands of years old. I fired again into the same spot. At the second shot he did not collapse but climbed with desperate slowness to his feet and stood weakly upright, with legs sagging and head drooping. I fired a third time. That was the shot that did for him. You could see the agony of it jolt his whole body and knock the last remnant of strength from his legs. But in falling he seemed for a moment to rise, for as his hind legs collapsed beneath him he seemed to tower upward like a huge rock toppling, his trunk reaching sky-wards like a tree. He trumpeted, for the first and only time. And then down he

came, his belly towards me, with a crash that seemed to shake the ground even where I lay.

12 I got up. The Burmans were already racing past me across the mud. It was obvious that the elephant would never rise again, but he was not dead. He was breathing very rhythmically with long rattling gasps, his great mound of a side painfully rising and falling. His mouth was wide open—I could see far down into caverns of pale pink throat. I waited a long time for him to die, but his breathing did not weaken. Finally I fired my two remaining shots into the spot where I thought his heart must be. The thick blood welled out of him like red velvet, but still he did not die. His body did not even jerk when the shots hit him, the tortured breathing continued without a pause. He was dying, very slowly and in great agony, but in some world remote from me where not even a bullet could damage him further. I felt that I had got to put an end to that dreadful noise. It seemed dreadful to see the great beast lying there, powerless to move and yet powerless to die, and not even to be able to finish him. I sent back for my small rifle and poured shot after shot into his heart and down his throat. They seemed to make no impression. The tortured gasps continued as steadily as the ticking of a clock.

13 In the end I could not stand it any longer and went away. I heard later that it took him half an hour to die. Burmans were bringing dahs and baskets even before I left, and I was told they had stripped his body almost to the bones by the afternoon.

14 Afterwards, of course, there were endless discussions about the shooting of the elephant. The owner was furious, but he was only an Indian and could do nothing. Besides, legally I had done the right thing, for a mad elephant has to be killed, like a mad dog, if its owner fails to control it. Among the Europeans opinion was divided. The older men said I was right, the younger men said it was a damn shame to shoot an elephant for killing a coolie, because an elephant was worth more than any damn Coringhee coolie. And afterwards I was very glad that the coolie had been killed; it put me legally in the right and it gave me a sufficient pretext for shooting the elephant. I often wondered whether any of the others grasped that I had done it solely to avoid looking a fool.

VOCABULARY

supplant (2)	garish (7)
prostrate (2)	conventionalized (7)
despotic (3)	resolute (7)
labyrinth (4)	pretext (14)
squalid (4)	

QUESTIONS ON CONTEXT

1. What is the author's attitude toward the Burmese? Toward the British Empire?
2. In paragraph 7 the author says that the white man "wears a mask, and his face grows to fit it." What does he mean by that?

3. Why does the author shoot the elephant?
4. What is the attitude of the other Europeans?

QUESTIONS ON FORM

1. The author writes: "They had not shown much interest in the elephant when he was merely ravaging their homes, but it was different now that he was going to be shot." What tone is he using here?
2. Why does the author use Latin phrases? What purpose do they have in the story?
3. The story is told in two tenses: the past and the present. What effect does this have on its telling?
4. Orwell encloses some remarks in parentheses in paragraphs 4 and 8. Why are these remarks set off thus?
5. What analogy does Orwell use in paragraph 10 to describe his feelings about the crowd gathered to see him kill the elephant? Is this an appropriate analogy? Explain.

SUGGESTIONS FOR WRITING

1. Analyze and discuss "Shooting an Elephant" as a story about the abstract versus the particular.
2. Write an essay entitled, "I wore a mask, and my face grew to fit it."

KATHERINE BUTLER HATHAWAY

from THE LITTLE LOCKSMITH

The American novelist Katherine Butler Hathaway (1890–1941) was born a hunchback. In this excerpt from her autobiographical novel *The Little Locksmith,* she writes in a lyrical style about her closeness with her brother, and how her deformity affected their relationship.

1 At this time of secret confusion it was lucky for me that I found my brother Warren. He acted as if he did not even see my disguise. He never mentioned it, he never explained how he felt. He merely treated me as if he saw in me the growing-up proud person that I felt myself to be.

2 In spite of my new fierceness I was shy and inarticulate, which he was not. He was a Harvard undergraduate then, and he had just found for himself the exhilaration and joy of intellectual exercise. He loved argument and discussion, and he loved also his own uninterrupted discourse. He could talk brilliantly and he loved to arouse and excite an admiring listener with his talk. He had the intellectual young man's favorite passion for influencing and molding another mind, especially a young docile feminine mind, since that was the sort of mind which lent itself most willingly to be molded. He gave me such a strong impression that he was always right in his opinions that I never doubted that he was, and I felt lucky and proud to be molded and influenced by him.

3 He never showed off to me as he did to some of his other feminine listeners. After my father died we lived in a small countrified town outside of Salem, called Danvers, where there was almost no conversation and no intellectual life, and the only appreciative audience he could find were his former high school teachers and their sisters and friends, all women. He chose this audience first because there wasn't any other, but for some reason he seemed to get some sort of very necessary nourishment and satisfaction from their uncritical worship of him. He used to love to dazzle and astonish those intelligent yet easily dazzled ladies, and he let me see that sometimes half the fun he got out of it was to start an intellectual discussion going and then laugh up his sleeve at his former teachers as they innocently fell into the trap of his arguments, and never guessed that he was amusing himself at their expense. Their generous, radiant admiration of his ability was not enough. He had to make them a little ridiculous in order to enjoy himself fully. I did not understand this need of his, but I noticed how, in great contrast, he always treated me with a humility and quiet comradeship and a cherishing in which there was never anything but the utmost deference, as if he had singled me out of all the world as the only one whom he could love simply and completely. After one of the sessions of talk and argument in a spinster schoolteacher's New England salon—which might be her back porch covered with a thick green curtain of Dutchman's-pipe or her kitchen where we sat around the kitchen table and ate doughnuts—he and I would walk home together and a sudden silence would fall on us while he held my arm caressingly with his rough blunt hand. Among the women he knew, the intellectual spinsters and their admiring sisters and friends, I understood that I was his favorite. For a long time I knew that I was the only one who really mattered to him.

4 Yet I never could learn to talk easily with him. I do not know why it was. A fear and shyness as hard as iron barred my most important ideas and feelings out of all conversation in spite of my will and my enormous need to share them. Whenever I tried to talk I was always embarrassed, and what I said was painfully clumsy and ineffective compared with what I felt within me. Every time after we had been together I suffered unbearably from my pent-up feelings and thoughts which his companionship had excited and roused to such a pitch and which my shyness had prevented me from expressing. In order to relieve this feeling I began to write to him every week as soon as he had gone back to Cambridge. For I was always at ease in writing. On paper nothing embarrassed me, nothing was too difficult or too emotional for me to try and express. But as soon as I had mailed the letter I would begin to grow hot and cold because of the things I had written. I hungered for emotional intimacy and yet when I had invited it and felt it coming toward me I was panic-stricken. I remember the real agony I felt after the first time I had written to him, whenever the postman rang, and the almost unbearable feeling when his letter actually came, and I took in my hand the heavy, fat, cream-white envelope with the crimson seal of Harvard on the flap. Opening the letter and reading it gave me a pleasure that seems strange indeed as I remember it now, because of the intensity which made it two-thirds pain. My

first experience in grown-up friendship was like an awful miracle, an expansion of myself that had something of the pain of birth in it.

5 His letters, so cherishing, so responsive, seemed to me almost like love letters, and our meetings like lovers' meetings. Every Friday or Saturday he came home and, after we had begun to write to each other, he always called my name as soon as he got inside the door, as if the only thing that mattered about coming home was to know that I was there. Thus I knew then how it felt to have my company very much desired by an eager young man. And I knew the pleasure of adoring and worshiping him in return. I thought to myself very solemnly: nobody will ever love me or marry me, and so it is all right for me to feel as if this were a love affair, as it almost seems to be.

6 On those week-end evenings we sometimes borrowed Betty, my sister's horse, and her open buggy that had rubber tires and square kerosene lamps attached to the sides. With these dim and elegant little lights bobbing on each side of us, we drove along pitch-dark roads, out into the wide and fragrant night, out under the stars, moving slowly and, compared to the way we move now, almost imperceptibly.

7 Being young, we had just discovered the wonderful charm of night, night away from houses, night moving along country roads, noiseless silken wood roads, black bumpy roads of pastures and farms, and the soft, misty, sweet-smelling roads with old wooden bridges where we stopped to listen to the gentle Ipswich River. Night was a new element that we had marvelously discovered. Yet curiously it was the same element that had been only a year or two ago nothing else than a tall policeman to us, the negative tiresome dark that put an end to all our pleasures, and which my revengeful imagination had filled with insane horrors. Now we were grown up, and by the magic of transformation the great welcoming night had become our partner and our friend, the only element that was really congenial to our new selves and our new emotions.

8 The country round us was benign and safe for our night wanderings. It was a country of small towns and quiet villages where nobody sat up late except when there was a meeting of the local historical society or the grange. We drove past the sleeping barns and farmhouses of North Beverly and the yellow-lighted houses of Putnamville, and out onto our favorite and lonely Valley Road to Topsfield where the street lights stopped and there was nothing but the vague dark shape of trees moving slowly past us on either hand and Betty's ears bobbing up and down ahead of us, sometimes dimly visible and sometimes vanishing altogether in the darkness. With only Betty's light footsteps and the spindly wheels of our little ambling carriage to disturb the silence we were nearer to the slow clouds and the stars then in those roads than we ever have been since on any other roads. We could hear every rustle of leaves along the roadside and even the soft sound of wind in ferns. Betty carried us along with a dreamy motion and a pace that was very nourishing and kind to our mood of intimate companionship. In that dreamy silence my own stillness and shyness were no longer a handicap. We both were still, both

feeling the night and listening to the night, each aware of the other's awareness and happiness as if we were two parts of the same person. Once, after such a silence, I heard my brother say, "Sometimes I wish you were not my sister."

9 Five or six times since I was born I have heard a sentence spoken that sounded as if it were made out of an entirely different substance from the substance of ordinary sentences, as if it were carved out of a piece of strange foreign wood. These sentences had no visible connection with what had been said before or with anything that came after them. They were undecipherable fragments, like meteorites from another world. For, as I think I have already said, I grew up in a family where a certain kind of intimate personal emotion was all so carefully hidden that it sounded to me when I heard it like a foreign language; while at the same time that it shocked and frightened me it sounded more familiar and more real than anything I had ever heard before. Those sentences were made of what George Meredith, on one crucial page of *The Amazing Marriage,* called "arterial words." They spurted out of the body involuntarily, coming from some hidden and much deeper source than ordinary speech. In our family those arterial sentences were instantly treated as if they had not been spoken. They were not answered, never repeated, and never referred to again. They were something not wanted, and something terrifyingly alive. They were foundling sentences, left on a doorstep in mid-air. We all looked the other way, we pretended we hadn't heard, and those parentless sentences we left to starve and perish, because, picked up and warmed and fed, they might have had the power to change our whole lives.

10 When I was young I blindly imitated the family tradition of ignoring those bursts of intimacy—I caught the contagion of our family's fear and disapproval of them. But even without the fear and the disapproval, since I was utterly inexperienced and untaught in the language of intimacy, although I felt a great hungering for the emotion and experience of it, I never in the world would have known what to do or to say in response to them.

11 So, when my brother said to me, after a long silence, that night when we were driving across a dark starlit place somewhere between the woods and the sea along the Beverly shore, "Sometimes I wish that you were not my sister," I recognized it for one of those strange sentences. It fell at my feet out of an unknown sky.

12 And I did not know how to stoop and pick it up and hold it in my hands. This strange thing was meant for me, and for no one else, but I had absolutely no skill or grace to receive it. It was like a letter sent to a person who hadn't any name, or any street and number. I was powerless to claim it even though I knew it was mine. It set up such a commotion inside me that I could scarcely breathe.

13 At the first impact of it I thought he meant he hated me, and wished he never had known me. Swiftly I thought that must be because he had found at last that, although he had tried very hard, the truth was that he could not enjoy being with a deformed person, and he wished he did not have a deformed little sister to go out driving with.

14 "Sometimes I wish that you were not my sister." I turned it over and over in my mind, terribly wounded and dumb, and then slowly another interpretation came flooding into me. Another meaning, and if it was the true meaning these were arterial words. For if my second guess was right then what he had said to me was a very amazing thing. It was a confession that had spurted out of his body. It was not a cruel repudiation of me, but the very opposite.

15 Then I hastily remembered that this was something I could not let myself believe. I could secretly pretend that I had a lover in him, but I could never risk showing that I thought such a thing was possible for me, with him or any other man. Because of my repeated encounters with the mirror and my irrepressible tendency to forget what I had seen, I had begun to force myself to believe and to remember, and *especially* to remember, that I would never be chosen for what I imagined to be the supreme and most intimate of all experience. I thought of sexual love as an honor that was too great for me— not too great for my understanding and my feeling, but much too great and too beautiful for the body in which I was doomed to live. I had heard people laugh and talk about grotesquely unbeautiful women who had the absurd effrontery to imagine that men were in love with them. Even the kindest people seemed to feel that for that mistake there should be no mercy, and that such silly women deserved all the ridicule they got. In my secret meditations I pitied them because I understood, what nobody else could have guessed, how easily they could forget the cruel discrepancy between their desirous hearts and their own undesirableness. There was a curious and baffling law of nature or human nature which was very hard on them and on me. If a girl or woman was pretty her function of loving and being loved was treated seriously and sympatheti- cally by everyone. But if she was awkward and homely and nevertheless eager for love that function seemed to be changed into something mysteriously comic and shameful. I had sworn that I never for one instant would forget the fearful discrepancy in my own case. I never would for one instant be off my guard. I never would be caught either pathetically or ridiculously imagining that anyone was or ever could be in love with me.

16 But I was very suspicious of my own amorousness. It was an unknown quantity in all human beings and I knew, although I had not heard of Freud then, that unknown quantity, from being forever repressed and denied, would be always waiting to trick me and betray me and make me behave without ever realizing it like one of those poor creatures. So now I sharply told myself that my sudden conviction that my brother meant he wished he could be in love with me was only one of those tricks of my own amorousness, and that I must have nothing to do with it.

17 With all this wild confusion packed inside my head I sat very still beside my brother in the little carriage. We were drawn slowly forward side by side in the starlight, all alone by ourselves in the sweet, lonely night. But after he had spoken we were as far apart as if I had been a wild animal whose distrust and fear of men even the love and good will of a kind master cannot cure.

18 In my sudden isolation I felt as if it were all unreal. Had he said that extraordinary thing, or had I imagined it? There was nothing in our silence to tell me. Everything seemed the same as before he had spoken. I waited, half expecting him to say a little more, so that I could be sure. But that was the end, he never said it again. He never told me what he was thinking and feeling that night, or what he thought my silence meant, that it kept him from saying any more. Perhaps he thought he had shocked me, or perhaps he decided merely that I was too immature to understand him. That foundling sentence of his died of my neglect, an atom of naked truth that was not wanted. But it never died in my mind. It never even grew misty or vague. Whenever I thought of it, even long afterward, I heard it again, as clear and startling and as incomprehensible as the first time. For it is that kind of an unanswered sentence that never does die. It stays always in our minds, ready to be remembered on the slightest provocation. It stays there always, even though it may turn into something altogether incongruous and irrelevant as our life grows and changes, a queer outlandish memento, like a piece of lava from Vesuvius lying on the parlor table.

19 It was a long time before that particular sentence changed into a petrified souvenir in my mind. That night when we had come in and I was alone in my room I felt a smug satisfaction because I had escaped the pitfall of making myself ridiculous or pathetic, as I was sure I would have done if I had spoken. But later on I began to be troubled by a more generous open-hearted feeling. A faint, faint, persistent surmise kept coming over me that he might really have meant the grave and tragic thing that my instinct had told me he did mean. What then? Then my shameful caution and ineptitude had killed his crucial impulse to take me fully into his confidence and to tell me all about his feeling for me, whatever it was. Perhaps I had failed him in what I painfully suspected then and surely believe now is the worst way in which one person can fail another.

20 If I did he took it without a word or a sign, and ever afterward it was as though our usual understanding of each other had never been interrupted. Perhaps he had offered me something that was too potent and too strong for me, considering how deeply moved I was just by the ordinary tenor of our relationship. That was anything but ordinary to me. Just to be out alone with him in the night, to feel myself his unspoken favorite, was as thrilling a thing as I could bear perhaps. Our love of Nature and of the night was such a newly discovered love that it alone seemed, for me at least, to constitute a passionate intimacy between us. But whatever the real meaning of it was, that evening's episode was a turning point at which I took the wrong turn. At that moment, when my brother reached out to me and wanted perhaps to tell me the miraculous, the unbelievable thing, that I could be desired if only I would believe it—I missed the way. By my miserable silence I elected to keep on carrying the secret burden of my ignorance and despair which was to grow with time to such terrible proportions. In that moment I let my body's injury begin to infect and cripple my life.

VOCABULARY

inarticulate (2)	repudiation (14)
exhilaration (2)	effrontery (15)
deference (3)	discrepancy (15)
imperceptibly (6)	repressed (16)
benign (8)	incongruous (18)
spindly (8)	outlandish (18)
ambling (8)	surmise (19)
undecipherable (9)	ineptitude (19)
foundling (9)	tenor (20)
contagion (10)	

QUESTIONS ON CONTENT

1. What are "arterial words" (paragraph 9)? Why did the narrator's family ignore them?
2. How does the narrator react to her brother's words: "Sometimes I wish you were not my sister"? Explain this reaction.
3. How would you characterize the author's image of herself?

QUESTIONS ON FORM

1. Reread paragraph 9. What technique does the author use to describe "arterial sentences"?
2. There are numerous descriptive passages in this selection, especially in paragraphs 6, 7, and 8. How does the author present descriptions? Give examples.
3. In her descriptions, which senses do the author's adjectives appeal to? The sense of sight, smell, hearing, or all of these?
4. What analogy does the author use in paragraph 20 to describe the choice she made in not responding to her brother's words? What is the significance of this analogy?

SUGGESTIONS FOR WRITING

1. Assume the saying "Style is the woman" to be true. Describe the woman behind the style in this selection.
2. Describe an experience that you have had with "arterial words" and how you responded to them.

WILLIAM FAULKNER

A ROSE FOR EMILY

This is a story about Faulkner's famous fictional county of Yoknapatawpha, Mississippi. It is the account of a bizarre Southern aristocrat and her macabre reaction to unrequited love.

I

1 When Miss Emily Grierson died, our whole town went to her funeral: the men through a sort of respectful affection for a fallen monument, the women

mostly out of curiosity to see the inside of her house, which no one save an old manservant—a combined gardener and cook—had seen in at least ten years.

2 It was a big, squarish frame house that had once been white, decorated with cupolas and spires and scrolled balconies in the heavily lightsome style of the seventies, set on what had once been our most select street. But garages and cotton gins had encroached and obliterated even the august names of that neighborhood; only Miss Emily's house was left, lifting its stubborn and coquettish decay above the cotton wagons and the gasoline pumps—an eyesore among eyesores. And now Miss Emily had gone to join the representatives of those august names where they lay in the cedar-bemused cemetery among the ranked and anonymous graves of Union and Confederate soldiers who fell at the battle of Jefferson.

3 Alive, Miss Emily had been a tradition, a duty, and a care; a sort of hereditary obligation upon the town, dating from that day in 1894 when Colonel Sartoris, the mayor—he who fathered the edict that no Negro woman should appear on the streets without an apron—remitted her taxes, the dispensation dating from the death of her father on into perpetuity. Not that Miss Emily would have accepted charity. Colonel Sartoris invented an involved tale to the effect that Miss Emily's father had loaned money to the town, which the town, as a matter of business, preferred this way of repaying. Only a man of Colonel Sartoris' generation and thought could have invented it, and only a woman could have believed it.

4 When the next generation, with its more modern ideas, became mayors and aldermen, this arrangement created some little dissatisfaction. On the first of the year they mailed her a tax notice. February came, and there was no reply. They wrote her a formal letter, asking her to call at the sheriff's office at her convenience. A week later the mayor wrote her himself, offering to call or to send his car for her, and received in reply a note on paper of an archaic shape, in a thin, flowing calligraphy in faded ink, to the effect that she no longer went out at all. The tax notice was also enclosed, without comment.

5 They called a special meeting of the Board of Aldermen. A deputation waited upon her, knocked at the door through which no visitor had passed since she ceased giving china-painting lessons eight or ten years earlier. They were admitted by the old Negro into a dim hall from which a stairway mounted into still more shadow. It smelled of dust and disuse—a close, dank smell. The Negro led them into the parlor. It was furnished in heavy, leather-covered furniture. When the Negro opened the blinds of one window, they could see that the leather was cracked; and when they sat down, a faint dust rose sluggishly about their thighs, spinning with slow motes in the single sun-ray. On a tarnished gilt easel before the fireplace stood a crayon portrait of Miss Emily's father.

6 They rose when she entered—a small, fat woman in black, with a thin gold chain descending to her waist and vanishing into her belt, leaning on an ebony cane with a tarnished gold head. Her skeleton was small and spare; perhaps that was why what would have been merely plumpness in another was obesity in her. She looked bloated, like a body long submerged in

motionless water, and of that pallid hue. Her eyes, lost in the fatty ridges of her face, looked like two small pieces of coal pressed into a lump of dough as they moved from one face to another while the visitors stated their errand.

7 She did not ask them to sit. She just stood in the door and listened quietly until the spokesman came to a stumbling halt. Then they could hear the invisible watch ticking at the end of the gold chain.

8 Her voice was dry and cold. "I have no taxes in Jefferson. Colonel Sartoris explained it to me. Perhaps one of you can gain access to the city records and satisfy yourselves."

9 "But we have. We are the city authorities, Miss Emily. Didn't you get a notice from the sheriff, signed by him?"

"I received a paper, yes," Miss Emily said. "Perhaps he considers himself the sheriff . . . I have no taxes in Jefferson."

"But there is nothing on the books to show that, you see. We must go by the—"

"See Colonel Sartoris. I have no taxes in Jefferson."

"But, Miss Emily—"

"See Colonel Sartoris." (Colonel Sartoris had been dead almost ten years.) "I have no taxes in Jefferson. Tobe!" The Negro appeared. "Show these gentlemen out."

II

10 So she vanquished them, horse and foot, just as she had vanquished their fathers thirty years before about the smell. That was two years after her father's death and a short time after her sweetheart—the one we believed would marry her—had deserted her. After her father's death she went out very little; after her sweetheart went away, people hardly saw her at all. A few of the ladies had the temerity to call, but were not received, and the only sign of life about the place was the Negro man—a young man then—going in and out with a market basket.

11 "Just as if a man—any man—could keep a kitchen properly," the ladies said; so they were not surprised when the smell developed. It was another link between the gross, teeming world and the high and mighty Griersons.

12 A neighbor, a woman, complained to the mayor, Judge Stevens, eighty years old.

"But what will you have me do about it, madam?" he said.

"Why, send her word to stop it," the woman said. "Isn't there a law?"

"I'm sure that won't be necessary," Judge Stevens said. "It's probably just a snake or a rat that nigger of hers killed in the yard. I'll speak to him about it."

13 The next day he received two more complaints, one from a man who came in diffident deprecation. "We really must do something about it, Judge. I'd be the last one in the world to bother Miss Emily, but we've got to do something." That night the Board of Aldermen met—three graybeards and one younger man, a member of the rising generation.

14 "It's simple enough," he said. "Send her word to have her place cleaned up. Give her a certain time to do it in, and if she don't . . ."

"Dammit, sir," Judge Stevens said, "will you accuse a lady to her face of smelling bad?"

15 So the next night, after midnight, four men crossed Miss Emily's lawn and slunk about the house like burglars, sniffing along the base of the brickwork and at the cellar openings while one of them performed a regular sowing motion with his hand out of a sack slung from his shoulder. They broke open the cellar door and sprinkled lime there, and in all the outbuildings. As they recrossed the lawn, a window that had been dark was lighted and Miss Emily sat in it, the light behind her, and her upright torso motionless as that of an idol. They crept quietly across the lawn and into the shadow of the locusts that lined the street. After a week or two the smell went away.

16 That was when people had begun to feel really sorry for her. People in our town, remembering how old lady Wyatt, her great-aunt, had gone completely crazy at last, believed that the Griersons held themselves a little too high for what they really were. None of the young men were quite good enough to Miss Emily and such. We had long thought of them as a tableau; Miss Emily a slender figure in white in the background, her father a spraddled silhouette in the foreground, his back to her and clutching a horsewhip, the two of them framed by the back-flung front door. So when she got to be thirty and was still single, we were not pleased exactly, but vindicated; even with insanity in the family she wouldn't have turned down all of her chances if they had really materialized.

17 When her father died, it got about that the house was all that was left to her; and in a way, people were glad. At last they could pity Miss Emily. Being left alone, and a pauper, she had become humanized. Now she too would know the old thrill and the old despair of a penny more or less.

18 The day after his death all the ladies prepared to call at the house and offer condolence and aid, as is our custom. Miss Emily met them at the door, dressed as usual and with no trace of grief on her face. She told them that her father was not dead. She did that for three days, with the ministers calling on her, and the doctors, trying to persuade her to let them dispose of the body. Just as they were about to resort to law and force, she broke down, and they buried her father quickly.

19 We did not say she was crazy then. We believed she had to do that. We remembered all the young men her father had driven away, and we knew that with nothing left, she would have to cling to that which had robbed her, as people will.

III

20 She was sick for a long time. When we saw her again, her hair was cut short, making her look like a girl, with a vague resemblance to those angels in colored church windows—sort of tragic and serene.

21 The town had just let the contracts for paving the sidewalks, and in the

summer after her father's death they began the work. The construction company came with niggers and mules and machinery, and a foreman named Homer Barron, a Yankee—a big, dark, ready man, with a big voice and eyes lighter than his face. The little boys would follow in groups to hear him cuss the niggers, and the niggers singing in time to the rise and fall of picks. Pretty soon he knew everybody in town. Whenever you heard a lot of laughing anywhere about the square, Homer Barron would be in the center of the group. Presently we began to see him and Miss Emily on Sunday afternoons driving in the yellow-wheeled buggy and the matched team of bays from the livery stable.

22 At first we were glad that Miss Emily would have an interest, because the ladies all said, "Of course a Grierson would not think seriously of a Northerner, a day laborer." But there were still others, older people, who said that even grief could not cause a real lady to forget *noblesse oblige*—without calling it *noblesse oblige*. They just said, "Poor Emily. Her kinsfolk should come to her." She had some kin in Alabama; but years ago her father had fallen out with them over the estate of old lady Wyatt, the crazy woman, and there was no communication between the two families. They had not even been represented at the funeral.

23 And as soon as the old people said, "Poor Emily," the whispering began. "Do you suppose it's really so?" they said to one another. "Of course it is. What else could . . ." This behind their hands; rustling of craned silk and satin behind jalousies closed upon the sun of Sunday afternoon as the thin, swift clop-clop-clop of the matched team passed: "Poor Emily."

24 She carried her head high enough—even when we believed that she was fallen. It was as if she demanded more than ever the recognition of her dignity as the last Grierson; as if it had wanted that touch of earthiness to reaffirm her imperviousness. Like when she bought the rat poison, the arsenic. That was over a year after they had begun to say "Poor Emily," and while the two female cousins were visiting her.

25 "I want some poison," she said to the druggist. She was over thirty then, still a slight woman, though thinner than usual, with cold, haughty black eyes in a face the flesh of which was strained across the temples and about the eye-sockets as you imagine a lighthouse-keeper's face ought to look. "I want some poison," she said.

26 "Yes, Miss Emily. What kind? For rats and such? I'd recom—"

"I want the best you have. I don't care what kind."

The druggist named several. "They'll kill anything up to an elephant. But what you want is—"

"Arsenic," Miss Emily said. "Is that a good one?"

"Is . . . arsenic? Yes, ma'am. But what you want—"

"I want arsenic."

27 The druggist looked down at her. She looked back at him, erect, her face like a strained flag. "Why, of course," the druggist said. "If that's what you want. But the law requires you to tell what you are going to use it for."

28 Miss Emily just stared at him, her head tilted back in order to look him eye for eye, until he looked away and went and got the arsenic and wrapped it up. The Negro delivery boy brought her the package; the druggist didn't come back. When she opened the package at home there was written on the box, under the skull and bones: "For rats."

IV

29 So the next day we all said, "She will kill herself"; and we said it would be the best thing. When she had first begun to be seen with Homer Barron, we had said, "She will marry him." Then we said, "She will persuade him yet," because Homer himself had remarked—he liked men, and it was known that he drank with the younger men in the Elks' Club—that he was not a marrying man. Later we said, "Poor Emily" behind the jalousies as they passed on Sunday afternoon in the glittering buggy, Miss Emily with her head high and Homer Barron with his hat cocked and a cigar in his teeth, reins and whip in a yellow glove.

30 Then some of the ladies began to say that it was a disgrace to the town and a bad example to the young people. The men did not want to interfere, but at last the ladies forced the Baptist minister—Miss Emily's people were Episcopal—to call upon her. He would never divulge what happened during that interview, but he refused to go back again. The next Sunday they again drove about the streets, and the following day the minister's wife wrote to Miss Emily's relations in Alabama.

31 So she had blood-kin under her roof again and we sat back to watch developments. At first nothing happened. Then we were sure that they were to be married. We learned that Miss Emily had been to the jeweler's and ordered a man's toilet set in silver, with the letters H.B. on each piece. Two days later we learned that she had bought a complete outfit of men's clothing, including a nightshirt, and we said, "They are married." We were really glad. We were glad because the two female cousins were even more Grierson than Miss Emily had ever been.

32 So we were not surprised when Homer Barron—the streets had been finished some time since—was gone. We were a little disappointed that there was not a public blowing-off, but we believed that he had gone on to prepare for Miss Emily's coming, or to give her a chance to get rid of the cousins. (By that time it was a cabal, and we were all Miss Emily's allies to help circumvent the cousins.) Sure enough, after another week they departed. And, as we had expected all along, within three days Homer Barron was back in town. A neighbor saw the Negro man admit him at the kitchen door at dusk one evening.

33 And that was the last we saw of Homer Barron. And of Miss Emily for some time. The Negro man went in and out with the market basket, but the front door remained closed. Now and then we would see her at a window for a moment, as the men did that night when they sprinkled the lime, but for

almost six months she did not appear on the streets. Then we knew that this was to be expected too; as if that quality of her father which had thwarted her woman's life so many times had been too virulent and too furious to die.

34 When we next saw Miss Emily, she had grown fat and her hair was turning gray. During the next few years it grew grayer and grayer until it attained an even pepper-and-salt iron-gray, when it ceased turning. Up to the day of her death at seventy-four it was still that vigorous iron-gray, like the hair of an active man.

35 From that time on her front door remained closed, save for a period of six or seven years, when she was about forty, during which she gave lessons in china-painting. She fitted up a studio in one of the downstairs rooms, where the daughters and granddaughters of Colonel Sartoris' contemporaries were sent to her with the same regularity and in the same spirit that they were sent to church on Sundays with a twenty-five cent piece for the collection plate. Meanwhile her taxes had been remitted.

36 Then the newer generation became the backbone and the spirit of the town, and the painting pupils grew up and fell away and did not send their children to her with boxes of color and tedious brushes and pictures cut from the ladies' magazines. The front door closed upon the last one and remained closed for good. When the town got free postal delivery, Miss Emily alone refused to let them fasten the metal numbers above her door and attach a mailbox to it. She would not listen to them.

37 Daily, monthly, yearly we watched the Negro grow grayer and more stooped, going in and out with the market basket. Each December we sent her a tax notice, which would be returned by the post office a week later, unclaimed. Now and then we would see her in one of the downstairs windows—she had evidently shut up the top floor of the house—like the carven torso of an idol in a niche, looking or not looking at us, we could never tell which. Thus she passed from generation to generation—dear, inescapable, impervious, tranquil, and perverse.

38 And so she died. Fell ill in the house filled with dust and shadows, with only a doddering Negro man to wait on her. We did not even know she was sick; we had long since given up trying to get any information from the Negro. He talked to no one, probably not even to her, for his voice had grown harsh and rusty, as if from disuse.

39 She died in one of the downstairs rooms, in a heavy walnut bed with a curtain, her gray head propped on a pillow yellow and moldy with age and lack of sunlight.

V

40 The Negro met the first of the ladies at the front door and let them in, with their hushed, sibilant voices and their quick, curious glances, and then he disappeared. He walked right through the house and out the back and was not seen again.

41 The two female cousins came at once. They held the funeral on the

second day, with the town coming to look at Miss Emily beneath a mass of bought flowers, with the crayon face of her father musing profoundly above the bier and the ladies sibilant and macabre; and the very old men—some in their brushed Confederate uniforms—on the porch and the lawn, talking of Miss Emily as if she had been a contemporary of theirs, believing that they had danced with her and courted her perhaps, confusing time with its mathematical progression, as the old do, to whom all the past is not a diminishing road but, instead, a huge meadow which no winter ever quite touches, divided from them now by the narrow bottle-neck of the most recent decade of years.

42 Already we knew that there was one room in that region above stairs which no one had seen in forty years, and which would have to be forced. They waited until Miss Emily was decently in the ground before they opened it.

43 The violence of breaking down the door seemed to fill this room with pervading dust. A thin, acrid pall as of the tomb seemed to lie everywhere upon this room decked and furnished as for a bridal: upon the valence curtains of faded rose color, upon the rose-shaded lights, upon the dressing table, upon the delicate array of crystal and the man's toilet things backed with tarnished silver, silver so tarnished that the monogram was obscured. Among them lay a collar and tie, as if they had just been removed, which, lifted, left upon the surface a pale crescent in the dust. Upon a chair hung the suit, carefully folded; beneath it the two mute shoes and the discarded socks.

44 The man himself lay in the bed.

For a long while we just stood there, looking down at the profound and fleshless grin. The body had apparently once lain in the attitude of an embrace, but now the long sleep that outlasts love, that conquers even the grimace of love, had cuckolded him. What was left of him, rotted beneath what was left of the nightshirt, had become inextricable from the bed in which he lay; and upon him and upon the pillow beside him lay that even coating of the patient and biding dust.

45 Then we noticed that in the second pillow was the indentation of a head. One of us lifted something from it, and leaning forward, that faint and invisible dust dry and acrid in the nostrils, we saw a long strand of iron-gray hair.

VOCABULARY

cupolas (2)	calligraphy (4)
spires (2)	dank (5)
lightsome (2)	temerity (10)
encroached (2)	diffident (13)
obliterated (2)	deprecation (13)
august (2)	tableau (16)
coquettish (2)	spraddled (16)
edict (3)	silhouette (16)
remitted (3)	vindicated (16)
perpetuity (3)	pauper (17)

livery (21)
jalousies (23)
imperviousness (24)
cabal (32)
circumvent (32)
virulent (33)
tranquil (37)
perverse (37)

bier (41)
sibilant (41)
macabre (41)
acrid (43)
pall (43)
cuckolded (44)
inextricable (44)

QUESTIONS ON CONTENT

1. What revelation is made in the final paragraph of the story?
2. What kind of society serves as background for the story?
3. What are the concrete signs of Miss Grierson's aristocratic heritage?
4. What ambivalence does the town show toward Miss Emily?
5. What epoch in Southern history is symbolized by the love affair between Miss Emily and Homer Barron?
6. What happened to cause Miss Emily to kill Homer Barron?

QUESTIONS ON FORM

1. What is the point of view of the narrator? How does it contribute to the story?
2. Faulkner is noted for his technique of foreshadowing events. What are instances of foreshadowing in the story "A Rose for Emily"?
3. Some of Faulkner's best descriptions of Miss Emily are couched in figurative language. What are some examples?
4. How would you describe Faulkner's style?

SUGGESTIONS FOR WRITING

1. Create a five-hundred-word portrait of Miss Emily. Begin with a dominant impression and then supply details that support this impression. Use language that will not clash with Faulkner's conception.
2. Choosing another story of your choice by Faulkner, do a five-hundred-word analysis of Faulkner's style. Deal with such matters as sentence structure and variety, connotation, imagery, and symbolism.

CHAPTER WRITING ASSIGNMENTS

1. Based on all the articles and stories in this chapter, formulate and explain your views on style. Quote from any of the selections in this chapter to support your opinions.
2. Examine and describe the techniques of description used by Orwell and Hathaway. Characterize the differences in their techniques.

part 3
Special Assignments

ten

The Research Paper

model

The Bilingually Handicapped Child

by

Elynor Baughman

English Composition

Fall, 1973

1

Thesis: Early compensatory education can enhance the achievement of the bilingually handicapped child.

I. There is empirical evidence that bilingualism adversely affects a child's speech development.

    A. There are several kinds of bilinguals.

        1. Coordinate bilinguals speak two languages independently of one another.

        2. Compound bilinguals tend to mix the words of one language with another.

    B. Bilinguals have difficulty with tests involving vocabulary and concepts unknown to them.

II. A child in a bilingual community in the United States is under double strain.

    A. Speakers of a foreign-language community are the slowest to acquire facility in the dominant language.

        1. They have limited contact with English.

        2. They have a sentimental attachment to their mother tongue.

        3. They have a conflict of cultures and are faced with prejudice.

    B. Every individual needs some degree of proficiency in the dominant language.

    C. The parents' role is important in helping their children in language facility.

III. There are several approaches to early compensatory education.

    A. Programs for teaching English as a

2

                    second language have some drawbacks.

B.   The Bilingual Program is the most
        innovative.

C.   Preschool education programs would give
        the bilingual child a head start.

D.   Television programs are being planned to
        provide general education for the bilin-
        gual child.

E.   Early compensatory language education
        should be given a very high priority.

3

The Bilingually Handicapped Child

Inability to communicate in English initially discourages school achievement. If a child has to use one language at home and another at school, he must be able to express himself adequately in both languages to avoid censure.[1] There are approximately five million children in the United States who attend public schools and speak a language other than English in their homes and neighborhoods.[2] Many of these children are handicapped in communication and thought processes and have to repeat the first grades in school several times. The bilingual child is usually unable to conceptualize in the English language taught at school since he is from a different cultural and language background and many begin to lag behind. Early compensatory educational programs would give the bilingual child a head start and he would be better prepared for handling schoolwork.

The acquisition and skill in their use of two languages, in an environment where two languages are necessary, often imposes a considerable task upon a child.

[1] Joyce O. Hertzler, A Sociology of Language (New York: Random House, Inc., 1965), pp. 432-33.

[2] "Bilingual Education," School and Society, 100 (Summer 1972), 290.

4

Simultaneous learning of two languages definitely
influences the speech development of a child unfavorably. "If two languages are spoken in the home, or if
the child is forced to learn a foreign language while
he is still learning his mother tongue, he gets confused
and his skill in both languages is retarded."[3]

In a study of bilingual Chinese children in Hawaii
and monolingual children in the United States, "it was
found that in either language the bilingual group was
below the average of monolinguals of the same age."[4]
Only "the superior bilingual child," who is more adept
at concept formation and has a greater mental flexi-
bility, is capable of performing as well as or better
than the monolingual child.[5]

A bilingual person is usually one who is able to

[3]Clifford T. Morgan and Richard A. King, Introduction to Psychology (New York: McGraw-Hill, Inc., 1966),
p. 66.

[4]Catherine Landreth, Early Childhood Behavior and
Learning (New York: Alfred A. Knopf, Inc., 1969), p. 194.

[5]Landreth, p. 194.

5

understand and speak two languages with native-like
control, but there are varying degrees of bilingualism.
The true or "coordinate bilingual" has two distinct and
separate sets of speech habits. He speaks the two languages independently of one another. The "compound bilingual" tends to mix the words or constructions of
one language within another.[6] Many American immigrants
are compound bilinguals. They gave up the use of their
native language and learned English imperfectly, and
therefore speak neither language well. A "bilingual
experience" is a situation where children who speak
English hear a foreign language spoken in the home.[7]

Children who come from homes where little or no
English is spoken have considerable difficulty in correctly answering test items involving vocabulary. When
children have to function in two incompatible systems,
it is necessary to take this into consideration when
evaluating their test performances.[8]

In many European countries children master several

[6]Donald Dugas, "Bilingualism and Language Learning,"
School and Society, 95 (Summer 1967), 294.

[7]Leonard V. Kosinski, "New Look at the Bilingual
Student," Senior Scholastic, 4 Oct., 1963, 14T.

[8]Landreth, p. 195.

6

languages with ease, but there is no marked cultural
discrimination involved and the several languages are
used with seemingly equal facility in the community.
Acquiring native-like control of several languages
without great social or psychic strain is not difficult if the conditions for learning them are consistent.[9] If the language and values expected at school
are different from the ones expected at home, the child
is under a double strain in most bilingual communities.
These dual values seem to be detrimental to success.

Americanization has been much easier for non-Eng-
lish-speaking people who have not resisted accultura-
tion.[10] Many Mexican-American communities in the
Southwestern United States adhere to their own language
for sentimental reasons and they desire to maintain
their ethnic identity.

A division of communities into contrasting groups
leads to a lack of understanding of the other and
prejudicial attitudes usually develop. In the Southwest,

[9]Faye L. Bumpass, Teaching Young Students English
as a Foreign Language (New York: American Book Company,
1963), p. 4.

[10]Thomas P. Carter, Mexican Americans in School
(New York: College Entrance Examination Board, 1970),
p. 1.

where these groups have had a "heritage of conflict,"
cultural differences tend to keep them apart and they
have a limited contact with the English language.[11]
If a child has inadequate stimulation in the language
he is being taught at school, his speech development
will result in definite deficiencies.

Proficiency in the dominant language is important for the welfare of both the individual and the
community. Every individual must not only prepare to
earn a living in the society in which he lives, but
must be able to communicate in the dominant language if
he is to obtain a job and function effectively.

Parents are a major influence in shaping the language facility of their children. They can strongly
encourage their children to master the language taught
in school and address them in English some of the time.
Limited early contact with English and inadequate
stimulation results in deficiencies in the language.
If there is insufficient or no verbal interaction in
English between the parents and the child, the child
will hesitate to use the language. If two languages

[11]Herschel T. Manuel, Spanish-Speaking Children of
the Southwest (Austin, Texas: University of Texas Press,
1965), p. 12.

are spoken in a home it is better for the child to
hear one language exclusively from one of the parents. The importance of children hearing English in
the home was determined in a Los Angeles school study
in 1968. The study revealed that "the exclusive use
of English contributes consistently and positively for
Mexican-American pupils at all grade levels."[12]

There are several early compensatory programs
designed to help the bilingually handicapped child.
Many of these programs are funded by the federal government. Most of the compensatory programs are teaching
the bilingual child English as a second language.

In the English as a Second Language programs, the
child's first language is used until his ability in
English permits the use of both languages.

Although much of the new language duplicates words
and concepts the child already knows in his first
language, there will be many words and concepts that
will not carry the same cultural meaning.[13] Some translations then will be like mutations that go off in

[12]Carter, p. 19.
[13]Carter, p. 109.

9

different directions. There are some words, such as
simpático in Spanish, that have no literal translation
in English. Bilingualism is accompanied by bicultural-
ism, and translation from one language to another impairs
bilinguals' ability to communicate because they are
unable to understand the translations of many words that
have specific meaning only in their language.[14] Shifting from one language to another in school may confuse
a child and he will be slow in acquiring facility in
the new language. The bilingual child will not use the
new language in his thought processes if he is given
equivalent words in a language he already knows.[15] There
is a tendency to translate rather than to think in the
new language. Encouraging the exclusive use of English
in the classroom would benefit the bilingual child since
practice insures fluency in a language.

Federal funds are enabling the University of Michigan to experiment with a bilingual education program in
which the curriculum is taught in two languages.[16] Draw-

[14]Hertzler, p. 428.

[15]Manuel, p. 128.

[16]Dugas, p. 294.

ing the curriculum from American and foreign cultures
and having both English and non-English students attend
may achieve a more complete liberal education.[17] There
has always been some social hostility toward people who
speak a foreign language in our country and perhaps
bilingual programs such as these would widen every student's
horizon culturally as well as linguistically. Facility
in several languages will be desirable and probably
necessary to function in a world that is getting smaller
very rapidly.

Preschool education programs provide formal school
opportunities prior to entrance to the first grade. A
close relationship exists between oral language ability
and the successful development of reading skills. There
is some evidence that preschool programs enhance a pupil's
potential for success in the first grade. "A study in
nine New Mexico towns found that first and second graders
with a year of preschool language instruction achieved
much better than the control group that had no such
experience."[18] Preschool programs can pave the way for

[17]"The Argument for Bilingual Education," Saturday
Review, 29 April, 1972, p. 54.

[18]Carter, p. 152.

production later by developing speaking vocabularies,
an interest in books, and communication and listening
skills.

The first national bilingual, bicultural Spanish-
English educational television program will start next
fall.[19] The program will be geared to preschool children and up to eight years of age. A good television
program could serve as a stimulating linguistic environ-
ment--one that could offer good language models. A
child's speech habits are very flexible in his early years
and he can produce sounds almost correctly by imitation.
He would have the advantage of seeing the instructor's
mouth and facial movements on the television screen when
words were being pronounced. Television has the potential
of helping children learn a foreign language without
making it a chore. Children love repetition. They
have a plasticity and a lack of inhibition, and if they
could be motivated by a good television program, they
would be able to learn almost by osmosis. Motivation
has always been important in learning--the more eager
a child is to learn, the greater his chance of success.

[19]Bella Stumbó, "Nueva Programa for Children of
Two Cultures," The Los Angeles Times, 24 Nov., 1972,
part IV, pp. 1, 20.

12

Perhaps in the near future, the television media will
present a deluge of good educational programs on the
screen to help the bilingually handicapped child.

According to Bloomfield, "the bilingual acquires
his second language in early childhood--after early
childhood few people . . . reach perfection in a foreign language."[20] Young children have keen auditory
perception, few inhibitions, and eagerness, which
enable them to learn a new language more easily. The
first impact of any language on a child always comes
by way of a conversational approach and most children
have mastered the fundamental rules of grammar by the
age of four without any direct training.[21] A child's
progress in language during the preschool years is
astounding and for this reason early compensatory education for the bilingually handicapped should be given
a very high priority. Introducing a new language before
speech habits are formed has many psychological advantages and will enable the child to speak without an ac-

[20]Leonard Bloomfield, Language (New York: Holt,
Rinehart and Winston, 1961), p. 56.

[21]Paul Henry Mussen, John Conger and Jerome Kagan,
Child Development and Personality (New York: Harper and
Row Publishers, 1969), pp. 252, 320.

13

cent.[22]

There have been very few studies that treat the
linguistic development of children from the point of
view of bilingualism. Much of what has been written
about any phase of bilingualism seems to be based on
speculative thinking and it is doubtful whether some
of the assumptions are sound. Most of the programs
offered to aid the bilingually handicapped are at the
first and second grade levels and may be too late to
help the child. Early compensatory education offered
at the preschool level would bring bilingually handicapped children up to a level where they could be
reached by existing educational practices. If the
oral phase of learning a language can be mastered before a child starts school, the other interrelated
phases (reading and writing) follow with ease.

[22]Manuel, p. 123.

14

BIBLIOGRAPHY

"The Argument for Bilingual Education." Saturday
    Review, 29 April, 1972, p. 54.

"Bilingual Education." School and Society, 100
    (Summer 1972), 290.

Bloomfield, Leonard. Language. New York: Holt,
    Rinehart and Winston, 1961.

Bumpass, Faye L. Teaching Young Students English as
    a Foreign Language. New York: American Book
    Company, 1963.

Carter, Thomas P. Mexican Americans in School: A
    History of Educational Neglect. New York: College
    Entrance Examination Board, 1970.

Dugas, Donald. "Bilingualism and Language Learning."
    School and Society, 95 (Summer 1967), 294.

Hertzler, Joyce O. A Sociology of Language. New
    York: Random House, Inc., 1965.

Kosinski, Leonard V. "New Look at the Bilingual
    Student." Senior Scholastic, 4 Oct., 1963, 14T.

Landreth, Catherine. Early Childhood Behavior and
    Learning. New York: Alfred A. Knopf, Inc., 1969.

Manuel, Herschel T. Spanish-Speaking Children of the
    Southwest. Austin, Texas: University of Texas
    Press, 1965.

Morgan, Clifford T., and Richard A. King. Introduction
    to Psychology. New York: McGraw-Hill, Inc., 1966.

Mussen, Paul Henry, John Conger and Jerome Kagan. Child
    Development and Personality. New York: Harper and
    Row Publishers, 1969.

Stumbo, Bella. "Nueva Programa for Children of Two
    Cultures." The Los Angeles Times, 24 Nov., 1972,
    part IV, pp. 1, 20.

We have chosen as our model a paper put together by one of our students. It is the kind of paper that a conscientious college student ought to produce. Notice that the student has successfully accomplished the following:

1. The paper is well organized, following the direction provided in the outline.
2. The paragraphs support a clearly stated thesis.
3. The student has synthesized the material from her reading sources and has absorbed it into her own style.
4. The student has documented her sources, avoiding plagiarism.
5. The student has followed the MLA Style Sheet for proper footnote and bibliography form.
6. The student has expressed herself clearly and with a degree of polish.

advice

B. L. SMITH

THE RESEARCH PAPER

B. L. Smith asserts the importance of the student research paper as an assignment and offers ten steps leading to the proper execution of such a paper.

1 At some point in any course given in the department of English you almost certainly will be assigned the writing of a paper. Whether your teacher calls it a "critique," an "essay," an "essay examination," a "term paper," or a "research paper," he expects a performance that will fulfill at least three basic requirements. He expects you to demonstrate, first of all, that you have read a body of material; second, that your reading has led you to an understanding of it; and, third, that you have the facility in the use of English to communicate your understanding effectively to the reader of your paper. You will save yourself unnecessary grief if you recognize that all three requirements are of equal importance. To put it another way more bluntly, it is not enough to demonstrate that you have read: you must in turn have something to say about what you have read, and you must be able to say that "something" at least clearly, and hopefully even gracefully.

2 The research paper is the most complex writing assignment, for it requires you to find the materials you will read and write about. It means that you must first decide on a topic that can be researched in the libraries available to you. It also means that you must keep a record of the materials that you found. And it means further that you must present a selected portion of that record so that your reader may evaluate your judgments accurately. This is basic scholarship. If you do well you will have certain rewards. Of course you will earn a respectable grade, but that may turn out to be the smallest of the gains from

your effort. Most rewarding should be the knowledge that you have come through a difficult task stronger than you were when you went into it. You will have judged yourself self-reliant.

3 But recognize at the outset that much of what your friends have told you about the research paper is nonsense. A research paper is not an assignment that calls for inordinate numbers of footnotes spiced with Latin abbreviations: footnotes are to be used when they are necessary to document what *must* be documented. Nor is the research paper to be an accumulation of quotations: quotations, paraphrases, and plot summaries are—at best—useful forms of evidence for supporting generalizations that you make. And, perhaps most important, the research paper is not the record of an enormous number of books skimmed: it does require the use of sources, but the topic and your approach to it will determine how many sources are appropriate and which sources are necessary. The point is that it is wrong to turn useful tools of inquiry into the dumb-show of pseudo-scholarship.

4 What, then, is a research paper? It is the presentation of the results of an independent investigation of a specific topic. The topic itself must be of a special kind if the paper is to have any significance at all. No simple statement will be a suitable topic; no declaration, no form of communication other than a *question* will result in the basis for a successful research project. You will recognize the point quickly and finally in one brief example. Write your name on a slip of paper. Now think of how you might suggest this to a friend as a possible research topic. Simply telling him your name will be of little use. You would have to devise some question about it, or any of its elements: "What is the origin of my last name?" "What is the symbolism of my first name, and how did that symbolic reference accrue to it?" It is to a question, then, that the research paper must direct itself.

5 The stages involved in preparing a research paper are:

1. Understanding the assignment
2. Defining the topic to be pursued
3. Recognizing the questions implied by the topic
4. Determining the kinds of materials needed to answer those questions
5. Gathering the materials
6. Abstracting notes on those portions of the materials relevant to your topic
7. Organizing the notes into a meaningful and relevant pattern geared to answer the questions implied by your topic
8. Writing the paper
9. Revising the paper so that it clearly and effectively communicates both the problem and its resolution
10. Proofreading and checking the format of the total paper (text, footnotes, and bibliography) to insure accuracy and completeness of presentation.

6 So a research paper is not a series of diary-like entries of the things you have thought, nor a travelogue of the books you have seen, nor a record of the

library shelves you have visited. Your professor's purpose in assigning it is not to catch students cheating or tripping over footnote format. It is a legitimate and a necessary assignment designed to give you practical experience in using the library, in gathering material, in taking systematic and helpful notes, and in efficiently organizing your judgments in the writing of a long paper. Ideally, you can demonstrate simultaneously your knowledge and understanding of both your subject and the writing process. If all goes well, what you have done will be a research paper: it will present the questions implied by your chosen subject, the answers to those questions and the information on which you have based your answer.

VOCABULARY

critique (1)
evaluate (2)
inordinate (3)
paraphrases (3)
pseudo-scholarship (3)
devise (4)
accrue (4)

implied (5)
abstracting (5)
format (6)
legitimate (6)
systematic (6)
simultaneously (6)

discussion

W. H. AUDEN

THE UNKNOWN CITIZEN

In this poem by W. H. Auden (1907–73), the research described is of a kind most of us are subjected to in growing amounts. It has become part and parcel of our technological neurosis.

(To JS/07/M/378 This Marble Monument Is Erected by the State)

He was found by the Bureau of Statistics to be
One against whom there was no official complaint,
And all the reports on his conduct agree
That, in the modern sense of an old-fashioned word, he was a saint,
For in everything he did he served the Greater Community.
Except for the War till the day he retired
He worked in a factory and never got fired,
But satisfied his employers, Fudge Motors Inc.
Yet he wasn't a scab or odd in his views,
For his Union reports that he paid his dues,
(Our report on his Union shows it was sound)
And our Social Psychology workers found

That he was popular with his mates and liked a drink.
The Press are convinced that he bought a paper every day
And that his reactions to advertisements were normal in every way.
Policies taken out in his name prove that he was fully insured,
And his Health-card shows he was once in hospital but left it cured.
Both Producers Research and High-Grade Living declare
He was fully sensible to the advantages of the Instalment Plan
And had everything necessary to the Modern Man,
A phonograph, a radio, a car and a frigidaire.
Our researchers into Public Opinion are content
That he held the proper opinions for the time of year;
When there was peace, he was for peace; when there was war, he
      went.
He was married and added five children to the population,
Which our Eugenist says was the right number for a parent of his
      generation,
And our teachers report that he never interfered with their
      education.
Was he free? Was he happy? The question is absurd:
Had anything been wrong, we should certainly have heard.

VOCABULARY

saint	eugenist
scab	absurd

QUESTIONS ON CONTENT

1. Who is the "he" referred to in line 1?
2. What is the basic problem exposed in this poem? Can you cite some examples of this problem in your own experience?
3. The protagonist of the poem works at "Fudge Motors." What does this name suggest?
4. What is the "modern sense" of the word "saint"?
5. The poem lists several items necessary to modern man. Does the list give you a clue to the date of the poem's authorship? What additional items might be included? Are there any other clues to the time described?
6. What is the meaning of the final line?

QUESTIONS ON FORM

1. How does the poet make his style harmonize with the subject discussed? Refer to specific examples.
2. What is the significance of the parenthesis in line 11?
3. Why are so many words capitalized throughout the poem?
4. What is the significance of the repetition of "and" at the beginning of several lines?

SUGGESTIONS FOR WRITING

1. In a three-hundred-word essay answer the questions posed near the end: "Was he free? Was he happy?"
2. In a well-developed paragraph explain the meaning of the line: "And our teachers report that he never interfered with their education."

example

JAMES NATHAN MILLER

THE BURNING QUESTION OF BROWNS FERRY

On March 22, 1975, a nuclear plant at Browns Ferry, Alabama, was damaged by a seven-and-a-half-hour fire. This article researches the causes of the fire, and ends by making a recommendation for the improvement of safety in nuclear plants.

1 Last year in March, electricians were engaged in a risky job at the Tennessee Valley Authority's brand-new Browns Ferry nuclear generating station near Athens, Ala. Two of the plant's three huge, billion-watt reactors were operating at full power, and the electricians were working in a room that was critical to both of them: a long, low, tightly packed space through which all the control cables for the two reactors' thousands of valves, motors and sensors were funneled on their way to the control room directly above.

2 If any part of the plant could be called its Achilles' heel, this so-called "cable-spreading room" was it. Eleven feet high, 35 feet wide, and 180 feet long, it was almost a solid mass of electrical cables—tens of thousands of shiny black snakes resting on track-like, galvanized-iron "cable trays" that crisscrossed through the room, filling it almost from floor to ceiling. The electricians' job was to seal the holes in the walls through which the cables entered the room.

3 Two things made the job risky. The sealant they were using—polyurethane foam, the same spongy material that's used to stuff pillows—is a highly combustible plastic. And the way they tested each seal was to hold a lighted candle to the hole and observe whether the flicker indicated that a draft was still coming through. During the couple of weeks before the big blaze, there had been quite a number of near-misses, in which workers set fire to the foam but managed to snuff the fire out before it could spread.

4 At about noon on March 22, a worker ignited a hunk of foam and couldn't put the fire out. Within minutes the splattering droplets of burning polyurethane had spread the fire to the highly combustible plastic coverings of cables in the neighboring, close-packed trays. Soon, more than a thousand cables were burning furiously.

Where There's Smoke

5 Let's pause here to ask several questions. First, why did inspectors permit the use of candles so close to flammable materials? It is a standard industry seal-testing technique, which the NRC[1] did not regard as dangerous. Why did the inspectors permit *any* construction job in such a critical room of an operating reactor? They simply did not know that such work was going on.

6 NRC inspectors rarely inspect plants. In fact, there is no record that an NRC inspector ever visited the spreading room. "The licensee is supposed to do his own inspection," says Donald Knuth, then NRC's director of inspection. NRC relies on plant operators to report to it all their safety problems. But TVA hadn't regarded the candle-testing job—or the small fires it had caused— as worth reporting.

7 What, then, do NRC inspectors inspect? Paper work, mainly. They spend virtually all their time not in the plant, but in its administrative offices, spot-checking its records—schedules showing how many fire drills have been held, the procedures used for qualifying welders, etc. Admits Norman Moseley, the NRC regional director of inspection who was responsible for Browns Ferry, "Our inspectors look at less than one percent of what goes on in a plant."

8 One more question: Why did NRC permit highly combustible cable coverings to be used at Browns Ferry?

9 NRC didn't know how combustible they were. The agency has no combustibility standards of its own and makes no tests of its own. It relies on equipment manufacturers and plant builders to set their own standards and do their own testing. It was not until after the fire that NRC made its own tests on the cables. The tests showed that many of the cables were so flammable that they "could serve as more intense initiators [of a fire] than open gas flames."

10 An important fact to note here is that the cables used at Browns Ferry are standard equipment that is widely used by the industry.

11 Now, back to the fire. As it began to spread, workers tried to get at it with backpack extinguishers, but they found that the crowding of the trays in the spreading room made this impossible. This difficulty of access to a critical, fire-prone area was a violation of elementary safety-design principles.

12 Many other violations quickly became apparent. The spreading room's chemical-foam extinguishing system was not designed to be triggered automatically. When the workmen running about the building finally found a hand switch, they discovered that it was covered by an unremovable metal plate. When they aimed a hose at the fire, they found that its spray nozzle could not make the water reach the flames. When they tried to phone in an alarm, they discovered that the alarm number posted on the plant's emergency placards was the wrong number. When they attempted to get through the smoke to battle the fire, they found that the plant was short of both the necessary breathing apparatus and the compressed air to refill it. How could *that* many violations have escaped NRC's fire inspectors?

[1]Nuclear Regulatory Commission.—Ed.

13 NRC has no fire inspectors. It relies on private-insurance-company inspectors. But the company that insured Browns Ferry insured it only for liability to outsiders, not for fire damage. So it had made no fire inspection. After the fire, when the company did make an inspection, it concluded that the spreading-room congestion was "inexcusable," and that unless a proper sprinkling system was installed, "a loss beyond imagination should be anticipated."

Danger: "Melt-Down"

14 As the blaze continued unchecked throughout the afternoon, a single grim question began to take on growing importance: Would the plant's operators be able to knock out the fire before *it* could knock out the valves and pumps that controlled the water-cooling system of the huge steel vessel that contained the uranium core of Unit One? Even though the nuclear reaction in the core was turned off early in the fire, there remained the danger that the fire might cause the most feared of all nuclear accidents—a "melt-down." The reason was this:

15 When the actual atom-splitting action inside a reactor's core is turned off, the heat in the 100-ton mass can*not* be turned off, and for months afterward the uranium pellets *must* be kept covered with cooling water. Without adequate cooling, the water would boil away and the uranium mass would melt, burning through its six-story-high steel container and releasing a large amount of radioactive gases and molten metal. Nobody knows precisely what would happen then, since there has never been such a melt-down in the brief history of atomic reactors. But the generally held assumption is that some of the gases would drift over the countryside with the wind. The number of deaths they would cause—whether a few dozen or many thousands— would depend on unpredictable variables: how much gas escaped, how big a city was downwind, etc.

16 As the blaze ate through the Browns Ferry cables, knocking out more and more of the vital valves and pumps that were designed to keep the core cooled, it forced the operators to improvise a desperate, unplanned defense. They called in as many off-duty employes as they could reach by phone (150 people showed up to assist the 17-man crew) and assembled them in and around the control room. As different pumps and valves conked out, these men were rushed to critical spots about the plant where, in effect, they could operate the reactor *by hand*—throwing emergency switches, turning the big wheels that opened stuck valves, phoning back instrument readings to the control room.

17 Behind this frantic extemporizing lay the worst of the safety lapses at Browns Ferry: the violation of one of the NRC's most sacred safety concepts, a principle that's supposed to be built into the basic design of every nuclear plant. This is the principle of "separation," which demands that all the plant's backup emergency devices *and their controls* must be spaced well apart from one another, so that no one event—fire, earthquake, pipe rupture, explo-

sion—can disable them all at once. The violation of this principle—by the jamming together of all the control cables into a single spreading room—enabled the blaze to knock out one, two and even three levels of Browns Ferry's defense almost simultaneously.

Achilles' Heel

18 How had so basic a compromise of so important a safety principle escaped NRC's notice when it approved Browns Ferry's design?

19 It had not escaped NRC's notice. The agency knew about it, but permitted it anyway. In fact, all 56 of the nation's already completed nuclear plants—plus all but 13 of the 142 plants now being built or in the blueprint stage—have the same Achilles' heel: the bunching together of all their control cables in a single spreading room.

20 The reason goes back to a fundamental mistake that Congress made 22 years ago. In 1954, when Congress set up the Atomic Energy Commission (AEC), it gave the agency two mutually contradictory assignments: to *promote* atomic development (which mainly meant finding ways to keep the costs of atomic plants down) and to *regulate* its safety (which mainly meant demanding expensive safety systems that drove the costs up). During the 1960s, it became apparent that this system was not working. Under pressure from the industry and its lobbies in Congress, the AEC gradually began to make promotion its dominant function; increasingly, when a compromise had to be reached between cost and safety, it was the latter that was compromised. Observe, for instance, how the AEC reached the compromise that allowed all U.S. plants to be built, like Browns Ferry, with a single spreading room.

21 Starting in 1965, a number of serious cable-tray fires in nuclear plants alerted the AEC to the fact that, to save space and money, plant builders were squeezing the trays so close together that a fire in one could quickly spread to others. So dangerous was this practice that the agency assigned an "A-plus" priority to the job of drawing up a tough "separation standard" to force builders to provide safe spacing between trays. One of the agency's most important aims was to make each plant separate cables between *two* spreading rooms, so that a fire in one room could not disable them all.

22 Though the AEC had the authority to issue such a standard on its own, it didn't do this. Instead, in 1971, it asked an industry group, the Institute of Electrical and Electronic Engineers (IEEE), to write a separation standard for it. Explains Robert Pollard, a member of the AEC group that worked with the IEEE on the separation standard, "When we draw up a new standard, an important aim is to make sure it's acceptable to the industry." But the idea of two spreading rooms was *not* acceptable to the industry. The reason: two rooms cost more than one. So the IEEE refused to okay the idea.

23 The AEC protested bitterly, predicting that a fire precisely like Browns Ferry's would result from the IEEE's refusal. But the protests did no good. In 1974, after three years of arguing with the industry group, the AEC gave in. It adopted a standard that permitted single spreading rooms.

24 Throughout the 1960s, the AEC was forced into many other, similar compromises. Finally, in 1974, in response to growing protests that the agency had become the industry's captive, Congress decided to rectify its 1954 mistake. It set up a brand-new agency, the Nuclear Regulatory Commission, with a new chairman and a new order: forget promotion, just regulate. But there was a catch: the new agency was not new. It was the old regulatory branch of the AEC—the same staff, same regulations, same administrative practices—under a new name. "All they did was change the stationery," says Pollard, who resigned from the NRC in February. Admits NRC's Knuth, "I can't put my finger on any basic changes we've made since the AEC days." As a result, almost all of the 142 plants now being built or awaiting an NRC okay have the same kinds of extinguishing systems as Browns Ferry and the same spreading-room congestion, and they are all subject to the same kind of less-than-one-percent inspection.

Clearing the Air

25 But now back to the fire at Browns Ferry. At 7:45 p.m., 7½ hours after the fire started, the Athens, Ala., fire department managed to get a hose on it and put it out. Now, though the fire was dead, the plant went through its worst ordeal of the day: a 2½-hour period during which all its water-circulating pumps—both primary and emergency—were rendered useless. "At that point we didn't know what the hell was going to happen next," says Browns Ferry superintendent H. J. Green.

26 But the worst did not happen. It turned out that there *was* a pump whose controls had somehow escaped the blaze. It was not designed for cooling, did not have the capacity to keep the core covered indefinitely, and was not even included in the plant's emergency plans. But it worked until the men could get the regular cooling equipment back into operation.

27 What would have happened if the pump had not worked? No one will ever know. So complex was the breakdown and so chaotic the situation in the control room that, depending on what you want to prove, you can shape the would-have-beens into a scenario that leads to either salvation or disaster. "The plant came pretty close to a melt-down," says Sen. Clifford Case (R., N.J.), a member of the Joint Congressional Committee on Atomic Energy. Not so, says NRC chairman William Anders; he insists that this "unfortunate and serious occurrence" actually proves the basic soundness of the safety system, since no one was injured and no radiation escaped.

28 But the question that the fire leaves unanswered is less important than the fact that it proves: The NRC, under pressure from the industry, has allowed serious compromises with safety to creep into the design, construction and operation of U.S. nuclear plants. As a result, the country has no present way of knowing how safe or unsafe its nuclear program is. Because all past studies of the safety question have been made under AEC and NRC auspices, they have started from a basic premise which Browns Ferry has proved to be fallacious:

the assumption that U.S. nuclear plants are built and operated to the highest possible safety standards. Nowhere do these theoretical studies give serious attention to such "real-world" factors as combustible cables, inadequate sprinkling systems, the effect of candle flames on polyurethane foam, spreading rooms that invalidate the principle of separation, or inspectors who look at less than one percent of what's actually happening in their plants.

29 Therefore, Congress should *immediately* appoint a top-level study commission—men and women of the highest possible technical expertise, integrity and independence—to get the answer to the fundamental questions raised by Browns Ferry: How safe is our atomic program, and how urgent is the need to make it safer?

30 Few question the profound importance to the U.S. economy of developing a strong nuclear-energy program. But before we commit ourselves to hundreds more plants like Browns Ferry, it is essential that we make sure that their safety standards are acceptable not just to the industry that builds them, but also to the public that has to live next door to them.

VOCABULARY

initiators (9)	scenario (27)
improvise (16)	auspices (28)
extemporizing (17)	fallacious (28)

QUESTIONS ON CONTENT

1. Why is the "cable-spreading room" the Achilles' heel of a nuclear plant?
2. What started the fire in the Browns Ferry nuclear plant?
3. What, according to the author, do Nuclear Regulatory Commission inspectors spend most of their time doing?
4. Why were combustible cable coverings used at Browns Ferry?
5. What was the worst safety lapse at Browns Ferry nuclear plant? Why was it committed?
6. What mutually contradictory assignments did Congress give the Atomic Energy Commission?
7. What would have happened had melt-down occurred at Browns Ferry?
8. What recommendation does the article make?

QUESTIONS ON FORM

1. How does the author switch the essay from a narrative on the fire to a recounting of safety violations?
2. What kind of evidence does the article mainly rely on?
3. Examine paragraph 12. What technique of phrasing does the author use to impart emphasis?
4. What is the function of paragraph 17?
5. Examine paragraph 11. What transition sentence does this paragraph use?

SUGGESTIONS FOR WRITING

1. Research and write an essay on the advantages and disadvantages to the United States of nuclear-generated energy.
2. Write an essay that analyzes and assesses responsibility for the near catastrophe at Browns Ferry.

TERM PAPER SUGGESTION

Write a term paper on the controversy over the safety of nuclear plants in the United States.

CHAPTER WRITING ASSIGNMENTS

Write a research paper, following the format suggested by your teacher. Above all, choose a topic in which you have a genuine interest. The following titles and restricted theses are presented to activate your own investigation:

Title	*Thesis*
"A Look at Thomas Wolfe"	The inconsistencies in Thomas Wolfe's writing can be directly attributed to constant family conflicts, to his doubts concerning his country's economic stability, and to his fear of not being accepted by his reading public.
"American Architectural Development"	The development of American architecture was greatly attenuated until the eighteenth century because of the pioneering stage—the lack of adequate transportation and manufacturing facilities, and the fact that city life had not formed until that time.
"Wordsworth and Coleridge: Their Diverse Philosophies"	Although Wordsworth and Coleridge were both Romantic poets, they believed in two completely different philosophies of Nature.
"Why Jazz Was What We Wanted"	This paper deals with the various influential trends that led to the rise, development, and recognition of jazz as a contribution to American musical culture during the nineteenth and twentieth centuries.
"The Influence of Imagism on Twentieth-Century Poetry"	Imagism, a self-restricted movement, has greatly influenced our twentieth-century poetry.

"Automation and Employment"	The current fear of man's being displaced by machines, or what alarmists term the "automation hysteria," seems to be based on unsubstantial reports.
"Needed: A New Definition of Insanity"	Our courts need a better definition of insanity because neither the M'Naghten Rule nor the psychological definition of insanity is adequate.
"The Proud Sioux"	In this paper I shall prove that the proud Sioux Indians, while confined to a shabby reservation, still fought on peacefully against their captors—the white man and his hard-to-accept peace terms.
"Women's Fashions after World War I and World War II"	World War I and World War II had a significant effect on women's fashions in America.
"Charlie Chaplin"	This paper deals with the various factors that led to the rise, recognition, and influence of Charlie Chaplin as the master of the silent movies.
"The Funnies"	The funnies today reflect a change in America's attitude toward violence, the minorities, and ecology.
"The Decline of the Mayans"	The four most popular theories that have been advanced to explain the abrupt end of the Mayan civilization are: the effects of natural disaster, physical weaknesses, detrimental social changes, and foreign influence.
"Relief Paintings in Egyptian Mastabas"	The relief paintings found in the Egyptian mastabas depict the everyday life of the Egyptian people.
"Athena"	The goddess Athena bestowed her favors not on those who worshipped her, but on those who fought for what they believed.
"Goldfish"	Originally from China, goldfish have been bred into one of the most beautiful and marketable species of fish.

Writing About Literature

advice

DOUGALD B. MAC EACHEN

ANALYZING A PLAY

> The following three selections consist of general questions designed to guide the student through his reading and analysis of these three genres of literature.

One of the major problems of the student who has to read a poem, a play, or a novel is what he should do with it. Until he has been given specific directions he doesn't know what he should look for; he doesn't know how to divide and conquer. If he is told to go to the reserve shelf and consult some lengthy book on the art of poetry or drama or fiction, he soon finds himself lost in an overabundance of instruction. He now has a double problem: what to do with the literary work and what to do with the manual on the particular art form. A battery of mimeographed questions can provide the student with most of the direction he needs. The question form of analysis gives him the pleasant feeling that he is being granted complete independence and not being made the prisoner of a closed system. The following set of questions on the drama may at the very least inspire a better one.

Characters

1. Who is the protagonist or main character? What are his or her main character traits? His or her chief weaknesses and virtues?

2. What are the special functions of the other characters? Do any of them serve to bring out certain aspects of the character of the protagonist? How do

452

they do this? Is there a character in the play who seems to be the special vehicle for the author's own comment on the play?

3. Who is the antagonist, if there is one? Is he a complex character, a mixture of good or bad?

4. If the play is a tragedy, what is the main character's "tragic flaw" or weakness? A moral defect, an error of judgment? What part does chance or accident play in his downfall? Is he of sufficient nobility of character, no matter what his social position is, to win our admiration and sympathy in spite of his shortcomings?

5. What means does the playwright use to characterize? Stage directions? Self-revelation by monologue or conversation? Actions? Comments of other characters? Characteristic habits, such as the repetition of some cliché or a little eccentricity? Does the playwright try to create his characters in depth or does he merely give one or two facets of them? Are there type or stock characters in the play?

Plot

1. What are the main elements of the plot? Into how many "chapters of action" is it divided, regardless of the act divisions? Can you summarize each chapter of action after you have finished reading it? Is the progress of the action clear or confused?

2. Is the plot of sufficient scope and importance to engage our deepest interest?

3. What brings on the dramatic conflict? At what point does the play begin?

4. Are the incidents well and plausibly connected? Is there sufficient causation supplied?

5. Is the resolution sufficiently inevitable, or is the denouement brought about by arbitrary coincidence?

6. Is there dramatic irony present? To what degree? What does it achieve in each case?

Setting

1. What is the setting? Does it change? If it does, does the change weaken the play in any way? Is the change of setting a necessary and natural one?

2. How does the setting contribute to the theme and characterization? Is the particular setting important to the play?

Theme

1. What is the moral or human significance of the play? Does it have universal significance through its theme, plot, and characters? Does it stimulate thought about any important problems of life? Does it supply answers by implication or direct statement?

2. Does the play clearly reveal any overall view of the universe on the part

of the dramatist? Is his view sentimental, romantic, Christian humanist, cynical, etc.? Does he content himself with showing evil and leave the conclusions up to the reader, or does he use devices to help form the reader's conclusions?

Language

1. If verse, what kind? Is the dramatist hampered by his verse forms?

2. Is the language elevated, or close to that of real life? Is it swollen, bombastic, stilted, artificial?

3. Does it contribute significantly to enjoyment of the play?

4. Is the language used by each character specially adapted to him, used to help characterize him?

General

1. Does the author observe the unities of time, place, and action? Does his play gain or lose by the unities he observes?

2. Would you like to give the play a second or even third reading? Why or why not?

ROBERT W. LEWIS, JR.

ANALYZING A NOVEL

(This version has been slightly modified by the author since publication in *College English*.)

This outline is merely a tool of analysis, and being put in the form of questions, it should constantly remind its user that only he or she can provide the answers. We hope we can talk to one another about literature and exchange informed and reasoned opinions about it, but if a given work of fiction is to mean anything to us, if we are to feel and know it completely, we must at one stage wrestle with the work bare-handed, without others as guides or informants. If one were to answer in detail each of the following questions, one would most certainly understand and, I hope, feel the work thoroughly. Not every question is relevant to every work; and in many cases complete answers will overlap with other ones. Also the good reader may well devise new questions to help one examine special kinds of fiction such as science fiction or black humor. The short story, while like the novel in many respects, is a distinct form for which all these questions will not be relevant. In general, however, these questions should alert the reader beforehand and afterward help one to verbalize or conceptualize one's thoughts and feelings, whether of the short story or the novel.

Only in section I, the questions about historical background, would the reader need any source other than the work itself to arrive at answers. And this section should clearly and emphatically be considered as what it is: mere background to the work itself. For some critical purposes, these questions can be ignored altogether, and in other cases such questions might be answered *after* a thorough analysis based on the other sections. Quite often, an introduction or preface will provide answers to these questions, but literary reference works, histories, and biographies, as well as the author's own comments in his journals, letters, essays, or autobiography, may sometimes provide useful information that may then be tested against the integrity of the work itself as the reader understands it.

To paraphrase Socrates, "The unexamined story is not worth reading." These questions should help one to answer the larger and older questions that, for all their commonplaceness, are still fundamental: What is the author trying to do? How has he done it? and Was it worth doing? Ultimately, we should not shun judgment of the story, but we should be certain through our analytical but sympathetic inquiry that we have opened our minds to a unique creation and tried to understand it and feel it on its own terms.

Analyzing Fiction

I. HISTORICAL BACKGROUND

A. When was the work written? What relation or significance does this date have to preceding, contemporary, and succeeding events—biographical events, literary publications, and important political, economic, or social occurrences? Is the author qualified to treat the subject? Is he or she biased or inaccurate?

B. Does the story significantly relate to the work of other writers or to source materials?

C. What place does the story hold in the author's total work?

D. Are any circumstances of special interest associated with the composition of the work? Do these circumstances in any way aid in the better understanding of the story itself?

E. Does the author make any useful comments concerning this story or his or her work in general in his or her letters, essays, journals, autobiography?

II. PLOT

A. Can you give a brief synopsis of the story?

B. Does the plot grow out of the characters or out of chance or coincidence? Within its own terms, is it logical and believable?

C. Is there a well unified beginning, middle, and end? At the beginning do we learn what happened, to whom it happened, when it happened, and where it happened?

D. Is there a strong center of interest and how is it determined: by the author's statements (but beware the "intentional fallacy"[1]) or by space, emphasis, and recurrence? Is there a central crucial episode or is the plot episodic with no one outstanding event?

E. If there is more than one action in the story, which is the main plot and which the subordinate plots (sub-plots)?

F. Is anything seemingly irrelevant to the main plot? If so, does it serve any purpose?

G. What is the nature of the conflict (or conflicts)? Are there complications to the main problem? Identify the protagonist and the antagonist. Where is the climax or turning point?

H. Is our curiosity aroused? How?

I. What of dilemmas, irony, foreshadowing, flashbacks?

J. Is the conclusion satisfactory? Does the story end with a bang or a whimper?

K. Is the title a good one? Is it helpful in any way?

III. SETTING

A. What is the historic time, place, and social background of the story?

B. Has the setting any influence on plot or characters?

C. Are any scenes especially appropriate for the action that takes place there?

D. Is there any use of symbolism in the setting? (Cf. H.)

E. How much time does the action cover? How does the author treat time gaps?

F. Which are the most interesting, striking, or important scenes? How does the author handle them?

G. How is the setting presented? With photographic detail? Impressionistically through a few suggestive details? Indirectly through thoughts and actions?

H. Is the setting detailed or generalized? Realistic or stylized? Is it thematically functional or casual, arbitrary, or atmospheric? (Would it make any difference if the story were set someplace else?) Is the setting allegorical or symbolical or merely literal?

IV. CHARACTERS

A. Can you sum up the appearance and important characteristics of each major character?

B. Are there any marked similarities or contrasts among the characters? (Cf. F.)

C. Are they "masters of their fate" or "victims of circumstance"?

D. Which characters change as the story proceeds? Do they change for the better or the worse? (Cf. H.)

E. Which characters are distinct individuals (round) and which are types (flat)?

---

[1]The "intentional fallacy": judging a work by the author's stated intention.—Ed.

F. Does every character have a function in the story? What are the functions of the minor characters? (Any foils?) Are these minor characters interesting in themselves?

G. How are the principal characters presented? By the author's description and comment? By representation of the thoughts and actions of the characters themselves? By observations and comments of the other characters?

H. Are the characters at once realistically consistent and also sufficiently motivated for whatever change occurs in them?

I. Toward which characters does the author show sympathy? Toward which antipathy?

J. Are the characters' names suitable or in any way significant? (Characternyms?)

V. STYLE

A. What are the outstanding qualities or features of the style?

B. How would you describe the author's style? Simple and clearcut, complex and involved? Smooth and graceful, abrupt and harsh? Richly suggestive and implying much, lean and direct? Poetic, sentimental, restrained? Literal or figurative? Concrete or abstract? Specific or general? Formal or informal or colloquial? Consistent or variable?

C. Does the author's style have individuality? Could another of the author's stories be recognized by style alone?

D. Is there any humor in the story? Is it quiet or broad?

E. Is the dialog appropriate to the speakers?

F. How frequent are dramatic situations? How are they reached, by anticipation or surprise? How treated, by suggestion or in detail? How rendered, by dialog or by description?

G. Are there any different rates of movement in the story? Where and why?

H. Do you note abuse of digression?

I. From what point of view is the story written? Is the point of view consistent? Could it have been changed for the better?

   1. Omniscient

      a. Editorial omniscient: author present as narrator and commentator who summarizes, analyzes, interprets.

      b. Neutral omniscient: author narrates but does not comment directly; but the author may use a spokesman character.

   2. Limited

      a. Third-person narration, but point of view of a single character; roving narrator, a variation.

      b. First-person narrator is the protagonist.

      c. First-person narrator is a minor character or merely an onlooker (Lubbock's "central intelligence").

   3. Wholly dramatic narration (effaced narrator—extremely rare). What are the discernible reasons for the choice of the particular point of view? The effects of the choice?

J. Are any of the sentences or paragraphs particularly striking, meaningful, or remarkable for their freshness or statement?

K. From the many possibilities, what materials has the author selected and what does the author's selectivity indicate?

L. What kind of action or scene does the author choose to expand? What kind to dramatize and what kind to narrate? What is the significance of his or her selection?

M. What effects does the author's style produce: atmosphere or mood (effect on reader); tone (author's attitude toward the material); irony; understatement; hyperbole; sentimentality?

VI. CLASSIFICATION

A. On what levels can the story profitably be read? (Plot, character, emotional effect, theme.) Is this a story of character with the primary interest being in personalities? Of action, primary interest in events? Of setting, primary interest in environment? Of idea, primary interest in thesis or ethical significance?

B. What is the theme or total meaning of the story? Do all the elements support that meaning? Are there other comments of significance—i.e., minor themes? Does the author raise questions or try to solve them? Is what the author says worth saying? (Beware, however, of reduction, distortion, or inflation of the story by a specific statement of theme.)

C. What is the ideological climate of the story? What ideas seem to be unconscious assumptions of the author and thus operate tacitly? What ideas become subject matter by being themes? And how are they presented, discursively or dramatically?

D. In what general literary tradition was the story written? Realistic: attempting to see life as it is with emphasis on the difficulties, absurdities, animalities, and ironies? Romantic: attempting to see larger truths beyond the literal and factual with emphasis on the imagination and sentiment? Naturalistic, fantastic, symbolistic, allegorical, picaresque, etc.?

E. Does the author make use of allegory, parable, symbolism, or myth?

F. Can you now make a judgment of the story?

ELEANOR BUTLER

WHAT TO SAY ABOUT A POEM

Even those students who feel competent to analyze a play or a story pale before an assignment to similarly analyze a poem. Perhaps it is too late to override the conditioning which causes a student to petrify when asked to analyze a poem; indeed, perhaps we must finally accept the mythology that poets are oracles and that poetry is too sacred to be sullied by any kind of formal analysis. However, pending the widespread acceptance of this idea, the on-the-line teacher is still faced with the daily chore of reading poetry to terrified students, and of goading them into some kind of critical commentary on its meaning. It is for this use that these questions are offered. I make no special claim for their helpfulness to others, except to say that for my own students, these questions have at least provided a consistent framework for talking about poetry.

1. TITLE

(The title of a poem will frequently synopsize its theme, or at least specify a starting point which the first line of the poem will abruptly take for granted.)

a. What is the significance of the poem's title? How does its title relate to the poem's theme?

b. Does the title specify a locale for the poem? (e.g., "Dover Beach.")
Does the title specify a person to whom the poem is addressed? (e.g., "To His Coy Mistress.")
Does the title specify some person or object about whom the poem is written? (e.g., "Ode to a Nightingale.")

c. Does the title specify an incident or action about which the poem is written? (e.g., "Auto Wreck.")
Does the title specify a dominant purpose for the poem? (e.g., "Elegy for Jane My Student, Thrown by a Horse.")

d. Does the title allude to some incident or event in literature which the poem assumes as its starting point? (e.g., "The Nymph's Reply.")

2. CONTEXT OF THE POEM

(Almost all poems assume a context based on some incident, event, action, or idea. Typically, this context is specified either in the poem's title or implied by its first line, e.g., "To His Coy Mistress" is based on the context implied by its title—the speaker is addressing his mistress who is being coy. The context of a poem partly explains its raison d'être; consequently, if a poem's context is understood, its content is frequently made plainer.)

a. Where is the speaker at the outset of the poem? Is he alone? Is there any significance to his being in that place?

b. Is the speaker addressing someone else? Is he addressing something? Is he talking to himself? Why?

c. What is the occasion of the poem? What, in other words, prompts the poem? Is the poem prompted by the speaker's encounter with someone, some animal, some object?

d. Is there a relationship between the poem's first line and its title? (Caution: once context is given in a title, the first line of the poem will take it as assumed and simply begin.) Does the first line lead naturally from the title?

3. SPEAKER

(Convention assumes that every poem has a speaker. However, while some speakers will simply function as an organizing point of view in the poem, other speakers are clearly differentiated. The highly differentiated speaker is called a persona, and may have all the multi-facetedness of a character in a play.)

a. Who is the speaker? Is the speaker a man or a woman? Is the speaker given a name? Does the speaker have a well-defined identity or does he function simply as an "I" point of view for the sake of the poem?

b. How does the speaker feel about the incident, idea, event, object, or person described in the poem? Does the speaker express any of his feelings in the poem?

c. Is the speaker differentiated as a person? Does he express any well-defined feelings or attitudes? Does the speaker express any peculiarities or idiosyncrasies?

d. What is the speaker's motive for feeling or thinking the way he does? Do the speaker's feelings or attitudes coincide with the way a "reasonable man" might be expected to feel? Or are his feelings and attitudes peculiar to him? (If so, the "I" is probably not merely an organizing viewpoint, but a persona or character.)

4. LANGUAGE AND IMAGERY

(Poetry uses imagery in a variety of ways: to reinforce a speaker's perceptions of the world, to underscore a subtle meaning, to limn a symbol.)

a. What kind of imagery does the speaker use in his descriptions? Do these images have anything in common? Do they cluster around a dominant theme or impression? Is there a common thread of meaning between these images?

b. How do these images color the speaker's perceptions of the world? Do these images suggest or imply any attitude peculiar to the speaker?

c. Is the imagery used to describe any object consistent with the way the object is typically regarded? Does the imagery suggest any special meaning for the object? (If so, the object may be functioning as a symbol in the poem.)

d. How would you characterize the diction of the poem? Does the speaker use slang words? Is his diction formal, or is it standard? What does the speaker's choice of words reveal about him?

5. RHYME, RHYTHM, AND VERSE FORM

(Rhyme, rhythm, and verse form are frequently deployed in a poem to underscore theme, and for that reason are well worth any attention you give them in your analysis.)

a. What is the rhyme scheme in the poem? Does the poem employ full rhyme, half rhyme, or no rhyme? Does the poem use inter-stanza rhyme? Is the rhyme appropriate to the poem's subject? If not, why not? (Possibly because the intent of the poem is satirical.)

b. Does the rhythm of the poem underscore its theme? Does the rhythm of the poem seem to run counter to the surface meaning of its words? (If so, satirical intent can be suspected.)

c. Is the poem written in any recognizable verse form? How many lines does each stanza have? Are the stanzas written in an equal number of lines and in the same rhyme scheme? What is the effect of the stanza arrangement in the poem? Is there any significance to the way the stanzas break? (Some poems will deploy their stanzas to add emphasis to an idea or theme. Some will even underscore an idea by breaking the stanza at a crucial point in the exposition of that idea.)

d. Examine the lines of the poem. Is each line a single unit of sense, or does its meaning run on to the next line? What is the effect of the arrangement of the poem's lines on its theme? (For instance, a terse summary sentence may be set off by itself in a line for the sake of emphasis.)

6. THEME

(It is customary in writing and talking about poetry to sum up the dominant meaning, effect, or characteristics of the poem into a statement of its theme. Once the theme is extracted from the poem, the purpose of analysis is to demonstrate that the theme is an appropriate hypothesis which can be supported by references to the poem itself. The analysis of poetry through the use of themes gives, at best, elliptical results. However. t is useful as a method of learning to think abstractly about literature.)

a. What is the theme of the poem? Does your version of its theme account for the major emphasis in the poem? (It must, if it is a good statement of theme.)

b. What proof can you adduce from the poem itself which supports your statement of its theme? Can you give specific quotations from the poem to support your version of its theme? (If you cannot, then your statement of the poem's theme is probably not appropriate.)

c. Is the theme you have inferred from the poem commonly found in literature? (e.g., *carpe diem* theme.)

d. Does the language of the poem, its imagery, rhyme, rhythm, support your version of its theme? Can you demonstrate that the poem technically underscores its theme? (An important consideration, since if your statement of the poem's theme is not supported by its use of language, you may be simply paraphrasing its surface meaning oblivious to a counter intention—perhaps satirical. Your theme must therefore be provable by reference to the poem's form as well as content.)

discussion

MARYA MANNES

HOW DO YOU KNOW IT'S GOOD?

Evaluation, whether of automobiles or art, implies the use of standards for judging. This article contends that criticism has abandoned the use of standards and that consequently the level of artistic competence has declined. It argues for the restoration and application of standards in judging all the arts.

1 Suppose there were no critics to tell us how to react to a picture, a play, or a new composition of music. Suppose we wandered innocent as the dawn into an art exhibition of unsigned paintings. By what standards, by what values would we decide whether they were good or bad, talented or untalented, successes or failures? How can we ever know that what we think is right?

2 For the last fifteen or twenty years the fashion in criticism or appreciation of the arts has been to deny the existence of any valid criteria and to make the words "good" or "bad" irrelevant, immaterial, and inapplicable. There is no such thing, we are told, as a set of standards, first acquired through experience and knowledge and later imposed on the subject under discussion. This has been a popular approach, for it relieves the critic of the responsibility of judgment and the public of the necessity of knowledge. It pleases those resentful of disciplines, it flatters the empty-minded by calling them open-minded, it comforts the confused. Under the banner of democracy and the kind of equality which our forefathers did *not* mean, it says, in effect, "Who are you to tell us what is good or bad?" This is the same cry used so long and so effectively by the producers of mass media who insist that it is the public; not they, who decides what it wants to hear and see, and that for a critic to say that *this* program is bad and *this* program is good is purely a reflection of personal taste. Nobody recently has expressed this philosophy more succinctly than Dr. Frank Stanton, the highly intelligent president of CBS television. At a hearing before the Federal Communications Commission, this phrase escaped him under questioning: "One man's mediocrity is another man's good program."

3 There is no better way of saying "No values are absolute." There is another important aspect to this philosophy of *laissez faire:* It is the fear, in all observers of all forms of art, of guessing wrong. This fear is well come by, for who has not heard of the contemporary outcries against artists who later were called great? Every age has its arbiters who do not grow with their times, who cannot tell evolution from revolution or the difference between frivolous faddism, amateurish experimentation, and profound and necessary change. Who wants to be caught *flagrante delicto*[1] with an error of judgment as

[1]Latin, "in the act, red-handed."—Ed.

serious as this? It is far safer, and certainly easier, to look at a picture or a play or a poem and to say "This is hard to understand, but it may be good," or simply to welcome it as a new form. The word "new"—in our country especially—has magical connotations. What is new must be good; what is old is probably bad. And if a critic can describe the new in language that nobody can understand, he's safer still. If he has mastered the art of saying nothing with exquisite complexity, nobody can quote him later as saying anything.

4 But all these, I maintain, are forms of abdication from the responsibility of judgment. In creating, the artist commits himself; in appreciating, you have a commitment of your own. For after all, it is the audience which makes the arts. A climate of appreciation is essential to its flowering, and the higher the expectations of the public, the better the performance of the artist. Conversely, only a public ill-served by its critics could have accepted as art and as literature so much in these last years that has been neither. If anything goes, everything goes; and at the bottom of the junkpile lie the discarded standards too.

5 But what are these standards? How do you get them? How do you know they're the right ones? How can you make a clear pattern out of so many intangibles, including that greatest one, the very private I?

6 Well for one thing, it's fairly obvious that the more you read and see and hear, the more equipped you'll be to practice that art of association which is at the basis of all understanding and judgment. The more you live and the more you look, the more aware you are of a consistent pattern—as universal as the stars, as the tides, as breathing, as night and day—underlying everything. I would call this pattern and this rhythm an order. Not order—*an* order. Within it exists an incredible diversity of forms. Without it lies chaos. I would further call this order—this incredible diversity held within one pattern—health. And I would call chaos—the wild cells of destruction—sickness. It is in the end up to you to distinguish between the diversity that is health and the chaos that is sickness, and you can't do this without a process of association that can link a bar of Mozart with the corner of a Vermeer painting, or a Stravinsky score with a Picasso abstraction; or that can relate an aggressive act with a Franz Kline painting and a fit of coughing with a John Cage composition.

7 There is no accident in the fact that certain expressions of art live for all time and that others die with the moment, and although you may not always define the reasons, you can ask the questions. What does an artist say that is timeless; how does he say it? How much is fashion, how much is merely reflection? Why is Sir Walter Scott so hard to read now, and Jane Austen not? Why is baroque right for one age and too effulgent for another?

8 Can a standard of craftsmanship apply to art of all ages, or does each have its own, and different, definitions? You may have been aware, inadvertently, that craftsmanship has become a dirty word these years because, again, it implies standards—something done well or done badly. The result of this convenient avoidance is a plenitude of actors who can't project their voices, singers who can't phrase their songs, poets who can't communicate emotion, and writers who have no vocabulary—not to speak of painters who

can't draw. The dogma now is that craftsmanship gets in the way of expression. You can do better if you don't know *how* you do it, let alone *what* you're doing.

9 I think it is time you helped reverse this trend by trying to rediscover craft: the command of the chosen instrument, whether it is a brush, a word, or a voice. When you begin to detect the difference between freedom and sloppiness, between serious experimentation and egotherapy, between skill and slickness, between strength and violence, you are on your way to separating the sheep from the goats, a form of segregation denied us for quite a while. All you need to restore it is a small bundle of standards and a Geiger counter that detects fraud, and we might begin our tour of the arts in an area where both are urgently needed: contemporary painting.

10 I don't know what's worse: to have to look at acres of bad art to find the little good, or to read what the critics say about it all. In no other field of expression has so much double-talk flourished, so much confusion prevailed, and so much nonsense been circulated: further evidence of the close interdependence between the arts and the critical climate they inhabit. It will be my pleasure to share with you some of this double-talk so typical of our times.

11 Item one: preface for a catalogue of an abstract painter:

"Time-bound meditation experiencing a life; sincere with plastic piety at the threshold of hallowed arcana; a striving for pure ideation giving shape to inner drive; formalized patterns where neural balances reach a fiction." End of quote. Know what this artist paints like now?

12 Item two: a review in the *Art News:*

" . . . a weird and disparate assortment of material, but the monstrosity which bloomed into his most recent cancer of aggregations is present in some form everywhere. . . ." Then, later, "A gluttony of things and processes terminated by a glorious constipation."

13 Item three, same magazine, review of an artist who welds automobile fragments into abstract shapes:

"Each fragment . . . is made an extreme of human exasperation, torn at and fought all the way, and has its rightness of form as if by accident. *Any technique that requires order or discipline would just be the human ego.* No, these must be egoless, uncontrolled, undesigned and different enough to give you a bang—fifty miles an hour around a telephone pole. . . ."

14 "Any technique that requires order or discipline would just be the human ego." What does he mean—"just be"? What are they really talking about? Is this journalism? Is it criticism? Or is it that other convenient abdication from standards of performance and judgment practiced by so many artists and critics that they, like certain writers who deal only in sickness and depravity, "reflect the chaos about them"? Again, whose chaos? Whose depravity?

15 I had always thought that the prime function of art was to create order *out* of chaos—again, not the order of neatness or rigidity or convention or artifice, but the order of clarity by which one will and one vision could draw

the essential truth out of apparent confusion. I still do. It is not enough to use parts of a car to convey the brutality of the machine. This is as slavishly representative, and just as easy, as arranging dried flowers under glass to convey nature.

16 Speaking of which, i.e., the use of real materials (burlap, old gloves, bottletops) in lieu of pigment, this is what one critic had to say about an exhibition of Assemblage at the Museum of Modern Art last year:

"Spotted throughout the show are indisputable works of art, accounting for a quarter or even a half of the total display. But the remainder are works of non-art, anti-art, and art substitutes that are the aesthetic counterparts of the social deficiencies that land people in the clink on charges of vagrancy. These aesthetic bankrupts . . . have no legitimate ideological roof over their heads and not the price of a square intellectual meal, much less a spiritual sandwich, in their pockets."

17 I quote these words of John Canaday of *The New York Times* as an example of the kind of criticism which puts responsibility to an intelligent public above popularity with an intellectual coterie. Canaday has the courage to say what he thinks and the capacity to say it clearly: two qualities notably absent from his profession.

18 Next to art, I would say that appreciation and evaluation in the field of music is the most difficult. For it is rarely possible to judge a new composition at one hearing only. What seems confusing or fragmented at first might well become clear and organic a third time. Or it might not. The only salvation here for the listener is, again, an instinct born of experience and association which allows him to separate intent from accident, design from experimentation, and pretense from conviction. Much of contemporary music is, like its sister art, merely a reflection of the composer's own fragmentation: an absorption in self and symbols at the expense of communication with others. The artist, in short, says to the public: If you don't understand this, it's because you're dumb. I maintain that you are not. You may have to go part way or even halfway to meet the artist, but if you must go the whole way, it's his fault, not yours: Hold fast to that. And remember it too when you read new poetry, that estranged sister of music.

19 "A multitude of causes, unknown to former times, are now acting with a combined force to blunt the discriminating powers of the mind, and, unfitting it for all voluntary exertion, to reduce it to a state of almost savage torpor. The most effective of these causes are the great national events which are daily taking place and the increasing accumulation of men in cities, where the uniformity of their occupations produces a craving for extraordinary incident, which the rapid communication of intelligence hourly gratifies. To this tendency of life and manners, the literature and theatrical exhibitions of the country have conformed themselves."

20 This startlingly applicable comment was written in the year 1800 by William Wordsworth in the preface to his "Lyrical Ballads"; and it has been cited by Edwin Muir in his recently published book "The Estate of Poetry."

Muir states that poetry's effective range and influence have diminished alarmingly in the modern world. He believes in the inherent and indestructible qualities of the human mind and the great and permanent objects that act upon it, and suggests that the audience will increase when "poetry loses what obscurity is left in it by attempting greater themes, for great themes have to be stated clearly." If you keep that firmly in mind and resist, in Muir's words, "the vast dissemination of secondary objects that isolate us from the natural world," you have gone a long way toward equipping yourself for the examination of any work of art.

21 When you come to theatre, in this extremely hasty tour of the arts, you can approach it on two different levels. You can bring to it anticipation and innocence, giving yourself up, as it were, to the life on the stage and reacting to it emotionally, if the play is good, or listlessly, if the play is boring; a part of the audience organism that expresses its favor by silence or laughter and its disfavor by coughing and rustling. Or you can bring to it certain critical faculties that may heighten, rather than diminish, your enjoyment.

22 You can ask yourselves whether the actors are truly in their parts or merely projecting themselves; whether the scenery helps or hurts the mood; whether the playwright is honest with himself, his characters, and you. Somewhere along the line you can learn to distinguish between the true creative act and the false arbitrary gesture; between fresh observation and stale cliché; between the avant-garde play that is pretentious drivel and the avant-garde play that finds new ways to say old truths.

23 Purpose and craftsmanship—end and means—these are the keys to your judgment in all the arts. What is this painter trying to say when he slashes a broad band of black across a white canvas and lets the edges dribble down? Is it a statement of violence? Is it a self-portrait? If it is *one* of these, has he made you believe it? Or is this a gesture of the ego or a form of therapy? If it shocks you, what does it shock you into?

24 And what of this tight little painting of bright flowers in a vase? Is the painter saying anything new about flowers? Is it different from a million other canvases of flowers? Has it any life, any meaning, beyond its statement? Is there any pleasure in its forms or texture? The question is not whether a thing is abstract or representational, whether it is "modern" or conventional. The question, inexorably, is whether it is good. And this is a decision which only you, on the basis of instinct, experience, and association, can make for yourself. It takes independence and courage. It involves, moreover, the risk of wrong decision and the humility, after the passage of time, of recognizing it as such. As we grow and change and learn, our attitudes can change too, and what we once thought obscure or "difficult" can later emerge as coherent and illuminating. Entrenched prejudices, obdurate opinions are as sterile as no opinions at all.

25 Yet standards there are, timeless as the universe itself. And when you have committed yourself to them, you have acquired a passport to that elusive but immutable realm of truth. Keep it with you in the forests of bewilderment. And never be afraid to speak up.

VOCABULARY

laissez faire (3)	disparate (12)
arbiters (3)	aggregations (12)
abdication (4)	depravity (14)
intangibles (5)	artifice (15)
baroque (7)	aesthetic (16)
effulgent (7)	dissemination (20)
inadvertently (8)	avant-garde (22)
egotherapy (9)	inexorably (24)
arcana (11)	obdurate (24)
ideation (11)	immutable (25)
neural (11)	

QUESTIONS ON CONTENT

1. What relationship does the author see between critical standards and art? Why are standards necessary?
2. Why are critics timid about making judgments?
3. How are standards acquired?
4. What, according to the author, is the prime function of art?
5. What are the keys to judging art?

QUESTIONS ON FORM

1. Why does the author end the first paragraph on a question? What do questions contribute to the phrasing of an argument?
2. The author writes: "For the last fifteen or twenty years the fashion in criticism or appreciation of the arts has been to deny the existence of any valid criteria and to make the words 'good' or 'bad' irrelevant, immaterial, and inapplicable." Why does the author use three words—"irrelevant, immaterial, and inapplicable"—when any one of them would have gotten her meaning across?
3. Reread paragraph 5. What is the purpose of a paragraph made up solely of questions?
4. Reread paragraph 6. What function does the analogy between "health" and "sickness" have in this essay?
5. How does the author support her contention that criticism has abandoned the use of standards? Is her proof adequate to her purpose?

SUGGESTIONS FOR WRITING

1. Are there absolute standards by which art can be judged? Take a stand on that issue and defend it.
2. "I don't know if it's good, but I know what I like."—Discuss the attitude implicit in that saying as it applies to art.

TERM PAPER SUGGESTION

Write a paper on the relationship between art and social class. Focus your research on the following queries:

(1) Does art reflect a class bias?
(2) Do different classes hold to different standards for judging art?
(3) Are these standards related to the ways different classes perceive the world?
(4) Is there a sociology of art?

ZBIGNIEW HERBERT

Translated by Czeslaw Milosz and Peter Dale Scott

EPISODE IN A LIBRARY

1 A blonde girl is bent over a poem. With a pencil sharp as a lancet she transfers the words to a blank page and changes them into strokes, accents, caesuras. The lament of a fallen poet now looks like a salamander eaten away by ants.

2 When we carried him away under machine-gun fire, I believed that his still warm body would be resurrected in the word. Now as I watch the death of the words, I know there is no limit to decay. All that will be left after us in the black earth will be scattered syllables. Accents over nothingness and dust.

VOCABULARY

lancet (1)
caesuras (1)

QUESTIONS ON CONTENT

1. What is the girl doing to the poem?
2. The poet writes, "Now as I watch the death of the words, I know there is no limit to decay." What does he mean by that?
3. In what time period does the poem occur? Does it occur only in the present? in the past? in both?

QUESTIONS ON FORM

1. What is the significance of the word "lancet" as it is used in stanza 1?
2. What figure of speech does stanza 2 end with?

SUGGESTIONS FOR WRITING

1. Discuss the idea, pro or con, that analysis destroys the beauty and appeal of poetry.
2. Write an essay outlining the way you read literature, whether analytically or emotionally or otherwise.

examples

W. H. AUDEN

DOING ONESELF IN

In this review of the English writer and critic Alfred Alvarez's book *The Savage God: A Study of Suicide,* W. H. Auden, himself a noted author and poet, appraises critically not only Alvarez's literary merits, but also his moral posture toward suicide.

1 Though I have been fascinated by this book, I am not sure that I am the proper person to review it. As a Christian, I am required to believe that suicide, except when it is an act of insanity, is a mortal sin, but who am I to judge, since at no time in my life have I felt the slightest temptation to commit it, any more than I can imagine myself going off my head or indulging in sadistic or masochistic acts? Of course, like everybody else, I have my "good" and "bad" days, but I have always felt that to be walking this earth is a miracle I must do my best to deserve. It would be most ungracious of me if I did not, seeing what an extraordinarily lucky life I have had. I was the favorite child of my parents; I have enjoyed excellent health; I am a worker not a laborer, i.e., I have been paid by society to do what I enjoy doing; I have been reasonably successful; and I have a number of wonderful friends whom I love dearly. This does not mean that I want to live forever: at present I feel that I would like *le bon Dieu* to take me at the canonical age of seventy, though I fear He will not.

2 I can imagine two situations in which suicide would be a rational act. If someone contracts a painful and incurable disease and knows, moreover, that the cost of medical treatment is going seriously to deplenish the estate he has to leave his heir, to put an end to his life would certainly be rational: whether it would also be moral, I can't decide. Then I think of the case of a French Resistance fighter who is arrested by the Gestapo and is afraid that, under torture, he may give away the names of his colleagues: in this case suicide would be not only rational but his moral duty.

3 Mr. Alvarez's opening and closing chapters describe personal experiences, one the death of his friend, the poet Sylvia Plath, the other his own, fortunately unsuccessful, attempt at suicide. I will discuss these later. The rest of his book is concerned with the history of attitudes toward suicide and the theories put forward to account for it.

4 In associating with the suicide the epic hero and the martyr, Mr. Alvarez seems to me to be stretching his net too wide. Though it is usually the fate of the epic hero to fall in battle, that is not his goal: his goal is to stay the enemies of his people, and by his valiant deeds to win immortal glory on earth. The martyr does not sacrifice his life for the sake of any particular social group, but for all mankind. He does not, incidentally, die by his own hand, but by the

hands of others. In the special case of Christ, the God-Man, he dies to redeem sinful mankind: the ordinary martyr dies to bear witness to what he believes (it can be Christian or Marxist) to be saving truth, to be shared with all men, not reserved as an esoteric secret for a few.

5 The Church from the beginning had always condemned the Stoic attitude toward suicide, but, during the persecutions, she discovered that there was an ethical-psychological problem which no one had foreseen, namely, that a man might insist upon getting himself martyred, not in order to bear witness to the truth on earth, but in order to win for himself immortal glory in Heaven. In other words, his real motive could be the pride of the epic hero. The Church found herself having to preach caution and discourage her converts from insisting upon martyrdom when it could possibly be avoided. Only when the choice lay between martyrdom and apostasy was martyrdom to be chosen. The paradigm was the story of the Passion. Far from rushing joyfully upon death, Christ, in the Garden of Gethsemane, prays in agony that the cup shall pass from Him.

6 The suicide proper dies by his own hand. This may be, as was the case with most of the famous Roman suicides, because he knows that if he does not kill himself he will be killed, and self-killing seems less degrading. But I would define a suicide in society as we know it as someone who for one reason or another finds his life subjectively intolerable. I stress the word *subjectively* because in circumstances that would seem to an outsider objectively intolerable, as in concentration camps or for sufferers from gross physical deformities, suicide appears to be rare. Mr. Alvarez quotes a very moving passage by the wife of Osip Mandelstam.

> Whenever I talked of suicide, M used to say: "Why hurry? The end is the same everywhere, and here they may even hasten it for you." . . . In war, in the camps and during periods of terror, people think much less about death (let alone suicide) than when they are living normal lives. Whenever at some point on earth mortal terror and the pressure of utterly insoluble problems are present in a particularly intense form, general questions about the nature of being recede into the background. . . . Who knows what happiness is? Perhaps it is better to talk in more concrete terms of the fullness or intensity of existence, and in this sense there may have been something more deeply satisfying in our desperate clinging to life than in what people generally strive for.

7 Money is an objective fact and when they lose it, some people, as during the Wall Street crash, kill themselves, but in such cases I suspect that money has become a private symbol for their personal worth. To those, like Chatterton, who have always been poor, this cannot happen. I think Mr. Alvarez is wrong when he says: "Suicide was a solution to a practical problem."

8 What we all ask from others is mutual understanding. In the case of physical pain, this presents no difficulty: we can all sympathize, that is, feel *with* someone else's toothache. We can also all share in another's happiness, for we are all happy in the same way. It is otherwise when we are mentally unhappy, for each of us is unhappy in his own unique way, so that we can never imagine exactly what another is suffering. Even two persons, both with

suicidal feelings, cannot, I think, completely understand each other. Mr. Alvarez's definition of suicide as *The Closed World* applies to all mental unhappiness.

9 In consequence, no theory, sociological or psychological, of why people commit suicide is satisfactory. For instance, in the case histories of many suicides it is found that they lost a loved one in childhood, but so have many people who do not kill themselves. Again, if, as Freud believed, there is a death instinct, which I rather doubt, it must be active in all men, yet the majority do not cut short their lives. Climate has been invoked as a factor, but though their climate is the same, the suicide rate is high in Sweden but low in Norway. Protestantism, it has been alleged, is more conducive to suicide than Catholicism, but Austria, a Catholic country, has the third highest suicide rate in the world. A pessimistic philosophy of life certainly has no influence. Schopenhauer[1] and Thomas Hardy[2] lived to a ripe old age.

10 If suicide has become commoner in this century than in previous ones, I do not think this can be attributed to our particular social and political problems, for social-political life has been very grim throughout history. What does seem to play a role in suicide as in art is fashion. (Think of the effect on the young at the time of *Werther*.) The late Middle Ages were grim enough, no anesthetics or plumbing, lepers, the Inquisition, plundering mercenaries, yet the poetry of the period, the writings of Chaucer, Langland, Douglas, Dunbar are happy. Today happy art is regarded by many as rather vulgar.

11 Mr. Alvarez's first chapter is an account of the last few years in the life of his friend, the poet Sylvia Plath. I understand that her husband, Ted Hughes, thinks it inaccurate, and I am in no position to judge. It does seem clear from the facts that she intended her successful attempt to fail, as her two previous attempts had. Mr. Alvarez says, and I agree with him:

> . . . for the artist himself art is not necessarily therapeutic: he is not automatically relieved of his fantasies by expressing them. Instead, by some perverse logic of creation, the act of formal expression may simply make the dredged-up material more readily available to him. The result of handling it in his work may well be that he finds himself living it out . . . when an artist holds up a mirror to nature he finds out who and what he is: but the knowledge may change him irredeemably so that he becomes that image.

The moral, surely, is that one should be very cautious in what one chooses to write about.

12 In our aesthetic judgments I think Mr. Alvarez and I would usually agree—one would not call good poetry what the other would call bad. But in our personal tastes, i.e., the writers we really take to our hearts, it is clear that we differ.

13 Reading those he calls the Extremist Poets, Plath, Hughes, Berryman, I greatly admire their craftsmanship, but I cannot sympathize fully with what they are doing. The poetry which is really my cup of tea, that, for example, to

---

[1]Arthur Schopenhauer (1788–1860), German philosopher.—Ed.
[2]Thomas Hardy (1840–1928), English poet and novelist.—Ed.

name two modern Americans, of Frost and Marianne Moore, whether tragic, comic, or satiric, is always firmly rooted in staid common sense. Mr. Alvarez's taste, whether in modern poetry or in the poetry of the past, seems to be for the extreme. For example, he obviously loves John Donne whom, great as he is, I find an insufferable prima donna; give me George Herbert every time.

14 Mr. Alvarez's concluding chapter is devoted to his own unsuccessful attempt at suicide. It is most moving to read but rather puzzling. For instance, he tells us that, as a child, he kept repeating endlessly to himself *Iwishiwere-dead,* but he cannot tell us just why this was so. The statistics, he tells us, show that:

> The incidence of successful suicide rises with age and reaches its peak between the ages of fifty-five and sixty-five. In comparison, the young are great attempters: their peak is between twenty-five and forty-four.

Mr. Alvarez was thirty-one and already established in the literary world before he swallowed forty-four sleeping pills, but at home, so that he was found by his wife just in time to save him. To the outsider an attempted suicide has about it the aura of a sick joke. (Cowper's account, quoted in this book, of his desperate and always thwarted efforts to kill himself is pure black farce.) Mr. Alvarez's reactions to his failure are fascinating and cheer my heart.

> The truth is, in some way I had died. The overintensity, the tiresome excess of sensitivity and self-consciousness, of arrogance and idealism, which came in adolescence and stayed on beyond their due time, like some visiting bore, had not survived the coma . . . I was disappointed. Somehow, I felt, death had let me down; I had expected more of it. I had looked for something overwhelming, an experience which would clarify all my confusions. But it turned out to be simply a denial of experience. . . . Months later I began to understand that I had had my answer after all. . . . Once I had accepted that there weren't ever going to be any answers, even in death, I found to my surprise that I didn't much care whether I was happy or unhappy; "problems" and "the problem of problems" no longer existed. And that in itself is already the beginning of happiness.

I congratulate him. That is what I mean by common sense.

VOCABULARY

masochistic (1)	paradigm (5)
canonical (1)	insoluble (6)
deplenish (2)	alleged (9)
Gestapo (2)	therapeutic (11)
epic (4)	dredged-up (11)
valiant (4)	irredeemably (11)
Marxist (4)	aesthetic (12)
esoteric (4)	satiric (13)
Stoic (5)	staid (13)
apostasy (5)	prima donna (13)

QUESTIONS ON CONTENT

1. A good review should give the reader an idea of what the book being reviewed is about. To what extent does Auden's review do this?
2. What is the purpose of the quotations from Alvarez in paragraphs 6, 11, and 14?
3. In paragraph 2, Auden proposes two situations in which suicide would be a rational act. What does he mean by "rational," and what are the two situations?
4. Do you consider all forms of suicide immoral? Give reasons for your convictions.
5. What is the difference between subjective and objective suicide? (See paragraphs 6 and 7.)
6. In paragraphs 9 and 10, what popular theories about suicide does Auden reject?
7. How do you account for the fact that Auden is cheered by Alvarez's account of his own suicide attempt?

QUESTIONS ON FORM

1. What is Auden's summary judgment of Alvarez's book?
2. In paragraph 1, what is the meaning of *"le bon Dieu"* and the "canonical age of seventy"?
3. Identify these allusions in the essay:
    (a) Thomas Chatterton (paragraph 7)
    (b) *The Sorrows of Young Werther,* by Johann Wolfgang von Goethe (paragraph 10)
    (c) Geoffrey Chaucer (paragraph 10)
    (d) William Langland (paragraph 10)
    (e) Gavin Douglas (paragraph 10)
    (f) William Dunbar (paragraph 10)
4. Paragraph 8 is developed by contrast. What verbal guidepost indicates the contrast?

SUGGESTION FOR WRITING

Write a five-hundred-word review of a novel of your choice. Include the following:
    (a) summary of the content of the novel
    (b) some quotations here and there to give the reader an idea of the author's style
    (c) an explication of the author's meaning or purpose
    (d) your critical judgment of the novel

GEORGE BERNARD SHAW

BUNYAN AND SHAKESPEARE

This review of a play based on Bunyan's *Pilgrim's Progress* is typical of the Shavian method—arrogance combined with insight and wit. George Bernard Shaw (1856–1950) was a well-known British author and playwright.

The Pilgrim's Progress: a mystery play, with music, in four acts, by G. G. Collingham; founded on John Bunyan's immortal allegory. Olympic Theatre, 24 December, 1896.

1 When I saw a stage version of "The Pilgrim's Progress" announced for production, I shook my head, knowing that Bunyan is far too great a dramatist

for our theatre, which has never been resolute enough even in its lewdness and venality to win the respect and interest which positive, powerful wickedness always engages, much less the services of men of heroic conviction. Its greatest catch, Shakespeare, wrote for the theatre because, with extraordinary artistic powers, he understood nothing and believed nothing. Thirty-six big plays in five blank verse acts, and (as Mr. Ruskin, I think, once pointed out) not a single hero! Only one man in them all who believes in life, enjoys life, thinks life worth living, and has a sincere, unrhetorical tear dropped over his deathbed, and that man—Falstaff! What a crew they are—these Saturday to Monday athletic stock-broker Orlandos, these villains, fools, clowns, drunkards, cowards, intriguers, fighters, lovers, patriots, hypochondriacs who mistake themselves (and are mistaken by the author) for philosophers, princes without any sense of public duty, futile pessimists who imagine they are confronting a barren and unmeaning world when they are only contemplating their own worthlessness, self-seekers of all kinds, keenly observed and masterfully drawn from the romantic-commercial point of view. Once or twice we scent among them an anticipation of the crudest side of Ibsen's polemics on the Woman Question, as in "All's Well that Ends Well," where the man cuts as meanly selfish a figure beside his enlightened lady doctor wife as Helmer beside Nora; or in "Cymbeline," where Posthumus, having, as he believes, killed his wife for inconstancy, speculates for a moment on what his life would have been worth if the same standard of continence had been applied to himself. And certainly no modern study of the voluptuous temperament, and the spurious heroism and heroinism which its ecstasies produce, can add much to "Antony and Cleopatra," unless it were some sense of the spuriousness on the author's part. But search for statesmanship, or even citizenship, or any sense of the commonwealth, material or spiritual, and you will not find the making of a decent vestryman or curate in the whole horde. As to faith, hope, courage, conviction, or any of the true heroic qualities, you find nothing but death made sensational, despair made stage-sublime, sex made romantic, and barrenness covered up by sentimentality and the mechanical lilt of blank verse.

2 All that you miss in Shakespeare you find in Bunyan, to whom the true heroic came quite obviously and naturally. The world was to him a more terrible place than it was to Shakespeare; but he saw through it a path at the end of which a man might look not only forward to the Celestial City, but back on his life and say: "Tho' with great difficulty I am got hither, yet now I do not repent me of all the trouble I have been at to arrive where I am. My sword I give to him that shall succeed me in my pilgrimage, and my courage and skill to him that can get them." The heart vibrates like a bell to such utterances as this: to turn from it to "out, out, brief candle," and "The rest is silence," and "We are such stuff as dreams are made on"; and "our little life is rounded by a sleep" is to turn from life, strength, resolution, morning air and eternal youth, to the terrors of a drunken nightmare.

3 Let us descend now to the lower ground where Shakespeare is not

disabled by this inferiority in energy and elevation of spirit. Take one of his big fighting scenes, and compare its blank verse, in point of mere rhetorical strenuousness, with Bunyan's prose. Macbeth's famous cue for the fight with Macduff runs thus:

> "Yet I will try the last: before my body
> I throw my warlike shield. Lay on, Macduff,
> And damned be him that first cries Hold, enough!''

Turn from this jingle, dramatically right in feeling, but silly and resourceless in thought and expression, to Apollyon's cue for the fight in the Valley of Humiliation: "I am void of fear in this matter. Prepare thyself to die; for I swear by my infernal den that thou shalt go no farther: here will I spill thy soul." This is the same thing done masterly. Apart from its superior grandeur, force, and appropriateness, it is better clap-trap and infinitely better word-music.

4 Shakespeare, fond as he is of describing fights, has hardly ever sufficient energy or reality of imagination to finish without betraying the paper origin of his fancies by dragging in something classical in the style of the Cyclops' hammer falling "On Mars' armor, forged for proof eterne." Hear how Bunyan does it: "I fought till my sword did cleave to my hand; and when they were joined together as if the sword grew out of my arm; and when the blood run thorow my fingers, then I fought with most courage." Nowhere in all Shake-speare is there a touch like that of the blood running down through the man's fingers, and his courage rising to passion at it. Even in mere technical adaptation to the art of the actor, Bunyan's dramatic speeches are as good as Shakespeare's tirades. Only a trained dramatic speaker can appreciate the terse manageableness and effectiveness of such a speech as this, with its grandiose exordium, followed up by its pointed question and its stern threat: "By this I perceive thou art one of my subjects; for all that country is mine, and I am the Prince and the God of it. How is it then that thou hast ran away from thy King? Were it not that I hope thou mayst do me more service, I would strike thee now at one blow to the ground." Here there is no raving and swearing and rhyming and classical allusion. The sentences go straight to their mark; and their concluding phrases soar like the sunrise, or swing and drop like a hammer, just as the actor wants them.

5 I might multiply these instances by the dozen; but I had rather leave dramatic students to compare the two authors at first-hand. In an article on Bunyan lately published in the "Contemporary Review"—the only article worth reading on the subject I ever saw (yes, thank you; I am quite familiar with Macaulay's patronizing prattle about "The Pilgrim's Progress")—Mr. Richard Heath, the historian of the Anabaptists, shows how Bunyan learnt his lesson, not only from his own rough pilgrimage through life, but from the tradition of many an actual journey from real Cities of Destruction (under Alva), with Interpreters' houses and convey of Great-hearts all complete. Against such a man what chance had our poor immortal William, with his

"little Latin" (would it had been less, like his Greek!), his heathen mythology, his Plutarch, his Boccaccio, his Holinshed, his circle of London literary wits, soddening their minds with books and their nerves with alcohol (quite like us), and all the rest of his Strand and Fleet Street surroundings, activities, and interests, social and professional, mentionable and unmentionable? Let us applaud him, in due measure, in that he came out of it no blackguardly Bohemian, but a thoroughly respectable snob; raised the desperation and cynicism of its outlook to something like sublimity in his tragedies; dramatized its morbid, self-centered passions and its feeble and shallow speculations with all the force that was in them; disinfected it by copious doses of romantic poetry, fun, and common sense; and gave to its perpetual sex-obsession the relief of individual character and feminine winsomeness. Also—if you are a sufficiently good Whig—that after incarnating the spirit of the whole epoch which began with the sixteenth century and is ending (I hope) with the nineteenth, he is still the idol of all well-read children. But as he never thought a noble life worth living or a great work worth doing, because the commercial profit-and-loss sheet showed that the one did not bring happiness nor the other money, he never struck the great vein—the vein in which Bunyan told of that "man of a very stout countenance" who went up to the keeper of the book of life and said, not "Out, out, brief candle," but "Set down my name, sir," and immediately fell on the armed men and cut his way into heaven after receiving and giving many wounds.

VOCABULARY

resolute (1)	strenuousness (3)
venality (1)	clap-trap (3)
unrhetorical (1)	tirades (4)
hypochondriacs (1)	terse (4)
scent (1)	exordium (4)
polemics (1)	prattle (5)
inconstancy (1)	Anabaptists (5)
continence (1)	soddening (5)
spurious (1)	blackguardly (5)
commonwealth (1)	copious (5)
vestryman (1)	winsomeness (5)
curate (1)	Whig (5)

QUESTIONS ON CONTENT

1. What is the real purpose of Shaw's critical review?
2. What does Shaw mean when he says that Shakespeare "never struck the great vein" (paragraph 5)? What reason does he give for Shakespeare's failure?
3. If you were to defend Shakespeare against Shaw's criticism, how would you proceed?
4. What criticisms does Shaw level at Shakespeare's fighting scenes? (See paragraphs 3 and 4.)

5. According to Shaw, what advantage did Bunyan have over Shakespeare with respect to background and experience?

QUESTIONS ON FORM

1. Shaw is noted for his witty sarcasm. What are some examples of this approach?
2. Who are the following people alluded to in the article? State why each of them is mentioned.
   (a) John Ruskin (1)
   (b) Plutarch (5)
   (c) Boccaccio (5)
   (d) Holinshed (5)
3. What purpose do the parentheses usually serve in this essay?
4. What is the purpose of the reference to Alva in paragraph 5? Who was he?
5. What is your judgment of Shaw's style? Comment on his sentence structure, choice of words, and tone.

SUGGESTIONS FOR WRITING

1. Choosing one of the following pairs of writers, write an essay in which you attempt to explain why you prefer one to the other. Be specific in your allusions to each author's work.
   (a) J. D. Salinger and Ernest Hemingway
   (b) Robert Frost and T. S. Eliot
   (c) Tennessee Williams and Edward Albee
2. Draw a five-hundred-word contrast between two poets of your choice. Choose poets from the same period and make sure that your bases of contrast are clear.

VINCENT CANBY

ERICH SEGAL'S ROMANTIC TALE BEGINS RUN

A noted movie critic tells why the film version of *Love Story* is more satisfactory than the novel.

1 What can you say about a movie about a 25-year-old girl who died?

2 That it is beautiful. And romantic. That it contains a fantasy for just about everyone, perhaps with the exception of Herbert Marcuse. That it looks to be clean and pure and without artifice, even though it is possibly as sophisticated as any commercial American movie ever made. That my admiration for the mechanics of it slops over into a real admiration for the movie itself.

3 I'm talking of course, about "Love Story," the movie from which Erich Segal extracted his best-selling non-novel, mostly, it seems, by appending "she said's" and "I said's" and an occasional "I remonstrated" to the dialogue in his original screenplay.

4 The film, which opened yesterday at the Loew's State I and Tower East

Theaters, is about a love affair so perfect that even the death that terminates it becomes a symbol of its perfection.

5 When, at the end, Jenny (née Cavilleri), the self-styled social zero from Cranston, R.I., the daughter of an Italian baker, is dying of a carefully unidentified blood disease in the arms of her husband, Oliver Barrett 4th, the preppie[1] millionaire from Boston, there is nothing to disfigure love, or faith, or even the complexion. It's as if she were suffering from some kind of vaguely unpleasant Elizabeth Arden treatment. Jenny doesn't die. She just slips away in beauty.

6 The knowledge that Jenny will—how should I put it—disappear not only gives the movie its shape (it is told in flashback), but it also endows everything—from a snowball fight in the Harvard Yard to a confrontation with snob parents in Ipswich—with an intensity that is no less sweet for being fraudulent.

7 Curiously, the novel, which I found almost unreadable (I think it might be as readily absorbed if kept under one's pillow), plays very well as a movie, principally, I suspect because Jenny is not really Jenny but Ali MacGraw, a kind of all-American, Radcliffe madonna figure, and Oliver Barrett 4th is really Ryan O'Neal, an intense, sensitive young man whose handsomeness has a sort of crookedness to it that keeps him from being a threat to male members of the audience. They are both lovely.

8 Then, too, Arthur Hiller, the director, has framed what is essentially a two-character story of undergraduate love with such seeming simplicity that nothing confuses the basic situation. He also associates his film and his characters with all of the good things in life. Jenny and Oliver fall in love in the snow (snow, clean and pure, is very important in the movie). They court in front of libraries, and they make love (nothing too explicit mind you) while doing homework.

9 When Jenny swears, she fondly uses a four-letter word that was shocking in the fifties, but that even mid-American matrons have heard now. When Oliver graduates from law school, he takes a job with an old, extremely respectable, New York law firm, but it's one that specializes in civil-rights cases. When Jenny is growing weaker, she can't remember the Mozart Köchel listings she once knew. Jenny and Oliver have (middle) class.

10 "Love Story" not only revives a kind of movie fiction that I'd thought vanished, it also revives the rich, WASP movie hero who rebels, but not too drastically, and it brings back the kind of wonderful movie aphorism that persists in saying nothing when it tries to say the most ("love means never having to say you're sorry").

11 Francis Lai's background score mixes Bach and Mozart and Handel with Lai, and resolutely avoids rock. Although Jenny does disappear at the end, everyone in the audience can take heart in identification—the ladies, because they can see how much will be missed, and the gentlemen, who will have the honor of being abandoned by one of fiction's most blessed females. I

[1]Prep student.—Ed.

might add that Oliver, though distraught, is also very rich, and he has promised Jenny to be a merry widower.

12 I can't remember any movie of such comparable high-style kitsch[2] since Leo McCarey's "Love Affair" (1939) and his 1957 remake, "An Affair to Remember." The only really depressing thing about "Love Story" is the thought of all of the terrible imitations that will inevitably follow it.

VOCABULARY

artifice (2)	explicit (8)
appending (3)	WASP (10)
remonstrated (3)	aphorism (10)
née (5)	resolutely (11)
fraudulent (6)	distraught (11)
madonna (7)	

QUESTIONS ON CONTENT

1. How would you summarize Vincent Canby's overall judgment of the movie *Love Story*?
2. The Herbert Marcuse mentioned in paragraph 2 is a university professor known for Marxist views. Why is he mentioned as one for whom the movie would have no fantasy?
3. According to Canby, what gives the movie its intensity?
4. Which does Canby judge to be superior—the movie or the novel? Why?
5. If you agree with Canby that the movie is "high-style kitsch," then what keeps it from being low-style kitsch? If you believe that the movie is low-style kitsch, then what makes it so?

QUESTIONS ON FORM

1. What is the significance of Canby's beginning?
2. In his title, why does Canby call the story a "tale"? What are the connotations of this word?
3. What is the tone of paragraph 6?
4. How much of the film plot does this review reveal?
5. What chance did Canby take at the end of his review?

SUGGESTIONS FOR WRITING

1. Write your own review of *Love Story*, beginning with your overall judgment of the movie and including summaries as well as explications of the key scenes.
2. Using a popular current movie of your choice, review the movie, beginning with your overall judgment and including summaries as well as explications of the key scenes.

[2]See Gilbert Highet, "Kitsch," p. 195.—Ed.

TERM PAPER SUGGESTION

Write a five-page critical analysis of one of Hemingway's novels. Use a minimum of five secondary sources to document your paper. (Your teacher may wish to substitute another author for Hemingway.)

CHAPTER WRITING ASSIGNMENTS

1. Discuss the role of scholarship in the evaluation of literature.
2. Write an essay in which you differentiate between talent and craftsmanship in literature.
3. Discuss the standards by which all art should be judged. Be sure to impose some organization on your essay.

twelve

Writing for the Sciences

advice

MORRIS FREEDMAN

THE SEVEN SINS OF TECHNICAL WRITING

This article discusses the seven most frequent errors in technical writing and
advises the student on avoiding them. Since these same errors are common
to all writing, the nonscience student should also find this article useful.

1 Let me start by saying at once that I do not come to you tonight just as a
professor of English, for, frankly, I do not think that I would have very much
to say to you only as someone expert in the history of the use—and misuse—
of the language. And any remarks on literature might be confusing, at least
without extensive elaboration, for the values and objectives of literature seem
so very different at first from those of technical writing—although fundamentally many of these values and objectives coincide. And I am sure that you are
more than familiar with such things as clichés, comma splices, fragmentary
sentences, and the other abominations we deal with in freshman composition.
These obviously have nothing to do specifically with technical writing.

2 But I want to say, before anyone thinks that I class technical writing
entirely by itself, immune from rules and requirements of communication that
govern other kinds of writing, that technical writing calls for the same kind of
attention and must be judged by the same standards as any other kind of
writing; *indeed, it calls for a greater attention and for higher standards.* And I
say this as a former science and medical writer for the popular press; as a
former writer of procedure manuals and directives for the government; as a
former editor of technical studies in sociology, statistics, law, and psychology;
as a former general magazine editor; as a writer of fiction, essays, and

481

scholarly articles; and, not least, as a professor of English. We can see at once why technical writing must be measured by higher standards, or, at least, by different ones, if anyone will not grant me that they are higher. Technical writing is so immediately functional. Confusing directions accompanying an essential device in a jet plane may result in disaster; bad writing elsewhere can have as its most extreme effect merely boredom.

3 Yet, while technical writing implicitly calls for great care, it differs from other kinds of writing in that its practitioners are, by and large, first technicians and only incidentally writers. And principally because of this arrangement, I think, technical writing has become characterized by a collection of sins peculiar to this discipline alone. I say the *collection* is peculiar to technical writing, not any one of the sins alone. Any newspaper, weekly magazine, encyclopedia, textbook, any piece of writing you might name, will contain one or another of these sins, in greater or lesser profusion. But I know of no kind of writing that contains as many different sins in such great number as technical writing, and with such great potential for danger. To repeat, the sins in the world at large—at least, of the sort I'm talking about—often don't matter much. And sometimes, too, they don't matter in technical writing. As my students argue when I correct them in informative writing: "You got the meaning, didn't you?" Yes, I did, and so do we all get the meaning when a newspaper, a magazine, a set of directions stammers out its message. And I suppose, too, we could travel by ox-cart, or dress in burlap, or drive around with rattling fenders, and still get through a day.

4 But technical writing in this age can no more afford widespread sloppiness of expression, confusion of meaning, rattle-trap construction than a supersonic missile can afford to be made of the wrong materials, or be put together haphazardly with screws jutting out here and there, or have wiring circuits that may go off any way at all, or—have a self-destructive system that fails because of some fault along the way in construction. Technical writing today—as I need hardly reiterate to this audience—if it is much less than perfect in its streamlining and design may well result in machines that are less than trim, and in operation that is not exactly neat. This is at worst; at best, poor technical writing, when its effect is minimized by careful reading, hinders efficiency, wastes time. Let me remark too that the commission of any one of these sins, and of any one of many, many lesser ones, is really not likely alone to be fatal, just as one loose screw by itself is not likely to destroy a machine; but always, we know, sins come in bunches, the sin of avarice often links hands with the sin of gluttony, one loose screw may mean others, and, anyway, the ideal of no sins at all—especially in something like technical writing, where the pain of self-denial should be minimal—is always to be strived for.

5 A final word before I launch into the sins (whose parade, so long delayed, will prove, I hope, so much more edifying—like a medieval tableau). The seven I list might be described as cardinal ones, and as such they are broad and overlapping, perhaps, rather than specific and very clearly distin-

guished from one another. They all contribute to making technical writing less clear, concise, coherent, and correct than it should be.

6 Sin 1, then, might be described as that of *Indifference,* neglecting the reader. I do not mean anything so simple as writing down to an engineer or physicist, although this is all too common and may be considered part of this sin. This writing down—elaborating the obvious—is one reason the abstract or summary has become so indispensable a part of technical reports; very often, it is all the expert needs to read of the whole report, the rest being a matter of all too obvious detailing. Nor do I mean writing above the heads of your audience either, which is a defect likely to be taken care of by a thoughtful editor. Both writing over or under the heads of your reader, or to the side, are really matters of careless aiming and, as such, of indifference, too. But what I mean here by indifference are shortcuts of expression, elliptical diction, sloppy organization, bringing up points and letting them hang unresolved, improper or inadequate labelling of graphic material, and the like. This is communication by gutturals, grunts, shrugs, as though it were not worth the trouble to articulate carefully, as though the reader didn't matter— or didn't exist. This is basically an attitude of disrespect: *Caveat lector*—let the reader beware. Let the reader do his own work; the writer isn't going to help him.

7 Here is the concluding sentence from a quite respectable report, one most carefully edited and indeed presented as a model in a handbook for technical writers used by a great chemical firm. The sentence is relatively good, for it takes only a second reading to work out its meaning (perhaps only a slow first one for someone trained in reading this kind of writing):

> When it is assumed that all of the cellulose is converted to ethyl cellulose, reaction conversion of cellulose to ethyl cellulose, per cent of cellulose reacted, and reaction yield of ethyl cellulose based on cellulose are each equal to 100%.

8 This is admittedly a tough sentence to get across simply, considering that "cellulose" is repeated in several different contexts. Yet two guiding principles would have made it much clearer: (1) always put for your reader first things first (here, the meaning hangs on the final phrase, "each equal to 100%," which comes at the end of a complicated series); and (2) clearly separate items in a series. (The second rule seems to me one of the most important in technical writing where so many things have to be listed so often.) Here is the recast sentence:

> If all the cellulose is converted to ethyl cellulose, each of the following factors is then equal to 100%:
>
> 1. reaction conversion of cellulose to ethyl cellulose.
> 2. proportion of cellulose reacted.
> 3. reaction yield of ethyl cellulose based on cellulose.

The changes are not great, certainly, but in the process we have eliminated the indisputable notion of a percent being equal to a percent, and have arranged the series so that both the eye and the mind together can grasp the information immediately. Sin 1 then can be handled, one way, by cutting out indirect Rube Goldbergish contraptions and hitting your points directly on their heads, one, two, three.

9 The remaining sins I shall discuss are extensions of this primal one, disregard for the reader. Sin 2 may be designated as *Fuzziness,* that is, a general fuzziness of communication—vague words, meaningless words, wrong ones. The reader uses his own experience to supply the meaning in such writing; the writing itself acts only as a collection of clues. The military specializes in this sort of thing. I recall an eerie warning in an air force mess hall: "Anyone smoking in or around this mess hall will be dealt with accordingly." It still haunts me. Here is a caution in a handbook of technical writing with which you may be familiar: "Flowery, euphemistic protestations of gratitude are inappropriate." We know what this means, of course, but we ourselves supply the exact meaning. It happens that a "euphemism" is "the substitution of an inoffensive or mild expression for one that may offend or suggest something unpleasant." At least, that's what *Webster's Collegiate* says it is.

10 Here are some other examples: "The intrinsic labyrinth of wires must be first disentangled." The writer meant "network," not "labyrinth"; and I think he meant "internal" for "intrinsic" and "untangled" for "disentangled." Item: "The liquid contents of the container should then be disgorged via the spout by the operator." Translation: "The operator should then empty the container." Here is a final long one:

> When the element numbered one is brought into tactual contact with the element numbered two, when the appropriate conditions of temperature have been met above the previously determined safety point, then there will be exhibited a tendency for the appropriate circuit to be closed and consequently to serve the purpose of activating an audible warning device.

Translation:

> When the heat rises above the set safety point, element one touches element two, closing a circuit and setting off a bell.

Prescription to avoid Sin 2: use concrete, specific words and phrases whenever you can, and use only those words whose meaning you are sure of. (A dictionary, by the way, is only a partial help in determining the correct and *idiomatic* use of a word.) English is perhaps the richest of languages in offering a variety of alternatives for saying the same thing.

11 Sin 3 might be called the sin of *Emptiness.* It is the use of jargon and big words, pretentious ones, where perfectly appropriate and acceptable small and normal words are available. (There is nothing wrong with big words in themselves, provided they are the best ones for the job. A steam shovel is right for moving a boulder, ridiculous for picking up a handkerchief.) We may want to connect this sin with the larger, more universal one of pride, the general desire to seem important and impressive. During World War II a high

government official devoted much time to composing an effective warning for a sticker to be put above light switches. He emerged with "Illumination is required to be extinguished on these premises on the termination of daily activities," or something of the sort. He meant "Put the lights out when you go home."

12 The jargon I'm talking about is not the technical language you use normally and necessarily for efficient communication. I have in mind only the use of a big word or a jumble of words for something that can be said more efficiently with familiar words and straightforward expressions. I have in mind also a kind of code language used to show that you're an insider, somewhere or other: "Production-wise, that's a high-type machine that can be used to finalize procedure. The organization is enthused." There is rarely any functional justification for saying "utilize" or "utilization" for "use," "prior to" for "before," "the answer in the affirmative or negative" for "yes or no," or for using any of the "operators, or false verbal limbs," as George Orwell called them,[1] like "render inoperative," "prove unacceptable," "exhibit a tendency to," "serve the purpose of," and so on and on.

13 Again, one can handle this sin simply by overcoming a reluctance to saying things directly; the most complex things in the world can be said in simple words, often of one syllable. Consider propositions in higher math or logic, the Supreme Court decisions of men like Brandeis and Holmes, the poetry of Shakespeare. I cannot resist quoting here Sir Arthur Quiller-Couch's rendition in jargon of Hamlet's "To be or not to be, that is the question." I am sure you all know the full jargon rendition of the soliloquy. "To be, or the contrary? Whether the former or the latter be preferable would seem to admit of some difference of opinion."

14 Sin 4 is an extension of 3: just plain *Wordiness*. The principle here is that if you can say anything with more words than necessary for the job, then by all means do so. I've already cited examples of this sin above, but compounded with other sins. Here is a purer example, the opening of a sentence in a technical writing handbook: "Material to be contained on the cover of the technical report includes . . ." This can be reduced to "The cover of the technical report should include . . ." Another example, less pure: "The front-mounted blade of the bulldozer is employed for earth moving operations on road construction jobs." Translation: "The bulldozer's front blade moves earth in road building." Item: "There is another way of accomplishing this purpose, and that is by evaporation." Translation: "Evaporation is another way of doing this." Instead of saying simply that "the bulldozer's front blade moves earth," you say it "is employed for earth moving operations," throwing in "employed" and "operations," as though "moves" alone is too weak to do this tremendous job. The cure for this sin? Simply reverse the mechanism: say what you have to in the fewest words.

15 Sin 5, once again an extension of the immediately preceding sin, is a matter of *Bad Habits*, the use of pat phrases, awkward expressions, confusing

[1]See "Politics and the English Language," p. 299.—Ed.

sentence structure, that have, unfortunately, become second nature. Again, I'm not alluding to the perfectly natural use of familiar technical expressions, which may literally be called clichés, but which are not efficiently replaceable. Sin 5 is a matter of just not paying attention to what you say, with the result that when you do suddenly pay attention, you see the pointlessness or even humor of what you have set down. Perhaps the most common example of this sin is what has been called "deadwood," or what may be called "writing for the simple minded." Examples: "red in color," "three in number," "square in shape," "the month of January," "the year 1956," "ten miles in distance," and the like. What else is red but a color, three but a number, square but a shape, January but a month, 1956 but a year, ten miles but a distance? To say that something is "two inches wide and three inches long" is to assume that your reader can't figure out length and width from the simple dimensions "two inches by three inches." I once read that a certain machine was 18 feet high, "vertically," the writer made sure to add; and another time that a certain knob should be turned "right, in direction."

16 A caution is needed here. There are many obvious instances when qualification is necessary. To say that something is "light," for example, is plainly mysterious unless you add "in color" or "in weight" or, perhaps, "in density" (unless the context makes such addition "deadwood").

17 I would include under Sin 5 the locutions "as far as that is concerned" (lately shortened to "as far as that"), "as regards," "with regard to," "in the case of" ("In the case of the case enclosing the instrument, the case is being studied"). These are all too often just lazy ways of making transitions (and, thus, incidentally, quite justifiable when speed of writing is a factor).

18 Sin 6 is the *Deadly Passive,* or, better, deadening passive; it takes the life out of writing, making everything impersonal, eternal, remote and dead. The deadly passive is guaranteed to make any reading matter more difficult to understand, to get through, and to retain. Textbook writers in certain fields have long ago learned to use the deadly passive to create difficulties where none exist; this makes their subject seem weightier, and their accomplishment more impressive. (And, of course, if this is ever what you have in mind on an assignment, then by all means use the deadly passive.) Sin 6 is rarely found alone; it is almost indispensable for fully carrying out the sins of wordiness and jargon. Frequently, of course, the passive is not a sin and not deadly, for there simply is no active agent and the material must be put impersonally.

19 Examples of this sin are so easy to come by, it is difficult to find one better than another. Here is a relatively mild example of Sin 6.

> The standardization of procedure in print finishing can be a very important factor in the efficient production of service pictures. In so far as possible, the smallest number of types and sizes of paper should be employed, and the recommended processing followed. The fewer paper grades and processing procedures used, the fewer errors and make-overs that are likely. Make-overs are time-consuming and costly.

20 Here it is with the deadly passive out and some other changes made:

To produce service pictures efficiently, a standard way of finishing prints can be very important. You should use as few types and sizes of paper as possible, and you should follow the recommended procedure for processing. In this way, you will make fewer errors, and have to re-do less work. You save time and money.

Associated with the deadly passive, as you might see from the two passages above, is the use of abstract nouns and adjectives for verbs. Verbs always live; nouns and adjectives just sit there, and abstract nouns aren't even there. Of course, there are a number of other ways of undoing the passivity of the passage I quoted, and of making other improvements, just as there were other ways of handling any of the specimens I have cited in the train of horrors accompanying my pageant of sins.

21 Finally we come to Sin 7, the one considered the deadliest by many, and not only by teachers of English but by technical writers and technologists of various sorts: *Mechanical Errors.* I don't think this sin the deadliest of all. It does happen to be the easiest one to recognize, the one easiest to deal with "quantitatively," so to speak, and the easiest one to resist. I suppose it is considered deadliest because then those who avoid it can so quickly feel virtuous. It can promptly be handled by good works alone. Actually most technical writing happens to be mechanically impeccable; not one of the examples I have used tonight had very much mechanically wrong with it. If anything, technical people tend to make too much of formal mechanisms. I remember working with a physicist who had much trouble saying anything in writing. While his general incapacity to write was almost total, one thing he did know, and know firmly, and that was that a split infinitive was to be abhorred. That, and using a preposition to end a sentence with. He could never communicate the simplest notion coherently, but he never split an infinitive or left a preposition at the end of a sentence. If Nobel Prizes were to be awarded for never splitting infinitives or for encapsulating prepositions within sentences, he would be a leading candidate.

22 There are a handful of mechanical errors which are relevant to technical writing, and these are important because they are so common, especially in combination with other sins. (Split infinitives or sentence-ending prepositions, need I say, are not among them.) These are dangling participles and other types of poorly placed modifiers, and ambiguous references. There are others, a good number of others, but the ones I mention creep in most insidiously and most often.

23 Here are some examples stripped down to emphasize the errors:

Raising the temperature, the thermostat failed to function.
Who or what raised the temperature? Not the thermostat, I presume; and if
    it did somehow, as the result of current flowing in its wiring, then this
    ought to be said quite plainly.

The apparatus is inappropriately situated in the corner since it is too small.
What is too small? Apparatus or corner?

Every element in the device must not be considered to be subject to abnormal stress.

What is meant here is that "Not every element in the apparatus must be considered subject to abnormal stress," almost the opposite of the original taken literally.

24 I should like to conclude by emphasizing something I glanced at in my introduction, that the seven sins of technical writing are to be avoided not so much by a specific awareness of each, accompanied by specific penance for each, as by a much more general awareness, by an attitude toward subject matter, writing process, and reader that can best be described only as "respectful." You will not help yourself very much if you rely on such purely machanical aids as Rudolf Flesch's formulas[2] for "readable writing," or on slide rules measuring readability, much as you may be tempted to do so. These can be devil's snares, ways to make you think you are avoiding sin. There are no general texts, either, at present that will help you in more than very minor ways. The only aids you can safely depend on are the good book itself, that is, a good dictionary (there are many poor ones), any of the several volumes by H. W. Fowler, and occasional essays, here and there, by George Orwell, Jacques Barzun, Herbert Read, Somerset Maugham, and others. And these, I stress, can only be *aids*. What is most important in eliminating sin in technical writing is general attitude—as it may well be in eliminating sin anywhere.

25 I repeat that technical writing must be as rationally shaped as a technical object. A piece of technical writing, after all, is something that is shaped into being for a special purpose, much as a technical object. The design engineer should be guided in his work by the requirements of function almost alone. (Of course, if he happens to have a boss who likes to embellish the object with useless doo-dads, why then he may have to modify his work accordingly to keep his job—as automobile designers do every day; but we try never to have in mind unreasonable situations of this sort.) It is as pointless for the design engineer to use three bolts where one would do (both for safety and function), to make an object square when its use dictates it should be round, to take the long way through a process when there is a short way, as it is for the technical writer to commit any of the sins I have mentioned. Technical writing— informative writing of any sort—should be as clean, as functional, as inevitable as any modern machine designed to do a job well. If I will not be misunderstood in throwing out this thought, I should like to suggest to you that good technical writing should be like good poetry—every word in its exact place for maximum effect, no word readily replaceable by another, not a word too many or too few, and the whole combination, so to speak, invisible, not calling attention to its structure, seemingly effortless, perfectly adapted to its subject.

[2] In 1943, Rudolf Flesch introduced a readability formula based on three factors: average sentence length, relative number of affixed morphemes (prefixes, suffixes, inflectional endings) and relative number of personal references.

26 If one takes this general approach to the shaping of a piece of technical writing, and there really can't be much excuse for any other, then there is no need to worry about any of the sins I mention. Virtue may not come at once or automatically, for good writing never comes without effort, however fine one's intentions, but it will certainly come, and perhaps even bring with it that same satisfaction the creative engineer experiences. Technical writing cleansed of its sins is no less worthy, no less impressive, an enterprise than good engineering itself. Like mathematics to physics, technical writing is a handmaid to technology, but like mathematics, too, it can be a helpmate, that is, an equal partner. But it can achieve this reward of virtue only by emphasizing the virtues of writing equally with those of technology.

VOCABULARY

implicitly (3)	diction (6)
profusion (3)	labyrinth (10)
reiterate (4)	idiomatic (10)
avarice (4)	locutions (17)
medieval tableau (5)	impeccable (21)
elliptical (6)	encapsulating (21)

discussion

MALCOLM COWLEY

SOCIOLOGICAL HABIT PATTERNS IN LINGUISTIC TRANSMOGRIFICATION

In the essay below, a well-known editor and author takes to task those sociologists who have become so engrossed with jargon that they can no longer express themselves in clear and simple English.

1 I have a friend who started as a poet and then decided to take a post-graduate degree in sociology. For his doctoral dissertation he combined his two interests by writing on the social psychology of poets. He had visited poets by the dozen, asking each of them a graded series of questions, and his conclusions from the interviews were modest and useful, though reported in what seemed to me a barbarous jargon. After reading the dissertation I wrote and scolded him. "You have such a fine sense of the poet's craft," I said, "that you shouldn't have allowed the sociologists to seduce you into writing their professional slang—or at least that's my judgemental response to your role selection."

2 My friend didn't write to defend himself; he waited until we met again. Then dropping his voice, he said: "I knew my dissertation was badly written, but I had to get my degree. If I had written it in English, Professor Blank"—

he mentioned a rather distinguished name—"would have rejected it. He would have said it was merely belletristic."

3 From that time I began to study the verbal folkways of the sociologists. I read what they call "the literature." A few sociologists write the best English they are capable of writing, and I suspect that they are the best men in the field. There is no mystery about them. If they go wrong, their mistakes can be seen and corrected. Others, however—and a vast majority—write in a language that has to be learned almost like Esperanto. It has a private vocabulary which, in addition to strictly sociological terms, includes new words for the commonest actions, feelings, and circumstances. It has the beginnings of a new grammar and syntax, much inferior to English grammar in force and precision. So far as it has an effect on standard English, the effect is largely pernicious.

4 Sometimes it misleads the sociologists themselves, by making them think they are profoundly scientific at points where they are merely verbose. I can illustrate by trying a simple exercise in translation, that is, by expressing an idea first in English and then seeing what it looks like in the language of sociology.

5 An example that comes to hand is the central idea of an article by Norman E. Green, printed in the February, 1956, issue of the *American Sociological Review*. In English, his argument read as follows:

> Rich people live in big houses set farther apart than those of poor people. By looking at an aerial photograph of any American city, we can distinguish the richer from the poorer neighborhoods.

6 I won't have to labor over a sociological expression of the same idea, because Mr. Green has saved me the trouble. Here is part of his contribution to comparative linguistics. "In effect, it was hypothesized," he says—a sociologist must never say "I assumed," much less "I guessed"—"that certain physical data categories including housing types and densities, land use characteristics, and ecological location"—not just "location," mind you, but "ecological location," which is almost equivalent to locational location—"constitute a scalable content area. This could be called a continuum of residential desirability. Likewise, it was hypothesized that several social data categories, describing the same census tracts, and referring generally to the social stratification system of the city, would also be scalable. This scale could be called a continuum of socio-economic status. Thirdly, it was hypothesized that there would be a high positive correlation between the scale types on each continuum."

7 Here, after ninety-four words, Mr. Green is stating, or concealing, an assumption with which most laymen would have started, that rich people live in good neighborhoods. He is now almost ready for his deduction, or snapper:

> This relationship would define certain linkages between the social and physical structure of the city. It would also provide a precise definition of the commonalities among several spatial distributions. By the same token, the correlation

between the residential desirability scale and the continuum of socio-economic status would provide an estimate of the predictive value of aerial photographic data relative to the social ecology of the city.

8 Mr. Green has used 160 words—counting "socio-economic" as only one—to express an idea that a layman would have stated in thirty-three. As a matter of fact, he has used many more than 160 words, since the whole article is an elaboration of this one thesis. Whatever may be the virtues of the sociological style—or Socspeak, as George Orwell might have called it—it is not specifically designed to save ink and paper. Let us briefly examine some of its other characteristics.

9 A layman's first impression of sociological prose, as compared with English prose, is that it contains a very large proportion of abstract words, most of them built on Greek or Latin roots. Often—as in the example just quoted—they are used to inflate or transmogrify a meaning that could be clearly expressed in shorter words surviving from King Alfred's time.

10 These Old English or Anglo-Saxon words are in number less than one-tenth of the entries in the largest dictionaries. But they are the names of everyday objects, attributes, and actions, and they are also the pronouns, the auxilliary verbs, and most of the prepositions and conjunctions, so that they form the grammatical structure of the language. The result is that most novelists use six Anglo-Saxon words for every one derived from French, Latin, or Greek, and that is probably close to the percentage that would be found in spoken English.

11 For comparison or contrast, I counted derivations in the passage quoted from the *American Sociological Review,* which is a typical example of "the literature." No less than forty-nine per cent of Mr. Green's prose consists of words from foreign or classical languages. By this standard of measurement, his article is more abstruse than most textbooks of advanced chemistry and higher mathematics, which are said to contain only forty per cent of such words.

12 In addition to being abstruse, the language of the sociologists is also rich in neologisms. Apparently they like nothing better than inventing a word, deforming a word, or using a technical word in a strange context. Among their favorite nouns are "ambit," "extensity" (for "extent"), "scapegoating," "socializee," "ethnicity," "directionality," "cathexis," "affect" (for "feeling"), "maturation" (for both "maturing" and "maturity"), and "commonalities" (for "points in common"). Among their favorite adjectives are "processual," "prestigeful," and "insightful"—which last is insightful to murder—and perhaps their favorite adverb is "minimally," which seems to mean "in some measure." Their maximal pleasure seems to lie in making new combinations of nouns and adjectives and nouns used as adjectives, until the reader feels that he is picking his way through a field of huge boulders, lost among "universalistic-specific achievement patterns" and "complementary role-expectation-sanction systems," as he struggles vainly toward "ego-integrative action orientation," guided only by "orientation to improvement of the

gratification-deprivation balance of the actor"—which last is Professor Talcott Parson's rather involved way of saying "the pleasure principle."

13 But Professor Parsons, head of the Sociology Department at Harvard, is not the only delinquent recidivist, convicted time and again of corrupting the language. Among sociologists in general there is a criminal fondness for using complicated terms when there are simple ones available. A child says "Do it again," a teacher says "Repeat the exercise," but the sociologist says "It was determined to replicate the investigation." Instead of saying two things are alike or similar, as a layman would do, the sociologist describes them as being either isomorphic or homologous. Instead of saying that they are different, he calls them allotropic. Every form of leadership or influence is called a hegemony.

14 A sociologist never cuts anything in half or divides it in two like a layman. Instead he dichotomizes it, bifurcates it, subjects it to a process of binary fission, or restructures it in a dyadic conformation—around polar foci.

The New Grammar

15 So far I have been dealing with the vocabulary of sociologists, but their private language has a grammar too, and one that should be the subject of intensive research by the staff of a very well-endowed foundation. I have space to mention only a few of its more striking features.

16 The first of these is the preponderance of nouns over all the other parts of speech. Nouns are used in hyphenated pairs or dyads, and sometimes in triads, tetrads, and pentads. Nouns are used as adjectives without change of form, and they are often used as verbs, with or without the suffix "ize." The sociological language is gritty with nouns, like sanded sugar.

17 On the other hand, it is poor in pronouns. The singular pronoun of the first person has entirely disappeared, except in case histories, for the sociologist never comes forward as "I." Sometimes he refers to himself as "the author" or "the investigator," or as "many sociologists," or even as "the best sociologists," when he is advancing a debatable opinion. On rare occasions he calls himself "we," like Queen Elizabeth speaking from the throne, but he usually avoids any personal form and writes as if he were a force of nature.

18 The second-personal pronoun has also disappeared, for the sociologist pretends to be speaking not to living persons but merely for the record. Masculine and feminine pronouns of the third person are used with parsimony, and most sociologists prefer to say "the subject," or "X——," or "the interviewee," where a layman would use the simple "he" or "she." As for the neuter pronoun of the third person, it survives chiefly as the impersonal subject of a passive verb. "It was hypothesized," we read, or "It was found to be the case." Found by *whom?*

19 The neglect and debasement of the verb is another striking feature of "the literature." The sociologist likes to reduce a transitive verb to an intransitive, so that he speaks of people's adapting, adjusting, transferring,

relating, and identifying, with no more of a grammatical object than if they were coming or going. He seldom uses transitive verbs of action, like "break," "injure," "help," and "adore." Instead he uses verbs of relation, verbs which imply that one series of nouns and adjectives, used as the compound subject of a sentence, is larger or smaller than, dominant over, subordinate to, causative of, or resultant from another series of nouns and adjectives.

20 Considering this degradation of the verb, I have wondered how one of Julius Caesar's boasts could be translated into Socspeak. What Caesar wrote was *"Veni, vidi, vici"*—only three words, all of them verbs. The English translation is in six words: "I came, I saw, I conquered," and three of the words are first-personal pronouns, which the sociologist is taught to avoid. I suspect that he would have to write: "Upon the advent of the investigator, his hegemony became minimally coextensive with the areal unit rendered visible by his successive displacements in space."

21 The whole sad situation leads me to dream of a vast allegorical painting called "The Triumph of the Nouns." It would depict a chariot of victory drawn by the other conquered parts of speech—the adverbs and adjectives still robust, if yoked and harnessed; the prepositions bloated and pale; the conjunctions tortured; the pronouns reduced to sexless skeletons; the verbs dichotomized and feebly tottering—while behind them, arrogant, overfed, roseate, spilling over the triumphal car, would be the company of nouns in Roman togas and Greek chitons, adorned with laurel branches and flowering hegemonies.

VOCABULARY

belletristic (2)	neologisms (12)
Esperanto (3)	recidivist (13)
pernicious (3)	preponderance (16)
hypothesized (6)	parsimony (18)
scalable (6)	debasement (19)
continuum (6)	transitive (19)
correlation (6)	intransitive (19)
commonalities (7)	coextensive (20)
transmogrify (9)	allegorical (21)
derivations (11)	roseate (21)
abstruse (11)	chitons (21)

QUESTIONS ON CONTENT

1. What is the relationship of the title to the content of the essay? Suggest a plainer title.
2. Why do you suppose Malcolm Cowley chooses a poet-turned-sociologist as his first example of linguistic transmogrification? Why not a historian or biologist?
3. Why do you think sociologists allow themselves to become immersed in "Socspeak"?

4. What are the reasons why sociological language is fuzzy?
5. What are the characteristics of Socspeak grammar?

QUESTIONS ON FORM

1. What is the purpose of using a satirical voice in taking to task the sociologists who have become fanatics of jargon?
2. Why does Cowley misuse the word "hegemonies" in his final paragraph?
3. In paragraph 20, what is Cowley's purpose in transmogrifying Caesar's words? As a class exercise, see if you can transmogrify one of the following familiar quotations:
   (a) You shall not kill.—Bible
   (b) There are no gains without pains.—Franklin
   (c) Life is a tale told by an idiot.—Shakespeare
4. Does the reference to George Orwell in paragraph 8 have any particular significance? Refer to Orwell's "Politics and the English Language" (p. 299).

SUGGESTIONS FOR WRITING

1. Write a one-page essay in which you relate a personal experience from the "I" point of view. Next, relate that same experience, deleting any pronoun that would suggest point of view. For example: "I had just bought a sack of potatoes" would become "A sack of potatoes had just been bought." Finally, write a paragraph commenting on the difference between the two accounts.
2. Write a three-hundred-word open letter to social scientists in which you accuse them of the main faults they commit in their writing and in which you also suggest cures for these faults. You may base your letter on both Cowley's and Orwell's essays.

MATTHEW ARNOLD

DOVER BEACH

Darwin and his theory of evolution posed an immediate challenge to the religious beliefs of Victorian England. In this well-known poem the Victorian poet Matthew Arnold (1822–88) broods on the decline of faith.

1 The sea is calm tonight.
The tide is full, the moon lies fair
Upon the straits; on the French coast the light
Gleams and is gone; the cliffs of England stand,
Glimmering and vast, out in the tranquil bay.
Come to the window, sweet is the night air!
Only, from the long line of spray
Where the sea meets the moon-blanched land,
Listen! you hear the grating roar
Of pebbles which the waves draw back, and fling,

At their return, up the high strand,
Begin, and cease, and then again begin,
With tremulous cadence slow, and bring
The eternal note of sadness in.

2 Sophocles long ago
Heard it on the Aegean,[1] and it brought
Into his mind the turbid ebb and flow
Of human misery; we
Find also in the sound a thought,
Hearing it by this distant northern sea.

3 The Sea of Faith
Was once, too, at the full, and round earth's shore
Lay like the folds of a bright girdle furled.
But now I only hear
Its melancholy, long, withdrawing roar,
Retreating, to the breath
Of the night wind, down the vast edges drear
And naked shingles of the world.

4 Ah, love, let us be true
To one another! for the world, which seems
To lie before us like a land of dreams,
So various, so beautiful, so new,
Hath really neither joy, nor love, nor light,
Nor certitude, nor peace, nor help for pain;
And we are here as on a darkling plain,
Swept with confused alarms of struggle and flight,
Where ignorant armies clash by night.

QUESTIONS ON CONTENT

1. Where is the speaker at the beginning of this poem? Whom is he talking to?
2. What does the "Sea of Faith" in stanza 3 mean? Why is its retreat "melancholy"?
3. What are the "ignorant armies" that "clash by night"? What do these have to do with the "Sea of Faith"?
4. Why does the speaker ask his love to be true to him? What does this have to do with the "Sea of Faith"?
5. What is the relationship between the speaker's descriptions of the scene and what he says? How are his moods projected into his descriptions? Explain.

[1]Sophocles . . . Aegean: In his play *Antigone* the Greek tragedian Sophocles compared the curse on the house of Oedipus with the force of the sea; the Aegean Sea is off the east coast of Greece.—Ed.

QUESTIONS ON FORM

1. What function does the title have in this poem?
2. Compare stanzas 1 and 3. What do they have in common?
3. How does the image of the sea function in this poem?
4. In the second stanza the speaker writes: "we/Find also in the sound a thought,/ Hearing it by this distant northern sea." Why does he use "we" instead of "I"?
5. Some poems can be divided into three parts: exposition, development, and conclusion. Does this division apply to this poem? If so, which stanzas correspond to which parts?

SUGGESTIONS FOR WRITING

1. Write an essay describing how science has affected your religious beliefs.
2. Analyze and discuss the theme of this poem.

example

PHILIP GOLDBERG

ARE WOMEN PREJUDICED AGAINST WOMEN?

WHAT HAPPENED WHEN COLLEGE GIRLS EVALUATED THE SAME ARTICLES— HALF WRITTEN BY "JOHN T. McKAY," HALF BY "JOAN T. McKAY"

This experiment attempts to measure whether women are prejudiced against other women, and comes up with some surprising results. It is an example of clear, jargon-free science writing.

1 "Woman," advised Aristotle, "may be said to be an inferior man."

2 Because he was a man, Aristotle was probably biased. But what do women themselves think? Do they, consciously or unconsciously, consider their own sex inferior? And if so, does this belief prejudice them against other women—that is, make them view women, simply because they *are* women, as less competent than men?

3 According to a study conducted by myself and my associates, the answer to both questions is Yes. Women *do* consider their own sex inferior. And even when the facts give no support to this belief, they will persist in downgrading the competence—in particular, the intellectual and professional competence—of their fellow females.

4 Over the years, psychologists and psychiatrists have shown that both sexes consistently value men more highly than women. Characteristics considered male are usually praised; those considered female are usually criticized. In 1957 A. C. Sheriffs and J. P. McKee noted that "women are regarded as guilty of snobbery and irrational and unpleasant emotionality." Consistent with this report, E. G. French and G. S. Lesser found in 1964 that "women who value intellectual attainment feel they must reject the woman's

role"—intellectual accomplishment apparently being considered, even among intellectual women, a masculine preserve. In addition, ardent feminists like Simone de Beauvoir and Betty Friedan believe that all men, in important ways, are superior to women.

5 Now, is this belief simply prejudice, or are the characteristics and achievements of women really inferior to those of men? In answering this question, we need to draw some careful distinctions.

6 Most important, we need to recognize that there are two distinct dimensions to the issue of sex differences. The first question is whether sex differences exist at all, apart from the obvious physical ones. The answer to this question seems to be a unanimous Yes—men, women, and social scientists agree that, psychologically and emotionally as well as physically, women *are* different from men.

7 But is being different the same as being inferior? It is quite possible to perceive a difference accurately but to value it inaccurately. Do women automatically view their differences from men as *deficiencies?* The evidence is that they do, and that this value judgment opens the door to anti-female prejudice. For if someone (male or female) concludes that women are inferior, his perceptions of women—their personalities, behavior, abilities, and accomplishments—will tend to be colored by his low expectations of women.

8 As Gordon W. Allport has pointed out in *The Nature of Prejudice,* whatever the facts about sex differences, anti-feminism—like any other prejudice—*distorts perception and experience.* What defines anti-feminism is not so much believing that women are inferior, as allowing that belief to distort one's perceptions of women. More generally, it is not the partiality itself, but the distortion born of that partiality, that defines prejudice.

9 Thus, an anti-Semite watching a Jew may see devious or sneaky behavior. But, in a Christian, he would regard such behavior only as quiet, reserved, or perhaps even shy. Prejudice is self-sustaining: It continually distorts the "evidence" on which the prejudiced person claims to base his beliefs. Allport makes it clear that anti-feminism, like anti-Semitism or any other prejudice, consistently twists the "evidence" of experience. We see not what is there, but what we *expect* to see.

10 The purpose of our study was to investigate whether there is real prejudice by women against women—whether perception itself is distorted unfavorably. Specifically, will women evaluate a professional article with a jaundiced eye when they think it is the work of a woman, but praise the same article when they think its author is a man? Our hypotheses were:

11 Even when the work is identical, women value the professional work of men more highly than that of women.

12 But when the professional field happens to be one traditionally reserved for women (nursing, dietetics), this tendency will be reversed, or at least greatly diminished.

13 Some 140 college girls, selected at random, were our subjects. One

hundred were used for the preliminary work; 40 participated in the experiment proper.

14 To test the second hypothesis, we gave the 100 girls a list of 50 occupations and asked them to rate "the degree to which you associate the field with men or with women." We found that law and city planning were fields strongly associated with men, elementary-school teaching and dietetics were fields strongly associated with women, and two fields—linguistics and art history—were chosen as neutrals, not strongly associated with either sex.

15 Now we were ready for the main experiment. From the professional literature of each of these six fields, we took one article. The articles were edited and abridged to about 1500 words, then combined into two equal sets of booklets. The crucial manipulation had to do with the authors' names—the same article bore a male name in one set of booklets, a female name in the other set. An example: If, in set one, the first article bore the name John T. McKay, in set two the same article would appear under the name Joan T. McKay. Each booklet contained three articles by "men" and three articles by "women."

16 The girls, seated together in a large lecture hall, were told to read the articles in their booklets and given these instructions:

"In this booklet you will find excerpts of six articles, written by six different authors in six different professional fields. At the end of each article you will find several questions. . . . You are not presumed to be sophisticated or knowledgeable in all the fields. We are interested in the ability of college students to make critical evaluations. . . ."

Note that no mention at all was made of the authors' sexes. That information was contained—apparently only by coincidence—in the authors' names. The girls could not know, therefore, what we were really looking for.

17 At the end of each article were nine questions asking the girls to rate the articles for value, persuasiveness, and profundity—and to rate the authors for writing style, professional competence, professional status, and ability to sway the reader. On each item, the girls gave a rating of from 1 (highly favorable) to 5 (highly unfavorable).

18 Generally, the results were in line with our expectations—but not completely. In analyzing these results, we used three different methods: We compared the amount of anti-female bias in the different occupational fields (would men be rated as better city planners, but women as better dieticians?); we compared the amount of bias shown on the nine questions that followed each article (would men be rated as more competent, but women as more persuasive?); and we ran an overall comparison, including both fields and rating questions.

19 Starting with the analysis of bias by occupational field, we immediately ran into a major surprise. (See box below.) That there is a general bias by women against women, and that it is strongest in traditionally masculine fields, was clearly borne out. But in other fields the situation seemed rather confused. We had expected the anti-female trend to be reversed in tradition-

ally feminine fields. But it appears that, even here, women consider themselves inferior to men. Women seem to think that men are better at *everything*—including elementary-school teaching and dietetics!

20 Scrutiny of the nine rating questions yielded similar results. On all nine questions, regardless of the author's occupational field, the girls consistently found an article more valuable—and its author more competent—when the article bore a male name. Though the articles themselves were exactly the same, the girls felt that those written by the John T. McKays were definitely more impressive, and reflected more glory on their authors, than did the mediocre offerings of the Joan T. McKays. Perhaps because the world has accepted female authors for a long time, the girls were willing to concede that the female professionals' writing styles were not *far* inferior to those of the men. But such a concession to female competence was rare indeed.

Law: A Strong Masculine Preserve

These are the total scores the college girls gave to the six pairs of articles they read. The lowest possible score—9—would be the most favorable; the highest possible score—54—the most critical. While male authors received more favorable ratings in all occupational fields, the differences were statistically significant only in city planning, linguistics, and—especially—law.

	Mean	
Field of Article	Male	Female
Art History	23.35	23.10
Dietetics	22.05	23.45
Education	20.20	21.75
City Planning	23.10	27.30
Linguistics	26.95	30.70
Law	21.20	25.60

21 Statistical analysis confirms these impressions and makes them more definite. With a total of six articles, and with nine questions after each one, there were 54 points at which comparisons could be drawn between the male authors and the female authors. Out of these 54 comparisons, three were tied, seven favored the female authors—and the number favoring the male authors was 44!

22 Clearly, there is a tendency among women to downgrade the work of professionals of their own sex. But the hypothesis that this tendency would decrease as the "femaleness" of the professional field increased was not supported. Even in traditionally female fields, anti-feminism holds sway.

23 Since the articles supposedly written by men were exactly the same as those supposedly written by women, the perception that the men's articles were superior was obviously a distortion. For reasons of their own, the female subjects were sensitive to the sex of the author, and this apparently irrelevant

information biased their judgments. Both the distortion and the sensitivity that precedes it are characteristic of prejudice. Women—at least these young college women—are prejudiced against female professionals and, regardless of the actual accomplishments of these professionals, will firmly refuse to recognize them as the equals of their male colleagues.

24 Is the intellectual double-standard really dead? Not at all—and if the college girls in this study are typical of the educated and presumably progressive segments of the population, it may not even be dying. Whatever lip service these girls pay to modern ideas of equality between men and women, their beliefs are staunchly traditional. Their real coach in the battle of the sexes is not Simone de Beauvoir or Betty Friedan. Their coach is Aristotle.

QUESTIONS ON CONTENT

1. What are the hypotheses of this study?
2. What, according to this article, is the definitive characteristic of anti-feminism?
3. How does prejudice affect our perceptions?
4. The author says that it is possible to perceive a difference accurately but to value it inaccurately. What does he mean by that?
5. Which hypothesis was not supported by the study? Which hypothesis was supported?

QUESTIONS ON FORM

1. Most experiments in social science manipulate a certain effect so as to test some group's spontaneous reaction to it. What effect is manipulated in this study?
2. What are the functions of paragraphs 2 and 3?
3. Every article reporting on an experiment will sum up the relevant research in at least one paragraph. Which paragraph in the article performs this function? Why is this necessary?
4. What significance does the Aristotle quotation have? Who was Aristotle? Why does the article begin and end with a reference to him?
5. What method of logic is this experiment an example of? Is it based on deductive or on inductive logic?
6. The language of science is typically neutral and unemotional. How would you characterize the language of this article?

SUGGESTIONS FOR WRITING

1. Discuss your attitude toward women and how you came by it.
2. Is it possible for women to be regarded as different from but equal to men? Or is this simply the "separate but equal" fallacy restated? Select a position on these questions and argue for it.

TERM PAPER SUGGESTION

Duplicate this experiment using your own subjects and write up your results.

CHAPTER WRITING ASSIGNMENTS

1. Discuss the notion that science is a "game."
2. Write an essay entitled "Why we need to send a poet to the moon."
3. Write an essay entitled "The answer to science is . . ." Say what you think the answer is, and argue for it.

thirteen

Writing Reports

advice

S. I. HAYAKAWA

THE LANGUAGE OF REPORTS

A report is an attempt to reflect accurately what has happened. The reporter tells what he saw, heard, smelled, and felt. In the selection that follows, the American semanticist S. I. Hayakawa describes report language and distinguishes it from the language of "inferences" and "judgments." (From *Language in Thought and Action*.)

1 For the purposes of the interchange of information, the basic symbolic act is the *report* of what we have seen, heard, or felt: "There is a ditch on each side of the road." "You can get those at Smith's Hardware Store for $2.75." "There aren't any fish on that side of the lake, but there are on this side." Then there are reports of reports: "The longest waterfall in the world is Victoria Falls in Rhodesia." "The Battle of Hastings took place in 1066." "The papers say that there was a smash-up on Highway 41 near Evansville." Reports adhere to the following rules: first, they are *capable of verification;* second, they *exclude,* as far as possible, *inferences* and *judgments.* (These terms will be defined later.)

Verifiability

2 Reports are verifiable. We may not always be able to verify them ourselves, since we cannot track down the evidence for every piece of history we know, nor can we all go to Evansville to see the remains of the smash-up before they are cleared away. But if we are roughly agreed upon the names of

things, upon what constitutes a "foot," "yard," "bushel," "kilogram," "meter," and so on, and upon how to measure time, there is relatively little danger of our misunderstanding each other. Even in a world such as we have today, in which everybody seems to be quarreling with everybody else, *we still to a surprising degree trust each other's reports.* We ask directions of total strangers when we are traveling. We follow directions on road signs without being suspicious of the people who put them up. We read books of information about science, mathematics, automotive engineering, travel, geography, the history of costume, and other such factual matters, and we usually assume that the author is doing his best to tell us as truly as he can what he knows. And we are safe in so assuming most of the time. With the interest given today to the discussion of biased newspapers, propagandists, and the general untrustworthiness of many of the communications we receive, we are likely to forget that we still have an enormous amount of reliable information available and that deliberate misinformation, except in warfare, is still more the exception than the rule. The desire for self-preservation that compelled men to evolve means for the exchange of information also compels them to regard the giving of false information as profoundly reprehensible.

3 At its highest development, the language of reports is the language of science. By "highest development" we mean greatest general usefulness. Presbyterian and Catholic, workingman and capitalist, East German and West German *agree* on the meanings of such symbols as $2 \times 2 = 4$, $100°$ C, HNO_3, $3:35$ A.M., 1940 A.D., $1,000$ kilowatts, Quercus agrifolia, and so on. But how, it may be asked, can there be agreement about even this much among people who disagree about political philosophies, ethical ideas, religious beliefs, and the survival of my business versus the survival of yours? The answer is that circumstances *compel men to agree,* whether they wish to or not. If, for example, there were a dozen different religious sects in the United States, each insisting on its own way of naming the time of the day and the days of the year, the mere necessity of having a dozen different calendars, a dozen different kinds of watches, and a dozen sets of schedules for business hours, trains, and television programs, to say nothing of the effort that would be required for translating terms from one nomenclature to another, would make life as we know it impossible.[1]

4 The language of reports, then, including the more accurate reports of

---

[1]According to information supplied by the Association of American Railroads, "Before 1883 there were nearly 100 different time zones in the United States. It wasn't until November 18 of that year that . . . a system of standard time was adopted here and in Canada. Before then there was nothing but local or 'solar' time. . . . The Pennsylvania Railroad in the East used Philadelphia time, which was five minutes slower than New York time and five minutes faster than Baltimore time. The Baltimore & Ohio used Baltimore time for trains running out of Baltimore, Columbus time for Ohio, Vincennes (Indiana) for those going out of Cincinnati. . . . When it was noon in Chicago, it was 12:31 in Pittsburgh, 12:24 in Cleveland, 12:17 in Toledo, 12:13 in Cincinnati, 12:09 in Louisville, 12:07 in Indianapolis, 11:50 in St. Louis, 11:48 in Dubuque, 11:39 in St. Paul, and 11:27 in Omaha. There were 27 local time zones in Michigan alone. . . . A person traveling from Eastport, Maine, to San Francisco, if he wanted always to have the right railroad time and get off at the right place, had to twist the hands of his watch 20 times en route." Chicago *Daily News* (September 29, 1948).

science, is "map" language, and because it gives us reasonably accurate representations of the "territory," it enables us to get work done. Such language may often be dull reading: one does not usually read logarithmic tables or telephone directories for entertainment. But we could not get along without it. There are numberless occasions in the talking and writing we do in everyday life that *require that we state things in such a way that everybody will be able to understand and agree with our formulation.*

Inferences

5 The reader will find that practice in writing reports is a quick means of increasing his linguistic awareness. It is an exercise which will constantly provide him with his own examples of the principles of language and interpretation under discussion. The reports should be about first-hand experience— scenes the reader has witnessed himself, meetings and social events he has taken part in, people he knows well. They should be of such a nature that they can be verified and agreed upon. For the purpose of this exercise, inferences will be excluded.

6 Not that inferences are not important—we rely in everyday life and in science as much on *inferences* as on reports—in some areas of thought, for example, geology, paleontology, and nuclear physics, reports are the foundations; but inferences (and inferences upon inferences) are the main body of the science. An inference, as we shall use the term, is *a statement about the unknown made on the basis of the known.* We may *infer* from the material and cut of a woman's clothes her wealth or social position; we may *infer* from the character of the ruins the origin of the fire that destroyed the building; we may *infer* from a man's calloused hands the nature of his occupation; we may *infer* from a senator's vote on an armaments bill his attitude toward Russia; we may *infer* from the structure of the land the path of a prehistoric glacier; we may *infer* from a halo on an unexposed photographic plate its past proximity to radioactive materials; we may *infer* from the sound of an engine the condition of its connecting rods. Inferences may be carefully or carelessly made. They may be made on the basis of a broad background of previous experience with the subject matter or with no experience at all. For example, the inferences a good mechanic can make about the internal condition of a motor by listening to it are often startlingly accurate, while the inferences made by an amateur (if he tries to make any) may be entirely wrong. But the common characteristic of inferences is that they are statements about matters which are not directly known, made on the basis of what has been observed.[2]

7 The avoidance of inferences in our suggested practice in report-writing requires that we make no guesses as to what is going on in other people's minds. When we say, "He was angry," we are not reporting; we are making

---

[2]The behaviorist school of psychology tries to avoid inferences about what is going on in other people's minds by describing only external behavior. A famous joke about behaviorism goes: Two behaviorists meet on the street. The first says, "You're fine. How am I?"

an inference from such observable facts as the following: "He pounded his fist on the table; he swore; he threw the telephone directory at his stenographer." In this particular example, the inference appears to be safe; nevertheless, it is important to remember, especially for the purposes of training oneself, that it is an inference. Such expressions as "He thought a lot of himself," "He was scared of girls," "He has an inferiority complex," made on the basis of casual observation, and "What Russia really wants to do is to establish a communist world dictatorship," made on the basis of casual reading, are highly inferential. We should keep in mind their inferential character and, in our suggested exercises, should substitute for them such statements as "He rarely spoke to subordinates in the plant," "I saw him at a party, and he never danced except when one of the girls asked him to," "He wouldn't apply for the scholarship, although I believe he could have won it easily," and "The Russian delegation to the United Nations has asked for *A, B,* and *C.* Last year they voted against *M* and *N* and voted for *X* and *Y.* On the basis of facts such as these, the newspaper I read makes the inference that what Russia really wants is to establish a communist world dictatorship. I agree."

8 Even when we exercise every caution to avoid inferences and to report only what we see and experience, we all remain prone to error, since the making of inferences is a quick, almost automatic process. We may watch a car weaving as it goes down the road and say, "Look at that *drunken driver,*" although what we *see* is only *the irregular motion of the car.* I once saw a man leave a dollar at a lunch counter and hurry out. Just as I was wondering why anyone should leave so generous a tip in so modest an establishment, the waitress came, picked up the dollar, put it in the cash register as she punched up ninety cents, and put a dime in her pocket. In other words, my description to myself of the event, "a dollar tip," turned out to be not a report but an inference.

9 All this is not to say that we should never make inferences. The inability to make inferences is itself a sign of mental disorder. For example, the speech therapist Laura L. Lee writes, "The aphasic [brain-damaged] adult with whom I worked had great difficulty in making inferences about a picture I showed her. She could tell me what was happening at the moment in the picture, but could not tell me what might have happened just before the picture or just afterward."[3] Hence the question is not whether or not we make inferences; the question is whether or not we are aware of the inferences we make.

Report	Can be verified or disproved
Inference	A statement about the unknown made on the basis of the known
Judgment	An expression of the writer's approval or disapproval

[3]"Brain Damage and the Process of Abstracting: A Problem in Language Learning," *ETC.: A Review of General Semantics,* XVI (1959), 154–62.

Judgments

10 In our suggested writing exercise, judgments are also to be excluded. By judgments, we shall mean *all expressions of the writer's approval or disapproval of the occurrences, persons, or objects he is describing.* For example, a report cannot say, "It was a wonderful car," but must say something like this: "It has been driven 50,000 miles and has never required any repairs." Again, statements such as "Jack lied to us" must be suppressed in favor of the more verifiable statement, "Jack told us he didn't have the keys to his car with him. However, when he pulled a handkerchief out of his pocket a few minutes later, a bunch of car keys fell out." Also a report may not say, "The senator was stubborn, defiant, and uncooperative," or "The senator courageously stood by his principles"; it must say instead, "The senator's vote was the only one against the bill."

11 Many people regard statements such as the following as statements of "fact"; "Jack *lied* to us," "Jerry is a *thief*," "Tommy is *clever*." As ordinarily employed, however, the word "lied" involves first an inference (that Jack knew otherwise and deliberately misstated the facts) and second a judgment (that the speaker disapproves of what he has inferred that Jack did). In the other two instances, we may substitute such expressions as, "Jerry was convicted of theft and served two years at Waupun," and "Tommy plays the violin, leads his class in school, and is captain of the debating team." After all, to say of a man that he is a "thief" is to say in effect, "He has stolen *and will steal again*"—which is more of a prediction than a report. Even to say, "He has stolen," is to make an inference (and simultaneously to pass a judgment) on an act about which there may be difference of opinion among those who have examined the evidence upon which the conviction was obtained. But to say that he was "convicted of theft" is to make a statement capable of being agreed upon through verification in court and prison records.

12 Scientific verifiability rests upon the external observation of facts, not upon the heaping up of judgments. If one person says, "Peter is a deadbeat," and another says, "I think so too," the statement has not been verified. In court cases, considerable trouble is sometimes caused by witnesses who cannot distinguish their judgments from the facts upon which those judgments are based. Cross-examinations under these circumstances go something like this:

WITNESS That dirty double-crosser Jacobs ratted on me.
DEFENSE ATTORNEY Your honor, I object.
JUDGE Objection sustained. (Witness's remark is stricken from the record.) Now, try to tell the court exactly what happened.
WITNESS He double-crossed me, the dirty, lying rat!
DEFENSE ATTORNEY Your honor, I object!
JUDGE Objection sustained. (Witness's remark is again stricken from the record.) Will the witness try to stick to the facts.
WITNESS But I'm telling you the facts, your honor. He did double-cross me.

This can continue indefinitely unless the cross-examiner exercises some ingenuity in order to get at the facts behind the judgment. To the witness it is a "fact" that he was "double-crossed." Often patient questioning is required before the factual bases of the judgment are revealed.

13 Many words, of course, simultaneously convey a report and a judgment on the fact reported. . . . For the purposes of a report as here defined, these should be avoided. Instead of "sneaked in," one might say "entered quietly"; instead of "politician," "congressman" or "alderman" or "candidate for office"; instead of "bureaucrat," "public official"; instead of "tramp," "homeless unemployed"; instead of "dictatorial set-up," "centralized authority"; instead of "crackpot," "holder of nonconformist views." A newspaper reporter, for example, is not permitted to write, "A crowd of suckers came to listen to Senator Smith last evening in that rickety firetrap and ex-dive that disfigures the south edge of town." Instead he says, "Between 75 and 100 people heard an address last evening by Senator Smith at the Evergreen Gardens near the South Side city limits."

Snarl-Words and Purr-Words

14 Throughout this book, it is important to remember that we are not considering language as an isolated phenomenon. Our concern, instead, is with language in action—language in the full context of the nonlinguistic events which are its setting. The making of noises with the vocal organs is a muscular activity and, like other muscular activities, is often involuntary. Our responses to powerful stimuli, such as to things that make us very angry, are a complex of muscular and physiological events; the contracting of fighting muscles, the increase of blood pressure, a change in body chemistry, clutching of our hair, *and* the making of noises, such as growls and snarls. We are a little too dignified, perhaps, to growl like dogs, but we do the next best thing and substitute series of words, such as "You dirty double-crosser!" "The filthy scum!" Similarly, if we are pleasurably agitated, we may, instead of purring or wagging the tail, say things like "She's the sweetest girl in all the world!"

15 Speeches such as these are, like direct expressions of approval or disapproval, judgments in their simplest form. They may be said to be human equivalents of snarling and purring. "She's the sweetest girl in all the world!" is not a statement about the girl; it is a purr. This seems to be a fairly obvious fact; nevertheless, it is surprising how often, when such a statement is made, both the speaker and the hearer feel that something has been said about the girl. This error is especially common in the interpretation of utterances of orators and editorialists in some of their more excited denunciations of "Reds," "pigs," "Wall Street," "radicals," "foreign ideologies," and in their more fulsome dithyrambs about "our way of life." Constantly, because of the impressive sound of the words, the elaborate structure of the sentences, and the appearance of intellectual progression, we get the feeling that some-

thing is being said about something. On closer examination, however, we discover that these utterances merely say, "What I hate ('Reds,' 'Wall Street,' or whatever) I hate very, very much," and "What I like ('our way of life') I like very, very much." We may call such utterances "snarl-words" and "purr-words." They are not reports describing conditions in the extensional world in any way.

16 To call these judgments "snarl-words" and "purr-words" does not mean that we should simply shrug them off. It means that we should be careful to *allocate the meaning correctly*—placing such a statement as "She's the sweetest girl in the world!" as a revelation of the speaker's state of mind, and not as a revelation of facts about the girl. If the "snarl-words" about "Reds" or "pigs" are accompanied by verifiable reports (which would also mean that we have previously agreed as to who, specifically, is meant by the terms "Reds" or "pigs"), we might find reason to be just as disturbed as the speaker. If the "purr-words" about the sweetest girl in the world are accompanied by verifiable reports about her appearance, manners, character, and so on, we might find reason to admire her too. But "snarl-words" and "purr-words" as such, unaccompanied by reports, offer nothing further to discuss, except possibly the question, "Why do you feel as you do?"

17 It is usually fruitless to debate such questions as "Is the President a great statesman or merely a skillful politician?" "Is the music of Wagner the greatest music of all time, or is it merely hysterical screeching?" "Which is the finer sport, tennis or baseball?" "Could Joe Louis in his prime have licked Rocky Marciano in his prime?" To take sides on such issues of conflicting judgments is to reduce oneself to the same level of stubborn imbecility as one's opponents. But to ask questions of the form, "Why do you like (or dislike) the President (or Wagner, or tennis, or Joe Louis)?" is to learn something about one's friends and neighbors. After listening to their opinions and their reasons for them, we may leave the discussion slightly wiser, slightly better informed, and perhaps slightly less one-sided than we were before the discussion began.

How Judgments Stop Thought

18 A judgment ("He is a fine boy," "It was a beautiful service," "Baseball is a healthful sport," "She is an awful bore") is a conclusion, summing up a large number of previously observed facts. The reader is probably familiar with the fact that students almost always have difficulty in writing themes of the required length because their ideas give out after a paragraph or two. The reason for this is that those early paragraphs contain so many judgments that there is little left to be said. When the conclusions are carefully excluded, however, and observed facts are given instead, there is never any trouble about the length of papers; in fact, they tend to become too long, since inexperienced writers, when told to give facts, often give far more than are necessary, because they lack discrimination between the important and the trivial.

19 Still another consequence of judgments early in the course of a written exercise—and this applies also to hasty judgments in everyday thought—is the temporary blindness they induce. When, for example, a description starts with the words, "He was a real Madison Avenue executive" or "She was a typical hippie," if we continue writing at all, we must make all our later statements consistent with those judgments. The result is that all the individual characteristics of this particular "executive" or this particular "hippie" are lost sight of; and the rest of the account is likely to deal not with observed facts but with stereotypes and the writer's particular notion (based on previously read stories, movies, pictures, and so forth) of what "Madison Avenue executives" or "typical hippies" are like. The premature judgment, that is, often prevents us from seeing what is directly in front of us, so that clichés take the place of fresh description. Therefore, even if the writer feels sure at the beginning of a written account that the man he is describing is a "real leatherneck" or that the scene he is describing is a "beautiful residential suburb," he will conscientiously keep such notions out of his head, lest his vision be obstructed. He is specifically warned against describing *anybody* as a "beatnik"—a term (originally applied to literary and artistic Bohemians) which was blown up by sensational journalism and movies into an almost completely fictional and misleading stereotype. If a writer applies the term to any actual living human being, he will have to expend so much energy thereafter explaining what he does *not* mean by it that he will save himself trouble by not bringing it up at all. The same warning applies to "hippies" and other social classifications that tend to submerge the individual in a category.

Slanting

20 In the course of writing reports of personal experiences, it will be found that in spite of all endeavors to keep judgments out, some will creep in. An account of a man, for example, may go like this: "He had apparently not shaved for several days, and his face and hands were covered with grime. His shoes were torn, and his coat, which was several sizes too small for him, was spotted with dried clay." Now, in spite of the fact that no judgment has been stated, a very obvious one is implied. Let us contrast this with another description of the same man. "Although his face was bearded and neglected, his eyes were clear, and he looked straight ahead as he walked rapidly down the road. He seemed very tall; perhaps the fact that his coat was too small for him emphasized that impression. He was carrying a book under his left arm, and a small terrier ran at his heels." In this example, the impression about the same man is considerably changed, simply by the inclusion of new details and the subordination of unfavorable ones. Even if explicit judgments are kept out of one's writing, implied judgments based on selective perception will get in.

21 How, then, can we ever give an impartial report? The answer is, of course, that we cannot attain complete impartiality while we use the language of everyday life. Even with the very impersonal language of science, the task is sometimes difficult. Nevertheless, we can, by being aware of the favorable

or unfavorable feelings that certain words and facts can arouse, attain enough impartiality for practical purposes. Such awareness enables us to balance the implied favorable and unfavorable judgments against each other. To learn to do this, it is a good idea to write two accounts of the same subject, both strict reports, to be read side by side: the first to contain facts and details likely to prejudice the reader in favor of the subject, the second to contain those likely to prejudice the reader against it. For example:

For	*Against*
He had white teeth.	His teeth were uneven.
His eyes were blue, his hair blond and abundant.	He rarely looked people straight in the eye.
He had on a clean, white shirt.	His shirt was frayed at the cuffs.
His speech was courteous.	He had a high-pitched voice.
His employer spoke highly of him.	His landlord said he was slow in paying his rent.
He liked dogs.	He disliked children.

22 This process of selecting details favorable or unfavorable to the subject being described may be termed *slanting*. Slanting gives no explicit judgments, but it differs from reporting in that it deliberately makes certain judgments inescapable. Let us assume for a moment the truth of the statement "When Clyde was in New York last November he was seen having dinner with a show girl. . . ." The inferences that can be drawn from this statement are changed considerably when the following words are added: " . . . and her husband and their two children." Yet, if Clyde is a married man, his enemies could conceivably do him a great deal of harm by talking about his "dinner-date with a New York show girl." One-sided or biased slanting of this kind, not uncommon in private gossip and backbiting and all too common in the "interpretative reporting" of newspapers and news magazines, can be described as a technique of lying without actually telling any lies.

Discovering One's Bias

23 Here, however, caution is necessary. When, for example, a newspaper tells a story in a way that we dislike, leaving out facts we think important and playing up important facts in ways that we think unfair, we are tempted to say, "Look how unfairly they've slanted the story!" In making such a statement we are, of course, making an inference about the newspaper's editors. We are assuming that what seems important or unimportant to us seems equally important or unimportant to them, and on the basis of that assumption we infer that the editors "deliberately" gave the story a misleading emphasis. Is this necessarily the case? Can the reader, as an outsider, say whether a story assumes a given form because the editors "deliberately slanted it that way" or because that was the way the events appeared to them?

24 The point is that, by the process of selection and abstraction imposed on us by our own interests and background, experience comes to all of us

(including newspaper editors) already "slanted." If you happen to be pro-labor, pro-Catholic, and a stock-car racing fan, your ideas of what is important or unimportant will of necessity be different from those of a man who happens to be indifferent to all three of your favorite interests. If, then, newspapers often side with the big businessman on public issues, the reason is less a matter of "deliberate" slanting than the fact that publishers are often, in enterprises as large as modern urban newspapers, big businessmen themselves, accustomed both in work and in social life to associating with other big businessmen. Nevertheless, the best newspapers, whether owned by "big businessmen" or not, do try to tell us as accurately as possible what is going on in the world, because they are run by newspapermen who conceive it to be part of their professional responsibility to present fairly the conflicting points of view in controversial issues. Such newspapermen are *reporters* indeed.

25 The writer who is neither an advocate nor an opponent avoids slanting, except when he is seeking special literary effects. The avoidance of slanting is not only a matter of being fair and impartial; it is even more importantly a matter of making good maps of the territory of experience. The profoundly biased individual cannot make good maps because he can see an enemy *only* as an enemy and a friend *only* as a friend. The individual with genuine skill in writing—one who has imagination and insight—can look at the same subject from many points of view. The following examples may illustrate the fullness and solidity of descriptions thus written:

> Adam turned to look at him. It was, in a way, as though this were the first time he had laid eyes on him. He saw the strong, black shoulders under the red-check calico, the long arms lying loose, forward over the knees, the strong hands, seamed and calloused, holding the reins. He looked at the face. The thrust of the jawbone was strong, but the lips were heavy and low, with a piece of chewed straw hanging out one side of the mouth. The eyelids were pendulous, slightly swollen-looking, and the eyes bloodshot. Those eyes, Adam knew, could sharpen to a quick, penetrating, assessing glance. But now, looking at that slack, somnolent face, he could scarcely believe that.
>
> ROBERT PENN WARREN, *Wilderness*

> Soon after the little princess, there walked in a massively built, stout young man in spectacles, with a cropped head, light breeches in the mode of the day, with a high lace ruffle and a ginger-coloured coat. This stout young man [Pierre] was the illegitimate son of a celebrated dandy of the days of Catherine, Count Bezuhov, who was now dying in Moscow. He had not yet entered any branch of the service; he had only just returned from abroad, where he had been educated, and this was his first appearance in society. Anna Pavlovna greeted him with a nod reserved for persons of the very lowest hierarchy in her drawing-room. . . .
>
> Pierre was clumsy, stout and uncommonly tall, with huge, red hands; he did not, as they say, know how to come into a drawing-room and still less how to get out of one, that is, how to say something particularly agreeable on going away. Moreover, he was dreamy. He stood up, and picking up a three-cornered hat with the plume of a general in it instead of his own, he kept hold of it, pulling the feathers until the general asked him to restore it. But all his dreaminess and his

ability to enter a drawing-room or talk properly in it were atoned for by his expression of good-nature, simplicity and modesty.

COUNT LEO TOLSTOY, *War and Peace*
(Translated by Constance Garnett)

VOCABULARY

adhere (1)	fulsome (15)
verification (1)	dithyrambs (15)
inferences (1)	extensional (15)
propagandists (2)	allocate (16)
reprehensible (2)	imbecility (17)
nomenclature (3)	induce (19)
logarithmic (4)	premature (19)
paleontology (6)	clichés (19)
armaments (6)	leatherneck (19)
prone (8)	beatnik (19)
phenomenon (14)	expend (19)
nonlinguistic (14)	subordination (20)
involuntary (14)	backbiting (22)
stimuli (14)	abstraction (24)
denunciations (15)	advocate (25)

examples

GEORGE ORWELL

A HANGING

The English writer George Orwell's story "A Hanging" illustrates the difficulty of distinguishing between objective and subjective writing. Whereas he only once explicitly states that it is wrong to take a person's life, his narrative nevertheless argues eloquently.

1 It was in Burma, a sodden morning of the rains. A sickly light, like yellow tinfoil, was slanting over the high walls into the jail yard. We were waiting outside the condemned cells, a row of sheds fronted with double bars, like small animal cages. Each cell measured about ten feet by ten and was quite bare within except for a plank bed and a pot for drinking water. In some of them brown silent men were squatting at the inner bars, with their blankets draped round them. These were the condemned men, due to be hanged within the next week or two.

2 One prisoner had been brought out of his cell. He was a Hindu, a puny wisp of a man, with a shaven head and vague liquid eyes. He had a thick, sprouting moustache, absurdly too big for his body, rather like the moustache

of a comic man on the films. Six tall Indian warders were guarding him and getting him ready for the gallows. Two of them stood by with rifles and fixed bayonets, while the others handcuffed him, passed a chain through his handcuffs and fixed it to their belts, and lashed his arms tight to his sides. They crowded very close about him, with their hands always on him in a careful, caressing grip, as though all the while feeling him to make sure he was there. It was like men handling a fish which is still alive and may jump back into the water. But he stood quite unresisting, yielding his arms limply to the ropes, as though he hardly noticed what was happening.

3 Eight o'clock struck and a bugle call, desolately thin in the wet air, floated from the distant barracks. The superintendent of the jail, who was standing apart from the rest of us, moodily prodding the gravel with his stick, raised his head at the sound. He was an army doctor, with a grey toothbrush moustache and a gruff voice, "For God's sake hurry up, Francis," he said irritably. "The man ought to have been dead by this time. Aren't you ready yet?"

4 Francis, the head jailer, a fat Dravidian in a white drill suit and gold spectacles, waved his black hand. "Yes sir, yes sir," he bubbled. "All iss satisfactorily prepared. The hangman iss waiting. We shall proceed."

"Well, quick march, then. The prisoners can't get their breakfast till this job's over."

5 We set out for the gallows. Two warders marched on either side of the prisoner, with their rifles at the slope; two others marched close against him, gripping him by arm and shoulder, as though at once pushing and supporting him. The rest of us, magistrates and the like, followed behind. Suddenly, when we had gone ten yards, the procession stopped short without any order or warning. A dreadful thing had happened—a dog, come goodness knows whence, had appeared in the yard. It came bounding among us with a loud volley of barks, and leapt round us wagging its whole body, wild with glee at finding so many human beings together. It was a large woolly dog, half Airedale, half pariah. For a moment it pranced round us, and then, before anyone could stop it, it had made a dash for the prisoner and, jumping up, tried to lick his face. Everyone stood aghast, too taken aback even to grab at the dog.

"Who let that bloody brute in here?" said the superintendent angrily. "Catch it, someone!"

6 A warder, detached from the escort, charged clumsily after the dog, but it danced and gambolled just out of his reach, taking everything as part of the game. A young Eurasian jailer picked up a handful of gravel and tried to stone the dog away, but it dodged the stones and came after us again. Its yaps echoed from the jail walls. The prisoner, in the grasp of the two warders, looked on incuriously, as though this was another formality of the hanging. It was several minutes before someone managed to catch the dog. Then we put my handkerchief through its collar and moved off once more, with the dog still straining and whimpering.

7 It was about forty yards to the gallows. I watched the bare brown back of the prisoner marching in front of me. He walked clumsily with his bound arms, but quite steadily, with that bobbing gait of the Indian who never straightens his knees. At each step his muscles slid neatly into place, the lock of hair on his scalp danced up and down, his feet printed themselves on the wet gravel. And once, in spite of the men who gripped him by each shoulder, he stepped slightly aside to avoid a puddle on the path.

8 It is curious, but till that moment I had never realized what it means to destroy a healthy, conscious man. When I saw the prisoner step aside to avoid the puddle I saw the mystery, the unspeakable wrongness, of cutting a life short when it is in full tide. This man was not dying, he was alive just as we are alive. All the organs of his body were working—bowels digesting food, skin renewing itself, nails growing, tissues forming—all toiling away in solemn foolery. His nails would still be growing when he stood on the drop, when he was falling through the air with a tenth-of-a-second to live. His eyes saw the yellow gravel and the grey walls, and his brain still remembered, foresaw, reasoned—reasoned even about puddles. He and we were a party of men walking together, seeing, hearing, feeling, understanding the same world; and in two minutes, with a sudden snap, one of us would be gone—one mind less, one world less.

9 The gallows stood in a small yard, separate from the main grounds of the prison, and overgrown with tall prickly weeds. It was a brick erection like three sides of a shed, with planking on top, and above that two beams and a crossbar with the rope dangling. The hangman, a grey-haired convict in the white uniform of the prison, was waiting beside his machine. He greeted us with a servile crouch as we entered. At a word from Francis the two warders, gripping the prisoner more closely than ever, half led half pushed him to the gallows and helped him clumsily up the ladder. Then the hangman climbed up and fixed the rope round the prisoner's neck.

10 We stood waiting, five yards away. The warders had formed in a rough circle round the gallows. And then, when the noose was fixed, the prisoner began crying out to his god. It was a high, reiterated cry of "Ram! Ram! Ram! Ram!" not urgent and fearful like a prayer or cry for help, but steady, rhythmical, almost like the tolling of a bell. The dog answered the sound with a whine. The hangman, still standing on the gallows, produced a small cotton bag like a flour bag and drew it down over the prisoner's face. But the sound, muffled by the cloth, still persisted, over and over again: "Ram! Ram! Ram! Ram! Ram!"

11 The hangman climbed down and stood ready, holding the lever. Minutes seemed to pass. The steady, muffled crying from the prisoner went on and on. "Ram! Ram! Ram!" never faltering for an instant. The superintendent, his head on his chest, was slowly poking the ground with his stick; perhaps he was counting the cries, allowing the prisoner a fixed number—fifty, perhaps, or a hundred. Everyone had changed color. The Indians had gone grey like bad coffee, and one or two of the bayonets were wavering. We looked at the lashed, hooded man on the drop, and listened to his cries—each cry another

second of life; the same thought was in all our minds: oh, kill him quickly, get it over, stop that abominable noise!

12 Suddenly the superintendent made up his mind. Throwing up his head he made a swift motion with his stick. "Chalo!" he shouted almost fiercely.

13 There was a clanking noise, and then dead silence. The prisoner had vanished, and the rope was twisting on itself. I let go of the dog, and it galloped immediately to the back of the gallows; but when it got there it stopped short, barked, and then retreated into a corner of the yard, where it stood among the weeds, looking timorously out at us. We went round the gallows to inspect the prisoner's body. He was dangling with his toes pointed straight downwards, very slowly revolving, as dead as a stone.

14 The superintendent reached out with his stick and poked the bare brown body; it oscillated slightly. "*He's* all right," said the superintendent. He backed out from under the gallows, and blew out a deep breath. The moody look had gone out of his face quite suddenly. He glanced at his wrist-watch. "Eight minutes past eight. Well, that's all for this morning, thank God."

15 The warders unfixed bayonets and marched away. The dog, sobered and conscious of having misbehaved itself, slipped after them. We walked out of the gallows yard, past the condemned cells with their waiting prisoners, into the big central yard of the prison. The convicts, under the command of warders armed with lathis, were already receiving their breakfast. They squatted in long rows, each man holding a tin pannikin, while two warders with buckets marched round ladling out rice; it seemed quite a homely, jolly scene, after the hanging. An enormous relief had come upon us now that the job was done. One felt an impulse to sing, to break into a run, to snigger. All at once everyone began chattering gaily.

16 The Eurasian boy walking beside me nodded towards the way we had come, with a knowing smile: "Do you know, sir, our friend (he meant the dead man) when he heard his appeal had been dismissed, he pissed on the floor of his cell. From fright. Kindly take one of my cigarettes, sir. Do you not admire my new silver case, sir? From the boxwalah, two rupees eight annas. Classy European style."

Several people laughed—at what, nobody seemed certain.

17 Francis was walking by the superintendent, talking garrulously: "Well, sir, all hass passed off with the utmost satisfactoriness. It was all finished— flick! like that. It iss not always so—oah, no! I have known cases where the doctor wass obliged to go beneath the gallows and pull the prissoner's legs to ensure decease. Most disagreeable!"

"Wriggling about, eh? That's bad," said the superintendent.

18 "Ach, sir, it iss worse when they become refractory! One man, I recall, clung to the bars of hiss cage when we went to take him out. You will scarcely credit, sir, that it took six warders to dislodge him, three pulling at each leg. We reasoned with him. 'My dear fellow,' we said, 'think of all the pain and trouble you are causing to us!' But no, he would not listen! Ach, he wass very troublesome!"

19 I found that I was laughing quite loudly. Everyone was laughing. Even

the superintendent grinned in a tolerant way. "You'd better all come out and have a drink," he said quite genially. "I've got a bottle of whisky in the car. We could do with it."

20 We went through the big double gates of the prison into the road. "Pulling at his legs!" exclaimed a Burmese magistrate suddenly, and burst into a loud chuckling. We all began laughing again. At that moment Francis' anecdote seemed extraordinarily funny. We all had a drink together, native and European alike, quite amicably. The dead man was a hundred yards away.

VOCABULARY

sodden (1)	servile (9)
wisp (2)	abominable (11)
desolately (3)	timorously (13)
Dravidian (4)	oscillated (14)
magistrates (5)	pannikin (15)
aghast (5)	snigger (15)
taken aback (5)	garrulously (17)
gambolled (6)	refractory (18)
Eurasian (6)	genially (19)

QUESTIONS ON CONTENT

1. The reporter in this event acts both as observer and as participant. Can you offer a reason for combining these two points of view?
2. Orwell offers few personal opinions on the hanging, but merely shows the spectacle in full detail. What is the advantage or disadvantage of such a method?
3. In what way does Orwell make clear his special purpose in reporting the hanging?
4. Why does Orwell include the incident about the dog (paragraph 5)?
5. Why does Orwell mention that the victim avoided a puddle (paragraph 8)?
6. We are never told the identity of the prisoner to be hanged nor what crime, if any, he committed. Why did Orwell leave out those details?

QUESTIONS ON FORM

1. What general mood is created by the opening paragraph? Pick out those words that contribute most to this mood.
2. Analyze the text for freshness of language.
3. In what two paragraphs does the reporter draw attention to himself? What reason is there for these shifts from "we" to "I"?
4. Does Orwell's method—one of showing rather than of telling—prove as convincing as a logical argument against capital punishment? Give the reasoning behind your answer.

SUGGESTIONS FOR WRITING

1. Write an essay in which you describe an event as an objective reporter, but choose only those details that support the general impression you wish to convey.
2. Relate a personal experience that taught you an important moral law.

KARL SHAPIRO

AUTO WRECK

In this poem the poet explores the nature of accident (chance) as it affects
human life.

1 Its quick soft silver bell beating, beating,
And down the dark one ruby flare
Pulsing out red light like an artery,
The ambulance at top speed floating down
Past beacons and illuminated clocks
Wings in a heavy curve, dips down,
And brakes speed, entering the crowd.
The doors leap open, emptying light;
Stretchers are laid out, the mangled lifted
And stowed into the little hospital.
Then the bell, breaking the hush, tolls once,
And the ambulance with its terrible cargo
Rocking, slightly rocking, moves away,
As the doors, an afterthought, are closed.

2 We are deranged, walking among the cops
Who sweep the glass and are large and composed.
One is still making notes under the light.
One with a bucket douches ponds of blood
Into the street and gutter.
One hangs lanterns on the wrecks that cling,
Empty husks of locusts, to iron poles.

3 Our throats were tight as tourniquets,
Our feet were bound with splints, but now,
Like convalescents intimate and gauche,
We speak through sickly smiles and warn
With the stubborn saw of common sense,
The grim joke and the banal resolution.
The traffic moves around with care,
But we remain, touching a wound
That opens to our richest horror.
Already old, the question Who shall die?
Becomes unspoken Who is innocent?
For death in war is done by hands;
Suicide has cause and stillbirth, logic;
And cancer, simple as a flower, blooms.
But this invites the occult mind,
Cancels our physics with a sneer,

And spatters all we knew of denouement
Across the expedient and wicked stones.

VOCABULARY

illuminated (1)	banal (3)
douches (2)	stillbirth (3)
tourniquets (3)	occult (3)
gauche (3)	denouement (3)
saw (3)	expedient (3)

QUESTIONS ON CONTENT

1. The poet's purpose in describing an auto wreck goes beyond the wreck itself. What larger purpose does he have?
2. In what way is death by war, suicide, stillbirth, and cancer different from death by accident?
3. What is the meaning of "deranged" in stanza 2?
4. Explain the meaning of the lines, "We speak through sickly smiles and warn/With the stubborn saw of common sense,/The grim joke and the banal resolution."
5. What is the "richest horror" referred to in line 9 of stanza 3?

QUESTIONS ON FORM

1. How is the effect of the ambulance's coming to a stop achieved? (See stanza 1, lines 6 and 7.)
2. Explain the metaphor "Empty husks of locusts" in the last line of stanza 2.
3. Identify and explain the images in the first two lines of stanza 3.
4. The word "wound" in stanza 3 (line 8) implies that there are two kinds of wounds. What are they?
5. What is the effect of repeating the pronoun "one" at the beginning of three lines in stanza 2?

SUGGESTIONS FOR WRITING

1. Draw a contrast between an accidental disaster and one that occurred as a result of a recognized cause. Use two specific examples to make the contrast come to life.
2. From your past experience of observing the scene of an accident, describe how onlookers tend to react.

CHAPTER WRITING ASSIGNMENTS

1. Reread Hayakawa's essay on the language of reports. Describe a house in your neighborhood, slanting your description with favorable details. Next, describe the same house with an unfavorable slant. Finally, write a description free from any kind of inference, judgment, or slanting.
2. Find a piece of writing loaded with inferences and judgments. Analyze it to show the purpose of the language used.

Appendix

The Five-Hundred-Word Theme: Some Annotated Student Examples

description
example
definition
comparison/contrast
division
causal analysis
movie review

description

GONE WITH THE WIND

The opening sentence states the dominant impression: "The town I grew up in is gone." The rest of the essay simply supports this dominant impression by supplying appropriate and specific details. No irrelevancies weaken the central notion of a vanished place.

1 The town I grew up in is gone. Now don't get me wrong, there is a town in the same geographical location, and it's still called Pismo Beach, but it's not the one I grew up in. My home town didn't disappear in a blinding flash, as did whole villages in the cataclysm at Hiroshima; rather, it slowly withdrew from existence under the double on-slaught of time and masses of humanity.

2 A few remnants of my old home town still exist. For instance, the public pier is still there, but it's a new, re-built pier. It doesn't shake and shud-der like the old one did when the mon-ster swells came rolling in from Hawaii and beyond.

Note the personification of the pier by having it "shake" and "shudder." Note, too, the personification of the swells as monsters. "Cotton-ball clouds" is an effective metaphor. The seagulls "wheel" and "soar"; they don't just "fly."

3 The foothills still slope gently -- grass green in springtime -- and the far hills are still painted purple by the

shadows of the cotton-ball clouds. The
blue Pacific is still blue and seagulls
still wheel and soar over the beaches,
but most of the pelicans are gone and
the clumps of driftwood on the beaches
have been replaced by bottles and cans
and white plastic jugs.

4 The bottom land just south of Pismo
has fallen to the great god Progress.
His bulldozer body and steam shovel arm
have ravished it. This is where I used
to hunt cottontails and jacks and ground
squirrels with my first .22. Now the
place is a shopping center and a mobile
home park, and the rabbits are mostly
fading stains on the nearby concrete
freeway.

5 On the west side of Highway One,
just south of the town, a hobo camp used
to lie hidden among the eucalyptus trees,
leaving traces and hints of a special
kind of rakishly free life, limited to
hobos only. But the hobos had to find a

Progress is personified as a god with bulldozer body and steam shovel arms.

Note how delicately the writer handles the rabbits being killed by cars.

new place to live because most of the

trees have been replaced by campgrounds

and gas stations and weekend people.

Here also the dune buggies are grinding

down the sand dunes faster than the wind

off the ocean builds them up, and the un-

muffled roar of internal combustion ob-

literates the crashing of the surf.

   6 Just north of town, expensive motels

and restaurants now perch atop the cliffs

where once sea birds made their nests

and where a kid could go fishing on a

blue and green summer day.

   7 I suppose children are still being

born and raised in this new Pismo Beach,

but they're not growing up in my home

town.

The use of "perch" is appropriate since the restaurants and motels have replaced birds.

The ending summarizes the nostalgic mood of the essay.

Humorous defini-
tion of *mayhem;*
examples illustrate
the definition.-

cause of our love of mayhem. <u>Mayhem</u>

designates absurd, gratuitous gore,

which I will explain by alluding to

Greek mythology. Sisyphus, we read, was

sentenced by the gods to push a boulder

up a steep hill for eternity. On reach-

ing the brow of the hill, the boulder

promptly rolls back down, compelling

Sisyphus to push it back up again. But

what if the boulder, on rolling down the

hill, should bash Sisyphus on the noggin,

spill blood, and knock him silly? That

would be mayhem.

5 Recently, in a game between Los An-

geles and Green Bay, I had the pleasure

of witnessing some authentic mayhem. A

linebacker from Green Bay was hit on the

blind side by a Los Angeles offensive

tackle and fell senseless as a cabbage.

Enough blood was visible to qualify the

hit as gory. But then something hap-

pened to elevate it to mayhem. The coach

ran onto the field, took off the injured

linebacker's helmet, and revealed the fellow's head to be perfectly bald! The mayhem was instantly clear, for it is tonsorial impertinence for the glabrous to play football. That little touch of blood and baldness was just deft enough to transmogrify ordinary gore into mayhem. The klieg lights blazed down, the fellow writhed with pain, the coach fussed with a tourniquet to stem the flow of blood, and shining implacably through all this frantic ministration was a sizzling, inglorious bald head. What a game that was!

6 Mayhem and gore, these explain why American men love to watch football on television. Satisfying our appetites for these is responsible for selling more television sets, automobiles, and indigestion medications than all the combined forces of soap operadom, cop stories, documentaries, thrillers, and miscellaneous voyeuristic tragedies.

Reiteration of thesis. The causes for the American male's love of football have been clearly established.

movie review

A REVIEW OF <u>SHAMPOO</u>

1 <u>Shampoo</u> is more than just a sexual
farce about the pitfalls and perils of
being a Don Juan. It is a time capsule
that will be worthy of study by future
generations of sociologists. It mirrors
the language, morals, and aspirations of
a large part of our society during the
late 1960s. It goes beyond entertaining
us to making us think about just how far
we have really come since then. The
movie begins as an outrageous chronicle
of twenty-four hours in the life of a
Beverly Hills hairdresser and grows into
something much more ambitious, in effect,
the decline of Western Civilization in
the vicinity of Beverly Hills.

2 Warren Beatty gives the most inspired performance of his career as
George, the handsome and desperately ambitious favorite of the "shampoo and

set" crowd at a fashionable Beverly Hills salon. George is envied by his coworkers and sought after by his homosexual boss. Our hero would like to buy a shop of his own, but cannot convince the bank manager that a motorcycle and his sex appeal are sufficient collateral.

3 Beatty's portrayal of George is thoughtful and tremendously appealing, and George's frantic quest is sadly tender and touching in the final outcome. The movie has a life of its own and stands as a genuine original. It is, for the most part, an excellent work of craftsmanship, and in coauthoring the screenplay Beatty has written some of the most bluntly outrageous one-liners ever blurted out. The playback of the language as it is spoken today provokes both shocked gasps and shrieks of laughter. It is both hilarious and horrible, tough and tender.

4 Only a serious-minded film maker

would have attempted such an ultimate
statement about the root causes of confusion in our society during the 1960s.
There are scathing examples of male ego
versus female ego, of backbiting and
bitchiness. In its use of irony, Shampoo surpasses entertainment and approaches art. While it is devastatingly
funny, it is also a most caustic attack
on the corruption of power and the immorality of affluence.

A memorable
scene is singled out
for detailed
comment.

5 One of the most memorable scenes in
the film is a dinner party that takes
place in a posh Beverly Hills hotel. It
is the last night of the Republican
National Convention and the diners are
celebrating the nomination of Richard
Nixon as their candidate in the coming
election. The scene is one of impending
disaster for George. All three of the
ladies he has made love to that day are
having dinner in the same room. A
thoughtful viewer will also perceive an

absurd parallel of imminent human disaster in Nixon's acceptance speech as it is being televised in the background.

The reviewer concludes by offering his final judgment.

6 Goldie Hawn, Julie Christie, Lee Grant, and Jack Warden give flawless performances. This movie does not seem to have been written, acted, or directed, but simply to exist from one moment to another with its own special verve. It is the most satisfying film of 1975.

G. P. PUTNAM'S SONS   For an excerpt from *The Coming of Age* by Simone de Beauvoir, translated by Patrick O'Brian. Copyright © 1972 by Andre Deutsch, Weidenfeld and Nicolson, and G. P. Putnam's Sons.

QUADRANGLE / THE NEW YORK TIMES BOOK COMPANY   For "Why I Am an Agnostic" by Clarence Darrow from *Verdicts Out of Court* by Arthur and Lila Weinberg. Copyright © 1963 by Arthur and Lila Weinberg. Reprinted by permission of Quadrangle / The New York Times Book Company.

RANDOM HOUSE, INC.   For "The Unknown Citizen" from *Collected Shorter Poems 1927–1957* by W. H. Auden; copyright 1940 and renewed 1968 by W. H. Auden. For "The Bird and the Machine" from *The Immense Journey* by Loren Eiseley; copyright © 1955 by Loren Eiseley. For "A Rose for Emily" by William Faulkner; copyright 1930 and renewed 1958 by William Faulkner. For "Auto Wreck" from *Selected Poems* by Karl Shapiro; copyright 1942 and renewed 1970 by Karl Shapiro. All are reprinted by permission of Random House, Inc.

THE READER'S DIGEST   For "The Burning Question of Browns Ferry" by James Nathan Miller; reprinted with permission from the April 1976 *Reader's Digest;* copyright 1976 by The Reader's Digest Assn., Inc. For "Why People Don't Help in a Crisis" by John M. Darley and Bibb Latané, as condensed in the May 1969 *Reader's Digest.*

D. L. ROSENHAN   For an excerpt from "On Being Sane in Insane Places" by D. L. Rosenhan from *Science,* vol. 179, January 19, 1973.

SATURDAY REVIEW   For "Are You Making Yourself Clear?" by Norman Cousins from *Saturday Review,* February 22, 1969; copyright 1969 by Saturday Review Co. For "I Am the New Black" by Thee Smith from *Saturday Review,* October 19, 1968; copyright 1968 by Saturday Review Co. Both are reprinted by permission.

SCOTT, FORESMAN AND COMPANY   For "Writing Successful Paragraphs" from *Strategies of Rhetoric,* revised by A. M. Tibbetts and Charlene Tibbetts. Copyright © 1974, 1969 by Scott, Foresman and Company. Reprinted by permission of the publisher.

SIMON & SCHUSTER, INC.   For "The Political Causes of the Decay of Rome" from *Caesar and Chrïst* by Will Durant; copyright © 1944 by Will Durant, renewed © 1971 by Will Durant. For "Some American Types" from *America as Civilization* by Max Lerner; copyright © 1957 by Max Lerner. Both are reprinted by permission of Simon & Schuster, Inc.

ALAN SIMPSON   For an excerpt from "The Marks of an Educated Man" by Alan Simpson from *Context,* I, no. 1 (spring 1961). Reprinted by permission.

THEE SMITH   For an excerpt from "I Am the New Black" by Thee Smith from *Saturday Review,* October 19, 1968. Reprinted by permission.

THE SOCIETY OF AUTHORS   For George Bernard Shaw's review of the play *The Pilgrim's Progress* by G. G. Collingham. Reprinted by permission of The Society of Authors on behalf of the Bernard Shaw Estate.

MAY SWENSON   For "Pigeon Woman" by May Swenson. Reprinted by permission of the author from *To Mix with Time.* Copyright © 1963 by May Swenson. Originally printed in *The New Yorker.*

HELEN W. THURBER   For "The Catbird Seat" by James Thurber. Copyright © 1945 James Thurber. Copyright © 1971 Helen W. Thurber and Rosemary Thurber Sauers. From *The Thurber Carnival,* published by Harper & Row. Originally printed in *The New Yorker.*

TIME   For "Baffle-Gab Thesaurus" from *Time,* September 13, 1968; copyright Time Inc. For "The Fine Print Translated" from *Time,* September 22, 1975; copyright Time Inc. Both are reprinted by permission from *Time,* The Weekly Newsmagazine.

TODAY'S EDUCATION   For "Stages of Dying" (originally titled "Facing Up to Death") by Elisabeth Kubler Ross from *Today's Education: The Journal of the National Education Association,* January 1972. Reprinted by permission.

TRANSACTION, INC.   For "Are Women Prejudiced Against Women?" by Philip Goldberg. Published by permission of Transaction, Inc., from *Transaction,* vol. 5, no. 5 (April 1968). Copyright © 1968 by Transaction, Inc.

UNIVERSITY OF CALIFORNIA PRESS   For an excerpt from *The Philosophy of Literary Form: Studies in Symbolic Action* by Kenneth Burke. Copyright © 1973 by The Regents of the University of California. Reprinted by permission of the University of California Press.

VIKING PENGUIN, INC.   For "Hell" from *A Portrait of the Artist as a Young Man* by James Joyce. Copyright © 1964 by the Estate of James Joyce. Reprinted by permission of Viking Penguin, Inc.

INDEX

B
C
D
E
F
G
H
I
J